BIKING ALONE AROUND THE WORLD

Travel! and thou shalt find new friends for old ones left behind;
Toil! for the sweets of human life by toil and moil are found:
The stay-at-home no honor wins nor aught attains but want:
So leave thy place of birth and wander all the world around!

—ARABIAN NIGHTS

ALSO BY J. HART ROSDAIL
The Sloopers, Their Ancestry and Posterity
The John and Leonard Hart Families

Lake Wanaka, New Zealand

Yours truly in Perth, Western Australia

BIKING ALONE
AROUND
THE WORLD

J. HART ROSDAIL

An Exposition-Banner Book
Exposition Press   New York

EXPOSITION PRESS, INC.

50 Jericho Turnpike, Jericho, New York 11753

FIRST EDITION

LIBRARY OF CONGRESS CATALOG CARD NUMBER: 72-86591

SBN 0-682-47541-6

Published simultaneously in Canada by Transcanada Books

To all those who
cannot resist the temptation
to see what is around
the bend in the road

Contents

Preface

When I graduated from college I had the normal young man's desire to see some of the world. I crossed the Atlantic by freighter, bought an old secondhand bicycle for seven dollars and set out to do Europe. Not having much money, I slept in Russian haycocks and Spanish jails and ate with the common man whether in Scotland or in Turkey. After ten months I returned home minus my $300 capital but with the scalps of 33 countries tucked under my belt. I had ridden the bicycle 11,000 miles and had eaten or slept in 220 different homes.

During the following years I seized all opportunities afforded by holidays and vacations from work to enlarge on my domestic travel experiences. Always camping out, I journeyed through all of the states and Canada, and visited practically all of our national parks and monuments.

However, it was not easy to break away for a second trip abroad. There was a job of many years' standing to leave, and by this time a family to be supported during my absence. But the world was put here for us to see and enjoy and I felt that the time to do it was now. Those few who attained success in the business world, it seemed to me, and who could presumably afford to travel were more tied to their jobs than ever before. Their responsibilities were heavier, and besides, 'uneasy lies the head that wears the crown.' If they waited until retirement they were usually too old to want to travel, or, if they did, it was only through limited, beaten-track areas with about half the enjoyment they would have had thirty years before. Then too I had become imbued with a little of the you-can't-take-it-with-you philosophy. In addition there were vocational usage possibilities in further travel experience which I wanted to explore. So the golden arrow seemed to point to my making a definite break—a pause to adventure.

With the same old bicycle I again set out this time to do Australia and Africa. It was a long trip; I was gone a year and seven months. During this time I visited 46 countries and traveled 67,000 miles, 11,600 of which were on the bicycle. My travels took me the length of New Zealand, around the continent of Australia, and two and one-half times the length of the continent of Africa, which I also crossed, in effect, at its widest part. As before, I roughed it, and many were the lonely camps in desert and jungle. On the other hand, I ate or slept in 380 different homes ranging from the most primitive African hut to the most palatial colonial mansion. Thus I obtained a good cross section of humanity.

It so happened that this second trip took me around the world and involved the crossing of three oceans. This cost me $1,200. But the total of all other expenses was less than $300. For example, my food cost me only $36; my passport and visas, $43; and my lodging, nothing.

I kept a running account of my experiences, endeavoring always to set them down while impressions were fresh. Thus my story grew to great length, and since I had been trained as a researcher, it often became almost documentary. Recipes for the housewife and methods of crop rotation crept between the pages. Deciding what people, material, and events to leave out has not been easy. However, I dare to hope that the result is the proper combination of action, description, and information for a good story of adventure.

BIKING ALONE AROUND THE WORLD

1

Wherein We Hear
a Good Tale and Set Sail

It was a year before my passport came. I could only mark time. Then one evening I arrived home from work and there it was, valid for "Australia, New Zealand, and the Continent of Africa." Great! Now there were things to do!

I applied for my Australian and New Zealand visas at the local British consulate in Chicago. They gave me no encouragement at all. I persisted. They asked for character references and then agreed to write the consular authorities in the East. Meanwhile I contacted the steamship companies. More difficulty. All space was taken for months in advance. For two weeks I hounded both the consulate and the steamship companies. When I did find a vacant berth on a freighter I ran into a hen-and-egg situation. The steamship company wouldn't issue my ticket until they saw my visas; and the consulate refused to issue my visas until I presented my ticket. They fought it out over the phone and the British won.

There was no doubt in my mind as to how I would travel on land. I didn't have very much money and knew from experience that the answer to this problem could be found by using a bicycle and camping out. In this way I had already taken a ten-month solo trip through 33 European countries at a total cost of only $304. Yet on that trip I saw more scenery, met more people, and got into more interesting situations than those who travel by conventional methods.

I still had the same old bicycle—Jacqueline by name. She had been resting patiently in the basement for a number of years with only a brief interlude in the Colorado Rockies one summer. It wouldn't do not to share further adventures with her. She was old, it was true—fifty years according to the estimate of an old Irish bicycle man. I had no way of knowing her age because she had no brand or number and had been purchased second-hand (for $7) in Germany. But old or not, she was tried. She had already carried me and my pack for eleven thousand miles. Besides, a new bicycle would cost money which I couldn't afford.

Now, as to Jacqueline's pack—well, I determined to increase it a little. Why shouldn't I have a few luxuries? Instead of one blanket (or no blanket) and the cold food on which I toured Europe, I would take a sleeping bag, a three-pound stove, and maybe even a tent. Eventually I came up with a master list of 134 items from rain cape to safety pins

3

covering all needs for travel in any clime. The sleeping bag I never regretted. It was the layer-cake variety and in some countries I would have to go to bed nearly nude on top of the bag, then later crawl in under the cover, still later under the top blanket, and finally, just before morning, I would scootch down into the center and pull up the zipper. The stove—well, that I later regretted. I cooked myself a warm meal every day for the first month of my travel on land, but then it just seemed I was more interested in miles, scenery, people, and sleeping than I was in cooking. Still I hung onto the darn thing for twelve thousand miles before leaving it in a corner of the Sahara Desert. And as for the tent—well, it was a good thing to have along for my peace of mind, but I always pedaled like heck for the nearest village if it looked like rain. Not that I stayed in hotels— I couldn't afford that—but there was usually a native hut or a shed to be found. And in good weather, if you are under a tent how can you see the stars?

I assembled all of my equipment, even the bicycle, in my living room. Sometimes I think that 50 percent of the enjoyment of any trip is to be had in sheer anticipation during the period of preparation. The thrills of conjecture, the queries of friends, the flights of fancy—how the mind races!

The smaller items of equipment—three food tins for vegetables, meat, and jam, stove, camera, extra tire tube, sou'wester, waterproof leggings, overshoes, etc.—I packed in a homemade, heavy canvas saddlebag having two pouches. In one of these I also placed a dark shirt, tie, and trousers tightly rolled in a piece of japarra. I rolled the sleeping bag up in the tent and placed the roll lengthwise on the rear luggage carrier. Then the saddlebag was placed over the roll with the pouches hanging down on either side of the wheel but opening inward. Two quart water canteens were carried in a pouch on the front handlebars. At the side of my pack I hung a leather shopping bag for current food items such as tomatoes, or bulky items like bread; or for my heavy army fatigue jacket, which might be exchanged for my rain cape in wet weather. The total pack weighed between 55 and 84 pounds, depending on how much extra water and food I might have to carry in sparsely populated country.

As for what to wear, experience in Europe had shown there was nothing better than overalls, work shirt, comfortable oxfords, and a dark workman's cap. The overalls were invaluable for comfort, the big and extra pockets, and hard wear. Roomy around the waist and hips, they did not bind, and were cooler than jeans and belt because the air was free to circulate. This roominess allowed the large hip and side pockets to hold traveler's checks, money, road map, etc., as well as a good-sized camera and a couple of oranges when desired. Passport and notebook were safe in the snap-button pockets of the bib. And the workman's cap, besides having the usual advantages of a cap over a hat, would substitute for the hot-country helmet when I folded my bandana inside.

On a spring evening in mid-April I left my suburban home and pedaled into Chicago. There were not many in the little bus station on State Street and since my baggage was about the first to go on the bus, there was no trouble about stowing Jacqueline. All aboard for New York and my ship to Australia!

By the time the bus arrived at the main station some blocks away the comfortable matron across the aisle was well situated on one and one-half seats on the aisle side with a mountain of packages on the remaining half-seat. The no-one-is-going-to-move-me expression was plainly written all over her face. But the little foreign-looking woman with the unpleasant face and the this-is-a-free-country-and-you're-not-going-to-step-on-me frame of mind had other ideas. She had already been up and down the aisle and there were other seats, of course, and nearby, but not for her.

"I'd like to get in there, please," she said icily, with a well-developed accent.

"No, you can't."

"Have you got two seats reserved? D-r-i-v-e-r!"

We only heard the first part of the last word, for she was out of the bus like a flash and berating the driver, who was superintending the luggage.

After a bit one of the passengers from the opposite side of the bus called to me, since I had a vantage point overlooking the battle: "What's she doing now?"

"You might know—she's talking!"

She finally made him take her luggage out of the bottom of the bus and we had to forego the pleasure of her company. The comfortable matron hung onto her two seats until the bitter end of the trip, when the driver had to pressure her to make room for another passenger.

The second morning we arrived in the heart of New York City. I packed Jacqueline and rode her down to Pier 61, where the S/S *Ten Sleep* lay readying for the long voyage to Australia.

The first thing of interest I noticed was the great number of watchmen. The piers were all roofed over, so it was like walking through great, nearly empty warehouses. No matter where I went, about every forty feet there were watchmen. Not one, but two, standing apart—one to keep the other from sleeping, don't you see. They popped out at me from behind tiers of oil drums or bales of this and that. Most of them had nothing in common but the big badge on the chest. Some wore caps, some hats. Some had heavy overcoats tightly buttoned and with collars turned up. Others had coats and suitcoats open and their hands thrust deep in their pockets. Exceptions to the usual run were the pier-gate watchmen. They looked and acted like retired army colonels. Attired all in khaki with army greatcoats and outside leather belts, great in stature and in front expanse, heavily jowled, stern of mien, their appearance alone was sufficient to put a droop to the shoulders of any ordinary mortal and a quaver in his voice.

But in all fairness, once a watchman was satisfied that I was permitted, he became a fairly sociable chap and betrayed the loneliness of his work. The long, lonely hours of the night, and those of Saturday and Sunday, in the most forbidding of surroundings: chill, dank, often smelly; dark, even in the daytime; bare rafters and concrete floors; and the disheartening sight of frequently seeing ships lift up their gangplanks and sail out into the sunlight bound for distant ports of adventure—such is the lot of the pier watchman. What are his thoughts as he stands alone during the long hours? In four days at the piers I never saw two standing closer than twenty feet. When I went up the plank for the last time our watchman took me by the hand.

"I say, lad, if you get to Melbourne will yuh see if you run across any 'Dinans'? I've got a couple o' brothers over there and I haven't heard from them for years. Will yuh, lad, huh? Dinan's the name. D-i-n-a-n."

Of course, there were cats in the warehouses too, and on occasion their wails broke the stillness. But their population was dependent upon rats and mice, so it could not maintain equality with the number of watchmen.

My time in New York was well spent. Jacqueline was ideal for transportation—no waiting for buses, no expense. Of course, riding up and down Fifth Avenue on an ancient bicycle and in overalls and beret might seem unusual to most, but I didn't receive the impression that it created much of a furore in New York. I rode down to lower Manhattan and up to the public library on Forty-first Street a number of times. Here I augmented my homemade guidebook until it bulged with information about seasons, temperatures, and prevailing winds of various areas; points of interest; first aid; symptoms of tropical diseases and treatment; and shipping companies and where they operated. I also made tracings of maps showing roads in Africa and Australia, where they seemed to exist. I was particularly careful in searching out points of interest, for it is far worse to miss something because you didn't know it was there than to miss it because of some physical factor beyond your control.

Late evenings when I returned aboard the *Ten Sleep* I became acquainted with the night mate, Captain Stousland. He had been an international hero in his day, a man who refused to give up his ship. I was to hear many a tale from seafaring men, but only three are worth the sharing. Captain Stousland's is the first.

Captain Stousland and the "Liberty Glo"

> He holds him with his glittering eye—
> The Wedding-Guest stood still,
> And listens like a three years' child.
> The Mariner hath his will.

My mariner was every bit as colorful as Coleridge's. He was certainly as ancient—eighty-three, he was; and his blue eyes shone brightly from under bushy brows and lids so heavy that at times his left eye seemed all but closed. And his tale was a twentieth-century counterpart of the famous "rime."

Captain John Ibsen Stousland was born in Skeien, southern Norway, about 1864. His mother was a Quaker and a sister of Ibsen, the great Norwegian playwright. He first went to sea when very young. He served in the Spanish-American War and was a high-ranking officer in World War I. A firm believer in discipline, he recalled his days with sailing ships when the captain held absolute control over his men, with the power to keep a man on board even after a voyage of 135 days from New York to Australia. He made a strong distinction between an individual's liberties and his right to do as he pleases. And he was stout in his denunciation of war.

Captain Stousland was short and stocky, with a tremendous chest, an erect carriage, and a healthy, tanned complexion broken only by a gray grandfather's mustache. He dressed neatly, almost jauntily. A black, heavy, turtleneck sweater accentuated his fine physique. Only the heavy veinings of his wrists made one conscious of his age.

Like the wedding guest, I was the sole listener to the tale of Captain John Stousland. We sat alone in the saloon of the S/S *Ten Sleep*, anchored in New York harbor, where he served as night mate following his retirement. We sat, nearly opposite, with a table between us. The portholes were closed, the city was far away. The saloon was but dimly lit. It was very late. The mariner began.

"In 1919 they were building ships under a new system at Hog Island Navy Yard. I rode down from New York on a train with the man in charge of the work. Instead of making one ship at a time, they had fifty ships—fifty ships, mister—building at one time. They would use the same part in all the ships, you see. Well, we looked over the work. They had a new method of riveting that interested me. The ships ran between eight thousand and ten thousand tons.

"Well, one of the ships was the *Liberty Glo* and they wanted me to try her out. I took her on a test run to Marseilles. In order to give her a good check I loaded her good. Then I put in a hundred and fifty more tons of coal than she was supposed to take. I wanted to test her. But she stood it. She came through fine. We got into a storm and when the water started breaking over her bow I called the engineer.

" 'Do you feel anything down there?'

" 'Not a thing,' he says.

" 'Well, the green water is breaking over her bow. Do you feel any quiver?'

" 'Don't feel a thing,' he says.

"On the next trip we were bound for Bremen and on the ninth of December, 1919, we hit a mine in a snowstorm in the North Sea. We were off the northwest coast of Holland and only about a hundred and fifty miles from our destination. This was the worst winter they'd had in ten years. Well, mister, that was an awful sight. The mine hit us just forward of midship and barrels of oil came right up through the steel plates of the deck right in front of my eyes. There was some force behind that, mister.

"Well, the men all made a rush for the boats, but I wouldn't let 'em cast off. I had the wireless operator send for help. I knew where we were. I had our position off a light. Well, a ship got our message and told us they were on the way. Meanwhile the forward part of the ship was breaking loose. That was a sight—to see those big steel plates tearing apart. And do you know where they were tearing? At one side of the rivets. The rivets were holding. I knew then that the method of riveting was a good one.

"We kept waiting for the ship to come. 'We can't find you, Captain,' they said. I couldn't understand it and I never knew till afterwards, when I read the message, why it was. But do you know what the operator had done, mister? He had become confused, you know, and had given our location on the wrong side of the light. He told them we were nine miles on this side here and we were really nine miles away on this side.

"Finally the front half of the ship broke clean away and the ship still hadn't come. I knew I couldn't hold the men any longer.

" 'You want us to go now, Captain?' they asked me.

" 'Yes! Go! Go on! Go!' I flung my arm at 'em. I was afraid I'd weaken, you see. I didn't want to be left alone. I wanted the third mate to stay with me. He was a good man, but I didn't have the courage to ask him. The [chief] engineer was the last to go.

" 'Are you coming, Captain?'

" 'No; she's still afloat.'

"He looked at the bulkhead. 'But she can't stand, Captain. You know that!'

" 'Well, she's still afloat, isn't she?'

"He came up to me and embraced me, you know, and kissed me on the chin. 'I knew you'd say that,' he said, with the tears starting to run down his cheeks.

"You see, mister [addressing me], there's a law at sea that says that anyone that finds a ship and there's no man aboard can have her; and nobody can claim against him. If there is a man on board and another ship tows her in, this man has a claim."

"Well, did you save the ship, Captain? What happened?"

"She went aground. Not on the mainland, but on an island near it. But she went ashore with the bulkhead first so she was protected from the sea."

"And you were the only man on her?"

"I was the only man on her.

"Well, I got off and went to The Hague and wired what had happened. Then I had to see about salvage. The people in Holland had a look at her. 'It can't be done,' they said. 'She can't be brought off.' 'I say she can,' I told them. Then I went to London and talked to the biggest people there; and to Scotland, to Edinburgh. 'She can't be brought off,' they said. Even the people in Ireland, in Belfast, the biggest company in Ireland, had a look at her. 'She can't be brought off,' they said. But I knew she could. I had been over every inch of her. Well, all these reports went to the Shipping Board at Rotterdam, head of all the shipping boards in the world; and telegrams to Admiral Sims in Washington. Then the Board called me down —a lot of big men. 'She can't be brought off,' they said. 'I know she can,' I said.

"You see, mister, England and America were vying for the seas at that time; and the other European countries too. They didn't want our merchant marine to prosper. I sent a long wire to Admiral Sims. It cost me an awful lot of money. 'There's something more in this than just one ship,' I told him. 'They don't think we can build ships and they don't think we know how to run 'em. I say the *Liberty Glo* can be brought off and I know how it can be done.' I had an idea, you see, mister.

"Well, then, I waited. Finally the answer came.

" 'Enter into contract for salvage.'

"Mister, that was something, I can tell you." The Captain took off his spectacles (which he sometimes wore) and set them on the table. He sat up straight and his blue eyes looked at me with the pride of achievement. " 'Enter into contract for salvage.' Mister, that was something.

"Well, I had a firm all picked out. It was the biggest one in Holland. I went to see 'em in Rotterdam. Two men were at the head of it. They were brothers. I showed them the telegram: 'Enter into contract for salvage.' 'But, Captain, you know it can't be done,' they said.

" 'Look here,' I said to them, 'Everybody in the world of any consequence has said the *Liberty Glo* can't be brought off. Now, if Holland and your company can do the job, think of what that would mean for you. Besides, I have a plan for getting her off.'

" 'What is your plan, Captain Stousland?'

" 'You sign that contract, and I'll tell you my plan.'

"Well, they were impressed, but they wanted to talk it over with their father first. So the next day I went back and talked to the old man.

" 'Why won't you tell us your plan, Captain?' he asked me.

" 'Because I want you to sign the contract first.'

"Well, he took a liking to me and they signed.

" 'Now then,' I said, 'take your biggest dredge. Take it down to_____

Company and have it fitted out as a sand sucker. Then bring it up to the ship.'

"I had taken soundings and knew the depth of the sand every foot of the way back to deep water. And we sucked out the sand. But somehow or other there was something I couldn't account for. It seemed like the sand sunk away in different places and left three bars we had to get her across. But finally we got her out. I was exhausted.

"But then another storm came up. It picked her up and put her back on shore further in than she was before. And this time the bulkhead was left toward the sea. 'Now you certainly can't get her out,' they said. By this time, you see, everybody in Europe knew about the *Liberty Glo.*

"Well, I left the boat and went down to Amsterdam and got me a room in the_____Hotel. I told the clerk I didn't want to see anyone, and that I didn't want to do anything but sleep and eat for twelve days. Then I went back to the salvage company."

"And I s'pose you had just as much trouble as before?" I asked.

"No. This time—well, you see, they had done it once. People could see that it was not an impossibility. Then I went back on board the ship. You see, I had to go out to this island each time.

"I had other troubles too. Fire broke out in the hold one time. The deck plates got so hot you couldn't walk on 'em. We couldn't seem to find the fire and everybody left. I was the only one that stayed. I got the cover off and found it was in some bales of cotton. How it started, I don't know. Some kind of combustion. I got some ice tongs and got them in a bale and tried to get one of the bales back on deck with a cable. But I wasn't man enough to do it. So finally I sent word that the fire was out. It wasn't out, but I told them so anyway. Then when they came back on board I had help to hoist out the bales. And do you know, some of that cotton had been in water but only about two inches of it was wet. It's packed that tight.

"Well, we got her off the sand again and then we had to take her down to Rotterdam. That was ticklish. When we went to tie her up, another man and I were on the rope. We had to be careful or we would smash her up. 'Heave,' I said. Well, we hove and we hove and we hove. When we got her hove to I collapsed. I went down. I was helpless. I couldn't move. This was what I had been working for so long. They had to carry me off the ship.

"Then it was to rebuild her. 'There is something more to it than the expense,' I told them in Washington. 'It isn't necessary to discuss whether it is practical or not. The *Liberty Glo* has become an international affair, the pride of the merchant marine, and our position on the seas is at stake!'

"Then came another telegram: 'Enter into contract to rebuild.'

"That was something too, mister. I went to the head of the biggest concern in Rotterdam. I told him there were two ways it could be handled. He could make me a contract price or he could use his labor as it was available and I would pay according to the hours spent. He was a man I knew could be trusted and I left the decision up to him.

"'I tell you, Captain Stousland. If I give you a contract price it will have to be a big one. Other ships may come in and need working on and I'll have to transfer one hundred men or two hundred men to them. I'll have to cover those costs. It's better to do it the other way.'"

"Did he speak English, Captain?" I asked.

"Oh, yes. As good as you. So I went over to London and got me some inspectors."

"Inspectors, Captain?"

"Yes, time inspectors. I asked them to give me a young man to supervise them—ab-so-lute-ly reliable! I got him. A fine man—one hundred percent trustworthy. And so we rebuilt the ship.

"When it was done I wanted to give a party on board. You see, the ship was so well known and I had even had pictures, motion pictures, taken of the salvaging. Those cost a lot of money. And there had been newspaper articles, and so on. So I called on the head of the company. 'I want to have a party,' I told him. 'I want you to invite the heads of all the big shipping lines in Holland. I want you to invite officials of the government, people of the press—invite everyone of importance who is interested in ships and shipping. Then I want you to make up a menu for a banquet and put on it every kind of wine, and whiskey, and champagne.' Those were prohibition days, you know, mister. So I told him to put on red wines and white wines and ales and everything in the book.

"'All right, Captain. We'll do it.'

"Later on he called me in one day. 'Captain,' he says, 'we have received a note from the head of the Shipping Board requesting that we serve only coffee and sandwiches on the *Liberty Glo.*' You see, mister, the Rotterdam Shipping Board hated me. They had hated me ever since I went above them about the salvage. Coffee and sandwiches! To celebrate something that had cost the United States two million guilders.

"'Well,' I says to him, 'who have you been taking your orders from?'

"'You, Captain,' he said.

"'Well, just keep right on. Go ahead as we planned.'

"After the affair was over, his daughter, a fine girl that I'd come to like, told me one day that the head of the Shipping Board had written a letter to Admiral Sims saying there had been drunkenness and disorder on the *Liberty Glo.* 'Well, all right,' I said to her. Then I had a list made of all the people at the party and I showed their positions. This one was head of that company, this one was an official of such and such department, and so on. Then I sent it to Admiral Sims with one of the menus.

"When I got back to the United States he sent for me. He showed me the telegrams from all those companies saying the *Liberty Glo* couldn't be brought off.

" 'We admired your spirit, Captain. That's one reason we sent you the telegrams to go ahead.'

"When I was about to leave, I said, 'Well, we didn't celebrate on coffee and sandwiches either.' "

The next day, at 5 P.M., we sailed—sailed on a trip of no less than 10,000 miles, of which 7800 miles, was over open water across the Pacific from Panama to Australia. The latter figure was larger than any appearing on my ocean communications map of the world.

Down the East River and past the Lady. We four passengers—two women and two men—huddled in fur coats and sweaters against the cold wind and watched the lights of New York go on. Captain Rank came down and introduced himself and chatted until the cold drove us all inside.

Recent bad weather had roughed up the sea and the S/S *Ten Sleep* pitched and rolled. Things banged and skidded all over the ship most of the night.

"First my toes were up in the air, then my head. It was an unhappy feeling," said Mr. Tubal, the Belgian passenger the next morning.

"Honest to gosh, I had to hang onto the edges of the bed to keep from being thrown out," echoed Sandra Moorcroft, the low-voiced Australian brunette.

Well, yours truly wrote until he became dizzy and commenced to sweat about the brow. He then wisely retired, knowing the symptoms from former experiences. But with the fan going and the porthole open, he managed to get by without reaching the danger point.

Delaware Bay was ours by morning and we proceeded up the river to spend the following three days at or near Philadelphia. Hundreds of fifty-gallon drums and five-gallon cans containing oil and oil products were taken on board, some refrigerators and washing machines, and other general cargo.

I spent my evenings with Mr. Tubal. He helped me with my French pronunciation and I reciprocated with his English. Besides French he could speak Russian and Polish fluently. He was a violinist and filled the ship with his fine music. He had been playing over the radio and hoped to make a living as a musician in Australia. He was good-natured and friendly and I liked him.

While Mr. Tubal and I were passing our time with languages, the women were being taken on a merry round of nightclubs by the ship's officers. Mrs. Moorcroft was a divorcee and her somewhat redheaded older sister, Mrs. Tyson, was a widow. They were not unattractive and while they dined at the passengers' table with Mr. Tubal and myself, we had lost out to the uniforms, titles, and ready money of the ship's officers ere the feminine foot had been four hours afloat.

Saturday we sailed, and at supper in the salon that evening I made the acquaintance of our fifth and last passenger, Mrs. Forne. She was a very interesting person. Travelers usually are, I find; or maybe it's just because I like to travel too. She was the wife of an Australian sheep rancher "outback" in New South Wales. Her ranch was umpty-nine miles from the nearest town. She met her husband in Hawaii, and had studied in both Germany and France. Called to America by an accident suffered by her mother, she had been just as suddenly called back to Australia by the illness of her husband.

Our passenger list and cargo now complete, the S/S *Ten Sleep* bore us southward toward the Caribbean Sea, the Panama Canal, and the great Pacific.

2

The Rolling Deep—Ulp!
And the Moonlit Jungle—Ah!

Nuts! Who was the guy that said "Oh, for a home on the rolling deep, a life on the ocean wave" or some such foolishness? And who were those doctors that are supposed to have prescribed a Caribbean cruise as restful? Peaceful man that I am, if any of these gazimbos were to show up right now, I'd shove them toward the rail and the ship would do the rest.

I am seated in the exact middle of the freighter *Ten Sleep*, port to starboard, and as near to the middle, bow to stern, as I can get. Nevertheless, the chair and I lean from side to side like a pendulum. If I look toward either rail, I can see it go down, down, and down until a good thirty feet of water is visible below the horizon. On the recovery the same rail traces a dizzy course up, and up, and up, past the horizon line and on up until a good thirty feet of sky is shut from view. Now, what these gyrations can do to your stomach, I leave to your imagination. As an Iowa farm lad, way out of his sphere, I can only say, "It's wonderful what the human body can endure when it has to."

You are thinking we are in a big storm? Oh, no! The sun shines and there is not too much wind—but you can bet there has been to get the sea riled up this way. The crew tells me the Caribbean is usually like this in spring and fall; and think of all the hurricanes drummed up in this part of the world.

Now, just in case my stomach might not already be acting up, the ship favors me with a lovely fresh odor of gasoline every twenty seconds. We have enough gasoline and oil as cargo on board this freighter to blow us all to you-know-where to say nothing of the fuel the ship burns. One of the sailors just measured the latter—wow! That last roll was a good forty feet— by lowering a weighted line through a hole in the deck while smoking a cigarette. He is probably in such shape he doesn't care what happens to himself or anyone else.

On either side of me are steel booms fifty feet long. They are supposedly fastened by steel collars attached to vertical steel girders; but I notice the latter give about a foot every time we roll, so if I am crushed . . . Ugh! That gas! Just ahead of me, and poised to fall right on me, is the biggest boom on the ship—a little number about a foot and a half through and sixty-two feet long. It can carry fifty tons all by itself if they can cook up enough power to operate it. Yowee! Over we go again!

Of course, the first few days of any voyage are the worst. There *is* such a thing as getting your sea legs. But there is also the possibility that you no sooner get used to a rocking side-to-side motion than the seas will run the other direction and your poor body will have to adjust to pitch, prow-to-stern activity. You may have both at the same time.

Methods of combating seasickness are legion, and what works for one may not help another. For those first days, or in rough weather, I found it best if I kept my eyes focused as far away as possible. I spent long hours on deck, often in foul weather, looking far across the waves. I rarely, if ever, missed a meal; or lost one. But it was sometimes nip and tuck to race away from the table and get flat on my back in my bunk before an up-heaval occurred. I am partial to dessert, especially pie; and if this were late in coming, I sometimes had a real struggle of mind over body to wait and eat it. My stomach would feel queer, and the table might start going places it shouldn't, before the meal was over. The thing to do was to lie down before dizziness gave way to the sweats of nausea.

On a freighter there is always some officer who is quick to notice a landlubber starting to get green around the gills. On my first North Atlantic crossing the first engineer loved to encourage us by describing how bad things *could* get. He told about a passenger they took to Europe one time who became horribly seasick. Nothing stayed down. He retched for days. Finally the poor devil dashed out into the middle of the midship deck, threw himself down, rolled onto his back, and flinging his arms toward the high heavens called out in anguish:

"Oh, my God, my God, show me some land! Show me some land if it's only in a flower pot!"

Whether on the Atlantic or the Pacific it doesn't take too much to make an 8,000- to 10,000-ton freighter roll. From 13 to 15 degrees is not un-common. I have devised an ingenious system which I am going to sell to Emily Post as the approved method of eating soup at sea. By this system you lower and crook the little finger of each hand so that it can hook the edge of the soup dish and tilt it to the proper level. Thus one can still keep the cracker in the left hand and the soup spoon in the right.

When the ship gets to rolling too much the mess boy wets the table-cloths. This keep the dishes from sliding from one side of the table to the other. Of course each table has a special railing to keep the dishes from going on to the floor.

After the meal you stagger down the passageway to your room. To enter is very simple. Just wait until the ship is rolling away from you and turn the key. The heavy steel door swings open like it had been hit by a cannon, you fall through the doorway and land on your bunk just under the port-holes at the far side of the room. Don't worry about closing the door. By the time you have picked yourself up the ship will have reversed its roll and the door will have slammed shut with a blam that fairly shakes the whole ship. I scarcely need to mention it would be suicide to try and take off one's pants while standing. You sit on the bunk or the anchored chair and pray that you can hang there until the operation is completed. Once asleep, you may awake in a few hours so dizzy you can barely make a trip to the head (toilet). And boy, does your back and stomach ache after ten hours in bed in rough weather! And after three days of squalls, when the ship pitches as well as rolls, you feel as weak as if you had been sick for a month.

Of course, these things happen just when you have a simple 15-degree roll. In a big storm the ship may roll as much as 40 degrees. Then life becomes much more simple. You don't eat, sleep, change clothes, and do all those other silly little things. You just grab onto something and hope that your grip will hold for about three days. Life is much simpler.

Meanwhile there is plenty of noise to keep you from getting bored. With the ship standing on her beam ends, the seas thunder over the midship deck at every roll. Mighty waves hit the side of the ship. B-r-r-o-o-o-m! The sound echoes through the holds like ten thousand great temple gongs. Your eardrums are tortured with the vibrations of steel floors and walls. In the engine room the chief engineer has taken over. As the ship pitches the propeller comes clear of the water. Power must be cut off at exactly the right time. When the chief miscalculates, the ship shudders violently from stem to stern. You feel as if it's about to fly to pieces. Oh, brother! Davy Jones, here we come!

But in all fairness, there is a much more pleasant side to ocean travel. Since leaving New York, with the exception of about three days, we have had a quiet sea and excellent weather. The scenes at night have been wonderfully beautiful—moonlight on the water, stars, and everything the poets write about. Mr. Tubal and I have sat on deck drilling in French and English. One day out of Philadelphia it turned warm and remained so. The blueness of the water, than which there is nothing bluer; the rise and fall of the waves; the whitecaps; the spray of the waves breaking over the decks,—these are some of the things which compensate for the discomforts of a voyage. The food, too, is excellent and plentiful, with oranges and apples to help keep things down. I had never eaten oranges at home if I had to peel them—too much trouble. But on board ship one soon learns that an orange is the best thing in the world to keep the contents of your stomach from coming up into your throat. I have noticed that other passengers seem to benefit by drinking lots of tea and coffee.

It was almost dark when we made landfall at Cristobal, Canal Zone. The ship was to bunker during the night, so everyone had a chance to go ashore. It was the first tropical night for several of us and Mr. Tubal had never before seen palm trees. There were many clouds and only occasionally did we see the moon. Light-colored shirts and trousers were sufficient to get into any cafe bar or nightclub. A gentle tropical breeze fanned our cheeks and moved the leaves of the palms as we walked through Cristobal and across the tracks into the city of Colon in the Republic of Panama.

Colon was very Latin American. Bars and shops with their fronts open to the streets, covered sidewalks, blocks and blocks of two-story stucco, many-family dwellings. Almost all the people had dark complexions, but in varying degrees. It was practically impossible to find a color line. The sailors had told us that most of the inhabitants were "high yellow"—that is, a mixture.

Well, Mr. T. and I made the rounds. During our strolls we were frequently propositioned by women, white, dark, and in between. A panderer with a taxi gave us a rosy picture of breathless beauty only five blocks away. If we did not like them he would bring us back and there would be no charge. But Mr. T. and I did the less commonplace—we window-shopped and strolled through the residential district. The street-level apartments seemed to be only one or two small rooms. These were so packed with furniture and other household items that it looked almost impossible for the denizens to squeeze through. Table, chairs, wall hangings, lamps, grandmothers knitting in rockers, odds and ends, all enough to fill a room fifteen by twenty feet, were crowded into a little place eight feet square. Our tour was pretty much in the shadows because of the covered sidewalks and no street lights except at intersections.

Toward midnight Mr. Tubal felt indisposed and we returned to the *Ten Sleep*. I undressed and sat on the edge of the bed. It was 12:45. I was not sleepy. I thought: In the morning at six we will leave on a voyage of eight thousand miles. For twenty-four days we will not see land—nothing but water. Outside there are palm trees, a moon, a gentle breeze, and an unexplored countryside beyond a teeming city. Below is Jacqueline, impatient to be abroad. But it will look foolish, dragging a bicycle up on deck to go for a ride at 1 A.M. I'd better forget it. Out with the light! But let's just take another look outside. Ah, how gentle the night!

I pedaled up through the city and out along the boulevard toward the Pacific. The street lights kept me company for about two miles and disclosed the Panama Railroad and various warehouses and oil-storage plants. Then all these were left behind, the forest gradually closed in upon the highway, and I was alone with the silence and beauty of the jungle night. How many times we have read those words, "beauty of a jungle night." We think we know what is meant but we don't. We imagine, but our imaginings fall short. We cannot feel.

Beside the road there was a small river. Or was it a river? It did not run, neither was the water stagnant. It was deep and seemed always to stay by the road like a canal. On the opposite shore, and very frequently between the water and the road, were all manner of trees. And what a picture these made outlined against the face of the moon—the black lines of the empty branches crossing its pale yellowness. It was the moon, of course, that made the picture; and I repeatedly turned my face up to it like a cultist or a coyote without voice. And I exulted in loneliness.

I stopped finally and turned around. But the gentle breeze with just a touch of coolness, and the road stretching away in easy curves under the frequent moonlight—why, it was impossible to turn back. How could I have even thought about it?

Further on the jungle closed in, around, and over the road so completely it was like riding through a tunnel. Then indeed did I get the smell of the jungle, not something dank and stinking, but rather sweet and intriguing with suggestions of all the ferns and mosses and creeping vines that I could not make out in the shadows but knew were there—just there.

Then the jungle weakened and I passed into more open rolling country. Now the setting of the moon drew my attention. The great arch was mostly dark, yet the blue-black clouds made slow haste to leave the moon's face when they were so indiscreet as to get in the way of his light.

About 2 A.M. a patrol car, which I had really been expecting, drew alongside just as I had arrived in the vicinity of the famous Gatun Locks. The lone officer was very polite and after a short explanation on my part—during which he muttered something about my being better off out here than in the fleshpots of Colon—he offered to take me for a ride about the works. It was quite a tour. There was Silver City, where hundreds of colored canal workers lived; and Gold City, where the white supervisors and officers lived. Then the locks themselves with a walk underneath the great archways just at the base of the huge gates.

I returned to Colon about 4 A.M. Everything was still open. The junior third mate, who had been on watch until midnight, was just getting a good start with a gorgeous blonde that he had found in some cafe. Back on the ship I found most of the passengers and officers were still in town. But as for me, I was dog tired and went to bed.

3

Our Shipboard Comedy

We had a pleasant trip through the canal. The highlight for me was not the locks, as it was for most, but the quiet cruise through the narrow valley approaching the great Gaillard (formerly Culebra) Cut. We were very comfortably seated on easy chairs on the forward part of the main deck, but in the engine room the temperature was 130 degrees. From our chairs we watched the pleasant scenery, and, for diversion, the antics of a couple of soused sailors (no work while going through the canal) trying to catch beautiful black butterflies with their caps.

One of the most amazing things about the Panama Canal is the variation in its vital statistics. These statistics were given us in the most solemn and unequivocal manner, solicited or unsolicited. Thus we found that the Atlantic Ocean is higher than the Pacific Ocean by three feet, while the Pacific is higher than the Atlantic by forty-six feet. Most remarkable! Our authorities included the chief mate, the chief engineer, the second mate, the first assistant engineer, the second assistant engineer, etc. All authorities, you see—been through the canal many times. One said it wasn't big enough for the *Normandie* and the *Queen Mary*; another said it was. One said the boats are lifted up forty-three feet, another eighty-six feet, another ninety-three feet, another—well, you can see it is a most remarkable canal.

The next morning found us landless, out on the surface of the broad Pacific. A succession of seemingly endless days at sea had begun.

"All the world's a stage" and "What fools these mortals be," sayeth the immortal bard. And here aboard the S/S *Ten Sleep* there was a far better chance for observing human nature than in the most gossipy country town in America. Counting the officers, crew, one other passenger and myself, there were nearly fifty men on board. One woman on such a ship is like having a time bomb in the saloon. But we had *three* women! One was a divorcee, one a widow, and the third a married woman on her own. And a ship out for thirty-five days is very little different from the well-fabled desert island. Gossip, rivalry, scandal—the entire human comedy was supremely played as we sailed alone across the greatest wilderness of all—the sea.

The characters in this moving drama were diverse, even international. There was the purser, a polished, sandy-mustached Englishman who must have had the world's easiest job. He was required to take up the tickets at the beginning of the voyage and with five passengers, this took him five minutes. In the weeks following, his duties consisted in taking sunburn creams and aspirin from his cabinet when the gals had need of them. This left him plenty of time for mischief, or the pursuit thereof. He usually wore a short-sleeved shirt and white shorts, thus exposing an unathletic figure and a lot of skin which he vainly hoped would tan but which never did anything more than turn a pale red and peel.

The second mate was a rogue of the first water, or should I say the third water. The first mate was the handsomest man on the ship, but notwithstanding this, I figured he was a pretty straight shooter. He showed us pictures of a very attractive wife and a little son who was his spittin' image. So I was surprised one morning in the saloon when the third engineer asked: "Say, Don, weren't you the guy who said he was goin' to be true to his wife?"

Don laughed. "Well, I'm going to be good when we get to Brisbane, though. You wait and see!"

Actually only two of the ten officers ever admitted to having been married. Life at sea is not compatible. I remember a chief mate who had been on the sea for twenty-five years since his marriage but had been able to spend only a total of eighteen months with his wife.

The captain on the *Ten Sleep* had a wife who lived close to the dock in New York yet he always slept on board. At sea his door was always closed, and since he ate at the stroke of the galley bell, the passengers and other officers rarely talked to him. Yet he was obviously pleased when I requested a tour of the bridge for the passengers one day. He talked about his $3-million-dollar modern ship with pride and said his cargo was sometimes worth half that amount. This reminded him of a ship he had once commanded which carried $500,000 in gold ingots from the United States to India. It had been delivered aboard by an armored truck and fifteen armed guards. The guards didn't go ashore until the gangplank was being pulled up. When the ship arrived in India two cart drivers called for the gold and went off with it in a high-wheeled cart drawn by a bullock, with no guards at all.

In contrast to the captain, the chief engineer always had his door open. This was just outside the saloon, so he had callers and plenty of friends, particularly since he was always quick to fix drinks. But when we asked for a tour of the engine room, he turned us over to the first engineer. Maybe this was because the first had a voice like a foghorn and it could be heard above the noise of the machinery.

Then there was Halloran, the second engineer. Halloran was the ship's storyteller. There is a chief yarn-weaver on every ship and there ought to be an office or a title for it. He is like the bards of ancient time who handed down their lore by word of mouth. Their stories lived on after their names were forgotten. And the chief storyteller on a ship will be remembered long after the faces of the captain and chief engineer have slipped into oblivion. He may have much less education than any of the officers, yet he can have an audience any time he wishes; and he can hold its attention better than a Sabatini with a string of degrees.

Halloran was an Irishman with curly hair and an enormous bay window. He wore medium-weight heavy underwear with short sleeves and never wore a shirt except at table—the captain always required a necktie at table. Sometimes Halloran didn't wear the underwear and it was a bit disconcerting, especially to any women about, to see Halloran seated on a bottom rail with his great bare paunch hanging over the top of his belt almost in the lap of his nearest listener.

Among the passengers in our moving drama, Mr. Tubal and Mrs. Forne were the most interesting. Mr. Tubal had been in Russia and escaped from that country into Poland when he was a child. He recalled living behind closed shutters for many weeks during the Russo-Polish War of 1920, while fighting raged in the streets below. He peeked out one time and saw a soldier aiming a gun at his window. The bullet struck just above Mr. Tubal's head. A machine gun was operated from the roof for a time, and on one occasion a bomb was dropped in their courtyard. However, it fell in the snow and did not explode and was gingerly removed.

Later Mr. Tubal and his baby brother and mother effected their escape from Russia. They were taken by a smuggler in a covered sledge. The contraband was nails carried in a false bottom. When nearly to their destination across the line in Poland, they had to cross a river. The ice was too thin for the weight of the nails and the sledge sank through, dragging the horses after it. The driver pulled Mr. Tubal and his little brother up out of the water and rescued their mother, but their papers and money (the family had been quite wealthy) were all lost. They crawled back up the steep bank to the town they had just left, but the inhabitants were all scared to help them, and they had to stand for a long time freezing in the middle of the street.

Mr. Tubal was short in stature, round of face, and often wore a broad smile and a beam in his eye. He was a musician with concert experience and an artist with a thoroughly French background. Now in his early thirties, he was bringing his European culture to pioneer a completely new life in a far corner of the English-speaking world.

Mrs. Rupert Forne, thin in feature, thinner in body, and jittery by nature, was a central figure in our shipboard comedy. She could soak up liquor like a sponge and could talk more in one hour than any other woman in four hours. The purser took her ashore in Panama and reported: "She talked steady for five hours on every subject under the sun and drank vermouth, gin, and rye until the place positively reeked—and it never fazed her."

I believed him on both counts. I overheard her talking to Mr. Tubal on Beethoven, Wagner, Tschaikovsky, *Parsifal,* the *Valkyrie,* and so on until

I was convinced she knew more about music than the violinist himself. In the next breath she spoke of Huxley, Wilde, and a host of others, not just by name but by their works and the vein and interpretation of each. She had been to all the places in the world ever visited by steamboat tourists, knew all the lines, could name the eight railway stations in Paris, and so on. She spoke in short sentences, each a complete point in itself. A sentence once started allowed no hesitation before it was finished. And she often threw out such bon mots at unexpected times.

Now, while Mrs. Forne was quite weak in the department of sex appeal, such was not the case with the other two members of the feminine contingent. Mrs. Tyson, the widow in her early thirties, had a cute figure, was somewhat redheaded and was vivacious in the bargain. Her favorite observation was: "Oh, I'm full of beans today!" Her sister, Mrs. Moorcroft, a soft-spoken brunette, had a well-rounded figure and was ten years younger. Both were Aussies returning home after the termination of their marriages to American GI's.

Since Mrs. Forne lived in the Australian outback, I approached her early in our voyage for some information on the country.

"Oh, the big problem in Australia is cooking. You can't get any cooks to stay with you. Why, we've had twenty-eight cooks—*twenty-eight!* I've seen the time when we would take one cook to the train and meet the next one coming on. Of course, it's partly my husband's fault. They expect him in for dinner at twelve and he may get tied up with the stock and come in at three. I have to pitch in, of course—carry wood and all that. There are always so many to cook for: mechanics, breeders coming to look at the sheep, and so on. We have a ram stud and breed fine rams. But the cooking —that's all we ever talk about. When I get together with my neighbor— of course, she lives a long ways away—I never get to talk about clothes and such things. It's always how many cooks have left us and so on. And the Australian women don't know how to cook anyway. There are three hundred ways of cooking potatoes, but they only know of one way—to peel them and put them in with the meat. And the eggs—they cook them in butter and they come out all greasy and—ugh! But they resent any suggestions as to their cooking, so now I've given up and just say, 'Fine, yes, it's fine.'

"Of course, there's an awful dearth of women in the country. All the women go to the cities where they can have the luxuries. Consequently a lot of the men have to batch it and they live on pork in cans and have an awful time. And in the cities there are five women to every man."

"Yes," chimed in Mrs. Tyson. "That's why we have to go on board ship to get our men." (Haw-haws from the officers in the saloon.)

"Climate?" Mrs. Forne went on. "Well, it's either dust or mud. Right now we're having an awful drought. I don't know when we've had such a drought. Some say that it's a lack of trees, some that we should try contour farming. Much of the land is worn out. It takes two and one-half acres for a sheep and that means a lot of acres. Of course everything is subsidized in Australia and that's why our taxes are so heavy. My husband pays sixteen shillings out of every twenty he makes to the government. We can't raise chickens because we can't get wheat and they just die off. But about the drought and the dust: I've seen the time when we had to keep the doors and windows closed for three days, and at night breathe eau de cologne. In the daytime with everything closed all you could smell was tobacco, smoke, and beer. And then we have grasshoppers too—they even get into the house. Did you see *The Good Earth*—how the locusts came and ate up all the wheat? I've seen grasshoppers just like that.

"Ranch life is pretty rugged. And it takes a stocky type of woman; not like me. Why, a woman gets so busy she doesn't even have time to stop and pet a cat."

Hardly more than a week after sailing, it could be said that the players in our human comedy were well settled in their roles. The stage was principally the boat deck—because the captain had decreed that there were to be no women visitors in the men's rooms and vice versa. He need not have worried about the latter because all three women were in the same stateroom and no one of them would have vacated the premises to afford another a private place for entertainment. There was too much rivalry between them. Below the stage—back of the footlights if you will—sat the audience. It was not a large audience, only Mr. Tubal and myself. But we sat there on the cabin deck every evening practicing his English and my French. Of course, we faced forward, but whenever we turned to starboard and glanced upward, we perceived the purser attempting embarrassing indiscretions with Mrs. Forne. Should we have turned to port, there was the second mate having better success with the Widow Tyson. But for what strange unfathomable reason was the purser attempting to cultivate some physical attraction for himself in the heart of the slender Mrs. Forne?

One of the strangest things about all this was that the most attractive of the three women, and the youngest by quite a few years—the brunette divorcee Mrs. Moorcroft—was the only one without a permanent suitor. It was like the wolves were afraid of the lamb. But the lamb was obviously put out; and all the charm of a bare midriff, bright-red bathing suit, and a frequent dark-hair-over-shoulders appeal seemed to do nothing for her predicament. In fact, she was occasionally reduced to short associations with the crew, or even a turn on the deck with Mr. Tubal and myself.

Being immersed in my French, I did not really tumble to these situations until Mr. Tubal approached me one evening on deck.

"Woman is a very strange creature, Mr. Rosdail."

"Mais oui, Mr. Tubal."

"You have observed the teengs that go on here, then?"

"Why, ah, no. You mean the purser and the second mate?"

"Oh, no, more than that. Have you not seen the zhelowszee that exist between the women? You see, I observe many teengs. You will be discreet, no?" This with a glance over his shoulder to see who might be about.

"Yes, of course."

"Well, last evening there was—you know what means to be discreet, yes?"

"Yes, I know."

"Well, last evening there was some intimasie [Mr. T. pronounced many English words as he would in French] between the purser and Mrs. Forne. And now, the other two, they are zhelous."

"Oh, no!"

"Yes, really, it is so. I see these teengs."

After that I noticed a number of little incidents which led me to believe he was right in his observations. There were whispered conversations between the sisters at table when Mrs. Forne was mentioned, or porthole conversations between them. About two evenings later Mr. Tubal came on deck and drew his chair close to mine.

"This evening there is also something afoot with our ladies," he said with a broad smile. "You say 'afoot'?"

"Yes. Why?"

"Well, only just now I was by the stair which go up on top, where we are not allowed, and Mrs. Tyson and her sister were going up. I could see their feet and legs. I said, 'Allo.' And they both stopped still on the stairs. But they did not answer to me. So I go, just quick, down the other stairs."

"Well, now, look, Mr. Tubal," said I jovially, "why don't you get in there and pitch? as we say. We know Mrs. Moorcroft, at least, is lonesome. I am married and anyway, you know I am a romanticist, and to me they are just three women who have been married and are therefore not interesting. But you are in a different position."

"No, Mrs. Forne is the only one that interests me and she—it is only the mind, you see. She is so pale and so, so . . ." He groped for words.

"Yes. You mean, no sex appeal."

"And Mrs. Moorcroft. We do not . . ." He meshed his fingers together. "Her mind—it is like I say to her: 'This [touching a winch control box nearby] is black, or brown, or gray.' Then she say to me, 'No, it is soft.' You see?"

One afternoon the purser, Mrs. Forne, Mr. Tubal, and I were on the boat deck enjoying a calm sea and fine weather in the shade of the bridge deck above us. The purser's face, both above and below his sandy mustache, was recuperating from a bad case of sunburn. He was attired in shorts, Mrs. Forne in light blouse and skirt. Mrs. Moorcroft drifted in and out in her red bathing suit. Mrs. Tyson was topside in her blue suit. Mrs. Forne knew better than to wear a bathing suit, but she covered this up by frequent remarks as to how sunburn just exhausted her and would we just see how her ankles were swollen already. Besides, the sun grayed her hair, really it did, just see. And then we commenced to wonder if her hair really was that dark. But anyway, Mrs. Forne got back at the other two women by constantly having a man in tow, that is, the purser. They were never apart.

The purser and Mrs. Forne sat, as usual, very close together on one pillow, his arm around her shoulders or waist. Occasionally he gave her a meaningful squeeze, to which she always responded in the same manner that one of the ship's booms responded to the steel collar which held it in place. But she was very gifted in repartee and always had something to say. Occasionally the purser would say, "Isn't she the most talkative wench you have ever seen?" To which she would reply, "He knows I just loathe being called a wench!"

Being a bit uncertain as to how to address a married woman—going home to a sick husband, too—with another man's arms about her, I thought it best to say, "Miss Forne."

"Oh, no! Not that!" interrupted the purser. "G——, no. Not Miss—Mrs.! Mrs.!—Mrs. Rupert Forne."

This afternoon Mrs. Forne had volunteered to mix us drinks. I had visions of some lemonadelike concoction, or a Tom Collins. It turned out to be one half vermouth and one half gin, straight. I never got past the first swallow and Mr. Tubal made such a wry face trying to be polite and say that it was good that we all had a good laugh.

Mr. Tubal told us a couple of his European jokes, and I have to laugh yet when I think of them. Here are the jokes and you will see it was not the jokes that were funny.

"Once there was a crazy one—how you say, foolish? Well, one foolish was standing on this [he walked over to the steps leading up to the bridge deck]—what do you call it, *l'escalier?*"

"Stairs," I supplied.

"Yes. Well, he was standing like this [he stood on the third step and reached upward toward the ceiling to make the gesture of painting it] and making with a . . . a . . . pencil—"

"Brush," I corrected.

"Ah yes, brush. And so a second foolish come and say, 'Wait a minute. I'll pick up the stairs for you.' "

Mr. Tubal now stepped back off the stairs and with a broad grin on his round face cast a somewhat anxious eye toward his audience. There was no registry. "Oh, I tell it not right." He gestured despairingly with both hands, and sat down.

His good-natured discomfort and the naiveté of the joke was too much for me. I howled in glee.

"See," said Mrs. Forne, "he gets it. It's all right. You know he's the smartest one of us. Tell another one."

Thus encouraged, after a little while, Mr. Tubal tried again.

"There was one foolish who was trying to drive a . . . a . . ."

"Nail," supplied the purser.

"Yes. And making with a . . . a . . . hammer, so." Mr. T. got up and went through a wild, hammer-swinging pantomime toward an imaginary wall. "But it wouldn't go in, you see. So the other foolish says, 'Here, try this wall over here.' "

All in all it was a most successful afternoon.

The next day was May 10 according to the "Officers' Daily Observations" posted on the bulletin board. This edifying little slip of paper also stated that we were only 5,000 miles from Brisbane, having come 2,800 miles from the Panama Canal. "Egad," I thought. "Think of it! Five thousand miles to go *yet*. I've already been on this boat three weeks and have two more weeks ahead."

Day after day we plowed on. But we might as well have been like Coleridge's mariner:

> Day after day, we stuck
> Nor breath nor motion
> As idle as a painted ship
> Upon a painted ocean

because there was utterly no visual consciousness that we were getting anywhere. The great majority of our people, who never take a long sea voyage, have no idea of the enormity of our aqueous sphere. Just then I was quite sure you could tumble the whole of the United States into the Pacific Ocean and it would make only a good-sized splash. But one thing! After a long voyage like this you can really appreciate land when you get to it. The air traveler who comes in just a few hours can never have such appreciation.

One night the officers and passengers decided to go on a binge and they all got a little percolated from the captain on down. The captain, it seems, had quite a time finding the third mate on watch, although the third claimed he had been on the bridge all the time. The captain got mixed up in fresh paint and some wire. I received comments on his condition from four different quarters, both passengers and crew. Mrs. Tyson had wanderitis. Mrs. Forne and the purser matched drinks all evening, but the purser couldn't make it to breakfast the following morning. Mrs. F. came down as chipper and fresh as a daisy.

Mr. Tubal had a little misadventure about three o'clock one morning. His bathroom was across the passageway, and with his eyes half closed with sleep he stepped out to visit it. The ship, of course, rolled and slammed his door behind him, locking him out. This was not so unusual, but Mr. Tubal sleeps *à la Freud,* that is to say, in the nude. In this sad predicament he lurked about the deserted passageway for more than an

It was 35 days from New York to Australia.

The mess boy looks at the world's greatest desert from a deck chipped free of rust.

hour. At long last a sailor hove into view and Mr. Tubal beckoned from behind a corner. The sailor reported to the officer in charge that there was a naked man running loose about the ship. Even then it was more than a half hour before they could locate a key.

There came a day when Mrs. Forne gave up her dignity and donned a bathing suit. The crew had rigged an attachment on one of the fire hoses, hung it on a boom on the after deck, and pumped aboard great quantities of sea water, which was surprisingly warm. There were all kinds of monkey-shines with everyone throwing cups or pails of water on everyone else, whether they wore swim suits or not. Mrs. Forne remained on the side lines for a long time but when the purser joined the fun, it was too much for her to see him out there with her two rivals. She got into a stick-candy, two-piece bathing costume from about 1890 and to the amazement of all, went under the hose. She soon looked like a drowned rat of indeterminate sex. Her act must have been a tremendous effort, considering that she worried constantly about any minutiae that might affect her appearance and well-being. Even a slight breeze would cause her to hang onto her dress and hair with such concern it was actually painful to watch.

Of course anyone out of the ordinary, whether superior or queer, always invites the practicing joker. The junior third and Sparks (the radio oper-ator) had only to pretend they had some sort of electric-shock apparatus in their hands when walking about the saloon, and Mrs. Forne was in near hysteria in no time. If there was a cloud in the sky the third mate would come around in a life jacket, whereupon one or more of the officers or passengers would comment about the time the storm was expected to hit. Mrs. Forne would get into a dither and eventually remark, "Oh, I must go and brush my teeth before it comes." If we didn't know her better we would think she surely must be joking. But a member of the crew would then be sent around to close her porthole against the "impending storm." And so it went.

By mid-Pacific we did work out of the good weather and had squalls, cooler temperatures, and high winds. Several different kinds of birds were seen, including the giant albatross with its tremendous brown wings and white underbody. One morning two white gulls crashed into the ship and knocked themselves breathless. Mrs. Tyson babied one in the saloon for a while. It had been carrying a small squid in its mouth and had just swallowed a small fish. Both were left on the deck.

During the last half of the voyage things were pretty well routinized. I walked four times around the ship after breakfast, before and after dinner, and before supper—a total of about three miles per day. In between times I studied French or played pinochle whenever there was a game possible. The third engineer, Sparks, and Halloran provided the threesome or the foursome. Sometimes we just sat and listened to Halloran.

Halloran could spin tales from his experiences on land as well as on the sea. He had been in the salmon-fishing business in Alaska and had misadjusted the weights on the owner's instructions in many a deal. He knew all about fishing laws, nets, and Indians' fishing rights. In World War II he had been in the jack-rabbit business in our Northwest. With two partners he had caught rabbits during the meat shortages, skinned them, and sold canned rabbit. He owned a cattle ranch in Washington and told of deer eating hay with his cattle in the wintertime, and of other experiences.

"But the biggest circus in the world is to pin down a rattler. You cut a forked stick or else split the end of one and lash it onto a stick about ten feet long. Then pin him to the ground just back of the head. He'll turn and twist and throw himself and kick up the ground until it smokes. But finally he'll give up and just lie there."

After I had told a wilderness story involving a mountain lion, Halloran had a turn.

"Well, I tell you, I was goin' through the woods one day when I saw one of these here cougars sleeping on a fallen tree. The tree had stuck on another one so that it was about six feet off the ground. Well, he was sure sound asleep and I had 'im all picked out for a rug I was going to make out of 'im. I took aim, you know, right for his eye. And I was a long time at it—I didn't want to put a hole in the hide. Well sir, I missed but I hit the log just in front of him so that it kicked up a lot of bark, wood, and stuff right into his face. Well, I never saw anything so funny in my life. He was so scared he jumped straight up into the air. And when he hit the ground his feet were already a-goin'."

"Like a bat out of hell, eh?" I interrupted.

"Boy, you can say that ag'in. It was so comical and I was a-laughin' so much I never even thought to fire another shot at him."

Halloran also recounted his escape from King's Hospital in Hawaii during the war.

"They couldn't find out what was the matter with me. I was so damned dizzy all the time. The doctors looked at me and they took X-rays. Finally they came around and told me they were going to have to operate and take out one of my kidneys. Boy, that scared me. I lost a week's growth right there. I didn't say anything but just laid there looking up at them. But I thought to myself, 'Boy, I'm gettin' out of here!'

"But they had my clothes locked up in one place and my sailor papers and money locked up in another. Well, I figured I'd better get the sailor papers and the money first. So I got up like I was goin' to the toilet or sumpin', but I was so darn dizzy I could hardly walk. Well, I was staggerin' around out in the hall and one of them nurses asked me what I was up to. I told her I wanted my sailor papers. Well, what for? Oh, I told her I just wanted to look at 'em for sumpin'. So she got 'em for me and my money was in there too.

"Well, I knew 'twarn't no use askin' for my clothes, so a little later I managed to stagger down to the corridor on the first floor near where people go in and out. I sat there on the bench and saw where the phones were. So I watched my chance and made a phone call for a taxi. There was an old gal at the desk and she was kinda eyein' me, and there were a couple other nurses around her and I could see 'em kinda talkin' and eyein' me and wonderin' what the hell I was up to. I knew the old gal had seen me makin' that phone call, but of course I was still in that there nightshirt arrangement they make you wear and—"

"Didn't you have any shoes on or anything?" someone asked.

"Not a damned thing. I was barefooted and that damned shirt only comes—well, it only reaches halfway to your knees. Well, I kept a-settin' there and I was so damned dizzy I didn't know how I was goin' to walk out to the taxi if it did come. The nurses finally got suspicious and one of 'em came over and asked me what ward I was from. So I mumbled somethin' about down the hall and she said I'd have to go back now, that I couldn't sit out there; and she started takin' me by the arm. But I was watchin' for that taxi and out of the corner of my eye I saw it a-comin'. So just as it pulled up front I broke out the door and across the little kinda court they had and staggered out to the taxi and got in and told the driver to get the hell out of there, and fast."

"Well, what did the driver think with you in your nightshirt?" I interjected.

"Oh, he—flabbergasted, I guess. But I was so damned weak I was blind anyway. I was so sick by that time that he actually had to lead me when we went to buy a pair of shoes."

"Well, but you didn't go into a shoe store in your nightshirt?"

"No. I'd give him money and he'd gotten me a pair of pants and a shirt, but he'd had to dress me. I was too weak.

"Well, then I had this guy take me to a doctor. The first one wouldn't touch me as soon as the guy told him where I'd been, but then I got to a Dr. Birch. Meanwhile the hospital had called the police, and the civil police and the military police and everybody else was a-lookin' for me. And by George! they just caught up with me at this Dr. Birch's. But of course it was too late then because I was under a physician's care and I'd already told him I wouldn't go back to that hospital.

"Well, Dr. Birch was a pretty square guy. But he couldn't find anything wrong with me. Yet I was still so g——damned dizzy I couldn't even see. So he wanted to know if they took any X-rays of me at the hospital. I said yes, they'd took every kind of picher possible—inside and outside. But the hospital wouldn't let him have the X-rays. So he had to go before a judge and get a writ to get them there pichers. Meanwhile he took me to a hotel and got me in a room."

Here Halloran paused to go into the officers' galley to get another cup of coffee.

"Well, that g——damned hospital kept them there X-rays just as long as they dared—seventy-two hours. When Dr. Birch got 'em he came up to me and—"

"How did you eat all this time at the hotel if you couldn't go out?"

"Oh, they sent stuff up to my room. I didn't have much appetite anyway. Well, this Dr. Birch says to me that these pictures showed that from the middle of my back right down and around up to the middle of my belly, I was just plain rotten. 'Is it that bad?' I says to him. Then he started askin' me a lot more questions and he was particularly interested in what kind of probes had been used on me in the past. Then he got the idea it was prostate trouble and when he put a finger on that gland, I'm tellin' you I never had such pain. It went through me right to the roots of my hair and I thought it was goin' to lift my scalp right off.

"Well then he knew what to do. He put me in a bathtub and said I was to live there in just as hot water as I could stand for just as long as it took to get that corruption to a head. Well sir, he kept that water so damned hot I was like a broiled lobster. And he called on me two or three times a day and if I wasn't sittin' in that damned bath when he popped in, I got holy hell. Well, after nearly a week of this, that damned thing broke and you never saw such puky filth and corruption in your life. And when it happened I—well, I was practically well right away. And those damned doctors at King's Hospital had been goin' to take out my kidneys."

Meanwhile our desert island, the S/S *Ten Sleep*, moved on into its fifth week. Thrown constantly into each other's company, we five passengers and the officers inevitably became too familiar. And whether familiarity breeds contempt or not, man's morality seems to descend in such conditions. The books that were read and the records that were played, echoing naughtily through the saloon, were only a few steps above what was then known as the gutter. And the men lost all restraint and told dirty jokes in feminine company. But one should not entirely blame the men. The women were so anxious to be good sports that they laughed encouragingly and often threw in a few innuendoes even the men had missed. There were even digs at the female figures present. One afternoon Mrs. Forne suddenly said to the purser and myself: "This is an awful ship! I don't know what any decent woman would do on this ship, really. Why, she'd shut herself in her room."

Thirty-five days after I had boarded the ship in New York, and on a Saturday morning, I lay awake in my bunk in expectation. This was the day when the long ride was to be over and there was to be land. Suddenly the engines stopped the high-pitched hum they had maintained twenty-one days and 7,800 miles from Panama. I piled into my clothes and was on deck in a jiffy. Ah—how beautiful! Australia at last! Our destination. There is no thrill on earth quite like the thrill of landfall after a long sea journey—whether it is home soil or foreign soil.

Our first view of Australia was in early morning sunshine and showed the odd-shaped peaks of the coastal regions to good advantage. The pilot soon came aboard and we started the trip to the north in order to enter the mouth of the Brisbane River. Ere long Mr. Tubal showed up on deck, actually jumping up and down in glee at the sight of the land which was to be his home for the future. It was about fifty miles before we got into the river and far enough so we could see our dock, and everyone was so land-hungry that no one stayed at table any longer than was necessary to gulp food. Going up the river, we met a boatload of excursionists and I was reminded with a pang of memory of the excursion boats I had seen on the Weser as we approached Bremen, Germany, on my first foreign trip nearly thirteen years before.

As we approached the wharf, an interesting and very appropriate bit of spice gave a finishing touch to the voyage. As you remember Mrs. Forne had told us she was returning to a sick husband at her home west of Sydney; but she had nevertheless become very intimate with the purser. The purser had told us her husband had taken up with another woman and wanted a divorce, and that was why Mrs. Forne was returning. At any rate the intimacies between her and the purser had become so commonplace as to descend to the table where the billing and cooing was a regular post-breakfast or postprandial affair. It was mostly on the part of the purser and at first Mrs. Forne had tried to escape by such devices as eating her dessert or salad while standing up in the middle of the room while the purser occupied the place he had just scootched her out of. But the last days of the voyage she had tolerated his advances, and even remarked when some gossip came up about the other two women being overly friendly with everyone: "Well, at least I have stuck to one man."

Anyway it happened that Mrs. Forne and the purser were in each other's arms on the boat deck, the purser's back to shore. Coming out of a long kiss, Mrs. Forne happened to glance over his shoulder to the dock toward which we were easing only a few feet away.

"Oh, my G——, there's Rupert!"

And sure enough there was her husband standing suavely on the edge of the dock and looking at the whole procedure. She had not told him that she was landing at Brisbane before going on to Sydney, nor had she even told him the name or the date of the ship on which she was returning. But there he was!

4

In Which We Fossick
the Great Reef
and I Capture a Shark

It was afternoon by the time I cleared the Australian customs and pedaled uptown. First impressions of Brisbane, capital of Queensland, were its peacefulness, its somewhat tropical beauty, its hilliness, and the street-side piles supporting houses whose porches were enclosed by latticework or bamboo curtains. Poinsettias and sunflowers were in bloom (it was May), and the tiny front yards of most homes were enlivened by the reds of the former. Picket fences or stone walls seemed to keep the yards from falling onto the sidewalk. In the streets there were streetcars (trams) running on narrow-gauge tracks, and the middle seats were open to the air. Half of the autos were of the small English variety—just room enough for two people and a little luggage behind them. Of course, all cars traveled on the left.

For two days I developed my cycling legs on the hills of Brisbane and Mount Cootha, the vantage point for overlooking the city. Then the following morning I got up at 5:30 and took my leave of the ship. The junior third, the second engineer, and Mr. Tubal, who happened to be up for something, made up my farewell party. The former boxed my breakfast and gave me a few supplies from the ship's larder.

Packed up and off! I was at the edge of the city before it got light. The open road at last! Hooray!

After lunch a big enclosed truck overtook me and offered me a ride. We rode up hill and down dale. Then we rode up mountain and down mountain. The roads became atrocious—narrow, rocky, rough. As the afternoon wore on and we didn't stop, the situation began to strike me as funny. Here I was covering all this ground—all these tremendous hours of work for a bicycle—and the ride was still continuing. What luck! Next to me in the truck were two dogs in a high board pen, a gas drum, an embroidered screen, and a small trunk. At one gas stop, one of the three men in the cab casually told me the trunk on which I was sitting contained a body. I never did find out what kind of body, but it developed that evening that the men were in the sideshow business and followed the carnivals. The older dog, a female, was a freak with two rear ends and a fifth leg. She was their main attraction.

It was nearly dark when we at last arrived in Gympie and camped in the fairgrounds. My night spent in the company of these men was an experience. I had never in my life heard such filthy language. Only one word out of three would be printable, and the terms were indiscriminately applied to man, beast, and object. Yet there was never one instance of sacrilegious speech, and when we were all turned in for the night, one of the men said: "Good night. God bless ye, lads."

Early the next morning I left Gympie and pedaled on northward. Much of the road was washboardy and very rocky. The country was not quite so rugged, but there were still plenty of hills. Nevertheless, I enjoyed myself. It was a new country. The trees were different, the animals were different. Tall, bare-trunked gum trees peopled the landscape. Forests were not dense, and it was usually possible to see out across the hills. Occasionally low coastal ranges had to be crossed. The birds made such unearthly sounds! More than once I turned my head at the sound of a pack of dogs yelping down the road behind me, only to find that the road was quite empty. I finally located the sound in the trees, coming from the kookaburra, the national bird. What a shock that was!! Magpies were plentiful, and their caws had some resemblance to those of our crows but frequently sounded like gurgles.

Houses were practically nonexistent, so I rode for hours through the solitudes of the forest. As always, the most enjoyable thing about the journey was the smell of early morning. This is such a delicate combination of aromas and nostalgia for aromas of early mornings in other lands that their impression upon me is truly bittersweet. One cannot describe these things—they are too intangible.

The small Australian town was quite different from its counterpart in America. The business houses and grocery stores were scattered blocks apart in different sections of town instead of being all bunched together on one main street. The houses too were scattered all over the township instead of being as close to the main street as possible. I sometimes sat on a curb to watch the inhabitants, my feet spread out in the dirt of the unpaved street. About two out of every eight men were barefooted, and the rest looked as though they'd like to be. The village girls were not unattractive. Bicycles were in common use, and small children sat on pillows tied on luggage carriers behind their mothers. The German *hausfrau* carries hers the same way, as I recall.

I passed through sugar-cane country and into a heavy forest. While toiling up a hill I met a man on horseback. He was a government conservationist whose duty it was to mark certain trees with a number and place his brand above it, if he felt they were suitable for cutting. His was rather a lonely job, but he seemed to think mine was far lonelier.

"I think I'd like a mite [mate]," he said several times.

He had scarcely left me, when one of these pint-size English cars pulled up and the young couple inside asked me if this was the road to Gin Gin. I told them it was and we chatted a bit.

"Say, aren't you the man we read about in the paper who's touring Australia on a push bike?" said the missus.

I admitted such was the case.

"And you're leaving a wife and five children in America?" put in the husband. "My aunt was telling me about it."

So I suppose the number of my children doubles for every hundred miles of distance from Brisbane.

I spent the night with a sugar-cane farmer, whose wife made the most delicious rozella jam. The next night I was on a lonely ranch near a river crossing. The following night I camped alone in the bush—the first of many lonely camps. A quiet little creek, soft sand for a bed, a lovely moon, boiled potatoes, cooked rice, beef, bread, and jam. What more could a feller want?

At a little seaport called Gladstone I had a real stroke of luck. One of the wonders of the world, the Great Barrier Reef, is to be found off the northeast coast of the continent. There seemed to be no regular service out to the reef, and even if such had been available, my finances were very limited. Yet as I was loitering wistfully about the docks, what should come in but a fifty-foot pleasure craft up from Sydney called the *Zane Grey*. I volunteered to help her dock—there was no one else around—and found out she was to take a group of Sydney men and their wives out to the reef that very afternoon. The cruise operator was quite willing to take me along as a sort of supernumerary, and not only that, but he would be returning to Gladstone for supplies in one week and I could come back with him. Boy, was I lucky!

About 1:30 P.M. I helped load the Sydney people. They had luggage enough to start a colony. Both plump dowagers and bay-windowed seniors were in shorts. The party included a gynecologist, an ophthalmic surgeon, a natural-history and press photographer, a marine biologist, a chemist with all manner of deep-sea fishing gear, a hotel owner, a pharmacist, the owner of the biggest carrying (trucking) business in Sydney, a rice grower, a confectioner, a cinema owner, and a few unattached secretaries and clerks. I could learn all about Australia without traveling farther.

All aboard! We passed smoothly out of the harbor and were soon on the breast of the broad Pacific, or, more specifically, the South Coral Sea. The boat did not pitch much and no one was seasick. The afternoon wore on. We were bound for Northwest Island, and there was quite a bit of talk as to whether we would find it or not. It seemed that the skipper had the not at all reassuring nickname of Sandbank Hodges and as I watched him scanning the horizon, obviously worried, I thought maybe the nickname was deserved. Anyway, we were all relieved when we sighted the island about 7 P.M.

The excitement and thrill of landing made us forget that it was past dinnertime. Never will I forget that sight. There was a brilliant moon, and it showed the coral plainly through ten feet of clear green water. (We came in at high tide.) It was necessary to row ashore in two small boats, one of which they called the dingy and the other a flattie. I was really at the height of happiness. Just imagine landing in a small boat by moonlight on a South Pacific desert island and over sea-green coral up to a long white beach of coral sand!

Many trips were necessary to get everyone, plus all that luggage, ashore. It was about a quarter-mile row each way, and I did the rowing some of the time. Tents were erected just beyond the beach and open-air cooking arrangements made for the chef and his assistants.

After a good supper I took my sleeping bag down the beach a ways and was soon asleep, with the waves almost at my feet across the white sand. Talk about your paradise. Brother! The little tree over my head did not shut out the brightness of the moon, which was waxing and only two days short of the maximum.

Subsequent days on the Great Barrier Reef can be described with only one word: fascinating. When the tide was out most of the reef, it seemed, was completely uncovered and there was no need for glass-bottomed boats. Wearing tennis shoes to protect our feet from the sharp coral, we hiked at will and went fossicking, as they called it. The beauties of the coral and the wonders of the marine life have been featured several times by *National Geographic* magazine. I found the deeper pools on the very edge of the reef to be clear and green and similar to Emerald and Turquoise pools in the Yellowstone, it being possible to see to great depths. When one of these pools contained a large mushroom of coral formations in the center, it was a beautiful sight indeed. And there were small cascades of water where the water ran off the edges of the formations into the ocean, perhaps a foot or two lower.

As might be expected, the marine life was more interesting than the coral. Green and blue fish darted about, and it was possible to catch them by hand or spear in the shallow pools or near the formations of coral. We overturned the coral groups sometimes to explore their undersides or to chase fish. To merely say that these fish were green or blue is inadequate. They were multicolored, and I can only refer you to the tropical-fish department of your nearest aquarium. The little boxfish interested me the most. Their bodies are almost completely encased in hard cartilage, but they could dart around anyway. I caught two, as well as a cod, and when I also found the first bala, the whole camp was convinced I was the head fish-catcher supreme. The bala had just finished digesting the inside of a clam, and still had within the compass of its body a huge shell. How wonderful, yet how relentless is nature! We had to toil with a heavy knife before we could open one of these large clams, yet the bala had done it without a knife. The bala is like a huge snail eighteen inches long over its back and perhaps a foot wide. The shell is salmon-colored inside and the flesh adjacent to it resembles the skin of a tiger for about an inch of width. The strip of inch-wide flesh is very beautiful. The women of the party were particularly thrilled with the balas, which are rare and much desired for use as lamp shades. We also saw a carpet shark, a mottled, brightly colored thing, and several eels, one of which was poisonous.

On the sand beach we found remnants of a turtle-soup factory the Japanese had built in the twenties. In fact, we found some very young turtles, recently hatched, about two inches across the back. I was told these would grow into giants four or five feet in length.

As we took our daily excursions I learned to like my Aussie companions. I was struck with the childish enthusiasm of some of them. I had been raised far from the sea, and the reef was a radically new experience for me. But the Sydneyites had visited islands before, some for long periods, and some had been on the reef before. Yet their enthusiasm far outdid mine. One chap put wet, slimy specimens of marine life into his pockets and even into his hat. He would hold them against his shirt, not caring if they wet it through. The owner of a large business establishment darted about like a boy and at the close of the first day remarked several times too all and sundry: "I say, we had a real full afternoon. It was quite all right!"

I never saw any suggestion turned down, or any modification proposed, no matter how scatterbrained or unapropos it was. If someone wanted to stumble about the turtle holes amongst the trees in the middle of the night, with two-inch red and yellow spiders suspended from every other tree, in order to dig up some soil samples—why, all right! Let's go!

The highlight of my trip to the Great Barrier Reef was my battle with the shark. I was wading ashore alone one evening at low tide and spotted a tan-colored shark about four feet long lying in about a foot of water fifty feet from shore. I didn't have any spear so I marked the spot on shore, hurried down to camp and got Bert's spear. I went back alone and found my markings.

Wading quietly out, I spotted the shark still lying in the same place. I was scared but determined. I crept up on his flank, grasped the spear firmly in both hands, took careful aim with the point not a foot from his back and let him have it. Wham-o! Things began to happen! He went around and around and turned himself over and over. In less than a minute he had torn the metal spear out of its wooden shaft and swam off with it. I took a general note of his direction and groped in the water for the spear, not realizing he had swum off with it in his back. When I couldn't find it, I hunted around for the shark. He was swimming around not far away carrying the spear.

Then commenced such a game of tag as I'd never had before. Back and forth, up and down. When I got near enough, I would take a crack at him with my spear shaft, but the water was too deep for him to feel it. Usually it would just confuse him and he would go in another direction. Sometimes he would come straight for my bare legs, and since there was then a swirl of coral sand about those valuable members, I couldn't be sure what was going to happen. All I could think of was how terribly sharp a shark's teeth were and what horrible things they could do to a man. He swam between my legs or right by them at least three times.

I was about petered out and actually gasping for breath from running in a foot of water, when Mr. Shark decided to slide under a big rock. I immediately ran up, put my spear shaft underneath and pried. He didn't move, so I thought I had him, although all I could see of him was about eighteen inches of tail. Then I took counsel. I didn't have nerve enough to grasp the tail yet. I seemed to recall that fish could inflict nasty cuts with their tails. Finally I took hold and gingerly felt the edges. It didn't seem to be bad. But there was the matter of his teeth. What to do? There was no one in sight, and camp was too far away to yell. I had no spear. Well, I couldn't stand there all night holding a shark's tail, that was certain. So I eased my stick out. He didn't move. H-m-m-m. Maybe I could puncture him with the stick. No luck; he was too tough. Then all of a sudden out he came. Zowie! Too scared to think, I ran for the beach but kept hold of his tail. He twisted and turned, and I slashed at him with my stick but never hit him once. He would twist and turn over so as to bring his mouth, which was working back and forth, up to within about four inches of my elbow. Oy! I never knew when he was going to succeed. I dragged him to the beach at last. I hammered at him but could only occasionally hit his underjaw, which of course didn't bother him at all. Finally I broke my shaft and then had to use the longest piece.

Eventually it was over and I was the winner. But I was so exhausted I could hardly stand. I gasped weakly for breath and my head ached. I was soaked to the waist. When I had recovered a little, I noticed in his back he had bent the iron spear into a big U in our first encounter. I carried him to camp, and that was a big job. One of the men helped me string him up just back of the tree under whose branches we ate our meals. So at supper that night I was quite the hero and was occasionally asked to recount the battle.

My farewell from Northwest Island was more touching than I had ever dreamed. Everyone came down to the beach to see me off. Although I had already entered the dingy, the girls made me come back and I was properly kissed as a Yank should be. It's too bad there was no picture, but the picture taker was one of the kissers. Then, as the little boat bore me away, everyone sang "Farewell" and "I Sailed Away from Treasure Island."

The sea was very, very rough on the return to the mainland and the little *Zane Grey* wallowed heavily. Still I managed to keep from getting really seasick. We fished from the rear of the boat, and I caught a tuna weighing about thirty pounds.

5

We Break an Axle and Ride Herd in the Great Outback

Pedaling northward along the Queensland coast, I reached Rockhampton. It was Sunday, and eight young people of the Salvation Army were holding a street service. I was glad of the chance to chat with one of them, for Sundays, even for a traveler, can be lonesome. Later I went to the Methodist church, seating myself discreetly in the back anteroom, as I had no Sunday clothes. Nevertheless, the pastor and several of the congregation hailed me after the service for friendly chats.

One of the strangest things I had noticed in Australia was the false-teeth situation. Not since England and Scotland had I seen anything like it. Young men, clerks, businessmen, post-office employees, all had false teeth. What on earth did these people lack in their diet? Eighty percent of all the people on the Barrier Reef cruise had false teeth, and a number were no older than myself. It was beyond me. Fine, healthy-looking lads of twenty to twenty-five did I see, but they had false teeth.

Travel can certainly be a great teacher if you are slogging along on a bicycle. For example, within a few days I was offered rides by a boiler inspector, a pharmaceutical salesman, and an ambulance driver. With the first I visited a coal mine, from the second I learned what the Aussies thought of the Yanks, and the third told me all about socialized medicine. The miners, who seemed to be all Scotsmen, had just killed a big snake and were debating its variety. They told me there were sixty-four kinds of snakes in Australia and forty-three were poisonous. The tiger snake and the black snake were supposed to be two who would lie in wait for a man. The deceased, it was decided, was a black snake and poisonous.

In the Goagingo Mountains I was surprised to find pear cactus growing as trees of medium height. I was told that a variety similar to our American cactus had once been imported with the idea of providing dry-country feed for stock. It overran the country, so they imported one of its natural enemies, an insect called the cochinella. (Perhaps this was the scale insect *Coccus cacti*, whose body provides the dye cochineal.) This failed to keep the cactus in check, so they brought in *Cactoblastus cacquorem*, which really did the business. With a name like that the cactus was probably scared to death. Anyway, my informant said there was even a monument to it somewhere in Australia.

As I proceeded westward the country became drier. Half of the trees were dead and much of the soil was red and dusty. The track I was following usually had dead grass in the middle. I crossed the Drummond Mountains, the principal dividing range in Queensland.

Jacqueline had been equipped with a two-speed shift and a New Departure coaster brake. I had been warned that too much tightening of the rear-axle bolts would pull the axle in two. I had avoided this, I thought, but the rear wheel tightened up and I panicked into a railway-station area and got a couple of young fellows to work on it. We freed it up, but when I tested it, the pedals locked tight. In freeing them one of the chaps used a little force and something cracked in the rear hub. That was the end. I had to hitch a ride in a ballast train of empty dump cars for the twenty-two miles to the nearest town, Alpha.

It developed that the mechanics in little Alpha were "five-eighths mechanics," that is, self-taught mechanics without too much experience. I went to see one and regretted it the minute I walked through the door. You never saw such a mess of a shop in your life. There were tools of every kind, parts of autos and bikes, oil tins, boxes, tires, bolts, nuts, strewn all over the floor. It was almost impossible to walk. Such a chap, I thought, must be shiftless and a poor workman. But although Jacqueline's operation was very vital to me, I tried to smile and treat him as though he were the best mechanic in the world. Well, we only got the bike torn down by closing time, and I left with visions of Jacqueline's parts lost among the thousands of objects on the floor by morning.

It was cold in Alpha. The inhabitants shivered in the evenings and shivered in the mornings. Therefore they stayed in bed until the sun was high enough to give warmth. Like all other crazy Australians they practically camp out, sleeping on open porches; or, if they have a room they might close, they sleep with the windows wide open anyway. They don their pajamas in the evenings, put a topcoat over them, and sit and shiver. Just before bedtime they brew themselves a British measuring cup full of cocoa or other hot drink in a desperate effort to get warm. But close a window or a door—never! Horrible thought! Man was meant to shiver! Let the night breezes blow!

The young mechanic and I worked all the next morning. We had to heat a part to get it off the axle and then he welded the axle. He rode the bike around the block—my hopes had risen with the sun—and returned with the axle broken again. My hopes vanished in one short second. But he absolutely refused to take a cent of pay for nearly a day's labor.

Alpha lacked steel for a new axle, and I had to hitch a ride with a salesman to Longreach, where the Qantas airline shops were located. There I met employee Kevin Barr, who, two minutes later, invited me to supper by the simple expedient of announcing to his wife as she passed by, "Tea for three tonight."

Thus commenced a friendship with Kevin Barr and his pretty wife,

Dulcie. Kev was small in stature but big of heart and spoke with a voice full of tone and feeling. They had a strikingly marked tiger cat of which they were quite fond, and a pretty bird in a cage. Almost every family had these grass parakeets or "love birds." Some are wild but live all right in captivity. Some folks also had canaries.

Kev played the drums in a five-piece band much in demand for dances. As in our own West, distances to be covered were great. He might leave at 5 P.M. for a town eighty miles away, where supper would be served to them. They would play until ten and stop for tea. At midnight there would be soup, and tea again at 2 A.M., and then breakfast just before they left for home. "Tea" as used in this sequence is just tea and biscuits or cake, not the full meal.

When dishes were done, Kev, Dulcie, and I drove out to look over the town. The highlight of our tour was the borehead, a sort of small dome on the hillside a short distance out of town. Here a huge pipe brought hot artesian water out of the ground. The pipe was too hot to hold my hand on it. Later in Kevin's home I used some of this water for washing clothes. It is excellent for this. No need to heat water for a bath in Longreach. In fact, you might have to let it cool. All this would not be so amazing in an area like Yellowstone or Iceland, but here in western Queensland there is no other sign of thermal activity. One bore served the entire population of Longreach (3,147). Eighty miles away in Barcaldine there was a bore, but the water was not hot and it was drinkable. Longreach used rainwater or river water for purposes other than washing or bathing.

The Barrs fixed a bed for me on their veranda. Like true Australians, they complained how cold it was but slept with every door and window in the house wide open. This included the double doors to their bedroom and the double doors to the parlor. A cold wind swept through the house all night.

The machinist turned out a new axle for Jacqueline the next forenoon, and I was soon ready for the road. But Kev insisted I stay for dinner first. In Australia they don't seem to eat family style, and everything is put on your plate by the hostess in the kitchen. There was corned beef with a white onion sauce, pumpkin (our squash), mashed potatoes, beans, and peas. The Aussie pumpkin is cooked as we cook our Hubbard squash and seems to be a favorite. I can understand this because it tastes twice as good. Our dessert was baked custard with grated pineapple and passion fruit. Aussie meals are tops with me because of the generous quantity of the desserts, which are served up in soup plates, believe it or not. I asked Dulcie for a favorite recipe to take home and she gave me one for treacle pudding. Treacle is dark cane syrup.

I was pedaling steadily out into the wide-open spaces of western Queensland when a little Hillman pickup stopped alongside. Percy **Strand** told me later the reason he stopped was the small size of my canteen. He claimed it was 120 miles to the next town and absolutely no water and I guess he was right, although I did see two windmills far, far off the road as we rode along. Mr. Strand, a wool classifier, was a methodical man who, like many Aussies, worried about his car. Every hour just as regular as clockwork he would stop, lift the hood, put in a cup or two of water, check the oil, check the tires and guzzle a glass or two of beer. Every third stop he took a glass of rum. Meanwhile and in between, he kept up the following:

"What does the speedo [speedometer] say?"

"Do you think the engine is running hot?"

"Do you think that tire will hold?"

"Did the cut seem any wider when you last looked?"

"What's that rattle?"

"I believe I'd better stop and let her cool off."

"We should be in at about five past two."

"Isn't this a bloody awful country?"

"Look at this awful road. Isn't it a disgrace?"

"Now, where would you get water through here?"

"You haven't seen any other cars, have you?"

"Your bones would have been left along the road. I'll show you some graves later on where people perished."

"Now I know this bloody-awful country backwards and forwards and you take my advice. When you get to Cloncurry, you get on the train and get back out of this nigger country. It's not even fit for the niggers."

"What does the speedo say?"

"What did it say when we left?"

And so on, and so on, all over again.

Although the country was flat and desolate, there was a little dry grass, good nourishment for sheep. At every station (ranch) boundary there was a "run-through" of some sort, to prevent stock from running through to the next man's property. This was a gap in the fence which might be filled by a gate (I was always getting out to open a gate); or a grid of small poles; or simply an opening with the two approaching car tracks forced into a short figure S, and lined at intervals on either side by bits of cloth or tin. It seemed that this arrangement spooked the stock so they would not cross through.

These run-throughs were usually many miles from the station headquarters, which were not to be seen. We did, however, occasionally pass a stockman (sheepman) driving perhaps a dozen horses, one of which would be carrying two water drums. A mile or so ahead would be the tucker (chuck) wagon. Percy explained the outfit would be going after sheep and the drovers would ride the horses.

I got to meet some of the local sheepmen when Percy stopped at a place called Kynuna for beer. I was amazed at the prodigious amount of beer these men drank. They told me the Aussies were the greatest beer drinkers in the world, and I seem to recall this later and verifying that only the Austrians beat them in per capita consumption. It was 11 P.M. when Mr. Strand finally called a halt to the guzzling and gossiping, which had mostly involved other sheepmen and horse racing. We drove westward over the plains, desperately groping for the trail that followed the telegraph line, the only real guide we had. Meanwhile I saw my first kangaroos, including a little "joey," in front of the car's headlights. "'Roos" are a menace to motorists at night and the Hillman already had a broken headlight from contact with one. 'Roo hunters got 4/6 (70 cents) per pound for skins, and a skin weighed about 1½ pounds. We camped on the open plain.

Percy had a terrific hangover the next morning, and things looked very, very dark indeed. The country showed grass and lots of red or white furze, flowers from the latter frequently fallen to the ground. We saw a wildcat, our second. They are about the size of an ordinary housecat or larger and in color are a strawberry blond with a yellow background. They feed on emu eggs, and it was through here I saw my first emus—big brown-gray ostrichlike birds with no tails. They have been timed running at forty miles per hour. An emu stands about five feet high and except for the ostrich is the largest bird in the world. The plummage is thick—two plumes growing from each quill. Wings are useless and so tiny they are not seen, being covered with body plumage. The rough green eggs are laid in a shallow nest scraped in the sand or dirt.

After a time we ran into trees and anthills. The road—a bush track—as always, continued to be "disgraceful," with deep gullies, rocks, and sand. A yellowish bush like our greasewood appeared.

"People in the cities of Australia have no conception, even in their wildest flights of fancy, of what this country is like," said Percy. "I try to tell them and can see the disbelief written on their faces. They think I'm romancing."

Percy reached his turnoff, and we parted in the middle of nowhere. He again admonished me to get out of the country, and added: "Besides, you are just now getting into the flies."

I realized this as I wrestled with the rocks and stones that afternoon. I could write an essay on these flies. They are small and swarm about you in droves. Utterly undaunted by brushing, they crawl all over your face, poke in at your ears and nostrils and especially delight in getting into the inner corners of your eyes. This is a very, very popular spot with them, and they tumble all over each other trying to get into this heaven. I recall pitying the cattle on the farm back home when their eyes were full of flies, but now I know how they felt. The flies will sometimes drown themselves in your eyes and will roll up like paper wads under your fingers as you try to brush them out. But if you are cycling in the bush, the occasions will be rare when you can take your hands off the handlebars, because you must look ahead and watch and jockey the wheels around and between the sharp stones, up out of the ruts, into the side gullies, etc. There are two enemies of this fly—the wind and the cold. He sits on the lee side of you and won't bother you much before 9 A.M.. But in respect to the wind you are caught between the devil and the deep. If the wind is behind you, it gives the bike a tremendous advantage and you just sail along, even up and out of the gullies. But meanwhile the flies crawl through your eyebrows and everywhere else on your face. If you go against the wind the flies are up behind where they won't bother but it is quite a low-gear fight to make any headway.

I camped that night near the tent and truck of a concrete contractor, who, I'm afraid, had ulterior motives. He wanted to hire me. Young fellows didn't want to work anymore, he said. He couldn't get any men to work for him. He had more jobs waiting than he could handle—the construction of stock tanks and the like—and there was an excellent profit. He was seventy-three, looked strong as an ox and could still do a full day's work. Although he had already eaten, he gave me an account of his daily menu, rightly surmising it would seem attractive compared with my own. He had a very bright carbide lantern hanging in his tent, and I wrote in there until midnight while he read a book, the white bark of a huge gum tree at the entrance reflecting the light. Once he broke out: "A wonderful country, this. All it needs is someone to work it and give it some attention. The bloody Australians won't do it. Right where you're settin' the soil with a little water would grow pumpkins and melons you couldn't lift—and tomatoes the size of a quart cup. A little rain and the grass pops up two feet high."

Cycling the next day was extremely rough, the worst yet! Sand, rock, dust up to six inches deep, with rocks, sharp and numerous, underneath the dust; and all this plus heat and a headwind. It was really tough. And I saw only one car all day long.

I worked westward into cattle country, an area of huge ranches, or "stations," as they call them here. I came to the turnoff to one of these called Devoncourt. Nearby was a large granite tombstone, of more than usual interest. It stated that here reposed the ashes and documents of Thomas Kennedy and his wife. He was born in Scotland in 1837 and came to Australia in 1861 as one of the first passengers on a certain ship. He died in Brisbane in 1936 in his ninety-ninth year. The stone listed at least five stations he had owned, Devoncourt being one of the more recent. I learned later that it was twelve miles wide and thirty-one miles long, so you can get some idea of his holdings. Devoncourt was unusually well chosen because it was almost completely surrounded by low hills.

It was late afternoon and I was in need of water to make camp, so I turned in. Mrs. Cameron, wife of the manager, was very friendly; and after we had chatted a short while, she invited me for dinner and to stay the night. Being a guest on an Australian ranch was a sort of event for me, and I washed, shaved, and brushed my shoes and clothes in preparation. I wasn't just sure whether I was to eat with the men or the family, but it developed I was to be a real guest. Mrs. Cameron had a severe limp, so I carried the huge dish and food tray from the cookhouse through the covered passageway to the family dining and living room. Soup dishes and plates had been carefully preheated, I noticed, and all food was covered.

There was another guest for dinner, a Mr. Wall, manager of a neighboring station, who was "attending" at Devoncourt. This term applies to a manager, or a man he appoints, who goes to his neighbor's "muster" and "drafting" (sorting out) to help and to spot his own cattle, if intermingled.

Relaxing in big, long, low camplike chairs near the table, we talked until 10 p.m. There was much discussion of stock and ranching methods, and I recalled what I could of our own Western life for comparison. They seemed particularly interested in my accounts of caring for stock in zero weather, and in blizzards, and of my experiences on Mount Rainier's glaciers. This was natural, since snow was unknown to them. The following odds and ends came out of the conversation:

The cowboy in Australia is the novice about the house who milks the cow (they keep one or two for this purpose), makes the butter, chops the wood, takes tea to the men, etc. The chap corresponding to our cowboy is the "ringer" or "stockman."

Calves are branded before weaning because certain areas are unfenced.

They raise mangoes and chocos, which grow on a vine and hang down like pears. They have yellow pumpkins called cattle pumpkins, and have our acorn and white scalloped squash.

The big problem in Australia is cooks, as Mrs. Forne had said on board ship. Mrs. Cameron spoke of having to be very careful to humor the cook. For example, she has to wash the dishes. The Devoncourt cook was a man, receiving top wages.

Blacks are very sharp on stock. They can't get lost in the bush and can trace cattle where a white man could not.

The ranch house had once been raised on piles, but the ants had eaten these and so now the house rested on concrete, which proved to be fairly cool.

During the course of the evening Mr. Cameron asked me how I was in the saddle. I told him I was green, but he offered to let me ride out in the morning and help with the drafting. You may be sure I accepted.

The first gong was sounded by the cook in the darkness at 6:30 a.m., and I was ready for breakfast by the second bell at seven. Everyone was promptly at table, but it was still so dark we had to use the carbide light we had used the night before. Mr. Cameron served porridge, a big soup dish of good oatmeal. Then came two enormous corned-beef fritters, each a meal in itself. When I remarked that I thought them good, there was laughter.

Eastern Queensland, Austra-lia.

Bowling on the Green—Longreach, Western Queensland, Australia.

"Drafting" on a "station," i.e., riding herd on a ranch—Western Queensland, Australia.

"Every cook in Australia serves corned-beef fritters for breakfast," said Mrs. Cameron. "It's an old standby."

Mr. Cameron had quite a time to fit me out. There was an extra saddle, but he had to beach the cowboy to get a bridle. I had told him that probably an hour or so would be enough for me to bother him as a tenderfoot, but he said not to worry about that. I wished afterward I hadn't been so modest about my riding ability, as the horse he picked for me out of the stockyard (corral) was certainly not ambitious. After I had saddled up and started to ride, I felt handicapped by not being able to talk to the horse. Aussie horses go by a kick in the ribs and don't know our Midwestern "get up" and clucking sounds.

While I spent only the better part of the forenoon helping with the drafting, it was really an experience to remember. We kept the mob fairly close together, each rider, including myself, holding a portion of the line. There were about six to eight hundred head. If a bullock broke out, one of us had to race after him at full lope. If a cow and a calf broke out, after we had allowed enough time for the cows to find their calves, we let them go. This holding operation was done in a paddock, a tremendous fenced area running perhaps miles on a side, after the cattle had been let out of the stockyard. After an hour or more of this the actual drafting commenced. This was done only from the front of the "camp" (mob) and consisted in a black riding in amongst the cattle, under the eye of Mr. Cameron, and working a bullock suitable for sale, or one belonging to the man attending, Mr. Wall, out to the edge and into the open paddock. At ten o'clock there was tea, brought out by the cowboy, boiling hot, in large billies (cans), along with pans of biscuit (good fresh pieces of raisin bread), and cake.

The second night after leaving Devoncourt found me within a few miles of Mount Isa, an important mining community. I camped by a windmill, as it was time to do some washing. Luckily there was a shanty nearby and I was able to borrow a big basin and laundry soap. I heated water on my little three-pound camp stove. There were some large vines about, and I stretched one between a couple of trees and so had a clothesline for drying. Meanwhile I did my cooking, eating and dishwashing, which usually took about two hours. I often had fried potatoes and onions, or boiled potatoes. I made soup: two bouillon cubes to two-thirds pint of water; and gravy from a mix I carried. For dessert there was always excellent Australian bread, butter, and jam. You see, this was relatively early in my travels and I had not yet found out I could get along without cooking. It was to be many thousand miles before I was to abandon my stove and live only on cold "bread and tin."

At Mount Isa I called at the police station to get some information about water holes along my route and found the constables friendly and talkative. In fact I wrote in my diary there until midnight tea. They had a galah in a cage and were very fond of him—in fact, everyone seems to keep birds. The tailor in town had six different kinds. The diversion of one of the officers was 'roo hunting. Hunters park their car perhaps half a mile from a windmill ("bore") and wait until they hear the 'roos hopping in for water. Then they flash a big spotlight on them and get them with a 303 service rifle. The light blinds the animals and it is possible to walk up and hit them with your fist unless they hear you and hop off. They are hard to kill, however, and will go several hundred yards with their entrails out. Hunters may get forty or fifty in one night. The skinning is done the following morning. The skins are pegged out to dry, and a mixture of arsenic and caustic soda is painted on the hide to keep out insects and weevils and to deter the dingoes. Hides averaged out to about 1½ pounds and the value at $1.60 per pound.

In Mount Isa I had more trouble with my bicycle but was lucky in meeting a couple of chaps at the bike shop who gave me a lot of free work and companionship. They also gave me a strong used luggage carrier for my old one. Harold was a veteran of the New Guinea jungle campaigns in World War II and well knew the horrors of being under fire. Yet it must be human nature to marvel at, or admire, something beyond the individual experience. For I was amazed when Harold said to me in regard to my lonely desert traveling: "You have more bloody courage than I would ever have."

After I had left town, I realized I didn't have enough bread for the long trek ahead, so I stopped at the nearest house to buy some. The chap did not understand English, so I asked him what language he spoke.

"Finnish."

"Oh," said I, happily recalling my experiences with Jacqueline in Finland. "Olen Americasta. Minna em osa Suormaya. Maxa leipa?"

I soon had my bread and an invitation to tea. There were about forty Finns working in the mine, and they had not bothered to learn English.

6

A "Real Damned Mad" Crosses Australia's Northern Territory

About 5 P.M. I reached a road workers' camp and stopped for water and directions. The ganger (road boss) made me at home at once, inviting me to supper and to camp there for the night. I wrote in my diary until dark. Supper! Oh, boy! All the slices of good, still warm, lean bullock I could cut out from the huge roasting skillet, plus good bread, several kinds of meat sauces, a huge warm potato still in its jacket, and some small cakes for a sweet finish. The ganger then offered pen, ink, and a table, and with a lantern for light I sat in the mess tent and wrote until midnight.

One of the men was very much under the influence, it being Saturday. This chap was like the bogie man in a horror movie. He had a heavy barrel chest and long arms. His complexion was a sickly white with red lips and swellings. One eye was completely closed, and I felt it was probably empty. The lid of the other was puffed so that he saw with difficulty. The lid was an angry red. His entire face was bloated, and he was bald. He grunted and roared incoherently or called for a drink in the early part of the evening, but later on fell asleep in his adjoining tent, only to holler periodically, "That's right! Yes, that's right!" His snorts and the distant howling of the dingoes kept me company on my midnight vigil, the ganger having retired early.

The next day's work was long and hard. My legs were not used to high-gear work on a level road, and even though the wind was partly helpful, I was really dead tired when I came to Wooroona Creek, sixty-five miles from the road camp. It was dry, of course, but my instructions were to turn up the bed to the right, follow along for a mile and a quarter and I would find water. Never were water and rest more earnestly desired. After a hunt, there she was! My first real desert water hole. It was deep and lined on three sides with smooth flat rocks of great length, similar to those seen so frequently in southern Utah. So enraptured was I with the place that I attached a string to the camera and snapped a picture of myself engaged in camp duties. During the process my blanket roll fell into the water, but it floated long enough for me to fish it out, and it didn't get wet either. Dingoes howled around my camp during the night.

I had not been on the road long the next day, before a man named Greb hailed me down from a parked truck. He apparently just wanted to talk, as he was a bit tight, but he invited me for breakfast. He had a fine, intelligent black man with him. The latter had already placed three large tins of small sausages and spaghetti under the fire, and using the usual, sharp knife for a can opener, emptied the entire contents of one into my pan. I couldn't eat it all and gave some to Greb, who was eating nothing. Bread and a yellow raisin-and-cherry pound cake completed the meal. When I left, the black man insisted on my taking the rest of the cake. I did not finish this cake until halfway across Northern Territory—two thousand miles from the place where it was baked. Meanwhile my white host was talking.

"For God's sake, come out and teach us how to run this country. Give us a kickoff, you fellows. You know how. We're way behind.

"You must have a lot of bloody guts to travel this country."

"Oh, I don't know," I replied.

"Well, you must have something back of you."

I was to hear these comments again. The Aussie was much impressed with Yank efficiency during World War II. He liked to tell the story about the Yank and the Aussie who happened to start to build an airplane at the same time. After three weeks the Yank called the Aussie on the phone.

"Well, how are ya doin'? I've got one more nut to put on and she'll be ready to fly!"

"Well," responded the other. "I've got one more form to fill out and then I'll have all my applications done so I can make a start."

At the same time the Yanks were considered by the Aussies to be "overfed, oversexed, and overrated." The second term refers to the inclination of the Aussie sheilas to ditch their Aussie boyfriends and go out with the tall strangers from overseas.

I camped one night at Soudan, an outpost station of Alexander Downs. This was the second largest cattle station in the world, with an area just under twelve thousand square miles. The stockmen were not in camp at first, so I got acquainted with the intelligent aboriginal cook. It was far from suppertime, and I ate my own meal in the light of his carbide lamp while he was up to his ears in huge tubs of flour and dough. As always I praised the good quality of Australian bread. The camp was on the bank of a small river which had water in it and showed its muddy color in the moonlight. Still I had learned that this water is usually better than bore water, which is frequently odd-tasting or brackish. When the cook finished his bread, he dragged out a huge tarp for me to sleep on and we folded it together. The stockmen showed up, and after a chat we all turned in. I enjoyed the thrill of all the strangeness of my surroundings for a few minutes before I dozed off.

I had told the cook I'd probably be leaving at daybreak, so I really believe he got up earlier than usual to give me a good breakfast. Certainly the stockmen were still rolled in their blankets even after I had eaten. I will not forget that breakfast in a hurry. Huge steaks three-quarters inch by six inches by eight inches rolled in seasoned flour and fried in deep fat. Oh, boy! Plus fruit chutney, tomato sauce, Worcestershire sauce, and sweet piccallili; and of course, this excellent bread. When I finished it was light enough to take a picture, and I snapped the cook amongst his huge black bread pans, skillets, and billies, and his two fires, while he was finishing his breakfast steaks. These he was placing in iron pots with lids to keep warm until the stockmen got up. He had some little sweet cakes of which he seemed proud. They were like scones. When I was about to leave, he told me to take some along. I picked up two or three, but he said, "Take a lot. Take a lot of 'em."

It was fifty miles to the next water, so I filled both of my canteens and a beer bottle besides. It was after lunch when I reached Wonirah, or Repeater, Telegraph and Telephone Station. The lonely man there, after asking if I had had tea, took me about the place. He was trying to raise vegetables but without much success. He found a small cantaloupe and gave it to me, but I talked him out of giving me a New Guinea bean—they are two or three feet long and six inches in diameter. He was concerned about where I would get water on my trek; and I had been told there was one waterless stretch of 134 miles. He said frequently there might be ten or twelve days without a car on the road. So he called his two neighbors to the west, one 74 miles away and the other 183 miles. Neither was on my road, but they would know about the water. Of course, when he told them there was a bicycle going through they wouldn't believe it, and when he was stumbling for words to explain, I supplied: "Tell them a crazy American on a push bike."

"Yes, a crazy American—a real damned mad," he laughed into the phone.

You see water might be obtainable at government bores. At one time wells and windmills had been put along the route for stockmen and cattle, but maintenance had fallen off and most of the mills, which had enormous wheels and gears, had simply run themselves out of grease and broken down. In fact, the first one I came to was in this condition except that water was still to be found at the surface of the ground. It was all mixed up with little stones, so I dug some holes and then found all the tin cans I could and scooped up the water, mud and all, and left it to settle.

Eventually I came to the approximate center of Northern Territory, which is about the size of Alaska. Here I traveled for some miles on the new north-south road, constructed as a wartime measure. Needing water, I turned off on a lonesome bush track, unmarked, in the hope it would lead to the Phillips Mission, one of the aboriginal inland missions. I really did not know where I was until I stumbled onto a bunch of native camps. These were simply brush lean-tos built to protect fires from the prevailing easterlies. One woman had gotten hold of a bit of flour and was mixing it with liquid fat, preparatory to frying it. Women and children were barefooted and barelegged. Hordes of dogs were about and flies galore. The only sounds I could get out of the women were those trying to quiet the dogs. No one spoke English, but when I thought to say "white man," they pointed in the right direction. But now would be a good time to set down some of the lore later imparted to me by the missionaries.

The woman I saw mixing flour was making a puftaloon, a food learned from the Aussies. But the aborigines' natural food is practically anything that moves, and a lot of other things: frogs, lizards, snakes, grubs, ants, worms, mice, rats, cats, birds, grass seed, roots. Grubs, worms, and the like are eaten raw. Aborigine children may spend hours taking ants from an anthill, pinching them, and building up a pile, enough to make a meal. Birds, if small, are eaten whole, after the feathers are pulled off. Small meat objects may be simply laid on coals, but the natives are not fussy if things don't get done.

The aborigines in the vicinity of the mission are occasionally given bullock meat. This is provided by a cattleman under a yearly lease from the mission, which in turn leases the land from the territory. (All land in the territory is said to be leased.) The cattleman and his men, with perhaps a few blacks, run a bullock under a tree, kill it and cut up the carcass. When the aborigines get anything big, such as a bullock's head or a kangaroo, they will first dig a big hole, put in stones or an ant bed (hill) and lay a fire on top. Later they take off the fire, take out the stones cover everything over with bark (or a piece of galvanized tin if they have acquired such) and seal everything with dirt to keep the heat in. They then leave the meat until it is baked, if they are not too hungry. They eat absolutely every part of the bullock except the hooves and bones, and the grass in the stomach. They have no set time to eat, just whenever food is handy. Water was formerly in good supply, but now the cattlemen have it and don't want the blacks around because of their dogs.

There are ceremonial dances for everything from kangaroos to flies. There are death dances. The deceased is placed on a platform in a tree until the flesh rots and drops off. Stones are placed around the tree and each one represents a man of the tribe. An old man, or certain person, watches these stones. If a piece of rotting flesh falls on one, that person is deemed responsible for the death and they go for him, i.e., they kill him. They don't believe in death by natural causes. Following a death, many of the Warramunga tribe go dumb for a time. But most of the aborigines use a sign language anyway. Speech is not necessary to them.

Aborigines know their family relationships very well. Many are great-grandfathers. Fathers' brothers are also fathers; mothers' sisters are also mothers. Fathers' sisters are aunts, and mother's brothers are uncles. Girls are promised in marriage in certain directions. A man may have two or more wives. The old men take young wives to care for them. When an old man dies, his wife or wives go to younger brothers, so in that way a young man may get a young wife. Sometimes an older woman is given to a young man. However, the young men are mostly unmarried and promiscuous. There are two tribes in the area, the Warramunga and the Wailbri. Women of one tribe go over to the other, perhaps on a business or fight settlement. Such are the social obligations of earth's most primitive peoples.

When I left the aborigines' camp, I found it was not very far through the bush to the mission. Here I was made welcome by a group of native boys and girls and three missionaries. In the evening I went to a sort of Sunday school meeting held in a rough building with open screened sides. The one Coleman lamp seemed inadequate. The children sat on benches at tables, and I later learned that this was also their school. There was no accompaniment for the songs, but they knew the tunes and sang very well, I thought. Most of them sang from memory, but a few had tiny songbooks and apparently knew how to read. Singing and instruction were in English.

The next morning when we looked in at the boys' dormitory, I found that the aborigines sleep late. The school-age group live entirely within the compound, but they are still wild and cannot always be found in the dormitories at night. The boys were sleeping side by side on the hard cement with only a thin covering above and below them. Food is made available to them at times and the missionaries told me of one of their early attempts to get them to eat oatmeal with spoons and bowls. The kids had decided it was more fun to use the spoons to throw the food at each other than to eat it. The natives still have many taboos. My host pointed out a little girl standing in his yard.

"She is a prisoner, you see. She can't look at a certain man, and he is standing by the gate."

"Well, why can't she close her eyes and walk out?"

"Oh, he might look at her."

I left the aborigines and worked over a hilly road as I headed north. A truck stopped and offered me a lift. I was grateful for this, even though the driver seemed to be stuck at the astonishing speed of fifteen miles per hour, very little above biking speed. There were four gold prospectors returning empty-handed from the Tenants Creek area to their homes in Darwin. Two of them were pretty well pickled, but the driver was sober, and the fourth chap could apparently hold his liquor. I was in the back with the two, who literally drank one bottle of beer after the other without stopping, for hours as we poked on northward. To keep things livelier there was a dog named Bootlace who would play with us one minute and bite us the next. He jumped all over the place, often on top of us.

Meanwhile I learned the lore of the gold prospectors. One of the four had once struck it rich. He had been the first into a new gold field about fifteen years before (although "color" at Tenants Creek dated back sixty years) and had once owned a mine and 25,000 quid (about $80,000). Prospecting was formerly done with camels, and some of them were still around. The best time was after the rains, when water stayed in the depressions. There was ordinarily no water, and of course no roads, for several hundred miles to the west of Tenants. The four men had just driven the truck about and made their own roads. They had been out in the bush for three months.

We poked along into the night. At about eight the driver came back and opened up the tucker box and I really waded into the good cooked beef. About nine we stopped and rolled out on the ground for the night, each having his own swag. This usually included a mattress. Mosquitoes plagued the place and we fought 'em all night. Gus, the worst toper of the lot, filled the darkness with his curses. My own netting was ineffective, so I got up and put on my head net in addition. But there was humor in the camp when we rolled out at daybreak. Bootlace had run off with Gus's false teeth; and the Yank was trapped in his head net because he couldn't get the neck knot untied. We finally found the teeth.

The prospectors drove on into a crossroads place called Newcastle Waters, where there was a sort of inn and a place to buy a meal. I took my leave of them sitting on the steps. They were all four worried about me, since I was leaving the highway and going on west. Newcastle Waters was the jumping-off place, and several knew the country I was planning to go through. So these four grizzled graybeards sagely wagged their heads.

The driver's last words were: "That's quite a thing you're taking on, you know."

At first there was no sand on the road to the west, and the two parallel tracks, although quite rough, made fair going. When darkness came, the moon came out so promptly to light the tracks that I kept on traveling. I ate a good supper by moonlight on the banks of Bucket Creek, which I had been following. This creek had the muddiest of yellow water, drying up in pools, yet the water was good, cool, and regularly used. Many hoofprints of cattle were to be seen; indeed, this was the eastern end of the famous Murranji Trek, over which the longest dry trek in history had been made by the Farquharson brothers. They had driven a thousand head of bullocks from Top Spring to Bucket Creek, a distance of 125 miles, and lost only three. Two were poisoned, and the third got to the creek but died on the bank.

I pedaled on through the moonlight until ten o'clock, something very unusual for me. It was a unique experience with a scattering of trees on an open landscape throwing odd shadows as I went along. At one time I came to a government bore, put in, of course, since the famous dry trek. I prowled about the windmill in a vain search for water and nearly stuck my face into a spider as big as my fist. Ugh! After about thirty miles or so, I turned in under a little tree on the open prairie.

Aboriginal cook preparing fresh beef steaks (6″ × 8″ × ¾″) for my breakfast on the world's second largest cattle station—12,000 square miles.

A lone windmill and water tank 40 miles from the nearest human. It was at one of these that I had a narrow escape from a bull.

The next forenoon was tough, very tough. Two tracks wound through the sand and dead trees. The road had never been surveyed or formed. There was sand and more sand. At 1 P.M. I estimated I had walked the last ten miles with no chance to ride, usually taking little mincing steps in the deep ruts of sand, either pushing or pulling the bike. But in the afternoon there was unexpected relief. The stillness of the bush was broken by a welcome sound, that of a motor coming in the right direction. I pulled off, and around a curve came a big diesel semitrailer loaded with steel. It stopped. The young driver grinned and we chatted a bit.

"Well," he said finally, "would you like to hoist the bike up behind?"

"Those are sure welcome words, mister."

Roy Peterson, of Swedish descent, and I stuck to that truck for the rest of the afternoon. We shared tucker and motor troubles. Our speed was hardly ten miles per hour, and a good bit of the time we were stopped, working on the truck. When Roy got dirty with fuel oil and grease, he would say, "It's a terrible dirty job, this."

The next forenoon we ground up and down a number of gullies. The truck had twelve speeds and used them all. Roy was trucking for the department of the interior, which hauls for cattlemen at sixpence per ton mile, a rate which keeps out private cartage.

When our routes parted I pushed on to Monteginnie, an outpost station of Victoria River Downs, commonly referred to as V.R.D. This was the largest cattle ranch in the world. Its area was thirteen thousand square miles, equal in size to the states of Connecticut and Massachusetts together. It was sixteen times larger than the King Ranch of Texas. However, negotiations were under way to sell three thousand square miles, so the crown for size would pass to Alexander Downs, the station where I had helped herd cattle some days before. Victoria River Downs ran 150,000 head of cattle and might overland 20,000 head in one year; that is, they would be driven over the Murranji and on across to the railheads in Queensland.

Monteginnie outpost station was sprawled about in tropical fashion. Certain working areas had brush roofs to break the heat of the sun, and the meat house had a thatched roof. Gins (aborigine girls) kept the covered areas and the whole yard neatly swept with brush brooms and quite free from stones. There was no grass of course. Everyone seemed to move slowly, and I recalled being told that one's blood thickened after years in the tropics and he was never good for temperate climate thereafter. In summer they work up till 9 A.M. and after 4 P.M. There was an adobe oven in the yard, and I noticed that the open semicircle took account of the fact that the winds are prevailingly from the east.

From Monteginnie I only had a short run of fifteen miles to Top Spring, the western end of the Murranji. This was a beautiful desert oasis with what I took to be palm trees closely hemming the green water. Actually they were pandanus trees.

I had been told to be sure and stop at Jack McDonald's out-camp at Garibaldi Creek because "he's an old chap all alone with a bunch of blacks and no one to talk to." I would not see this camp from the trail, but if I watched for a certain scattered group of trees and then stopped and fetched a shout or two, I'd get an answer. Well, I really didn't have any confidence that such Robin Hood proceedings would have any results, and since I hadn't seen any humans or even cattle for miles, I felt kind of foolish stopping and shouting in the wilderness. So I was quite surprised to hear, after only my second try, a response to my yell, "Ho, Jack." I followed the direction of the sound, off through the trees, making my own trail. Did I ever mention that the "bush" is singularly free of bushes?

And so I came to Garibaldi out-camp, whose only mark upon the landscape was a small windbreak. Mac had thinning gray hair and gray whiskers, but he was only thirty-eight. He lost no time in persuading me to set down a day in his camp, enticing me with prospects of a good photo of the bronchoing operation the second morning. Meanwhile he grabbed a shovel, laid a couple of huge steaks about an inch thick on it, and proceeded to grill them over the coals of his fire. He had already eaten, and both steaks were for me. I ate until I was in misery. There was bread, honey, and cakes in the bargain.

Mac was up and off the next morning at break of day. I should have joined him at breakfast but was not hungry and waited until eight o'clock, then ate the two steaks he had left in the skillet near the coals. I was way behind in my diary, so I wrote steadily until 1 P.M., when Mac returned from mustering up a mob to be bronchoed. He had a big bunch of horses and about fifteen aborigines in his camp. The wives of two of them did his camp duties. In the afternoon Mac and his men remounted and drove the mob into a paddock. I washed clothes, using the water the women had lugged from the creek.

Garibaldi out-camp was still on Victoria River Downs and was based on Monteginnie outpost station. You see, there might be several out-camps, perhaps as much as thirty miles from the outpost; and the outpost in turn might be eighty to a hundred miles from the main station headquarters. A day's camp routine at Garibaldi ran about as follows.

At forty-five minutes before daybreak one of Mac's men would come up to his tent, put some wood on his fire, and call him.

"Is the star up?" Mac would query back into the darkness.

"Yeah, she's up."

Whereupon Mac would roll out and put on his breakfast steaks. Then he would cut bread from sections of the huge circular loaves two feet in diameter, enough bread for each man. He told me he had to ration in this manner or rations would disappear too fast.

"Right-o!" Mac would holler out into the darkness.

Soon dark faces, shining on one side from the glow of Mac's fire, would file in out of the darkness, take their bread and silently go back to their own campfire, where their own meat would be in readiness. There were a couple of youngsters, ten or twelve years of age, who worked along with the men. They always wore smiles of pride at taking their rations and places with the men.

By daylight all men would be catching their horses out of the mob that were hobbled in a group near by. The process took quite a long time, as the horses were rested and didn't want to be caught. If the men were back by noon, the feeding process was repeated. Meanwhile the two women heated dishwater and washed up the breakfast and supper dishes. The left-over loaves of bread would be placed in huge pack bags, very carelessly closed. However, the bread has a thick protective crust, and they bake almost every day. The women fill the big heavy-gauge, galvanized-iron, aluminum-colored canteens, and the big black billies, from the creek. The canteens have a hole in one corner, and any pouring out must be done while they sit on the opposite end.

In the evening the feeding process is repeated. Mac sits around his camp-fire behind his windbreak; and two other campfires in the middle distance show where the men and the two women have their respective fires.

Since the bread is excellent and provides half of the diet, you may want to know how it is made. Mac makes the dough in the evening, using a tall drum eighteen inches in diameter and three and a half feet deep, and mixing with a paddle. The gin does the baking the next day. She first gets her ashes, coals, and a little wood fixed up in her camp "oven" in the ground. Then, with all her round pans and their lids, both scorched quite black, she retires to a place on the ground near the raised dough. She lays out a large piece of white canvas, pours out huge batch of dough, and kneads it. She puts three loaves in each pan with a small loaf in the center. Since each pan is over two feet in diameter and nine inches deep, the finished loaves have some real size. The lids are put on the pans, all go in the oven, and ashes are put on top. I don't recall ever tasting any better bread.

Mac was quite a character. He had run away from home when only thirteen. He had seen the most rugged types of service in the war, and swore they would never get him into another war. He had been in the 18th Australian Brigade, which had 95 percent casualties, the worst per-centage of casualties in the Australian army. Like other Aussies he had a gripe against the Yanks taking credit for capturing islands when the Aussies had actually done the dirty work and the Yanks only the mopping up. In the army he had cooked, with eight assistants, for 130 men. When Mac grilled four steaks on a spade in Garibaldi out-camp, and I tasted them, I

Aboriginal woman baking bread at an an outpost station of Victoria River Downs, world's largest cattle ranch—13,000 square miles.

had no doubt as to his experience. He also made an excellent raisin cake. The second evening I was there he had "curry," which really means an Irish stew—potatoes, onions, plenty of beef, and a little curry. All this fresh beef gave me what is known in this country as the "fresh beef trots," so that wasn't so good. But I will never forget the cooking.

While staying with Mac, I learned a lot more about cattle. Bullocks are in good condition on Garibaldi, but if they are driven five hundred miles to Wyndham, for example, they will develop muscle and lose vitamins, and the meat will be tough. To drive cattle the other way, overland to Queensland, is to "drive inside." Sometimes the cattle are held there at railhead to fatten on different grasses. During the first six months the bullock turns the paddock to powder trying to get out and go home, but in another two months he is slick and fat. Some yard feeding is also done near the cities, as we do in our Middle West.

Early the second morning I watched the bronchoing. They use a broncho panel, two short sections of post fence end to end, with perhaps a foot of space between. The top of one section is straight, the other has a slope. Two riders on heavy horses lasso a bullock from amongst the mob. They use a heavy braided rope, almost like a cable. One end is fastened to a heavy breast strap on the horse. The riders pass on the side of the panel opposite the bullock, dragging their ropes over the sloping section to the center space, where they drop down. Next a man on each end of the panel gets a rope on the far leg, front and rear, and snubs it around the end posts. This throws the bullock into a shallow hole by the panel. The horseman's rope is taken off, and he goes for the next bullock. Mac then takes over and saws the horns half off, alters the animal and earmarks him.

After leaving Garibaldi, I stopped at the second bore. There was a windmill and three tanks. There were no cattle about except a sick bullock—or so I thought. I had occasionally seen skeletons near the bores, and I felt sorry for this bull. "Poor old fellow," I said aloud. "I s'pose you've crept in here to die." I was overdue for a shave, so I started toward the watering trough with my equipment, which included my boy scout fold-over-handle aluminum skillet, which I was using for a washbasin. I was surprised to see the bull get to his feet and start walking toward me, but thought nothing of it. He had extremely long horns too. However it suddenly became apparent that he was after me when he started to run at me with head lowered. I was so surprised that I banged him on the nose with my pan and then turned tail, he after me. Like a fool I stumbled and fell. Why I fell I'll never know, because there wasn't even a pebble on the ground. Quite coolly I thought, "His horns will enter my back any second now." But he stopped when I fell—surprised, I suppose; and then when I scrambled up, pursued me to the nearest tree on the run. Here we played tag. He got his head down close to the tree and ran around it trying to reach me. For a minute or two I was pretty dubious how it would come out. Then we squared off, the tree between us. He glared at me, and I— well, somehow or other I was uninterested in the landscape just then. After a little he retired, and so did I, all my sympathy for him quite evaporated. My pan was bent, my mirror broken. Blood had spurted from my cut hand onto my cap and gear. I washed and shaved at the trough, keeping a wary eye on my adversary. I had been around cattle many times but had to come all the way to a deserted windmill in Australia to be chased by a bull.

I worked westward following the stock route. This was the greatest stock route in the world, stretching from the Kimberlies in Western Australia up through Wave Hill (cattle station) and Newcastle in Northern Territory, and down to the Queensland railheads. From forty to fifty thousand head yearly went over this route, and the motion picture *The Overlanders* was made to dramatize it. I was occasionally made conscious of this when I met a great mob of cattle. I respected the black drovers, who spoke straight across the board and did not use the white man's obscenity and profanity. When the mob shied at my bicycle, I said to one of them, "I guess they don't see many bicycles around here."

"No, it's been years since I've seen one."

"Where you from?"

"Ord River [a place on the Western Australia line], bound for Morestown, Queensland."

I mentioned having come from Newcastle, and one of the men said, "She's an awful lot of bush, that Murranji!"

"Boy, I'll say. And sand too!"

The stock had gummed up the road so badly I could hardly move or even find the road when I went to leave the next bore. Hoofprints and dust made me walk or crawl in low gear. Where the ground was rocky, the tracks were filled with loose rock. But I cooled off with the reflection that if it were not for the stock, I wouldn't have water every fifteen to twenty-five miles.

Nevertheless, I made dry camp that evening. It was warm in the desert. Cloudy. Not a breath stirring. No grass; just dust, gravel, and the scattered trees, under one of which I was camped. Although my digestive system was still off, I made soup and ate a good meal. Then, using my flashlight, I wrote for two hours.

Eventually I came to a place I'd been hearing about for many miles: Wyeville. I was a bit shocked to discover the name was really Wave Hill. It was a large station, third largest in all Australia. Here within a neatly kept and well-arranged rectangle was a complete living unit settled down in the desert. The buildings were painted red and were along a road curving around three sides of the rectangle, the fourth side being the "main road." There were the manager's house, the bookkeeper's house and office, the store, the post office, quarters for certain men, the cook's quarters, the kitchen, the tea or smoke-o room, the saddler's shop, and the blacksmith shop. ("Smoke-o" is the midforenoon or midafternoon pause for tea and cakes.) The bookkeeper and the manager's wife made me welcome and wanted to get me something to eat, even though it was not mealtime. I settled for "a drink of milk," and the cook provided me with three and a half glasses of ice-cold milk. Right off the road, and two months and two weeks from my last glass of milk, I don't think I ever tasted anything so delicious.

Two bush contractors had driven their truck 280 miles to Wave Hill to get some blacksmithing done. They offered me a lift, and I rode with them 130 miles to the next station, Inverway. It was a wild night ride over rocks, gullies, and sand, all mixed in with trees, bush, spinifex clumps, and whatnot. At 2 A.M. we stopped outside the yard fence and tumbled off the truck and into our swags.

Daylight, and I rolled out.

"Has the gong rung yet?" asked Tom. He was referring to a heavy piece of iron suspended and struck with another piece of iron to announce a meal or smoke-o. The hospitality in this country was tremendous, and it was assumed travelers would come in for meals. In fact there was a washbasin and water just inside the fence.

The gong rang and we went in to breakfast.

"Mr. Rosdail, meet Mr. Farquharson, owner of Inverway."

An old chap of eighty-six, a red kerchief on his head, with red-rimmed watery eyes, Mr. Farquharson had been in the area since 1902. He had started to buy cattle and to hunt for gold at the age of twenty-four, way in the east. He had come overland from Quensland by bullock cart. He and his brother, as I mentioned before, had been the first to dry-trek cattle over the famous Murranji—one thousand bullocks and 125 miles. It was a privilege to talk to this old pioneer.

After porridge, steak, bread, and jam, our conversation turned to death by thirst. They said a man could go four days without water but only one day if he was walking. They spoke of one chap they found who had pulled off all his clothes—it seems they develop a fever. Then there was another case where the man had done the same thing before his mate left him but had his clothes back on when they found him dead.

Traveling with the two contractors, I saw all over again the relationship between the aborigines and the whites. When a stop is made at a bore for a meal, the blacks build a fire outside the enclosure (if there is one), grill the beef and make the tea. These they bring over to the whites, who have their own canvas spread out for eating. It seems like the slave system of the United States all over again. The blacks are given tucker, clothes, tobacco, rides. They are happy and in return do the white man's dishes, open his gates, do much of his cooking. If the boss is tired when evening comes, they unload his swag from the top of the truck at his order. They milk the goats (I was getting into goat country) and so on. In Northern Territory you must pay them a wage, but in Western Australia at this time only a license was needed to keep them. The Aussie occasionally mentioned that the race was dying out, and I had the feeling that maybe he was a little afraid of it. But the black apparently demands respect from his white boss, because I heard comment concerning a drunken white's verbal abuse of a gin who was doing his kitchen work. She walked straight out of the kitchen and refused to return except on managerial persuasion.

"Oh, you can't abuse 'em," said Les. "They won't do a thing if you do."

7

Wherein We Get Lost and Hunt for a Water Hole After Dark

Pedaling into Western Australia, I found rugged country. There was a fringe of low, red mountains on the north and west, and these I eventually crossed. Then I came to a tin shack and some tropical-looking trees on the trail. Mr. Cameron, an old bachelor with quarters in corresponding condition, greeted me. He was "terrible crooked up" in his legs, he said.

"If you're going in to town, tell Johnson, the storekeeper, to send me out some castor oil and some Epsom salts. I haven't been to the lavatory for ten days, going on eleven. I've got a dead feeling in my legs and am pretty crook. Maybe Martin, the policeman, will bring it out."

The town he referred to was Halls Creek, and it would be my first in about six hundred miles of travel from Newcastle Waters. Although there would be nothing there but a tiny "hospital" with two nurses, a pub, a store, and a police barracks, it was still a town in the great outback.

No car had been by, said Mr. Cameron, in at least five days. So I promised to try and get into town that evening, even though I was pretty tired already. He then invited me to eat, saying that anyone was welcome there.

"He's welcome to share what I've got for a day, or a week if he cares to, or a fortnight if he's out of a job."

He raised chickens, but when I asked him how many, he started telling me about the snakes poisoning them and eating them (the little ones). He didn't get many eggs because the snakes got to them in the grass before he did.

Although there was a road of sorts, travel was pretty rugged. I went up steep grades and down steep grades, and there was all manner of rocks and stones. About 5 P.M. I came to the other "hermit of Halls Creek," an old soldier prospecting or living in an adobe and red-rock hut quite close to the road.

Here was a hermit just the opposite of Mr. Cameron. He was neatness and cleanliness itself. Dressed only in shorts and a heavy graying beard, he was sitting in his little cookhouse playing chess, with his books and odds and ends in ready reach. A beautiful, freshly baked loaf of bread was resting on the table. He said he fed his burro bread also—and he showed me the highly polished hoof of a burro that he had owned. Near his hut he pointed out some gold-bearing rock, and he even washed a little gravel in a pan to show me the fine gold remaining.

Shortly after it got dark my troubles commenced. The rear tire started to rub and I fussed with rear-wheel adjustments. No results, so I finally stopped and unpacked, and found out that the underinflated tire was coming out of the rim. Then I couldn't get air through the pump. The moon came up, and I stopped work and ate. Then I worked by moonlight. What a time I had! I wore myself out pumping, which, since the air wouldn't enter, was a more tiring process than pedaling. Time and again I was ready to give up and roll in, but I kept thinking of my "mission of mercy." By 10 P.M. I felt the bike was fixed at last, and I rode on in the moonlight. It was really a hair-raising experience, on a strange mountain road of very steep drops through deep ruts, over roots and rocks, into unexpected gullies, etc. There was supposed to be a well halfway between hermit number two and Hall Creek. But at night every anthill—yes, even every tree—became this well. Finally, when I estimated I had passed this well and had only a couple of miles to town, the tire came out again. Too tired to struggle with the pump a second time, I took a canteen and a couple of little cakes, and started to walk to town, leaving Jacqueline.

I was tearing it off at a good clip, when all of a sudden there was the well. Hell's bells! Well, how far was it to town then? While debating what to do, I windlassed up a bucket of water. I remembered that no one in this country really knew distances (too few cars and those had broken speedometers) and since it was already after midnight, I decided to give up. I probably wouldn't have done so even then, but Mr. Cameron had said morning would be O.K.

Astir at daybreak, I spent more than an hour on the tire, ate a bite at the well and proceeded into town. Mr. Johnson agreed with me that we should have some kind of medical advice, so I went to the hospital. The two nurses there had no patients, so it was no great decision for them to take their cross-country vehicle and go out to see about Mr. Cameron.

Leaving Halls Creek, I traveled through a section of small stations relatively close together. Hostess at one was a half-caste I first took to be an aborigine. I was very favorably impressed. She was dressed neatly and in excellent taste, and I'm sure she hadn't been expecting company either. She played the role of hostess in as charming a manner as any American housewife and looked after the dressing and bringing to table of her children besides. Two of these could have passed for white.

Another station maintained a fine garden. Here is a list of the things they were raising: pear tomatoes; shallots; chilies; sugar cane; Indian copper corn (which looked like kafir corn); ironback and other pumpkins; garlic; pe-tsai; cress; Kentucky beans; a kind of cabbage which raises little heads after the main one is cut and then substitutes for Brussel sprouts; soup celery, which grows only three inches high; seven-year beans, which must be cut back after seven years so they may take a fresh start; the ordinary gamut of beets, lettuce, onions, etc.; English potatoes, bananas, and figs; and marigolds and other flowers.

In the bush I saw one of the most unusual birds in the world. This was the brolga, or native companion. It is a large bird like a flamingo or crane, more gray than red. One time I saw a group of them behaving like soldiers on drill. There was a long row of birds a few feet apart facing a leader who stood perhaps ten feet in front of them and in about the center of the line. At some signal which I could not detect, the leader and the entire row advanced a number of paces, keeping a quite straight line. At another signal they all stopped, then reversed direction until they had attained their original position. This would almost have to be seen to be believed. The Aussies referred to it as "set dancing," comparing it to our square dancing; and it may be that the brolgas perform more intricate patterns than the one I saw.

I learned other quite interesting lore in this section of the great outback. The kangaroos I saw through here were really euros, or hill kangaroos. They have hair instead of fur, and the current market for the skins was $.96 a pound as compared with $2.25 per pound for the regular red or blue 'roos. At one station the boy had a little joey (baby kangaroo) for a pet, and I noticed it lapped up milk like a cat. Abos (aborigines) will take a 'roo, draw out the entrails, discharge the contents, punch holes in the hide, and sew it up again with the entire gut inside. Then they place the 'roo in a hole and roast it until it's about one quarter done and then eat it. When an abo dies, his friends hit their heads to make themselves cry. Gins may show up for work with great welts on their heads. The huge anthills I saw are still active. In buildings the ant may be, and often is, deterred; but he is really unstoppable. Legs of a wooden cabinet may be set in little lids or cans of oil or water, but the ant will build up a rod of earth around the receptacle and go up through a hole in the center of it. Ants have been known to go through concrete and even rubber.

Camp. Stars. A full moon. Silhouettes of trees. Sudden flutterings of wings. Loneliness—yet no loneliness, none that I felt, at least. Sleep. The morning star. Light. The trek. Two paths through sand, spinifex, and tall grasses. Spinifex resembles an enormous tumbleweed with many sharp points—it's really like a big pincushion. Occasionally the golden wattle, a sort of bushlike tree, deposits its yellow blooms (Australia's national emblem) on my cap and shoulders.

My stops at stations for water would invariably be met with offers of hospitality: place to rest, tea and cakes, meals, tucker (food) for my pack. At a place called Bohenia (after the tree), I commented about this.

"I can't get used to the hospitality in this country—the way you folks feed a chap passing through, and all that."

"Well, you won't get it in the south, you know," said my host, "especially around the cities."

"No, I suppose not. It seems to be a curse of men in the city areas that hospitality is lacking."

"Yes, and the ones that have never traveled are the worst."

Bohenia had hogs, which ran wild in a few years; and 220 goats, the heaviest ones up to 70 and 80 pounds. So I had goat's milk, yellow goat's butter, and salt pork. The pork gave me a terrific thirst, and on the trail I consumed an imperial quart of water in less than an hour's time. There was often sand too deep to even push or pull the loaded bike through. At such times I would follow a cow path or make my own, dodging anthills from six inches to six feet in height, clumps of spinifex, deadwood, and trees.

At another station I met a minister who had the largest pastorate in Australia, possibly in the world. He was a Presbyterian with the Australian Inland Mission, a traveling padre visiting his parish, which extended from Broome to Mount Isa and included all of the north except the immediate vicinity of Darwin. Rev. Mr. B. and his wife were being entertained at this station by the cook, the manager being absent. It is a common joke that the cook thinks he is the most important man on a station, and this one spent the evening windbagging in high gear. I don't suppose the padre and his wife were much edified by the cook's accounts of his barroom escapes, his falling down a well while drunk, and the antics and language of all the drunken people he had ever known. I felt it would be very difficult to be a minister in the outback, where there were no churches or assemblies, and the people seemed to treat Sunday like any other day. But maybe they have more serious thoughts of God than I imagine.

Australia's famous flying doctor service originated with the A.I.M., Rev. John Flynn being its proponent. The first one was at Cloncurry in 1934. The Aussies took to it, and others outside the church wanted to contribute, so Rev. Flynn, with difficulty, persuaded the church fathers to let the service pass outside the church. Flynn and another man also developed the famous (and still much used at that time) pedal wireless. The latter kept the cook busy the following morning at breakfast. He was getting the gossip, a custom at all stations this time of day. It works out just like the old party-line telephones in the States.

I came to a station called Chestnut at 10:45 A.M., expecting to confirm some directions I had received on how to get to the next station, Gogo, forty miles away. But Chestnut was deserted, it was too early to stop for the day, so I sallied forth again. There were forks in the trail, or so I fancied in my memory after I had got a couple hours past them. Then my direction changed from west to north, and even northeast. Having never been able to obtain a map of the area, and having seen only one, old and inaccurate, I allowed my memory to recall trails such as the one I was following, leading way north into the bush not far from the sea and having no outlets. I found a water hole of muddy water by following some bullock tracks, and I think this helped me to keep sane. Then I hit a long stretch of sand with the usual endless horizon. It would seem that I was approaching a river—an uneven line of trees greener than the others. But then I discovered that no matter where I looked I could pick out such a line. In fact, there was a perfect circle of "river" about me. Not since I had been lost in the mountains of western Norway had I felt so desperate. I felt angry with everyone for not having given me better directions; yet in the same minute I called on the Lord for guidance. It was such a long way back to Chestnut, I would have the wind to buck, and I was tired. The chap at Chestnut might not come back for several days, and what would I do for directions? But the thing that really made me decide to go back was my failure to see the padre's car tracks—or any other tracks, for that matter. And as I turned back it seemed the trail really was an old one. And then the long, long dreary miles back to Chestnut, arriving after dark.

The mechanic had returned to Chestnut. He said I had been on the right road after all. I argued and went over my check points. I had thirty miles to traverse a third time the next day.

One day on my travels I came to what I had been told was "pindown" country. Well, I was *pinned down* all right. Deep red sand for hours. Most of the time it was out of the question to even walk in the tracks, they were so narrow and deep. And red was the color of the sunset that night, with the trees strikingly silhouetted against it. The land was as flat as a floor, and each tree stood just far enough from its neighbor to steal its share of the flaming great arch of heaven. Even more, the trees were grouped as in the wings of a mighty theater, with the center of the stage open for nature's greatest spectacle, the setting of the sun.

I now commenced to go through a string of five sheep stations. Cattlemen, by tradition, distrust sheepmen; and I had been told I wouldn't get the hospitality I had been receiving. But I didn't find this to be the case. At Nooncombah I had a fine hot lunch and the offer of all the tucker I needed for the trek ahead.

As evening approached I had visions of a fine supper with this new provender. But these were blasted along about dark when I came to the sad realization that I had not filled both canteens at the last water hole and here it was dark and I hadn't reached the next water hole and I did not have enough water to last the night. To make matters worse, the road ruts got so deep and sandy that riding would have even been impossible in the daytime. I moaned aloud into the silences.

"You idiot! Oh, what a dumbbell! Thought you'd reach Broken Wagon water before dark, did you? Won't you ever learn you can't rely on this country? Now where are you? Up to your neck in sand and you can't even see where to walk. How are you goin' to find water even if you do get to that run-through? Anyway, do you know how far that is? Have you come eight miles from the last landmark? What a blithering ass you are! What a FOOL!"

Just as I reached a good climax I came to the run-through. Then I felt a bit contrite at such chastisement. But now, how was I to find the water hole? My directions were that there were tracks leading off to the left. But how see those in the dark? And would they be just inside the run-through, or, as was more likely, would they be a few hundred feet, or a quarter mile, or a half, beyond?

I took off the bike light to use by hand but found the sand too heavy to push the bike while hunting, so took it back to the run-through. Glory be! There were a couple of old tracks off the trail just inside the opening. I tried to follow with my weak light, but I lost them when I reached hard ground. I continued in the general direction but had no luck, so started to return. At this point I should say that the thirst of a thirsty man, already fired by sand and dust as was mine, automatically increases tenfold when he starts hunting for water. On my way back to the road I walked in darkness to save my batteries. Wham-o! I fell smack over an anthill and sprawled in the grit. I had forgotten the blasted anthills couldn't be seen in the starlight any more than the clumps of spinifex.

On my next trip I walked up the main trail for a long way, hoping to see other tracks or come to signs of a watercourse. What a torture of decisions I went through trying to decide whether or not to go on to the next clump of trees before turning back! On my way back to Jacqueline I stopped to listen. In the distance and in the right direction from the road I heard the raucous cry of a bird. One cry, and nothing more.

"That bird is by a water hole, I'll bet my bottom dollar," I said aloud.

On my third trip I had brains enough to take my empty canteen along. I headed out in the direction of the cry of the bird. This time I went much farther. Suddenly realizing I might get lost, I turned and took bearings by the stars and certain trees, though I knew I couldn't really rely on the trees. Soon I knew I was approaching water. How did I know? Well, it's something one can't describe. I didn't smell it, though I sniffed. It was just a sort of sixth sense. Presently a ravine, then a declivity, and shortly the blessed stuff lay before me faintly reflecting a tiny bit of starlight. A good deep hole. I thanked the Lord and drank greedily, prone at the edge. No, I'll be honest. I drank first and then gave thanks.

The station buildings of Upper Liveringa were handsomely located on the shelf of a small mountain range above the Fitzroy River. The bookkeeper instructed me in the lore of the sheep country.

Upper Liveringa had the largest wool clip in all Western Australia: 1,000 bales per year with a maximum of 1,500 bales. This is from 70,000 to perhaps 100,000 sheep. However in the current year they had lost 15,000 sheep from corkscrew grass, locally called grass seed. This goes in the wool, curls and penetrates the skin of the throat or elsewhere. It takes thousands of them to kill a sheep and the difficulty arises only about every twenty years in a wet season. Sometimes the grass is found in the cooked meat.

The map of Liveringa showed it was divided into paddocks of from 7,000 to 32,000 acres, all fenced. There were bores at alternate corners so that one bore provided water for four paddocks. Bores were from 50 to 400 feet deep, and a complete expense record was kept on each. Paddocks marked "stud" on the map were for breeding rams only; but it had become cheaper to buy good rams than to breed them. Sheep dogs were not used on Liveringa, and handling was done quietly on horseback. Sheep are not "driven." You move among them and get them started.

At another station I saw a huge bullock wagon in a shed. I was told it was a ten-tonner (the rear wheels were higher than a man) and that seventy-six donkeys had been used to haul it. I rather discounted this until I visited the next station, which happened to be a cattle station again. Here I was told that some stations still use two- and five-ton wagons and may hitch as many as thirty donkeys to one. They were used to carry posts or rails, or to drag a fireplow. However the practice was dying out and the donkeys were running wild, so that they were a menace by stampeding cattle during a mustering. Donkeys originally cost the settlers about $160 each; now they were shot.

By this time I had nearly completed my trek across Northern Australia, but I now came to a 112-mile stretch of sand I had been warned about as far east as Newcastle Waters. I took the greatest pains to set down directions for this stretch, as I well knew there would be no one to ask about the waterholes along the way. Even so I found that I missed waterholes because I was unable to identify "a bit of a creek" or even a "definite creek crossing." The land was level, and these "creeks" were hardly more than dry, sandy depressions, frequent and barely recognizable.

Nillibubbica—Nillibubbica—a name and a place I knew I should never forget as long as I lived. The water from the mill dropped from the pipe into a clear saucer-shaped pool, and bubbles of air rolled back up to the surface. The pool, though shallow, seemed to reflect the blue of the sky. All around was sand and scattered trees: bush, the endless bush, miles and miles of bush. From Nillibubbica I knew I should have to plunge into deep sand and heaven only knew when I should find water like this again. And so I drank . . . and drank . . . and drank some more. Then I filled both canteens, a beer bottle, and a little food can; and then I drank some more. I started out, pushed the bike through deep sand for scarcely ten rods, panicked, left the bike, walked back . . . and drank some more!

It was heavy going all right. But at one time they had marked out the track with a grader, and there was room outside the sand ruts to walk with the bike and hold it steady. I walked for four hours or more without a letup, figuring that I had done twelve miles by camp time. It was hot and dusty. My throat was dry. Yet I did not sweat a great deal, just walking; and this new experience seemed to hold my throat in abeyance. Perhaps I exercised will power but I seemed only to be dry, rather than thirsty, and when darkness came I ate my whole meal and went to bed, having consumed only my beer bottle of water.

The second day the trek continued about as before. The tracks usually ran straight as a die, but might go slightly up hill and down dale. Apparently I calculated my walking speed fairly well, because I completed a certain seventeen miles at about the time I figured. I hadn't really arrived anywhere then. It was only a sign which pointed in a vague direction off into the bush: "Yalleroo Well, 4 miles." Hunt as much as I liked, I could see no trail leading to this water. I gave it up and passed on. The going was a bit better. Later I found a pit containing water.

During the afternoon I was forced to walk out into the bush, as the road was too soft, even on the shoulders. This meant dodging fallen trees and getting the bicycle over all kinds of fallen bush. The front fender would frequently catch in the twigs, and I would have to bend down and free it. Meanwhile twigs from other brush would jab me in the neck and back. Sticks would get caught in the spokes too, and this didn't help any. Some trees (small, about three inches thick) lay one way and some another, usually broken about a foot off the ground so that I had to lift first the front wheel and then the back one to get over them. It seemed as though I had to walk three miles to get one mile. Besides, I made three sallies into the bush for water. I found none. Nor was there any water in the water hole I did find. So I was good and thirsty when I came to a well after dark. Then I drank too much, got a bad case of cramps, and got sick in the bargain.

Broome at last. For hundreds of dry and sandy miles I had been promising myself that when I reached Broome, one of the most remote towns in Australia, I was going on an ice-cream binge. This would be to celebrate, not only my first thousand miles, completed long before, but my crossing of the continent. And so it was with a sinking heart that I pedaled about the sprawling, tropical town, realizing there was no ice cream to be had.

Broome is noted for its great tides (34 feet) and its pearl shells. I ate lunch one day near a pearling lugger and a pearl-shell warehouse, where a couple of the workers gave me a pair of nice shells. There was a big boom in the industry just then, and one of the 225-pound bags of pearl shells just unloaded from the lugger was worth about $270. Before the war there had been over three hundred luggers in the pearling fleet, but many were sunk for defense or other reasons and now there were only nineteen left. Each carries a full crew as well as perhaps two divers and mechanics to handle the diving gear. Clams are removed from the shell on board the boat, and the shells are packed. In the warehouse I watched Old Chris, a black, as he expertly classed these shells from bins. They would be transshipped to coastal boats, taken to Freemantle, and transshipped again for America. Emory stones polish the outside of the shells, which may then be made into brooches or fancy wares. However, most shells are used for buttons.

I eventually found a place where they had ice cream. The proprietress

"Bronchoing" on the world's biggest ranch. A bullock has just been thrown inside the broncho panel. Note branding iron.

A picture cannot do justice to the wonders of a sunset seen from a lonely camp in the bush.

The never-never country— dry, hot—bush!

was a Creole, or half-caste aborigine, or a Malay, or a Chinese, or some such mixture, but there was nothing wrong with the mixture of her ice cream. She had never before sold it in bulk and was amazed at my consumption.

And in Broome I got a telegram. They found me at a garage repairing Jacqueline. The notice scared me half to death. I pedaled madly to the post office and found it was not bad news from home but a congratulatory message from the Elliott Cycle Company way down in Perth, a thousand miles away. It concerned my "epochal trip across Australia." I never did find out how they knew about it.

8

Incredible Encounter
on Ninety-Mile Beach

From Broome I turned south and west in the direction of Perth. I had a ride with a station manager for the first stretch, but although he had driven over the road a number of times, he chose a wrong turn and got lost. There was such a crisscrossing of tracks with no set road that even the locals got mixed up. We stopped at a station called Thangoo, where Jack Willis had his "harem," as he called them, of young gins prepare us a steak dinner. Jack was "bloody crook" in bed with some kind of fever he hadn't been able to decipher. However, he arose and dragged a set of boomerangs and two shields out of a drawer and offered them to me. I took one of each when I found they would be shipped home for me. The return type boomerang will come back from as far as 400 feet if thrown by an expert. The war type boomerang can be thrown as far as 750 feet, farther than any object can be thrown at ground level.

There seemed to be very little diversion or recreation available to the people on the stations. There was no card playing to speak of, perhaps a little gambling. There were no dances or sociables because there were so few women. Only a few young nurses seem to have risked going out into this "never-never country," and they were not long unmarried. I saw no church activity. The men occasionally go the long distances to the "towns" for supplies, and then stand around the bar in the pub guzzling great quantities of beer. Consumption of beer may average as high as fifty gallons per capita. Pubs were open daily but on Sundays only from seven to eight and ten to twelve in the morning and after four in the afternoon.

Ninety-Mile Beach is a deserted, shadeless, nearly waterless plain along the edge of the Indian Ocean. I was about thirteen miles out, when I saw something coming on the track in the distance. I couldn't identify it at first, but as I came a little closer it dawned on me that the object was a man pushing a wheelbarrow. Then I remembered hearing about a thousand miles earlier of a man pushing a wheelbarrow around the continent and that I would meet him. I had only about half believed what I'd heard, yet here he was.

With this, I was all prepared to meet up with my rival for popular attention and say, "Well, this calls for a celebration." But when he got closer and stopped opposite me—two lonely souls in one of earth's most God-forsaken areas—I almost gasped in astonishment at what I saw. Here was no kindred adventurer but the most disreputable tramp I had ever laid eyes on. His trousers had great holes on the knees and seat about four inches wide and six inches long. In these, in a haphazard manner, he had tied, yes, tied with string, patches that were not large enough to lay over the edges of the holes. The patches thus hung like pendulums in the holes. In addition one trouser leg had been ripped at the front, starting just below the crotch, so that his nakedness was barely concealed. There were no underclothes. On his head was a dilapidated, bandless felt or skin hat of the kind Robin Hood is supposed to have worn—in fact, there was even an old feather attached to it.

And his equipment! You wouldn't believe that either! The wheelbarrow was a disreputable old iron one with the wheel so askew on the axle that it leaned at a 30-degree angle; or perhaps it was that the axle had fallen down at one end. On the wheelbarrow were some items of junk, but only three were recognizable enough to stay in my memory afterwards. One was an old, old dirty, worn-out brown grip (country-doctor kind) with one handle hanging by one end only. The second was an old, smoked-up dirty lantern with a broken glass, only one jagged part of which remained. The third was a light-colored quart bottle, filthy inside and out, containing about two cups of liquid, and having no cap but a small, inverted rusty tin can.

I was simply too dumbfounded to start the conversation. So he began.

"How far is it to Anna Plains?" He took a swig from the bottle and spat it on the ground. I gathered this was to impress me how little he cared for the desert traveler's most prized possession.

"Oh, about . . ." Here I paused to study my watch. "Oh, about thirteen miles. You'll come to a gate in about eight miles, and then another in five more miles, and then you're practically there."

"Well, I won't make it today!"

"Why not? A man can walk three miles an hour!"

"I only make seven or eight miles per day." Another swig from the bottle, which sat right out in the hot sun. But he didn't spit this out. "I had to go about three miles off the road to get into that last mill. Have you got any smokin'?"

"No. Don't happen to smoke. Say, be sure you get good directions at Anna Plains. There are a lot of trails; and then there's a couple stretches of pindown—you know what pindown is?"

"Nope. You mean spinifex?"

"No. Pindown is stretches of red sand so deep you can't move through it and have to walk out in the bush and dodge brush and fallen trees. It's bad east of Broome. Are you going east of Broome?"

"Buggered if I know!" was his response.

"Well, I suppose you are used to people telling you that the road ahead is worse than the one you have come over."

"No. Can't say that I am."

About this time I got the idea that he looked on me as a grandfather does a young whippersnapper. So I kept still.

He picked up a shoulder strap from the right handle of his wheelbarrow and said, "Well, I'll be movin' on."

Again I was amazed. Here was a guy more anxious than I to keep on the move.

"Have you got everything you need?" I asked.

"Yes, except smokin'," and he moved off. The wheel on the barrow turned to a certain point, held a moment, then groaned on over, giving ample evidence of lack of grease. Tilted as it was, it looked terribly hard to push.

"I've got a wrench. Would you like me to help you fix your wheel?" I yelled after him.

"No, she's right."

He continued on down the north track, leaving me nothing to do but continue on the south track in my own direction.

Never will I forget that incredible encounter. I heard much later on my travels that he perished on one of the desert stretches I had been over. I was forced to believe the rumor, since the one about my meeting him had certainly been correct.

The going was pretty good on Ninety-Mile Beach. There were some rough stretches where stock had stepped in wet weather, but I was so happy to be out of the red sand and be able to ride at all, I did not mind much. It was about forty miles to first water, the usual brackish (salt-sweet) stuff found close to the sea. Nevertheless I took time out to walk a mile or more over to the summit of the hills lying toward the sea and paralleling the road. I couldn't even then see the sea itself, but I was rewarded by a view of the sea beyond more hills. Here was real loneliness. And this was the Indian Ocean, a new ocean for me.

During the afternoon I made note of some of the desert fauna and flora. There were hundreds of little lizards that raced along the track ahead of me. Even in high gear I could not overtake them, and their tiny feet seemed to go so rapidly they hardly touched the sand. Among the plants was a pretty, delicate pink blossom shaped like a cattail. Then there was pigweed, a weed of variegated greens and pinks, also called sand fire because of its appearance at sunset. I examined the little bulblike leaves of this plant and found that each of the tiny bulbs was chuck-full of water, sweet and good to the taste.

Near the end of Ninety-Mile Beach I came to a station called Nalgi, where I was made royally welcome. A special treat was a bowl of very white, quite thick cold cream. This was made from cow's milk, but I had also eaten it made from goat's milk. The separator is set for very rich, and the cream is kept in the icebox. The cream is best spread on top of jam. Delicious.

Aboriginal girl on Nalgi station.

Crossing the infamous "90-mile beach," northwestern Australia. There was no shade in which to eat meals on this stretch.

When I arrived, the station operator's two children were "in school." They were excused in honor of this strange visitor from a far-off land. School was a little room, more like the end of a hallway, where both children could listen to their teacher many miles away through wireless headsets. There were books and exercise papers on their desk just as if they were in a real school.

It was only fourteen miles to another station, Wallal. Here I had the opportunity of seeing the culmination of Australia's leading industry, a sheep shearing.

The shearing shed was just that, a shed, unpainted, long and low and with a gable roof. The sheep came into the pens on one side of the shearing shed, and the shearers worked in a rather narrow aisle on the other. A shearer would go into his pen, grab a sheep by the forefeet and drag it out with its back between his legs and its head and forefeet at about his waist. It was amazing how quiet the sheep were resting awkwardly on their bottoms, their backs bowed between the shearer's legs as he sheared. The mechanically driven shears hung down from an overhead drive shaft powered at one end of the building. The arms and propelling belts for the shears were like those for a dentist's drill. The shearer started on the sheep's belly and worked down and onto the hind legs and then up the sides until the coat lay in a pile, one piece, at his feet. He worked swiftly and surely. One man who was supposed to be the champ of northern Western Australia could do over two hundred sheep in an eight-hour day. Sitting on the rail of one of the pens was the "expert," who had to see that everything mechanical was working properly. When the men stopped work he sharpened the shears, which resembled a barber's clippers, by using two giant emery wheels turning at high speed.

While the shearers worked, a lad in shorts and a duster (a cap such as American housewives sometimes wore for cleaning) picked up the pile of wool, tore down the aisle with it and placed it on the classifying table at the end of the shed. Here three young men sorted the fleeces under the watchful eye of the classifier, who was really the boss of the outfit. The boss explained to me the meaning of such terms as crimp and tensile strength. Nearby was a boxlike machine which forced the wool into huge bales contained in burlap and weighing over 200 pounds each. These bales would be three feet square and perhaps four feet or more in length.

Shearers are called kings of labor because their wages are good and they eat well. The basic wage for nonshearing labor was then five pounds seven shillings per week, but shearers averaged twelve pounds ($39). Each outfit worked on a contract basis, carried its own cook, tents, etc. The shearer got two pounds, five and one-half shillings for each one hundred sheep shorn. He worked an eight-hour day and a five-day week.

The shearer's supper was the biggest meal I have ever been served. It began with a huge bowl of soup, well supplied with barley and meat and eaten with several slices of bread. My main plate was covered with meat somewhere on the bottom, but I had to eat down through practically a whole can of peas and a great heap of cooked pumpkin to get to it. There was honey to go with the bread. Then came sweets, a great bowl heaped with prunes and custard pudding. No one but a shearer or a crazy American cyclist could make away with such a mountain of food. Yet, I was told later, "some jokers make away with two of those meals of an evening." It seems they can't eat very much for their other meals, as they have to bend over the sheep all the time and too much in the stomach would not allow this.

On a station called Pardoo I was given good mutton chops and sheep's brains for breakfast. The latter are considered a delicacy, and I'll admit they were good. While here I was introduced to a Mr. Peterson.

"That sounds like a good Swedish, Danish, or Norwegian name," said I. "Norwegian."

"Yah. Kann du snacka Norske?"

He broke out into a smile, and we were friends at once. He had run away from home when he was fourteen. How many other Norwegian boys did the same? There had been a family of eleven children. The pattern was familiar: too many children for the hard-working mother to give much individual attention or sympathy. He had gone to sea, as was natural. He had visited America, liked it and even fought for us in the Spanish-American War. In South Africa a captain had promised to land Peterson and others of the crew on the west coast of North America but had double-crossed them and gone to Australia. Communication with home? Yes, one sister, heard from just before the war. "She was five when I left home." How little of later family ties this man had experienced! He had never married; bachelorhood is as common as false teeth in Australia. Now he was sixty-seven, native tongue almost forgotten. A blacksmith on a lonely station. There could be only a few associates, perhaps no real close friends. I later inquired what would happen when old chaps like Peterson passed on. The body would be brought in to Port Headland, the nearest town, and there the priest would read a burial service. Or if the man was of different faith, or of no faith, the clerk or justice would read the service. People would drive in from the station to attend. So thus will this lonely son of Norway find a resting place far from his native land.

Near Pardoo I turned south to take the inland route to Perth. People could not understand why I was taking this route because it meant nothing but miles and miles of barren deserts—the "madman's trek"—whereas the coast route, although much longer, went through a number of towns. But the inland route went more through the center of Western Australia, and thus would give me a better idea of the country.

At the start I had the wind against me for the first time. Nor was I yet out of the pindown, so I did quite a lot of walking beside the trail. In late afternoon I detoured briefly to an open well. Here I lowered my Aussie canteen on a long wire but still could not reach the water. There were some bits of ledges on the inner circumference of the well, and I descended part way in order to get the canteen in. You can bet that I was m-i-g-h-t-y careful—and nervous—for it might be weeks before the next guy left the road to visit this particular well. Not that it would matter if I slipped.

There are a few rivers in this part of the world, but they flow for only a couple of months of the year. One of these is the DeGrey, and I found it almost dry. First there was a quarter of a mile of dry bed. Pebbles and sand were so deep that wool and spinifex and pieces of heavy wire netting had been laid on the tracks. When I had waded through that, I came to a line of big trees, in the shade of which and about whose roots were some good-sized pools of water. I found that by laying my canteen down in the middle of each pool, I could step across without getting my feet wet. Thus I was literally fording the river on a canteen of water. On the far bank, desert or not, there was a grassy place, and I sat there amid very picturesque surroundings and enjoyed a good breakfast of bread, cheese, meat, eggs, sugar, and jam.

I worked south through Marble Bar, known as the hottest place in Australia. It once endured 160 days with the temperature above 100 degrees. Then on to a station called Mount Edgar, very neat and trim with white buildings and many flowers, even though the blacks had run off "yandying" for tin. There were zinnias, jacarandas, jacket bushes, chinteals, date palms, poinsianas, yellow-flowered tecomas, and oleanders in bloom. Of flowers in this area, the Stuart's pea, a sort of shrub, is the most striking. The flower resembles that of the tiger lily but is red in color with two large black eyes like those of a dragonfly.

"Oh, how wonderful is nature! Come and gaze upon her glories!" I shouted aloud into the mountains the next morning. I was witnessing the sunrise through the clouds in the mountains above Nullagine, following a similar sunset the preceding evening. The skyline was a truly serrated one, and it mattered not that the peaks had little altitude. The mountains were red, red in color; also the stones and the road. The road had improved so that cycling was pleasant and thrilling in spite of Jacqueline's defective rear axle. There was very little bush. There were some of the bright, white gum trees, and the usual—no, the word is ill-chosen—*unusual* desert flora. For the desert always has been and always will be the most interesting place in the world. Here was a beautiful azure-gray—or was it silver?—bush with a bright-yellow flower. There was a green plant with a purple-pink cattail blossom. And over there was a little one, the softest of pale lavenders with suggestions of white. And there was a black and white swallow skimming so close to the ground he almost touched it.

One of the divisions in the pinion-bearing race of the driving hub had broken, and sometimes I had no power from the chain. Occasionally I had no brake. As if all this weren't enough, I seemed to spend about an hour every day changing and fixing tires.

I was eating breakfast one morning near one end of a watering trough. I looked up and was amazed to find five big emus within twenty feet of me. What a chance for a picture! Curses! The camera was in my pack on their side of the trough. Moving slowly, I tried to reach it without scaring them away, but they ambled off. I settled back to eat but with my camera handy, and another group of about fifteen came out of the bush on my side of the trough. I waited patiently and was rewarded by two shots of the birds drinking, within some twelve to fifteen feet of me.

This morning I got one of the luckiest breaks in my travel career. I got a long, long ride of eight hundred miles to the nearest bike shop—at Perth. I didn't realize how lucky I was until I found that the axle was broken quite in two except for a tiny sliver of metal. Meanwhile I rode steadily southward with Sam and Arnold, who had driven some government officials into the north and were returning after a two weeks' absence.

The first night we arrived at the railhead in Meekatharra. I spent quite a bit of time talking to the railroad men there. They spoke of a train carrying arsenic, and when I expressed surprise, they told me that arsenic and antimony are by-products of gold. They talked of the famous Murchison gold fields, where our President Hoover was once a mining engineer. I heard of mines like the Great Fingal, formerly the largest in Australia, and still the richest at ten ounces to the ton of ore. There was another mine from which 400 tons was expected to have a value to 40,000 pounds. Certain mines yielded a product with a value of 12 pounds of standard gold per ounce, compared with 10 pounds, 10 shillings for ordinary gold.

On the afternoon of the second and last day of the trip the bush took on a greener tinge due to a rain. We entered an area where there were great fields of everlasting flowers. First there were fields of white ones, then fields of pink ones, then yellows, then all three kinds together. These flowers are so named because they will keep a "twelvemonth," having very dry petals. They are hung with the heads down for about a week, and then they may be displayed in more conventional fashion. Sam and Arnold took time to stop and pick great bouquets, in spite of their hurry to get home. Some of the mulga was also in yellow bloom. We saw two emu hens with four chicks each. Then there was the salmon gum tree bursting into bloom, the blackbutt tree, and the gimlet tree. The last is a twisted affair with a cross section like a four-pointed star. This tree is not liked by white ants and is therefore of great value.

Nearly two hundred miles from Perth we came out of the bush and into the area of green cultivation at last. Here was my first wheat field, lovely and green, where the land had been cleared of its original bush. Soon we entered an area of mixed farming: wheat, sheep, and possibly a few pigs. Nearby were fields lying fallow, and I was told these might be

Curious emus approached my breakfast spot at a lonely watering trough in northwestern Australia. Emus are about as large as the ostrich.

disked several times to keep the weeds down. Other fields appeared white from a distance and turned out to be full of bleached stalks from the preceding year's wheat. (It was now early August.) Other fields had the green spring wheat already knee high. Sheep may be turned onto the stubble just after the harvest.

My long ride ended at my request on the outskirts of Perth. As I was casting my eye on my tucker bag a fisherman (the Swan River was just near) turned up a face of inquiry from below the bank of the road. I introduced myself, and then in a minute or so he called up that he had a bed on the veranda of his house just close by and that I should bring my stuff down. When this was done, he invited me to sit inside by the fire and eat; and maybe you think that fire didn't feel good in the cold dampness of the river bottom.

So with this hospitality I arrived in Perth, capital and really the only city in Western Australia. I had been on the road for more than three months and had completed a huge northern semicircle around the continent from Brisbane on the east. And what experiences I had had!

9

Among the Cockeys
of the Southwest

One of the first things I did following my arrival in Perth was to go to Elliott's Cycle Shop. Here I took Jacqueline apart and found that the axle was literally just hanging together by a thread of metal. Imagine! Talk about luck in getting that long ride! There was nothing to do but put on an English Sturmey-Archer three-speed gear in place of my American two-speed coaster-brake assembly. This meant that new spokes were required, and this in turn meant a new wheel rim. But Mr. Elliott was most generous and helpful, and I was soon fixed up in good shape. In addition, I was a dinner guest at his home that night.

I spent several enjoyable days in Perth, often "at home" with "Pop" Wright, the man who had called me down to his house from the road embankment that first night. He and his wife had lived there for forty years, raising a family of seven children, all married except Celia, living at home. Celia was a great comfort to her parents and did a great deal for twenty-two nieces and nephews. She also helped the American adventurer with such things as his sewing and ironing. Her hobby was the royal family, and the walls of the small living and dining room were covered with framed pictures of all vintages of various members of the family. You could have scarcely driven a nail anywhere without striking a king, queen, or princess at some stage of their development.

When I objected to the Wrights' feeding me as well as sheltering me, Pop would say: "Now as long as you're here, you eat with us."

Pop could tell of several cases where he and Mom had helped passers-by from their little "house by the side of the road." He had a really generous heart and a genial disposition. At one time he had raised and sold flowers, so I learned a great deal about the ins and outs of the flower-vending trade, cemetery markets, street markets, store markets, bobs and pence per dozen, and whatnot. In his back yard on the river bottom he had orange and lemon trees with ripe fruit on both, and since he sometimes sold from these, I learned about their market while eating one of the oranges. He kept a horse and a two-wheeled cart which he had used to cut and sell wood, so I learned about the wood market. He had always been a fisherman and his nets were hung just back of the house. He made his own nets and showed me how it was done and about the kinds of string used and methods of treating it. Then followed a lengthy and interesting account of

84

fishing laws and of various game wardens through the years, and of trials before solicitors, and of proper methods of getting along with such people; and of which parts of nets could be retained under legal confiscation, of the kinds of fish caught, their lengths, weights, percent of bone, etc.

Pop also kept a calf, which he fed chaff (chopped straw), and a number of pens of chickens. In one was a rooster all by his lonesome. He was being fed exceptionally well "so that he'll make good eggs when I turn him in with the hens." In a second pen were young hens; in a third, old hens; in a fourth, young hens and roosters; and in a fifth, roosters. The only reason I could see for not running them all in together was that then Pop wouldn't feel he had any chores to do, not having to crawl through all those gates. The chickens all received the same feed—wheat; and of course I got a history of the wheat market.

In his garden Pop grew shallots, leeks, onions, and more shallots, leeks, and onions, a few beet roots (beets), swedes (Swedish turnips), spinach, and even cape gooseberries. These last greatly resemble our ground cherries, but the fruit is a bit larger and has a sweeter taste. A spring on the hillside flowed out through channels cut around the vegetable beds, and so to the river about four rods away.

Celia left with a sister for a week's holiday, and from then on I ate with Mom and Pop alone. Back in America I had lived much with my grandparents, and here I was with such similarity that I had to remark about it. Pop even had a mustache like grandpa's and had the asthma just as badly. Both liked to get up early. And meat and eggs were the staple diet for both.

The children liked to come home to Pop and Mom's. There were only three in the immediate area, but they liked to show up either with or without their families. They would just sit and talk to Pop while Mom would listen but never miss a thought. Then there was a young chap of about thirty called Sam. Sam was just a friend but around as much as the children. He was smart as a whip, a detail-minded researcher, but he liked to talk to Pop. I felt that his presence was a tribute to Mr. Wright's character.

With these companions and in this environment we shared our seven meals a day in the little room with the fire at one end. The royal family looked down on us from the walls, and the seven children and the twenty-two grandchildren peeked at us from the pictures crowded onto a table in a corner near the fireplace.

Mom made a fruit pudding for Sunday dinner. First she measured into a bowl one and one half cups of flour, one pound of mixed fruit (raisins, currants, peel, etc.), two eggs, a tablespoon of dripping, and a cup of sugar. She mixed these. Next she took one pudding spoon (nearly a tablespoon) of "essence of coffee and chicory," put it in a cup, added a little boiling water to dissolve, then a bit of cold milk, and then stirred the lot into the pudding. She next dipped a pudding cloth in hot water, placed the pudding in the cloth, and tied it up. Both were then put in a pan of boiling water and boiled two hours. It was later served in slices with custard poured on each.

In Perth I got much of the lore of the city and country from an American. He had married an Aussie girl after the war and elected to stay. We roamed the city's pride, Kings Park, and talked. From Mount Eliza we looked out over the city with its red brick and white stone front buildings, and down to Perth Water. The ferries on the latter plying over to isolated Mills Point seemed so very tiny and so far away below us. Wide reaches of the Swan lay peacefully to the right, and the course of the popular rowing races could be seen. There was no commercialization, no dirty docks to mar the view.

"Now you see, Hart, why I love this place so much," said Dick. "The funny part of it is that I feel at home here—more so than in my hometown." And he made his point firm by telling me with animation, a wealth of lore about Perth and Western Australia.

From Perth I went to Freemantle, the real seaport, and then turned back east on the long, long road that was to take me a second time across the continent of Australia.

On the second day I came into an area of very pleasant farms. Here lived the "cockeys," or farmers of the Southwest. Contented cattle, mostly Jerseys, grazed on the greenest of grasslands amongst the great trees still standing on the partly cleared land. There were frequent showers, and it was feasible at night to ask the nearest farmer for the use of a shed to place my sleeping bag. The place sometimes turned out to be a covered porch with an old bed on it.

I was invariably asked into the house to share the evening meal. They never served family style, and mom dished up the portions on the plates. On two occasions I was taken into the house by the husband after the portions had been laid out. In one case they took from six different plates to fill mine; in the second the oldest daughter gave up her plate, much to my embarrassment.

After the meal we would all sit around and talk. But at eight o'clock sharp, kids of all ages were sent to bed. They obeyed without a murmur, even though it was very unusual to have an American globetrotter in the house. A girl of twenty would go along with the rest, but in some homes a boy of even eighteen would be allowed to stay up until nine. Such a lad would be already minus some teeth, and his parents very probably would be using false ones. Dad and I would continue talking until nine (which was considered bedtime), while mom listened or dozed tiredly nearby. All housewives work side by side with the men doing the chores, so no wonder they are tired. As soon as the milking and separating are done, mom rushes into the house to finish up the supper.

Fred Stephens had a 400-acre farm with 180 acres under cultivation. He raised some corn, but a bit differently than back home in Iowa. He cultivated his maize land several times before planting so that there would be fewer weeds. He then made trenches six to eight inches apart and four inches deep with a plow (moldboard type). The kernels were sowed by hand and covered by the making of the next trench. The corn was never cultivated. When it tasseled out, it was harvested and used as a green feed, stalk and all.

People along the way were most friendly. The following is typical and came from three workers building a house about seven rods from the road.

"Where are you bound?"

"Oh, I don't know. But I can tell you where I've been."

"Oh, American, are you! Well, good on you, Yank! Good on you!"

In a town called Kirup I had breakfast in the home of the mailman. He said he had been living in Kirup for thirty years.

"What kind of country is it south of Bridgetown?" I asked him.

"Well, I really can't say. I've never been beyond Bridgetown."

"Oh! How far is it?"

"Twenty-five miles."

I was too shocked to make any further comment after that.

In this part of Australia the eucalyptus tree was well represented by the jarrah and karri trees. The jarrahs are great towering giants which provide one of the world's finest hardwoods. It is used for railroad ties and the underwater piles of docks and wharves. To see the karri trees I had to go south of Bridgetown to a place called Manjimup. Near there was a sawmill.

The Jardee Mill worked almost nothing but karri. The foreman took me through the plant and I marveled at the huge vertical saw (the only one in Western Australia) and the twin travelers, two six-foot circular saws one above the other in the same vertical plane and almost touching. Karri is hard, heavy, and very stringy. I was surprised to see that they worked the great logs, some eight feet in diameter, clear down to fruit-box lumber. Of course there are other uses, like bridge building overseas where there are no white ants, or truck bodies, and arms for telegraph poles. The box lumber, even the small side and end boards, were wet and heavy. The foreman said if one of the boards were left on its end overnight, there would be a pool of sap underneath in the morning. Perhaps the frequent rains are responsible. The mill had no sawdust burner but burned waste in an open pit.

A few miles away was a great karri tree with a lookout built on the top. This must have been between 180 and 200 feet above the ground. It was reached by a wire and wood ladder going around the tree in an ascending spiral. Like our redwoods, the branches of the karri start from 80 to 120 feet above the ground.

I spent the night with Jock Lamb, construction boss on the railroad that brought logs to the mill. The railroad had to be "shifted" and extended from time to time as new areas were readied for the mill. Jock had been a cockey until he lost his wife.

"Ye canna carry on much wi' the farmin' wi'out a gude woman," he explained.

As we sat before the fire Jock got up to show me how he pressed his clothes. His shirts were neatly folded inside two towels and he sat on them each evening.

"Me granny used to do it this way back in Scotland and it saves me ironin'."

Traveling toward the eastern edge of the cockey country, I came to the farm of Phil Tuckett, forty-three miles from the last town and fifty miles from the next farm. Phil turned out to be one swell guy. He was about forty, his wife thirty. They had three children, the oldest about ten, and were expecting another. Phil was hewing some small karri logs for a stockyard when I arrived and his wife and young hired man were managing the cows and milking machine in the "dairy."

The first thing I noticed was the way they stalled the cows. Instead of having stanchions, they tied a rope tightly around the hind part of the cow to keep her well forward in the stall. This also kept her tail in place so stripping could be done without interference. The cow's kicking leg was also usually tied. When a cow had been milked, a long wooden lever was pushed. This opened a door just ahead of her, and she walked out into the yard. Then the next of the twenty cows was driven in from a small yard in the rear.

Calf feeding also was different from back home in Iowa. In place of letting one or two calves come to a slightly opened gate to drink out of a pail while you beat off the others with a club, Phil had little stalls for the calves. In the front of each was the bottom third of a five-gallon petrol can. When he opened a gate from an adjoining yard, five little calves trotted quietly in, each one found a stall, and drank the milk with no trouble or fuss. Then the next bunch of five was driven in. Their milk had a cup of "pollard" and a teaspoon of fish oil added for each five gallons. Pollard is a term applied to the second covering of wheat, the first being bran.

Water for washing the separator and pails (five-gallon tins fitted with bails) was heated in a sort of outdoor brick fireplace. Phil did the washing while his wife went into the house to fix tea. The skimmed milk left after separating was dumped on the ground, Phil remarking he had no hogs to feed it to as in America. A "weaner" (little pig) cost about two dollars, and feed would erase any subsequent profit.

When we went into the house, it was almost like going into the barn back home in the wintertime. The house looked O.K. both outside and in, nicely plastered and finished off; but there was no ceiling, just the corrugated iron roof. The cold drafts came in under the eaves and right down into the rooms where it struck you on top of the head and shoulders. Mrs. Tuckett, barelegged, had a severe cold and could hardly breathe or talk; and the children had colds. One of them sounded quite croupy. Phil and I sat at the corners of the old-fashioned cook stove because it was in an alcove (as usual in this country) and his wife had to work from the front. Phil had been swinging an axe and sweating like myself, so he noticed the cold and even occasionally reminded the children to close the outside door. This is unusual for an Aussie, who will sit with the door open for ten minutes or an hour in the middle of the winter and never notice it.

The children were fed first: cold breakfast food with hot milk, and toast if they wished it. As was the custom, toast was made by placing a large slice of bread in front of the stove door where the wood was put in. While the bread blackened quickly, the toast was good. Then the kids had to take baths, and I shuddered at the thought; for the bathroom was drafty and unheated, the temperature was about 40 degrees, and there were no signs of hot water. But they went barefooted and barelegged outdoors, so maybe they were tough. When they reappeared in pajamas and dressing gowns, dad combed the hair of the two girls and sent them to bed. It was scarcely 7 P.M., but where else would they keep warm?

When we adults shivered to table, it was to two poached eggs on toast. I was to learn that this was standard inner Southwest diet. I recalled Phil had remarked when I first arrived that I was welcome to tea but they had no meat. But there was plenty of good homemade yellow butter, and cream for a spread, and jam, so things weren't too bad. If only they didn't cut the bread so thin! How different from the huge thick slices of bread I had eaten on the great cattle stations!

In spite of the cold we sat up late around a big fire in the stove and talked on, even after evening tea. Phil had been all over Australia and believed that Southwestern Australia was the only place where one could start up without capital. He had been there eleven years and had cleared the land; that is, he had chopped and burned the smaller trees and ringed the larger ones. It takes the latter fifteen years or so to fall down. He was pioneering just as our own forefathers did.

I slept soundly in spite of cold sheets because the good bed was heavy with blankets. The next morning I left before breakfast, although Phil called me back to give me a pound of good butter and to be sure I knew the road.

Pedaling steadily eastward, I worked out of the cockey country and into an area where the farms were even farther apart and more like stations. There was bush, bush, and more bush; a lonely, lonely trail. Mile upon mile of rolling upland country, and one afternoon I became more conscious of my surroundings than ever before. It was a cloudy day with occasional spatters of rain. But, I said to myself, why think of loneliness or the sun that was well hidden and had been for days? Let's just stop and take a look at the beauty about us. And here are the on-the-spot jottings from my notebook.

Alone under the dark, cloudy vault of heaven. A few tiny patches of blue if you hunt for them. All around me the bush. Green of every imaginable shade with dull red, orangey, and yellowish blooms. Few bushes higher than a man. Green shrubs with gray stems. Little white- and yellow-blossoming shrubs. The variety of the scene is beyond imagination. Green berries, gray ones. Little cones on tiny evergreen-tree shrubs. White-star blossoms with rust-colored stems. Tiny white flowers. Shrubs with blossoms like Dutch clover. Yellow burs on thistlelike shrubs. Greenish-white bells and cups on bushes as high as a man. Tiny blood-crimson and a few salmon-colored heart-shaped petals on tiny green shrubs. White needles on green evergreen-tree shrubs. Dark-green plants shaped like big redwood cones. Pale-green, broad-leafed bushes with acornlike nuts. Tiny pink shrubs. Others with gray-blue ball-shaped nuts. Red-berried bushes. Velvety, heart-shaped, yellow petals with crimson-magenta and orange-shadowed centers on still other small shrubs. Dark pinks. Plants with red tripartite petals and a jack-in-the-pulpit petal just opposite. Purples with yellow centers. And so on, and so on. And here it is still winter. What must the bush be like in the spring?

Nevertheless, even in such lonely country, when night came there was a bush farmer. Ridge Reid had carved himself a home in the wilderness more than fifty miles from a town. His last visitor had been thirteen weeks before, his womenfolk hadn't been off the place in six months, and they sometimes went ten weeks without mail. It was not surprising that I was treated like a king and given a spare bedroom. But I was so tired from the long hills that I had difficulty keeping up the conversation a good guest should provide.

At a town called Ravensthorpe I had been asked to visit the school. The twenty pupils all stood up to say, "Good morning." I was the first American they had ever seen. After I had given them a little talk, the teacher showed me a rare qualup bell flower and a fine spray of boronia. She then excused the boys, who, she said, were "bicycle crazy," to go out with me to see the bicycle.

Ahead of me lay an even longer between-habitations trek than those I had encountered in crossing the north of Australia. This was approximately two hundred miles to a place called Norseman, over an old trail, much of it sand, which hadn't been used in seven years, according to local folk. I spent much time getting direction from a man who had traveled over the trail by car a number of times during the war in order to court his girl at the other end. So he had had love to guide him. I had no such advantage.

At his suggestion I made a detour of twenty miles to a store in the hope I might get more recent information. While I was there a mailman drove up with a load of people on a route which crossed mine. But not one of them had been over the trail or could tell me much about it. The store people said only two or three cars per year ever went over the route. My spirits sank to a new low when even a grizzled old-timer said: "Well, it's been about eighteen years since I was over the road, but there used to be water just this side of the rabbitproof fence on the old snake road. Just about two hundred yards this side but on the old snake road."

So it was with rather a worried mind that I set out on my undertaking. The directions I had written down were to go twenty miles on a line to the rabbitproof fence, then along it two miles, right two miles; then there would be a fork; go on a straight line for fifteen miles; left on a line, except for a deviation around a dry lake, for thirty-five miles to a government water tank; then right thirty-five miles on another line; then five miles of rough stones on an angle to a Y; then eight miles to a smooth rock; then seven miles to the Norseman-Esperance road; then thirty-four miles to Norseman. There was supposed to be a lot of sand on both the thirty-five-mile stretches.

As I reread these directions I was reminded of an old cartoon I once saw in *Collier's*. An aviator, empty parachute on his back, had bailed out of his plane onto the snow-covered, treeless wastes of Siberia. In this vast expanse of white snow he had found an Eskimo and was asking directions. The latter was saying:

"Novobisoffovisk? Go north 2,000 miles to a pile of walrus bones, then west 3,000 miles to a burned cabin, then . . ."

How could I ever describe my ride or the hundreds of thoughts that crowded through my mind, especially on the first couple days? It seemed impossible not to think of the road and to try and calculate speed by frequent consultations with my watch at every change from riding to walking in light sand or to plodding in heavy sand. The wind was against me too.

"Now don't fight the road so hard," I kept telling myself. "You'll get through. You've been in the bush before—many times. You've just got out of practice recently by staying with all those cockeys. Don't worry about the water. Look, there's even some in a puddle. You could drink it in a pinch."

Although it was cloudy and spitting rain most of the time, the sun shone briefly just before it sank, and this flooded the bush ahead of me with a peculiar and rather foreboding red. Anxious to be on the road every available minute of light, I kept on until I couldn't judge the sand and then hurriedly ate because there was no twilight in this country. Then, taking my camp axe, I cut a lot of bushes for a windbreak. In the darkness I had to be very careful not to get lost from Jacqueline, because twenty feet away from her the bushes all looked alike. In cutting all around the base of a particular cluster of bushes it was easy to become confused as to directions. It would have meant spending the night in the wet without a sleeping bag. I did lose one pile of brush for a time. I put in a fairly comfortable night, although it did rain some. I used my raincoat for a cover, but in the morning it was wet on the underside.

Daylight, sudden as usual. Before breakfast I reached the rabbitproof fence—my first real marker of distance. But I had hoped to reach it the night before. It's strange how warm and friendly a thing like a fence can be. But here *man* had once been. I admired the sturdy construction, soliloquized on its long and lonely trek—even lonelier than mine—through the solitude, and even took a picture of it.

The forenoon passed, and it was lunch time before I came to the first thirty-five-mile stretch. I gave up all thought of reaching water that night. During the afternoon I had miles of very heavy sand. However I didn't actually have to leave the road as I had been forced to do in the north and could usually wade through the high narrow center between the ruts. It was still discouraging work, and I hoped for hills to get out of the sand. But when I found hills, I still had the sand. Then there were other worries. The fork of my bicycle cracked alarmingly with the awful strain, and I had visions of a broken fork and the impossibility of steering at all. It later proved that I was correct, that my fork was actually broken, and the encasing stem too. You see, I would often try to mount and ride. In the narrow rut, partly filled with sand, I would have to twist and turn the front wheel violently; and the heavy pack, throwing like a snake's tail behind, would create a further strain. The same process would be repeated when I hit sand when once mounted. As an added worry I found I had not provided enough meat and cheese to get me through to Norseman, and the prospect of just bread for the rest of the meals was not a happy one. I needed meat for strength.

It was cold that evening and during the night, and I felt the need for more under me. I had some protection from the wind by crawling deep into low bushes.

Daylight! And eventually the government water tank. How welcome it was! A large roof of corrugated metal had been erected on a rise, the roof sloping inward to a trough and the trough draining into a concrete tank underneath. This was brimming full of dark, deep, ice-cold, fairly good rainwater. The top of the tank was so near the roof and I had been thinking about water only for drinking purposes for so long, it never entered my head to wash my face and hands until I was about three sandy miles down the trail. But on that road I would not have turned back even one quarter of a mile, no matter how much I needed a wash.

Only the footprints of the dingo and the emu broke the sandy surface of the ruts I followed. The dingo's prints were, of course, like those of a dog. As for the emu, I marveled at the great length of his stride and measured it with the bike. It was longer by twelve inches than the extreme tip-to-tip points of the tires. Perhaps it had been a big emu, or maybe he had been running away from the dingo. Who could say?

Now I had many miles where the two ruts were so filled with sand they were little more than depressions. Dead leaves and twigs had collected in them, and there was not the slightest indication any car had been over the route in months. Yet what was that reflection far down the road ahead of me. Incredible! It couldn't be! Yet, it was! A pickup truck! I had to believe it! I crawled out of the sand and off the trail, for certainly the truck was pinned in by the bordering dead trees. The young driver piled out.

"You're damned game, aren't you?" he said in admiration.

"Oh, I don't know."

"Don't you know it's prohibited to even travel this road by car—or at least not without notifying them at the other end you're coming through?"

"No, I didn't know that."

"We were drunk when we started out."

His older companion was still drunk. They gave me a tin of beef and some bread and insisted I take the latter because they had nothing else to give me. They had brought no other food and, worst of all, not a drop of water. Knowing what was ahead of them, I didn't even want to take the meat. But the younger man insisted, and since he was now sober, I accepted. I warned them of the deepest sand sections, twice as deep as where we met, and where brush in the ruts well blown over with sand gave evidence that the last motorist—in dim months before—had been stuck, and well stuck. But it was true they were only about sixteen miles from the tank (their big concern), according to my calculation.

By evening I had fought through to rather high timber country and comparative freedom from sand. This was my third night in the bush, and my cold experiences of the preceding night made me use towel, newspapers, Eisenhower, and similar expedients to keep out the ground cold. Then the night turned out to be warm, and I nearly cooked. But I beat daybreak in the morning.

This day I had other troubles instead of the sand. The rear tire developed a slow leak. Then I found another broken spoke. This did not surprise me, because I had been hitting a great number of small trees fallen across the road; and also kerthumping down from tree roots in the track. These roots were many, and on each decline the sand had washed full above them, but holes had washed out below. It was impossible to avoid them completely by going along on the edge of the rut.

But pretty flowers offered some compensation. There was one in particular. It was to be seen on an often dead-looking shrub only about six inches high. The flower was shaped like a bullet with a long bayonet on the pointed end and with a frizzly fringe around the base. The color was crimson throughout, and you can imagine the contrast with the gray stem of the shrub from which it dangled.

At last a made road! In a few miles I came to a newly erected wood-cutter's shack. Here were two men who echoed the opinions of the truck driver.

"You've got more bloody guts than Ned Kelly."

"Who's he?"

"Oh, he's . . ." The speaker groped for words.

"A sort of legendary character like our Paul Bunyan, I suppose," I volunteered.

"Yeah! What would you do if the bloody dingoes attacked you? Ask this bloke. He won't sleep in the bush with me; he'll sleep atop the bloody truck. One guy, all they found was his buttons."

Later on he again referred to the trek. "I won't go through there even in a truck unless I let 'em know I'm comin' at the other end."

Having reached signs of civilization, I had suddenly and peculiarly become very tired. I even threatened myself with an hour's nap as I pedaled on into Norseman. This I reached at about five o'clock in spite of a very washboardy road—thirty miles in a little more than three hours. Ah! Sweet, sweet destination!

10

Storm on the Skittleball Plains of Tasmania

In Norseman I looked up an acquaintance from Perth, Tom Fuller. Besides offering me excellent hospitality, Tom did three things for me: took me to a bike shop, introduced me to the Granny Smith apple, and arranged a three-hundred-mile ride. At the shop they had to replace the front-wheel fork but refused to take any pay whatsoever. The Granny Smith apple is not just an apple but an institution. It is sweet and juicy, and some are four or five inches through. I have never seen such large apples in the States nor tasted any as good.

Riding eastward in the warm cab of a big semitrailer rabbit truck, I learned about the rabbit industry. There are millions of rabbits roaming the plains of Southern Australia. About forty trappers were then working for the Western Rabbit Company Limited in the region centering on a point 302 miles out from Norseman. These chaps live in isolated tents and work singly or in pairs. One lucky man has his wife with him. Ordinary steel traps are used at the entrance to burrows. Small trucks operating from the base at milepost 302 go out into the bush and take supplies to the trappers and pack up the gutted rabbits. At the base the rabbits are placed in "friges," large but portable refrigeration units, and frozen.

The frozen rabbits are taken by the big semis into Norseman—an average of over three trucks per week. The bigger trucks carry ten tons of rabbits or between 4,000 and 4,500 pairs. They are carried in the open on stringers of young gimlet trees about two inches in diameter. Although the grain turns, these trees are straight and without branches for ten to fifteen feet. Rabbits are hung on these by their hind legs in pairs. From Norseman the bunnies go by rail to Coolgardie, then by Kalgoorlie express to Perth in a total rail trip of twenty-four hours. If the fur market is firm the rabbits are then skinned and the carcass is refrozen and held for shipment to England. If the market is unfavorable, the skins are left on. There is also a market in Singapore.

Two starved young chaps with heavy beards were huddled by the fire when we arrived in camp about midnight. They were trappers waiting for their orders (for food), having nothing to eat until our truck came in. I felt sorry for them, as they looked anything but prosperous—hatless and dressed in old army castoffs—and so I helped my driver try to locate their box of supplies. We had a bad time, as the boxes were all mixed up and some had no dockets. Food is transported very carelessly in the outback,

Two days out on an abandoned road. Would I ever get out of the sand and be able to ride? Did I have enough water for two more days?

The "outback" country of Southwestern Australia. In such country I traveled from one to four days without finding a house. But the flowers of plants and shrubs were fantastically varied and beautiful!

Ten tons of frozen rabbits leave the Nullabor Plain on the long journey to the coast.

and it nearly makes me weep to see nice fresh bread riding unwrapped out in the open, or thrust in half-closed burlap bags. When we finally got the men some food to gulp, my driver took me into the cook tent for his group, where a swell stew of rabbit, potatoes, etc., had been saved for us.

The next day I made rounds with a supply truck and learned some more about rabbits. They were then in general migration from east to west—a phenomenon occurring in good seasons. Burrows are found chiefly in open country (there was quite a bit of bush scattered about). A doe may have only one kitten the first time but an old doe may have up to six. Before season (winter) is over, her first kittens will be having kittens of their own. Breeding is affected by food and water; rabbits won't breed in summer unless there is plenty of water.

My first station after leaving the rabbit camp was Madura, where genial and hospitable Scotsman Robert Mackie made me welcome. Madura had a million acres, and Mr. Mackie had another place in the north of 500,000 acres. The cattle he ran seventy miles north did well on saltbush, bluebush, and other semiarid herbiage. His nearest neighbor to the west was 212 miles, to the east 52 miles. He said there were only six people in 500 miles and 60 million acres of territory, but if the government could be persuaded to develop it with bores and let up on the intolerable taxes, thousands of people could live there.

In the yard at Madura I was amazed to see a big bull camel. Mr. Mackie said he had returned just that day after an absence of nearly four years. Camels were originally imported into Australia by early explorers and ranchers and turned loose when they ceased to be of use.

At Madura I again came in contact with aborigines. Mr. Mackie was much interested in their welfare. I had been warned by the rabbit trappers that I should be sure to speak of them as natives rather than "bungs" when at Madura. Now I found one of them at table with us. He was a young lad whom Mr. Mackie had brought down from his land in the north. My host pointed out how he handled his knife and fork and understood some English.

"Pretty good for only six months, don't you think?" he said proudly.

He spoke of nursing some of his natives back to health and of the easy hours he gave them. Yet I got the impression that he had no real control over them and that his courtesies, such as cigarettes and a lantern for their bush excursions, were things they had come to take for granted. But this is human nature! He had a room for them in the house but they spent many nights wild or peaceful in the bush. They also trapped rabbits.

I worked on eastward over the transcontinental highway, really the only road across Australia. The road was not too bad, but traffic was unknown. In six days of travel I saw exactly one car making the trip in either direction, and it was one that I met. The road leads across the Nullabor Plain and is level and fairly straight. It more or less parallels the transcontinental railroad, but that is about seventy miles to the north. The line has the longest straight stretch of track in the world, 297 miles without a curve, and gives good proof of the kind of country I traveled over. Lonesome? Oh my!

Although I was not far from the Great Australian Bight, I saw only its blue expanse at one point. This was from atop some sand dunes near an old telegraph station called Eucla. I passed one night at a small sheep station called Koonalda. The attractions here were the wonderful hospitality of Don and Dorothy Gurney, and Koonalda Cave, explored and publicized in *Walkabout* (magazine) in May, 1947, and possibly one of the largest in Australia. With the children we were seven to table in the tiniest of houses. The meal was good, and the bread the best I had ever tasted outside of Sweden. The children stuffed themselves on the bread, and it was so good that really we didn't know when to stop. Mrs. Gurney admitted fresh bread really upped consumption. I inquired as to her recipe: ten to twelve pounds of flour, handful of salt, cup of yeast, four to six pints of water, but don't mix too stiff. Knead it a lot, and keep it warm.

Supplies have to come from Fowler's Bay about 180 miles away. They are brought to that point at sporadic intervals by ship from Adelaide. Mrs. Gurney gets a ton of flour, six sacks of sugar (100 pounds each), and fifty pounds of tea at a time.

The Nullarbor Plain! The "greatest amount of nothing spread over the greatest amount of nowhere"! Endless stretches of straight road only slightly rolling. Stock ramps with white sides. Almost no trees (null arbor), just scattered ones, and seldom in groups. Bluebush, saltbush, and a little herbage of other kinds. Light-blue skies. Cold winds that make it imperative to keep on the move, and require instant donning of cap and coat when I stop for breakfast and lunch. Variable winds that may boost you on the right shoulder in the morning and hold you to a straining hour-after-hour low gear on your left shoulder by late afternoon. Progress markers like this: 17 miles to a vermin fence, 22 miles to shed tanks, 18 miles to vermin fence, etc. Scurrying rabbits. Wombat holes, often in the road. Mirages, and moving mirages, which look like animals across the plain. Of all these things are composed the famed plains of Nullarbor and the areas skirting them.

I might explain that the wombat is an animal with claws like a mole, head like a woodchuck, and hair, skin, and coloring like a wild boar. It apparently lives in burrows like the rabbit.

At a station called White Wells I was treated to puftaloons. The missus had given me her last loaf of bread (and a whole shoulder of cooked mutton) to pack in my tucker bag the night before, so there was nothing left for breakfast but to make puftaloons. And boy, were they ever good! Here is the recipe: a sifter of flour about two thirds full, a heaping teaspoon of baking powder (unless self-rising flour is used), and one half teaspoon of salt. Roll out like a biscuit, round or square, to a thickness of one quarter inch, and drop into a pan of hot deep fat. Fry about five minutes. We ate them with a thick golden syrup. Delicious! In addition we had lamb chops and good gravy.

I worked on into central South Australia. There was rain and wind and I was often wet and uncomfortable. But the hospitality of the farmers— I got into farming country—never changed, and I had chances to dry out and to eat tons of good food. Most of my hosts were "good talkers," and I learned a lot about them and their problems. And for a big change, I even got into mud. This was so sticky that both wheels gummed up and refused to move. I took to the brush, but that was not too satisfactory, for there was mud there also.

Port Augusta West marked my real return to "civilization." Here I had some people to visit, a result of my hobby of genealogy. They were descendants of a Norwegian family that had been on the first immigrant boat to America, along with my own great-grandparents. I was entertained most royally in Port Augusta West.

Beyond Horrocks Pass I came upon beautiful farming country. There were fruit trees, cows, and many little stone and corrugated-iron farmhouses. One woman milking some cows gave me a quart of milk, and a man gave me some mandarins. One farmer had some hogs: Tamworths and "Large Whites." He had to keep the chooks (chickens) shut up or the foxes would get them. There were long hills. It was wheat, oats, and barley country. Farms consisted of six to eight hundred acres. Sheep were raised.

I spent two days in Adelaide and was sometimes recognized on the streets as the round-Australia cyclist who had been in the newspapers. A pretty city. I enjoyed particularly the pretty homes with their flower-bordered walks and great well-trimmed green hedges. I had not seen anything prettier in either Florida or California. The yellow or white stone house with a recessed red-stone border about the windows is popular both in the city and in the country. Going out of the city to the east, I ascended a long hill. With its horseshoe curves and magnificent sweeping views, this was one of the finest mountain drives to lead above a city it has been my good luck to see. Higher up there were fine canyons, all green and wooded, and views down over the Adelaide plain and eastward to Mount Lofty, capped by the monument to Kingsford-Smith.

Since I was now on a road with a fair amount of traffic, I was offered a number of rides. This meant a saving in days on my trek to Melbourne.

At Melbourne I boarded the *Taroona*, a fine vessel, bound for Tasmania. The forecast for the trip was "rough." It wasn't really; yet if I hadn't crawled into my bunk in a hurry I would have lost a good ship's dinner. I was in such a hurry that I dared not take off my clothes, so I slept in them for the first time on my entire trip. This was rather ironic when you think of all the times I'd slept in the open on the ground and still donned my pajamas every night. Here on the ship I had a fine bed but slept on top in my clothes. When I awoke at 2 A.M., I felt O.K., but it was a false feeling. The w.c., as they call it, was up a flight of stairs, and by the time I was at the top I was dizzy and nauseated. I just barely made it back to my bunk and got flat on my back in time to keep from heaving. A close call!

At 6 A.M. we sighted land and proceeded up the Tamar River estuary to Launceston. It was a beautiful ride, and the boat passed slowly along in order to negotiate the turns in the river. The green hills and little hamlets were very close at hand all the way.

Headed south on my trusty Jacqueline once again, I found Tasmania strongly reminiscent of old England. The land was gently rolling and quite pretty. There were hedges and estates. When I crossed a jolly little river with a castlelike house on one bank, I said to myself, "This is England." My opinion was strengthened after I had passed a night as a guest in one of these English houses, for the owners were as English as their castles.

The next day, with the wind behind me, I worked southward through rough country. About forty miles from Hobart, the capital, I was offered a ride by a chap who was fixing a tire on a load of wood. It was gumwood from his "farm" (whose only product was wood) and he was trucking it in to Hobart to be sold at about nine dollars per ton.

The drive was very beautiful. Long hills, partly wooded slopes, and the usual Australian tree-and-shrub-in-bloom landscape. This is certainly something we don't have in America. There were broom and the prickly goss— low, yellow-flowered bushes; the brilliant yellow wattle—great trees of it; and old, old scraggly hawthorn hedges with red berries. Then there were orchards in bloom—the white blossoms of plum trees and the pink of peach and apricot. Along the highway, perhaps every three rods, the government had planted thousands of poplar trees and a few pines, each one still young and protected by a high wooden cage. These trees had sometimes been planted along adjacent paralleling ravines. Along lanes or around homesteads were the most interesting pine trees. One type grew no taller than a man and the branches stemmed upward from the trunk just like a huge fern. The color was yellow with the undersides of the branches shading off into green. Another type had a normal trunk but had been cut across the top with sufficient frequency so that it also branched upward from the trunk but came to a flat top about twenty-five feet above the ground. Beside the pines there were windbreaks of huge red gum trees with long streamers of smooth reddish bark hanging from the trunks or lying around at the foot. Finally, along the watercourses some weeping willows were to be seen.

Besides the houses I mentioned there were other buildings of interest. Every six miles were old freestone stagecoach inns; and there were stone churches looking like old English abbeys; and in the towns, rectangular, white freestone two-story houses. Then there was one great, old red-brick mansion of twenty-seven rooms. This had been built by a chap for his bride, and then he had died soon after his marriage. She still lives there, alone with the servants.

Further impressions of Tasmania included the rather good-sized eight-wheeler steam engines on the narrow-gauge railroads. The speeds are very low, and I was told the main-line passenger train takes two hours to go forty miles, and sometimes the trucks go off the tracks.

There was human interest along the highway also. It was Saturday, and the bike-race-conscious Aussie was out struttin' his stuff. A round-trip race from Hobart to St. Peter's Pass, fifty miles out, was in progress. The first group we met were closely bunched struggling up a hill. No, I shouldn't say "struggling"—that is a term more applicable to me. My wood-selling friend said that when they could stay bunched they broke the wind for each other. Near the foot of the hill was one lone geezer pumping along like mad. He looked a bit weak to me, but I was told there were sprint men, who have a handicap and start later. We met three more groups of cyclists. Bike races are held on weekends, when there is less traffic.

Hobart is a hilly city of red iron and red-tile roofs. Red-brick walls and high and broad green hedges keep the inhabitants and their front yards from rolling into the streets. There were more wood houses than I had noticed before. Most had long porches with corrugated iron roofs.

From Hobart I turned inland to the northwest to see some of the center of the country. The second day on the route was Sunday, but I was in the saddle before daylight. For who can sleep out when you're on the road and the wonders of the world are waiting to be seen? A beautiful Sabbath! The great hills disclosed snow-covered peaks to the west, and I gloried in all of them. Close at hand were more English-manor estates. I never seemed to tire of my daily travels.

One reason for this was the good food. If I did not have the abundant hospitality of the Australians, I had my roadside lunches. I enjoyed the one as much as the other. When I ate alone on or near the road, I could pick the most lovely picnic sites imaginable. The hours were 7:30 A.M., 1:00 P.M. and 6:30 P.M., and no going hungry and getting grumpy because I was miles from a place to buy a hot meal. I never missed such; and having never learned to like coffee or tea, I never missed those either. My meals consisted of three big slices of good bread spread thick with good butter, and accompanied by big spoonfuls of "beefsteak pudding," or "mutton and peas," or "lamb and vegetables," or "camp pie," or "cottage pie," or "beef and vegetable stew," or "baked beans," or "Irish stew"; hunks of mature cheese; and for dessert, golden syrup or raspberry jam, or plum jam, or honey, or loganberry jam, or apricot jam, or even sugar —all on bread, of course; and finally an orange plus a couple bites of chocolate. It may have been living on "bread and tin," but each meal on the open road was like a banquet.

, Two young chaps with a motorcycle and sidecar insisted on giving me a lift for two miles—a rough ride. Then I worked into the mountains, the scenery being not unlike that of certain parts of Colorado, say around Slumgullion Pass. The bicycle is not too bad a means of passport, even in the mountains, when compared to other means. A car went by but offered me no lift, as it was quite full. One mile later I passed it with a flat tire. The folks were all jolly, and the ladies seated on a log called: "Now you have the laugh on us!"

A couple of miles further on there was a lone motorcycle leaning against a stump beside the road, and several miles farther I came to a mountain garage. Here were two chaps sitting impatiently at the door waiting for the garageman to eat dinner. They hailed me, and it developed one was the owner of the motorcycle.

"I can't get her out of intermediate," he explained. "She locked on me."

"Oh well," I consoled, "you can go in intermediate, can't you?"

"Yes; but now I can't get her started."

The other chap also had a motorcycle, which he offered to sell me cheap.

"I can't get the bloody petrol to feed out of the tank," he explained.

These remarks reminded me of motorists way back in Queensland who had been stranded for repairs.

I will stick to Jacqueline.

The road continued up and down, but always high up in forested mountains just like the road west of Gunnison, Colorado. The trees, however, were much bigger, and I was moved to take pictures of their majesties. Really, they towered upward nearly as majestically as our California redwoods, perhaps because they frequently stood partly isolated. Then, in the depths of a canyon of giants, I saw beautiful Kenmere Falls. Toward dusk the road became quite shaded but not overly cool. I enjoyed the peace of the great forest and reveled in the fragrance of wet logs and ferns and mosses, and water dripping over exposed rocks.

Since I had to schedule my travel to catch a weekly ship, I continued after dark. I'll never forget my night walks and rides through that Tasmanian mountain forest. This night was beautiful and clear, fairly calm, and the stars and the Milky Way were out in full splendor. But the great trees were the attraction. They had a peculiarly small amount of foliage, and that was mostly high in the air—perhaps 150 feet. The darkness of the night made the smaller branches invisible, and thus I looked up at great wreaths suspended in midair. There were circles, rectangles, squares, huge question marks, and other shapes. Through these frames I could see the stars.

But the next day I paid the penalty for such peace and beauty. I worked down out of the mountains and onto spurs which jutted out into a plain. There was a strong northwest wind, but this I expected as it was the direction of my route and I was trying to make a ship. Mountains, sand, wind,

The eucalyptus may reach 300 feet—Tasmania.

rain, mechanical difficulties—these always seem to appear to belabor a poor traveler when he has a ship or train to make. It started to rain as the morning wore on. The wind continued and the forest giants swayed violently. Still they offered me much protection from the wind. But gradually I had to leave them for more open stretches, and then the full fury of the storm hit and buffeted me so that I had to walk. I had donned boots, raincoat, and sou'wester and had put my Eisenhower in my leather tucker bag for protection.

It was not long before I was pretty wet. The water from my hat went onto my raincoat, joining with water there to flow on downward into my overalls just below the knees. I fought the usual losing battle trying to keep the raincoat over my knees and keep the direct rain from soaking me above. But the water line kept creeping up. Ere long I conceived the idea of wrapping my water bag canvas about my windward leg and thus funneling the water outside my boot. Although done tardily, the idea worked fairly well. But before I completely left the shelter of the trees, I felt the water in my lee shoe and knew I was getting pretty wet. By the time I had reached the shores of the Great Lake I was jolly well soaked from the waist down and there was water in both boots.

There was a mile or two of good protection along the lake after I first hit it. Beyond it was all open, and I hesitated. It was 11:30 and too early for lunch, and I had covered only twenty of the sixty-four miles I had allotted for the day. Not only that but there were mountains beyond the lake and the road had been closed by snow only five days before. And so I pushed on, and up a hill . . . out . . . out . . . out . . . onto the unprotected plain— directly in the teeth of the howlingest, fightingest gale I have ever experienced

"This is a bad move, Rosdail," I told myself. "You are in no condition to go out here."

No man can describe the ferocity of a storm he has experienced to another man who has not experienced the same storm. Perhaps it would be better to say that he can describe it, but his reader or listener will not understand. The wireless sets in Australia that evening would talk of the seventy- to ninety-mile-per-hour gales that had swept across Tasmania, but the listeners snug beside their fireplaces conceived nothing of the drive of the icy water through the clothing and into the skin of the American battling almost inch by inch across the plain by the Great Lake. I learned later the area was called the Skittleball Plain, and the wind thereon was like a permanent barrier.

I walked on, bent nearly double against the gale. My hands on the handlebars were numb with cold and bleached white by the rain. I lacked control over them and once let Jacqueline fall over in the mud. The rain never seemed to hit the ground—the wind was too strong for that. Yet I saw little balls of sleet forming all about me. My feet, in their icy castles, crunched the sleet, yet I could not hear the noise, only sense it.

Breathless, numb, I fought on. Gone was my do-or-die determination to reach Burnie in time for my ship. There was only one thought now—self-preservation!

There came a time when I approached the far edge of the plain and could see a house. Soon there would be people and a fire. It would take me two hours to dry, I reasoned. But . . . horrible thought! The place looked deserted.

"Oh, no! Not that!"

But I knew that such was the case even before I found a way to cross the ditch lying between the road and the house. And as I drew near I could see the padlock and chain around the door. But in the back of the house was a tiny room to which the door was open. I crept in out of the storm. But there was no heat. What should I do. Should I put on my Eisenhower? It might still be dry. My prime need was to catch a passing car. But were there any? None had passed all day. I could not see the road. Should I take my bike out and lay it across the road? My mind raced.

"Easy now, Rosdail. Don't get panicky!"

I shed my wet raincoat and put on the Eisenhower. It was not very wet—only a spot or two. But horrors! my fingers were too stiff for the buttons. How shiveringly painful was the long process. Ah, how cold I was! Should I dance? No, that only makes me feel the icy wetness filling my boots. Well, I'll beat the goose. Yes, that's better!

Come! Out to the road! Gosh, how cold it is! Put on your gloves! They'll be soaked in two minutes, but put them on anyway. Let's go. But first a quick prayer: "Dear Lord, please get me out of this."

Once on the road I gained the lee of my first trees. Could I possibly ride? Every bit helps. You'll keep warmer. Come! You must! Don't fall now! Almost did that time. Try again. Steady! Ah . . . !

Hardly a mile had I gone, when a new Ford came up behind me. I barely heard it in time to hail it. Was my facial expression more eloquent than my words? Or was it the fury of the storm? Anyway, Jim Booton was more than willing to lift me out of my predicament if we could load the bike without damage to the car. We did. Once inside he insisted I wrap myself in a nice rug (car blanket), wet though I was. And even when I leaned over and a half bucket of muddy water ran out of one of my boots, he said not to worry.

And so soon we were off. I had the same saved-from-drowning feeling I'd had thirteen years before (almost to the day) in the high Alps in Switzerland. Then I had teamed up with the season's last motorist to fight across the mighty Grimsel Pass, already half closed, in a raging blizzard. I remarked about the similarity to Mr. Booton and waxed voluble, as any saved man will do.

11

The Worm With Twenty Fish Lines

Back from Tasmania, I continued my travels through the settled section of Australia, the Southeast. Here was the "population" of the vast island-continent, and with Jacqueline, on the road and in the cities, I came to know almost every segment of this population. There were well educated and formerly well-to-do Jewish refugees from Europe and less educated but equally warmhearted immigrants from Italy. There were run-of-the-mill office workers with whom I had lunch in the cities, and even executives whom I met while arranging for passage to New Zealand. There were bread-cart drivers who told me of their wages and costs of living; and no end of truck drivers who offered me rides on the road and told me of their overloading to make money and consequent fear of the "bulls" or "Johns" who patrolled the roads to catch them. I yarned at length with electricians and railway clerks and government employees, watched or played cards (euchre and five hundred) with hotel transients and householders, and talked with dentists and policemen.

And with all I found friendliness and hospitality, perhaps not to the extent of those in the great outback but more than adequate. And I continued to learn the unique Aussie vocabulary until I had compiled a list of 350 words and expressions either unknown or used differently in the U.S. (There were only four of our words they didn't seem to have: cookies, crackers, potato salad, and sauerkraut.)

Pronunciation I learned the hard way. For example, one day in the Tax Department building in Melbourne I suddenly noticed my watch differed widely from the clock on the wall back of the inquiry clerk. Seeing another employee with a button similar to this clerk's, I approached him, saying: "Is that clock right?" This drew a blank even though I inclined my head toward the clock.

"Is that clock correct?" I tried again.

"Why, yes, he's all right."

It then dawned on me he thought I meant the "clark" (clerk) under the clock. ("Clerk" is pronounced "clark" by the people in the British Commonwealth.)

The method of phrasing a question is also to be watched. While inquiring the way to the Melbourne suburb of Elwood, I slowly pedaled up to a fat gentleman idling on the curb waiting for a tram.

"Elwood straight ahead?" I queried.

This seemed to draw an utter vacuum in the gentleman's mind, so as I was abreast of him, I said: "Straight ahead to Elwood? Elwood?"

But it was not until I was two rods past him and had given up hope of receiving an answer that he shouted after me: "Straight ahead—oh, yes—straight ahead. That's right! Elwood is straight ahead!"

I was told later I should have asked simply, "Which is the way to Elwood?"

From Melbourne I journeyed northeast to Canberra, Australia's capital. Like Washington, it is located in its own federal territory, which lies entirely within New South Wales. Like Washington also, it was planned from the beginning (1911) to be a city worthy of a great nation. Canberra is "the City Beautiful," but at this time is was really yet to become a city. Laid out on a magnificent scale, there were miles upon miles of lovely pines and flowering peach and plum trees. It was the second day of spring and the fruit trees, most of them very small, were masses of bloom—dark pink, light pink, and white. I was certainly visiting the place at the right time.

"Canberra in the spring, tra-la-la-la, tra-la-la-la," I kept singing as I pedaled along the fine concrete and bitumen drives and admired the trees.

The Parliament House and the great War Memorial were the two largest structures. Office buildings and residences were arranged along the avenues and trees so that it was impossible to see any one of them from the lower windows of another. The Capitol had not yet been built, but a great central circle had been arranged for it.

A few days later, when I arrived on the outskirts of Sydney, I turned aside to pay a visit to the famous Jenolan Caves. Since my time was short before sailing to New Zealand, I took a train to a place called Katoomba, leaving my faithful Jacqueline in the baggage room of a station until I should return.

The scenery was really very fine. The double-tracked railway line into the Blue Mountains had been built along the mountainside overlooking deep paralleling gorges or crossing the ends of side canyons. The line had been cut through solid rock for much of the way, and I could recall no place in America where there were such long stretches of "straight-up" rock lining a railway or road. These man-cut cliffs rose thirty feet or more on both sides and sometimes ran a quarter of a mile without a break. Once we were on top of the range, the line twisted and turned to hold its position.

Meanwhile, with no effort on my part, I had become acquainted with Mrs. Geneva Dalton, one of the six people sharing my compartment. She was an outgoing friendly person who had mothered no less than seven sons, the youngest, then four, being fifteen years younger than his next-oldest brother. Mrs. Dalton got off the train a little before Katoomba but not until she had invited me back to spend the night on a spare couch in her home.

At Katoomba I walked in approaching darkness to the far end of town in order to visit Echo Point and see the Jamison Valley and the Three Sisters, the combination of the three being the principal attraction in the Blue Mountains outside of the Jenolan Caves. From the point, floodlights played at intervals on three huge monoliths at the end of an adjacent peninsula jutting out into the valley. These formations resembled those in the Colorado National Monument. The most impressive thing, to my way of thinking, was the sheer drop below my feet at Echo Point. Here was no sloping cliff for one to bounce onto, as is the case with so many observation points. Here there was absolutely nothing but empty space—1,100 feet of it, I found out the next day.

After a good sleep at the Daltons', I got better acquainted with them the next morning. Mrs. Dalton, having had five sons ahead of Allan, then nineteen, was of grandmotherly age and appearance. Allan, and apparently his brothers before him, were habitually great kidders and pals to "Mum." When something came up about Peter being so far behind the others, Allan said: "Well, you know it was during the war years and we still aren't sure!"

He was making jovial allusion to the fact that both his parents had been traveling during the war, Mum as matron on big boats plying from England to Australia and Mr. D. as a technical man with an officer's rating in case he fell prisoner to the Japs.

When I showed the pictures of my family to Mum and Dad on the back steps that morning—we were all getting warm in the early sun—I of course asked about their family. Mrs. Dalton listed only Peter, Allan, and another son in Sydney, who, she said, was pretty much of a nervous case. Thank goodness I had the sense not to ask about the others. I supposed they had drifted away and let it go at that. But later, Mrs. Dalton spoke to me in the dining room, when Dad was not around.

"You see, you mentioned Norway out there on the steps. That's where we lost one of our boys in the war. I saw Dad's jaw drop, and so I didn't dare say anything then. We lost two boys in the war—one was shot down over Germany and the other in Norway. We don't know much about what happened to them except they had to feed the one in Norway. And then this one . . . [with a nod toward little Peter]. It looks as thought there must be something. . . ."

We were six passengers and the driver-guide in the old Cadillac sedan which was to take us on the 100-mile round trip to the Jenolan Caves. The day was fine and the air bracing—too bracing, in fact, to have the window open. But those fresh-air-bred Australians—even the old and middle-aged women, mind you, sat directly in back of the driver's open window with never a murmur. On the opposite side, in the front seat to get some protection, the American buttoned his Eisenhower and unbuckled his knapsack so it would cover more of his knees. He'd only slept out in the open a hundred nights or more and wasn't tough enough yet.

The unique thing about the drive to Jenolan Caves was the way the road clung to the crest of two mountain ranges for the greater share of the distance. I don't recall anything like it in my travels. It surpasses the Skyline Drive near Canyon City, Colorado, and is longer than the one to Hat Point, Oregon. The road was a great horseshoe along two opposite sides of a great valley, the largest in Australia, The views were extensive and magnificent. Some of the road had been built by convict labor in the very early days of Australia. On a natural connection between two mountains they had built a hand-cut rock bridge. It was a hundred years old and had never been altered or repaired, even though no concrete had been used to hold the stones together.

We arrived at the caves through a great natural archway which must have been three to four hundred feet long, and curved. A stream flowed alongside, and tame wallabies hopped about ready to eat from the traveler's hand.

There was a choice of five caves to visit. I chose the Lucas and found it quite comparable to any of our American caves: Wind, Morrison, Mammoth, Carlsbad. The Lucas is not as big as Carlsbad, but I found the coloring as rich and as varied, and the "characters," such as the Bishop, as interesting. The Jenolan Caves excel, I think, in the size and beauty of their shoal formations, i.e., the folded curtains of orange and white limestone which hang from sloping ceilings. Lighting, though not concealed, was very effective with the Jewel Casket, and in depicting sunrise, noon, and sunset in the windows of the Cathedral.

Back in Sydney again, I pedaled about sightseeing and making arrangement for my passage to New Zealand. Cities do not move me as much as the wide open spaces, which I much prefer, yet I well appreciated the beautiful harbor and the magnificent bridge of which Sydneyites are so proud. There is quite a rivalry between Sydney and Melbourne, I found. Sydney is a little larger. "Our harbor" is contrasted with "the miserable little Yarra" which flows though Melbourne.

But the Sydneyite may admit: "Of course, Sydney is an old city and its streets are quite narrow and they run every which way, but in Melbourne the streets are all wide and laid out nicely at right angles, aren't they?"

Well, now that he mentions it, the heart of Melbourne is prettier and more modern than the heart of Sydney. I never did get the straight of a "Sydneyite's Prayer," written, I suppose, by a Melbournian; but the Lord's Prayer is supposed to start out:

"Our Father, we thank Thee for our harbor and our bridge. . . ."

From Sydney I took passage on an honest-to-goodness ocean liner for New Zealand. The ship had been converted to a carrier for three thousand troops in the war. I was rather surprised to find the same problems of seasickness as on a freighter carrying only six passengers. The difference was that my troubles were here shared by hundreds of other mortals. Following are some on-the-spot impressions set down on the third day of the voyage.

The passengers, poor souls, go around—if they are able—like lost sheep searching for a fold, a fold where the motion of the ship is not felt quite so much. No one speaks to anyone else. Everyone is too miserable. The ship is like a tomb of lost ghosts.

The majority of the passengers, however, make the meal table, because most of them know they must eat if they are to cope with the situation at all. They sit close together at long tables so narrow that noses of opposite parties are only two feet apart (one foot, ten inches in my case); yet by some miracle of the eye muscles everyone avoids everyone else's gaze. There are two reasons for this phenomenon. First, one feels so miserable he doesn't want to be looked at; and second, one might get spoken to and have to reply, and think how horrible that would be! So the dinner tables are the quietest places imaginable. Everyone has a single thought: get it down as fast as possible and get out of here. The women are as pale as death, but the men are all flushed—rather a strange contrast. When the ship lurches, eyes are instantly raised to some distant part of the room, but quickly averted en route if the gaze meets that of someone across the table.

On the deck only the children and the aged seem to be anywhere near comfortable. Yet can the latter really be comfortable? If all the verve, the sparkle, the enterprise of youth are stilled by the monster *mal de mer,* how can the aged nerves and organs adjust? One feels distinctly he would want to do all his traveling before he gets old, and yet. . .

There is one girl in particular on board the ship whose seasick countenance is enough to turn the heart of the most valiant. Although her complexion is not blemished, the withdrawing blood has left it somewhat splotchy. Her mouth, one would surmise, naturally turns down; and in her deep malady the lower lip has sunk about ten degrees more. Her eyes, you cannot avoid, and they greet you with all the feeling of a whipped dog who was sick before you whipped him. This face you cannot stay away from because . . . oh, my gosh! It has just this minute entered the writing room where it stands over me with a handkerchief covering the mouth and nose, ready to "whup," I suppose. Well, I was going to say that this face draws you like a magnet from all over the ship—but my appetite for this subject has now vanished.

Another character on board is a doting papa with a two-year-old toddler in harness, a little redheaded girl. Although seasick himself, he trails her all over the deck, hour in and hour out, and she never seems to tire. At night he has to take care of her in the men's quarters, for mama is too seasick to move from the deck chair. At mealtimes she may be seen mouthing dry toast or bread and butter, the crumbs dropping away from her dry lips.

The dear lawmakers, deep in the heart of whatever nation, who passed the law requiring lifeboat drill the first day at sea had never, I fear, been to sea themselves. When the announcement came over the loudspeaker, I did not hear the inward moans of anguish, but I knew they were there just the same. Of the four men in my tier of bunks, only one, J. Hart Rosdail, was able to make it to boat drill. One of them called out in a quavery voice, "St-e-w-ard, st-e-w-ard! Do we have to go if we're sick?"

He was quite unmindful of the fact that the announcement came over the public-address system and the steward and all his assistants were two decks above him and well out of earshot.

I have found that the reading room is the most comfortable place on the ship. It is well aft and seems to pitch very little. My stomach has become adjusted to the location, and when night comes I see no sense in forcing it to become used to another motion elsewhere. So I sleep on a couch here rather than in my bunk.

After three days I landed in Auckland, New Zealand's largest city. Then I commenced a journey around what was to become my favorite among the 250 countries I eventually visited.

In the country I first noticed the green grassy hillsides dotted with white sheep, a scene which would be repeated many times until it became for me a New Zealand trademark. The second thing I noticed was the high percentage of new and modern-looking homes. They were usually of wood siding with varicolored tile roofs and lots of windows. Hedges, flowers, and nice walks enhanced their appearance. Then I noticed windbreaks of tall pines scattered about the hills. A beautiful country!

A curious thing to me was the small pens at the edge of the road beside the gates into the farms. These were for little calves ("bobbies") which were marketed by the farmers when three days old or sometimes younger. A truck (cart) came by about twice a week and picked up these calves.

In early evening I came to the world-famous Waitomo Cave and took a guided trip through. It was entertaining to pick out the forms suggested by the guide and to see the lighting effects. When shown his effigy, George Bernard Shaw is supposed to have quipped: "You see, they even thought of me three million years ago."

The guide was a good one and teased the ladies with his stories about the Sheik's Bedchamber. He also sang to us in a room noted for its acoustics.

The outstanding part of the trip was the Glowworm Cave—a cavern unlike anything else in the world. That alone, I believe, is worth a trip from America to see. It is magnificently unique.

Our party entered a boat on the underground river which flows through the glowworm grotto. The guide propelled us along by pulling on wires strung on the walls. The ride was a weird and eerie experience, and all the poets who have written of underground rivers, or the river Styx in the depths of Hades, never imagined anything better. Overhead, hanging from the roof at odd angles, were a number of huge round-nosed rocks, some so low as to almost knock us out of the boat.

However, the greater part of the roof over the underground river was free of such formations. Here it was that millions of glowworms gave forth their bluish lights. As we proceeded in utter silence, our eyes became accustomed to the diffused glow. We first made out the figure of our boatman in the prow of the boat. Although he was standing, he kept well hunched over to maneuver the boat along the wire, and you can imagine the effect of his hunched silhouette. Eventually we could discern enough from the light so that, just to test its value, I could see the outlines of the road map I carried in my pocket. But apart from this curious moment, my eyes, like everyone else's, were on the sapphire-studded ceiling of the cave.

The Waitomo glowworm is the larva of an insect, the female of which lives thirty-six hours and the male twelve hours. The reproductive rate is controlled by the space available on the roof of the cave when the eggs are to be laid. There are no seasons for this, as the temperature of the cave, about 49 degrees, varies less than one-half of a degree throughout the year.

In its larval stage the insect is about an inch long. Its light is present even before it reaches this stage. It is a cold light, being 98% cold and only 2% heat. It is controllable, and the glowworm can switch it through all gradations from bright to clear out. If the worm is disturbed, the light may be switched off, and both sound and a stronger light will cause this to occur.

The worm is carnivorous. It weaves a hammock about five inches long out of a sort of silken or weblike material which it makes. From this hammock, which it fastens to the roof of the cave, it suspends 20—not 19 or 21 but 20—silken strands. Small flies or midges coming into the cave strike against these strands and become stuck. With the aid of the guide's flashlight we actually saw this happen and could see the worm hurrying along its hammock trying to find out which of its 20 fish lines had been successful in catching some dinner.

We rode to where the river emerged from the cave. It was raining outside and we stayed only briefly, discerning dim outlines of trees and massed ferns in the darkness. We then reentered the cave and rode slowly back to our original point of embarkation, heralded by the drip, drip, drip of water from the ceiling onto the river.

Two days later: a new day! The sun was shining, and the odors of early morning and the mists hanging in the valleys made cycling most pleasant. It was hilly but the road was excellent and I didn't have to walk too much. By midafternoon I was convinced that New Zealand was just one big lawn. All the hillsides were the most vivid green and the sheep and cattle kept the grass as close-cropped as though a lawn mower had been run over it. And there seemed to be no mudholes or other disfigurements to mar the green sward. The grass is kept thriving by the rain and the applications of superphosphate. The cattle and sheep thrive on the grass, but they are also given chowmoller, which is something like a huge Chinese cabbage, and Swedish turnips (swedes). The stock are turned into small fields (breaks) of swedes and eat the tops and whatever part of the roots they can get at. The farmer then disks out the rest of the roots for the stock to eat.

I came one day to the Rotorua hot-springs area and entered the native Maori village of Ohinemutu. Near the central square was an old Church of England church handsomely decorated on the inside with Maori carvings. The church was located almost on the edge of Lake Rotorua.

Since it was lunch time and raining intermittently, I inquired at a Maori house if I might eat my lunch on their porch. I thought it was the back porch, since it was on the opposite side from the central square, but later found it was in front of the only entrance. I was immediately invited inside and asked to sit at the table and partake of the food they had left from lunch: cheese, butter, bread, and jam. Meanwhile mama packed the kiddies —there were four of them—off to school. Each had a complete rain outfit.

Rangi Mitchell and I then had a good get-acquainted chat. Petite, well-formed, Rangi had been a Maori beauty and still retained a great deal of her chic and charm. She was smart and a lively conversationalist, a good hostess, and hospitable. She insisted I take a whole packet of cheese for my tucker and wanted to give me most of a jar of her own homemade tomato preserves.

Her home consisted of one room only. There was a double window on the side of the square. Adjacent to it in one corner was a fine bed, well made up with nice pillows and fine blankets. In the other corner was a wardrobe with a curtain in front. At the foot of the bed was a dresser and at the opposite side of the room a fireplace. Near the dresser was the table, located just under double windows looking out on the porch. Clean sugar sacks were laid about the room and in front of the fireplace to serve as rugs.

After I had finished eating, Rangi and I sat in front of the fire while outside the rain beat upon the roof.

"This is where the Maori spends most of his time," mused Rangi. "He has become lazy and shiftless since the white man came. His health is not good and he has to have false teeth. Too much soft white man's food. But he can no longer catch fish for himself; the laws won't let him."

She taught me a few words of Maori.

"The Maori is too lazy to even use his own language. I am proud of the fact that I can speak it—but I had to learn it. Now when we speak in Maori they won't answer except in English. They know what I say but answer in English."

Occasionally we stepped to the windows looking over the choppy waters of Lake Rotorua.

The Maori guide on the left entertained me in her home—New Zealand.

"It looks like more rain. That's where all our bad weather comes from —from over the lake."

When I requested some hot water to wash out a food tin, Rangi threw a coat over her shoulders, grabbed a wire soap holder and a kind of string dish-mop on the end of a wire, and bade me follow her. Not five feet from the house was a concrete trough about eight inches wide, two feet long, and one foot deep, nearly filled with boiling hot water. Through a hole in one end an overflow of considerable volume escaped toward the lake. Rangi explained that the trough was kept constantly full by a duct leading from the main geyser not more than twenty feet from the end of the house and at one edge of the village square. It was well protected with concrete and stones. Just a few feet away some short planks covered a steaming pothole, and on these some wet sugar sacks were lying. She explained that when she had a pot of anything to heat she set it on the planks and covered it with the sacks to keep the heat. In a few minutes the steam would boil the contents of the pot.

"Oh, yes, the poor Maori doesn't even have to build a fire to cook by and make him ambitious. And the white man gives him social security so he doesn't want to work."

Although I had been told by a white man that the Maori were considered equals, Rangi denied this. She said they were looked down on. A truck driver later corroborated this statement with the remark they were shiftless and lazy.

"The children don't know anything but to cadge pennies off of you," was one of his comments. "And now that they have been paid for some of the land, more and more claims are being laid by the tribes. Of course, it's right in a way; but the Maori took the land from the Maoriori [their predecessors] and never paid them anything—killed the poor buggers off, in fact.

"But I'll admit," he added "the Maori have been spoiled by politicians who were after their votes."

But to return to Rangi. She had a key to the main Maori council hall situated at one side of the square. When the rain let up she took me over. Maoris work most excellently in wood, and the carvings were intricate and full of history. Rangi pointed out some of her own handiwork in the woven wickerwork sections on the walls. They had all had a hand in building it. Women are not allowed to speak in Maori council chambers, but the precedent had been broken by Eleanor Roosevelt.

On the central pillar of the house there was a carved figure holding a sort of billy club. When I remarked about this, Rangi asked me if I had seen a green stone. When I replied in the negative, she took me back to her own home and dug out a large collection of green stones, carved and polished to varying degrees and cut in the shape of an oval paddle from eight inches to one foot in length. They were quite beautiful and were

Photographer's reward for patience. A boiling mud bubble at the split-second of its bursting! Geyserland, New Zealand.

"patus," or symbols of authority. This particular green stone was translucent, although the middle thickness must have been at least one half inch. Rangi also had a collection of "tikis," good-luck charms made from the same stone and shaped like little men. The "tiki" with the biggest tummy was the most valuable.

Leaving my new friend, I pedaled two miles south of Ohinemutu to the Whakarewarewa thermal area. Here the Maori were living in somewhat dilapidated houses almost on top of steaming vent holes. They had channeled hot water into bathing pools, and the children and a few grown-ups were having a glorious time. When tired of the water they would lie on the lean-to roof of a nearby house until they got cold and then go back into the water. They did not all wear bathing suits.

At Whakarewarewa there were blowholes, boiling mud pools, and geysers in that order of importance. The mud pools were in the nature of Yellowstone's paint pots and there were a dozen at least, each showing a different mud and boiling to varying extent. The geysers played to a height of only a few feet.

The next day I cycled along "government plantations," where the mountainsides had been planted with thousands of pine trees. These were now grown and very tall, and since they were quite close together they presented a magnificent front along the road. In most areas the forests had been divided into great blocks separated by roadways or firebreaks from eighty to one hundred feet wide. Nevertheless I found many of these blocks devastated by fire, and I was incredulous that a fire had been able to jump across such a wide firebreak.

The Waiotapu Thermal Area was interesting but not as good as Yellowstone. There was a small river of cold water made tepid by the inflow of boiling water from pools where the temperatures were labeled up to 226 degrees. There were a number of rather large steaming craters, including a real "Dragon's Mouth," and small, brilliant yellow, sulfur vents. One rather large steaming lake resembled Yellowstone's Prismatic Spring. It was called Champagne Pool and was 301 feet deep. The overflow eventually fell over a terrace of white and yellowish green—really pretty—called Bridal Veil Falls. There was one geyser, the Lady Knox, but as she had to be soaped, and soap cost 2/9 per box, her prowess could not be enticed for the benefit of less than five onlookers.

12

An Earthquake in the Rickety Isles, and Where Was I?

New Zealand is made up of two large islands—the North and the South. Perhaps the finest scenery is on South Island, so I bought a steamship ticket from Wellington over to a place called Nelson. I went on board the *Matangi* about 6 P.M. Rain as usual.

I put in a fairly comfortable night, although the ship was a small one and rolled all over the place. The sea was so rough we were three hours late arriving at Nelson. This made it incumbent upon the ship to serve tea in the corridors and rooms. I was only interested in the bread and butter that went with it and used cheese from my pack to make out a breakfast. While munching this, I was not far from the crew's mess and the bosun came by and said, "Is that the best you can do?"

"Well . . . uh . . . uh . . ."

"Would you like a little binder? Here, let's see what's left."

So I was set down to mashed potatoes, kidneys in gravy, smoked fish, and all I wanted of the usual accessories. I buttered my bread American fashion, rather thinly; but the bosun couldn't stand that: "Smear it on—go on—plenty of it. Aw, put it on!"

When the ship docked, Jacqueline was hoisted out of the hold and I set out southward. A southwest wind. Slow progress. Mountain scenery. Cool to cold air. At 5 P.M. I stopped for road information. The family was having tea and I was set to table: mashed potatoes, carrots, meat, pickled beets, pieplant sauce, and a curious combination for dessert—macaroni and custard. Besides the parents there were three little boys, and when I commented that they were one ahead of me, as I had only two children, I was told that the three were only the youngest of eleven. I later stayed the night with three bachelor brothers and had further experience with the boundless hospitality of New Zealanders.

Toward the close of the next afternoon I was pedaling past a little "house by the side of the road," when its owner hailed me from the door. I stopped and he came down the walk and through the gate to the road where I had stopped. Almost immediately, on discovering I was an American, he launched out into international affairs, wars, and related subjects. At seventy-one Mr. Guildford had been in three wars, the first being the Boer. He told me a few things about World War I that I'm sure never got into print. In France he fought near a group of Yanks and saw them take Germans surrendering with their arms raised and run them through with bayonets while crying, "Remember the *Lusitania!*" Before Guildford's regiment went into a battle one day, their British officer told them he wished he was going with them.

"The men you are going up against," said he, "are of the regiment from which the men were picked who shot Nurse Cavell."

"So when we took German prisoners," said my companion, "we said, 'Remember Nurse Cavell' before we shot them."

I could not help but recall the righteous indignation felt by Americans after World War II when Germans shot American prisoners in Belgium and Italy. And I was not surprised when Mr. Guildford said we had no right to try the Germans at Nurnberg.

"We should have let their own people deal with them."

"And that atomic bomb!" he vouchsafed later on. "We should never have dropped that. We outlawed poison gas, and this was far worse."

I was asked in to tea and to spend the night, but it was only 5 P.M. and I pushed on.

Later I was picked up by dentist Bill Keesing of the west coast town of Westport. During the war he had been the only dentist for about nine thousand people. As we traveled together along the Buller River he proved to be a gold mine of information about the old sluicing-for-gold operations and ghost towns through which we passed.

When we arrived at Westport, I was invited to Bill's home for the night. This was a very large one-story house with fireplaces and fires in both the dining and living rooms. After a big dinner we joined Mrs. Keesing in the living room in order to help entertain two lady visitors. The women being in the majority, the talk was mainly of cooking. Mrs. Keesing had recently made a pieplant pie from an American cookbook recipe.

"And, my dear, it is simply marvelous. You've *never* tasted anything so delicious." And dutiful Bill copied off the recipe for the guests, who were anxious to try it.

We had supper at 10:30, but we didn't finish the discussion on angel food cake until 11:30. However, I'll have to admit I did as much talking about American foods and ways of preparation as the women. But the point was that poor Bill and I were planning on getting up at 5 A.M. to go whitebait fishing.

When that delicate hour arrived, it was surely hard to roll out.

"Would you like something to eat?" Bill called from the kitchen.

"Not unless you do," I rejoined.

So he broke a raw egg into each of two glasses and added some Worcestershire sauce and other ingredients. "Here you are," said he.

Long experience on the road with food of many countries has hardened my stomach to nearly everything, so I hardly blanched. I gave it a go, but couldn't get the yolk, as yet unbroken, down the hatch. "How do you get the yolk down?"

"Oh, just kind of munch it." It is remarkable how many people have never made the acquaintance of a "prairie oyster." Yet in a poached egg, the yolk may be practically raw. This gives your stomach the most wonderful, contented feeling.

We picked up a cobber of Bill's and drove out about four miles along the Buller to the sea. On a long rock and earth pier we secured two nets and hurried along the rocks. Bill's favorite spot had already been taken, but there was room elsewhere. The net is nearly as finely woven as cloth and is tied on a wooden loop about three feet in diameter, affixed to a rather heavy ten-foot pole. This was quite cumbersome to handle and in addition it rained, making the rocks slippery. We stuck it out until 8:15 and had moderately good luck.

Whitebait is considered a great delicacy along the west coast, and it is well known in Europe and elsewhere. It is a small fish which looks as much like a big flat white worm as a fish. It is transparent and gutless but has a mouth and two prominent eyes. Commonly it is the young of herring or sprat and enters the mouths of rivers by the million. When we got ours home, Bill repaired to the kitchen and fixed up his favorite self-concocted whitebait recipe. Whitebait is usually made into patties with eggs and flour, and I found it very good. Lemon juice improves the flavor. There are jokes about closing your eyes when eating so you won't see the fish heads and eyes.

It sprinkled most of the following afternoon, and there were mists over the mountain passes. I felt in good trim and walked in long strides up the long grades and around the curves. Toward evening the sea came into view and the road stayed near its edge. The sea, where it has rocky shores and jutting headlands, is impressive at any time, but particularly so on a stormy day. I had views of it from many heights, and its roar as it fought with the stubborn land was always in my ears. At these times man is moved to words; he is impelled to expression. I poured out unwritten masterpieces of description covering ranges of vision from the mists on the upper reaches of the headlands to the fishing vessel and the coast steamer out at sea. But I couldn't stop in the rain to transcribe these masterpieces and now the descriptive words seem dull and flat. All I can say is that it was very wonderful; and the fact that everything was dripping water—ferns, nikau palm trees, sheep, and I—did not dampen my appreciation of the scenery.

The next day around noon a chap on the road invited me down to his house for lunch. This was a real break because it gave me a chance to learn more of the life of the real coaster (resident of the west coast). He showed me his gold, both the pure and the amalgam. The latter means that the quicksilver used in gathering it in the washing process had not yet been separated. He said his gold came from the sea and that the millions of mussels making the rocks black below his cabin would yield gold. He was going to demonstrate this, but one of his neighbors (he had only two) dropped in to go crayfish fishing with him. To catch crayfish (like a small lobster) they had a kind of crocheted sack that would have fitted over five inches of broomstick. In this sack they put the bait—usually small fish—and the crayfish would cling to it when it is lowered into the water on the end of a fish pole.

My host had two cats, one of which killed ferrets and weasels. However, opossums were the big pest. He claimed they had been imported into New Zealand and now overran the country. He said they were full of curiosity, and a trap could be placed almost anywhere and baited with only a little bit of paper, and it would be successful.

I continued to work south along the coast. One day I had rain, and although I had a sou'wester on my head, a waterproof cape, waterproof leggings up to my hips, and four-buckle boots, I got good and wet. I never could figure out how this happened. One forenoon I got a ride on a small log truck. This was picking up logs from the cockeys (farmers) who lived in the occasional clearings in the forest. Gum was the most plentiful timber, but there was also much *kaihikatia*, or white pine. The *mati*, or black pine, was not so plentiful, but we loaded one log which must have been between four and five feet in diameter. It is excellent for ballroom floors, as it takes a high polish. It is also good for firewood.

The mountains to the south were very impressive. There were many square miles of snowfields through which jagged, snowy peaks jutted into the skyline. Meanwhile I crossed wide-bedded mountain rivers and skirted beautiful lakes, such as Wahapo and Mapourika. At Waiho I visited one of these rare-in-the-world mountain-view churches. The great Franz Joseph Glacier could be seen through the church window in back of the altar. There really could be no more impressive backdrop for the worship of God than the view of the glacier framed above the cross by green trees.

To reach the Franz Joseph I had to ford seven watercourses. At the end of the auto road I took to the trail and it was a thriller. Much of it was on the face of a precipice overlooking a lake once formed by the glacier. There was a high footbridge just below a fine waterfall, and the water plunged on down over a second precipice which I could not see until I descended to the flat between the lake and the glacier's snout.

As I walked out toward the latter a great mass of ice detached itself from the glacier's edge and crashed to the valley-floor. If only my camera had been ready! When I reached the snout of the glacier, I carefully crawled around on the great chunks of ice until I could take a picture of the Waiho River as it emerged from under the ice. When I clambered in closer for a better look, I happened to look up, and the proximity of the overhang of tons of blue and white creviced ice made me decide to move in a hurry. I *could* be under the next avalanche. After all, even if there was no adjacent rock cliff, those blocks of ice I was clinging to must have fallen down some-time.

The other great west coast glacier, the Fox, lay sixteen miles to the

Loading a Karri log, South Island, New Zealand.

Snout of the Franz Josef Glacier, and start of the Waiho River, New Zealand.

south. Over this stretch I got a ride with a truck driver named Johnnie. Jacqueline was put in the back with a bunch of wobbly-legged little calves and some chickens. Johnnie thought he was a race-car driver, and I got one of the wildest rides of my life. Up the long grades he could only toil in gear, but down the mountains we fairly flew. If there was even a suggestion of a straight, Johnnie let her go and didn't wham on the brakes until the last possible moment. Between watching for the curves to keep from getting car-sick and worrying about meeting a car, I tried to enjoy the scenery. This was absolutely tops. The mountains and mountain ridges were between three and four thousand feet above us, and the valley walls were sheer. Yet there was a tremendous amount of vegetation clinging to them: trees, ferns, vines, and bushes of great variety. Far above, snow clung steeply to jagged summits. It was awe-inspiring and I was very much impressed. I had never seen valley walls that steep which carried such vegetation. It looked as though all that greenery was hanging in midair.

The end of the ride and the Waheka Hotel. Johnnie approached a cobber.

"Say, could a bloke ride north with you in the morning?"

"Who?" queried driver Ed Kirby, seated at tea with his back towards us.

"Oh, a bloke," said Johnnie enlighteningly.

So I introduced myself, whereupon Ed replied, "It's O.K. if you get me a pair of overalls like those you have on."

From this point I pedaled the few miles remaining to the Fox Glacier, which, in the late afternoon, showed as a ghost's finger reaching down the mountain into the darkened forest. Returning, I again crossed a new suspension bridge over the river which issues from the glacier. The bridge floor was of concrete slabs about three feet wide with fillers of tar between. These fillers were either lower or higher than the slabs, and as I crossed I was listening fearfully to the thud, thud, thud of my tires and wondering if one was flat. And that, gentle reader, was how I missed the great New Zealand earthquake of 7:40 P.M., 13th of October. Just across the bridge were some road workers' tents and a shack. Outside the latter a man was half squatting, groping around in the grass and weeds, picking up pans and looking for stuff of some sort. A kitchen work bench stood nearby.

"Quite a shock, that!" said he.

But I, having felt nothing, could not understand the sense of such a remark, and watched more or less open-mouthed at the queer antics he was going through. It was not until the following day when Ed Kirby told of dishes falling off the shelves in the hotel, the chandeliers swaying, and his expectations of seeing the walls fly apart that I understood what had happened. There were even headlines in the papers—and where had I been? Of all places, smack in the middle of a suspension bridge with bumpy flooring.

A day later in a forest along the Taramakau River, I had a flat tire. A young bicyclist with a rifle stopped to help me. He was alert for deer, which are considered pests in New Zealand and can be shot anytime, anyplace. He invited me to his house for tea and for the night, but when the tire went flat again I made him go on home so his wife, who usually came down the road to meet him, would not be kept waiting. Meanwhile I changed to a spare tube—a fairly long operation.

What a lift such offers of hospitality gave me! Here, late in the day, alone in the forest, with no otherwise certain knowledge of where the next habitation would be, it was solidly comforting to know that ahead, on the road, I was expected and welcome—that there would be a hot evening meal and a roof. Having been away from home for six months, and frequently thinking of it late in the afternoon, the friendliness at another's fireside was a wonderful thing.

It was just a tiny one-and-a-half-room cabin by a sawmill. In the one room at the back Arthur Jones and his wife Shirley, and two tiny girls, Helen and Jennifer, had their beds. The narrow half-room at front was a kitchen and dining room. There was a range, and dishes were few and un-matched.

"Honestly, we're glad to have someone with us of an evening," said Shirley when I mentioned how good it was of them to ask me in. "We sit here alone evening after evening and never do anything."

And in the morning when I went to leave, Shirley stopped me with, "We just wouldn't *ever think* of letting someone go away without break-fast." And so I sat down to three sausages and two fried eggs. Arthur left to hunt deer before going to work, and I left shortly afterward.

The next day I tackled Arthur's Pass and the Otira Gorge. The ascent was very steep. Bill Keesing had said he had barely made it in low gear with an eight-cylinder Hupmobile. A road sign warned that low-horsepower cars would experience difficulty in crossing. But Jacqueline and I went over. It was inch by inch going though, and I had to partly carry the bike by keeping one hand under the seat. To make it even harder there was loose "shingle" all the way to make my feet slip. Shingle is river-bottom rock or gravel, and differs from other crushed rock, which is called "metal." Neither transport truck nor bus dared to try Arthur's Pass, but there is a railroad tunnel underneath, no less than five and a quarter miles long. It took me about three hours of steady work to reach the first summit. In the saddle there were fine views of the wild, nearly snow-filled Upper Otira Gorge. Very fine indeed—tremendous summits with snow clinging to the topmost pockets and filling the side canyons wherever they were not too steep.

Down from the pass and out from the mountains I came to the region of the east coast and its attractive cities of Christchurch, Timaru, Oamaru, and Dunedin. Here was a land of plains and gentle hills, of farms and open spaces; quite in contrast to the mountains and snow-filled canyons, to the glaciers and great forests, of the west. There were still beautiful trees, but they were in groves, or "plantations," of evergreens (*Pinus insignus*) dotting the countryside as windbreaks for homes and fields against the northwesters. Then there were hundreds of gorse hedges, brilliant with deep-yellow bloom, crisscrossing the land, marking the fences. This gorse is a kind of boomerang. It covers the fence, grows steadily and keeps in the stock so the farmer never has to repair the fence proper. This he promptly forgets. But the gorse branches way out from the fence line unless trimmed, and this is an awful job. The stuff is as sticky as anything, and the branches are thick, perhaps several inches through. Some farmers get disgusted and set fire to the stuff, but it only comes back to thrive better than before. Besides the pines and the gorse, there are long rows of fine poplars to be seen; and weeping willows along the watercourses. These are wide gravelly washes like those in southern California. The whole countryside would be bathed in sunshine, and back in the distance were the snow-covered ranges of mountains. In contrast, to the east, the broad Pacific appeared, with here and there some fine beaches.

The farmsteads usually put to shame most of their contemporaries in midwestern America. There were no unsightly sheds or rusty machinery visible. All was green grass, flowers, flower-bordered walks, and neatly painted bungalows. On occasion there was even a fine old English mansion; I stayed the night in one of these. And the cities such as Oamaru were full of beautiful homes with flower- and shrub-bordered terraces. I felt that the beauty of southern California homes was commonplace in New Zealand.

I spent one night on a poultry farm with white leghorns and black Orpingtons (Australorps). But my hosts, Mr. and Mrs. Hobart Johnson and son Desmond, saw to it that I did not sleep with the chickens. There was an excellent bed all freshly made up with clean sheets and pillowcases, nice "robes," and an "eiderdown" (silk-covered comforter). The Johnsons had to go to a neighbor's that evening, and Desmond—only seventeen and thus still in possession of his teeth—took off for a dance. Yet they left me alone without the slightest qualm and with a good fire. Can't you just picture an American family leaving *any* stranger alone in their home after one hour's acquaintance? Well, there I had a swell chance to write in my far-behind diary without any obligation to tell of my travels and make polite conversation. The light was good, the room was nice, and there was a fire. But dang it all, I was so tired from cycling against those New Zealand winds that I kept falling asleep and had to go to bed!

Toward Dunedin it became quite hilly but over the last hill I got a ride with a couple of Scots in a 1932 Hudson. They at once appointed themselves my guides, and we stopped at several vantage points. Otago Harbor is thirteen miles long and locked in by high hills. It was a sight to compare with Wellington, Oslo, and the much touted Naples. Then there were the botanical gardens, said locally to be the best in the Southern Hemisphere.

"Would ye like a wee walk through?" asked Mr. Beveridge.

"Sure, if you have the time."

So we parked the car.

"Do you have a tire pump on your bike?" queried Angus.

"No; it's in my pack," I replied.

"Ah, good. The Scotchman's fingers stick to other things besides what's in his pockets, ye know," said Mr. Beveridge.

"Well, the Scotch humor is certainly not dead," I laughed. He was indirectly referring to the fact that Dunedin is largely peopled by Scots.

We had trouble with the car before he got home, and I became much impressed with the patience and cheerfulness of my two friends. This was evident in their homes also. Mr. B. insisted on getting up early the next morning to prepare my breakfast.

"And what would ye like for breakfast? I'll cook ye anything ye like."

Knowing that the Scotchman's heart is bigger than his larder, I replied, "Oh—what have you got?"

"Would ye like a rasher of bacon and an egg?" he responded brightly.

"Swell," said I, knowing that was probably what he was sure to have.

The next day I had more trouble battling the wind. Even when I changed directions, I fought the wind. But on the positive side of the ledger I got several rides from farmers. The last was from Mr. Angus Kay, who, when we arrived at Balfour, bade me wait before unloading.

"Look," said he returning a few minutes later, having obviously just called up his wife. "Your road lies there to the west, but I live two miles south of here and you can have a bach there for the night if you like."

I thought about those two extra miles against the wind and that I could probably find shelter without leaving the road. But then I sensed that he hoped I would come with him. I accepted his invitation, and I will never regret it. For Mr. and Mrs. Kay were people than whom there are none finer. While she was drumming up a superfeed, I bathed and shaved. Then I got on the outside of three big chops, potatoes, eggs, gravy, bread, and cookies. Ah, boy! It was real hospitality I have come to associate with people who have had big families and have seen how children eat and have grown bighearted with much living. Yet the Kays, though married for twenty-five years, had had no children. After the meal they bundled me off to bed—and I know it was not because they wanted to retire at nine but because they could see I was dog tired. And in the morning I had an enormous dish of porridge, bacon and eggs, and more. Finally, for my pack, Mrs. Kay gave me a tin of the popular cream-colored solid honey, filled my butter tin to the brim and give me a big sack of her homemade and most excellent cookies. (I would be back for another visit, undreamed of, later.)

I wanted to visit New Zealand's famous Southern Alps, so headed off toward the west coast again. Mountains and trees eventually tempered the wind and made cycling a bit easier. Eighteen and a half miles north of a place called Teanau there was a bridge under construction. One chap obligingly helped me by carrying the bike high over his head while we walked across the bare girders.

"Well, that bicycle has ridden over the crupper of a horse and has even ridden in an ambulance," I commented to the boss, "but this is the first time she's been carried over an unfinished bridge."

Near here I visited my first New Zealand sheep station. Sheep here have different problems than in the great dry outback of Australia. One of these is snow. A sheep caught under the snow may be found after perhaps twenty-four hours, as the heat of its body will melt a hole. If it is still not rescued, it will eat its own wool, which will cause stomach balls and ultimately death. New Zealand sheep have a great deal more moisture than Australian, and their wool lacks the fine quality to be found in Australia. But all this green New Zealand grass makes for better grazing and better mutton, which is the country's main export. At the Canterbury Freezing works (Christchurch) I had seen the long ramps leading from the sheep pens up to the second-floor slaughtering area. Three well-trained decoy sheep led the rest up the ramps to their doom. Such sheep were necessary because the others smelled the blood and would not go. The sheep were then handled on a production line, each man doing only one operation. One man cut throats. They put a new man on one day and he cut the throat of a decoy sheep. He was given the sack.

The next day I pedaled up the beautiful Eglinton Valley with snow-covered ranges on either side and jagged peaks poking their black faces up through the snow fields. Later a steel truck lifted me into the magnificent Hollyford Valley, then past a road camp and a spectacular waterfall and through a gorge nearly as wild as the Seljestad in Norway. Clouds of mist filled the upper portions but occasionally passed to reveal summits and several blue and white hanging glaciers. Water streamed and plunged from the great black wet precipices in a dozen waterfalls at least fifteen hundred feet high.

From here I walked Jacqueline up about three miles of steep grades to the mouth of the Homer Tunnel. This had been put through about eight years before, but the entrance to the tunnel, a concrete snowshed affair, had completely collapsed. Now all was in ruin and disuse. The trail now wound about and entered the tunnel from a hole at the side of the collapsed shed, just at the mouth. Dirt and rocks from avalanches and melted snows were all about.

It was supposedly eleven to thirteen miles from this point through the tunnel and down to Milford Sound, one of New Zealand's most famous attractions. I didn't know how long the tunnel was, but I had been told it was full of water. Well, there was plenty of water all right. It poured or

New Zealand scenery is little short of perfection.

Milford Sound country, New Zealand.

Milford Sound.

ran from the roof and down the sides in hundreds of places. Not that I could see these places. It was as dark as Hades, a spooky and uncomfortable place. My feeble light was inadequate, especially before my eyes became used to the darkness. It wouldn't have been so bad if there had been any certain footing underneath, but the floor was uneven, there were rocks both loose and round, slippery boards, and puddles with slippery rocks at the bottom. There was even abandoned machinery to avoid. I stumbled along. Man does not belong underground, and I was not particularly happy. The sound of water filled my ears as I progressed, and the floor fell away rapidly in front of my feet—too rapidly for any sense of security. I thought that all this water must practically fill the lower end of the tunnel. Still further in, the two-way arch became one and gave me a better sense of location. Finally I glimpsed a bit of light at the far end. That was encouraging. And before very long I was taking off boots, raincoat, and hat at the exit.

A great view! The enclosing cirque was deeper at this lower end of the tunnel. The weather too was better, and the sun and light clouds played above the mountains and ridges as I descended. The trail (one couldn't call it a road), having no traffic, was rough and stony. The stones were round and treacherous. I used the brake to carry the weight of the bicycle and thought back to down-mountain walking I had done in Norway with no rear-wheel hand brake to take the weight from my aching feet. Higher and higher rose the canyon walls. Light rain. Waterfalls. Moss and lichen-covered trees. Roaring, boulder-filled mountain streams. But finally the lower levels and eventually the end of the road.

Here was the great Milford Sound at last, with the towering Lion Peak and Mitre Peak, so often reproduced in New Zealand halls and tourist literature. Mitre Peak ascends 5,560 feet from the water. Here was the valley of the Arthur River leading into McKinnon Pass. Here was the beautiful arch of Bowen Falls. Still the fjord was not as impressive as Norway's Naerodal and Naerofjord, because the peaks were separated and leaned back more from the water.

I found an abandoned road worker's cabin for the night: double walls, table, chairs, a soft cushion, and a bed of ferns with plenty of sacks on top. A big storm came up toward morning. The wind roared through the trees and shook my little cabin to its foundations. In my snug bag I could feel the whole cabin give and come back before the wind. Several times I thought it was going to blow me right out of the canyon.

The next day I toiled upward on the return to the Homer Tunnel. At a sign marked "The Chasm," which I had missed before, I took a trail through the wet bemossed and belichened forest. It was not far to where a young river boiled and plunged in a chasm only a few feet wide fifty feet below the trail bridge. The spectacle ranked with Colorado's Box Canyon or Switzerland's Trummelbach.

13

In Which Stinker, the Thar, Jumps Into the Skillet

Again I was battling the wind—the northwester. After twelve miles my route turned at a full right angle. Did the wind lessen? It did not. It was worse than ever. But along came Stewart Kirkland in his Ford and offered me a lift.

Stewart, a manual-training instructor, turned out to be a regular guy. He saw to it that I visited all the points of interest in and around Queenstown and he and his wife entertained me in their nice new home for two days. The house was situated on a hillside about thirty feet above the level of Lake Wakatipu and had the most wonderful view from its wide and spacious windows. On the left across the water were the Remarkables, a jagged sky-lined range to out-Teton the Tetons, though without the latter's glaciers. Every shoulder of the Remarkables showed a razorback, nearly precipitous ridge. The mountains rose probably six thousand feet above the lake. And near at hand, between the house and the lake, was a sloping grassy lawn holding four beautiful cypress trees.

When I finished my visit, the Kirklands gave me a big lift on my way. We drove the mountain route to Arrowtown, which resembled certain towns in Utah with its many poplar trees, a river, and mountains. There were switchbacks over a barren hill with high barren mountains all around. Later we climbed the Crown Range over a grade like the Whitebird in the Salmon River country of Idaho. At the top was the sign: "Summit Crown Range, 3676 feet above sea level, highest motoring road in N.Z." In making our farewells they took a picture of Jacqueline and me in front of this sign. (We never dreamed this picture would later appear in the *Guinness Book of World Records* with an account of my travels.)

The next day I had rain and snow as I cycled toward the Mount Cook area of the Southern Alps. As I was changing a plugged tire valve, a big road-grader stopped and the driver offered me a five-mile ride. This was a new experience. Eventually I came to Glentanner, one of the largest stations in South Island. Its sheep ran up the slopes of Mount Cook itself. It was on a corner of Glentanner that the first thars (or tahrs) were released. This animal is a kind of mountain goat, and a few were given to New Zealand by an Indian prince from the Himalaya regions. They have multiplied so that they are a menace to sheep by taking their grazing, and the government had hired four men to hunt them and keep them in check.

New Zealand Alps are a world wonder as this picture testifies.

The Remarkables, New Zealand.

Taken in my favorite country, New Zealand.

Canyon of the Shotover River.

Looking toward Mt. Cook (12,349 feet) from the Tasman Valley.

"It's absolutely remarkable the way they can jump on a precipice. You wouldn't credit it," said my host on Glentanner.

The next day I traveled in a young blizzard, and the visibility was almost nil. But the weather let up as I followed along a lateral moraine of the great Tasman Glacier, reputed to be one of the longest in the world. Eventually I reached a mountain hut not far from the Ball Glacier. Here I had companionship: a girl mountaineer and guide, Junee Mulvay, and two thar hunters, Des and Jim. In the evening as we sat around the great stove we discussed the various climbs we had made. Cold and snow without, and cold inside if we got away from the stove. Occasionally Stinker, the pet thar, would knock at the door. All of us cast anxious eyes from time to time toward the barometer, but it held steady. Junee had offered to take me out on the ice in the morning if the weather permitted, so I hoped it would clear off. Her predictions were clear weather, but the thar hunters were not so sure. They planned on setting up an outpost tent over on the Murchison the next day. Meanwhile if we stirred to the adjoining room where the dishes were washed, we froze, and beat a hasty retreat to the kitchen proper. We turned in about 10 P.M.

Junee was to roll out at 5:30, but I was up first at 6 A.M. We let Stinker in, and as you might expect of a mountain goat, he jumped up on the table occasionally. This wouldn't do, so Junee and I put him out, but when Jim came in later, he let Stinker in also. Like a flash he jumped up on the stove, thence to the high back, down again smack into the skillet with all four feet together, and then back to the floor spilling the skillet of hot grease all over the place. We caught him again—he wasn't much bigger than an overgrown lamb—and put him out for good. After breakfast Junee fixed him a bottle of milk, and we went out and enticed him from the tin roof near the chimney, where he usually hung out.

A fine day! Ice! Snow! Brilliance! This was a break; for Junee told of numerous cases of folks who had saved money for a vacation of mountain and ice climbing and then had to waste it all sitting day after day at the hotel waiting on the weather which never cleared. She told of the time she and Harry (another guide) had planned on spending three weeks at climbing and had clear weather for only three days. Even in summer the weather was uncertain.

With a pair of Junee's boots and wool socks, which had adorned my feet since arrival the preceding day, and with an axe, I followed her down a precipitous loose-shale declivity to the face of the great Tasman Glacier, eighteen miles long. Small rocks tumbled down around us because Stinker was following us on the cliff above. We were worried that he would dislodge more substantial stones, but he presently decided not to follow us farther.

We walked up the Tasman to the base of the great Hochstetter Icefall. I hadn't been on the ice since Mount Rainier and enjoyed every minute

Working up the Hochstetter Icefall. New Zealand scenery rivals that of Norway and Switzerland.

Just after a sudden snowstorm at the edge of the great Tasman Glacier, New Zealand.

"Stinker," the thar, is in no hurry for his bottle. The first thars were gifts from the Himalayas. Their surefootedness is amazing.

of it. Junee was a good guide, experienced, cautious, attractive. Fresh snow covered many a small water-filled crevasse, and constant probing with the ice axe was necessary. It was most challenging to plot a trail among the ice pinnacles, valleys, and hummocks, cut our own steps up ice cliffs and balance ourselves along sharp ridges and ice overhangs. Meanwhile there were the most glorious views imaginable of the great Hochstetter, Ball, and other glaciers, and of the saddles, cols, and ridges of the giants, Mount Cook and Mount Tasman. What a world of ice and snow we were in! Ninety-five percent of all the surfaces we viewed were dazzling white in the sun. Even Junee kept remarking about the good weather and the fine views. For a climax we saw three avalanches on the Hochstetter.

From the Mount Cook area I headed back northeast to Christchurch. Here and in the nearby port of Lyttleton I spent ten days trying to arrange for a ship to Africa. Meanwhile I had much time to take the pulse of New Zealand.

Among the half dozen families that entertained me, I spent the most time with the George Murthas. I had actually been directed to their door by an office friend of mine in America, whose daughter was a pen pal of young Coleen Murtha. The Murthas had a corner store, and they lived in back of it. Sometimes they had to get up from the table to wait on trade.

One Saturday afternoon George and I went to the horse races. Although there was racing in New Zealand every Saturday of the year, and sometimes on Fridays, this particular Saturday was special because it marked the competition for the New Zealand Cup. For me, it was my first horse racing; and it was the first day following the completion of a five-month journey around Australia and New Zealand.

"Oh, New Zealanders are great on sports," said George. "Don't come to New Zealand if you're not interested in sports." He claimed horse racing was the favorite, but cited figures showing that in cities such as Christchurch and Dunedin from one-third to one-half of the population attended football games.

After we parked our car we took a box we had brought from home to stand on and walked through the gates. We left the box by a ticket taker so we could walk around through the crowds unencumbered, but just before each race we would get the box and stand on it just in back of the rows of people lining the track. Before I knew anything about it, George had placed a ten-bob bet ($1.60—the minimum) on one of the horses for me. This was Highland Fling, the winner of the New Zealand Cup, the major race, and it paid me well, 2½ to 1. There were other races and other bets, and I came out ahead for the day by nearly five dollars. It was impossible to get George to take back even his initial investment, let alone the winnings. Each race was a thrill. Horses would frequently act up at the start and lose a great deal of time. George knew in advance which ones would be apt to do this and took cognizance of it in his betting. Sometimes

Upper end of Lake Wanaka.

New Zealand is one of the world's most beautiful countries.

New Zealand's Alps are not soon forgotten.

two or more horses would be bracketed because they had the same owner or trainer. In this case, if one of the horses was winning, the other horse would be held back. If one won, and the other placed, and you had money on them in that order, it would be winning a double.

I learned how to place bets. If I had a pound note and went to the window bearing the number of my horse, and I wanted to put ten bob on this horse to either win or place, I would say "both ways, once." If I didn't say "once," I wouldn't get ten-bob change and the entire pound would go on the horse. If the horse won, I would get the rate shown on the tote (totalisator) for the horse, and if he got second or third place I would get that rate. "Rate" refers to the amount a horse pays for every one-pound bet. If my bet was just for the horse to place, and he won, I would collect my bet at a separate first-place window.

An overall tote showed the total amount of bets placed on the various horses as they were placed. A tote is an enormous blackboard with speedometer windows, visible for a considerable distance. Total bets for the day were forty thousand pounds and there were forty thousand people present.

That evening we went to the New Zealand Industries Fair. One exhibit involved our attending a movie on the value of proper dental care. The nation is conscious of the fact that most of its people have very poor teeth. To an American visitor it seems that most of the people have no teeth of their own at all. I have commented on this before. I recall visiting in one home where the daughter was nineteen and her brother twenty-one. She was as attractive a girl as I've ever seen, with plenty of sex appeal, but with a complete set of false teeth. Her boyfriend had an upper plate and part of his lower teeth were missing. The son also had a complete set of false teeth; his girlfriend had a complete upper plate and had just had the remainder of her teeth pulled. Consequently her gums were sore and she could hardly eat. One wonders if the problem is not connected with the national diet of tea and cake.

After the fair we went to the "pichers." Seats had to be reserved, and there were no continuous performances. I had yet to learn this is typical of most countries outside America. The program opened by the screening of a picture of the King of England, on which appearance all the people stood up. Next came the shorts. Then there was intermission during which people went out to buy ice cream or to smoke. Next came the feature, an English comedy, which I was surprised to find enjoyable.

When I crawled into bed, after a midnight snack, I found a hotwater bottle. But, as you have guessed, the window was wide open. It never occurs to the Aussie or New Zealander to shut out the cold night air.

Sunday afternoon we went to the motorbike (motorcycle) races. This was also a new experience for me, but I didn't get the thrill I expected. This was possibly because one doesn't realize the speed at which the machines travel. The track was sod—crooked but not overly hilly. There was only one spill, and I failed to see that. I spent most of the time near the judge's car to get a close-up of the winners in the biggest races. Most of them were in their twenties; only two seemed to be older. I looked at them intently and pondered how impossible it was to tell from the look of the eye or the turn of the jaw whether a racer had that certain quality of calculated daring sufficient to make him a winner.

We enjoyed an "old-fashioned evening at home." George sang, while his wife accompanied him on the piano. She also played two pieces on the organ and two selections on the violin. Little Carmel, so cute in her manner of speech, gave a fine performance of a child's prayer. Coleen, quite bashful, was persuaded to let us hear her very fine voice. And what was the American's part in the entertainment? Well, even though I've been told I can't carry a tune in a bucket—with a lid on it—I finally agreed to "Carry Me Back to Ole Virginny" and "Jingle Bells."

Monday I pedaled over to the seaport of Lyttleton to try for a work-away passage to Africa. My return ride was along steep hillsides far above the water. But there was some walking, and as I walked past a house almost hidden by hedges and bushes, high on the steep bank above me, I heard a voice say, "How much further do you think you are going tonight?"

As a mater of fact I was intending to make my own camp that night. The weather was fine, and I had bought three potatoes in anticipation. It took me a minute to shake this idea and to realize that here was an invitation right off the road to spend the night.

"Well, I was thinking about pitching camp pretty soon," I said to the middle-aged lady above me.

"There's an empty room here we're not using."

And so shortly I was exploring the garden and grounds of Miss Mulligan, who lived there with her cats and a gentleman by the name of Grant. The latter, it developed after he came home, was from Scotland, and Miss Mulligan had nursed him when he returned wounded from World War. I.

Here was a strange alliance—or was it? Two lonely souls had teamed up. Long since settled in their ways, they will probably live out their lives together in this house. Mr. Grant was an extremely spare man, and there was no problem in counting his ribs when he took off his shirt. His body was full of silver plates and whatnot, but he had a keen mind. Miss Mulligan had a rather weather-beaten countenance, wore a sacklike, gray-home-spun, torn-sleeved dress, and her bare chapped legs rose stolidly out of Clementine shoes.

The house was somewhat consonant with its mistress. Miss Mulligan mulled about without any seeming direction—one of those persons who talk while they work, yet not being able to do both, concentrate on the talking. The housekeeping showed the result. There wasn't any house-keeping. She admitted this, saying she finally had decided there was no special need for it. Things were not particularly dirty; they were just untidy.

And of course there were cats everywhere; and all spoiled. The Scotsman spoiled them as much as the spinster. If they jumped onto the table or the sink—and they did—they were never punished but were lifted carefully down and talked to the while. A mother cat nursed three kittens smack in the middle of the triangle formed by the table, the stove, and the sink; yet two meals were prepared and served and mama kitty only got talked to.

This meal business was peculiar. When it was an hour past teatime, I said I'd dive into my tucker bag. Miss Mulligan asked me if I'd like a cup of tea and I declined. Then, when I was in my room and just getting started, I was stopped by the Scotsman.

"Don't eat that. She'll fix your tea."

"Well, uh—uh—."

"Yes, she'll fix your tea."

"Well, uh—uh— how do you know she will?"

"Oh, she'll fix it."

Well, at his request to fix some tea, she gave us tea and bread, butter, cheese, cake, and jam. I filled up, thinking this was the evening meal. After I had finished and Mr. Grant had taken himself off to bed Miss Mulligan announced she had better go and milk the cow and then fix tea. It was already nearly 8 P.M. and about dark, and I was aghast.

"But Mr. Grant has already gone to bed and you don't need to fix anything for me," I protested.

"Oh, I always serve him his tea in bed," she explained. "It's been that way for over twelve months now. And I have a stew already made up."

So about 9 P.M. she had succeeded in clearing to one side the debris from the 7:30 meal, and we ate real "tea." Of course, the cats got as much of the stew as we did.

Back in Christchurch I often ate my lunch on the banks of the Avon River. Flowing at times right around the edge of the business district, the Avon is a mecca for the clerks at lunch time. There is a quiet charm about the river, and the banks are absolutely idyllic. Between the bridges weeping willows bend slightly to let their riverward boughs dip their leaves in the swiftly passing waters. The grass is kept trimmed right to the water's edge. Smaller trees have been planted in the parklike areas not far from the water, and a few well-placed park benches are available for those who are not inclined to accept the invitation of the green slopes. Often, as I ate, the wildlife put on a quiet but interesting movie at my feet. A sparrow might hop up for crumbs from my bread. Papa, mama, and little Sammie wild duck would swim about just a few feet away. One minute they might be paddling to keep "bottoms up" while they searched for food on the river's bed; the next minute they might splash the water in a rapid takeoff on a flight to the next bridge a block away. But Johnny Trout and his friends could put on a good show too. One day a black trout and a speckled trout, each over a foot long, were—well not being versed in trout lore, I don't know what they were doing. Perhaps they were fighting, perhaps playing, perhaps making love, but anyway it was interesting. The stream was clear and free from debris. I could see the many islands of moss patterning the bottom and refusing to be dislodged by the friction of the waters.

Not being able to get a workaway to Africa, or indeed even a paid passage, I took a ship called the *Port Hobart* from Christchurch (Lyttleton) back to Sydney, Australia. The trip was fairly comfortable, with some pitching but relatively little roll. Still most of the first-class passengers and a few of the tourist class were seasick.

In Sydney I had no better luck in getting passage to Africa. There were very few ships, and berths on those were all booked up well in advance. Finally there was a cancellation on a British India freighter called the *Palikonda,* but its departure was delayed for repairs and it was actually five weeks before I left Sydney. Although I had friends there, I did not wish to impose on them and spent most of my nights camping in the breezeway of a schoolhouse. With a diet based on a loaf of bread and a "tin of bully beef," there were times when I lived a whole week with no more outlay than $1.25. Meanwhile I became as well acquainted with the big-city Aussie as I had with his brother in the great outback.

One of my friends was Fred Dorock, who had gone fossicking with me on the Great Barrier Reef. I met several of his family, including two sisters, Freda and Mrs. Grant. As soon as Freda found out who I was, she said: "Well, I never! I lost a whole night's sleep over you and that battle with the shark. Fred told it, you know, and my two small lads took it all in. Loch was sleeping with me and he kept asking me questions about it. At two o'clock in the morning he was still at it. 'Mama, why didn't the shark bite him?' 'Oh, I don't know,' I said. But then it was, 'Mama, did the shark try to bite him?' 'Oh, blast him,' I said, 'and the shark too!'

"But I never expected to meet you," concluded Freda.

On another evening Freda and her sister told about their experiences with the Americans during World War II. Although there was pathos, the stories for the most part were very funny, and tellers as well as listeners got a big kick out of them.

"There I was," Freda began, "with Loch just learning to talk, and Peter, on the dock; and it was after I had been divorced, and you know how kids get ideas in their heads; and Loch was going up to this man and that and askin' 'em, 'Are you my daddy man?' And this big American sailor was one of them. I think he was quite a bit older than I, but he was real friendly and he didn't seem to mind, and he picked Loch up and we talked. He was lonesome, you know, and he wanted someone to show him around and would have liked a place to stay. I told him he was better off staying on his ship because, oh, the Aussies were treating them badly, and taking their money, you know. But I promised to show him around a little.

"Then once when we went to get off a train he said, 'Here, hold this

for me and I'll take Peter by the hand.' He gave me an envelope with a
handkerchief wrapped around it, but I paid no attention to what it was,
you know, and just dropped it into my handbag and forgot about it. Well,
later on I took Loch and went into a ladies' restroom to wash and freshen
up a bit, and I put my hand into my purse for something and out came
this handkerchief and envelope and fell on the floor; and I don't know
how much it was, but a big roll of money came out. And all the women
in the place looked at me and then at the American money. And, well, I
picked it up, and I picked Loch up by one arm so fast I jerked him clear
off his feet and I got out of there and I went outside to where Charlie—
that was his name, Charlie—to where Charlie was waiting with Peter, and
I said, 'You big, silly idiot.' And oh, I lit into him and I told him how
would he know that I would bring it back. And he just grinned. And when
I stopped to catch my breath he told me he had been some kind of a
criminal investigator in New York and knew I would return it. He said
he could tell an honest person every time, but he hadn't expected me to
find it before the next day, and that way he thought he'd see me again,
you see. But there I was in that roomful of women, all looking at me and
that money. It's a wonder I didn't break Loch's arm. I got out of there, I
tell you.

"Well, I got quite fond of Charlie after that, but he went off and he
was real good about writing. But then I didn't hear for a long time, and
I used to tell Edna [her niece] when she'd call up about her Yank, 'I
haven't heard from my Charlie either.' And then I got this nice letter from
the chaplain that he'd been killed and had left word with him to notify me."

Mrs. Grant's story was principally about the Yanks and her daughter
Edna.

"Well, the Yanks came to Sydney, and it was before the war—one of
these goodwill tours, you know. And Edna was only sixteen, and I had
made up my mind they weren't going to get *her!* And then I came home
from shopping this one day and here was this tall sailor. He was from
Kentucky—have you got a place like that? And well, I told him, 'Now, see
here, you're not coming around here after my daughter. She's not home,
and I hope I never see you again. Now, go on. And, well, he looked so
sort of pained and uncertain, but I said, 'Off with you now!' But then he
asked me if he could leave a note; so he wrote it out on the wall with
me glaring at him. And here I didn't even know she'd ever been near a
Yank.

"Then the next day just as I was coming home, here they both were
coming along together. And I sailed into both of them; but he had tickets
for the theater and he showed them to me, and—well, he was nice, mind.
And so I said finally, 'Young man, you have my daughter home at eleven
o'clock and not a minute after!' Well, eleven o'clock came and went and
then a quarter of an hour, and I went to bed. But almost right away I

heard some footsteps tip-tapping along and it was, 'Mum, could you come to the door?'

"I said, 'No! Now, see here, young lady, you're a quarter of an hour late!'

"But then it was, 'Mum he won't go home until he sees you.' He wanted to explain about that quarter of an hour, you see.

"Well, then, the next day, it was, 'Mum, he's coming for tea tonight.'

"And so I was at the door when he rang and I told him to get off. 'You're not going to steal my daughter.'

"He looked so awful and said, 'Your daughter invited me to tea.' And just then Jim, that's Edna's brother, came out and said, 'Well, hello friend! Come right in!' And he said, 'You *are* a friend of mine!'

"Well, I even went to the American consul after that—I did! And he was very nice to me too. And it was then I commenced to decide that maybe Americans weren't so bad after all. 'Madam,' he said, 'I appreciate your concern but your daughter cannot leave Australia until she is twenty-one.'

"Well, I went home then, but all the neighbors knew about it and they asked me, 'Did you have an American at your house last night?' And not only that, but she had worn his . . . those little white things they wear on their heads. She must have had that on on the train, because the neighbors told me about that —some of 'em had seen her, you know. And she still has it—all wrapped up in tissue paper. And when she was twenty-four, I still caught her sighing over it.

"And then when the Yanks came out again—that was a time. 'Edna,' I says, 'you're not to go near the waterfront.' 'No, mum,' she says; but she did. And they were here three weeks. And when they left she wanted to go down and see them off.

" 'No,' I said, 'you're not going near the wharf!'

"But she kept at me. So I said, 'I'll go with you.' And a friend of mine and I went with her. But then it was, 'Mum, can I go on the *Rodney?*' You see, it was going alongside to see the boys out of the harbor, and all the girls were going on it. 'No,' I says, 'you cannot.' But the next thing I knew she had slipped away, and so we came home in a taxi and I had to tell her father. I didn't know for sure where she had gone to.

"Well, then, when we heard about the accident . . . the *Rodney* turned over, you see, with all the girls running to one side . . . and they were telling about the bodies recovered over the radio; and we sat there listening to the descriptions—we knew what she was wearing you see—they came to one with a blue dress and white shoes and grasping a white bag.

" 'That's her,' said Jim (my husband's name is Jim too). 'Let's get right down to the morgue.'

" 'No, we'll wait awhile,' I said. But it wasn't long before Dorothy, her married sister, came over. 'Did Edna go on the *Rodney?*' 'I don't know,' I said.

" 'Well, come on, we're going to the morgue,' she said.

"And so we started out; but we had to wait for the tram, and just before it came . . . there was about a minute before the tram going down and the one going up . . . here came the other tram. Well, you know, I suddenly felt faint and I—well, I had to sit right down. And do you know! She had been up on the headland watching the boats go, and she didn't even know there had been an accident.

"Then, when the Yanks were here during the war . . . well, she had been going with Bill for two years—engaged in fact—and she broke it off. She took him out on the porch and told him. 'Yes,' she says, 'go on now; skiddoo. I'm going out with a Yank this evening.' "

"Oh, no; she didn't tell him that!" I interjected.

"Oh, yes, she did. And she told him that she'd said she'd be late 'cause she had to break off with Bill."

"Talk about your international situations." I laughed.

"Poor Bill. He came inside to tell me about it, and I felt so bad, and we both felt so bad. . . . They were perfect on the ballroom floor together. Well, we felt so bad that we both sat down on the couch and cried together. And her uncle came home—he liked Bill and was almost like a father to him—and he almost cried too. But it was the uniform, and the nice ways, and so on. The Aussie boys used to stand in groups on the corner and see their tabbies go by with the Yanks."

14

The Happy Life of Riley

Fred Dorock operated a kalsomine factory and I learned about aspirator hammers, and saw how silica sand (nearly as hard as carborundum or diamond) and limestone blocks were ground into a fine flour. And when I finished my visit with Fred, I went to see Les Poynter, another friend from the Great Barrier Reef trip. Les owned a candy factory, and as I watched his operations I learned how they get those little tiny stripes in the round and rectangular pieces of Christmas candy. This was a fascinating process —in fact, I took enough notes in both factories to be able to go into business for myself.

Although Les had a physical handicap, he was quite an eligible bachelor and very popular. Friends of both sexes kept his phone busy and his evening-to-evening plans were very uncertain. He had a nice personality, a car, a yacht, a flat, and a factory; so what more could a girl want? I went out with him one evening, and went yachting with him one Saturday.

With his friend Lillian and his brother and his girl friend, we were five on the yacht. Still it was quite comfortable. I was groggy from lack of sleep and expected to be seasick, but though we were out six hours, I got along fine. It was too wet to sail, so we used the motor. Part of the afternoon we spent at anchor in the Kuring-gai Chase National Park, reading, talking, and watching the rain. Later in the afternoon we saw a racing yacht cross the finish line near where we cruised.

The next day I watched a cricket game. This is too slow for me. It takes hours, even days, to play one game. Still it's really the national sport, I guess. Even the women play. Our pitcher's wind up is nothing compared to the Aussie bowler's. He takes a run and a half step and delivers the ball overhand without bending his arm. And the pitcher can never argue with the umpire over a strike because they have some pieces of wood back of the plate called a wicket and if a ball hits this, and sort of disorganizes its posture, the pitch is a strike and no mistake, and the batter is *out*. This elimination of the batter-umpire fight possibly detracts from the interest of the game as compared with baseball. The batter wears leg protectors like a baseball catcher. When he is out, he walks off the field, undoes the straps and passes the protectors to the next batter, who puts them on. Each batter is allowed two minutes for such shenanigans. Now what they want the pads on for, I don't know, because the ball does not cross the plate anywhere near as fast as a baseball, and it's seldom a batter gets hit even in that game. But in a big cricket match or "test" game, as they call it, I understand they have four sets of pads, so there may be fewer delays.

On Sundays I always went to church, and sometimes Sunday school. Church attendance was very poor. What courage the ministers must have to face that emptiness Sunday after Sunday! The few faithfuls—the minister must know in advance just who will probably be there—valiantly attempt to scatter about and make the place look less empty. The pamphlets he has printed for the day's service and midweek events lie largely undistributed after the congregation has departed. The minister not only has to keep up his own morale over the low attendance at Sunday services but needs to convince the members of his congregation that each of their lives touches many others and the church has thus a larger influence than is apparent. I became acquainted with a few ministers and came to believe that their lives have been so full and rich in varied experiences that they have this for a foundation for the belief in God and in the innate goodness of human life. Thus they sustain themselves and encourage others.

One night I returned to my schoolyard, only to find my breezeway occupied by a male and female of the species Homo, but whether young or old I couldn't tell from the light of the cigarette that greeted me. They said they were leaving soon, but I couldn't be bothered waiting on the whims of love, so prepared to squeeze through the fence to enter the adjacent shelter. Then I was surprised to hear footsteps on the bitumen. (most Australian school grounds are paved.)

"Hello," I thought to myself. "Here's where the police run us all out." But no, it was a young soldier.

" 'Scuse me for buttin' in like this, but did you see a digger and two sheilas walkin' around here?"

I hesitated. Had his mate run off with his girl, and should I help him by mentioning the folks in the dark shed behind us; or should I keep silent? I decided on the latter course.

"Why, no . . . I didn't."

But he wanted to chat a bit. Meanwhile I couldn't hear a sound from the couple, who were only about twenty feet away. But the soldier must have heard something, for he suddenly said, "They aren't in there, are they?"

"Why don't you look?" said I, curious as a cat.

"Well, I hate to . . . it might not be . . . but . . ." and as he spoke he went up the steps and struck a match, which lit up the whole place.

"Excuse me but . . . aw, I see . . . you're not . . . I was looking for someone and . . ."

The man was already on his feet, but it was the woman who said, "That's all right. We understand."

The soldier left and I went to bed. The couple left before I went to sleep. The place was evidently too popular for love to flourish.

I spent a lot of time in the library reading up on Africa, but sometimes ate and relaxed at the concrete checkerboard tables in Randwick Park. There, early one Sunday morning, I met an Irishman named Murphy.

When Murphy found out I was from America, he opened up on how he was kept from going there by an offer of three thousand pounds. He was an ex-prize fighter and apparently a pretty good pug in his time, having defeated some champion. This champion had fought all over the world, had gone to London and then been lost at sea while attempting to rescue a woman who had fallen overboard. Murphy was now sixty-four, but looked forty-four. He had been an "educated pug" rather than a "tough guy." Ship captains sometimes took fighters to America to fight, and one of them had offered Murphy the chance, saying he could arrange fights for him in Frisco. Murphy was all for going, but an "auntie" who had taken an interest in him had offered him her shares in a certain Colonial Sugar Company if he would remain. One uncle had gone to America in the fighting game and never returned, so she was not going to lose Murphy. The shares were worth three thousand pounds. At this point Murphy went into the histories of all the sugar companies that had ever sprung up in Australia. But when the auntie died, a cousin informed him that he, not Murphy, had received the shares in the will. Murphy felt the auntie was incompetent at the time and wanted to contest, but his mother persuaded him not to. Murphy's only consolation was that his cousin had lost the money afterward.

Murphy had to show me his scars. He moved his nose so I might hear the "bones" creak, improperly fitted after a fight. There were supposed to be markings from a dozen stitches over one eye, and I nearly went blind tryin' to find 'em. There was one scar on his temple I could see. It had been caused by an opponent in the nineteenth round. Gloves in those days were used over and over again until they became hard, and anyway, perhaps this one had lead in it. His opponent came rushing out of his corner with left arm straight out in front of him like a ram. Murphy was surprised, and then the bloke brought up a terrific right that downed him for the count— and, in fact, until he got to the hospital. The crowd gave Murphy no sympathy whatsoever, because he had had the fight up until that point, and so they thought it was fixed. Pieces of Murphy's skull slithered out through the wound above his eye for several months after that; so Murphy decided he had had enough of fighting.

Murphy was also a fine singer, as was to be expected of an Irishman. He was at the top of the heap so far as repertoire was concerned. In competition in the old days it wasn't always who could sing the best but who could sing the most songs. Murphy had won one competition by singing forty-four Irish songs. Not long after that a pub owner asked him if he could sing sixty songs, and Murphy felt that he could. Arrangements were made for him to sing fifteen songs on two succeeding Friday and Saturday nights. But an opposition pub owner bribed the cops, and they called off

Murphy on the ground it would draw too large a crowd and thus the brawl would be bigger than usual. Murphy sang four of his sixty songs for me, and I enjoyed them very much. He then hastened off to church like a good Irishman, joining scads of other Catholics headed in the same direction.

Before the day was out I met Irishman number two. He had been a sailor but was mild-mannered and well educated, the type who had taken trips into the country rather than make for the nearest pub. He was something of a philosopher, and I set down a few of his sayings.

"The Aussie has become slow and easygoing. . . . 'If I don't do it today, I'll do it tomorrow'; or, 'If I don't do this, I'll do that.' "

"There's no school in America, nor in Australia, nor in the world, that will teach you as much as you'll learn on the road."

"You [meaning me] are never alone because you're always with your own thoughts; and that's something that no one else in the world but a traveler will ever understand."

During weekdays I sometimes talked to men on the job. Strikes always came into the discussion. The wharfies (stevedores) have exploited this tactic to the point of blackmail. They are the disgrace of Australia, and everybody knows it. The ministers even mention it in the pulpit.

"A mate of mine is a wharfie," a telephone linesman said to me one day. "Last week they were out and so I says, 'What are you out for now, matey?'

" 'I don't know; but we're not going back till we get it.'

"They don't know what they're out for half the time . . . don't care, really. Well, he says: 'I can get enough work in three days to support me the rest of the week, so why bother. If I do work more, the government just takes it in taxes.' "

The wharfies work just about when they feel like it. The day before New Year's they worked one and one-half hours but received pay for the full four hours. If a sprinkle of rain comes up, they knock off, especially if it is within a couple hours of quitting time. If a job is one requiring stooping, they get extra pay—"stoop money." One man does nothing but relieve men who want to go to the washroom, but he gets a full day's pay anyway. But the worst thing is that the men know they rule the roost. They make no pretense of respect for the cargo. Boxes are broken, flour bags are split open, and the waste is great. The chief mate on the ship can only walk the deck and fume inwardly. If he so much as opens his mouth, they may take offense and walk off the job. If a winch needs fixing, the chief engineer practically has to kowtow. Meanwhile ships lie around in ports for weeks and the owners lose thousands of pounds. And the stevedores' union even decides how many are allowed to work. There are a thousand men who would like to work on the docks but cannot, and probably two thousand are really needed.

Australians are world-known for their swimming and surfing, the surf at Sydney being especially suited for the latter sport. The surf boards I saw at Marouba and Bondi looked like a very shallow boat enclosed on top. The surfer carries it down to the water on his head, shoves it in, crawls on top, gets on his knees and paddles with his hands. The operation is supposed to work the board out past the incoming breakers. Two of the three chaps I was watching made it O.K., but the third never did succeed. It must be thrilling as both board and rider often go right through the breakers. Some surf boards are managed by a two-bladed oar. You may stand on a surf board and ride the waves in; or you may go body-surfing and have no board at all.

One of the men explained about undertows and lifesaving. An undertow is really a current that is strong enough to sweep you out to sea, perhaps around some promontory. It is impossible to swim against the current, but you can sometimes swim across it. If you are unsuccessful, the thing to do is to hold up your hand. The lifeguard, or someone, is supposed to see you. It would do no good to yell, because of the noise of the waves. On the beach are canvas belts attached to ropes, which are wound on a drum in a red container. The lifeguard puts on one of these belts and swims out to the distressed swimmer. Then someone on shore pulls them both in.

At long last the shipping company said the S/S *Palikonda* would definitely leave for Africa. And sure enough, the day before Christmas we sailed. Two other passengers, Charles B. and Marian E., and myself were taken out to Cockatoo Island and put on board. There was help with the luggage, but I trusted no one but myself to carry the precious Jacqueline up the steps. We sailed almost at once.

For a day or so the ship went fairly steady, and this made it possible for us to enjoy Christmas Day. The food was good and varied. The boys had decorated the tiny saloon with streamers of all colors and designs. Purple, red, yellow, and green were visible everywhere. Stars had been put on the walls by pasting up parts of streamers. Balloons and bells hung at streamer intersections. On the two tables were two three-story cakes, frosted, and decorated effectively.

I mentioned the boys. These were actually Indian men from Goa assigned to wait table for the officers and passengers. There was one of them for every two of us. They placed the menu in front of us before each course, took our orders and went out for immediate and personal execution thereof. All food was brought in by them in serving dishes, presented at the diner's left, and held while he helped himself. My "boy" I found, watched me so closely that I never had to wait for anything. He seemed to sense when I was in need of butter, another piece of toast, or whatever, and he would have it in front of me almost before I was aware of wanting it. For someone who was used to months of self-help from "bread and tin," I

New Zealand homes often show masterpieces of shrubs, flowers, and hedges.

Not all the tall trees are in California. These are in Victoria, Australia, and reach 301' 6", the tallest hardwood trees in the world.

found this quite a change. The officers, in their relationships with these men, followed, I suppose, English colonial tradition. There were no pleases or thank-yous. They called for their boys by simply calling out "boy," with a peculiar kind of pronunciation which made you think the word must be spelled b-u-o-y. They referred to them with such statements as:

"My *buoy* ought to know what I mean. He's been with me a year and a half."

"Hasn't your *buoy* shaved off his mustache?"

By Christmas Eve the ship had started to pitch a little, and since my resistance to such is very low on an empty stomach, I was unhappy until the meal was served. Marian had acquired some new war-discovered seasickness pills proved effective with Canadian soldiers on the Atlantic. She said these were supposed to be 90 percent effective and so, psychologically, she was quite all right and didn't expect to get seasick. We both passed the evening O.K., but the next morning was a different story. The boat was pitching quite a bit, the sea having been roughed by a storm. Instead of arising at 6:30 when our boy brought us tea, I slept on until nearly nine which is our awfully late hour for breakfast. Then, when I got up, I was as dizzy as a coot and by the time I was shaved—*w-o-o-o!* Nevertheless, I got through breakfast and made it on deck, where continuous strolling with my eyes far out to sea, plus the fresh air, kept things at least under control. Marian, with the confidence of her 90 percent seasickness remedy, sailed into, though not entirely through, a good breakfast. Retiring to her cabin afterward, she was suddenly surprised by losing her entire meal.

The *Palikonda* stopped at Melbourne, and since we were to be there for at least a week, I decided to take a four-day excursion into the hinterland with Jacqueline. Early one morning I secured some butter from the butler, which is what they call the steward, and some cold tongue and turkey, the better part of a loaf of bread, and some cheese, and set off to see the tallest trees in Australia.

I had a fine excursion. There was beautiful weather and fine forested mountains. There were "rosy-fingered morns," grassy, dew-wet valleys, and mountain streams. No use denying it, I like the "rugged outdoors." Memories of American camping trips with my family and with friends came back to me. These were no doubt fostered by all the Aussie campers I saw on the road or camped near. Most of them had old touring cars—Hudson, Chevrolet, and the like of the years 1920-26. I visited two areas of tall trees, the first requiring a forest hike of about twelve miles. The second was relatively near the road, but it climaxed an uphill walk with Jacqueline of more than four hours. Here in a sample acre the undergrowth had been cleared so one could admire the trees: twenty-seven giant mountain ashes, the tallest in the Southern Hemisphere. A sign on one tree read: "Height 301′ 6″. Girth at 10′, 16′ 5″. This specimen is the highest known living tree in Australia and the tallest hardwood tree in the world." These trees compare with our own *Sequoia sempervirens*, the branches starting very high above the ground. There are very few leaves on the ash and one wonders how they could grow so tall.

My road returning from the big trees followed the crest of a mountain ridge for thirteen miles, yet all of it was slightly downgrade. There were glorious views of distant forest ranges and adjacent valleys, all in fine sunshine and under a cloudless sky. But the next day at lower levels I had much up and down work, and finally a terrific dust storm as I worked into Melbourne. When I returned to the ship, I really appreciated a hot bath and a good big dinner. The total expenses of my glorious four-day outing had been a bit less than four cents.

New Year's Eve brought a big party in the second engineer's cabin. The crew were all attired in flowing white robes, colored caps, and whatnot. They gave serenades; the butler played the violin. All the ships in the harbor blew their whistles. Then the officers and passengers settled down to singing and the passing of the flowing cup. The majority of the lads were Scotch, and there were some very fine voices. The American was called on for songs and suggestions, but distinctly was not "in voice," a rare event in any case. Still I contributed my bit, and we all really got going on "Clementine." Marian was the life of the party but insisted on dancing barefoot, which required the rest of us to take off our shoes. By and by we rigged up a light and radio on the boat deck and danced up there. Eventually, around 4 A.M., we all got hungry but couldn't find anyone with a key to the pantry. I never could stand waiting, so I went to bed, and the rest soon followed.

The next day I visited my old friend of S/S *Ten Sleep* days, Irvin Tubal. He had given several violin concerts, and critics had been kind to him. He had become engaged and I met his charming fiancée. On following days I visited the botanical gardens, the public library, and other Melbourne friends, and also went shopping or wrote. Meanwhile I was enjoying fine meals on board ship. Life on a freighter is really the life of Riley. Nothing to do but eat and sleep or take excursions ashore as the spirit moves you. The bicycle is an ideal adjunct.

Before we left Melbourne, another passenger came aboard, a sandy-blond school secretary returning to Tanganyika for service there. We had a fine voyage to Adelaide, where we docked not far from a tiny beach that afforded us chances to go swimming. In Adelaide we acquired two more passengers, a saleslady and a minister-missionary. So now as we started the first leg of our journey, across the Great Australian Bight, we were six passengers to table. And as the days went by we became well acquainted. Although the *Palikonda* was a freighter, we still had deck sports like deck tennis, rope skipping, and badminton, by making use of the forward hatch cover. And in the evenings we played five hundred and occasionally bridge, or argued with Charles on all manner of topics.

Charles was the character among the passengers. In essence he was an artist, but he had many other pursuits. His first forty years were spent in New Zealand. He became an admirer of Beethoven and made a special trip to Europe for a Beethoven festival in Vienna. He steeped himself in the haunts of the famous musician and secured some valuable relics. He then spent ten years in London but made excursions nearly every year to most parts of Europe. He traveled as an artist, sketching from train windows or stopping at little villages in remote mountain areas to paint this scene or that as the spirit moved him. His pictures showed a marked attention to detail, and this I liked. No blotching in of landscapes—every leaf, every cloud, every crack in a stone wall, are there. The contrast of his colors is sharp.

He had now been living in Sydney for eight years. There he decorated his apartment with Beethoven souvenirs, antiques, Moorish arches, and Arabic inscriptions. He worked as a bookbinder's jobber and also transposed music for the special needs of others. Artists and music lovers reveled in his decorations, but Sydney produced no close friends for him. He became disgusted with the "knavery, crooks, thievery, cheating, selfishness" of the metropolis, dismantled his room, and shipped everything to Cape Town, where he hoped to start life anew. This was really a courageous step, because he must have been in his sixties. He had gray hair, was balding badly, had one leg bandaged because of poor circulation, and was slightly deaf. He spoke much too loudly and was overly jovial and bombastic. Imagine his deep voice speaking of one of the jolliest of the officers.

"You can feel the beam coming along and you're full of joy before you know it. Oh, the twinkle in his eye—a song without words. By Jove! What you don't meet up with on board a ship! But the thing I can't stand is wowsering—a rank, sour wowser!"

But Charles was argumentative and intrusive, and often turned out to be the very wowser he despised. He was one who never admitted being wrong, and his ideas were final. Food was a natural subject, as we were all together at table.

"No pork for me!" said Charles. "I've seen pigs eat. The filthy, dirty beasts!"

When eating dessert one night, I said, "This is called jello in America instead of jelly."

"Jello! Well, who ever heard of that. Of all the silly names!"

"But you make no distinction between real jelly and this," I pointed out.

"What do you mean, 'real jelly'? This *is* real jelly."

The others at the table had already caught the point and helped explain. But of course Charles had the last word.

At another meal I said, "Well, it's a long time since I've had chicken."

"What do you mean? A chicken is a little thing. This is a hen or a rooster. This is no chicken!" blasted out Charles.

"Oh, well, maybe you call them 'chooks,' " I responded, recalling the Australian term.

"No, and we don't call them chooks either. But a chicken is a little bit of a thing. Don't try to tell me what a chicken is. I know what a chicken is!"

Charles had an abnormal fear of being left out of anything. A group conversing or planning a card game had to be extremely careful not to offend him. He refused to recognize that most of the passengers were little more than a third as old and were bound to prefer company their own age. The officers who ate at his table were extremely young—ruddy cheeks, dark curly hair, even dimples. And so Charles was sometimes openly cross and upset.

In speaking of his Sydney friends, he said. "Oh, yes, they all want me to write them. But it's only to give them a little amusement. They aren't really interested in me as a friend."

He was unctuous with the women and admitted he had always wanted to marry, "goodness knows." "The hand has always been out," said he at table, holding out his open palm at arm's length. "But I must do something at Cape Town. I'm tired of this single business."

But we were all afraid his lonely life would continue. One of the women summed it up one night just after his complaint about the selfish and unfriendly Australians.

"I'm afraid you're going to find people like that wherever you go, Charles."

Quite in contrast to Charles, in her effect upon the passengers and officers, was the lively and colorful Marian. She was always on the go and full of ideas. Her *joie de vivre* also found expression in the vivid colors of her attire. She matched her fresh eager face with reds and yellows and vivid greens found in striped sweaters, long-tasseled dwarf caps, burnooses, odd slippers, and the like. Although unpredictable in dress, you could predict the outcome when she played games like deck tennis. She usually won, even though the game was fast and required catching and throwing with accuracy. But, like Charles, she had a few strange hang-ups. Coffee had to be very hot and very black. Ordinary cut-up lettuce leaves would not do; she had to have a special serving of the full leaves. Lemon for fish had to be quartered in a certain way. Toast had to be sliced very thin. Marian's "boy" had to make many an extra trip to the galley.

Among the officers, two, the purser and the chief mate, spent time with the passengers. The purser, an Indian, was an intelligent chap, quick of perception and well educated. He sometimes played five hundred with us, and one evening he told our fortunes by reading our palms. He said I would always find people agreeable, no matter what kind they were. He had just become a father for the first time, the little girl being named Marouk after the moon. She had been born January 5, but the telegram did not catch up to him until January 20, when we were in Perth. He had had two extra weeks of worrying, and now he wouldn't be able to see his daughter for a whole year. Boy, you can take the life of a seaman—I wouldn't want it.

Speaking of childbirth, the chief was telling us of an embarrassing experience. He was the mate on an Indian coastal ship one time with three thousand deck passengers. The passengers did not always use the facilities provided, and the ship's scuppers were full of filth in spite of efforts to keep the ship clean. Making an inspection one dark night, he espied a figure squatting in the scuppers against the rules and angrily fetched it a kick. It turned out to be a woman in childbirth. Among certain poor classes, Indian women may not stop work for a day to have a baby, perhaps not even for an hour. The chief claims to have seen them carrying coal, step out of the line for a few minutes, have their child, tie up its cord, cradle it on their back and keep on working. Well . . . could be!

Once across the Great Australian Bight, we rounded Cape Leeuin and headed north. The change in direction brought us into the wind, and the ship had to take the swell broadside instead of bow on. This caused considerable movement aboard, and not a soul suggested cards that evening. The next morning all the dishes slid off the table opposite us and there was a big crash as the artillery, with which we were brilliantly supplied, followed suit. At our own table we succeeded in keeping our crockery out of our laps, but Charles' fish wound up in the sugar bowl, his toast on the floor.

Drowsiness is almost as bad a disease to fight on a sea voyage as seasickness. It is a peculiar phenomenon. The body seems to require twice, even three times, as much sleep on board a ship. It not only requires extra sleep, it insists, it demands. All of the *Palikonda* passengers succumbed except the young minister and myself, who resolved to pursue a normal schedule. He had his texts and Greek to study, and I was drilling myself in Swahili and Arabic. But it was no use. We lost. Our hearts, our whole beings, seemed to get into a kind of deep torpor—so deep that it made us unwell. This feeling usually reached its worst just before lunch or dinner. A good meal would temporarily alleviate it. We could only conclude that the motion of the ship caused our bodies to expend tremendous energy for adjustment.

And talking about adjustment, when we did arrive in Freemantle and the ship's motion ceased, some of us actually felt sick. It was a most peculiar, a sort of dizzyish feeling; and after a full night's sleep in the bargain. But it seemed as though the ship still ought to be wallowing in the waves. Mr. Chittleborough noticed this phenomenon even when downtown in Perth, but I never felt it after leaving the ship.

At Freemantle three hundred passengers walked on board—all sheep. They had been herded into the town, and onto the dock alongside, by a herder and one dog. The dog did most of the work as the sheep climbed a long and rather steep special gangplank to the main deck, where pens had been built for them. We had been outbound only a day or so, when the chief walked past our groups of passengers on the way to look after his sheep.

"Chiefee!" called out Marian. "Have you met our new passenger, Miss Coxon?"

"No," said the chief without looking around or thinking how it would sound. "I'm afraid I'm not much interested in her. I've got three hundred sheep on the after deck."

The chief was the ship's storyteller. He was a big man and always wore a big broad smile on his ruddy countenance, which extended well past where the top of his forehead was supposed to be. He would sometimes stop on the boat deck to be with us for an hour or so in the afternoons, and we had a yarn with him almost every evening. Several of his best stories had to do with cats, but to understand them some words of explanation are necessary.

Shipboard Cats

Apart from their usefulness as ratters, cats are often valued on freighters for the companionship they afford lonely men. Seamen talk of them with a great deal of affection. And cats learn to adopt a ship as home and stick with it through voyages long and short.

In port, like a seaman, they take shore leave at the first opportunity, trotting down the gangplank without a qualm. But unlike the seaman, who usually returns aboard each night, the cat will usually remain ashore until the last few hours—even minutes—before the ship sails. It is uncanny how they seem to know when this will be, for it is a date even the chief officer may not know until the day before. And the ship may have been in port for two weeks.

A ship is required by law to keep track of its cat. If one should be lost in port, the Australian customs levied a fine of 50 pounds (about $160), as part of a program for the control of communicable disease. To avoid such a fine the ship's officers will have to fabricate a story of the cat's death and actually make an entry in the ship's log to substantiate it.

The *Palikonda's* cat was a big black and white tom named Whiskey. Between Sydney and Melbourne, Whiskey had a wife aboard; but in the course of nature she had become pregnant and gone ashore in Melbourne to have her kittens. Knowing the habits of such creatures, the chief had been at pains to secure a new mate for Whiskey, giving him a divorce on the grounds of desertion. He secured a lovely Tiger Girl, and when Whiskey paid a visit aboard about a week before our departure, the chief made the introduction in the chart room. This was not at all successful. The chief, Marian, and I went up to see how the young couple were getting along in their honeymoon chamber. It was obviously no go. Tiger Girl was seated on the couch all right, but Whisky was at the porthole meowing to get out in the most worried manner possible. Tiger Girl was peeking at him affectionately from around a corner. Choice tidbits from the table had been left uneaten on the floor. So Whiskey was let ashore the following morning, and Tiger Girl said goodbye a couple of days later.

A week after this, at noon, just four hours before we sailed, Whiskey came trotting up the long gangplank. The chief told us of the time they had used ramps to load coal and Whiskey had gotten in the habit of going ashore over one of them. After they had pulled up the ramps to sail, Whisky returned. There he stood, lonely on the dock where the ramp had been, meowing at top voice, scared to death that the ship was leaving without him.

But there came a day, in Adelaide, when Whiskey failed to come up the plank before sailing.

"We'll sure miss Whiskey," said the chief.

"I'm surprised he didn't come aboard," said I. "Cats are usually so uncanny about coming aboard just before sailing. But I didn't see him come aboard at Melbourne either."

"Oh, yes. He came aboard all right—just ten minutes before we pulled up the plank. But someone got him in Adelaide! It's a bloody shame too. He had been with us ever since the ship was launched. The old man [captain], the chief [chief engineer], Whiskey, and I are the only ones that have been aboard her right along. A bloody fine cat, that Whiskey!"

"That Amber was a fine cat too," inserted the fourth engineer.

"Yeah, but she left us before Whiskey did—to have her kittens, I think. And then when I told the customs man that I saw her jump out of a lifeboat after a sea gull one morning at six and go overboard, and he said, 'That's your story and you're going to stick with it, eh?'"

"So I put on a long face and said, 'If you're implying that I am prevaricating from the truth . . .'"

We were all in stitches by this time, picturing the ridiculousness of a cat making a pass at a sea gull, when we knew they never come closer than five rods of a ship at sea; and this coupled with the extreme unlikelihood of a cat ever losing its footing!

"But no more bloody cats. After I had to put an entry in the log book that I opened up number one hold and found Whiskey down there with a broken back and had to toss him overboard . . . No, sir! Arthur Prater is not going to perjure himself any more over bloody cats even if it does save the company fifty pounds."

"But aren't you supposed to cut off their tails for proof?" put in the fourth engineer again.

"Oh, yes. But with Amber—well, she went over the side, so I couldn't get hers. And with Whiskey—well, I forgot his! But no more bloody cats!"

Starting with a burst of laughter, the chief continued: "I'll never forget the time we thought we had a mate for Whiskey. A fine, big ginger cat came on board, you know—a helluva fine-looking cat. Well, I only got a look at it 'bow on,' you know; so I told the boy to take it up to the chart room. Then when I went up a little later here was the old man [captain] down on his hands and knees with his belly almost on the floor, crawling along with a bit of cake. 'Come, puss, nice puss, puss, puss. Bloody fine mate you got for Whiskey here, Chief. Here puss . . .'

The chief had to stop for laughter.

"Well, just then the cat turned around on both of us and we got a full view of his rear, and oh boy! Ha, ha, ha!"

"And the old man jumped up and said to me, 'Where in the hell did you get your education?' And all I could do was to splutter that I'd only looked at him bow on. Ha, ha, ha!"

When the laughter had died down and we were all lost in our own thoughts, the chief went on.

"There was another time I'll not forget either. It was when I was mate on the Burma run. We used to make Chittagong, Akyab, Sandoway, Rangoon—all those places. We carried the mail, you know, and I'd have to take it ashore in a small boat at some of the towns where they didn't have a harbor. So I'd just left the ship at some small place, and 'the old man called out after me, 'Pick up a kitten while you're ashore.' 'Oh, O.K., sir!' So when I got ashore I asked this Burmese postmaster if he had a kitten. Well, no, he didn't; but he'd fix me up next trip and I could pick it up then. So that was áll right. Well, then the next time I went ashore I saw sort of a barrel, or a cask, really, there. And there was a meowin' comin' from it; and so I said to the postmaster, 'What's that you got there?'

" 'Oh, that's your cat.'

"So I had the boys roll this cask down the jungle path to the ship. And I thought there was an uncommon amount of spitting' and noise comin' out of it. Well, we got it aboard, and I told the tingle [boatswain's mate] to carry it up to the chart room. When the old man wanted to know what it was, I told him it was the kitten he wanted.

"So: 'Well, let's get the lid off.'

"So we got it off all right; and no sooner was it pried loose than out came seventeen bloody jungle cats—ft-f-f-ft-ft-ft-f-f-ft-ft—all covered with offal from being in there so long and rolled around in it, you know. And they cleared out of there so fast all we could see was a lot of bloody yellow streaks goin' through the air—"

"What do you mean? Wildcats?" I interrupted.

"Yes, wild as hell. They're long yellow-and-red spotted ones—half again as long as an ordinary cat. This postmaster had had his boys catch them in the jungle, you see. Seventeen bloody wildcats!"

"They sure took the rats off that ship, though. But whenever we walked around after that near some lifeboat, or any corner, there would be a bloody

A vigilant sheep dog holds 300 sheep in position for loading on the Palikonda. They kept us company for 3,235 miles.

Crew inspection: Goans on the Palikonda.

yellow claw reaching out at you and *ft-ft-ft-f-f-ft* [The chief used gestures here]. G—, it was funny!"

For many days we ploughed westward across the south Indian Ocean. It was a most pleasant voyage, and here are my notes to prove it.

Every afternoon from four to six we play deck tennis on the top of number three hatch, using a rope quoit. Several of the officers join in, and we have some rousing good games. The captain and the chief look down from the bridge, and the fours waiting for the court cheer the players on. The exercise is great and keeps us fit. In the evening we play five hundred or carroms.

Late forenoons and early afternoons are spent relaxing on deck. There is a shelter over the top deck, and there we passengers sit by the hour in solid, cool comfort. Each pursues his own fancy. Most of us study or read. We all listen to Marian's record player. Imagine listening to *Tales of the Vienna Woods* or *Largo* and then lifting your eyes to look out across the peaceful blue waters of the great deep. *C'est magnifique!* The weather has been perfect with only an occasional fresh wind or light shower. Day after day the sea is perfect, and since we are long ago accustomed to the slight rolling and pitching of the ship, there is nothing to mar our enjoyment.

Blue! Vast! Restless! These are the three words, arranged in proper order of impression, which describe the Indian Ocean in summer. There seem to be two main moods the sea displays. Today its surface is quite smooth and puckered only by small waves and wavelets; but these are borne on the breasts of calm but great surging swells. On other days the swells are huge waves that rise to peaks and sharp ridges. On such days, paradoxically, the ship rides more gently.

Today a great sense of peace comes from watching the sea. I think of our great isolation from the world—the clangor of its cities, the puny strivings of its people. Land is 2,500 miles behind us, and the waters, as I look out to the south, reach about 3,300 miles to the Antarctic. In the opposite direction it is 2,000 miles to India, while to the west it is 500 miles to a tiny island called Mauritius. Our ship moves on and on—a wonderful moving islet or magic carpet, whose effortless functions rarely intrude upon our thoughts. Ah, paradise! And with Tchaikovsky's Concerto No. 1 in B Flat Minor moving my heart in unknown ways, I am almost inclined to agree with some of the passengers who wish that the voyage might go on and on forever.

15

Island World

We hung over the rail and with glasses studied the rugged outlines of the island as we approached. Mauritius is of strategic importance on the Africa-Asia water routes, but we thought only of the thrill of a new and "undiscovered" land at the end of a long voyage. But it was afternoon before we glided past some tiny offshore islands and into the horseshoe harbor of Port Louis, the capital. Here we cut the engines, and two hawser boats, each rowed by four men standing up and leaning on their oars, carried the *Palikonda's* ropes over to well-anchored buoys. But we found there was no going ashore before the following morning, and it was with the greatest impatience that we awaited that event.

After breakfast the company launch landed us at the strip of concrete along the water's edge where the customs officers functioned under an open-sided shelter. The streets just ahead were quite narrow, but the Place d'Armes to the right was a wide thoroughfare, strongly reminiscent of Panama City with its tropical setting of tall feathery palms.

I walked straight ahead. On either side shops lined the street, but they were little more than cubbyholes, and even Barclay's Bank, when I reached it, was scarcely more impressive. It was less pretentious than the average Australian corner pub. The floor was just one step up, and there were no pillars or marble floors. The offices of the five big shipping agents—my first day's objective, since I was concerned with later passage to Madagascar —were part of the same picture and one of them was in a warehouse.

The Englishmen on the *Palikonda* had asserted confidently and with the pride of empire that the people of Mauritius spoke English. So it was disconcerting to find in each shipping office several dark-complexioned chaps in khaki, perhaps wearing a red fez, not one of whom could speak English. I was obliged to dig up my latent French. Back of the counters at dimly lighted desks were chaps of varying shades of white and black, but no matter how white a chap might be he spoke English only reluctantly and with uncertainty, if one could lure him into attempting it at all. Back at the Treaty of Paris in 1910 when Mauritius, then Ile de France, passed to English ownership and government, it was provided that the inhabitants might retain their own religions, customs, and language. More than one hundred years later they were still clinging tenaciously to that privilege. But I was later to find not one Englishman who would admit that anything but English was the language of the island; and at the hospital the matron,

Corn on the island of Mauritius. South Indian Ocean.

Cooling drinks, droll stories by the first officer, Tchaikovsky's Concerto No. 1 in B Flat Minor, pretty girls! 11:00 A.M. on the Palikonda.

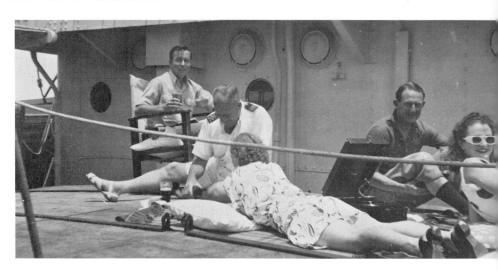

addressed by me in French, assured me stiffly, "I speak only English."

As I strolled about the city in work shirt, overalls, and jockey cap the good people of Mauritius apparently found me as amusing and interesting as I found them. This was my first contact with Asian culture—more than half the population stems from India—and my first acquaintance with the Creole. The Indians had been first brought over as coolie labor after the British freed the native slaves. So now here were Indian women, well rounded and often attractive, dressed in saris of bright pinks or yellows, topped with a colorful jacket (*badjong*). Many were barefooted, others wore sandals, and most of them wore small buttonlike ornaments of brass or silver fastened neatly to the lower part of the left nostril, adding a certain charm to the wearer. Over her head each woman had draped a light cloth which she adjusted from time to time if one's scrutiny became too obtrusive.

There was one anachronistic note. Here and there were a few withered old ladies dressed in black—black skirt, black jacket, black stockings, and little black hat. They were not unlike the little old-fashioned lady one saw now and then back home in the U.S.A., the one people speak of as a "bit queer." How these little old ladies have managed to retain their idiosyncrasy in the midst of the colorful folk of Port Louis is beyond me. And where did they come from?

The native businessmen and the young men who idly lounged about the street corners or doors of shops were dressed in suits of white cotton or in khaki, with the shirt collar open. The sparingly clad laborers—the men on the lighters that loaded and unloaded cargoes, or the men struggling with head, shoulders, and feet against the heavy wooden carts—wore a pair of undershorts, over those a pair of khaki shorts, and an old hat, and sometimes a shirt. If the white undershorts showed through a great rent or rents, it did not bother the owner thereof. Yet the ragged laborer was the exception, for the needle is well known in Mauritius. Most laborers' clothes were sewed and patched to perfection, and sewed even where there were no patches, just as a precautionary measure against the day when there might be a need for patches.

There were several crippled hags crouching on the sidewalks, two chaps with stump hands, and a nearly legless cripple sitting in a little cart such as a small boy would make and dressed in a white suit and black fez. A black boy occasionally picked up the tongue of the cart and hauled him to a new location. But outside of these five or six people there were no beggars to be seen all the time I was in Port Louis, which was not bad for the heterogeneous population of eighty thousand.

At a shipping office I discovered there was a ship in port, the S/S *Hoeveld*, bound for Madagascar. This was a godsend. I hired a couple of chaps to row me out to the ship and persuaded the captain to sign me on as steward for the trip at the old customary wage of an English shilling

(20 cents) a month. I ran into a snag with the company itself, however, which said I could go only as a passenger for 125 Mauritian rupees ($38.50). The captain was called into the office, but he stood by his agreement. So again I was lucky, for the days of "workaways" are unhappily gone from the shipping lanes of the world.

With business finished, I took Jacqueline from the hold of the *Palikonda*, said goodbye to my friends and was soon pedaling inland from Port Louis. The road led upward, a long and steep climb, to Curepipe, elevation 1,800 feet. Buses loaded to the gills went by me every few minutes. The road was never deserted. There was always at least one Indian or Creole woman in view, accompanied by a child, and often carrying a five-gallon can of water on her head. There were occasional bicycles also, some ridden by native police in helmet and full khaki uniform. With coat buttoned tightly around the neck and a belt in the bargain, I don't know how they stood the heat. Except for my undershirt I was stripped to the waist and sweating like a Turk.

When I asked one of these policemen the way to Tamarind Falls, highest on the island, he seemed amazed I was going so far. Yet it was not more than eight miles. This reminded me that one of the customs men had referred to a place as "very far away indeed," yet it was actually only about twenty-five miles. In other words, this Mauritius, this tiny isle, was a world to the inhabitants. A great distance was not five hundred miles or a thousand but twenty-five miles. In trim I could probably cycle around it in one day. No one had any idea of the distance to America, and the average Creole, of whom education was not required, had not even heard of us.

Above a thousand feet the island was much cooler. At Curepipe I stopped by previous invitation at a home to pick up a map of the island. It was a fine residence with hedges and flower beds. Phillipe du Coudroy not only greeted me warmly but invited me in for tea. I was suddenly plunged into fine company and a jolly time with a gay little group of Mauritians, speaking French, of course. One of the group later conducted me through the filtration plant that supplies practically the whole island with water. On my subsequent tour around the edge of the island I was impressed to see that I was never more than a mile from a roadside faucet.

My campsite that night was by a fine stream flowing merrily over rocks only a few feet from my head. Trees, grass, and a few clouds—and only one mosquito. In fact, the pests seemed to be very rare. In the morning I visited Tamarind Falls, not spectacular but in a beautiful setting. Back on the road, whenever I stopped to rest, someone was sure to come along and pause for a chat. Since the Creole language is a patois, differing in pronunciation and style from French, and especially from mine, it was amusing to see which of my listeners, young or old, would catch on to what I was saying in answer to their numerous questions. When I was nearly across the island, I felt so pervaded by the warmth and hospitality of the people that I stopped at a house to rest.

"I am an American traveling around the world on this old bicycle," I introduced myself. "It is hot, and I would like to sit down here for a little while. May I?"

"Oui, monsieur," said the short, dark-complexioned Creole. Then addressing the oldest of his children, "Bring a chair."

"America, it is very far from here?" he asked politely.

"Yes, very far. About fifteen thousand kilometers."

Then he stepped inside and brought out a large coconut and lopped off one end with a knife. One of his children brought a glass, and he poured out a clear fluid as delicious as any soft drink I ever tasted.

"What do you call this?" I asked.

"Coco, monsieur."

"It is the first time for me. It is very, very good—and good for the thirst also, is it not?"

"Yes. Would you like some more?" commencing to pour another glass.

"Ah, no . . . please. Give it to your children there. I have enough."

A little later the family brought out a *mangue* (mango), a yellow and green fruit with a huge stone in the center. This was also new to me, and it pleased them when I told them as much. They showed me that I was to peel it and gave me a knife for the purpose. The fruit was delicious and had the color and somewhat the texture of the inside of a muskmelon.

Leaving my kind host, I descended to the sea. Having crossed the island, I was now at the south end. It was surrounded by coral reefs, and thus the surf and breakers were a long way offshore. This left a series of beautiful lagoons. After lunch and a shave on the beach I lay down on the sand in the shade of a tree and slept. When I awoke to languidly gaze out upon the distant breakers canopied with a blue sky and a few fleecy white clouds, I thought it was about as near paradise as it is possible to get on earth.

I made a circuit of half the island on my return to Port Louis. En route I was surprised to find corn growing as well as in my native Iowa. As before, there were plenty of people to visit with along the way. But I most enjoyed the children at the Champ de Mars back in Port Louis. I had settled myself on the steps of a small pavilion and in true housewife fashion had laid out my sewing; overalls, food bags, and pack were all in need of repair. Idle young men playing cards and checkers had paused to chat with me, but when the children got out of school, I found what it was to really have an audience. They never deserted me, and when I had to walk over to the bicycle for supplies, at least a dozen trooped after me. They were mostly from five to eight, and all were boys except two Chinese

Disembarking the 300 sheep at Mauritius. Into the basket and . . .

. . . when five sheep are inside, a winch hoists the basket over the side to the waiting barge.

girls. Some of the lads were quite bright, and eager to try the few words of English they had learned at school.

One evening on the way out of the city to pass the night, I stopped to visit a Hindu temple, one of several I had seen. It had been built by the Tamils, people from the south of India in the vicinity of Madras. The priest was small of stature (as are all the Tamils), wore the usual white, draped pants, and had a very meager knowledge of French. I managed to make him understand I wanted to see the interior of the temple, and he motioned for me to take off my shoes.

There were six-armed figures painted bright green, yellow, and red; figures of kings in yellow robes; tapers and little piles of chalklike substance; dark chambers and arches; and even a huge black, blue, and white hobby horse. In front of the main part of the temple was a little red pagoda with a kind of black couchant lion inside. Overhead were tiny bells on a special pole of their own. Only when the wind blew hard did these ring.

When the tour was over, I put on my shoes and bade the priest goodbye, explaining to him by signs and a few French words that I proposed to sleep on the edge of the wood not far away. But when I wheeled Jacqueline across to the place designated, he motioned me to come back and made it clear he was inviting me to sleep in the courtyard on the stone veranda adjoining his own quarters. Sleeping in a Tamil temple appealed to me and I accepted, whereupon he squatted stoically on his doorstep, occasionally smoking a cigarette but paying no further attention to me. I preempted a small bench at hand and ate my supper of bread and "tin," occasionally offering him some, but he did not accept. I had bought a mango or two and was eating one of them, when he suddenly went inside and brought me out a nice big ripe one which put mine decidedly in the shade. Later he followed this gift with a ripe banana.

He remained the perfect host. There were a few electric lights about the temple and one on the priest's porch. Under the latter I wrote in my diary until 9 P.M. while he reclined on his bed inside and watched the stranger from far lands. But as soon as I stirred toward bed, he came out and arranged several mats for my use. In spite of the high wall around us, sufficient breeze came in to make me pass a pleasant night. In the morning I was invited to stay for coffee. It was presented in a handleless tin cup and was very good, though a bit murky. In the kitchen there was a huge iron kettle underneath a smaller one, which in its turn was underneath a tap. The water from the first kettle overflowed into the larger kettle, which was a good three feet across. At one side of the room a few bricks enclosed some hot coals, and here was where my coffee had been prepared. I parted from my firmly silent little priest with the feeling I should never forget the experience.

Came the day to leave Mauritius. With Jacqueline laid across the prow of a longboat, I was rowed out to the S/S *Hoeveld*. She was a coal burner and stevedores had been busy for days carrying baskets of coal up long jiggly planks from barges. It was said the ship had already served forty years on the Gold Coast. The engineers' quarters were on the afterdeck over the poop, and the captain had a little room on the bridge. Just under this small bridge was the saloon, flanked by narrow passageways, beyond which were two heads and a small room for baths. There was no shower and no tub, but one could get water in a pail. Under the saloon there were small cabins for the three officers and a cabin for passengers, if any. The new steward, Hart Rosdail, was assigned the cabin.

16

Laughter in Madagascar

There is was. Another African island. Madagascar, a French possession larger than France. But it did not look at all like an island, because a thousand miles of coastline stretched away north and south into invisibility. It might have been another continent instead of the fourth largest island in the world.

Madagascar the mysterious! For the island's origin is uncertain. It has produced fossil remains of the African hippopotamus, and some of the people show that their forebears came from Africa. But 240 miles of ocean ten thousand feet deep now separate Madagascar from the mainland. Scientists believe that some stupendous cataclysm of the past tore the island from the side of its mother. Ethnologists have discovered that the leading race, the Hovas, descended from the Malays and that there are traces of Melanesians on the island. Madagascar might once have been a bridge to Asia but how could people have come from the South Pacific?

We arrived in the port of Tamatave on a Saturday evening but could not dock until Monday morning. However, there was a fast launch service ashore for all ships, and on Sunday evening one of the mates invited me to do the town with him as his guest. As we started out he handed me all his money as a precautionary measure. This was not too startling, especially after I saw he was able to establish credit wherever we stopped. Cognac, pernod, whiskey, claret, and beer were produced in quantity and in bewildering succession. He not only established credit but actually succeeded in borrowing a thousand francs from a man whose acquaintance he had picked up on the street only five minutes previously. And this man held an important position in one of the local shipping offices, I found out the next day. He sat at table with us and was treated on his own borrowed money to an excellent dinner and more and more drinks, while we watched the dancers. The music gave me itchy feet, but alas, there were no unescorted girls, and our companion said those present would not dance with strangers.

The hostess was quite attractive and most efficient. As we were leaving the mate went back to speak to her. While he was a bit unsteady in his walk by now, he seemed to remain polite and debonair. I turned back to get him, and so saw them together, as could everyone else in the room. He did not touch her so far as I could see, but in a moment he strode past us without looking to either right or left and with the hostess shouting after him. It was too much French for me to understand. I started after him, but she ran past me still shouting. There were at least fifty people about the doorway, and they all looked after the mate, who was striding down the middle of the street. Our chance friend ducked discreetly into the shadows. I decided to follow the mate. The hostess was still shouting after him, but I assumed the affair was closed.

It was a good three blocks before I caught up with the mate, who was just signaling a passing car for a ride, probably thinking it was a taxi. The car stopped all right, and at least six young men popped out and in a twinkling he was surrounded. Then I saw the girl was with them. She jumped out, slapped the mate's face a couple of times and went on with her tirade. He took it but finally walked away, ignoring me, probably to disassociate me from his embarrassment. Again I thought the incident closed as I started to follow him. We strode along the promenade, and he began to make an explanation. Then he stopped and said softly, "They are coming again."

"No, surely," said I.

"Yes, they come again."

Not one car but two suddenly pulled up to the curb. About a dozen young chaps piled out and made a rough semicircle around the mate. The girl apparently had plenty of friends, all anxious to avenge her for whatever had happened. She slapped my host's face again, still lashing him with her tongue as well. One of her champions took a poke at him, he retaliated, and fists flew, while she, who had apparently not bargained for this, covered her face with her hands and cried, "Oh! Oh!" Meanwhile the mate had fallen down with another chap still poking at him. I decided it was time to intervene and succeeded in getting him out of the arena.

"They are too many for you," I said. "Come."

We eventually gained the customs outpost and the wharves. But the mate, possibly expecting another attack, refused to take the launch, and so we parted. He boarded the launch at a place farther on. Back on the ship I went to bed thinking he must have manhandled the girl or insulted her in some way. It was not until the next day, when I asked our friend of the evening, that I discovered all she had accused him of was trying to kiss her. Evidently Madagascar was no place for a wolf on the prowl, even a mild-mannered one.

It was hot in Tamatave. As long as I rode the bike and got a little breeze everything was O.K. But when I stopped and entered an office, I broke out in a wilting sweat. All offices and stores closed between 11 A.M. and 2 P.M. During these hours it is even uncomfortable under a tree, so I was grateful for an invitation to lunch at the de Charmoys', relatives of Mauritius friends. We ate in a large room with French doors opening toward the sea and letting in the ocean breeze. We lingered over lunch in the French manner, that is, with much vivacious conversation, all of which was in French and put quite a strain on my attainments. The Malagasy boy who served us probably also did the cooking. Whenever he moved away from the table and off the carpet, he placed his feet on two felt cloths and walked with a peculiar shuffling gait in order to polish the floor.

In the evenings a good breeze blew off the sea, and the whole city turned out to enjoy it along the promenade, which encircles half of the harbor. The children played games in the sand; the young men and women rode bicycles up and down or played ping-pong on the veranda of a nearby club. The rest of the people strolled by in pairs or sat quietly looking out to sea and at the ships anchored off shore. The white girls were very chic in cool prints and wide-brimmed hats, but the native girls dressed more plainly. The Anglo-Indian girls wore their long silks and adjusted their headpieces whenever they thought a man might be looking at them. The men were in khaki or white shirts and shorts, some with white knee socks and many with sun helmets. And always there were the French sailors with the red topknots on their white caps. Then there were the Mohammedans in long white or yellowish coats, trousers, and red fezzes; and a few Chinese and native Malagasy boys. All types were to be seen on the grand promenade at Tamatave.

In Madagascar I found the last word in postal red tape. I brought ashore with me from the *Hoeveld* two small properly wrapped packages which I wished to mail home. One was Jacqueline's old bell, which I wanted to send to a bell-collector friend in Chicago, the other a roll of exposed film.

At the post office I laboriously filled out forms to cover the mailing. So far, so good. But then I was told I had to get a customs permit. After a couple of tries I located the proper building and waded through six inches of sand across the yard to the steps. Thence to several offices on the first floor and finally to the right one on the second. Here an assistant told me I must first get a customs permit for the entry of the parcels into Madagascar.

So down the stairs and across the sand to Jacqueline again. After two or three tries I found the right building and of several entrances available fortunately chose the right one. In due course, after explaining my past history, contents of parcels, why I was sending a bell home, etc., etc., I got stamps on my parcels. These were then taken to a higher authority for initialing. Ah! Now back to bureau number one for the exit permit.

Well, it seemed that Monsieur Jilong, the director of this particular bureau, had to sign the permit and he was absent. "When will he be back?" I asked.

"Oh, I don't know, monsieur. He is ill."

"Well, who signs in his absence?"

"Ah, no one, monsieur."

"But there must be someone. Things don't just stop when he's not here, do they?"

To this I got a shrug expressive of "Yes, that's the way it is!"

"Well, will you keep these two parcels until he returns?"

"Ah, yes, monsieur. I'll put them right away in the safe."

Two days later I called again. "Has Monsieur Jilong returned?"

"Ah, no, monsieur."

"But what am I to do? I'll be leaving Madagascar in a few days. How long has Monsieur Jilong been ill?"

"Since last Monday. He is very ill, monsieur. He has a fever."

"I am sorry." Then a sudden thought. "But who is his superior? He can sign the permit, can he not?"

"Yes, but he is in Tananarive."

The next day the countenance of my friend in the export-permit office showed he had some news to report. "I have been to see Monsieur Jilong myself," he began, "and it is not possible for you to send your bicycle bell and films. You see [showing me a pamphlet], here is a list of the things permitted for export. There is honey, and these items here, and . . . but no bicycle bells or exposed films."

"But that is for things manufactured in Madagascar," I protested. "You don't manufacture bicycle bells and you don't even have films."

Long pause. "Oh, well, let me have the parcels." I was suddenly afraid that if I pushed the matter further, they might not even let me embark with the packages.

Later I outlined my mailing problem to an immigration official, a young and friendly chap. He stuffed the parcels in his pocket, put me on his motorcycle, and when he found out it was my first ride on such a vehicle, broke all the speed records getting to the export office. Here he got the proper stamps, and we tore off to the residence of Monsieur Jilong for his all-powerful signature. Jilong was really ill (malaria), but his wife admitted us. When he sat up in bed and we shook hands, his skin felt like a piece of metal that had been lying in the sun. In view of the listed exportable articles, he did not want to sign, but at my friend's urging, agreed. Then a new crisis arose. No one had a pen. But hold! I had an indelible pencil. We got the signature.

An anticlimax was a twenty-minute wait in the sweltering mob at the post office. A receipt for every letter and parcel had to be stamped in duplicate, whether registered or not. The poor clerks were swamped. Then it took my clerk a while to find a spot not covered by string, stamps, and signatures where he could affix the postage stamps. But at last the red tape was finished and the packages were mailed!

In Tamatave I was invited to spend some time in the home of one of the French consular officials. Both my host and my hostess gave very vivid accounts of the then recent Malagasy rebellion. They felt they were still sitting on a powder keg. They had bars on all the windows and always kept the doors locked. When the rebellion had started, there were only a few guns in the city and no ammunition. My host made torches and acquired gasoline to throw on any mob. They had spoken German in front of the Malagasy servants, since this was not understood. In all seriousness my host stated there was much talk that America would like to seize it before Russia took over. Later I talked to one of the educated Malagasy, who carefully characterized the uprising as "the resistance of the Vichy regime." Fifty years before, the government of the leading tribe, the Hova, more or less enlightened, had been crushed by the French. Several of the leaders had been executed, the prime minister banished, and their Christian queen exiled. Now in the period of unrest and uncertainty brought about by World War II, it was not strange that Madagascar should feel the stirrings of nationalism. These were abetted by vacillating policies of the French government, black-market extortions, high taxes, and the like. The initial rebellion had been quelled, but it left in its wake apprehension on the part of the French population and hate and a desire for revenge among the natives.

One night I found an excellent campsite outside the city. Heretofore I had crawled into the thin outer covering of my sleeping bag and covered my face with a mosquito net. But in Madagascar heat any covering at all was enough to make me sweat. I decided to try putting up my little pup tent and lying on top of my bag. It worked perfectly. I left the flap of the tent open and pinned my net across the opening. By morning it was cool enough to crawl under the cover of the bag.

My camp was near the hut of a native Malagasy. The owner called for a chat, and I invited myself over for water for shaving. They gave me a huge cupful and a little chair to sit on outside. The man knew just enough French for me to identify myself properly. When I returned the chair and cup, he had gone, but the wife and a little boy of three greeted me with smiles. Since it was my first visit to a Malagasy home, I took careful note of everything. In one corner was an open hearth. On a metal framework about fourteen inches above the coals was a kettlelike skillet holding grease. Opposite the fire was a tiny table with bottles and miscellany. On the floor was a dish of rice from which the small boy and the cat alternately helped themselves. The boy used a spoon. In the other half of the room was a canopy of some diaphanous material suspended by cords and reaching to the floor. Inside was another, young woman, possibly a sister; and a little girl baby and two dishes of rice. In addition there was a baby not more than two weeks old. The proud mother cuddled it and put on a little white bonnet and white wrap especially for my benefit. I found the mother would smile and nod to whatever question I put, so I gave up on conversation.

I wanted to visit Tananarive, the capital, near the center of the country. Everything was still under military control, and cycling was prohibited, but there was a train. A *laissez-passer* was necessary for the trip, and my friend from the immigration had to do a lot of talking with the top military authorities before I got it. Once more we raced about town on the motorcycle, cutting corners lying down, and stopping on a dime.

The trip to Tananarive was a memorable one. The scenery was superb, the company most agreeable, and there was humor and laughter aplenty. What more could a traveler want?

I was in a compartment—there were four to a carriage—with four French soldiers and a young and pretty Malagasy miss who may have had a good dash of French in her blood. Again she may have been a true native because the Hova, for example, except for their dark skin and black hair, sometimes more closely resemble the European than the Negro. At any rate her presence added just the necessary spice to the party. She was the only one who had a reserved space on a seat, and several times when the train stopped she was given fruit through the window by someone at the station. I could never figure this out, because she never seemed to ask for it or pay for it. Nevertheless, our compartment soon commenced to look like a storehouse with great bunches of bananas and oranges all over the place. En route we read French movie magazines and had a lot of fun teasing our modest companion, who took it all with a great deal of charm. The soldiers could never get her consent to pose for a picture.

The scenery was like that of Florida at first—level country with rivers hemmed closely by tropical trees. After about seventy miles we began to climb, trees and vegetation disappeared, and we traveled rolling hill country similar to western Dakota or Wyoming. We then entered a forested area and passed slowly around a bridge blown up in the rebellion.

We followed a great river which may have been the Yoni, the Ikapa, or the Rioriua. No one seemed to know. It was beautiful, flowing slowly and deeply. Later a few cascades and rapids appeared. These soon increased in size and number, the mountains increased in size, the valleys in depth, and even the heat of the sun in intensity. Wild, wild country! No wonder the Malagasy were able to strike suddenly and disappear in a trice. With the railroad the white man had only made a wee track, winding ever upward, sometimes making long detours up adjoining valleys to gain altitude. Most of the passengers stood up a good part of the way in order to watch the scenery. We passed two fine waterfalls where the whole river plunged over a ledge of rock and ploughed around great boulders in its descent. The river was in flood, so it was quite a spectacle.

I have spoken of the railroad as a wee little track, yet it was wonderfully constructed. I have never seen an American railroad which gave such an impression of solidity. All bridges, tunnels, embankment walls, and drainage chutes were built of granite blocks, carefully cemented. Everything looked as though it were there to stay until eternity. The bridges reminded me of those in Switzerland. One made it possible for the railroad to pass over itself.

Boys of Tamatave, Madagascar, the world's fifth largest island.

Railroad station scene in eastern Madagascar. Apples, potato pancakes, oranges, bananas, etc., are for sale.

It was engrossing to look out the window and watch the sturdy little locomotive with its four sets of drivers, never faltering, no matter how steep the grade. We could always see the engine, because we were always going around a curve. I have traveled on our own principal mountain railroad, the Rio Grande. There we have a veritable giant of a locomotive and long heavy cars with all their plush gadgets and comfort. The train crawls and groans up the grades! One feels that he must get out and help push. Yet the jolly little train in Madagascar with its six small carriages rushes merrily along without half trying. It had a shrill little whistle and toot which seemed to say: "Come on, let's go! Aren't we having fun? Let's see what's around the next curve."

At a small station I saw evidence that the rebellion was still in progress. Two Malagasy attired in the usual burlap shirt were seated on the platform with their hands tied behind their backs. The older had been wounded, and there was a great deal of blood on the side of his face and on the floor. I was told he was a lieutenant in the rebel army and the other was his aide. Both were being abused by the Senegali guards, who occasionally made a pass at them with bayonets. The faces of the prisoners were passive, but the older lurched or lunged forward in a rather peculiar manner from time to time.

The train continued on into the interior. Toward midafternoon an adjutant joined our little group in second class. He turned out to be a wit, and we had a circus! He started to imitate my slow method of talking French, and I laughed and gave him back as good by appropriate remarks, so that the laugh was often on him. Of course, too, there was always the struggle to sit next to our fair young Malagasy companion to protect her from the rest of the wolves. The adjutant showed her his ring by way of promotion, and she kept it. This started more fun.

They all got a huge kick out of my old joke about the sense of humor of the Germans, English, French, and Americans. First we spent about fifteen minutes establishing the French word for "joke." I failed to secure comprehension of the word I wanted with "une petite histoire pour fair on rire," and was getting desperate, when I happened to think about the French edition of the *Reader's Digest*, one being at hand. I picked out a joke and demanded a name. After palaver they decided it was "une humeur."

"Bien," I said. "Attention. Listen to me."

And so there they all sat—six of them around me in a circle with grins of expectancy on their faces. The American was going to tell "une humeur" involving Frenchmen.

"When a German hears a joke," I began, "he laughs twice: once for politeness and again when he thinks he understands. He never does get the point.

"When the Englishman hears a joke," I continued, "he laughs three times: the first time for politeness, the second time when he thinks he understands, and the third time when he actually gets the point.

"When the Frenchman . . ."

"Non, non—l'Américain!" There was a chorus to the interruption.

"No, the Frenchman."

"Non, non, l'Américain, l'Américain!"

But I persisted. "When the Frenchman hears a joke, he laughs only once. He gets the point right away." (Cheers and laughter)

"Et l'Américain?"

"Well, when the American hears a joke, he doesn't laugh at all. He's already heard it."

And in laughter we came to our destination. Here was Tananarive—Tana, capital of an area nearly as large as Texas. Tana, the magnificent, I thought, for it surmounted a great hill in the midst of a broad valley. At night it was very well lighted and cosmopolitan. The French had seen to that. There was a great tunnel near the heart of town, and a pretty lake, Lac d'Anoisy. The steps on the hillsides in the central district were really magnificent affairs, twenty-three feet wide and handsomely colonnaded and bricked at the sides. The Place de la Pergole was crowned with a colonnaded pergola looking out over the slopes below. And the Tana market was one of the most colorful to be found anywhere.

On the return trip to Tamatave I had two companions in my compartment, both planters, one French, the other Malagasy. The only difference I could notice was the livelier spirit of the Frenchman. Between the two I learned a great deal about the country.

In the lowlands rice was being raised in fields called *rizieres*. Little ridges of land or small ditches demarcated various owners. There was some terracing. There were also manioc, unhappy-looking corn, and a sort of hillside sage brush. Everything was green, but I was told it would dry up later on. But green or dry, sheep do not thrive in this region, and cows will give only three liters of milk per day. On the other hand, the grassy slopes of western Madagascar produce excellent beef, and there are plants for commercial canning. The country raises coffee and vanilla. In the forested area we saw eucalyptus trees, not as large as those in Australia but usable for planks and furniture. There were raffia trees in clumps on the hills. Raffia is native to Madagascar; in fact the name comes from a Malagasy word, *rafia*. The raffia is a palm, and the fibers from its leaf stalks are used in making baskets and hats. Native villages were made up of houses built of reddish clay, sometimes two stories high. Roofs were thatched and steep to shed the frequent rains.

The afternoon following my return to Tamatave, I embarked on the S/S *Grigua* for Mombasa on the African mainland.

That night there was a full moon over the Indian Ocean as we rode off the Malagasy coast. The sea was superb. I studied it carefully as it rolled away from the bow of the ship. At last I came to the conclusion the only

Vegetable market, Tananarive, Madagascar.

Flower market, Tananarive.

proper words of description were "molten obsidian." If you have ever seen a picture of coal-black, glassy-smooth obsidian, you will know what I mean. The moonlight on the water was a thousand flashing lights that danced and played, appeared and disappeared, with the shape and motion of the waves. These lights were eerie; they seemed to exist, yet not to exist. They were like ghosts with wet garments, disconnected—yet they moved as units just under the surface of the water. I marveled. Occasionally a gray cloud obscured the Queen of the Night and my eerie lights sank from view. In the distance above the Malagasy coast, blood-red lightnings flashed from behind dark cloud masses.

The *Grigua* was a Dutch-built ship flying the British Mauritian flag and manned by a French-speaking crew. The tonnage (1,400) was about the same as that of the *Hoeveld*, but she was a much trimmer tramp designed to accommodate passengers. There were two of these, neither full-paying: the captain's niece and myself.

The meals and manner of eating on board the *Grigua* were the strangest I had ever encountered. Only two meals were served, one at 9 A.M. and the other at 6 P.M. A horrible schedule. The officers with whom I ate apparently ignored the fact that the human stomach is empty after three or four hours, regardless of the amount eaten, and so attempted to make up for the nine-and fifteen-hour fasts between meals by eating such an enormous amount you wouldn't credit it. I never knew the human stomach had such capacity.

Here is the minimum consumption per meal for each person, including the captain's niece. For breakfast: first, a plateful of steak and potatoes. This alone was more than an ordinary man eats in the States for dinner. Bread without butter was eaten also. Second, a plateful of rice, curry, and some cooked vegetable, usually beans, navy or brown. Now, when I say a plateful, don't visualize a normal helping, two normal helpings, or even three. The rice was spooned off a platter two feet wide by two and a half feet long, and each person completely buried his full-size plate to a depth of two inches! Yes, two inches! And this depth was not just in the center— it was all over the plate to the very edges. On top of this was placed one or perhaps two pieces of very hot curry, usually fish. Around the curry, but of course also on top of the rice, were ladled three or four oversize tablespoonfuls of beans. Now they were ready to get down to business, the steak and potatoes having been only the appetizer, you see. So with a big spoon and fork used together, they waded in. The food went to the mouth in this oversize tablespoon—and *it was heaped!* But the spoon returned to the plate *empty!* In remarkably quick time the plate too was empty.

At dinner the same two courses were preceded by a consommé covering chunks of beef and bits of vegetables. Everyone ladled up plenty of these items from the bottom of the tureen. Most people could make a meal out of this course alone.

Breakfast and dinner were followed by eating an orange, green-colored and rather sour. They had not learned the fast and unmessy way of eating an orange—by quartering the skin and peeling alternate quarters back from each end. Instead they quartered the whole orange, and using both hands, tried to force the skin back from each end of the quarter by pressure in the middle. The mouth was then opened over each end and then the middle, and attempts were made to bite or tear away the flesh. A second method, which some also used, was to peel the orange like an apple, in a circle. This left most of the white inner covering still on. It was then painstakingly removed with knife and fingernails in a process that took at least five minutes. The orange was then split along natural lines and eaten.

For our entire voyage the sea was almost without swell—just a few small waves. There was almost no roll or pitch to the *Grigua*. One day as I was on the foredeck the captain shouted down, "What do you think of the lake?"

"I've never seen anything like it," I replied. "Is it always like this?"

"Nine months of the year it's like this."

I made a mental note to take all of my late-life pleasure cruises at the north end of the Mozambique Channel.

17

Lion Country.
Which Way Is the Wind Now?

We came to the mainland of the Dark Continent early on a Saturday morning. Mombasa, Kenya, looked picturesque from the sea. Cliffs lined the shore of the long island on which the port is situated. Ahead of us on a hill was the reddish-yellow Fort of Jesus flying the red flag of the Sultan of Zanzibar, from whom the British leased the coastal area. The fort was built in 1593 by the Portuguese, those early adventurers who left their mark on so many places around the world. Mombasa harbor is comparatively shallow and used chiefly by dhows from Arabia. We passed on and anchored in the main harbor, Kilindini, "the deep place."

Shortly after going ashore I went to the passport office to get a visa for another country. Here was a regular battle-axe in a high position—super-efficient, white starched dress in perfect condition, shiny silver letters on one shoulder saying "Kenya Police" and on the other "Passport Control." The atmosphere was very hot outside, but in her office it was plenty chilly—b-r-r-r! I was dust under her feet. She knew everything and was obviously furious I had dared to set foot in Kenya without her express permission.

"This is no visa!" she iced out, examining my Kenya visa but not even deigning to look at me. "Wherever you got it I don't know. There's not even a number on it."

Now I knew perfectly well that "Commonwealth of Australia" was printed in capital letters on the first line and highly legible numbers were printed after the words "Visa No. ——." But I had learned not to argue with a woman, especially one in authority. So I moused a low "I see" and waited. Eventually I got the visa I was after, but only in combination with a new visa for Kenya. I don't know why the British tolerate these old-maid tyrants.

Mombasa proved to be a combination of old and new. Some buildings had been built by the Arabs, some by the Portuguese, and the more modern by the English. The older section of the city was a maze of irregular streets and lanes with overhead passageways and carved woodwork to add color. But the area containing the European residences was as spacious and attractive as one could wish. The population was given as 28,000 natives, 13,000 Anglo-Indians, 8,000 Arabs, and 1,000 Europeans.

I hunted all over Mombasa trying to get a map of Kenya roads. But when I finally found the residence of a man with a map, I had a surprise bonus. For he lived next door to Gordon Plante, F.R.G.S., big-game hunter and solo roamer over much of East Africa on foot and motorcycle. He had maps and could correct them, add distances, sources of water, etc. He knew a great deal about the wildlife, told me what to do when I met my first lion and my first elephant and where to expect them. I learned how to feel the wind and determine from what quarter an attack might come. The buffalo, Gordon said, was probably the most dangerous animal.

The next morning, not without some trepidation after this interview, I set out toward the interior. For a while there were natives to watch along the way. A boy climbed a tall palm by simply walking up the trunk. The women wore nothing above the waist. They were mostly unattractive except for one young belle in a red skirt and headpiece who was fully aware that she was a belle. The natives were friendly and hospitable. When I stopped for a drink of water, I got a banana and a cup of tea.

The road was uphill, it was hot, and I sweat a few bucketfuls. Then I had tire trouble and hailed a passing car for another valve or a different pump. Neither did any good, but the motorist, a farmer, formerly from South Africa, offered me a lift and I accepted. He had an attractive fully dressed young native girl in the front seat and a colored lad in the rear of his delivery truck. After we were well along, he asked me if I minded sitting by a colored girl. I replied in the negative.

"I don't know if you know the Bible or if you're religious at all," said he, "but do you remember who Moses' wife was?"

"Well, no, but I think she was colored," said I.

"Yes, she was an Ethiopian. And you remember what happened to Marian when she criticized Moses for taking an Ethiopian to wife? She was afflicted with leprosy. So who am I to say something different than what was in the Bible?"

After all this I concluded he was married to the girl; but later he said: "I suppose you are wondering, but the lady is not my better half."

The road was washboardy, but we kept going at a good pace.

"I can't drive as fast as usual," he said. "I've got no brakes."

I noticed that the car also had an Australian speedometer—that is, one that didn't work. Nor did the heat indicator indicate heat.

My route left the main road at a place called Voi, so I saw no more of the folks in the truck. It took me two hours to fix my tube, even with the help of four or five natives. When I left, the only one who spoke any English warned me to be careful of lions. This confirmed Gordon Plante's remark that from Voi to Taveta was lion country.

As I cycled along I don't deny I was nervous—especially as darkness approached. About this time I realized I was not very far away from a place called Tsavo, the locale of a book entitled *The Man Eaters of Tsavo!* Lovely thought! Well, I watched all the bushes and wondered how I could escape from a lion when all the trees were thorn trees with thousands of great long spikes. I particularly watched those bushes downwind from me because wild animals impute to man the same sense of smell and reasoning they follow themselves. "Which way is the wind now?" I kept asking myself and raised a freshly wetted finger. But while I saw no lions, I was rewarded by glimpses of my first African wildlife: the tiny deer called dik-dik and some monkeys. Just at dark it was my good luck to come to a place where the road crossed a little-used branch railroad and there were two wood and tin huts to provide some security for the night.

The next day was very hot, the road was still uphill, and the country was all dry bush. By 5:30 P.M. I came to a long white adobe structure on a railroad. Although it lacked an hour before darkness, this was still lion country and discretion suggested shelter while it was available. The building had been constructed for the section workers, and I belabored my poor Swahili to the ganger. He showed me to one of the eight rooms. They had certainly been designed for protection from the wild beasts. The two tiny windows would have made even a housecat think twice, and the ganger showed me how the heavy door could be bolted from the inside.

There was no furniture of any sort in my cubicle, so I sat down outside to write in my diary. I was promptly served with an enormous cup of something my host called "chai." Since this is an Asiatic word for tea, I expected that, but it proved to be a sort of unsweetened thin porridge. I sneaked in some sugar and ate it with bread. When it got too dark to write, the ganger showed me into his cubicle, where there were lantern, chair, and table. On the table there was a hodgepodge of everything from tools to old newspapers covered with dust. Of personal possessions he had three: the Bible in Swahili, a nice book in which he took great pride; the time sheet for himself and his men; and his identification paper. This showed his tribe, subtribe, date of circumcision (aged 16), and thumbprint.

While I was writing, I noticed him quietly sifting flour. So I was not surprised when he presented me with a great heaped bowl of what appeared to be white mush. It was little more than a solid flour-and-water concoction, without taste, and it seemed to be the solid variety of what had been given me earlier. (I was told later that it turned into "concrete" in one's digestive tract.) There was also a dish with meat and gravy in it, but this was as tough as all get-out and I suppose only half cooked.

The next day I crossed the line into Tanganyika Territory and before long found myself on the southeastern slopes of Mount Kilimanjaro. This is Africa's highest mountain, rising 19,340 feet above sea level and about 17,000 feet above the surrounding plain. Here I ran into a populated area with natives looking just like the Negroes of the southern United States. Everyone was barefooted. The young men wore shirts and shorts, but the older ones wore a blanket draped like a toga and used a long walking stick. The women wore a single-piece, below-knee-length skirt sometimes tucked in at the top of the breasts in the manner of a bath towel. They also wore a sort of turban, and both it and the dress were often colorful. There was no evidence of sewing, yet I often saw a little house or shop beside the road with a man seated on the porch running an old noisy Singer.

Of course the women did all the work. They carried huge branches of bananas, banana leaves for thatching, a great bunch of grass for feeding the cows, or just their big, hoelike digging spade. The men had a long tradition of not working. The headmaster of the Marangu Teachers Training School told me that milk for the school was obtainable farther down the mountain, so he had set up the rule that the boys were to go and fetch it. This lasted only a few days because the boys said they could not be seen doing women's work.

The natives I met were all friendly and cheerful. The men usually said, "Mjambo" ("Hello") or, "Mjambo bwana," and the older ones raised their hats respectfully. Some placed a hand to the temple and dropped it as a salute of respect. The little boys never failed to say, "Mjambo bwana," and a group would continue to say it smilingly as long as I could answer them. Some of the small boys spoke a little English; they go to school for at least four years, but the girls do not. The women were quite shy, and most would not speak unless I spoke first. If they saw me coming, they would frequently get clear off the road or even up a bank and out of sight. When I came upon a group suddenly from behind, or even sounded my bell from a distance, they jumped like startled rabbits, heavy head burdens and all. The young ones would then giggle with embarrassment. Some of the young coquettes I met, however, gave me a greeting first; so perhaps emancipation is beginning.

Near the base of Mount Kilimanjaro was a town called Moshi. Here I met Chlotahlas M. Pahl, one of the many Anglo-Indian businessmen handling the commerce of East Africa. He invited me to take lunch with him, but it was already 11:30 when I came back to his office to accept.

He smiled. "You do not give me much time."

"Oh!" I said. "Perhaps we had better forget about it."

"Oh, no. I will be glad to have you, only it will not be possible to prepare variables."

I do not know what "variables" he had in mind because when we went out to his home about 1 P.M., there was, for me at least, plenty of variety. Perhaps this was because it was my first Indian meal.

His small daughter, pretty as a picture and aged about eight, brought in two brass platters or salvers about eighteen inches in diameter and rounded to a vertical lip of an inch and a half. The inside seemed to be hammered silver. These huge salvers were placed in front of us on a bare oversized card table set up in the center of the room. On one side of the salver was a shallow, hammered-brass bowl about six inches in diameter, half full of a yellow liquid which turned out to be a curry sauce. In making this, milk is allowed to stand until it forms curds, and these are then broken up and flavored with curry. On the other side of the salver was a helping of warm potato salad. (The warmth may have been partly due to the chili and salt with which it was seasoned.) There was also a liberal helping of string beans, or *gewar*, too highly seasoned for me to enjoy. Finally there were two thin pancakes called *paranthas* which we broke, dipped into the curry, and ate with the fingers.

Served to us separately were two other items. The first was a very thin, quite transparent wafer the size of a pancake, called *mathias*. It was made —fried, I think—out of pulse. The second was a somewhat sweet pastry made from gram flour, potatoes, and bananas. These tasties, which I thought the little girl would never stop heaping on my plate, were called *bhajas*. With this course we had cold water served in two large silver tumblers. The "hot" food and the metal containers made the water doubly enjoyable.

When my host and small daughter were quite sure I had had enough of everything, especially curry and bhatas, rice and two supplemental dishes were brought in. Of the latter, *dall* was a yellowish product resembling rice and made from the seeds of the toover plant, split into two parts in grinding and mixed with a yellow flavoring called *haldi*. The second dish was cooked butter, or ghee. The dall was placed on top of the rice with a serving spoon, the ghee was poured over it, and we mixed the lot thoroughly with our fingers. However, we ate it with our spoons, the only utensils provided for the entire meal. We cleansed our fingers finally by holding them over the remains of the curry and pouring water over them from our tumblers.

After the meal we chewed soybean seeds and betel nuts. The former were served in a long glass dish after the table had been cleared and were for the purpose of cleansing the teeth. The betel nuts I did not care for. They were cut up by my host into very thin slices and bits with an instrument resembling a nutcracker. Meanwhile my host's wife, in keeping with Indian custom of the time, never put in an appearance.

In the town of Moshi I also met Phil Pegg, English planter, and accepted his invitation to visit his *shamba*. It was a forty-five-mile ride, and the Bedford pickup was loaded to the Plimsoll mark with Phil, his wife, a neighbor, myself, Phil's big dog Rusty, his "boy," Jacqueline, and scads of supplies from grapefruit to stovepipe. The truck had oversize balloons that really smoothed out the ever present corrugations. Between the front wheels was only one transverse spring acting as both spring and axle. The car performed well, but Phil was trying to sell it, as he had succeeded in getting a new Ford pickup.

"It isn't that there aren't any buyers." Phil grinned. "There are plenty of them. But I just can't find them!"

We arrived at his place, to find a long, semicircular one-story ranch house with Negro servants everywhere. That was my first impression. On both sides of the semicircle were wide verandas full length, stone in front and wood and stone in back. At the rear of the house was a nice flower garden with grass and hedges—all very beautiful. The rooms were large, nicely furnished, and well kept up. It was, I suppose, like an old American Southern plantation. For a Northerner, unused to servants, it looked like a wonderful life. Neither master nor missus had to lift a finger. All physical work about the house or farm was done by natives under native overseers. Setting the table, cooking, washing, ironing, taking care of the car, preparing and planting the vegetable and flower gardens—all this was taken care of. What fun it would be just to plan this or that, knowing you only had to go out and watch it grow!

Phil and his wife were moving over to another farm, and Phil drove me over to see it. It was called Endarguai and had been started by the Germans when Tanganyika was German East Africa. This shamba was more palatial and more beautifully situated and laid out than the first. The flower beds in particular made me think the African planter makes much better use of his black labor than does the Australian station manager with his aboriginal. The view out across a vast low-lying scrub and farm area to majestic Mount Meru (14,979 feet) was really superb. Endarguai was operated by Mr. and Mrs. Kerr, both tall and lanky, typically British.

Mrs. Kerr, attired in slacks and smoking a cigarette, took an active interest in the cattle. She showed us around the barnyard in spite of the manure which picked up on her shoes. (Of course, the boy would clean them.) It was milking time, and the "wogs" (natives) were milking the good old-fashioned way but without milk stools. The barn was just a shed with a few stanchions. Milk production from the forty to fifty head had dropped to twenty gallons per day due to hoof-and-mouth disease but had now recovered to a normal of thirty-five gallons. The market was twenty-seven cents per gallon. The breed was a mixture of Holstein, Guernsey, Shorthorn, and the native humpneck. Occasionally a lion took one. Phil had just recently shot his first lion.

The next day Phil and I came back for a real tour of Endarguai. It had rained overnight, so we were not able to drive "up top" to see a new wheat farm laid out at six thousand feet using modern American machinery. But there was much else to see. Coffee plants were irrigated, and water flowed in furrows everywhere. The berries were green but would turn yellowish and later reddish. The natives got five cents for every five-gallon "debby" when picking. After washing and drying, the berries would be worth about $400 per ton. Phil had about forty-five acres with a top-yield expectation of one-half ton per acre.

Land was plentiful, so there were no definite lines around or between fields. Here in a clearing was a field of coffee; then, walking through a little scrub, we would come to a field of corn; and cutting across through more scrub, to a clearing containing pawpaw; and so on. In one field two blacks

The Indians have been the commercial architects of East Africa.

Getting juice of the papaya —Kenya. A razor at the end of the stick "bleeds" the fruit. "Milk" drops onto canvas and congeals; later it is dried and shipped.

were plowing with three yoke of oxen even though the red ground was nothing but mud. In an adjacent patch corn was just showing through the ridged ground. This corn had been planted by hand; no harrow had graced the seed bed, and as the corn plow is unknown, it would be tilled by hand, that is, by swinging, picklike, the big three-cornered hoes called *jambes*. In a third field, corn was in the prime of full growth with stalks and ears as good as those in Iowa, although the stand was not as even. Corn was hand-snapped to sacks, dumped in oxcarts, and husked later. It could be grown the year around.

General wages for the natives varied from 12½ bob per month for pawpaw-fruit cutters to 50 bob ($10) per month for houseboys. The leading natives were given their own shambas—little plots on which to build huts and plant gardens.

Pawpaw (i.e. papaya) trees were planted amongst the corn and marked by green sticks. Some were just showing. Nearby was a field of mature pawpaw, and I had the good luck to see the natives harvesting the juice, Phil referred to this as pepsin, but I think the juice contains papain, a digestive enzyme resembling pepsin; and it is used in chewing gum and perhaps medicinally. The United States was the big buyer and preferred the pepsin from the slopes of Kilimanjaro. The pawpaw fruits grew up to eight inches in length and four or five inches in diameter before they were cut for juice. They hung around the trunk of the tree like Brussels sprouts, about five feet from the ground. Now, after a rain, the natives were going along with a sharp piece of tin embedded in the end of a stick and making three, four, or more vertical slashes on the outside of the green fruit. At once a milklike fluid ran out and dropped onto inverted canvas umbrellas which had been placed closely around the trunk. This solidified into milky strings and masses which would be taken to a drying house. Since the pawpaw trees may grow too high for convenient picking, interplanting is done to start new trees. The latter are first grown in a nursery along with young coffee plants.

The drying house for the pepsin had a fire flue running under the full length. A big screen in the center held the pepsin. The dried product was not unlike sweet-corn seed. The market was then about $3.60 per pound, and the crop would run around one and one-half pounds per day for ten months in each year from twenty acres.

18

With My Stomach
on Africa's Highest Summit

Mount Kilimanjaro had been many times in my thoughts across those thousands of miles of ocean approaching Africa. The highest mountain in all Africa! What a thrill it would be to climb it! It is 19,340 feet high—almost 5,000 feet higher than any mountain in continental U.S. It is so high that even though it rests nearly on the equator, it bears a crown of snow the year around. What would it be like—jagged like the Alps and the Tetons, or isolated and supreme like Mount Rainier? But more important, would I be able to climb it? My homemade guidebook said that the law required a guide and safari at 250 shillings, and where on earth was I to get fifty dollars to climb a mountain?

I had my first view of Kilimanjaro not from across the plain many miles away but from the lower part of the forest at its base. The clouds hiding its snow-domed summit had drifted away, and from the clearing where I stood I could see this giant among the world's mountains. For it was not just one of a close group of peaks that was a little higher than the rest but a gloriously isolated giant standing head, shoulders, and trunk above the vastness of Africa.

If the height of a mountain be judged by the number of feet it rises above its base (instead of above sea level), then Kilimanjaro, in rising approximately 17,000 feet above the plains, could probably claim to be the second highest mountain in the world. At any rate I knew I had to climb it.

Kilimanjaro actually consists of two peaks, Kibo and Mawenzi. Mawenzi is less than 17,000 feet high and is far enough from Kibo to be regarded separately, so that Kilimanjaro becomes Kibo and vice versa. According to the Masai, Kibo is Ngaji Ngai, the "House of God." On the southwestern side of Kibo, glaciers and snow descend to an elevation of 12,500 feet, but on the northern, or equatorial side, only to 18,700 feet. Below the snow line lies a wide belt of sparse, short vegetation; and below 10,000 feet are the forests. In these dark and somber forests, according to my book, elephant, buffalo, and rhinoceros roamed at will.

I'll admit I thought about these big beasts the first night I slept out under the trees. But I knew there were some natives living not far away down the mountain, so I did not feel the area was too dangerous. I shall never forget that particular night, for the African moon was at its fullest. The little glade I chose to sleep in was so brightly lighted that I sequestered

Mt. Kilimanjaro, 19,340 feet, highest mountain in Africa.

myself in the shadow of a bush along one side. Not even a whisper of a breeze stirred through the jungle, and there was not a sound of bird, beast, or man. Was this another world and I the only being in it? But the African moon rode high, and Kilimanjaro rested from her volcanic past and kept guard over all her vast domain. I was a speck floating up and up to view her eternal snows and pass on out into the abyss of time. . . .

Daylight. And having failed to dream myself up the mountain, I set about making arrangements for a safari. The headmaster of the Marangu native teachers training school generously agreed to act as interpreter, but he had not been too long in the country and his Swahili was not of the best. No member of my prospective safari spoke a word of English; nevertheless, we got things fairly well understood.

The requirements of the mountain club and the government were that there must be a guide and three porters. They of course required a cook, so there were five to go. Three of them went with me to a nearby Indian *duka* (Anglo-Indian store) to buy provisions. The trip was to last five days, and the estimated needs were one pound of meat per person per day, two pounds of flour per person per day, a total of three bottles of ghee (native butter), salt, tea, two pounds of sugar, and five packages of cigarettes. This came to thirty-two shillings, or six dollars. Then there was something about blankets—one for each man, each to be kept. This sounded crazy to me, but I told them I would get blankets and later that evening borrowed five from the native hospital, the school being short of blankets. I also got a large cooking pan, and the headmaster supplied a lantern and some miscellaneous articles.

The following morning, about 8:30, the head guide and four other natives arrived. When I explained that the blankets must be returned, they objected. I walked up to the school with the *kiongozi* (head guide) to get an interpreter. I knew the regular blanket charge was one shilling (20 cents) per day per man, or twenty-five shillings if they furnished the blankets. But the leader refused such, and it looked black for yours truly going up the mountain. I was stubborn because he had a slip of paper showing that five blankets would cost 14.30 shillings apiece at the duka he wanted to patronize. The interpreter said to me: "It is too much. I don't know why they always charge Europeans more than natives, but they do. It's too bad you have not more time. One of the teachers could get blankets for you for nine or ten shillings."

Meanwhile time marched on, and I, who had always started all major trips at 5 A.M., wondered if it soon wouldn't be too late to start at all. Nevertheless, as we started for the *kiongozi's* store, I put my tongue in my cheek and grinned to myself. Now at last I was experiencing what other travelers had written about hiring guides for safari.

On our way we passed another *duka*, where I knew I could get blankets for 7.50 to 12.50s. The *kiongozi* did not want to stop, and I was glad that

I had studied Swahili and could argue a little. But I wound up by buying at the *kiongozi's duka* after all. Here I succeeded in refusing Scotch plaids at 17.50 and in buying four blankets at 9.50s and one at 7.50s. I expected a terrific yowl from the guides, but they never objected in the slightest.

We loaded up at the headmaster's. Fifty pounds of flour was put in a gunny sack and twenty-five pounds of meat in a "debby." The latter is a five-gallon can with the top cut out and perhaps a round piece of wood across for a handle. The debby was put in a box with the ghee, an extra bottle of kerosene, and my canteen. One man carried this; another, the flour and a couple of blankets. My pack, sleeping bag, and a sackful of miscellaneous stuff were bound tightly together by a strip of bark rope from some tree and hoisted to the top of his head by the smallest porter of the lot; he seemed little more than a boy. The *kiongozi* carried a big wicker basket on his head, and the cook—well, I don't remember what he had, but my sack of coats and bread were carried by someone. And so we were off. I only regretted that my kodak was tied up. The headmaster's wife wished me Godspeed and said she'd been praying that I could succeed in getting my arrangements made and make the trip.

Our cavalcade filed up through the school grounds, and of course all the students *would* be out at recess. I felt somewhat self-conscious at the head of my first safari, especially since the bwana (me) carried absolutely nothing. Across the athletic field we passed. Then up and up, steeply, along a well-populated trail. We went by some native wood sawers at work. They had a log on a scaffolding, and one man was above and the other underneath as they operated the crosscut. Further on we heard a drum, like the beat of the tomtom, and soon we passed the yard of a small school. Here we saw the drum being beaten by a girl of about eight years. Still further along we met several women with corn, and the *kiongozi* and a porter bargained for some. Everyone was cheery and full of laughter, especially when the *kiongozi* started to stuff ears of corn in his porters' packs. They all objected, and one or two took theirs and stuffed them in the leader's basket. Lots of fun! It seems to be the nature of the people. Even during our altercation over the blankets, I don't think the *kiongozi* ever lost his smile for more than thirty seconds.

We hiked right along. They wanted me to take the lead and set the pace, so I did. The way led largely up through heavy forest—one God had planted, as the headmaster had said. There were heavy accretions of moss on all the trees, and it reminded me of the Milford Sound forests of New Zealand. I stopped for my lunch at the usual time, but the boys did not eat until we had arrived at Bismarck Hut, around 3:30 p.m. I thought it was a shame to waste the rest of the day, without going on, but I made the best of it by writing in my diary. I pulled the hut table over to the door into the sunlight and wrote overlooking the valley far below. This view was really tremendous, and I am convinced I could see half of

Tanganyika Territory. I was at nine thousand feet, and the plains below were little more than two thousand feet. It was a view similar to that from the Knife Edge Road in Mesa Verde, only more spectacular. There were two lakes, one large and rectangular and one small. They were far away and far below and looked to be muddy green in color. Isolated mountain peaks and ranges were lost in the haze of distance. Fields, or rather vast areas, of yellow and green checkerboarded some parts of what appeared to be the valley floor. What vastness!

To pass the time I went down the trail with the porters to the nearest wood and helped to carry up some firewood. They had a small separate building like a big chicken coop constructed out of corrugated iron. They did their cooking over an open fire near the door. In the opposite end of the building, boards had been laid on the ground and covered with hay. But I had the big Bismarck Hut all to myself. I would have been less lonely and had warm meals if I had been with the porters, but of course the old color bar is so strongly established there was no use thinking about it. The cook was apparently "my boy," and I don't suppose he had ever had anyone who required less waiting on. I did not want a fire, I did not want tea; I had no dishes to wash; I had no bed to make; and so on. However, he kept me company during the evening meal, and I hinted pretty strongly that I enjoyed it. Of course, our conversation was all one way. With my homemade vocabulary of *Palikonda* days, I could usually get my ideas across. But not having a Swahili dictionary, it was just too bad when poor Fuataidi said anything.

I let the boys set their own starting time each day, as it was only about four hours' continuous hiking between huts and it was no fun having to sit in one place for half a day. I knew they would start late—8:30 or 9:00— and this would shorten the day. This second day was largely through open upland country affording fine views, all hinting of the vastness which is Africa. The herbage could have been that of any western state in the United States—a similitude of silver bush, sagebrush, greasewood, and clumps of grass with occasionally a few flowers. I set a good pace, and we arrived at Peters Hut, 12,500 feet, by 12:30. I would have liked to go on to Kibo Hut but could not persuade the guides. Secretly I felt it was just as well. The theory is that one should spend a day at each elevation in order to become accustomed to the rarer air.

Peters Hut was not in as good condition as Bismarck, and I had to put a piece of corrugated iron over a broken window. I had the same kind of bunk, however—boards with a little hay on top. Luckily I was used to sleeping on hard objects. A short time after eating I felt a dull discomfort at the pit of my stomach, just as in seasickness. I think mountain sickness— about which I read in nearly every climbing report recorded in the hut registry books—is probably much the same. Although I thought the afternoon would drag, I was agreeably surprised that my diary kept me quite

My bearers for the climb up Mt. Kilimanjaro.

Two of my porters resting on the third day of the climb up Mt. Kilimanjaro. Above is Mawenzi, 17,000 feet.

busy. The cook built me a fire about 5 P.M., and by its warmth I wrote or read climbing reports until after nine. The lantern gave me the needed light. Before I retired the cook called me out to see the lights of Moshi almost directly below us, about 10,500 feet.

On safari the next morning at nine, we journeyed on up the mountain. There was a long, long climb up to the broad saddle between Kilimanjaro's two peaks, Mawenzi and Kibo. Although Mawenzi is the shorter of the two summits by 1,600 feet, it is the more spectacular. Its skyline is jagged and needlelike at nearby points, and the glaciers hang steeply to the precipitous ravines. To study the peak's configuration was tremendously inspiring, especially for a mountain lover, and I could hardly turn my eyes away. Occcasionally light clouds covered parts of the peak as we marched along, but they seemed to come from nowhere, as the day was clear, cold, and sunny.

This day on the trail we were far above the forest area in open upland country. When we arrived on the saddle, the vegetation largely failed so that we crossed a gravel and rock desert. The porters as usual would have liked to go on to Kibo Hut before stopping for food, but I stopped at 12:45. I could not see any sense just using up half a day when one could spend more time on the trail and really enjoy it. I was quite content to snuggle down on the lee side of a big boulder and enjoy my lunch. But the porters thought it a cold and miserable place, for we were well above 15,000 feet and even an equatorial sun at high noon failed to give enough warmth to counteract the wind. So I told the porters to go on; however, the cook and my personal bearer remained. The latter covered himself completely with his blanket and curled shiveringly on the ground. There was another blanket handy, but he refused my suggestion of using it. Meanwhile there were such good cloud effects on Mawenzi that I snapped a picture with my blanket-shrouded porter in the foreground.

By 3:30 P.M. I had finished my amble up the long desert slope to Kibo Hut, the last of the three shelter huts provided. It was far above timberline, and wood and water had been carried all the way from Peters Hut. Kibo was at the 16,000-foot level. "Sixteen thousand feet—just think of it," I said to myself. "That is fifteen hundred feet higher than the highest mountain in continental U.S. and I still have not commenced the final assault." I recalled the headache and throbbing temples and eating difficulties in the Rockies after exertion at only 11,000 feet and marveled that at 16,000 feet I still felt fairly comfortable. A little soreness in the temples, but nothing to speak of.

As the *kiongozi* and I were to go on alone at 2:30 the following morning, I wanted to get to bed by 5:30. But it was nearly an hour later by the time I had fixed up three lunches for the climb and crawled into my sleeping bag. Since the guide had no watch, it was up to me to do the calling; but I would have taken that responsibility anyway because on such an important occasion I would not want to rely upon anyone but myself. This robbed me of some sleep, for I checked the watch at 9:15, 11:15, 1:15, and 1:55. At 1:55 I dressed, called the guide and returned to my cabin to eat one of my lunches. At about 2:25 I went to the porters' tent, thinking he would be ready. But no such luck. He was just in the middle of dressing. They had a fire going, but there was no place for the smoke to escape. I couldn't stand it and waited outside. Yet I did not want to start up the mountain with cold feet. So I was 'twixt the devil and the deep and alternately roasted my feet and stepped outside to cool my eyes.

And what was the guide doing all this time? Well, Saidi Keli, being of black skin and tropical clime, was putting on as much as he could, not only to protect himself from the cold of the high reaches of the earth's atmosphere but, I suspected, also to wear what he thought a best-dressed guide should wear. At any rate he had already donned shirt, sweater, and full-length pair of khaki trousers. Next he put on two pair of heavy wool socks, then his big shoes. These were big enough to encase feet that had run around barefooted for probably thirty years, so you have some idea of the size. These shoes had to be laced with heavy cord from the bottom up and this took time. But I thought the end was surely near when this had been accomplished. But no, out of the mysterious basket that he had been lugging for three days, he took a roll of khaki the soldiers use for puttees. This he laboriously wrapped around one ankle very tightly and then continued to wrap until the long tie had also been used up. Meanwhile I was groaning with impatience. When the second ankle was finally finished, I'll be darned if he didn't produce a band for his head. Over a stocking cap pulled down over his ears, he wound the band around and around and then down over his neck and over his chin and back up around his forehead until nothing was visible but his nose and eyes. Over the latter he placed a pair of goggles. In place of gloves he doubled over a long pair of wool socks. He donned a greatcoat, a sort of raincoat, and we were ready. The only concession I made for attire was to retain my pajamas and put on a pair of wool socks I had brought from the hospital. I took along my regular socks to double over my mittens, and, oh yes, I had folded my towel to act as a head scarf and keep my ears and the back of my head warm. I had an alpenstock, but Saidi carried only the lantern.

Well, we set out! My predecessors' accounts spoke of the terrible scree and how good it was to get over so much of it before daybreak so that it would not appear quite so disheartening. This scree is nothing more than loose gravel, but you do sink in and ofttimes it seemed that I took two steps forward to advance one. The going was mechanical. At first I took the lead, but after a misstep or two Saidi took the lantern and hung it on his right arm, the hand of which he kept in his pocket for warmth. This kept part of the light shielded by his coat, but I had not the heart to insist on an arm-length carry. A few steps up and then a short rest. More steps up—perhaps as many as a dozen or more sometimes—I never counted. My criterion for rest was solely the pounding of my heart. When it was too much, I called a halt and remained quiet until it subsided. Thus we went on like two automatons.

"*Ngoja* [wait]." The two big shots with the khaki-encased ankles just above me stopped still.

"*Kwenda* [to go]." The feet moved on again.

"*Ngoja*"—the feet stopped—always partly buried in the scree. I was glad my overshoes kept the stuff out of my shoes.

"*Kwenda.*"

"*Ngoja* "

"*Kwenda.*"

Once in a while I couldn't think of "*kwenda.*" "I've heard high altitudes curtail the mental process," I said to myself. So I just said, "Safari."

There was a cold wind, and I was soon chilled to the bone. This made me a little peeved because I had wanted to bring my raincoat as a windbreaker but Saidi had said it was not necessary. I got even now by taking my rests in Saidi's lee. But I could not keep out all the wind, and my legs began to tremble uncontrollably every time we stopped. How I longed for the dawn and the warm sunlight!

It must come—soon!

It came as I knew it would, directly behind us to the east.

It was the most fantastically weird sunrise I have ever beheld, or ever hope to behold. We must have been at approximately 17,700 feet and thus were above the summit of Mawenzi's jagged ridge. Behind that silhouette was the redness from the unrisen sun. That alone would have been spectacular. But the black clouds on the horizon seemed bent on assuming shapes as fantastic as those on the mountain. One of these in particular was like the end of a golf club. This was to the left of Mawenzi, as if putting. To the right was a whole series of dark outlaws and back of them the increasing redness. Above, lighter clouds, and about them the lightening sky.

It was too much! Cold as it was, I made Saidi hand me my little sack. It hung under his left arm by a tiny rope over his shoulder. With fingers that soon became numb with cold I untied the string and got out the camera for a silhouette shot.

About 7:20 I called a halt for breakfast. Saidi, I know, thought I was nuts; yet when I offered him a slice of buttered bread with meat and beans on it, he did not refuse. There was not enough heat to keep us warm, and there were one or two inadequate boulders for wind protection. Yet I knew my stomach.

As the morning progressed I occasionally looked upward. Nothing met my gaze but the interminable scree. Later heavy boulders appeared. This, I supposed, precluded a short ridge following which would be a second scree slope to negotiate. It never occurred to me that it was the edge of the actual summit. And so I was most agreeably surprised when at 9:15 A.M. we crawled up to a little tin box containing the achievement register for Gilman's Point. We had made better time than I expected.

It was a "point" all right. A point of space, just about big enough for one person to stand. There were boulders about to prevent one from falling off and it gave the effect of a natural pulpit on the tip of a mountain. Looking ahead and down, one could see long ridges of ice with precipitous ledges. This was the old volcanic crater of Kibo. Gray scree slopes on the bottom of the crater separated these long, high iceberg islands. Then my gaze wandered along the south rim of the great crater to the far side. There were several points, bare, grim, and overhanging the crater's depth. One of these would be Kaiser Wilhelm's Spitze, the highest point. I looked at Saidi, pointed and said in Swahili: "Kaiser Wilhelm's Spitze. Let's go! I feel fine." This I demonstrated by beating my chest.

But Saidi objected. He said something to the effect that there was too much snow and ice and that we had to get back to Peters Hut. I knew, too, he was thinking that most people were satisfied to reach Gilman's Point and why should I be different? But, more than that, when he did start to follow me, I saw that he had not been beyond Gilman's Point before. For whenever there was a possibility of two routes, he seemed uncertain and was quite willing to follow my suggestion rather than his own. I then recalled that I had not seen his name listed as guide for any of the stories of ascent written up in the hut account books. Oh well, I believed I could lead without a guide. It was not too hard a task, and we got along fairly well. The ice hung close on the south edge of the mountain, and we had to decide before passing each small peak on the crater rim whether to take the precipitous crater side and run the risk of sliding down the scree and off over the edge or whether to pass out on the bare ice on the outer edge of the mountain and run a risk equally as great. Sometimes we had to descend quite a lot, and it was heartbreaking to think we had to make the climb back up again.

Since arriving at Gilman's Point we had become enveloped in a cold gray cloud that shut in our vision to a few hundred feet. Now it began to snow in addition. Yes, even though we were almost on the equator it was snowing—swift white flakes that shot at us suddenly out of the gray and drove rapidly away into the yawning crater below. This was one of the very few places in the world where it is possible to experience a snowstorm at the equator.

Rock and ice climbing is not easy, and above 19,000 feet it is exceptionally difficult because of the rarity of the atmosphere. I had always wondered what mountain sickness was like but had never been able to find any description in writing. Now I found out on Kilimanjaro, and for the benefit of the medical profession and future mountain climbers, I do here set down that mountain sickness is evidenced by nausea, stomach upset, and panting spells similar to those preceding a faint.

Toward noon we reached a second and higher point on the rim of the crater. But there was still the highest point to attain, and I pushed on without stopping. Around one o'clock I reached the true summit; Kaiser Wilhelm Spitze and Saidi arrived soon after.

And so I had reached the top. I was too tired to feel elated and too unhappy with my stomach to regret that the clouds and snow continued to block out nearly all view. Yet the deep satisfaction of achieving a goal gave me a sense of mental well-being. I had succeeded. I was 19,340 feet above sea level! I was on the highest point of a great continent! Kilimanjaro was mine!

19

Life on the Somalia Mail

The second day following my descent from Mount Kilimanjaro, Jacqueline and I found ourselves cycling through the country of the Masai. The Masai are usually considered to be the most warlike of all African tribes. They formerly killed a man to signify arrival at the much desired state of warriorhood, but now they managed to content themselves with a lion. They also underwent training to become warriors, and during this period—from the age of seventeen to twenty—they drank a mixture of hot blood and milk and ate half-raw beef.

The Masai were tall and fairly handsome, being a mixture of Hamite and Negro. Both men and women were fond of wearing ornaments, and I took particular note of those worn by two men I saw. Since they wore only a short burlaplike tunic, there was an excuse for some adornment. Around the left arm were three bracelets. Two were small coiled sticks of brilliant purple, and the third, the one resting midway between the other two, or halfway between wrist and elbow, was of links of gold. Around the neck was a tight band of pink buttons, divided by bars of purple, and fixed in a framework. Suspended from the top of each ear was a coiled stick ring of bright purple about four inches in diameter. A similar ring was suspended from the lower part of the ear. Also suspended from the lobe were two rather heavy, gold, bell-like ornaments united at the lobe so as to appear like a spread clothespin. In their right hands these Masai dandies carried a long walking stick.

Days continued to be sunny and not too hot. Mornings were inclined to be cloudy, and when I rolled up my tent I found it wet with dew.

I passed out of Tanganyika and into Kenya on the slopes of Longido Mountain, where the first African battle of the 1914-18 war had been fought. This was my second visit to British Kenya, a country considerably smaller than Tanganyika but nearly as large as the state of Texas. The land continued to be hilly, and I had some long and arduous pulls with the bicycle. Heavy bush, with a sprinkling of good-sized trees, surrounded me at all times. The ground was dry, and it looked like water would be hard to find. Yet I occasionally met Masai with herds of cattle. They were the champion cattle breeders of East Africa, it seemed, and were said to have a million head of the native humpneck, or zebu.

Although these cattle were very important to the Masai, he did not treat them with the best of consideration. When bloodthirsty he would tie a leather thong around an animal's neck and shoot an arrow into a distended vein. As the arrow was withdrawn the blood would be caught for drinking. When a Masai wanted a choice steak at a feast, he would cut it from the living animal, taking care not to cut any main arteries, and would be quite indifferent to the beast's suffering.

Cattle were also used as purchase money for wives, and a wife with a good figure might cost a Masai warrior as many as four cows and bulls. He has had plenty of time to acquire wealth to buy a wife, or two, or three, because he did not marry until nearly thirty. Meanwhile the very young girls of the tribe had been keeping house for him and other warriors, in separate bachelor quarters. These girls might commence at the tender age of seven but return to their mothers at the time of puberty. The female head was often shaved very closely and eyebrows and eyelashes pulled, as only the warriors were supposed to have hair. Youths pulled out their beards until they became warriors.

The Masai I saw that particular afternoon all carried great long spears. I sometimes observed groups of two or three unconnected with cattle, walking parallel to the road at a distance of about a hundred yards. It was pretty wild country, so they may have been hunting lions. They were tall and had striking physiques and with those long spears must have appeared formidable even to a lion. Now a Masai warrior was not supposed to speak to an elder until the elder spoke first, but probably one friendly chap who hailed me from the side of the road figured that I was not his elder. Anyway, I had a good opportunity to examine his equipage.

To match his giant physique he displayed the usual African set of good white teeth. He was dressed in a chamois-colored shirt affair like his less sociable fellows. This single-piece garment extended fore and aft from the shoulder to below the knees. On either side it was entirely open so that one could get a full view of black skin from arm to foot. There was a sort of strap around the upper thigh, but I could not see that this did much toward keeping the shirt in place. He carried a long orange gourd about two feet by seven inches in diameter, and I figured that this was for water. But the most interesting item was a sort of big quirt with a black eight-inch-long horsehairlike brush. My thought was that it was probably used to keep off the flies, but I suspect that it was made from the mane and tail of a lion and that its main purpose was to demonstrate that the owner, having killed his lion, had become a warrior.

The country continued to be hilly, and by 5 P.M. I was almost too tired to proceed. While resting under a tree I debated falling asleep, since it was big-game country and somehow I kept looking off downwind. But I could see there was to be no habitation for umpty-nine miles, so felt I might as well resign myself to my surroundings for the night.

But fate decreed otherwise. Just before dusk my astonished ears heard the sound of a motor. A bit later a big old army truck came along, and I

A Masai with his herd.

Masai youngsters—Kenya.

Masai women.

soon found myself in the cab jolting along toward Nairobi with two British soldiers, one sick with malaria. Guineas and foxes scurried out of our way as we lumbered into the dusk. We slept in the truck that night and in the morning traversed a great plain teeming with antelope of various sizes and colors, and with wild buffalo. By 8 A.M. we had roared into Nairobi, capital of Kenya and metropolis of British East Africa.

This ride was a big break for me, as it gave me Saturday forenoon to buy supplies and would not require my remaining over Sunday. I had decided to go to Italian Somaliland (later Somalia) and was anxious to get started. But I was still to realize how big a break the ride was.

Nairobi I found to be quite a busy cosmopolitan place laid out on supposedly modern lines. I say "supposedly" because it seemed to me that the traffic circles hindered the heavy flow of traffic instead of facilitating it. There were nice hotels, fine public buildings, and up-to-date shops. It seemed incredible to step out of the wilds and onto the paved thoroughfares of a modern city.

At Nairobi I disclosed to the Royal East African Automobile Association agent that I wanted a map for a bicycle trip into Somalia. He was amazed that I would even contemplate such an adventure through five hundred miles of what he vehemently characterized as "absolute nothingness—thorn and shrub," but he offered to trace off some of his maps for me. I then chased off to the Civil Affairs Headquarters to see Major Pither and get permission to travel to Somalia. You see, the former Italian colonies were managed by the British, pending a decision of the UN, and there was talk that the natives had been promised they would never be returned to Italian rule. The situation was particularly touchy, as they had just had a big riot in Mogadishu (Mogadiscio), the capital, in which there was much looting and fifty-two Italians were killed.

Major Pither turned out to be a chap with whom I had already chatted in the post office. He thought he could fix me up, though he was worried whether I could get through into Somalia before the rains. The last or second to the last Somalia Mail Convoy was being dispatched that day. If the one did not go next week and I got bogged at Garissa, near the frontier and 225 miles out, I'd be in a spot, because there would be no vehicle behind me. Also Colonel Turner controlled things, and he might want to wire Mogadishu. In this case there would be a delay of several days.

The colonel did want to wire, nor could he promise that I could proceed from Garissa if I pedaled out there ad interim. He could give me a pass on the Somalia Mail Convoy, but it would cost me twenty dollars to Mogadishu. I protested, but said I could probably pay from Garissa over the border. He said it would still cost me twenty dollars. However, he went out to talk it over with the major and they decided that I might have a special rate of twelve dollars to Kismayu (Chisimaio), just across the border, but I must report to the authorities there. It looked as though I had better accept, and I did. The colonel was really a friendly chap, and I felt that he was acting in my best interest. The major had said that when the road beyond Garissa got wet, nothing moved; and I believed him. It was March 13 already, and the preceding year the road had closed on the nineteenth. It would have taken five days by bike to Garissa.

The colonel told me to be back in one hour, as the mail left at noon. I rushed around combing the town for films, changing a traveler's check, buying bread without coupons, etc., but I made it; and at 12:45 the Somalia Mail Convoy—a bus and a truck—pulled out for Kismayu, Somaliland, 575 miles away, with me on board. There were three Somali sergeants and three Somali soldiers on that bus, one of the sergeants being armed. There were an Italian driver and a Somali helper for both the bus and the truck; there was a British captain in charge; and myself. So in less than five hours after I roared into Nairobi, I roared out again. Truly no man knoweth what strange turns fortune will take. Without my ride into Nairobi I would have been delayed a week and might have never seen Somalia and the Horn of Africa at all.

We stopped at a place called Thika not far out of Nairobi while young Captain Allan Cullimore said goodbye to a couple blondes. He, like the Somalis, had been over to Nairobi on leave. While waiting, the Somalis, the American, and the Italian driver carried on a conversation of sorts to get acquainted. Somali, Swahili, Italian, and English sputtered and groped all over the place, but as usual the whites had to rely the heaviest on the blacks—the supposedly inferior race. Two of the sergeants knew English. They were members of the Somali Youth League, and one showed me his card. He said it was like the Boy Scouts. One of their objectives was an independent Somalia. Still, they said they would be glad to have America take over. Their Somalia would include former Italian Somaliland, British Somaliland, and those parts of Ethiopia and French Somaliland where the Somalis are of numerical importance. This would mean an area of about 300,000 square miles and a population of 1,750,000.

Sixty miles out of Nairobi a few isolated peaks and rock outcroppings appeared. The country was fairly well wooded, but there were almost no villages. At eighty miles, the trees petered out, but a scattering of little ones, really bushes, continued. There was a sparse growth of dry grass and green weeds and the country continued to be rolling. Occasionally we saw herds of native cattle, perhaps fifty head, with two natives in attendance. The road was badly corrugated, and there were many gullies.

We traveled on until dark, when we reached a native village situated on top of a hill. Here the captain called for *chai* (tea) and the purchase of some eggs, which a couple of the sergeants went off to get. There was a big assembly of natives gathered on the hill slope at one edge of the cluster of huts, awaiting darkness to see some motion pictures. Meanwhile a sound truck entertained the assemblage with western cowboy songs and hillbilly yodeling. When the pictures started, they showed the visit of the King and Queen to Basutoland. The Basuto riding their ponies brought much laughter.

At about 8:30 we stopped for more *chai* and supper. The captain had brought double rations for fear we would be hung up by the rains and could not get through. He and I stuck together in assembling and preparing our food. It was surprising, though, how much he seemed to rely on me. One of the sergeants said he could cook and we had eggs but no grease to fry them in. I had to supply the grease. Our larder contained canned beef, peas, potatoes, carrots, grapefruit, butter, and jam. A number of the captain's cans bore familiar United States labels, and so did the sergeant's gun.

We drove until midnight and camped. Allan and the Italians had cots, but the Somali and I rolled on the ground. Remembering the dew, I slept under the gary, the local term for lorries and buses.

The thorn became more and more lifeless as we approached Garissa. The country was a desert of sand and thorn trees with arroyos to be crossed. After traveling sixteen hours by bus, I looked forward to Garissa—255 miles out—as the metropolis of eastern Kenya. Actually it turned out to be little more than an oasis in the desert, situated at the crossing of the river Tana. This was a deep and wide muddy affair coming down from the slopes of Mount Kenya, visible from the road the day before. Across the river a tiny mud village lay baking in the sun.

Allan reported to the district commissioner, who lived in a two-story building made of bricks (which had been molded in the vicinity), and of modern architecture. There were no trees about, but it was comfortable enough inside. The D.C. said the temperature had dropped considerably from that of preceding days and was now only 102. (We were nearly at the equator.) In such temperatures and in such a desert of thorn it had never occurred to me that there would be any game; but the D.C. spoke of having killed a lion at the bridge only the night before and told of elephants being in the vicinity.

In Garissa we also called at the police post. There were 24,000 square miles in the police district and only one man, a British officer, to look after it. Imagine one policeman patrolling the entire state of West Virginia! The Garissa officer was about to start up country after a man and I gathered that he was not relishing the idea.

After reporting here, we found the trucks and ate lunch in deep shade. When we were almost ready to leave, the Kenya counterpart of the Somali Youth came around with free tea, served in real cups and saucers, and some biscuitlike fritters. The men were dressed in long white robes with red fezzes.

We rolled away from the Tana under a blazing sun and were again surrounded by never ending stretches of sparse, scrubby thorn trees. In less than a mile I saw my first camel, and we soon chased several of the stupid, ungainly, hobbled beasts. There was muddyish, yellow water along the road from the recent rains and for many miles we met groups of white-robed natives. Most wore nothing on their heads against the sun, and it fairly made one shudder. Their skins were so shiny black that faces and heads actually glistened. We saw one cluster of mud huts—a village, that is—with not a vestige of shade in the place. In fact, the huts were only as high as the thorn.

Later in the afternoon we came across the opposite edition of the Somalia Mail stuck in the sand. A group of curious natives had gathered and since we stopped to do some sidewalk superintending, there was an opportunity to really absorb the local color. I was surprised to find the natives so small in stature. They were quite a contrast to the giant Masai I had seen two days previously. Their features were more like the Arabian and bore practically no resemblance to the negroid. This group had draped part of their white dress over their heads and carried spears. One let me examine his spear and threw it for us by way of demonstration. On the business end was a piece of metal like a dull chisel. The whole spear was about five feet long. I found that these natives were friendly, modest, and accommodating, and engendered in me a certain undefinable sense of understanding.

Later that afternoon I saw my first giraffe. I couldn't have missed him because he stood, head, neck, shoulders, and body above the scrub. What an anomaly! That long neck had been created to reach high up into trees for tender, succulent leaves. Here it stood ten feet taller than anything else in the whole dome of heaven.

We made camp early. There was rain ahead, and we debated about driving on. For supper we had liberal portions of fried eggs, fried potatoes (my suggestion), and peas. The Italians treated us also to some delicious spaghetti, and the Somalis added dates; so we had plenty to eat! And I should not forget the enormous cup of tea. This was usually served first thing, and after drinking just half of it (my first experience), I actually felt full and as though I did not want anything to eat. Now I understood why the Somalis and the British were sometimes able to pass up a meal completely.

We were off at daybreak. After one mudhole we waited for an hour for the following lorry and then started back after it. We found that the delay had been occasioned by Mario dropping a box on his wrist. It must have been his unlucky day because shortly afterward he got stuck, although the truck was the higher and more powerful of the two vehicles. We had a time, I can tell you. It was a case of maneuvering the bus around and through the soft spots so as to get a pull with the big tow chains. Great ruts had to be filled with wood, of which there was plenty. Routes were studied and debated; shovel and pickaxe were used. What we needed most was someone to take charge. The Italians did not seem too certain. Two of the sergeants were willing but uncoordinated. I looked to the captain to order them to get wood and so on but he took an easygoing attitude to-

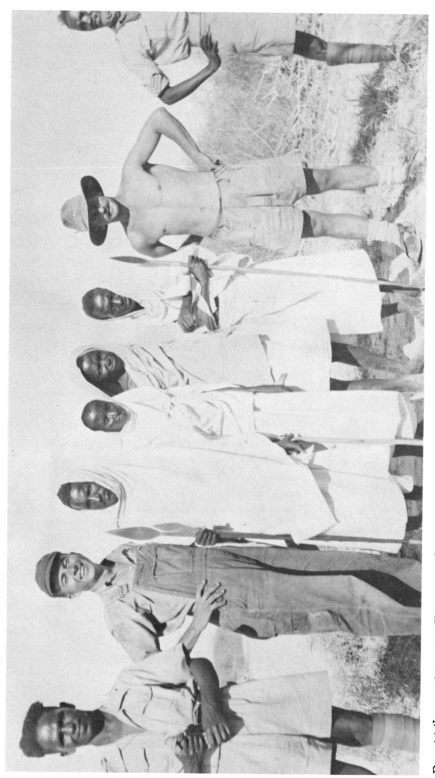

Desert tribesmen in eastern Kenya near the Somali frontier.

ward them and I suppose he could really do nothing else, because they were on leave like himself. Everyone was willing to do just a little—like throwing in a bit of wood. But then they wanted to stop and see what the truck would do by itself. To me things necessary seemed obvious, and little by little it appeared that I should direct the operation, particularly after they failed to follow my advice for the bus and it got stuck. Things did look bad then, with both cars stuck. The last tow truck was 350 telephoneless miles behind, the next 420 equally communicationless miles ahead. But I called for more wood, setting the collecting example. Eventually we got out and engineered the bus for a front pull instead of rear as formerly; and we finally made it. Everyone congratulated me, even the bus driver. I suppose they still think Americans can do anything.

Later on, the pitman arm of the truck fell off, and this was a delay. From time to time the carburetors had to be dismantled.

"Life on the Somalia Mail," I sang.

Then we hit Somaliland, and Italian road construction seemed to be better. Nevertheless, there was one section where the road was often under water for long stretches. One of these was pretty deep and water came up through the dash and flooded us. The driver was soaked to the waist and had a small lake under the pedals. This I named *Lago di la Autista*, and we all had a laugh. Big rains seemed to be ahead of us, but after they cleared we thought going would be O.K. Then we hit a muddy stretch and had to stop for the night. The big lorry could not stay on the road, now graded for the first time. It was pitiful and silly. Neither vehicle had chains. Their answer to my accusation of oversight in this respect was that the road board would fine them five hundred to a thousand shillings for tearing up the road by using chains. Anyway, we stuck, in one-half inch of mud.

We camped right in the middle of the road, and the Somalis put their sleeping bags down on the mud, ignoring the miracle of stretches of grass on the bank.

While seated around these campfires in Kenya and Somalia or jolting along on the Somalia Mail, Allan told me a great deal about the Somalis, the Italians, and the Mogadishu riots. He had been in charge of the police station in Mogadishu at the time. It was during a UN visitation, and about six thousand Somalis were parading. The Italians hired Somalis to parade for them, and things would have gone all right but someone threw a bomb. Since Somalis were killed, they started raiding Italian homes in retaliation. Knives and guns were used, and fifty-two dead resulted.

Many Italians took refuge in the cathedral and wanted the police to send lorries for their possessions. This was done, but there was lots of trouble about it. Meanwhile there was looting of the houses. Allan went up an outside stairway at one place to stop it, and the thieves came down on top of his bayonet. Another, he had to club. The Italian men did not wish to return to their homes to see if their wives and children had escaped unless they had police escort, even though it was necessary to wait for it. On the other hand, the Italians were sometimes willing to run risks for their animals. One man left the protection of the cathedral and walked to the police station, a very dangerous thing to do, and asked for an escort to go see about his horses. They had been left shut up, and he was afraid the Somalis would not look after them and they would have no water. He could not remain safe while they might be suffering. Allan gave him not only the escort but the use of a lorry as well.

Further as to the Italian character, I noticed that our two burly drivers had bought a big bunch of carnations in Nairobi. These were carefully husbanded through 770 miles of desert and nearly five days of travel to Mogadishu. They had them well wrapped and each morning helped each other carefully change the water, wash the stems and repack. You would not see an American male take that much care of mere flowers.

In Somaliland I was to meet quite a few British officials in both the police and military departments. Some were concerned about future riots; others pooh-poohed the idea. One chap was obviously worried and did not seem to be able to dismiss from his mind the slow method of death the Somalis had inflicted on one or two Italians.

The road had dried out by morning, and we proceeded. Many baboons, ostrich, and a species of animal looking exactly like history-book pictures of eohippus, were to be seen. The country continued flat and dry, with here and there a greener stretch where hit by recent rains. Late in the afternoon we struggled through sand over an old rock-block Roman type road into Kismayu.

Kismayu has an interesting history. I think the Portuguese may have been there once, but the British came in about 1860 and received concessions from the sultan of Zanzibar to settle in Giubaland. Their old fort still stands in excellent condition across the plaza from the district commissioner's offices. They worked their way up the coast, won a battle or two, but decided things were too hot and retired back to Kismayu. Eventually, when the Italians became established in Somaliland, they complained of not having any harbor in the south. In World War I, Britain promised Albania to Italy and when that failed to materialize, she gave Kismayu and surrounding area to Italy. Now Britain again governs it pending UN decisions.

In regard to the latter, the D.C., who invited the captain and me out to his house for lunch, told us some rollicking stories. While we all laughed, I know enough of natives to know they were true, at least in spirit.

A UN commission—a Frenchman, an American, a Russian, etc.—traveled through the country to determine what sort of rule the natives would prefer.

"Would you like British rule in Somalia?" one chap up-country was asked.

"No. No, I don't want the British—but the English would be all right."

"Would you want the Abyssinians to rule the country?" another native was asked.

"Well, it would be all right if the English said so."

"Would you like French rule?"

"Ah—well, I suppose it would be all right if the English thought so."

Perhaps you would like the Italians to come back and rule."

"Ah, no, I don't think so. But it wasn't so bad. Well, maybe it would be all right."

In Kismayu the village idiot came up to the commission.

"Do you like the British rule?" he was asked.

"Oh, no! Very bad, very bad, indeed," was the reply.

"Yes, yes, tell us more," said the Russian eagerly. "Why don't you like the British command?"

"Well, you see those ships sunk out there in the harbor [two freighters]; and you know that island down the coast?"

"Yes," said the Russian.

"Well, they belong to me, and the British commissioner won't give them back to me."

The D.C.'s residence, built many years before by the Swedes as a mission, was an enormous stone affair, cool and comfortable inside. Allan, although only twenty-two, had succumbed to the African habit of a nap after lunch, and so I strolled downtown alone and made a tour of all its sandy streets. Kismayu was a city of blazing white under an equatorial sun, and at two o'clock in the afternoon was nearly deserted. Coal-black Somalis sprawled in the shade of its porticoes, a blanket, often ragged, draping their lower bodies as a long skirt. An oxcart creaked slowly past. A Somali police sergeant and his assistant lazed on the steps of the police department building and jail, and tried unsuccessfuly to look alert. The plaza was deserted except for an old hen and a miserable-looking chick. These gave some evidence of movement occasionally, as did the British flag which moved in the sea breeze that tended to make the town livable.

At 3 p.m. I gathered up the bus driver and sergeants and picked up the captain at the D.C.'s. We were off after tea. We paralleled the Giuba (Juba) River for nearly fifty miles, making one stop at the farm of an Italian. He grew Indian rice of a Karachi variety that looked very much like oats before threshing. He raised plenty of bananas and gave us three bunches, but they had green skins, and unlike the Mauritian banana, could not be eaten until they had been kept awhile. He also grew some corn but said it was too much work considering the result. The river was low and not much wider than twice the length of the cable ferry on which we crossed.

The next morning we passed two or three great ridges of sand dunes. This reminded Allan of the time when he had spent five days hunting for a body among the dunes. The man's enemies had tied a cord around his neck in a loose loop and then pulled on the two ends until his head was nearly severed. Accompanied by some relatives, Allan had found the twenty-eight-day-old remains, which they gathered up in a blanket and returned.

At 12:30 we turned off on a side road which was paved. As we crossed a reddish sand dune toward the sea, a fairy city appeared before my astonished eyes. It was the fairy city of Merca—a curious *Arabian Nights* city—a combination of old Portuguese, old Arabic, and modern Italian architecture overlooking the sea in the Italian manner.

In the city piazza we found the gendarmerie headquarters and the genial, experienced Captain Crowther living overhead. After lunch we repaired to a balcony over a wine shop across the square, and there we met the D.C., Mr. Keats, and his wife. These three people constituted the English white population of the place, and you might know, starved for company as they were, that we soon had invitations to spend the afternoon and night.

I was asked to stay at Captain Crowther's. He had spent twenty-one years in China and Malaya, so I did not venture to exercise my two years of school Chinese. He spoke of interesting though unpleasant experiences in a Jap prison camp. Having been delegated the job of commanding the camp, he had been able to smuggle his wife from the women's section to live with him. This was fortunate because she had been ill from malnutrition. Mr. Crowther said his own stomach shrank so that a couple tablespoons of food and a cup of tea would make him feel full.

I washed out some laundry and toured the town in the afternoon. After supper we sat in the captain's living room just off the second-floor balcony, from which he watched the flow of life in the piazza or reviewed the parade of his troops. Our view commanded the evening, the sea, and the stars; and the young moon smiled down on the curious Portuguese-Arabic-Italian buildings around the square. Verily the place was like a paradise.

By and by we joined Allan and the Keatses on the British-reserved balcony across the way. Young Mr. Keats was one of those types who loved an audience. After five years in isolated Somali posts without one, he had become a bit of an eccentric. He wore his thick curly hair long in the back and had grown an enormous handlebar mustache, whose ends he continually manipulated while spinning his long yarns. He was a good mimic, and his imitation of crows was perfect.

Recounting the English experiences with the Somalia riots brought out some good laughs. During the telling of one tale Keats said the most common sight was that of orderlies carrying coffee in and out of police headquarters. Then Allan, in all innocence, was relating an account: "And so here were all these people armed with sticks and stones and bricks going past the gendarmerie—we could see them through the window—"

"Yeah"—I broke into laughter—"through the window." And so we all had a good laugh.

Lacking pretzels with the beer and vermouth, Mr. Crowthers provided roasted peanuts. These were shelled and still warm and were practically all consumed by the American in order to drown the taste of the liquor, which he doesn't like (excepting champagne). And there sat Allan, forced to do all that social drinking on an empty stomach, for the Keatses had not yet eaten. When my stomach is empty, anything to drink, even a glass of water, makes it feel deucedly uncomfortable. As the hours wore on I heard Mrs. Keats whisper softly in her husband's ear during his lengthy storytelling: "Darling, remember this man hasn't had anything to eat."

Finally we adjourned to the Keatses, who lived in one of the villas outside of town, situated on a slope overlooking the sea. The table was set, the black servants at attention. "Now at last Allan will get some food," I thought. But no, Mr. Keats got started on some of his drawn-out stories and time went on until 11:40. "Surely soon," I said to myself, recalling that the hostess had said they frequently did not eat until midnight and also remembering that all lights in the town went out at that hour. But no, the lights went out and we carried on by flashlight. At 12:20 I dragged Captain Crowther off for a cool walk home under the stars. I never knew how much longer the storyteller held forth with his reduced audience. Perhaps they were so weak from the lack of food they could not help themselves.

In the morning Captain Crowther and I stood on the balcony and watched his men take their physical exercise in front of headquarters. They went past in rank on a good half-run, clapping their hands in unison as they went along. This was at 6 A.M., and the captain said it was largely for his benefit—to prove that they were on their toes. Speaking of natives, even his orderly was only a few months out of the bush, yet he could laboriously peck out English characters on a typewriter. But Captain C. said they were a long, long way from education and self-government. He thought a British ten-year mandate was the solution, but in the present state the British did not feel like making an investment.

On the way out of town the next morning, we stopped to pick up Allan at the Keatses'. The D.C. was just getting out of bed wearing a big bright-red skirt reaching down to his ankles. The hostess was up, and in the absence of her husband, had asserted herself enough to get Allan up to the table.

We passed through rather dry red desert country with some Utah-like erosion near Merca, and about 10:30 A.M. arrived in Mogadishu, capital of Somalia. It was a sprawling, fairly modern, white desert city in which the Italian construction was more prominent than the Arabian. We cleared the customs in the port, and I once again mounted my faithful steed, Jacqueline. My ride on the Somalia Mail was over.

20

"And Besides, There Is a Lion!"

I cycled out of Mogadishu northeast, through a rolling desert country of red sand. There were lots of Navaho-like stick hogans along the road for some distance, and a great many people walking on the road. The women carried heavy burdens upon their backs, supporting them by headbands. Cute little burros plodded along with their loads of sticks, hay, or what have you, and ungainly camels moseyed along near the highway, both singly (being led by ropes) and in a caravan.

Thus here on all sides of me was the life of a people—the Somali, a pastoral people, a nomadic people, counting their wealth in their herds and flocks as did the people of the Bible. And in this dry and inhospitable land, grazing rights were of such importance that tribal wars and blood feuds were not uncommon. And these nomad Somali looked with disdain on those few of their brethren who were trying a precarious agriculture where moisture permitted.

People along the way became fewer and fewer as I progressed inland, but scrub thorn, red desert, and for a time, distant views of the sea kept up my interest.

At dusk I stopped for the night at Balad. The young proprietor of a roadside "hotel," who was an English-speaking Somali, took me in tow at once and gave me tea and two hard-boiled eggs. I ate these seated outside, with a crowd of about forty men and boys around me watching every move. Shortly a big lorry and trailer pulled up, and one Daud Mohamed descended, elbowed his way through the crowd and commenced to chat a bit in English. In a couple minutes he offered me a ride to Dagabur, Ethiopia, several hundred miles away.

It was simply too good a break to be true; and so I was not too surprised to run into trouble on the road a couple hours later. The lorry had stopped for water outside Villagio Duc d'Abruzzi, when the local gendarmerie requested that I report to their boss for a check. It seemed that the Balad policeman, a Somali, arriving at that roadside hotel, after I had departed, had wanted in on the act, and never having heard of a gunless traveler on a bike, had phoned the man in charge up the road at Villagio. And now it seemed that this Villagio police bloke lived so far away from the road that it would take an hour to see him. Daud said he would be unable to wait for me. Of course, I set up some loud protests about such foolishness, but the Somali were firm, although friendly. Finally Daud said he would wait a half-hour.

Away we tore through the night. The two Somalis struggled valiantly to walk as fast as the American. On over a footbridge, over a shortcut through a factory—on and on. After fully eighteen minutes of very fast walking we arrived at the policeman's house. Thank goodness he was an Englishman; and after one look at my red face and on hearing that I was in danger of losing a ride, he saw the light and set about making amends. He and his wife hauled out a bottle of ice-cold beer and tried to get me to settle down in the parlor for a bit. I declined, and he, after considerable trouble, got his four-by-two, as they call a 1,500-pound jeep, agoing and we all raced for the place where Daud's truck was waiting. The policeman and his wife made me take the beer, and I thought I would treat the boys in the lorry for waiting on me. There were four of them, but when I offered it, Daud said they were Mohammedans and did not drink. So that was that! I dumped the balance out of the back of the truck later.

Forty-seven people of all descriptions piled on the lorry at Villagio. I carefully husbanded a full sleeping space on the floor of the truck, and since the road was good and the pace slow, slept a full sound eight hours as we went on through the night.

The next day Daud treated me to a big dinner (which included goat liver) at a roadside place on the Somalia-Ethiopian border. It was run by two Italians and the native wife of one of them, and such a questioning they gave me! Daud, who spoke Italian, was the showman interpreter. I received the usual warnings of bandits, beasts, etc., and was told I had to carry a gun. "How could I, being an American, not know anything about guns, or not be rich?" That was the native attitude. The Italian proprietor gave me a big bottle of wine, but I managed to get the rest of the patrons to drink nine-tenths of the punk-tasting stuff. We rested both at FerFer and on up the road through the heat of the day. The country was desert—much like northeastern Utah—with low, flat-topped hills either near the road or in the distance.

Once in a great while we passed a well by the road. This was a huge, concrete affair with a monument for a top—the Italians are great for monuments—and was usually situated at the end of a fine concrete bridge spanning an arroyo. Although we had left the oiled road at the Somalia boundary, the Italians had put in a good foundation of hand-laid rock on this section in Ethiopia. You've got to hand it to the Italians for building roads instead of using some for houses. However, this road was as crooked as heck. Instead of cutting straight across the desert floor, it clung to the base of the bordering foothills. In and out, in and out, following each valley way in to the upper end, then out around the bend and into the next valley. Daud said that it had been built during the war and the workers needed the protection afforded by vantage points on the hills above them.

Many people in other countries never know when to eat. I followed

The fairy city of Merca, Somaliland (Somali Republic).

An anthill in the Ogaden, Ethiopia.

Uardare, Ethiopia, was an important junction for camel caravans.

the practice of adjourning to the rear of the truck for supper at 6 P.M. After supper I would spend an hour watching the road ahead, the desert, the stars, and the growing moon. I would then roll out my sleeping bag on the floor of the truck, and in spite of very rough roads, would sleep like a log. This particular night I was awakened at midnight.

"Hart, are you asleep or awake?" It was Daud Mohamed.

"Uh. . ."

"Do you like macaroons in oil?"

"Why, ah, yes, I guess so."

"Have you a plate?"

But when I got the dish he filled it with macaroni. And it was good —even in the middle of a night's sleep.

The next day the hills disappeared and we crossed a flat open semi-desert, another part of the dry inhospitable Ogaden. Sometimes I rode in the back of the truck with a nice middle-aged Somali with a Vandyke beard. He wore a turban, a European corduroy jacket, and a skirt. The skirt was held to his legs by black garters, as I noticed when they fell to his ankles at one time (a Somali's calves are too skinny for garters anyway). The men in this country when resting sit with their knees up, but always wrap their skirts so well that modesty is never shocked. And speaking of modesty, they are very careful to go far away when attending to natural functions, both of which are performed in a squatting position.

There were also a divorced woman and her small son sitting in the back of the truck. The lad was a cute, active little chap for whom I made a paper cap. His mother did not seem to be very interested in him, either when he wailed or when he was in danger of falling out. He had diarrhea, but his mother gave him no personal attention in that respect either. Of course he was clad only in a short shirt, which was more than adorned his little playmates who cropped up miraculously out of the bush every time the truck stopped in the desert. His mother was attractive and wore long, silk print pantaloons, flared at the bottom, underneath her skirt. On her head was a cloth worn Madonna fashion. She had been divorced.

Daud said Mohammedan divorce was very simple. The man just sends his wife home, which was where my traveling companion was going. However, he usually thinks twice before doing this because according to custom he cannot ask her to come back until she has passed one night with another man. The husband may select this man himself; it may be his best friend. But even so, the practice is quite enough to deter a normal man from divorcing in a hurry.

Marriage was not so simple as divorce, Daud explained, still speaking of his own customs. I cannot set down the exact proceedings, but it involves a lot of money and red tape. The father of the boy, frequently about fifteen years of age (Daud's age when he married), speaks to the father of the girl, and they come to a monetary agreement. If the lad's father is dead, he must get four or five wise old men to go with him to the girl's father. First he must find out if he can approach the father and make an appointment for the wise men. The wise men extol the lad's virtues. In either case the girl's father consults with the girl's mother. During all this the lad has still to see the face of his bride-to-be for the first time.

On the wedding night the bride's mother and other women bring the bride to the lad's home, and there is a feast for which the groom must pay the mother. Then, when the young couple are alone, the groom must offer the bride money to see her face.

"You must give her some money so that she will be happy, you see," Daud explained. (Brother! What a system!)

This sum may be two or three hundred shillings (around $50), but if she is not a virgin, the groom need pay her nothing when they settle accounts the next morning. He can send her home. In fact, according to another educated Arab I met later on, the man can kill his wife if she is not a virgin, and there is no law to punish him. On the other hand, if the groom, in company with his mother and the mother of the bride, finds that she is a virgin, he takes the blood on a handkerchief and rushes outside to show it to all the people who are waiting to see. Then they all cheer and go away happy. To encourage premarital chastity, the clitoris of girl babies is removed. The birth of a girl baby is considered a great disgrace to a man anyway, and he sets up a great howl.

For the first weeks or so after marriage, according to Daud, the bride does nothing in the way of cooking. I think he said her mother cooked for them both, and this would imply that they lived in the bride's home.

Daud Mohamed had had five children. Three were living, the oldest being twelve. Daud himself was twenty-seven and president of the Local Born Young Arabs' League in Mogadishu. Like many other natives, he spoke Arabic, Italian, and Somali fluently, and could speak English and Swahili quite well.

At last we came to a place called Uardare—a place in the Ogaden! A squat, sprawled-out place—uninviting, yet intriguing! A place unimpressive, yet romantic!

In the great open space between the village proper and the police post, hundreds of camels and their owners made an unforgettable scene. Some were in herds, either grouped quietly or being driven about in the midst of clouds of dust and rolling stones. Others were in long well-laden caravans coming in from the direction of British Somaliland, Somalia, or the Sudan. Others were being assembled into caravans for departure. Still others were bellowing protests as their owners with sticks and ropes and foul language belabored them into kneeling positions so that they might be loaded for the trail. Camel cargo in the Horn of Africa consists of millet, coffee, hides, skins, cotton, salt, ghee, gums, resins, indigo, myrrh, and frankincense. The Somali lands are the Terra Aromatica of the ancients.

The village was a thick cluster of square, smooth-walled mud huts. At one edge was a one-story battered and scarred Mohammedan mosque surrounded by stones and rubble and giving much evidence of disuse. On the opposite side of the camel area were a few one-story buildings where a British policeman and an Ethiopian customs officer looked after affairs of government. Here also two Italians did a little commerce.

We lay over the better part of a day at Uardare. I was the guest of the British policeman, Inspector Hill, "out" for three months and fed up with everything. The country was just a great emptiness, he was lonely, and the standard article of diet was goat's liver, it being taboo for the Mohammedans. Goat's milk or camel's milk had to be mixed with canned milk for tea, and to top it off the inspector did not know the language sufficiently to do anything about the menu his houseboys prepared during the absence of the cook.

Hill had a pet antelope that would come into the house to be stroked when called. It had tiger markings like a dik-dik but was much larger and had tiny horns. Outside the house two prisoners were drawing water under the watchful eyes of an armed sentry. The well was very deep, and they lowered a five-gallon tin on a long rope slung over a pulley. They drew up about two gallons at a time, and during the process the two men sang in unison as is their custom. Hill said he once asked some natives what they were singing. They were on a job where they had to alternate the direction of pull. The words were: "Now pull toward Nairobi, now pull toward Mombasa."

We left Uardare before 4 P.M. because it was prohibited to leave later. There had been shifter activity (banditry) up the road, and it was required to traverse this section before dark. With us Hill sent an armed *askari* (native soldier), largely because I was along, I felt. A preceding truck had been shot at.

At four the next morning Daud woke me to say we had arrived at Aureh, a junction where I was to leave him for Hargeisa, military capital of British Somaliland. The men were loath to leave me in the pitch blackness in the middle of nowhere and thought I had much courage to proceed alone by bicycle.

"It is a hundred miles, and there is no water or people and there is a lion," Daud said.

Daud and one of the men held Jacqueline while I saddled up, meanwhile urging me to proceed with them to Dagabur. I did not want to bypass British Somaliland but could not help wondering myself if the inky darkness around us harbored any more bandits or even the lion Daud spoke about. After the truck departed, I walked Jacqueline cautiously along in a direction where Daud had said there were some huts. In this dark hour before dawn I was lucky to avoid bushes and holes in the sand and still luckier to find the huts.

Through a tiny crack in the door of one I saw a light, knocked and asked permission to wait outside until daylight. When it got a little lighter, I was surprised to see a truck standing nearby, and conversation disclosed that the owner was going to Hargeisa also.

The truck was stacked high—and I mean high—with sheepskins, and it never occurred to me there would be room for Jacqueline and me. Besides, there were a half dozen shrouded Somalis squatting silently beside the hut waiting for the takeoff. But the owner said I was to come also.

We had quite a time getting Jacqueline and my gear on, but everyone was helpful. When we were ready at 5:30 a.m., and were just able to see the road, the owner gave me a heavy blanket to use. I protested, but afterward it proved most welcome.

What a load that was! Wow! But the driver was careful, the road was excellent—graveled, believe it or not—and the truck worked perfectly.

Shortly after crossing the border from Ethiopia into British Somaliland, the thorns and bush gave way to sheer desert. The soil was red and herbless, even when the thorn started to appear again.

The Somaliland Protectorate was set up by the British along the coast of the Arabian Sea in 1884. In an area about the size of Oklahoma lived 350,000 Somali Mohammedans, mostly uneducated. The capital was Berbera on the edge of the Gulf of Aden, terrifically hot, arid, and unhealthy. But now after sixty years the government had awakened to the fact that the interior plateau was more comfortable. The military section had already transferred to Hargeisa and expected the political section to follow suit.

The Somalis in Hargeisa and surrounding area were great thieves—from economic necessity, I was told. At any rate, I found that the immigration official, Captain Fry, did not want me to go on alone, as there had just been an attack on a chap from India who was walking around the world. Only forty miles from Hargeisa and along my road, he had been attacked by two natives and robbed of money and passport. He was even then in the hospital. The police told me it was with a head wound, but an English-speaking Somali who had seen him said they had slit his ear. He felt that the robbers had done this only because he resisted them. So the captain arranged for a truck to take me to Jijiga (Giggiga) in Ethiopia. I had already seen a lot of Haile Selassie's kingdom but had not visited any good-sized towns, so I offered no objection.

A young Somali named Mohamed and his friend were in charge of the old Ford truck. It was what is called a trade truck and bore a canvas cover on the hood, on which were shown tiny blue and red pennants in a sort of V-shaped design. Other drivers had decorated their canvas covers according to their own tastes. My consorts in the front seat were lighthearted chaps and like others of the dark race were usually laughing and joking. If not doing this, they were singing the Somali national anthem—at least, that is what it seemed to be. There were two lines of it which were sung over and

Feeding a tame dik-dik in eastern Ethiopia.

over again—sung so much in fact that it seemed to be a subconscious thing.

The SYL, Somalia Youth League, was very prominent in both Somalias and far into Ethiopia, and there was no love lost between the Somalis and the Ethiopians. In some places the Somalis were so bold as to fly their own flag.

After crossing into Ethiopia (the second time for me), we soon entered what seemed by comparison to be the promised land. In place of desert country where great mirages shimmered and receded, here was a plain of grasslands for grazing; in place of great dust spouts rising thousands of feet into the air, here were hundreds, yes, hundreds of flocks of blackheaded sheep, cattle, and camels. Everywhere you looked and as far as the eye could see, there were herds and herdsmen. Somtimes the herders were small boys and girls, and they would make a wild run for the road to watch us go by. Occasional rows of large stones across part of the road indicated they had been up to other pranks. The men along the road walked with a long, quick, springy stride and frequently had their hands on the ends of a stout staff laid across their shoulders. Sometimes we saw little groups of huts, each shaped about like a loaf of bread. I assume from what I saw on the backs of some of the camels that these houses could be torn down, transported and re-erected.

In Jijiga I was invited to dinner by a British police official named Jones. When a couple of his boys were making up my bed in a guest tent near by, I asked them what time dinner would be served. It was already nearly 7 P.M. and I had been starved for an hour. They answered, "Seven-thirty," so I changed clothes and hustled over. Alas! I was yet new to British colonial customs. There was no dinner in sight, and Jones, another officer, and myself, and a caller, just sat around with drinks. British conversation is never vivacious, rarely stimulating, and usually stilted by American standards. On an empty stomach it is three times as bad. Eight-thirty came and went. Nine o'clock crept slowly around. There were long gaps in the conversation when everyone sat in silence. During these silences there was certainly nothing to hinder someone—just anyone—from saying something about dinner. By 9:15 I was so numb that I was no longer hungry—only outraged. I promised myself to leave at 9:30, but by then I was stubborn. Then I set a second deadline of a quarter to ten, and at that time as I was about to rise and excuse myself off to bed so that I could raid my food bag, Jones said we might as well eat because I had been traveling and might be hungry. Holy Jehoshaphat! Hungry! I had been stiff from starvation since six o'clock.

Early next morning, armed with my camera, I went down into the city to absorb the local color and to buy a loaf of bread. A woman was selling milk on a street corner, filling her customers' bowls, tin cans, or whatever as they were presented. At the district post the British-trained Ethiopian police displayed a very neat appearance. Their uniforms were spic and span, and shorts and shirts were starched and pressed to the nth degree. A bright-red cummerbund encircled each waist, and a black leather belt rested in the middle of it. Shoes looked like they were a recent innovation. Most of them were sandals of varied design, and I saw one pair of open leatherwork that looked like baby shoes except for size.

Later in the morning I was granted an audience with the Ethiopian provincial governor. He was a pleasant, well-bred gentleman, living in surroundings which strongly reminded me of Turkey and the Near East. He told me that one of the great barriers to national education and unity of the Ethiopians was the learning of their difficult language, Amharic.

While in Jijiga I visited the school. The headmaster was an American missionary, Keene Spitler, and we discovered that we were both ex-employees of Marshall Field and Company, Chicago. Keene's contract with the Ethiopian government had started six months before, but it had delayed his entry permit for three months. As yet he had received no pay at all.

Keene's charges included about two hundred and fifty youngsters of all ages, and the curriculum and schedule of classes looked like a crossword puzzle. Keene had studied Swahili in Aden but was trying to pick up Amharic, as Swahili did not seem to be of much use in Ethiopia. The Ethiopian school official whom I had the good luck to meet, helped Keene with the language, but there were no textbooks and Keene and the native teachers had to impart their own knowledge. Keene had cut up a few American picture magazines and was using those. Most of the pupils were Ethiopian in spite of the fact that the population was predominantly Somali. Most Ethiopian parents sent their children to school. The Somalis had no literature of their own and only one or two grammars had ever been written for them. Yet they aspired to be independent.

I was offered a ride out of Jijiga on a German-made truck that had apparently been used by the Italians, because the motto *Siempre corragio* had been painted just above the windshield. The driver was a passive, small-boned young Somali who wore an Arabian lacework cap. It was quite dark by the time we reached the junction at Nabadid (back in British Somaliland again). Here the native policeman fixed me up for the night in a room with a dirt floor at the back of his quarters. It was about six by six feet and had mud walls reinforced by sticks. He had a fire going in his outer room, and I had visions of being smoked out, but of course smoke rises and I got along O.K.

At 6 A.M. I wheeled Jacqueline out past the still-sleeping figures and the embers of the fire. How good it seemed to be on the bicycle again! It did not even bother me that I was scarcely ten miles from the spot where the Indian traveler had had his ear slit and his passport and money stolen.

I pedaled along as happy as a lark. I had ridden on trucks enough. What a help it had been though! In about nine days I had covered roughly fourteen hundred miles.

I finally left the plains, and the land became quite hilly. By afternoon I had worked into very rugged country, resembling that in western Colorado below Grand Mesa. Parts of the road followed the crest of a ridge and reminded me of one in the Pinal Mountains north of Tucson. Everything was very dry, a desert. I took a picture of the flora: great organ-pipe cactus, yuccalike cactus with curled-down leaves, and vines resembling pear cactus growing over thorn trees.

The next forenoon I tried to snap a picture of a small caravan of three camels led by three native women and their babies. The babies were carried in a fold of the mothers' garments and slung just in back of the left hip. The little tykes had their heads and shoulders exposed to the blazing sun, but I suppose nature had fortified them for that. A brown cloth garment entirely enveloped the women except for arms and shoulders, and they wore a string of bright-colored beads around the neck. Turbans covered their heads. Each carried a staff and a water jug as well as the baby.

When I turned to follow the women and their camels for a picture, they set up a shrieking and a man came running from a gully. He was carrying a spear and had a huge two-edged curved knife in an embossed brass scabbard carried horizontally at his belt. I tried to make this chap understand by signs that I wanted to take a picture. He seemed amenable, but when I actually got out the camera, the women uttered some screams and finished their job of scurrying away into the bush—camels, babies, and all. When I started off again, the man wanted me to give him my shirt, which I had taken off on account of the heat and had tied outside my pack.

I had worked into rugged country again. The mountains were close at hand, and their rough, sparsely covered slopes reminded me of the Cedar Mountains southwest of Great Salt Lake. Later I followed a dry riverbed. Then the country flattened out and the mountains receded. There was a continual succession of wadis (arroyos) to cross. After each steep little incline out of a gully, which usually required walking, there was a gentle grade up to a slight summit. Then came the declining slope until the sudden declivity of the next gully. On a good road in such country I could make use of the descent to negotiate the ascent on the other side, using low gear at the last moment. But here the road was full of rocks, and the bottom of the washes usually contained deep gravel. So by noon I was about bushed. This surprised me until I stopped to think that it was very hot; it was only my second day on the bicycle in a long time; and I had done sixty miles in rough country the day before. Further, there was a pretty stiff breeze against me, and apart from extra work, this dried up my perspiration very quickly. I knew from past experience that this combination of conditions could be very weakening.

A short rest before lunch, a long one after lunch, and still another after 3:30 failed to return much strength to my limbs. The ranges were farther away now—rather misty with dust and heat—and the plain, riverbed, and gullies were dry and wind-swept. Still, there was usually some shade to be found.

By 5 P.M. I could see a white building off in the distance. I could not be sure that it was inhabited, and people were so rarely seen that when I chanced on two camel herders I asked them for water. I had already consumed nearly three quarts. They supplied my needs from a brown vase with a narrow neck, carved like a vase from an Egyptian tomb. The neck was one and a half inches in diameter, but the hole from which the water issued could not have exceeded three eighths of an inch.

Ere long I pulled into Abdelcader—a police post and a few native houses. Here a chap about six foot six and a little fellow in white took charge of me. The big one wore the usual long blue-checkered skirt clear to the ankles, with an ordinary civilian shirt hanging on the outside like a bobby-soxer's. He was the policeman, and the other was the dispenser of medicines. The latter got me basin, soap, and towel, and I went to it. They gave me a clean room in the police-post building, and I wrote in my diary, explaining to my friends that I would talk more to them after night-fall.

Before I finished writing, I was interrupted by a delegation of three or four from the group of policemen and villagers who had been palavering about me at a great rate. The dispenser was the spokesmen.

"It is one hundred miles to Zeila. It is very dangerous for you. There is no water. You will die. There is much sand. You cannot go by bicycle. The natives are very bad people. They will kill you. And besides, there is a lion."

I tried to quiet them by pointing out that I had three bottles of water. I had traveled through sand before and so on. They retired only after I consented to take an extra bottle of water. But I was not too surprised when they woke me up at 1 A.M. They had found a lorry going through that would take me to Zeila. The driver turned out to be the same Mohamed who had taken me from Hargeisa to Jijiga.

Mohamed had a woman in the front seat with him this time. She looked older than he and acted as though she had some control over him, but whether she was his wife, mother, or mistress, I never knew. I slept out the rest of the night and had breakfast from my pack as we passed through Silal. This was a tiny village so filled with sand that it looked as though it was just able to keep its head above the drifts. Here and farther along several crews of natives were occupied in shoveling sand out of what passed for a road. At about 8 A.M. we arrived at Zeila, near the frontier between British and French Somaliland.

Desert landscape in British Somaliland (Somali Republic).

Gentlemen of Zeila, British Somaliland.

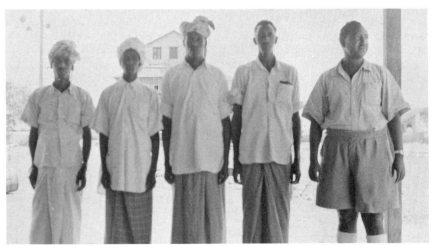

21

With a Cow and a Dhow
on the Gulf of Tadjoura

Zeila—a spot on the sand of a deserted strand on the horn of Africa, one of the world's most out-of-the-way places. Although the sun was very hot, it was cool and pleasant on the second-floor veranda of the district commissioner's residence. The pale-blue quiet sea, the tiny island offshore, the yellow sand, the sleeping native village, and the white government buildings made a charming picture.

I was at ease as a picnic-luncheon guest of a British doctor and his wife who had come down from the interior for a short vacation. They were "camping" in the unused D.C.'s residence, the only three-story building in all of British Somaliland. As we lazed on the veranda they spoke of a recent fishing trip with an old Arab guide to an island about five miles off shore. In a little creek and its inlet they were able to pull in the fish without a rod, one after the other. There is no doubt about the water being virgin.

I was offered a ride on a lorry over to Djibouti in French Somaliland. The lorry bore the usual heterogeneity, but a good many were government employees going over to celebrate their three-day Good Friday holidays.

One of the three English-speaking chaps on the bus was the most educated and intelligent fellow I had met in all Somalia. How he kept posted I don't know, but he read the *Reader's Digest*. This he regarded as American propaganda, though he admitted that it might be only private enterprise that gave it such world-wide distribution. He seemed to know more about the government of the United States than I did. Of course, he raised the Negro question, and he asked why with all the Negroes in the United States —and he knew the exact number—there were no Negro congressmen. He said that certainly was not representation, and he blamed the type of government. After we had battled each other to a standstill on a number of questions, I asked him what he thought the future of all Somalia should be. I was especially interested in his answer, since he was not a member of the SYL. He said the Somalis were not yet ready for or capable of self-government, and he thought it would be twenty years before they were. He thought British administration was O.K. ad interim. He said I must not forget that there was no school in British Somaliland prior to 1944. The first attempt was made in 1926 by missionaries, but when the Mohammedans saw that the people became Christian, they drove the missionaries out. A school was attempted a second time in 1938 or 1939 but with the same result. But in 1944 the people themselves asked that a school be set up.

I was the only one who knew any French, so the group asked me to translate for them at the French frontier. The young ex-soldier in charge was a jolly, good-humored fellow, so I think anything would have gone by. Well, we jolted and jerked on into Djibouti, for the French have built no better roads than the British, and comparing the areas, not as many. The Côte des Somalis Francaises (French Somaliland) was a neat little package as to size, embodying land on both sides of a big bay. But you couldn't even travel around it by road. What improvements the French had made were all in Djibouti, the metropolis of about two hundred miles of coastline. Even here they had gone no further than to pave the streets and build a sort of canal. Just as in Madagascar, there were no concrete sidewalks, and this makes any city look messy. The dust and dirt and rubble of the walks fall over the curb and onto the pavement and frequently hide it. At the base of the colonnades supporting the building porticoes, the concrete plaster and stone comes loose and adds to the rubble. Dirt spatters up on the colonnades and the building walls. Such cities look like unfinished jobs.

My second day in Djibouti fell on Easter. How strange to be so far from home! I envisioned the family going to services in the States. Meanwhile, with two lady missionary acquaintants, I attended the only Protestant church in Djibouti. This was a still different experience. The congregation was Malagasy and the service mostly in Malagasy, although a little was read in French. Both of the missionaries could speak Somali but no French or Malagasy. Nevertheless, they knew the tunes and could hum, and "Hallelujah" is a word which seems to remain intact in every language. The singing was especially fine, especially that of the young girl who led it.

The service was held in the front part of an empty building and was in a room partly divided by a double archway. Walls were of stone and two feet thick and the ceiling was twenty feet high, both things typical of hot-country buildings. We sat on chairs and benches on which flag-shaped reed fans had been placed for our comfort. There were about sixty present, including a number of soldiers on the back seats and three well-behaved little children. Both children and grown-ups were very well dressed. The women were partial to white, and some wore a broad white scarf across the shoulders. For the most part their dresses were the same as I would have seen in America, but after all, Djibouti belonged to the French. The men wore tropical suits of white.

The order of service and the behavior of the congregation were just about the same as in America. Differences were the black color of the skin, the lack of a minister, and the wiser taking of the collection at the close of the service. The minister's place was taken by the leader and five male members of the congregation. The former sat down or stood back of a table covered with a white cloth. The others read from a sort of pedestal pulpit near by.

While in Djibouti I stayed with three young men from India. I had already found the Indians I had met in Africa to be intelligent people to know and very hospitable. Laljee, Gudvantrai, and Shantilal did everything to strengthen that opinion. Laljee, who was big for an Indian, did the cooking. Gudvantrai, slender and dark, was something of a musician. Shantilal, still darker, was the shortest. In language and in race they were Gujarati from north of Bombay; in religion they were Jains, a sect carrying respect for animals to great lengths.

The three men lived in a three-story building occupying all six rooms on the third floor and all rooms (not counting the utility rooms) on the second floor. Completing the household were a little houseboy and a young girl. These two made tea and washed dishes and clothes.

When "at home" I followed the custom of my hosts in undressing for meals. It is a practice much to be preferred to dressing for dinner, especially in hot countries and when eating in the Indian manner. We each wore nothing but a pair of sandals and a skirt made from a sheet tucked around the waist like a towel. At table we squatted on the floor or on benches about four inches high with our knees up in the air and our feet hugged in close to keep them out of the huge brass platters where the food was. Just imagine if you wore pants how you would keep them from getting baggy in such a position. On the other hand, there were disadvantages. You could not bring the food up close and eat from between your knees because of that darn skirt; and of course you had no lap to put the food on. Finally, until you got used to the attire, you constantly worried about preserving modesty.

I enjoyed the Indian food. At my first supper we had the lightweight thin pancakes made of millet flour. Then there were potato patties made by taking sliced potatoes, rolling them in gram flour and frying them in a kettle of fat kept boiling over a primus. Then there were the round sort of cakes *(puri)* made in about the same way except that the center was of mashed potatoes. Although about two inches in diameter, they were very light in weight. The patties were dipped in finely ground red chilies. Tinned butter was supplied for the bread and spread on with a spoon, the only utensil in view. We wound up with betel nut to cleanse the teeth.

After supper—they do call it supper, and the noon meal is dinner—the four of us and two Indian friends took a long walk out to the end of the Djibouti pier. This was a nightly affair for these young men, and their quiet walk was not disturbed by the temptations of the bars and hotels we passed. For like Daud, the Mohammedan, they did not drink. Our conversation frequently turned to India, a country of which they were naturally quite proud and of which they spoke with obvious nostalgia.

In keeping with their Jain religion, my hosts did not eat meat, and even eggs were taboo. But even a completely vegetarian diet can afford variety, and dinner consisted of wheat-flour pancakes called *roti* and a stew composed of the following:

1. *Nuthia*—heavy rolls two inches long and one inch in diameter composed of mashed potatoes mixed with *methi,* a variety of a class of vegetable called *salad,* and rolled in gram flour (a flour made from the seed of certain leguminous plants such as the chick pea).

2. *Brindijan*—a vegetable like a small top-shaped eggplant.

3. *Haricots verts*—string beans.

4. Green and ripe tomatoes.

5 *Noog* oil, an Ethiopian cooking oil.   .

6. Flavoring of chilies and salt.

Our third course was rice over which we poured soup of *bhagi*—another variety of *salad*—swimming in plenty of noog oil and flavored with chilies and salt. Rice and soup were mixed together and eaten with the fingers.

In the evenings Gudvantrai occasionally played for us on the flute, or *wagon,* a Japanese six-stringed instrument. This affair had a keyboard like a typewriter and was minus five of its strings, but so far as I could tell, Gudvantrai made good enough music on only one.

I was six days in Djibouti before I could arrange passage across the Gulf of Tadjoura to the north. The captain of a tiny dhow agreed to take me over to Obok, from which a trail led across the desert to Eritrea. The cargo consisted of some dates and a cow. I was told we had to wait for the cow to eat and also for some of the crew. So it was five in the afternoon before the half-eyed captain escorted me over the long pier to his dhow. He was certainly a character to look at. His right eye was completely white, his left nearly so. He stuffed his embarkation permit into my pocket, as neither his calico shirt nor his short skirt had any pockets. On his head was a big calico turban. He was a Danakil, small, thin, and wiry like others of his race. He was kind to me, and I trusted him.

When we arrived at his *boute,* sure enough there was a little cow munching some hay alongside. The cows here never seemed to have very visible udders, and if they gave milk it must have been on rare occasions. Along about six o'clock a group of Danakil, mostly the crew, picked bossy up and rolled her over the side into the *boute.* This was just a big boat about eight feet in beam and forty feet long. Gudvantrai had come down to see me off and expressed fear I would get seasick in such a tiny vessel. It was made completely of wood with one mast and a long wooden pole at the bottom of which was rolled the one sail. Having no experience in such matters, I wondered how they unfurled the thing. But they had a block and tackle and hoisted the pole to the top of the mast and the sail came down to be made fast at either end by the rope along the bottom. And so we got under weigh and sailed slowly out of the harbor just at dusk.

The voyage was really an experience for me, though there was nothing unusual about it for the natives. I was a sort of honored guest, and they wanted me on the stern, the only place where there was a platform and I could be with them. Here also was a fire of charcoal built in one half of a

...key cart and old auto,
...bouti, East Africa.

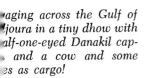

...aging across the Gulf of
...joura in a tiny dhow with
...alf-one-eyed Danakil cap-
... and a cow and some
...es as cargo!

small tin drum; and in a big well-blackened tin can they were making tea. Of course the boute gave more motion at the stern, so when the smoke from the fire became too thick for comfort I was glad for an excuse to sit on a beam just forward. From there I gradually worked forward, past the cow, to a point just ahead of the mast, where my stomach was more comfortable. The cargo of dates, packed in wicker baskets, rested in the same section of the boat as the cow and so was occasionally watered.

I found some clean packs of rushes near the bottom of the boat and lay down, feeling it unnecessary to bother with my sleeping bag. And there I slept the night. The sail was usually directly above me, and every time I awoke I could see it framing the stars in its curves. But the wind that would keep it swelled died during the after part of the night, and though the man at the rudder stick bestirred the sleeping crew to change it once or twice, we were becalmed about 3 A.M. Then, as I lay there looking up at the sail and the stars, I marveled at where I was. An Iowa farm boy on a Danakil dhow in the middle of the Gulf of Tadjoura on the coast of French Somaliland—names which would be entirely unfamiliar to 99 percent of my countrymen. Talk about Haliburton adventure! And the Danakils were supposed to be savage with leanings toward torture.

I awoke in the morning, dizzy as a coot. In keeping with my policy to always eat something, I managed to swallow a cheese sandwich, but that was my limit. Lucky I was raised on a farm, or the activities of the cow might have upset me still more. The sea was calm but rose and fell in gentle swells. I returned to my bed of rushes and slept until the captain called me at nine. A breeze had sprung up, and we were in Obok harbor. I really should not say harbor, because there wasn't any. The dhow stopped about one-eighth mile out in waist-deep water. I know it was waist-deep because a native lad waded out to us with his shirt held above his head. Since the natives of East Africa are careful about exposing their persons, he stood by the boat for about ten minutes embarrassedly attempting to cover himself with one hand.

They took me part way ashore in a small canoe. The oars used were like ping-pong paddles on the ends of small poles. When the canoe grounded, the boatman pushed me a short distance on the mud. I took off shoes and socks and with the help of one of the men packed Jacqueline in about ten inches of water. Once ashore I washed my feet and paid the captain for my passage. This cost me—you'd never guess—twenty-five cents. It was so little that I felt guilty and wondered if there was some catch to it. The only catch was that the captain had suggested *baksheeshi*, so I dug up fifteen cents more for a tip.

Obok, desert outpost, consisted of a government building, a few huts, and a total absence of trees or anything remotely resembling the color of green. What a place! Yet it was the last "civilization" I was to see in some time.

On the way up the bank I met the jovial, genial commandant, M. L'Arangé. He was driving a jeep out to inspect the boat and invited me up to his house. After sipping the usual drink and meeting his wife and two children, I received an invitation to dinner. The radio operator, the only agent of communication with the outside world, joined us for the meal.

I noticed that gazelle meat figured in two of the courses. Though anxious to get started, I stayed for after-dinner coffee (ugh!). Then came a surprise. If I would wait until 2 P.M., the commandant would give me a good start with his American jeep. It developed that this was to be a mutually enjoyable expedition since L'Arangé, his adjutant (the wireless chap), and a Danish friend were avid hunters. This Dane was engaged in constructing a great lighthouse on a nearby promontory, Ras Bir.

We stopped for the Dane at his lighthouse, and after a round of wine (hang the awful-tasting stuff!) we four men set out after a gazelle. This ride in a jeep was a new experience for Jacqueline, who had already ridden in everything from a buggy to an ambulance. The terrain was flat and gravelly with not many bushes, and so we just took off across the country as the fancy suited us. The method was to spot some gazelle and then stop the jeep close enough for a shot. If they ran away, we tried to head them off with the jeep. We missed a couple shots—the Dane and the adjutant had guns—and then we came on to a group of three in terrain suitable for close pursuit. So away we tore through thick and thin, Jacqueline and I hanging on desperately. Two gazelles veered away, but a shot had broken the left foreleg of one and we took after it. It could run as fast on three legs as four. The part below the broken knee flapped painfully, at right angles to its body as it tore along. The speedometer registered thirty miles per hour. Talk about thrills! We dodged thorn bushes, sand dunes, and what not. If we hit a few of these obstacles, what did it matter! When the gazelle made a turn and we tried to follow, I thought sure we would upset. Finally another shot from the Dane, in the animal's rump, tumbled our quarry, and we stopped. The gazelle gained his feet for a rod or two, and the Dane and I took after him on foot. We carried him to the jeep, and L'Arangé cut his throat.

"*Excusez-moi, mais . . . ,*" said the commandant with a shrug of his shoulders, expressive of, "It's the fortunes of life."

We tied our game on the back of the jeep and went on, cruising far and wide over the plain. But though we sighted more gazelles, we could not get near them. Finally we gave up and hunted for the trail which I was to follow off into the desert to the north. It was so ill-defined that we crossed it twice before we recognized it. My companions helped me pack up and then headed back toward the post.

Jacqueline and I looked out across the wastelands of the southeastern Sahara.

22

Prisoner in the Desert

Then I commenced a never-to-be forgotten desert trek. For a while I could ride my bicycle, but the sand deepened and forced me to walk until dark, when I pitched camp. Stars and myself, and a cool breeze from the Arabian Sea.

In the morning I traversed a second Monument Valley. It was most picturesque with odd-shaped hills and mountains rising in the distance. Sunrise and sunset make a monument valley particularly beautiful, and I enjoyed the morning as the strange shapes rose out of the haze.

This was Danakil country. I had been warned about Danakils by British authorities, Italians, and natives in Somalia, Ethiopia, and British Somaliland. They were a wild tribe avoided by white men because of the unspeakable mutilations and other atrocities they were said to perpetrate. They believed in djinns, or bad spirits, which might inhabit anything from a stone to a person—the traveler, for instance. In either case the djinns had to be expelled by violence.

By midforenoon my trail disappeared completely. I knew I was in the vicinity of the well, Ferom Kaato, but could not see the faintest trace of it. There was a scattering of palm trees about but absolutely no grouping to indicate an oasis. I pushed on, still walking. At last I saw a string of camels and headed off across the sand to follow them, feeling that they were probably going to the well. When I caught up, their owner was busy dragging water out of a small hole in the desert—quite unnoticeable until I was about fifty feet away. A man beyond that distance might perish from thirst with no knowledge of the presence of water.

The camel driver poured the water into dirt troughs, and the camels pushed against each other to get it. I saw that if I approached too closely I would frighten them away, so I dragged Jacqueline through the sand to one of the three or four trees in the vicinity and waited. By and by I took my empty canteen to the camel man, who left his watering and advanced to meet me with a smile and a handshake. Instead of going to the well, he took my canteen to where his womenfolk had seated themselves with a few possessions. Here he filled and returned it to me, and after I had drunk the contents he refilled it for the road. By sign language I then asked about the route. The sand had covered it over he indicated, but if I took off in a straight line toward a gap between two peaks on the far horizon, I would be O.K. There were several peaks to be seen, and I realized how desperately important it was that I understand the right passage.

I labored off through the sand. Fortunately the wind was directly behind me, and the sand swept by in clouds. Of all the places to be in the world's deserts, I had chosen one where the monsoon was raging! The monsoon is a continuous periodic wind, usually violent, and in this part of the Sahara and in Arabia, always dry. The northeast monsoon brings the dhows from Arabia to eastern Africa and when the southwest monsoon sets in, it drives them home again. This was April, the month when the monsoon starts changing around toward the southwest.

I had to walk, but there were stretches where the wheels of the bicycle would turn, so I only had to drag it part of the time. To drag Jacqueline I had to place my right arm across in front of the seat, and half bending, lift on the bar running from the seat to the pedals. It was slow work with eighty pounds of pack and bicycle.

How I studied the terrain! Where the barren desert seemed to lead to some place of pale-green herbage, I wondered if it would be wise to approach, since the sand was probably drifted about the clumps. But my route lay beyond, so I had no choice. For an hour or more I steered for a lone thorn bush, then for another hour or more for the gap in the mountains. But the relationship of the latter changed as I approached, and I did not know which side of the valley should be my objective. Eventually my surroundings became extremely wild. I was fairly close to the sea and the ever present gale raised the yellow sand high into the air between the two peaks. To my left were other small peaks. Rather a fearsome place for a lone traveler without a trail. But after a while . . . What was that over there? A line of stones across that rise? Sure enough! It marked the trail.

I managed to follow this for a long time, though sometimes it was very faint—just the track of a jeep—and only occasionally were there rocks for demarcation. I kept on until I found my first tree since Ferom Kaato. I had wanted to rest before, but there had not been a speck of shade nor even a place to lean the bike. Now I stopped for rest, choked down some food and slept for an hour or so with my black bag, flour sack, coat, and raincoat near my head to keep the sand from filling my hair and eyes. Meanwhile I realized how inadequately I was prepared in the matter of food. Instead of having cans of juicy fruit or vegetables in liquid, I had stuff like gazelle meat and cheese to stick in a dry throat. I had water but did not feel I had enough to drink unrestrainedly.

Again the trail disappeared; but in the gravelly washes I could still find a jeep track by scouting. There was no way of knowing whether it had been made on a trip to Eritrea or on a gazelle hunt. It was hard work dragging the bike and pack through the sand. The sun was hot. About four o'clock I spotted a shade tree and saw two Danakil approaching. They came up uttering respectful salaams, and we shook hands. I asked for water to drink, but they had none. However, the older sent the younger off across the desert, telling him to hurry. I had some water but knew I'd have to make dry

Gazelle bagged after a wild run-down chase in the deserts of French Somaliland (Afars and Issas).

Light sandstorm in the southeastern Sahara. (The bicycle bell may be seen at lower right.)

camp that night, and so was grateful when the man returned accompanied by another chap with one of these aluminum water bottles that must originally have been standard equipment for some army. It was covered with burlap and used without a cork. I wondered if the latter fact had anything to do with the coolness.

It amazed me to find how very, very tired I was. It was almost like being sick. I wanted to lie down, and the elder Danakil picked out a better place for me in the shade and occasionally smiled in understanding. I dozed for perhaps twenty minutes and opened my eyes to find they were still there. The elder indicated I should drink some more water and then they would go. He also asked me for a cigarette. After making it plain I did not smoke, I offered him twenty francs in place of it and for the water; but he declined this. They left me with friendly farewells, and I pushed on.

By sundown I came to a deserted hut by the sea. Near this there was supposed to be a well. I failed to find it, so made dry camp farther on. I ate very well—too well, in fact, considering my fatigue, and I realized it not fifteen minutes later. So it was a case of waiting until my supper came up.

I was on the road early the next morning and though weak, stopped in the shade of a sand dune to eat breakfast. Nourishment refused to stay with me. The more I traveled, the weaker I became. The yellow desert stretched away, vast and without end. I commenced to feel a certain desperation and jettisoned things from my pack to lighten its weight. The sun rose. I walked weakly on. The desert was now complete—yellow gravel and sand, nothing more. I thought once or twice of trying to ride, but knew I must cover distance and felt riding Jacqueline might tire me too much. After all, I must get to water, and it was strength for the long pull that counted. But how slow, how slow it was to walk!

Eventually I mounted my bike in desperation. To my surprise I found that I had the strength to ride. The surface of the gravel was often soft, but with a reasonable amount of speed I kept on top. How wonderful to put the kilometers behind. How far back I would be if still walking. But steady now! That last patch of soft sand almost threw me! Would I have strength to remount if I fell off? I uttered a prayer. It was a long time before I descried a small mountain barrier by the sea and a trail leading up to it. Weak as I was, could I possibly push Jacqueline up that? I felt I could hardly walk up myself.

I was on foot again before I reached the base of the barrier. It seemed an eternity. Further doubts assailed me. I had been told there was a post of six *askari* off my trail on the right at a place called Doumeira. "Doomer-a"—the very name was foreboding. Would it not logically be located on this barrier? Yet I had been unable to detect any main trail continuing to the left of the barrier. Where, then, was I?

At least here was a made trail. I started up. Little by little. It was worse

than my experience climbing above 19,000 feet on Mount Kilimanjaro. A
gale blasted and tore at me. At last, what I had thought to be the top; but
with a groan I found the road continued to go higher. I gave up, let
Jacqueline fall against the cliff and staggered feebly on. Would I be
crawling before I reached the top? Another fear entered my mind. Only two
poles were visible at the peak. No building of any sort. Perhaps there was
no post! I scanned the desert and seashore far below me, fearing I would
see a building and have to retrace. There was an empty boat in a little bay
but no hut on the beach between the peak I was on and the next. But what
would be over the top of the hill I was ascending? Why would they ever
construct a good mountain path wide enough for a jeep if it didn't lead
somewhere? Surely there would be shelter at least.

Praise heaven, there was! Just over the top was a low stone building.
Was that the form of a man sleeping on a mat inside? It was, thank God!
I staggered through the doorway and flung myself down in the middle of
a group of sleeping men. The wind, cool and wonderful, came in off the
sea through window and rafters. One of the men took off my shoes and
loosened my suspender belt. A small boy was dispatched to make tea or
coffee. The corporal felt my pulse. As I stretched out a thousand giant
needles pricked into my wrists and the pit of my stomach, where a great
knot seemed to form. Tears of emotion for being suddenly saved squeezed
from the corners of my closed eyes. How wonderful it was! How wonderful!

Soon came two cups of hot coffee heavy with camel's milk. Then sleep
for an hour; and repetition. Meanwhile two men had been sent for the
bike, as the corporal thought I might have better things for nourishment.
The very things I now needed badly for the first time in ten months of
travel—the dried soups, for example—I had thrown away in the desert only
that morning. What irony! But I had saved a tiny can of bouillon cubes.
They took one of these for broth but put it with some gazelle meat and
fish I had in order to make soup. The liquid all cooked into the meat and
I couldn't bring myself to eat it. But in the afternoon I managed to swallow
some rice and drank some camel's milk, sweetened to drown its sour taste.

During the afternoon and the following forenoon, Danakil came and
went. Out of the barren desert they came, sat awhile, and returned unto
the desert. They were courteous, gave the greeting "Sahaa" and shook
hands. A dirty skirt served as apparel. Usually each carried a wad of snuff
or some such under his lower lip or back of his left ear. He spat on the
loose-gravel floor and watched a game of cards in progress among the
askari. Up the hill out of the desert came a lad of perhaps nine with a stiff
leg and a cloth around the knee, and accompanied by his little sister of
about five. They drank water and tea, sat awhile, and went down the hill
into the desert again.

On this forbidding rock, this "Doom-er-a," the six *askari* did not live quite alone. Besides the small boy who cooked, there was the patient burro who for seventeen years had made the trip across the desert to get water. Also there were two cats—a tom and a tabby. They ate rice. How out of place they seemed here on a mountain promontory with the sea three hundred feet below on two sides and the desert on the third, stretching far, far away to the hazy mountains! On the seaward side—the Red Sea, I might add—barren, rocky mountain-islands were close at hand. Nowhere was there vegetation. The wind blew night and day without letup, whistling and howling in fury. You could feel it even inside the stone hut. It tore unceasingly at the flat corrugated-iron roof weighted down by heavy stones. Looking down on the sea, one could see the wild waves the wind created and watch them lashing the great cliffs. Or you could look far out on the desert and see the fury of the wind in the clouds of yellow sand. Never will I forget Doumeira—the tip of a continent, the end of the earth, the gates of hell, the place of my physical salvation; *and* the place of my physical incarceration! For, lo and behold, when I started to leave in the afternoon the *askari* refused to let me go. There was no violence, but Jacqueline was brought inside. I was a prisoner!

My passport had been properly visaed and stamped by the immigration authorities as being good to pass out of the territory. I even had a separate customs clearance. But the corporal couldn't read or write, nor could any of his men. In fact, the corporal could hardly speak French and understood only simple sentences. I couldn't blame him for detaining me. I had stumbled in out of the desert, half dead. Surely only a spy or an international escapee would tackle the desert alone. I suppose he thought he would wait to see if anyone came after me.

It was a hard thing to face, but I decided to accept my fate and be sensible. The men appreciated my effort; it was a tense time for them too. They did not want to restrain me. First, I suggested fishing, but they had only one too-small hook, and the only fish they ever got was brought in by an occasional boat. Then I suggested cards. They had the most worn-out, sorriest deck, thirty-two in number, that I have ever beheld. It was no longer possible to see the numbers, and very difficult to recognize and count the clubs, spades, diamonds, and hearts. It had long been impossible to shuffle them and just barely possible to pick them apart. A half inch of the edge had worn into dust. But anyway, another chap and I passed an hour playing a sort of honeymoon bridge.

I was fed well during my captivity. Plenty of rice and camel's milk. The milk was brought up every few days in unwashed skins of some small animal. I also ate durra, dry-country grain sorghum. The grains were rough and about three-sixteenths inch in diameter, brown in color; but when burst open with soaking, the meat was white. It required a great deal of chewing and tasted not unlike whole wheat cereal. Eaten with milk, it was nourishing, and I liked it. The *askari* ate from a great pan, but they dished me a separate lot in a cheese tin I had emptied. The durra was eaten from 11 to 12 A.M., no breakfast being eaten. About 2 P.M. rice was served and perhaps again just before dark.

Usually everyone except me was on his mat by 6:30. Without a light there was nothing for me to do but pet the tomcat (a new experience for him); or watch the light on Perim Island in the strait of Bab el Mandeb, off the Arabian coast. I sat in the lee of the hut and watched the lonely wonders of desert, sea, and firmament. The desert and the sea showed various moods under the moon because of occasional clouds. I was surprised to notice distant heat lightning.

During my captivity I made the acquaintance of the seashore below the hut. There were odd rock formations where the waves broke, and one very nice well-protected beach. Here I washed clothes and bathed. I chased the little crabs, poked at them in their shells, and had an interesting time. When I was wading, some queer little fish or crab would suddenly emerge from the white sand and scoot like lightning from the shore, burying itself again before I could examine it. On this beach the little boat I had noticed was moored, the captain being forced to await a letup in the weather. I made the acquaintance of some of the eight members of the crew and found them sympathetic when I told of my being held prisoner. They were pleased that I knew a few words of Danakil and made me repeat them. I watched one of the men catch crabs. He reached down into their holes, hauled them out and wrenched off the pincers and legs in a twinkling.

While at Doumeira I had ample opportunity to inspect the physiques and faces of the Danakil. They are of Hamitic stock, like the Tauregs, and are more akin to the Arab than to the Negro. I noticed they were all short, with ridiculously small legs, sometimes slightly bowed. No fat anywhere. The skin was almost a shiny black, in contrast to the gray-black of the *askari*. Features were quite small, with high cheekbones, prominent jawbones, thin lips, and narrow noses. Their faces mirrored their characters, I thought. With some, intelligence stood out at once; others were the faithful plodder type, made to follow. One of these helped me mend my black bag and notebook one afternoon. Some of the Danakil played cards with the *askari*, all acting like any American card players—arguing, joking, and yelling *"Trompe!"* with emphatic motions.

On my fourth day as a prisoner, the corporal surprised me by giving permission to leave at once or wait until the morning. I think he expected me to do the latter, but I stood not on the order of my going. All the men helped me pack. I tore down the mountain and out on the desert floor. Free! Free!

I crossed the line into Eritrea, my forty-eighth country, and stopped at a village named Rahaito to inquire the way. The sultan and three subchiefs had to be called from various houses to meet me. They were all so friendly and kind I felt guilty about pushing on. How welcome I would have been there!

A djinny dance had recently been held in Rahaito to expel the djinns from a pregnant woman who was sick. Although she was seven months pregnant, she participated in this wild dance. It took place in one of the small village huts. The Danakil made a circle around the woman and the village doctor. They clapped and sang in rhythm and the woman and man danced and danced in all sorts of wild movements and contortions. Sweat streamed, but they kept it up for hours. Most of the night this went on. Since she was no better the next day, they repeated the performance for two more nights.

Once again I rode out into the gravel and sand of the desert, now peopled with small bushes fighting it out with the dunes. Night, and what a pleasure to be camping once more on the road! A good supper; a nice bed on the sand; protection from flying sand by my pack and a big sand dune; and my old friends the stars: Orion, the Big Dipper, the North Star, the Southern Cross.

Off at daylight the next morning. The greater part of the road was still cyclable. What wild country! Flat desert—absolute desert again—with little mountains rising therefrom either close at hand or in the distance. These were rocky, with no vegetation, and it was easy to see where the Italians had obtained the boulders for the tracks I was following. Far to my right I occasionally saw the sea beyond the yellow sand. The wind was strong and it looked like a hard day.

I passed into an area of drifted sand and big dunes caught by clumps of bushes or a species of palm. It was very difficult to follow the trail. A native with a small scythe in his hand came up to the road. His expression gave me no clue to his intent. Mindful of all the horrible things that the Danakils were supposed to do with a knife, I greeted him with the Danakil "*Mahisi*" and the Arabic "*Salaam*" and extended my hand. There was no immediate response, and I held my breath. But all was well. He had delayed while marveling at the sight of the bicycle. He showed me the way to go for about an eighth of a mile.

I came into another palm and dune area. Apparently there had once been an old riverbed, but it was so filled with sand dunes and trees it was indistinguishable. This sort of thing had been too much for the Italian road builders, and the road had disappeared. I took a bearing and was lucky to hit the trail again. More dunes and palm clumps. There was no avoiding the dunes, and I had to struggle over them. The monsoon seemed to increase in intensity and there was much sand in the air. Near a palm clump I came across two native beds, although there were no huts in sight. These beds were made of a simple wood framework on which palm strands had been woven. It was nearly noon, and as I looked beyond the protecting clump and into the raging sandstorm I decided I had better rest. I propped myself between the boles of two palms and put my handkerchief over one eye to keep out the sand that even here occasionally drove through. I left the other eye uncovered to watch Jacqueline, since two little boys had appeared and seated themselves opposite. One of them got up and cut me a frond to rest against.

In about five minutes here came two native men lugging one of the two beds. By signs they told me to lie thereon. One brought a blanket and a canvas ground sheet, and we arranged them together. They asked me if I wanted something to eat or drink. By signs I told them I would eat from my pack in about a half-hour. Five natives had gathered by now and were resting on the remaining bed, except one chap who brought me a cone-shaped cup fourteen inches long made from palm strands and filled with as good a drink as any teen-ager ever got at a corner drugstore. It had a little froth on top and a beetle or two floating in it, but it was the most delicious, most refreshing drink I ever tasted. Since I knew I would need a thirst quencher after my meal, I saved part of the drink by sticking the point of the cup through a space in the weave of the bed. They called the drink *douma* and pointed to a nearby tree. The top had been cut off the bole and a cover put across. At one edge hung one of these cups. I learned later that some groups of natives nearly live off this douma, that when it has fermented it is intoxicating and that often whole villages get drunk on it. Taking it from the tree nearly kills the tree, so they have to be careful.

I rested with my eyes toward the bike but did not worry about losing anything. One of the men, perhaps the chief, for he was old, sent the two boys clear away from it, and even cautioned one of the men to come away when he was standing fully five feet from it.

A little later, when I started to eat, another chap offered me two small eggs. I didn't know whether they were raw or cooked. And as to the variety, I supposed it must be some bird, for how could chickens live in the middle of a sandstorm? My Samaritan broke off the ends of the eggs for me, and I sucked the contents. All I could say was, "*Meh eeyohapti*," which in Danakil means, "Thank you very much." By way of reciprocation I offered the men a taste of plum jam. I was low on food and had nothing else to offer. Four of them accepted.

When I pushed out into the sandstorm again, I had a soft spot in my heart for the Danakil. In place of a bloodthirsty savage against whom I had been warned, I had found a friend in need who practiced the golden rule. Did perhaps part of his reputation come from lack of contact? Man usually fears and distrusts that which he does not know. If all men were travelers would there be as many wars? I wondered.

23

In Which We Get Run Out of Town

The afternoon did not turn out as badly as I had expected. The monsoon continued, but the sand became part gravel and I was able to do some riding. Then, through the sand-filled air, I glimpsed one of Mussolini's great highways—the one from Addis Ababa in Ethiopia to Assab in Eritrea. Soon I climbed up on its smooth, black bitumen surface. This part of the world would never forget the Italians, because those highways were made to endure.

The highway changed my direction, but I was just able to ride against the monsoon because it did not quite catch me head on. Ere long I could see the Red Sea—Assab Bay—in the distance. This harbor was the first territory acquired by Italy in Africa. The neighboring district, with an area of 243 square miles, was sold in 1870 by some Danakil chiefs to an Italian steamship company to be used as a coaling station on the way to India. The Italian government took it over in 1880 and soon began to improve the harbor, build roads, and erect a lighthouse.

In less than an hour I was in Assab town. White walls in a blazing sun and a howling gale. Asaam and Massaua, the principle seaports for Mussolini's east African empire, had the reputation of being the two hottest, most inhospitable ports on the face of the globe. Assab was certainly bleak and forlorn-appearing, in spite of its grandiose construction. Building walls often showed large bullet holes. Crushed were Mussolini's dreams of empire.

As I made my way up the blinding street to the British Military Administration headquarters, I looked like a man from another world. There was a layer of sand over my face, arms, and shoulders. Only my red eyes shone through. The resident captain spoke with the pompous accent the movies tell us Britishers are supposed to use, but he was an O.K. guy and extended me a cordial welcome.

I had supper with the only other American in Assab, Mrs. Francis Mahaffy, Orthodox Presbyterian missionary. Her husband had just gone up-country on a trip, with a guide, and a camel to carry the supplies. Rental charges for a camel proved so high they had bought their own for sixty dollars. Mrs. Mahaffy had recently had a minor operation in an Italian hospital in Asmara. The Italians seemed averse to anesthetics, and she had had none. When children had their tonsils removed, they were strapped and held. Antiseptics were rarely used. A towel or baby's nipple dropped on the floor was not sterilized. The diet was also poor, largely rice. In Assab, Mrs. Mahaffy said, the Italian women fed their babies milk for only seven months, then gave them one or two meals of semolina a day until the age of two. Sometimes they also gave bread cooked in oil. Vegetables were given after two years.

We also talked about the expense of shipping goods out from America. The Mahaffys had shipped two boxes of baby food, each a foot square and sixteen inches long and worth about fifteen dollars. Freight to Djibouti, say about 6,000 miles, had been twenty dollars. But the charge from there to Assab, about 150 miles, had been forty dollars. Customs duties were charged on goods plus freight. There were charges for carrying the boxes off the ship to the customs, charges for opening the boxes (even if they weren't opened), charges for carrying them back, etc. In fact, the situation was so bad customs duties were charged in Red Sea ports between cities in the same country. The Mahaffy passage money from New York to Port Said, 5,350 miles, was less than from there to Massaua, about 1,000 miles.

The climate in Assab was not only hot, it was humid. A sheet put on a bed in late afternoon would be wet from humidity before bedtime. Daytime temperature *in* the Mahaffy home was 112 degrees, but one room could be kept down to a mere 96 degrees by hanging a blanket against the sun, mopping the floor heavily and running the ceiling fan. Ceilings were about twenty feet high. The rooms had plenty of cross ventilation with enormous windows off heavily shaded verandas. Later in the season they would have to give up mattresses and sleep on cots by the veranda portals, or even outside the house, with native mats on top of the cots. Prickly heat was hard to prevent and often progressed to pimples and even painful boils.

Late that evening I accepted Captain Campeon's invitation to visit him at the bowling grounds. Since there were just seventeen women in Assab (and only one was single), the Italian men looked to bowls for entertainment. It was played on a court about eight feet by sixty feet, constructed of an earth especially imported for packing. Four men played at a time and from the same end of the court. One, the previous high scorer, threw a ball, about the size of a tennis ball, to the opposite end. Each player (they played partners) took two balls, a little larger than croquet balls, and rolled them to the small ball. The one hitting it, or stopping his ball the closest, won. If a ball stopped directly in front of the small ball, a player might throw high in the air to hit the small ball without touching the ball in front. This was quite a remarkable feat, and it was surprising how often it was successful. The devotees of the game played every night up to midnight or 1 A.M.

There was a ship in Assab. A ship in port in this out-of-the-way place seemed odd. That it was ready to leave was unusual. That it was leaving for Egypt, the only country nearby for which I had a visa, was a downright marvel. It was April 10, the one-year visa expired April 22, and if I was to use it I would have to go on this ship.

The following morning I went down to the harbor to talk to Captain

*is a "fuzzy-wuzzy"
...king on the docks in Port
...n.*

*...e officers of the Arabian
...hter on which I worked
...ge the length of the Red
...(Eritrea to Egypt).*

Beuschen (a Russian) of the S/S *Yousuf Z. Alireza*. He would take me as
a workaway providing the agent was willing. Surprisingly enough, the
agent was quite agreeable. I returned to the captain and clinched the deal.
He was waiting for some more Ethiopian flour before sailing, and as I left,
truckload after truckload was coming in from Addis Ababa. And they were
still stacking flour on the hatches when I came aboard the *Yousuf* the next
morning. To see those little black men—Yemenis from the Arabian peninsula
—struggle up a loading plank with a 220-pound sack of flour on their
shoulders was a wonder to behold.

About 10 A.M. on Sunday we cast off. The wild green waves whipped
up by the monsoon could not have been greener, even if this was supposed
to be the Red Sea. I studied the ships sunk in the harbor during the war.
It was depressing to contemplate their superstructures, the only parts visible.
Underneath the water would be swirling through the holds and cabins.
There would be barnacles, rust, and fish, the great engines idle forever.
Once these ships had sailed the seas, officers and men proud of their re-
sponsibilities. Then had come man and his foolish wars!

The *Yousuf* was an Arabian ship, her home port being Jeddah, the port
for Mecca. Indeed, one of the main items of traffic in season was the pil-
grims to the Mohammedan shrine. She was a trim little craft with accommodations for about thirty people. Her tonnage was 1,061, the smallest I
had been on. She carried 400 tons of flour and was so loaded down in the
water that the sharks played old cat on her Plimsoll mark. When I stood
on the deck, I could almost touch the waves, and they were certainly level
with my porthole.

The crew was a composite of nationalities, but the majority were Saudi
Arabians. Most of them slept on the deck where it was cool. I found a nice
place just under a lifeboat; but if I rolled over too far in my sleep, I would
have dropped into the ocean. Every other man on board bore the name of
Mohamed. If someone called "Mohamed" down the well of the crew's
quarters in the forecastle, at least a dozen men would answer. They were
congenial company, and we played cards and ate well. Water and coffee
were between-meal refreshers, and sometimes lemonade. Most ocean travelers would think it queer to see the cabin boy entering the saloon with four
glasses of good cold water instead of beer or whiskey. The Mohammedans
are an abstemious people.

After a sweet little voyage we dropped anchor at Port Sudan in the
Anglo-Egyptian Sudan. The town was an agreeable surprise for a desert
coast, as I could see a large park with trees and flowers. Working on the
docks were my first real fuzzy-wuzzies. Black, long curly hair formed a
deep crown all over a fuzzy-wuzzy's head. Around his ears and across the
back of his head he had straightened out the long curly strands with dirt,
syrup, or cow dung and so had a straight fringe about six inches long
hanging like a curtain to the base of his neck. To add to the artistry he

had put sticks in his hair. The effect cannot be imagined. From a distance he looked like a woman. For clothes he had a wide strip of khaki, similar to canvas, though lighter in color, draped about his legs and up around his shoulders from the waist, then back again. I could sometimes glimpse a wide leather belt under the cloth.

The *Yousuf* left Port Sudan after bunkering and continued northward. I chipped rust from the deck with a hammer and scraper and thus did a little something as a workaway to pay for all the good food I was consuming. Among other things we had fish, liver, potatoes, greens, rice, macaroni, four different kinds of bread, and chocolate pudding.

At about 1 A.M. on April 20 I was sleeping soundly when awakened by a knock on the door. "Doctor!" We had arrived at Suez, and the quarantine official was already aboard. He demanded my yellow-fever vaccination certificate, and I could just feel Captain Beuschen hold his breath because he had not thought to ask me for this when I came aboard. The immigration officials aboard then cleared me, and there seemed to be no reason why I should not go ashore with the ship's agent.

On shore I had difficulty with an official and a police inspector who wanted first a large, then a smaller sum, of money, but claimed they had no change for my Egyptian note. Past them and scarce daring to breathe for fear of some other obstacle, I lit out. As is usually the case when one wants to get away from the police before they change their minds, I took the wrong direction. A dock hand put me right, but then I found there was another hurdle—the customs. Here a sentry with gun, fez, and greatcoat ordered me inside. A young Nordic-looking clerk took one look at my pack and indicated I could go; but the dark Egyptian aide and the sentry with gun, fez, and greatcoat were skeptical. There must be something wrong with me. Probably they thought me a Jew. I suppose I should have told them I wasn't. Anti-Jewish feeling was running high in Egypt because Palestine was then fighting for independence. At any rate the customs made me show this thing and that from my pack and when they found the camera they were triumphant. The "chief" said it was dutiable. I protested it was old, which was obvious, and an heirloom. He asked me to open it.

"Ah," he said, "it is new inside."

He asked to see my money. Then, though it was 2 A.M., he called up his boss to report my case—got him out of bed, I suppose. I figured there would be just one answer: "Hold him until eight A.M." After a bit of talk in Arabic the chap hung up. I resigned myself. But no, I was free to go. The sentry with the gun was amazed.

In the early morning I left the Suez Canal and pedaled out across the desert to Cairo. At one check post near a German prisoner-of-war camp, I met and chatted with some young Englishmen traveling in civilian attire. After I cleared the post, they offered me a lift to Cairo, and soon I was being taken merrily across the desert in a Ford station wagon, to be let out near a big army camp on the outskirts of Heliopolis, Cairo's principal suburb. Scarcely was I on my way again, when a truck loaded with Egyptian men in uniform passed and stopped. The men piled out and made me stop and began pawing my luggage in rather a vicious manner. A couple of officers got out of the cab to watch. Meanwhile I tried to answer everybody's questions and retain my good humor. I assumed, of course, that they were within their rights. I don't know what the chap fishing among my cans was expecting to find, but he was surely after it. Some got hold of some things, some were examining others, so my attention was divided. They even pointed at my pockets and I showed them some items, still trying to keep good-natured. But when one of them grabbed my watch, snatching it off and breaking the thong, I grabbed it back and gave him a piece of my mind. This stopped the fortune hunt, and they then indicated they would give me a ride. I declined, saying by signs I preferred to walk. They objected. They hoisted bike and all onto the truck. During all these goings on a motorcycle cop was alongside making no protest, and he followed as we entered Heliopolis. I was still in my undershirt, standing up with Jacqueline in the back of the open truck with the soldiers around me. As we arrived the one who had tried to take my watch asked me to show him the time. I indicated by signs that if he wanted the time he could look at the watch on one of the officers.

I wound up with Jacqueline in the private office of the head of the Criminal Investigation Department of the Heliopolis District of Cairo. It was two hours before that chap could clear me. He had to reach the top man of the police, the immigration, and finally a man he referred to respectfully as "the Governor." Meanwhile he filled two pages of paper in Arabic about my case and had me sign one of them. I decided to check over my stuff. A little drawstring pouch I had just made on the *Yousuf*, and of which I was so proud, had disappeared. It contained my knife, a spoon, a can opener salvaged from the Western Australian bush, and a little aluminum salt shaker. I reported this to the chief, who, I should say, had been both apologetic and sympathetic from the start.

"It is very regrettable that this has happened," he said for the second time. I suggested that he send a man with me to buy replacements, and I made it plain I expected them to pay for the stuff. He hesitated but shortly agreed. We succeeded fairly well; the new spoon was lighter weight; knife and can opener were new; and although the shaker was plastic, I even had it filled with salt.

I ate lunch in a nearby office. Everyone was courteous.

"I suppose what you write in your book about Egypt will not be very good," the chief said.

"Well, I'll admit I haven't been so manhandled in any of the fifty countries I have visited," I said, "but you have said you were sorry, and that helps a lot."

He had already asked me if I had had similar trouble before and I cited my good-natured run-in in Nazi Germany—where I had been treated with consideration. With all the reputation Egypt had for thieves among civilians, I had been robbed by soldiers under the very nose of a policeman. The chap said my first captors had probably thought me a Jew or a German. The proximity to Palestine and the Arab feeling on that question was probably back of the incident.

"He who hath not seen Cairo hath not seen the world," runs the saying. "It's soil is gold, its Nile is a wonder, its houses are palaces, and its air is soft, its odors surpassing that of aloes-wood, and cheering the heart, and how can Cairo be otherwise when it is the mother of the world."

Cairo is not ancient, like the pyramids standing nearby. There was nothing but desert and patches of cultivation before the Romans built two fortresses on the site. Then the caliph Omar drove out the Romans in 641 and set up his tent, and later quarters for his army. Since the Arabic word for tent is *"fustât,"* the town which sprang up was called by that name. However, the present Cairo was not actually laid out until 969 A.D, when a second Arab conqueror descended into Egypt. The story goes that he laid out an area a mile square on the desert just to the northeast, marking the edges with poles. A rope was run between the poles and bells were hung thereon so that when the signal was given all the workers could begin digging at the same time. Then the astrologers studied the signs in the heavens to determine the most propitious time. However, a raven alighted on the rope and started the bells to tinkling, so the workmen started to dig. The planet Mars—*Al Kâhir* in Arabic—was just over the horizon, and in spite of the fact the raven was a bad omen, its signal was held to be good and the city was called *Kâhirah* after the planet. From this word, which means "the victorious," the name Cairo was evolved.

In the Cairo I visited there was a multitude of impressions to crowd upon the stranger. One of the first of these was the modernity of the city. There were tall buildings of late architecture, there were wide boulevards, fine residential districts, and an abundance of very late model cars. When I learned these automobiles cost about three times as much as in the United States, I knew that Cairo was also a wealthy modern city.

Cairo was surely the noisiest city in the world. Most of the streets were narrow, and to clear them of people the motorist, the carriage driver, and the cyclist resorted to horn and bell. They did this on even the wide downtown streets, until the whole city was a bedlam. The cyclists had long since given up the simple little bell such as I had for big gongs; and most of them had graduated to two gongs. All this noise had defeated its purpose, for by now people were so used to it that no one paid any attention. There were plenty of collisions too.

During my days in Cairo I pedaled many, many miles about the city, exploring, absorbing, wondering. I saw an odd thing in the way of carts.

Port Sudan—the Mosque.

A load of dark-green hay moves slowly along a Cairo street. But downtown Cairo is one of the busiest and noisiest places in the world.

The wheels were fully eight feet high. Yet the body of the cart resting between these wheels was only two feet wide, three feet long, and two feet deep. Many of the burros pulling carts had our own jingle bells on their necks. Milk peddlers' bicycles had two five-gallon cans suspended from the rear-wheel luggage carrier. I found that Cairo had its dung peddlers as well as its vegetable carts. A constant hazard for the cyclist was the coachman with his whip. There were quite a number of hacks drawn by two horses, and just when the cyclist went to pass, the driver was quite apt to flip the long whip in his face.

Near the eastern edge of Cairo are some of its most interesting sights. Here is the Mosque of Sultan Hasan, covering more than two acres and with one minaret rising 267 feet, the tallest of the city's 250 mosques. When built, the work so pleased the sultan that he ordered the architect's right hand to be cut off so that he could never again design one like it. Just beyond the Hasan Mosque on a hill is the fortress called the Citadel, with outer walls built by Saladin in the time of the Crusades in the twelfth century. Inside the Citadel is the Mosque of Mehemet Ali, the crowning glory of Cairo.

Mehemet Ali was an Albanian who came to Egypt to help the Turks fight Napoleon. When that genius departed, Mehemet played politics with the Turks and a powerful ruling class of soldiers called the Mamelukes. When it suited his purpose, he betrayed the latter in one of the most treacherous massacres in recorded history. On March 1, 1811, he invited them into the Citadel, ostensibly to celebrate the appointment of his son to the command of the army. Entrance was by a narrow road flanked by walls. The wily Ali arranged to have Turkish troops both before and behind the unsuspecting Mamelukes, and as soon as they had ridden through the gate the massacre commenced. The victims were shot down from previously occupied vantage points, and those attempting to escape were slaughtered with the sword. Of 470 Mamelukes only one escaped—by jumping his horse over a wall into the moat. The spot was pointed out to me by a boy guide. It seems that the horse was killed in the fall but the man miraculously escaped.

The mosque built by Mehemet Ali stands on the highest spot within the Citadel and overlooks the entire city of Cairo. It is constructed of gleaming alabaster, and the impressiveness of the dome and lofty minarets as seen from the outside is yet surpassed by the vastness and colorful beauty of the interior. I recalled the mosques of Constantinople I had visited thirteen years before. The Mohammedan world holds its head well in the clouds with the Christian world in the majesty of its structures of worship.

Leaving the Citadel, I visited the tombs of the Mamelukes—a group of small gilt-domed monuments with fanciful networks of arabesque tracery located in a vast cemetery. People lived amongst the tombs and walls, so that often little one-story mud-brick homes alternated with small areas of perhaps fifteen feet square containing four or five tombstones. The latter were like a child's bed, with the old-fashioned rounded tops for head and foot boards.

I made the acquaintance of a young Egyptian who wanted me to go to the cinema with him one evening. I hinted I would rather visit the slum section of the city, so he took me to two of the worst areas. One was the Wesh El Berka. Here the harlots held forth. A few had rooms to themselves, but usually they sat in well-lighted entryways in groups of two to six. There were some perfectly enormous fat ones that would have appealed to no one except a man from the Near East. The women were less bold than those of Panama and seemed content to sit quietly and wait for customers. Often their next-door neighbor would be a patient craftsman working in wood or metal in his small shop, though it was already nine o'clock. When and where these artisans ate and slept, I never found out. The entrances to the narrow, tortuous streets of this red-light district were hard to see from the main thoroughfares and one had to go up inclines or even stairs. There was usually a sign saying, "Out of bounds to military personnel."

One afternoon I visited the Mouski, the bazaar section of the city. It was the most amazing thing of its kind I had ever seen. Shops, shops, shops —tiny ones with six- to fifteen-foot frontage on narrow streets so filled with people it was only by using low gear and the bell that I was able to proceed at all. More often I walked. Blocks and blocks—miles of bazaars. And on every other block a mosque, with shops continuing along its walls. Some of the mosques were old and dilapidated, some of the walls looked like remains of forts built in olden times, and over some doorways Kufic texts had been carved in stone. Tin shops, brass shops, carpet shops, perfume shops, herb shops, all kinds of shops, with the artisans crowded inside. There was barely room for the workers and their stocks, let alone the customers. More often the products were sold at separate shops.

If Cairo is the crossroads of Europe, Asia, and Africa, then the Mouski is the crossroads of Cairo. To the Mouski come the Turk, the Levantine, the Persian, and the Greek; the Arab, the Sudanese, the Berber, and the humble fellah; the Mohammedan, the Jew, the Christian, and the Copt. Mustaches, beards, and soft eyes walk in the Mouski as do skullcaps, fezzes, and turbans, the straight hair and the kinky, and not one but hundreds of Joseph's coat of many colors. People, people, people—color, color, color! No man can adequately describe the Mouski of Cairo; of that I am sure. I felt I could spend weeks in the place. I was not bothered by boys or beggars and in fact saw very few beggars, which was not according to Cairo's reputation. A policeman looked at my passport, a shopkeeper went out of his way to get me a drink of water. At an open place not far away two entertainers had captured a crowd with their antics. One was a strong man, and he was lifting two chaps at once and had everybody laughing. He swung the two round and round until he had them hollering for him to stop. His partner squatted nearby with his face chalked a ghostly white, so apparently he was the clown in the act.

While in Cairo I even saw the king. It was one morning on my way to the Egyptian Museum. I had noted soldiers lining a certain street, and later on wondered why traffic was held up. The king's cavalcade was headed by four motorcycles, followed by four jeeps all painted red and with four men in each. Then came a sedan with the king in the back seat and on my side so that I had no trouble in recognizing him. Then more jeeps, another sedan, and some motorcycles behind. I heard later that he was making a surprise visit to Alexandria. The king's popularity was just so-so, I guessed, because the folks I talked to spoke of his weakness for women.

One day I cycled across the Ismail Bridge and out to see the pyramids of Gîza and the Sphinx. It has been commonly believed that the pyramids were built with slave labor impressed by tyrannical rulers. Most people picture a long line of near-naked men groaning and fainting under a whip while pulling on a rope attached to an enormous stone. But research has now pointed out that the pyramids were probably built by the local peasantry more or less voluntarily and at an actual benefit to them. It is known that the Nile was in flood during three months of the year and since the ancient fellahs were unable to work their land, they could work for the Pharaoh and be fed by him.

Still it staggers credulity to think that the work of building the pyramid of Khufu (Cheops), for example, was accomplished by working only three months out of each year. There are 2,300,000 blocks of stone in this pyramid, and they had to be brought from a quarry across the Nile. The average block weighs two and a half tons and even after it was taken off the boat, it had to be dragged approximately six miles. Then it had to be taken up the not inconsiderable hill to the base of the pyramid, and thence by inclines to heights varying up to 480 feet, the original height of the pyramid. Allowing for twenty years' construction by 100,000 "slaves," it has been figured that the production rate must have been twenty-five blocks per hour or one block in place every two and a half minutes of each working day during all twelve months of the year. That's a lot of blocks, and King Khufu must have started his tomb a long time before he expected death. The Great Pyramid was the first of the Seven Wonders of the World.

I was surprised to learn that the pyramids were constructed by building a small pyramid and gradually enlarging it, instead of first laying out the complete base and then building up from it. Inclined planes on wide setbacks were used to get the huge blocks to the upper levels. Of course, by this method a Pharaoh would always have a nearly complete pyramid no matter when construction was stopped. King Khufu kept on building until he had a base 750 feet square.

As I climbed the Great Pyramid I noticed that about 150 feet up several blocks had been removed from one corner. It seems that the Egyptian government wanted to place a gun there during World War II but was unable to get it up the side of the pyramid. Apparently modern man needs to invent a few more machines for moving heavy objects or else take a lesson from the ancients. It is still a cause for world-wide astonishment that the Egyptians had the mechanical skill to quarry these enormous blocks, raise them to their proper levels, and set them in their proper places; and yet no indication of mechanical contrivances used for the purpose have been handed down to us. And modern man has unfortunately not shown too much respect for the monuments of his forefathers' fellow men. The smooth outer casings of stone on all the pyramids of Gîza have been removed and used, it is said, in the building of Cairo. The nose and beard of the Sphinx have been knocked off by the Arabs and Egyptians, who thought, in their zeal to promote Mohammedanism, that they were destroying a heathen god and that it made a good target for artillery practice.

Actually the Sphinx is a monument built by King Khephren and bearing his features. Built five thousand years ago, it is still the largest single sculptured figure on earth. The body is that of a lion couchant and is carved from a single piece of natural stone except for the forepaws, which are built of blocks. It is 240 feet long and 70 feet high. During the last two-thousand years the Sphinx was covered over by the drifting sands of the Sahara until only the head and shoulders were visible. For hundreds of years it has been regarded with great awe and deep mystery. But now that the excavations have uncovered the body and an adjacent temple, one can see that it was part of Pharaoh's plan. He wanted this Sphinx, which in his time was an emblem of grandeur and power, to stand by the temple opening of a walled causeway leading up the hill from the Nile to his tomb, the second pyramid.

I left Cairo early the next morning and soon found myself out of the city. For ten days I followed the Nile southward and there was always something of interest to see.

There were women with veils over the end of the nose and lower face and with a little gold ornament parallel to, and resting on, the bridge of the nose, suspended from across the forehead by a black cord. Other women wore veils shaped almost like a rectangle hanging from a point below the nose to the middle breast and covered with coins. Still others had vertical marks tattooed on their chins, giving them from a distance the rather disgusting appearance of having beards. These marks were supposed to prevent illness and make them good women. In a typical group of husband, wife, and child, the man wore a tight-fitting cap *(taakay ya)*, blue dress *(galabieh)*, and mustache; the woman, the usual black dress and head covering *(tarhah)*. Astride of father's neck was the small daughter. Sometimes she rode on a shoulder.

There were small boys playing jacks by the wayside, using stones; workers laboriously hand-weeding in the fields; and tiny girls, surely not

climbed the tallest, the great pyramid, and followed the Nile for 3000 miles.

he last word in slow motion—first the camel takes a step, then the cow, later on
e camel—if you watch closely you may see the plow move (Egypt).

more than seven years old, bearing great baskets of heavy wet manure on their heads. These baskets were at least two feet in diameter and loaded to a depth of one and a half feet. The little tykes in their long colored dresses had rested their burdens on the concrete block marking the end of an irrigation culvert. It was about half their height. Yet they somehow got under the baskets again, and staggered, yes, actually staggered down the road. When they got their balance, you could tell by the way they placed their little feet how heavy was the load. I would have thought twice before trying it, I assure you. And as I looked off toward where their next resting place would be, it was literally not in sight.

Sometimes I saw men walking hand in hand or bathing in the canal or canals paralleling the road. Some preserved modesty, some did not. Apparently the women never bathed.

The canal was used for washing clothes and dishes, swimming, and allowing the water buffalo to take his beloved dip. It was often hard for the lads or drivers to get these big animals to come out when once in. Always I saw women picking up fresh manure, liquid or solids, with their bare hands. Or mixing it or kneading it with dirt.

Along the road were burros or camels carrying baskets of dirt, probably to be used in irrigation, and oxen plowing with the crude old wooden plow and barely moving. As often as not one took a step and then waited for the other to take one. I saw one team composed of an ox and a camel and that really did break the speed records! Some native travelers were sound asleep in carts while their patient burros plodded on. Blind trust! A canal on either side, trees at the edges, and passing buses, camels, and people for hazards. These burros wore a placid half-smiling expression, even when switched about the ears, just as though they were the bosses, not their drivers or riders. The latter used no halter or bridle but stopped, started, and steered their mounts with the tap of a small stick. They rode well back on the sharp rump, and it looked deucedly uncomfortable.

The common position for rest of both sexes was the downright squat, but modesty was always carefully preserved. The men wore underdrawers, but usually wrapped their dresses under their upper legs as well. These dresses were protectors of modesty behind when performing the natural functions. Everything was accomplished from up front, and paper was unheard of. A convenient clod might be useful to the fastidious.

I saw threshing done by driving a team of oxen dragging a sort of sled riding on six discs. The grain was then piled up and winnowed by throwing small shovelfuls high into the air from the piles in which it had been placed. With all this going on around me there was never a dull moment.

Towards noon a car picked me up and took me for a visit to a nearby farm operated by Charles B. Feltes, a Christian Egyptian. Feltes had attended the American College at Cairo and spoke English quite well. His farm home was well built and rather pretentious for the squalid Egyptian countryside, but kept up like a bachelor's quarters. There were several well-dressed men about. One of them, the bookkeeper, had a dress made out of the pinstripe suiting then popular in the United States.

Buildings were of the native mud bricks, and so were the native quarters. We entered the home of one of the fellahin, as Charles wanted to show me how they lived. The old peasant, bearded, grizzled, and beturbaned, was seated on the floor eating his meager fare of native bread. He jumped up and kissed Charles' hand, which was hastily jerked away by its owner. He greeted the assistant and myself by taking our wrists and then raising to his lips the back of his own hand in lieu of ours. At the right of the door was a raised area eight by eight feet, two feet above the floor. A small hole on the side of this raised area, about one foot from the floor, and perhaps eighteen by eight inches in height, was an opening for an oven. Here he could bake, and in the wintertime lie on top and keep warm. Just to one side of the oven proper, and also in this raised area, was a rectangular well in which were kept chickens or other small fowl. This little well—about two by four feet—had a small door at floor level. To the left of the area in front of the door, and of the oven and pen, was a doorway leading into a dark room where the fellah kept his burro and his ox. Charles said these two animals were very dear to their owner, so he slept by this doorway in the summertime. According to Charles about 70 percent of the people of Egypt lived in just such a home.

I noticed piles of white stone for construction work. These had been brought from across the Nile by canal and boat. We saw two fine bulls of the zebu type in one of the barns. In these buildings there was an absence of efficiency. Mangers needing fixing, and piles of manure lay here and there. Yet Charles certainly had plenty of laborers.

The most interesting thing to me was the pigeon cote. I had been noticing these white fairy-castle buildings along the way but did not know their purpose. The one on the Feltes farm was about thirteen feet by twenty-five feet by twenty-five feet maximum height. The roof was terraced at heights of from three to five stories, and on top of the third, fourth, and fifth were rounded domes surrounded by small mud chimneys, in turn surmounted by pottery vases. Many holes were visible for ingress and egress. The outside walls were heavily splotched with white to attract the pigeons and guide them safely home in the evenings. I expressed a desire to examine the inside, so Charles sent one of the overseers to get the key for the single small door. It was dark inside, but I could soon distinguish a succession of thick walls reaching to the ceiling. In these no less than fourteen hundred good-sized pottery vases for nesting had been sunk flush with the surface. These were cleaned out every two weeks and the droppings used for fertilizer.

Out on the fields cotton was showing about two to four inches high. The land had been worked by hand into ridges ten inches high and eighteen inches apart, and the plants appeared about eight inches apart near the summit on one side of each ridge. At one o'clock a swarm of workers descended upon us. One of them came up to me and held out his arm horizontally across the front of my body. I did not know what he wanted. He kept saying something and emphasizing it by raising and lowering his arm. Finally he gave me up as a bad job and passed on to the other "big shots." They took his arm in a handshake. So when I saw what to do, I beckoned him back and gave the proper greeting.

Several of the fellahin had large baskets containing chemical fertilizer. The others had small plates, and these they filled with the circular white pebbles of chemical. Then with thumb and fingers—full measurement—they placed some of the chemical at the base of each and every cotton plant. A great job to test the back. The neat weedless ridges were crossed every two rods by small irrigation ditches. In summer they irrigated every ten or fifteen days. When the Nile was low, the government lessened the water allowance for cotton and so a large pump was used to bring it up from the water level fifty feet below. Cotton was planted in February and was ripe in September. The yield might be 1,500 to 2,000 Egyptian pounds (weight) per acre.

I examined the fertile Nile soil. The surface cracks open as does ours, and there are clods. But instead of rounded or roundable edges, the clods have angular corners. The three-cornered heavy hoe was used for ridging or mulching, though apparently little of the latter process was felt necessary. Wages, I learned later, were about seven piastres, or twenty-eight cents, per day, seven days a week. Charles said the wide gap in riches of the Egyptian people (he had a $6,000 car, for example) made the country ripe for communism.

I took my leave of Charles in the field, sitting on a chair which had been brought to him and still holding his cane of authority.

In late afternoon I stopped at the town of Wasta, where there was supposed to be an Evangelical congregation. Before giving me directions, two chaps in European clothes, but wearing fezzes, and who spoke a little English, examined my passport. Civilians in Egypt often took this responsibility, and they, as well as the police, asked my name several times and got the exact pronunciation. I had the feeling that in this way they were attempting to find out if I was a Jew. One of these two chaps showed me the Coptic cross tattooed on his wrist and seemed surprised I did not recognize that it meant he was a Christian.

They sent a young man with me to the shop of the humble shoemaker who headed the church group. He did not know enough English to converse with me but politely offered a seat near to himself and two men busily plying their needles. News of my arrival in the town spread rapidly, and in a very short time a crowd of boys and young men gathered in the street across the opening, perhaps ten feet wide, of the little shop. There was no place for us to get the bike out of sight, and the crowd continued to increase. Not only that but it refused to disperse and started to move into the shop. The poor shoemaker and his assistants worked faster and faster in embarrassment, not even pausing to look up. Tension mounted, and I, totally unprepared and not understanding such a reaction, was slow to recognize it. In the crowd was a young man who spoke a few words of English. He suggested, I think more or less in desperation, that we go to look at the church. I do not believe there was a church, but even I could at last see a move was necessary.

The young man turned me over to a small boy and disappeared. The lad seemed to know only enough English to say several times, "You want me to show you the American church, George?"

I tried to move the bicycle into the crowd, but they pressed so closely I made no progress. By this time I realized it was a mob, for there was yelling and hollering. The young man suddenly returned and suggested by signs that I put the boy up behind on Jacqueline and then "go quickly." After saying this he disappeared again and I felt rather desperately alone. The boy got up on my pack but fell off or was dragged off and this increased the mob's excitement, especially as it caused me to take a partial spill in trying to mount. Now I commenced to be conscious of a badly pocked, dark-bearded man in dirty black clothes who was shouting louder than the others. At first I thought he was an enemy, but suddenly I realized he was trying to help me. He carried a long heavy strap and started to swing it viciously about him, thus clearing just enough space in the mob so that I could mount.

But in the confusion I took the wrong direction and instead of returning whence I came, went the long way out of town right down the main street. The mob howled and swirled around me, and no speed was possible. Through the opening of a small shop I saw a soldier or a policeman, who turned to look but ignored my desperate gesture of appeal for help. I suppose he thought a Jew was being run out of town. Meanwhile it was all I could do to keep from falling over because frequently the dark man with the heavy strap running alongside would grab my handlebar. But his violent swinging of the long strap kept the nearest part of the mob from getting at the bike, and kept those in the rear at bay by hitting the pack with a resounding whack. Eventually his tactics discouraged most of the mob, and they fell behind. It was only then that he showed his teeth in a grin. Shortly afterward he dropped away, motioning me out of town in a hurry. I hurried!

During the whole procedure I had maintained a quiet good-natured grin, and I believed this helped. But I made up my mind never to risk such a happening again at the first sign of unfriendliness. It was fortunate for my peace of mind that I did not know an American was to be killed by Egyptians within a couple of weeks.

24

More Misadventures
With the Egyptian Police

I slept in a field of green hay. The ridges between the tiny irrigation ditches forced me to pad my bed with my coat. I was up and off at 5 A.M.

The road, lined with trees, followed the canal as always, and on the other side of the canal was the railroad.

That night as I was about to retire from the road to a spot I had picked out, two chaps in *galabiehs* came along. The galabieh is a sort of white sheet draped on the body to form a long dress. By signs they indicated that it was very dangerous for me to sleep alone, that they were soldiers and I should come to their place to sleep. It was a little hut five feet high and seven feet square with mud walls and some sugar-cane stalks laid across the top. I was soon sound asleep; but alas, not for long! A vehicle of some sort left two soldiers in uniform, and I was asked to go with them to their superiors. I figured this would be to the last village I had passed through. It was useless to explain that the traffic-control men there had already looked at my visa. Traffic men are stationed at every village. Usually they didn't bother me, being principally concerned with looking at the licenses of the passing cars and buses. But sometimes they called for my passport.

We had a long moonlight walk—or rather I had a ride on Jacqueline; but I had to crawl to keep pace with the soldiers. Arriving at the police post, we awoke the lieutenant, a friendly chap who decided it was a matter for the captain living next door. After some respectful hammering on the captain's door, he put in a pajama-clad appearance on his tiny second-floor veranda. There was talk, and we returned to the post, where I was told the captain would see me in the morning. I raised a howl about starting early and apparently the captain heard it, for he called us back from his veranda. I belabored my school Arabic. Suddenly he said: "Do you speak English?"

"Yes, you bet I do. Yes, indeed," said I with relief.

However, the captain had not had occasion to utter a syllable for six years, so I had to go easy on him. He promised to see me at 5 A.M., and I returned to the barracks satisfied. The lieutenant offered me his bed, but I declined in favor of my own. Before I could roll in, here came the captain fully dressed. He was a rather handsome cleanly shaven chap of about thirty, smiling and curious. He spoke carefully and slowly, thinking out his whole sentence before commencing it. He quizzed me for an hour or so, obviously more interested than inquisitorial, so I was not able to lose patience with him. He looked at every map I had and every stamp in my passport and the pictures of my family. At midnight he signed off but said he would have to make a report on me. I expressed hope that it would not delay me, and he agreed to let me know at six in the morning.

After I had dressed and shaved, I called on him. He was not ready, but I had expected that, so I wrote in my diary. One policeman insisted on getting me tea. The Egyptian takes his tea in a glass and his coffee, which is the more popular drink, in a tiny cup. The coffee is taken black and is very bitter. I can't take it straight, so I dilute it with a lot of milk, let it cool and the grounds settle, and then manage to get some down. Either drink is served boiling hot, and the Egyptians drink it that way. This amazing feat is accomplished by sucking up the fluid to the lips over the edge of the glass. The space between fluid and edge seems to be sufficient to cool it. The first thing the Egyptian does when you come into his presence is to ask if you will take coffee with him. The time of day is unimportant. On this particular occasion I let my tea cool and when the lieutenant had stepped out, gave it to the small boy who served it.

Another policeman asked if I would have something to eat and appeared with two hard-boiled eggs and some bread. The captain showed up at about eight, made out a report and said he would have to take me to his chief at Megagh, quite a ways back along the road. I asked him if he would go in a lorry, and I thought he said yes.

"Well, come on, let's go," I said.

But a few minutes later he changed his mind and said he guessed he would let me go.

"But the men really did you a service bringing you back here," he said. "There are many criminals about at night. Don't try to sleep out alone. People will think—"

"That I am a spy?" I put in.

"Yes, but I believe your papers are in order."

"I know they are."

"But there have been cases of passports being a . . ."

"False—forged," I volunteered.

Then, as I was about to go, he asked: "But your cap, is it not German?"

"No, I bought it in Australia. See, here, the label reads, 'Adelaide.'"

Toward noon I was given a short ride by Abdel Monem, Sanitary Inspector for the northern half of the Mudiriya of Minia. He said that the villages were without sanitary facilities but they kept a careful check on the people, testing water, etc.

On entering Minia we bought several Jews' mallows—the long cucumber-like melons—and in Abdel's office everyone had a section. Having had my lesson with coffee from a burned tongue, I asked for a soft drink when drinks were served. It was lemonade and good. At 1 P.M. we went to Abdel's house, where I was to be a guest until the morrow. There was a very plump young woman visible through a doorway shortly after our arrival, and Abdel said, "That's my wife in there."

That is as close as I ever got to the wife during my stay. If I suddenly entered a room where she was, she left at once. Egyptians treat their wives as greatly inferior. A man never speaks to one in the open and they never speak, unless their menfolk are not around.

Here's the menu for our two-o'clock dinner. All items were in the kind of dishes we use at home for cereal or soup.

1. Egyptian beans (yellowish black when ripe) chopped or ground fine and containing a condiment of onion cooked in butter.
2. Ground parsley and meat made into patties and fried.
3. Native bread, double pancake style, made from wheat flour.
4. A kind of cucumber melon called *aggor*—long and green and resembling the English mallow except in color. It was peeled, cut up into finger-sized pieces, and served with quartered onions in a pink liquid in which there was vinegar and salt.
5. Chopped leaves of the Jews' mallow, dark green in color, in liquid which dripped viscously. It was cooked in broth from pieces of water buffalo, delicious morsels of the meat remaining in it.
6. Sliced *aggor*—slices three-quarter inch thick and 3 inches in diameter.

After dinner I took a nap for an hour or so. Meanwhile at Abdel's suggestion, his servants were busy on my clothes. My underclothes were so stained with sand and sweat that I had been unable to get them white for months. Now my undershirt came back to me so white it was like a miracle. How they did it, I don't know. No detergents or bleach either!

Then we went for a walk around the city. The highlight for me was a shop where a man and a boy were turning sugar-cane stalks through a small rolling machine. I stopped to look, and Abdel bought us each a big glass of cold pure cane juice—delicious.

I had an early start the next morning. The canal I had been following since Cairo now assumed the proportions of a wide river, and large boats with long masts worked their way down with the current and without sails. Cable ferries crossed at intervals. Gray mud-walled villages continued to be frequent and were always built in a thick grove of palms. Streets were narrow and dirty. Houses were made of mud, nearly windowless, with small four-by-five-foot doorways disclosing dusty dirt floors—just an extension of the street. Outside, women squatted in the yellow dirt and children played in it. Fewer trees lined the road than formerly, and so the midday roadside sleepers were more bunched up. Traffic of burros, camels, and people continued. There were occasional buses but rarely a car.

Beyond Asyut the road twisted and turned on a ridge averaging about fifteen or twenty feet above the surrounding area. As always, the poor fellah was at work with his three-cornered hoe, swinging it up and down into the hard earth. If this was too hard, he sometimes turned in the water and worked in the mud. How those chaps work! I have stopped to write or eat lunch opposite hand-operated water lifts, and know definitely that they work without letup for at least an hour to an hour and a half.

These water lifts so necessary for irrigation are called *shadoofs,* and they are one of the oldest contrivances known to man. In a country like Egypt where water is life and all water must be raised from the Nile, it was only natural that the *shadoof* was one of the first inventions. It is like an old-fashioned well sweep with a weight on one end and a bucket on the other. The weight is a big stone, and the bucket is made of hide, shaped like the big end of an egg and fastened on a wooden hoop. *Shadoofs* are usually operated by two men who stand facing each other with their hands on the light pole connecting the bucket with the sweep. So it's pull down, bend over, push up, for the fellah, hour after hour, seven days a week. Not a particularly literary life, though a slightly musical one because each *shadoof* gives off a sort of resonant creak which no slow traveler through Egypt ever forgets.

The fellah has another, more modern invention for raising water which only dates from the days of ancient Rome. It is called the *sakieh* and may be described as an ox-driven water wheel twelve or fifteen feet in diameter. The wheel reaches the level of the Nile or a nearby canal in a deep, narrow trench. Its axle is connected by crude wooden gears to a large horizontal wheel turned by a cow tied to its perimeter. A boy sits on the wheel to prod the cow. The *sakieh* has its own music, but it is not as haunting as that of the *shadoof.*

At the town of Kena I enjoyed the flawless hospitality of Makram Makriky Habashy, oil and cotton merchant. It was not, "Dinner will be ready at nine," but, "When would you like to eat?" I could have said, "Right away," but I was polite and resigned myself to suffer until the late hour Egyptians eat. However, Makram took care of this danger by promptly serving me tea with plenty of cookies and bread.

Meanwhile a servant was put to polishing my shoes and washing my clothes. The educated Egyptian seems to be very conscious of cleanliness, and I was privileged to take a bath oriental style. First they heated a great brass vase of water over a primus. Then I was given a pint cup, a heavy tin basin with vertical sides a little larger than standard size, and another of about three feet in diameter to be used as a tub. I washed my hair in the smaller basin and used the larger for my bath. The handicap was in ladling out all the needed hot and cold water from the tap on the brass vase by means of a pint cup. It takes a lot of water to cover the bottom of a flat three-foot tub.

Mr. Makram put me in his own big room and his own bed, and in the morning sent me off on the road with four eggs, two loaves of bread, and other gifts of food.

That noon I shared lunch with two friendly road workers under the

Another method of Nile Valley irrigation. The cow walks in a circle turning a horizontal wheel, which operates a vertical chain of pots reaching down to water level.

Morning view from my bedroom window in central Egypt. My host gave up his own room for me. Americans have no conception of real hospitality!

Irrigation along the Nile. The huge stone at upper left is on the other end of a long pole from which hang the two small poles and the skin basins. It is daylong, backbreaking, monotonous toil.

palms. These workers lifted water from the canal to lay the dust and hold the dirt scraped into the holes. Thus they kept the dirt road in pretty good condition. For their lunch they had only heavy bread and onions. I gave them cheese, but they politely declined my offer of eggs. They eagerly accepted a share of a melon remaining from a purchase I had made that morning. These two chaps were as friendly and polite as one could ask. They had not intruded on my privacy without a smile and greeting of encouragement on my part. Indeed, most of the Egyptians were friendly, and as soon as I mentioned I was an American, they seemed pleased. On the other hand, the young hotbloods along the road were a bit of a challenge. One jumped up suddenly yelling, "*Ya hood*" (Jew) and made toward me in a vicious manner, while his mate further along struck his stick down on the ground in front of my bike. On a different occasion a young chap ran after me and laid his hand on my handlebar, thus detaining me without actually stopping me. When I looked displeased, he doubled up his free fist. But when I said I was an American, he freed me at once. Especially with the young chaps, therefore, I found it feasible to greet them with a smile and a "*saeeda*" (hello). Their training required them to reply with a fuller greeting, and this took their minds off suspicions until I was well past them. So with all the people on the road I uttered a string of saeedas. With the older chaps it was really a pleasure. Sometimes it was a struggle for them to reply. One old man I remember had a heavy load on his head which required the use of both hands. He had two corners of his skirt drawn up to his mouth and was holding them with his teeth so he could walk more freely. The indecision as to how to return my greeting was plain in his face, and I passed by before he could make up his mind.

I reached Luxor seven days after leaving Cairo. This is about three days faster than by steamer. Luxor is the most interesting site for the appreciation of monuments of Egyptian antiquity. There is more to see here than anywhere else in Egypt. Fortunately I was able to borrow a five-hundred page authoritative book covering the monuments, and armed with this and a detailed map of the area, I spent a day and a half touring the ruins.

It was nearly evening when I pedaled Jacqueline down the long row of ram-headed sphinxes in front of the temples of Karnak. This had been the ancient approach from the Nile, but now the river had moved away. Far inside the temple gates I met two American missionaries out to explore some unknown corners, and I was privileged to go along. Both were many-time visitors, and both knew enough practical Arabic to excuse me from attempting my school Arabic with the guide.

The huge columns of the Hypostyle Hall of the Temple of Ammon were a most impressive sight. I felt like a dwarf in a giant's castle. Now, how on earth did they ever raise those huge stones without differential gears? But the pharaohs had not relied on stones and size alone for glory.

The doorways of the Temple of Amenhotep III were in his time studded with gold and the forecourt was paved with silver. The excavations in progress—we talked with the gray-bearded Frenchman in charge of the work—were disclosing garden and terraces and sunken pools. At sunset we sat by the Sacred Lake, formerly used for washing sacrifices.

Jacqueline was a very important adjunct to my sightseeing. The customary method for tourists to visit the Valley of the Kings is to cross the Nile and take a donkey. The next day I was advised to do the same because it was a "pretty long and rocky road" out to the valley. But Jacqueline only cost me four cents for fare on the small sailboat across the river, whereas it was a dollar to rent a donkey. Not only that but it was only a half hour's easy pedaling through a desert valley to my destination. How thankful I was I did not have to broil in the sun on a slow donkey.

The word *valley* is really misleading, for to us it implies a stream, green grass, and trees, or at least one of these three. But the Egyptian kings had no opportunity to select such comfortable surroundings, and the Valley of the Kings is completely devoid of water, green grass, trees, or anything even remotely suggesting the color of green. Not only that but this valley of tombs is so completely and so closely surrounded by steep high hills that no breeze ever enters. It is actually in the edge of the Western Desert, and the brown gravels reflect the heat of the desert sun in a cloudless sky.

The tombs of King Tut, Rameses VI, and Seti I all unfolded their stories and mysteries to me. Without my borrowed book I would have only the guide's repetitious pointing out of the various gods depicted. But with the text I could understand the significance of the pictures as they showed the phases of the journey to the afterworld. Seti's tomb was especially interesting for the methods he had used in construction to foil subsequent grave despoilers. He was smart but not smart enough. A well, and a blind lead, had failed to protect him.

The Tomb of Tutankhamen is world-famous more for what was found in it than for its appearance or construction. Whereas tombs of the other kings had been despoiled by robbers, that of King Tut was found intact with all its priceless possessions when discovered in 1922. Some of these I had viewed in the Egyptian Museum at Cairo. Among the most important relics are the king's throne richly overlaid with gold; his personal jewels; his statue of black wood with its heavy headdress, arm band, bracelet, and skirt of beaten gold; and the handsome vases of pure alabaster with their exquisitely designed alabaster supports. These vases contained perfumed ointments for the use of the king in the "land of everlastingness." It is said that when the tomb was opened the fragrance could still be detected even though 3,272 years had passed by.

When a king or a noble died, as much effort as his constituents could afford was expended to bury him. A coffin was carved out of wood or stone in the likeness of the deceased so that it was both a statue and a coffin. The body was embalmed by a special process and then wrapped again and again in folds of linen previously soaked in a preservative. This mummy was placed in the statue coffin, and the coffin was then put inside a second coffin, made of stone or wood. This coffin was placed in a tomb, and around it, or in the antechamber, were placed baskets of food, vases of ointment, and whatever else of the deceased's possessions might prove useful to him in the afterworld. Sometimes wooden statues of servants called *ushabtis* ("answerers") were placed just outside the inner tomb so as to wait upon the spirits of the dead.

The walls and ceiling of the tomb room, the antechambers, and the long tunnel leading from the outside were almost always filled with carved and painted figures. These depicted scenes in the lives of the deceased— conferences, battles, the sowing of grain, journeys, hunts. In most of the panels were one or more of the Egyptian gods, carved with the bodies of men but with various heads. Khepre, a sun god, had the head of a scarabaeus, and Horus, another sun god, the head of a falcon. The fine coloring of the figures—the greens, the reddish browns, the ochers, the blacks—were remarkably well preserved for being three thousand years old.

Leaving the Valley of the Kings, Jacqueline and I pedaled around the Nile-fringing hills to the Terrace Temple of Queen Hatshepsowet. Surrounded on three sides by the towering cliffs of Deir-el-Bahri, this temple presents one of the most imposing man-and-nature pictures to be found in the world. The temple was constructed on two levels, the second further back toward the base of the cliffs, and each level was divided by an impressive flight of stone stairs. Queen Hatshepsowet was the stepmother of Thothmes III, perhaps the greatest of the pharaohs of ancient Egypt. She is spoken of as the world's first feminist, "the Queen Elizabeth of Egypt," and a "little minx," so she must have been quite a character. She kept things going at home while Thothmes was off in Asia making it hot for the Syrians and getting gifts from the king of Babylon. To get myrrh and incense for her temple, the queen sent an expedition to Punt, the ancient "Land of the Gods," believed to have been the Somalia coast. Both Punt and Ethiopia sent great quantities of ivory and gold to Egypt in the days of Hatshepsowet and Thothmes III. And how do we know all these things today? Well, they were no fools, those Egyptian rulers of three and four thousand years ago. They knew how easily time effaces the knowledge of names and events, and they insured the permanence of both by building lasting monuments of stone and deeply carving on the walls their records in pictures and picture writing.

But the pharaohs and their queen had other enemies besides time. A subsequent rival was so jealous of Hatshepsowet's fame that he ordered that all carvings of her be obliterated. Fortunately he was not thorough, and the guide unlocked a small alcove to show me two that had been overlooked.

The tombs of Egypt hold great fascination.

Egyptian fellahin at work.

It was high noon and the sun was blazing when I finished visiting the imposing Terrace Temple of Queen Hatshepsowet. The mountains of the Western Desert shut out what breeze there might have been. As I pedaled down the slope to the Tombs of the Nobles, I felt a little proud that the tan on my arms and shoulders could withstand the heat. The poor guides had to leave the scant shade which they had found and come and show me what I wanted to see. I had not planned on seeing the Tombs of the Nobles—had not heard of them in fact—but several in Luxor had recommended them as being more interesting than the tombs of the kings.

On the walls of the Tombs of the Nobles, "men plow, harvest, winnow, broil meat, pound grain in mortars, bake bread, tan leather, carry geese by the wings, build houses, build boats, and do a hundred other things just as they are done in Egypt today." The Tomb of Nakht was especially noteworthy for its brilliant coloring, which has not appreciably dimmed through three millenniums.

I ate lunch in the shade of the great pillars of the Rameseum, the work of Rameses II. Rameses II was apparently the greatest builder of statues of himself that Egypt ever knew. He built gigantic self-images in the ancient Egyptian capital of Memphis, near Cairo. And at the other extremity of Egypt are the four seated mammoths hewn from the solid rock cliffs rising just above the waters of the Nile at Abu-Simbel. Rameses II knew that all travel in Egypt would continue to be along the river for thousands of years, and he saw to it that they could never pass by without seeing his imposing visage. And at the Rameseum he carved the largest statue ever found in Egypt—weighing one thousand tons and with ears three and a half feet long and feet four and a half feet wide. Of polished red granite, the statue has fallen now and is broken in two, but it is none the less impressive. It is immense! This is the statue which inspired Shelley's Ozymandias:

> "My name is Ozymandias, king of kings:
> Look on my works, ye Mighty, and despair!"

One wonders if this man Rameses II was some sort of superegotist to build so many monuments to himself. But he seems to have led a life of merit and to have accomplished many worthwhile things for his people. When only ten years old, he went off to the wars in Syria and having thus become experienced, subdued the tribes of the upper Nile a few years later. After he became pharaoh he distinguished himself further when leading the Egyptians against the Hittites. By personal bravery when leading his own chariots he turned defeat into victory at the battle of Kadesh. Rameses II was also an able administrator, and Egypt prospered under his rule. He repaired and extended the irrigation canals and established the route to Ethiopia by setting up caravan stations. So perhaps he was entitled to his statues and temples.

Rameses II, incidentally, was the king who allowed Moses and the

Israelites to come in when there was famine in Canaan and then kept them in Egypt in spite of all the plagues of blood, frogs, boils, hail, and so on. "But the Lord hardened Pharaoh's heart, and he would not let them go." —Ex. 10:27.

Rameses III must have been a great hunter. The walls of his temple at Medinet Abu show him overcoming mountain goats and wild asses and wild bulls. And he must have had a weakness for the women, too, judging from the harem scene on the inside wall of a room in one of the towers.

In completing my day's tour I returned to the Nile by the Colossi of Memnon. These are two great seated statues no less than sixty-five feet high sitting lonesomely and oddly in the middle of a cultivated plain. I was amazed to learn from my guidebook that these statues of Amenhotep III and Tiyi, his queen, were all that remained of perhaps the most glorious Egyptian temple ever built. As I thought of the great temple of Luxor and the tremendous Hypostyle Hall with its towering columns at Karnak, I could not believe that here had been a structure even greater. What had happened? Why, there was not even a floor under the statues—only the green rock-strewn plain.

Late in the afternoon I recrossed the Nile on a sailboat so filled with Egyptians that I had to balance Jacqueline precariously on the prow and dodge the pole when the chaps changed the position of the sail.

En route to the post office back in Luxor an Egyptian policeman stopped me. A few questions and he let me go on. I forgot the incident, but shortly afterward I saw him back of the window at the post office, earnestly talking to the clerk. He did not want him to mail my parcel of films and my two letters until he had heard from the police. The clerk apparently had no respect for the police and listened with but half an ear. Nevertheless, I had to go with the policeman to the station, he leading the way through the streets on his motorcycle.

Those rascals kept me two hours. The policeman maintained that I had a wireless set. Where he got that idea I do not know unless from the front brake rod. The bike had only my waterbag on the handlebars—no other luggage to arouse his suspicions. The young head of the criminal investigation department and others kept coming in and out and occasionally asked me this question and that. Meanwhile, knowing they must have their fling, I filled in the time writing in my diary. They were quite nonplused to find I had been in Luxor one and a half days without their knowing. But I made one mistake in dealing with them. I let them know I wanted to get away by 6:30 to prepare for a 7 P.M. dinner invitation with my American friends. So they kept me on and on, once or twice saying I could go and then changing their minds. One man, more educated than the rest, saw through this and suggested I see the chief of police. I was amazed that I had not thought of this myself. The chief dismissed me after only a few words. Yet they stopped me again as I mounted the bike; the criminal investigation had not made its report. I complained to the chief of police, and he roared at them; but it was 7:10 before I could get away. Later the crazy policeman had the nerve to call my host from the dinner table and tell him I had a wireless set. Egypt was certainly a country where the government tried to be modern but the police force operated back in the fourteenth century, when travelers were supposed to register in each town and be police-controlled. I met several fine men on the Egyptian police, force, but others were biased and conceited. The criminal investigation head in Luxor told me that the Egyptian police force was the best in the world. He was surprised that I had not heard that before coming to Egypt. When I left, I told him an efficient force would have accomplished in fifteen minutes what they had taken two hours to do. I dared not say more because I had not yet left the town.

The next day was to be Easter in Egypt, and the Coptic Christians were commemorating the event that evening. I was surprised to learn that Christianity had preceded Mohammedanism in Egypt. But when the Saracens took over the land in the seventh century, the Mohammedan religion was established, and practically all of the fellahin are nominally of that belief. I say nominally because I never saw any of them praying, and it was said the real religion of the people was one of amulets, and of superstition that had been handed down for thousands of years. However, the artisans— tailors, jewelers, and the like—held to the Christian religion and were known as Copts. They numbered about one million, or one-sixteenth of the total population. They followed most Christian practices, such as taking only one wife. The Copts were the direct descendants of the ancient Egyptians, and the majority had kept the blood pure, with practically no infiltration from the Romans, Arabs, or Turks.

My host suggested I attend the Coptic service for a short time that evening. So about 10:30 I went over to their church. No need for a guide, as you could hear the singing from a long way off. There were incense and ritualistic proceedings similar to those in a Catholic church. The priest looked very similar to the pictures one sees of Greek Orthodox priests. The altar was visible through a doorway, and he marched about it occasionally, followed by a couple of boys. One of these held a portable microphone for him to chant into. The language was ancient Copt, spoken by the pharaohs but not understood by present-day Egyptians. The main floor of the large church was filled with standing men, but the women were up in the balcony. I found a place near the front but off in a corner. An usher spotted me and put me in the choir stalls on the front row, just in front of the congregation, and only about eight feet from the steps leading up to the altar doorway. Now, I had neither coat, fez, nor mustache; I felt more than conspicuous in my new position, and my embarrassment was heightened by the fact that there were only small boys about me. But I ignored the congregation, assumed a nonchalant air and eventually enjoyed the service. The little boys, and small girls too, looked so tired—as if they wanted to be home in bed. Yet when it came their turn to shout their a-a-a-a-a-a's in varying crescendos, they pitched in and made the whole city hear them. I was told later they really enjoy it and go on until one or two o'clock in the morning. On this final night, about 1 A.M., they closed doors, then brought in a picture of Christ, signifying his rising. Considering the strenuous service, I was not surprised there was no sign of life at the church the following morning.

However, the United Presbyterian Church had an Easter service, and I stayed to attend. Thus it was I attended two Easter Protestant services— one in Djibouti, French Somaliland, on March 28, conducted in Malagasy; the other in Luxor, Egypt, on May 2, conducted in Arabic. The observance of Easter was the practice of the Christian Church from a very early period, but a controversy soon arose between Jews and Gentiles as to the proper time. It was left to Alexandria, home of astronomical science, to calculate and set a universal time for the entire world. This was fixed on the first Sunday after the full moon following the vernal equinox.

In the Presbyterian church in Luxor there was a screen to separate the men and women. I could join in the service by humming the tunes, but my Arabic was not good enough to understand the sermon. One thing I noticed which we might copy in America: the collection plate was passed twice— the first time for coins only, the second time for paper.

Once more Jacqueline and I set out on the high road to adventure. For the first twenty-five miles we passed through more "cultivation," as the farming area along the Nile was termed in my route guides.

Burros and camels alike shied at Jacqueline. Sometimes a burro shied so quickly that the sacks of flour on his back or the driver himself was thrown off. The camels were liable to go clear off the road, and the drivers would dash madly after them. For that matter, little girls were often frightened and went screaming off, if alone. Little boys, on the other hand, spied me and came running from far off to chase or to look.

Often the faces of the babies and little tots were nearly covered with flies. Occasionally I saw mothers dispensing nourishment while on the march. Sometimes I passed camel drivers singing rather loudly with a finger deep in each ear. This seemed logical to me, a foreigner, but I had been at a loss for the native reason until Makram explained he thought it was because of a belief that too much noise was not good for the ears.

The first day out of Luxor I stopped to push Jacqueline across the ridged dry "cultivation" to where some farmers clad in short blue dresses were threshing on the bank of the Nile. I asked for *moya* (water), and a little maiden dressed in the usual feminine black brought me a red earthenware bowl full of cold water. Others asked me to sit down and rest awhile. One brought a blanket and another a small loaf of *aish* (bread). This was coarse, and I could still see the awns in it. It reminded me of bread I had eaten among the Russian peasants, only that was almost black. Either kind is more filling and keeps moist and edible longer than the white kind bought in either country. The chap who brought the blanket playfully wanted to trade hats with me, and I had to grab mine back. This taught me I could be overfriendly with the peasants, since they were really children and by their pranks might inconvenience or delay me.

About 3:30 P.M. I turned across the railroad out into the Arabian Desert. The crossing watchman gave me a loaf of bread as a parting gift. The desert was gravelly and thus gave a good surface to the old military road that had been marked out by some kind of scraper. There was utterly no vegetation, but I kept the cultivation in sight for a time. At dusk I pulled off amongst some great piles of rocks that had been excavated from several caves or tunnels leading into the side of a hill. I camped in the narrow, canyonlike entrance to one of these, trying to figure out if it was the work of archeologists or miners. The tunnel was full of bats, and as I ate and made my bed thousands of them wheeled and turned close above my head, occasionally brushing me or each other. It was not exactly a place of repose for the squeamish. However as soon as it was dark enough the bats got their bearings and flew away.

The next morning I found two big jugs of cold water by the wayside. Who maintained these for the thirsty traveler, I do not know, but it was a treat. From here I turned more directly into the desert and penetrated ranges of small mountains. No sign of plants, bird, or beast, or man either, and it seemed as though I was traveling through the deserts described in the *Arabian Nights*.

It was terrifically hot at 1:30 P.M., when I turned against the wind a quarter, I soon became very tired. Not a living thing was in sight, even when I passed from one heat-blasted valley to another.

Desolate and rugged mountains surrounded me. Not even a vulture soared through the dull blue-gray of a monotonous cloudless sky. In the wildest imaginings of the wildest dream there would have been no more dramatic natural setting for a lone traveler. And here was the real Egypt—not the Egypt of a mere four thousand years of man's known struggles along the Nile, but the Egypt of a million years ago, grimly desolate, grimly unchanged through eons of time. Here also was the forgotten Egypt —the Egypt beyond the Nile—the 90 percent of the country little known and little visited because of its desolation.

Though very tired I journeyed on and on through this fantastic landscape until I got a distant view of the cultivation. Even then it was a long, hard struggle against the wind before I reached the turnoff leading to it. Then I debated. I did not know how far it would be to the next cultivation, and although I had water, I had learned how much more efficacious was a good drink of cold water compared with a ton of warm water. Furthermore, my experience in crossing the desert near Doumeira was still in my memory. So I fought the wind head on for at least three miles to get to the edge of my cultivation. By then I really was all in—though not in such an exhausted state as at Doumeira. The natives drank the water from the irrigation ditch, and I was in no mood to be choosy. While I rested flat on my back, an old camel man ministered to me. Noticing a couple cows nearby, I indicated by signs that I would like to buy some milk. The old chap went and milked one of them. He did not get much milk, but it was fresh and surely tasted good.

Back on the main road once more, I crossed a range and found myself alongside the cultivation. How I bemoaned my useless expenditure of effort for that side trip to reach it! Later I camped in the sand amongst the wild rocks of the desert.

During the following forenoon I returned to the edge of cultivation and an irrigation canal. A donkey rider came along, and seeing I wanted water and had no place to lean the bike, hastily dismounted, hobbled his mount with a piece of rope and made two trips with my canteen and bottle across the ditch to a place suitable for filling. That is kindness for you. Still further along at another ditch I decided to get water again, knowing not when the road would reenter the desert nor for how long. This time a man indicated by signs that I should not fill from where I stood. He took off his undergarment, stepped into the ditch, waded to the middle with the water up to his thighs and took my bottle to fill from deep down in the stream. As a Mohammedan explained to me later, they believe if they do a good deed, someone else may later do something for them. But these natives did not appear to be selfish.

By 10:30 it looked as though I was really leaving the cultivation, so I stopped a a cane enclosure for more water. Seeing no one outside, I entered the enclosure, noticing two more enclosures beyond. In the third I saw a little girl seated on the ground by what seemed to be a well. She started shouting at me and was soon joined by an older woman. Who can say how old or how young? The two became very vociferous and ignored my request for water. They picked up things to throw, so I beat a retreat. As I did so a kindly-looking older man came from a hut not far from the woman and the girl. But his gesture of restraint toward them had no effect. It was lucky I kept watching them as I left because the woman threw a heavy jug which struck me on the leg; and as I reached the road she threw a good-sized rock which would have struck me on the head if I hadn't ducked.

A half mile farther on near an empty mud hut and at the edge of a village was a big water jug. I recalled seeing such a jug in other villages, so now I commenced to appreciate its purpose. There must be no excuse for a strange man to enter an enclosure where there are Mohammedan women.

I now turned out into the desert, hot as hades. About 1 p.m. I saw a tongue of palms stretching to within a half mile of the road. I decided discretion was the better part of valor and walked and rode over to the shade. I slept an hour, then ate and slept another hour. The shade was fair, but the breeze was negligible. I had to make several moves to keep in the shade. This waterless oasis surrounded by untold miles of blazing yellow sand was like something you see only in the movies.

When I reached Aswan, I was the guest of two Evangelical ministers to whom I had been referred by my host in Luxor. Reverend Mr. Faheem took me to visit his school. He had about forty boys and fifty girls. In one girls' class the teacher had them sing a song for me; and in a boys' class one showed his ability to read English. Mr. Faheem said that in the government schools English had been cut out of the primary department. Therefore students from mission schools such as his own were in a stronger position when transferring to higher courses, such as engineering, where the textbook would be in English.

The government schools were free and provided free meals. This put the Protestant schools at a great disadvantage, since they had to charge. Some of the children were Nubians, whose great-grandparents had been Christians until the religion had been stamped out. Now again Christianity was being discouraged in Egypt. I recalled American missionaries further down the Nile who had spoken of their unstable positions and the strong nationalistic spirit following the British departure from Palestine.

Out into the desert again, and to Shellal, where the steamer for Wadi Halfa in the Anglo-Egyptian Sudan awaited me. Shellal was the end of the road, except for especially equipped expeditions requiring a guide to negotiate three hundred waterless miles.

I had made the acquaintance of Taha Hasson Salih, the Sudan Railway agent, and he had ironed out my boarding and customs operations. The steamer *Britain* was like our Mississippi River stern-wheelers but had two large double-decked barges lashed on opposite sides. One was for mail, the other for third-class passengers and freight. The freight was carried on the lower deck on this barge, while a struggling mass of humanity occupied the upper deck. Salih arranged for me to take all my stuff and live below with the freight in solitary grandeur with plenty of privacy. He also made arrangements for me to have plenty of ice water en route and access to first- and second-class decks on the steamer.

So at last I was on a steamer making the famous trip up the Nile. We saw the Aswan Dam and the top of the submerged Temple of Isis on the island of Philae. I was surprised to see so many villages with their tiny one-story mud structures perched on the cliffs just above the water. Everything was devoid of life around them, so perhaps the dam had backed up water to cover their cultivated areas. Palms appeared at the edge of the river, but after thirty hours of travel their roots were still under water. I commenced to believe the water was backed up clear to Wadi Halfa.

Sometimes we went close to the palms, sometimes close to the cliffs. There were no lights along the shore, and since it was rather a dark night, I surely hoped the captain knew his river. Having just read *Life on the Mississippi* while on the *Yousuf*, I appreciated the voyage the more. But the wonders of the great rock temple of Abu Simbil, which we visited the next day, quite eclipsed anything to be seen on our own great river.

25

In Which I Hitchhike on a Camel

Sometime on the second night we reached Wadi Halfa, frontier post of Anglo-Egyptian Sudan. Here was a country of one million square miles, nearly one-third the size of the United States. It was a country eight hundred miles broad and twelve hundred miles long, which could present a contrast of flat barren desert and fertile semiforested hills, with a vast area of great plains lying between; a country which, like Egypt, was split by the Nile and whose economy was intimately connected with it; and a country with boundaries encompassing a thousand and one polyglot tribes of men of varying shades of black in addition to Arabs, Egyptians, and Englishmen.

We went ashore at 7 A.M., and I ran kerplunk into one of those narrow-minded English officials who have no imagination and don't try to have any. He could not or would not understand why I had obtained my visa at Port Sudan if I had not used it to enter the country there. I had anticipated just such an obstacle when I got the visa but had been unable to get the issuing official to understand why he should endorse it to show nonentry. And now this chap!

"How are you going to Khartoum? What class?" he bellowed.

"Why . . . uh . . . fourth class—or third if necessary." (I added the latter in alarm.)

"Then you can't go."

He said I would have to wait three days for the next train while he wired Khartoum. Of course, the visa was authorized by Khartoum in the first place. He doubted the visa of his own government.

"I've been on this job twenty-eight years," he roared. "If I'm wrong, I'll pay your hotel bill."

Humph! Of course, he was making a big show in front of a roomful of other people trying to enter the country. Unfortunately I was to find similar-acting English officials in the Sudan. But it was not until months later that I heard from British officials in other colonies that those in the Sudan had the reputation of being "highhanded and highbrow." And what a contrast it was to be with the fine treatment I later received from Portuguese and French colonial officials.

I asked my vociferous friend to whom I could appeal. He said the district commissioner. Then he took my passport and money and shoved a shore pass at me.

It was Friday and a holiday, and I had slim hopes of seeing the D.C.

But luck was with me, for the assistant district commissioner was just arriving at the port. He was a Sudanese, and I was to find that nearly all seconds in command in the Sudan were natives. He was entirely sympathetic and went at once to see the captain, or whatever he was, who was denying me entry. But that worthy raised such a stew that even the poor assistant D.C. was half convinced I should not be allowed in. But he finally prevailed. However, they took my passport for forwarding to Khartoum. The assistant himself saw it sealed and stamped and took it away. An English-speaking friend later told me he saw him get it registered and said it would go on the same train I did.

The next hurdle was to get them to sell me a fourth-class ticket. Salih had said the company had recently issued a ruling that Europeans could travel fourth class—"even the prime minister," he had added with a laugh. But Salih's light-complexioned assistant had disputed him. The officials in Wadi Halfa were also light in complexion, and the chief of the railway station was an Englishman. None of them wanted me to go fourth class; the prestige of the white man must be maintained, you see. I did not really sense this until after I had succeeded in getting a fourth-class ticket. It was ninety-two piastres (about $3.70), and third class would have been at least sixty more.

My fourth-class ride to Khartoum was really an experience. It's lucky I got my seat early, because I have never been so packed in. There were white galabiehs (the draped-sheet dress), white turbans, and dark faces. I was glad the faces were getting darker, for to me this betokened a second approach to the region of the cheerful, innocent, friendly black of central Africa. Seats were crowded, and people sat on the backs of them. The passageway was piled with baggage higher than the windows, that is to say, to a depth of four feet, and people sat on that. Baggage was stowed under the seats and between the seats to a level higher than the seats. There were woven baskets, both the ordinary kind and the cane kind, as in our clothes baskets. There were heavy, locked, tin boxes belonging to soldiers and large animal skins packed with possessions of natives; also huge fringed carpetbags in purple, yellow, red, and black. There were even four or five fuzzy-wuzzies in my car with spears in great carved leather cases pointed with carved silver. To go from one end of the car to another was to thread a maze of boxes, carpets, bare feet, sandals, blankets, and arms with phylacteries fastened by leather bands. A phylactery is a small square leathern box containing paper slips of Scripture, worn on the arm or forehead by Jews during prayer.

The trip was through the desert for the first 230 miles. The train stopped at lonely stations twenty-five miles apart. At some of these there were vendors of *chai* (tea), and many a hot glass passed through the windows.

Our speed was only about twenty miles an hour, but the antics of the people made the trip immensely interesting. Someone was eating every fifteen to thirty minutes, and as often as not food would be shoved in my direction. This was mostly native bread and white salty cheese. Sometimes there were Arabian pickles—carrots and turnips soaked in brine; or beans, apparently prepared in the same manner. With the beans, one had to press off the cover like a grape or suffer a bitter taste. An Egyptian traveler had some cookies. It was really a problem to dive into packs and come up with all these eatables. And when someone wanted a drink, it was more feasible to pass a tin can from the corner jug over a bunch of heads than to make a trip oneself. Naturally someone might drink the water en route so that the can would arrive empty.

Occasionally there were heated arguments and the participants stood up in various parts of the car to shout their views. I expected blows a couple of times, but there was always a peacemaker or two about. I noticed Arabs have a habit of cracking their knuckles when upset. I ate at the time appointed to Americans, sewed my overalls (a perpetual job), or socks (another perpetual job), or wrote in my diary.

After passing a station or two in the evening, the population thinned out just enough for the Egyptian and myself to half stretch out and sleep. I slept solidly for nearly eight hours. During the following forenoon we paralleled the Nile but with no letup in the sand, though there was some sparse vegetation. Sand blew in through the windows and added its quota to the dirt of nutshells, split bean hulls, and whatnot on the floor. But I managed to get some water in a soup dish, wash up, and shave.

Near Khartoum small boys did a thriving business selling tooth sticks through the train windows. These are small green sticks about one foot long and ten to a bundle. The end of one, when frayed a little, is rubbed over the teeth as a toothbrush. So the last few miles into Khartoum found everyone busy polishing his teeth.

On the day I arrived in the capital of the Sudan, the official temperature was 113 degrees in the shade.

The next morning, Sunday, I went to the passport office, worried for fear my precious passport had not come through safely. I hung around for three hours, half of the time in the office of the chief immigration official, writing letters home and inwardly chewing my nails. From long experience I am never without something to write when at a government office. The government's mail was supposed to be delivered at 10 A.M., and here it was eleven. Indeed, the post office had informed me that it would be delivered at 6:30 P.M. the preceding day. The chief himself became worried and set out to track it down. At last it came; but there was more red tape. They had to satisfy themselves that I was not writing articles—for then I should have to see the publicity director. Then they found I traveled by bike and said it was prohibited to travel by bicycle.

"Why didn't you tell us this?" I was asked.

But of course they had been told when I got the visa. Now I asked if I could appeal. Yes, to the civil secretary's secretary. This was my first Englishman. He said it simply was not allowed to travel by bicycle. Could I appeal from him? Well, I could see the commissioner of police.

First I saw the assistant to the commissioner; then the commissioner himself. I told all these officials that if they had not unnecessarily grabbed my passport at Wadi Halfa, I could have gone on by train the same night I arrived in Khartoum, made the fortnightly boat connection at Kosti (a point further up the Nile) and thus made them happy. I told them I just did not want to be held up; also that southern Sudan roads were better than a lot I had been over, and I touched on my experiences in deserts far worse than they had south of Khartoum. The commissioner finally said I could cycle as far as Kosti but from there I must use other means of transportation. Before I left, the immigration chief made me write out and sign a statement to that effect. This was really done under duress, for after all, I wanted to leave the country. But he did not rely upon my statement anyway because he said I had to check with the district commissioner at Kosti. Even until the end I had to override the chief's request to come back the next day for my passport. I finally secured it after six hours—at their 2 p.m. closing.

In Khartoum I was the guest of a young Sudanese whose great-grandfather had been the architect for all of the city's principal buildings. This indicates the Khartoum of today is not an old city; and therein lies a story which concerns some of the monuments and also the neighboring native city of Omdurman. I visited these places by bicycle with a friend.

Khartoum was established as early as 1823 under the wily Mehemet Ali. Its position at the great junction of the White and Blue Niles brought the city rapid expansion. While Egypt was under British control in the 1880s, the famous uprising under Mohammed Ahmed (the Mahdi) took place in the Sudan, and General Gordon was sent to Khartoum to evacuate the Egyptians. The Mahdists killed Gordon and razed the city, abandoning it for Omdurman across the White Nile. The British were in no position to take their revenge until 1898, when Lord Kitchener was sent up the Nile. He captured Omdurman and rebuilt Khartoum as the capital, drawing up the plan of the city himself. A fine esplanade fronts the Blue Nile, here straight as a canal, and behind it are the governor-general's palace and other public buildings of yellow stone and red brick surrounded by gardens and small groves of trees. Back of this section, which also includes the famous bronze statue of Gordon seated on a camel, is the main commercial district of the city laid out in blocks to represent the British flag.

Jacqueline and I slipped out of Khartoum bright and early one morning. The road tended to follow the railroad at first but soon veered away. It was just a track, occasionally through heavy sand, and the temperature was very high. By noon it was well above 110 degrees in the shade, but shade was scarcer than hens' teeth. In the afternoon I received a long ride in a truck.

The next day I continued southward along the Blue Nile—invisible off to my left. Far from any town I saw huge warehouses and bales of cotton and decided to stop in and see some of the industrial side of the country. Although there were Greek and Armenian supervisors, the only resident who spoke English was the inspector. He got into his little English-built Ford and personally showed me around the plant of Maringan Ginneries, Barakat, Blue Nile Province.

Barakat is a key name in the history of the British experience in the Sudan. Although they accomplished the defeat of the Mahdists in the name of Egypt and set up the Sudan as an Anglo-Egyptian condominium, the British found that the leaderless and considerably impoverished country had become their responsibility. In order to get some sort of profit from the land, a pumping station was installed at Barakat on the Blue Nile. With this, irrigation for cotton was begun on the Gezira, the term applied to the great triangle of land between the two Niles with Khartoum at the apex. By the close of World War I, a demand for more cotton and more income required the British to build a dam costing 7 million pounds. It was to protect this investment until return could be realized that kept them on in the Sudan either governing alone (1924-36) or with the Egyptians. Meanwhile history shows that they dealt fairly with the natives in the matter of the Gezira land.

At the Maringan Ginneries I saw four factories, each with a capacity of 270 425-pound sacks of cotton per day and 670 310-pound bags of seed. In ginning the cotton they used 1,200 handmade leather rollers per year. Strips of the best bullneck leather one inch wide were laid on edge, corkscrew fashion, around wooden rollers about four feet long and eight inches in diameter. The strips were glued together with the best English cascade glue. They were used until worn down to one-sixteenth-inch width. The purpose of the rollers was to draw the lint (i.e., cotton) underneath the top ginning knife. Static electricity was a big problem, and a key held an inch from a machine might make its cotton suddenly go up in smoke.

The cotton was baled, after a double wetting, by a huge press with two and a half tons pressure. All cotton went to Manchester. The seed was collected and sent through a rotating drum affair for sifting. Lint was taken from seed by another machine and used for cotton stuffing. Even the dirt and waste were cleaned and sold for such things as stuffing for donkey saddles. The seed was stacked for shipping and wound up as oil cake or fertilizer. I saw workers loading railway cars by carrying the 310-pound bags of seed—a piecework job paying twenty-five to thirty piastres ($1) per day. The factory proper was on a daily wage scale.

I saw seed to be used as seed, in the process of treatment. It was treated with mercuric oxide against the boll weevil, in a revolving drum heated by steam to a temperature of 65 degrees centigrade. After twenty-four hours' cooling it was stored until planting—August 15 to 20.

The plant was a vast one, and we drove about for several miles. There were houses for five thousand workers, located and sized to be in keeping with the job of the occupant. There were hundreds of family homes. Each one was round and the size of an overgrown silo. Brick walls to about the height of five feet were surmounted by a round, high, thatched roof. A whole city of witches' huts. The bachelors' quarters, however, were rectangular and resembled the bomb shelters in England from which their parts had been obtained. There was a jail to accommodate the many drunks, the inspector said. They made and drank their own brew. This was surprising to me and indicated a diminution of Mohammedan influence. There was a football ground and a place for an open-air cinema, which usually showed educational pictures.

After leaving here I traveled alongside a great canal. In the shade near some large irrigation gates, a very giant of a jug filled with cold water was standing. It mattered not that the water came from the canal and was not clear. The day was extremely hot, and the water tasted plenty good. Incidentally I stowed away prodigies of water these days. It was a marvel! But it kept my body temperature down.

The road followed the canal, but the dredgings formed an intervening parallel wall a good twenty-five feet high. I camped near the base of this that night. Early the next morning I reached Sennar, bought some bread and tomatoes and turned west to cross from the Blue to the White Nile. I followed the railroad across the plain, and I don't think either one of us made a curve in the entire seventy-two miles. The first water at station Jebel Moya I reached about midforenoon. With temperatures of 115 degrees in the shade and around 150 degrees in the sun, it is dangerous to be out after 11:30. But I felt I could not waste a couple hours' traveling time just because I probably would not arrive at the next shade by 11:30. So after a couple of drinks of *moya* (water) I pressed on to Jebel Doud, the next station. The road was good, but the temperature higher and higher and, believe me, I was glad to see the yellow-cement "witches' hat" of Jebel Doud sticking up beyond the shimmering mirage ahead. It was a good five miles away even then, and not a few qualms crossed my mind en route. What was it my first-aid book said about heat prostration and sunstroke? Is it sudden? Suppose I should have a flat tire?

The nice old stationmaster went away while I rested on one of the two beds in the station house and returned, after what seemed like ages to thirsty me, with a cool yellow drink. It held a lot of coarse brownish sugar in the bottom, and so I was not surprised after drinking some to see him dilute the remainder with cold water from a cup and bowl he had brought. I stayed in the station until 3 P.M. and found quite a few interesting and friendly folk. The quiet, modest, stationmaster had once studied English but remembered only a few words. One thing he did remember, however, was the child's poem entitled "Pretty Cow." This he recited to me in a low, pleasant voice without hesitation, and it was very charming. The last verse is as follows:

> Where the purple violet grows,
> Where the bubbling water flows,
> Where the grass is fresh and fine,
> Pretty cow, go there and dine.

I cycled on from 3 P.M. until 5 P.M., when along came a couple of Italian lorry drivers, and so I had a lift into Rebek and a fine dinner of macaroni and chicken. The truck boy was a Habasha from Ethiopia and prepared the two chickens *"poule Habasha,"* he said; but the Sudanese boy on the other lorry said it was also *"poule Sudanese."* I watched the process. The bird was plucked dry and singed thoroughly in the flame of the fire. Then one of the drivers held it. First the Habasha cut off the tip of the tail and the wing tips. The wings were cut off at the first joint and put into the pot, followed by the legs cut off at the body. The crop was extracted next and the fowl filleted. The middle wing sections were then grabbed and pulled off with great slices of meat following. More filleting. The canal was detached at the throat; the wishbone or breast was pulled down, thus splitting the body. While the assistant held the neck and the rest of the fowl, the waste portions were detached. The gizzard was put aside. A small kidney-shaped organ was cut in two for examination and placed in the pot. The fatty abdominal parts were cut off. The ribs were broken to each side, the lungs picked loose and out with the point of a bowie knife (the assistant still holding the neck) and the ribs picked out and discarded individually. The assistant grabbed the back, and the native cut the flesh away from the base of the neck and put it into the pot. The neck was then cut into three sections. The native next chopped with his knife down either side of the backbone and followed through. The wing stubs, no flesh remaining, were torn off and thrown away. Now only the wishbone remained with much flesh attached, and this was chopped in two as it was held point down. The leg and thigh were taken from the pot and separated. The final step was to clean the gizzard. The edible parts of the chicken were then washed three times and cooked with two huge onions, well diced.

Of course, while this operation was going on and chicken was cooking, I was starving. I would have been far happier to eat bread and "tin" at 6 P.M. than macaroni and chicken at 9 P.M.

There were several great "crab spiders" around the camp that evening. They dashed here and there very quickly, and both natives and the American were jumping all over the place trying to avoid them. They are not dangerous but are very unpleasant. One of the drivers killed one with a stick, and we examined the still-kicking corpse. It looked almost like a giant crab. It is called in Arabic *abu shenab*, according to the district commissioner for the region, but the camp-fire folk called it *karaba*.

Friday morning, the fifteenth, I pedaled through the sand, across the

White Nile, and over to Kosti on the west bank, and quite a way in on the road to El Obeid. This was to satisfy the police commissioner and chief immigration officer at Khartoum, who had told me to check with the D.C. at Kosti. Also to fulfill that crazy agreement they forced me to sign in Khartoum about using transportation other than the bicycle. I called on the Sudan Railways agent and inquired of merchants in the village but found there was no transportation south for two weeks. So far as I could see, that let me out of my agreement.

Nevertheless, I checked with the district commissioner as instructed. He had received a telegram concerning me from Khartoum but declined to hold me up. I thought the situation required a couple hours of political talk on my part, but I like to feel that he had the common sense to let me go on without any talking. But then it was too late to travel until afternoon, and the D.C. invited me for lunch. By the time I recrossed the river and pedaled back to Rebek in the sand, it was 5 P.M. I had lost a whole day trying to live up to the edicts of the Sudanese government.

The trail the next day was quite good and went through bush country not different in general appearance from some of the territory in north-western Australia. Toward noon I arrived at Gebelin, a rather large village on the banks of the Nile. Here I ate, shaved, and rested at the post office, and later at the dispensary on the invitation of the man in charge. When I left, there being no bread in the market, he supplied me with the thin Sudanese bread which is folded until each bunch looks like the leaves of a book. A better approximation is a large-size flat jelly roll. He sent his servant and a small boy a long way from the town, and on foot, to be sure I found the right road.

I spent the night under a friendly tree and a nice moon. There was hardly a breath of air, but a good breeze sprang up before morning. This breeze developed into a dry wind which blew against me as I traveled. In addition there was quite a lot of sand on the track, so by nine o'clock I was pretty much all in. While resting with a *Reader's Digest* in the shade of a bush, here came two camels with their riders. The camels shied off into the bushes, but I hollered to the riders, asking how many "kilos" to Geiger, the next town. The kilo is some sort of mythical measure of distance, the length of which I never learned; but since no one ever designed an odometer for a camel, no two people have the same idea of distance and there are no signposts, probably because the English officials do not want independent travel.

The two camel riders made their mounts kneel and let them off, and then led them over toward me. I indicated by signs that the wind was bad for cycling and I was tired, so how far was it to Geiger? They suggested that we put Jacqueline on one of the camels and all proceed to Geiger together. I could not believe this at first. Hitchhiking on a camel! What an idea! So I declined. But then the experience and novelty of the thing struck me and when they repeated the offer I assented. They made no fuss about forcing their camels to kneel and tying Jacqueline lengthwise on the pack of one. I tried to take a picture of the process under the handicap of obscuring branches. They tied my pack on the other camel, and the rider arranged his seat so that I might ride in place of him. I mounted, hanging onto the pommel, you bet, not knowing whether my new steed got up front first or rear first. When he was up, his owner handed me a sort of rawhide whip. The two men picked up their long spears, took their lead ropes in hand, and we were off.

This was my first camel ride. Only that morning I had been wondering how I would manage this part of my experience. I knew it would not do to go home without having ridden on a camel, and here was the answer to my wish.

We moved along at a camel's pace. Yes, that's right. I did not find it hard to get used to the rocking of my camel's gait, though Ahmed (my camel's leader) asked me by signs how I liked it. Both Ahmed and Mohamed did their best to read my wishes and please me. My camel was the hungry kind, and if a bit of dry straw or delectable green sprig of a thorn tree tempted, and if Ahmed was adjusting the other pack, my mount and I wandered off into the brush. At such times I held my breath, for I knew naught of camels' habits. He might kneel or suddenly decide to take a roll, for all I knew. Even on the march he would suddenly break stride to kick at a fly. Besides, I had slapped him a few times with my whip, and he occasionally looked around to give me a baleful glare.

While riding along, I often watched the great front foot pads of Mohamed's camel. After he set a foot down, the cushion above the sole would spread out beyond its edges as he applied full weight. How admirably adapted for his customary terrain!

At 11 A.M. we made for some shade not far from the road and not far from a small pond. We unpacked, unsaddled, and hobbled the camels to graze. Mohamed sewed, and I followed suit. Ahmed went through the motions of assembling a fire and looked questioningly at me. I thought he was offering me tea, so I said no. I had forgotten the incident until some time later when he returned from quite an absence and I noticed him rolling a stick upon a flat place cut on another, trying to start a fire. In embarrassment I said, "I'm sorry" and got him a match. He had probably gone a good way after wood hard enough to suit his purpose. I had to light the match for him, as he did not seem familiar with its use. Soon there was tea, and I shared, of course. They had only one glass and insisted I take it first. I set it aside for cooling, until I noticed them strangely silent. Then I insisted that they drink first, knowing they took their tea as hot as possible. This they did.

One of the camels tried to take a roll in the bog, even though hobbled. Mohamed ran down much excited and succeeded in driving him out. Incidentally we took our water from a muddy ditch dug near the open water, and since it was a thirsty time of day for me, I was not surprised that my stomach was upset later.

I ate at the usual time, offering my friends portions of beans and cheese. They politely declined, but when they ate about 2:30 I took a little of their main dish. Meanwhile they had each eaten a couple of raw onions without bread, to stay them over. Their main meal consisted of flour and a little water cooked in a five-gallon can cut down to a height of about six inches. Plenty of fresh milk, brought by a passing herdsman, was added to this. We dipped our fingers into the piping hot mixture, mixed the milk on top in with the gruel, and brought it to our mouths. I nearly burned my fingers. I was also given a big cupful of milk to drink, and it was much appreciated.

These people seemed to have no conception of countries and had never heard of America. So far as I could make out, they did not even know they lived in Africa. And when I say "these people," I mean not only the camel drivers, because a half dozen herdsmen visited our camp.

There was much politeness in these visits. Each greeting lasted a full two minutes, with the two parties talking alternately at high speed. When I arose for my greeting, the thing soon fizzed out because I could say nothing but "*Zayak?*" ("How are you?").

Although my friends said they would be in Geiger by nightfall, I doubt if they made it because it took me one and a half hours by bicycle and they had not left our camp by 3:30 P.M. Geiger was quite a little village and when I stopped for water and to buy bread at the leading "sidewalk cafe," I was very warmly received. I got not only the water and lots of bread but a big dish of okra with fine chunks of fowl in it. It was only 5 P.M., but I did ample justice to this early supper. Tea followed. They wanted me to spend the night with them, but I declined. These sidewalk cafes are a far cry from those in Paris or even in Khartoum. The walk is of dirt and the cover of thatching is supported only by bare poles. But I think the important difference is in the friendly interest in the stranger and the hospitable good will with which he is received. There was no thought of pay, and, as usual, I was waited on hand and foot. I did not have to carry my canteens and follow the boy after water. I was made to sit down at once, and a boy (in some cases the proprietor himself) took care of it. In such cafes I was always given a special stool or chair to sit on when I stopped, even before I introduced myself. And if I wanted to buy bread, I was made to sit still even though someone had to go all over town to get me some.

As I pedaled out of town I stopped to snap a picture of a couple of black dandies of the Dinka tribe. They wore coarse, gray, knee-length dresses draped over one shoulder, and crude sandals. Both had high chokers of white beads and two-inch headbands made in a design of white

Jacqueline and I hitchhike on a couple of camels in the Sudan. It was a welcome relief from sand and a stiff headwind.

Dinka dandies of the middle Nile are very allergic to work.

and colored beads. One had a string of large white triangular shells reaching from choker to belly. Both carried walking sticks with long points covered tightly with cowhide to which were attached oval flaps of the same material. Later on I found one of these sticks and sent the point home as a souvenir.

The Dinkas were the first of three Nilotic tribes to come to my attention. Like their relatives, the Shilluks and the Nuers, the Dinka men were extremely allergic to work in any form, although they would hunt and fish and herd cattle. The two Dinkas I overtook were indulging in a favorite pastime—dressing up in their best bib and tucker and going to town. The American woman does the same thing, only she expects to buy something, and usually does, whereas the Dinka had no interest whatsoever in acquiring products of civilized manufacture.

26

We Continue Unpopular With the British in the Sudan

I had been instructed by the district commissioner at Kosti to check with an assistant district commissioner at Renk. I found that he was absent, but his assistant, the *mamoor*, I unearthed by calling at his home. He was a Sudanese and friendly, and practically admitted, when I caught him off guard, that I could cycle to Malakal. But he felt bound to observe the letter of the telegram received from Kosti, a copy of which went to Khartoum. This said I could go only as far as Renk. I argued unavailingly. The mamoor was sure a lorry would be through by "tomorrow evening at the latest," and he promised to compel the driver to take me. I had my doubts, but what was I to do!

I washed clothes, and got acquainted around town. There was an Armenian trader there who treated me to coffee and gave me a giant can of apricots. This was a real present—worth around a dollar or more. We talked to each other in French.

That evening I joined the *mamoor*, the postmaster, the Armenian, and others at the town "club." This was in the open, outside the clubhouse, which was adjacent to the resthouse to which I had been assigned. These houses each consisted of two round silos with witches'-hat roofs, connected by a wide thatched and screened passageway. Entrance was obtained through another screened passageway at right angles to this one and required opening two screen doors. Floors were of concrete, but there was not a stick of furniture in the resthouse.

I passed the morning hours chatting with a native merchant and a lot of loungers. I munched peanuts—a tremendous quantity (at least a quart) having been purchased from another merchant for about two cents. My host treated me to a plateful of dates.

Dinkas with tin bracelets from elbows to wrists dropped by. These bracelets were never taken off even though the wrist might swell up from restriction of the circulation. They were worn by both sexes to indicate the wearer was of marriageable age. They had other adornments—bead rings in their ears, white shell dickeys, neck rings bearing strings of beads, arm rings, and spears. Some of the young men mixed cow dung and ashes and got a sort of crownlike section of their hair done up so that it looked like a white cap. To emphasize this they had encircled the crown with a chain of beads. Perhaps they might have a feather stuck in their hair.

I made note of the ornaments on the right forearm of one chap. Just above the elbow was a band of lightweight rope, then one of white beads, then two bands of white beads with black and red beads inserted in two places, then five more bands slightly different. Halfway up his forearm were two more bands of beads, and at the top, two more. On his wrist were two bands of wire about twice as heavy as No. 3, and a carved copper wire, and another bronze wire. It seemed to be the custom to also decorate the fingers of at least one hand. One chap had orange beads on his thumb, then another band of orange beads on his forefinger, followed by a wire with a four-inch extension shaped into two circles about an inch in diameter. The rest of his fingers were similarly decorated. Another chap had used old inner tubes to cut three-inch ornaments for each finger. These were split like a clothespin and had serrated edges. Wire circles or hooks suspended above the fingers held the end of a bullet, a short wooden dowel, and a small seed or core of a nut dyed red.

You may gather from all this that the Dinka men did not work. They sat, idled, and lounged generally, although looking after cattle was permissible as not being work. Some Dinkas wore a dirty cloth over one shoulder, falling fore and aft nearly to the knee. With no fastening, or very little, the attire was anything but modest. But most of them went around without a stitch on anyway. They would then frequently have just three ornaments: a chain of beads around the waist, a small earring of beads through a perforation in the top of the ear, and another through the bottom. The man dressed in numerous ornaments would usually have a spear or walking stick about three and a half feet long with an eight-inch cowhide tip. About halfway along on this tip were attached two pieces of cowhide in the shape of a slightly oblong circle. These were for ornamentation and were especially nice when the stick was used in dancing.

When I was aguing the *mamoor* into giving me prisoner's rations during my detention, the assistant district commissioner himself, Mr. Dulcer, an Englishman, suddenly returned after a few days' absence. Although only an assistant, he seemed to be in charge of the area, which I later found was part of Upper Nile Province. He was rather unprepossessing in appearance, slightly stooped, wore a several days' growth of beard, and never looked one directly in the eye. I started very respectfully to introduce myself but was interrupted: "Never mind. I know all about you. And I haven't time to talk to you now."

But he added a few other remarks. One was of the effect that I would have to go back to Kosti. Finally he said I could cycle on as far as Banjang.

"There are American missionaries there. You can stay with them."

"But I don't want to impose on them," I objected. I could not see what right he had to sponge me off on someone who did not know me without even asking them.

"You can have Faulkner [the American at Banjang] take you to Melut," he said. "Tell him I'll provide the petrol."

I heard the mamoor gasp and gathered that gas was a scarce article.

"I owe him that," explained Dulcer.

"But I would not want to ask Mr. Faulkner to take me," I protested.

However, I need not have worried, because Dulcer later informed him that he wouldn't provide the gas.

Meanwhile Dulcer took another tack.

"The first truck going through to Malakal, I'll have them pick you up. But you must wait there."

I pointed out that it might be several days before a truck came along. But that made no difference to Dulcer. Finally I said: "Well, if I wait at Banjang, you will require the first truck through to stop and take me. Is that it?"

Dulcer assented. So that was that.

While this palaver was in progress, the English soil-conservation chap for the province dropped in. I had just said something about being anxious to get on so I could complete my trip and get home to my family.

"Oh, you Americans are always in a hurry. It doesn't mean a thing," he interjected.

All in all, I gathered that Americans were not very popular in the Sudan.

Both the assistant D.C. and the mamoor were probably relieved to get rid of the importunate American. The mamoor sent his boy over to the resthouse with bread and a plate of scrambled eggs. It was then nearly 11 A.M. and the south wind was blowing fiercely. Thus both the heat of the day and the wind were against my departure, and the postmaster stood aghast when I indicated I would leave forthwith. But he did up a package of mail for me to take to the Americans at Banjang.

By midafternoon the heat had put me in need of a rest in shade and a drink of cold water. A chance for both was offered by a native village, baking in the sun. There were only women and children in the place. The Dinka's word for water is not *moya* but *pew*, so I suppose it was largely my gestures that brought a pint cup of water. This was not too cool, but a second try at another home a little later brought a big pint bowl full of quite cool water. I drank some more after twenty minutes and again just before I left. A little girl went clear across the village for it, so I gave her some peanuts. I also gave some to a tiny girl just past walking age. She was too shy at first to walk the eight feet over to where I was, but the older women seated in the group sent an older girl with her. The women, even the young girls, wore skirts. Their heads and eyebrows were shaved clean.

The country continued flat with alternate stretches of open, tall brown grasslands, and thorn tree and bush country. I arrived at Banjang about dark and was welcomed by the Americans Mr. and Mrs. Faulkner (Ruth and Glenn) and Miss Rosemary Chafey. Ruth was from Ponca City, Oklahome, Glenn from Salina, Kansas, and Rosemary from Sunnyside, Washington. Rosemary was the station nurse. Ruth was pretty much under the weather with pneumonia, and the heat made her lot unenviable. I too, was on the uncertain side with a light dysentery and flatulence. I was more troubled with the latter, and did not know whether it was amoebic dysentery—the general thing in these parts—or just an upset due to too much bad water. I carried a specific for the former—Entero Vioform—and decided to take it. If it was dysentery, that was the remedy, plus proper diet. And how good of the Lord to plant me where I could get the latter: good soups, hot cereals, eggs, milk, butter, etc.!

To my experiences I now added two days of life on an African mission. It was located among some of the most primitive tribes I saw on my whole trip.

The first evening turned to things religious—quite naturally, I suppose. Like very many people I had always assumed that when someone asked you, "Are you saved?" it meant they had been through some kind of very high religious experience, sudden and compelling. I learned that the questioner asked only if one personally accepted the fact that Christ died for one's sins, so that each sinner, acknowledging Christ and his own sins, realized he had been saved.

Breakfast at 7:15 was followed by devotions in the parlor. Afterward Glenn sounded a big bar of iron, and we went to the dispensary hut for worship with the Dinkas. In number these varied daily from one to twenty. There were about six present, including a subchief and a girl whose nose had been eaten away by syphilis. There were songs and a talk by Glenn, all in the Dinka language. Glenn was the most proficient in the language among those missionaries in a large area who had taken a recent examination. Then Rosemary changed her dress for a nurse's uniform and held clinic. Medicines were dispensed at cost. Natives were not allowed to take medicine away, unless it was very little, because they sold it to the witch doctors. They also had the idea that two treatments for any disease were quite sufficient. A baby suffering from dysentery was brought by its parents to one station. After two visits they refused to come again even though they had to wait for a week in a neighboring market for a lorry to take them home. When they left, the nurse could see that the baby was dying but there was nothing she could do.

A very high percentage of the natives had venereal disease, as evidenced by the noseless girl then getting better under treatment. Glenn spoke of the general promiscuity among the peoples of the region. A Shilluk woman, as soon as her firstborn arrives, must confess the name of any man with whom she has had relations. The villain is then fined one cow, which must be paid over to the husband. If there have been a lot of men in milady's life, she throws a handful of sand into the air and her mother is taken to task for neglecting her daughter's upbringing.

In the clinic on this particular morning was one chap with a bad tooth. There was no dentist, so the only thing the missionary could do was to pull it. This does not bother the native Dinka, for he tears out all his lower teeth anyway. Since the cow and other animals are nearly sacred, the Dinka does not eat meat, so teeth aren't much good. He usually pries them out with a spear or a large fishhook, tearing out pieces of gum, bones, etc., in the process. Hence it was a luxury to come to the station where Glenn pulled teeth with a good pair of forceps.

After the clinic I worked with Glenn on a combined kitchen and pantry building. The native labor was of the Nuer tribe—all stark naked and not a one under six feet. All of the three principal river tribes—Shilluks, Dinkas, and Nuers—took great care to stay far away from anything even remotely resembling work, but of the three the Nuers were the laziest. They did not even bury their dead. So I was much surprised to see that my fellow workers were Nuers. They walked about in a listless manner and made very halfhearted attempts to do anything, but one chap plastering the walls with mud, sand, and gum arabic was a good worker. Bricks were made in the vicinity. Cement was used for floors, and the final outside coating for mud-bound bricks. The roof framework was constructed of small trees bound together by pieces of rope, or twisted wire in crucial places. Bunches of long withes were tied horizontally at intervals around the roof. Finally it would be thatched. I wired in separate short rafters to extend over the edge of the building for eaves. This also would be thatched. All wood was hard —the window frames were mahogany, for example—so that the white ants would have tough going. A sheet of tin had been placed in the wall also.

There were many posts around the enclosure containing this and the main residence of the mission. These posts had been only partially set, and one of my jobs was to cut them off to proper lengths. Fortunately Glenn had a good saw for the hard wood.

Houseboys were often of the Shilluk tribe. They were identified by a string of raised places in the skin around the forehead just above the shaved eyebrows. These raised places were made by opening the flesh and pulling it out a ways, then treating it with mud or something so that it could not return to its bed. The process might be repeated. The features of the Shilluk, I noticed, were more like those of the Arab than of the Negro.

The Shilluks are unique among African tribes in having a history, or at least a sort of legendary hero whose fame has been handed down through the generations. He was called Nyakang and was the founder and first king of the Shilluks. He did not die like ordinary tribesmen but disappeared in a big thunderstorm, so today there are ten cenotaphs to his memory. Some of his divine spirit was inherited by subsequent kings, and according to tradition, whoever could kill a king and thereby take his place acquired the spirit. In later times the king was killed ceremonially with his own consent at the first sign of old age so that the spirit could carry on undiminished. A strong continuing spirit was very important because it was responsible for ensuring the good health and reproduction of both man and cattle and for prevailing upon the god of rain to water the crops.

Pens and watches failed to perform properly in the hot and sometimes humid Sudan climate. The expensive kind did not pay. Since electricity was unavailable, most iceboxes were of the kerosene variety. Some were not too efficient, and the Faulkners saved their ice cubes for afternoon tea. The cold-water problem was a big one for them. The river water was hauled by donkey cart and placed in three huge earthenware jugs, each about five feet high and with diameters of fifteen inches to two feet. Water dripping out the bottoms was thus filtered, caught in tin boilers, then boiled, and the boiling water poured into four small earthenware jugs for cooling and drinking. Our consumption was so great, however, that we could never allow it to get properly cool.

Dinner was served at 12:15. As I came in dressed in overalls and washed up, it seemed as though once more I was home on the farm in Iowa. We had potatoes for dinner, a treat for the mission folk, as it was the first in four months or more. They could get substitutes such as spaghetti and rice, and used dried peas and dried beans. Supplies were ordered for a whole year on account of the rainy season. When potatoes were in season in Egypt, it was possible to buy them for a little more than ten cents a pound. But three-fourths of the year, it was spaghetti and rice.

From 1 to 3 P.M. everyone rested, with the sun and wind deflected by judicious use of shutters. At about 3:15 we consumed two pitchers of iced tea with cookies.

In the afternoon Glenn and I went to the market and down to the river for sand for the cement. It was Ruth's birthday the next day, and we were both on the lookout for presents but had no luck. There was just nothing you could buy in these out-of-the-way places. Of course eggs were plentiful. Every time we stopped, there came girls and women with a few eggs. Glenn always bought—partly for reasons of diplomacy, I thought. I bought a dozen myself for the mission larder, but the outlay was only about six cents. As we drove about, plenty of local color rode along. Naked men were all over the car, carrying spears too. Glenn bought wood for building and was always good-natured in his bargaining. He was a fairly tall chap, but many of the natives were much taller, a height of seven feet being not uncommon. I felt small alongside. The Dinkas had a habit of standing on one leg, placing the foot of the other just above the knee.

We had supper at 6:30—soup, eggs, cake, leftover creamed chicken, etc. Visiting in the parlor, and to bed about 9 P.M. Such is life on an African mission.

On the afternoon of the second day, we learned a truck had gone

through for Melut without stopping for me. This showed that Dulcer had
not lived up to his part of the agreement with me. I therefore resolved to
leave by bike the next morning. But that evening we found that the local
wheat merchant was going to pick up some wheat near Galhak, the next
place south, and would give me a lift that far. This suited me because if
I rode in a truck I was apparently within the law. The trader consented
to wait while we made a hasty two-mile return to Glenn's for bike and pack.
It was a hasty departure, and a fast moonlight ride. Game—cow size—fled
across the road, and the trader blazed away with his gun.

When I was landed at Galhak, the trader saw that I had a bed and
helped me with my luggage. When I came up from the truck, I was not
sure whether or not the poor camel driver lying on the ground had been the
original occupant of the bed. Anyhow, I lacked the language to apologize.
A scratchy rash on my skin, plus mosquitoes, made my night an unhappy
one. The camel drivers left with their camels, which had rested only a few
feet from my bed, at 3:30 A.M. I was reminded of the mamoor's statement
when I asked him if there was an objection to my going on by camel. He
had said I would see no more camels because they could not exist south
of the 11th parallel.

I was on the road at 5 A.M. This was the day I was to negotiate the
driest and worst stretch of the road to Malakal, the threat of which had
been used as a deterrent by the office at Renk. Apart from the stiff head
wind, and an unusually rough road, I had no trouble. The longest stretch
between villages was only twenty-five miles. I met a truck about 11 A.M.
and was given the treat of plenty of cool water. I had a quart and a
half left of my own, but it was warm as usual. The Egyptian driver offered
me a ride to Malakal the next day when he returned from Renk. We made
an arrangement for him to pick me up at Paloich.

I found some shade at noon, and after eating had a good sleep. Then
I jounced on over a very rough road through the late afternoon—unk, unk,
unk—until my bottom was sore. I was traveling over a vast grassy plain,
almost devoid of trees, villages, or any other landmark. The road was the
type I had found in Australia and is typical of dry country where there is
no sand and the soil splits open in great cracks. Here they call it cotton
soil. It is impassable after a rain, as I soon learned. Just before dark I ran
into a section where there had been rain. The tires started to pick up, and
I turned back to a little group of deserted grass huts. Here I debated.
The sky threatened rain, and I had shelter. But there was a suggestion of
trees or a native village across the horizon. Could that not be Paloich? I
desired to be at my destination to be on hand for my ride the following
morning; and I also wanted to be with English-speaking missionaries who
could tell me of the road. So I went on. Soon I could only walk and drag
the bicycle. It started to rain, and then I could not even drag it because of

clinging mud. And so with reluctant heart I left poor Jacqueline on her side (not even a tree to keep her head up) on the highest clump of grass I saw.

By this time I could see that what I had noticed on the horizon was really a village. I plowed through the mud to it. It was Paloich. But how far was it to the white man's house? The word *American* produced no effect. So I uttered the Arabic word for "man," pointing to myself, and said, "Eck," the American's name. Then I said, "Eck effendi." This got a glimmer, and after I had a drink, three natives led me across the village to where we could see a distant flickering light. I was not sure I could get there, as it was black as pitch by this time except for occasional lightning and the light was not always visible. So I was glad when the three natives routed out a fourth and he started off to guide me. Mud, water, flashes of lightning, and rain. To a voyager from the deserts of six or eight countries, it was a new experience—ordinarily welcome. Finally we arrived, and friendly American voices from a dinner table bade me come in out of the storm and eat.

Mr. Marvin Eck, wife, daughter, and Miss Christine Scott of near Glasgow, Scotland, were the other diners. We had only a lamp for light, but the drinking water was cold, though tasteless. Meanwhile, outside, the heavens let loose. I thought of poor Jacqueline and my films and camera. After the meal, and when the rain seemed to slacken, we tried to organize a rescue party. Marvin's three boys balked. He and I decided to go alone; it was about three-fourths of a mile. This shamed one of the boys into coming along—braving the cold, for as Mrs. Eck said, the rainy weather was cold to them.

We found the orphan without much trouble. The black took the heavy pack; Mr. Eck took roll, flour sack, and lantern and went on. I started to carry Jacqueline. This shortly exhausted me, and I tried other expedients, such as carrying the hind wheel or dragging the bike. Even with a naked bicycle, it was hard work. Sometimes if the road was wet enough, one wheel would turn, rarely both. I cleaned out mud by the bushel from under the fenders. Toward the end of the trek the wheels were so stuck up I could only sort of throw the bike two feet at a time. I was so exhausted I could not lift it.

The Ecks were from Oklahoma and had a cute little girl named Sharon. Christine was full of good Scotch fun. Marvin's big worry at the moment was a well which he was digging. The rains looked to be setting in before he was through. The next morning I took a look into the well's depth, and when I saw him laboring away twenty-five feet below me at the bottom of an unshored hole, I surely did not envy him his position. He admitted that just around him was a layer of sand. He had built a collar of concrete at the bottom of the well and was digging out the mud and sand underneath the edge. Thus the collar sank of its own weight, but he had to be sure that it sank evenly. He had heard of the technique from another missionary. These missionaries have to be house builders, well diggers, surgeons, accountants, treasurers, bill collectors, and whatnot.

It was a dull, sticky, cloudy day. We didn't think the roads were drying out much, so when we were just ready to sit down and eat we were surprised to see a truck pull in and stop. It was my Egyptian friend who had offered me the ride to Malakal. But my joy was short-lived. He showed me a note from Dulcer which told him he was not on any account to give me a lift to Malakal. Apparently Dulcer was piqued because *he* had not arranged the transportation. The Egyptian said Dulcer had told him he was leaving twenty minutes later and would pick me up himself and take me to Malakal. The whole business sounded so screwy to me that I really did not expect Dulcer to come along at all. Consequently I took my time about digging the mud out of my pack and washing it up. Mrs. Eck kindly mended both pairs of my dilapidated shorts.

It did not dry out too much during the day, and the weather remained damp and sticky, but the following morning I decided to try the road. When I was ready to start, about 5 A.M., it was trying to sprinkle and most of the sky was cloudy. I washed and shaved, but the outlook remained the same, so I decided to chance it. After two miles I hit a stretch not sufficiently dry and had to return—just in time for a good breakfast.

The door to Christine's little house was not closing, and though it was Sunday, she was going to fix it. I took over the job and after getting it to close was fixing the latch, when I heard shouts of "Here comes a lorry!" I rushed over to the road and hailed a couple of Sudanese in an old Ford truck with a dozen or so sacks of wheat. They would be glad to take me, and soon we were on the way.

Of all the rides I have had, this one gave me the most doubts about an arrival. The starter was gone, and the crank would not hold. The sparkplug caps were gone, and the driver kept contact by twisting the wires around the tips and covering them with grease. I had always thought that grease had to be kept away from the plugs. A tin can sat over the opening where the air cleaner should have been. The radiator leaked so badly we put in five gallons of water every three miles. The connecting rod bearings got to knocking before the end of the trip. Lizzie wheezed and puffed, but by noon we had struggled through the mud to Melut on the Nile. The drivers hoped to get the truck fixed up and offered me a ride to Malakal. But to me such a venture seemed dubious.

There was lots of small grain (mostly durra) both loose and in sacks in a round mat granary on the river front. One white man was seated on one of the sacks. As I packed up he introduced himself as Bert Ellis, engineer on the ship, the *Nimr*, on which the wheat was being loaded. In jig time he had invited me on board to have lunch with him and had offered me a ride to Malakal, and the local postmaster had invited me to tea. The engineer is the big cheese on the Nile boats. The pilot is sometimes called captain, but he can't move the boat until the engineer gives the order to proceed.

I had not been on the boat long before who should appear but the mamoor from Renk. He said he was there on other business but that he had received a telegram from Dulcer saying he should take my bicycle from me and await further instructions. However, the mamoor who was basically a common-sense chap, told me he was going to wire Dulcer I was proceeding on the *Nimr*. I felt if I ever got through the Sudan it would be by the grace of God and the Sudanese. The namoor also said Dulcer had asked the English family and the American family to keep me with them in Melut. And the final straw was the earlier information from Ellis that the Malakal commissioner of police had waited for me in Melut on the province boat until 9 A.M. before going on to Malakal. He had waited on instructions from Dulcer.

An hour or so later, as I was strolling about, whom should I see but Dulcer himself. He was talking to the mamoor and another Englishman and I had a prickly feeling up my back that it was about what they were going to do with me. It seemed I was rapidly becoming important, what with chiefs of police, assistant district commissioners, and other dignitaries chasing all over the country after me. I stood off at a respectful distance.

"Oh, you here?" (Just as if he didn't know very well.)

"Yes, I'm here. I believe there's been a sort of misunderstanding, and I would like to speak to you about it when you are free."

"Well, I'm too busy to talk to you now." (That's what the fellow had said the first time he ever clapped eyes on me.) "I thought an American's word was as good as his bond, but, well, we live to learn."

He said this with a nervous turn, a scraping of his foot along the ground, and a complete avoidance of meeting my eye. He was unshaven as before, and his face was still flushed or sunburned around the center and pale around the edges.

"I don't feel that I've broken—"

"No, I don't care to talk to you any further. You're going on the *Nimr*, and you will be met at Malakal."

So that was that.

Later two houseboys called for me. I could not understand them but supposed they were from the postmaster. They took me to Mr. Holdman, the English missionary. He invited me to tea, but I had to decline, as I was due at the postmaster's. Then he asked me to dinner, and I accepted.

I had to take the postmaster's tea—a delicious, perfumed drink—on the run. For here I found Dulcer telephoning some important official about me. As he came out the post-office door he said the minister of agriculture (this other Britisher who had appeared on the scene) was going on into Malakal and had agreed to take me. The lorry would be leaving in a half-hour. Also

I could sleep on the minister's boat anchored at Malakal that night, for we would be arriving late. He made sure I heard him extract assurance from the postmaster that his telegram to the governor of the province had been received.

"You are to go and see the governor at Malakal," Dulcer instructed me.

His curiosity then being too great to restrain, he asked me if my visa said anything about my method of travel, and I was sorry to have to tell him that it did not, whereupon he *generously* said maybe the governor would let me go then.

So I said, "Well, don't be too hard on me to the governor."

At this time he expressed some fear as to what I might write in my book. When men start fearing what someone might write about them—well . . .

The eighty-mile ride into Malakal was a rough one. We were in a new Ford but had no brakes. I smiled about the dear Sudan officials worrying about my safety alone on the road with the bike on such long dry stretches as Galhak to Paloich; fifty miles of no water, they had said, whereas the greatest distance between native villages had actually been twenty-five miles. Also there were lions which mauled people, said they. But in a brakeless car with a wild driver I was quite safe apparently.

While irony is in my blood, I should say that about 9 P.M. we came across the Egyptian who had offered me the ride to Malakal. He had run out of gas the preceding evening twenty-five miles short of his destination and had been at that spot for twenty-four hours while a man walked into the town and got a truck to come out with gas. The truck had just arrived. So brother Dulcer had not really deprived me of time after all.

We went on board the province boat at Malakal about midnight. This boat was to bear the minister of agriculture on up the Nile the next day.

Then I slept on the deck and fought mosquitos. In the morning I saddled up and went ashore to get a haircut. After all, I had to look presentable for the governor. While I was roaming about, the police spied me, and I was not surprised when they asked me to see the mamoor, a Sudanese. He said the district commissioner wanted to see me and that if I was to visit the governor, he would take me. I told him I had to eat and change my clothes first, but there were plenty of excited policemen in sight while these things were being done. Apparently they felt I was a chap who might just disappear at a moment's notice. I bore it all good-naturedly! It was pretty hard to get mad at the Sudanese, and besides, they were only carrying out the Englishman's orders.

The district commissioner's name was Lane, and it seemed that he was more highly thought of than Dulcer. He was standing when I came in and was tall for a Britisher. There was no friendly introduction or handshake, just a remark to the effect that he thought I was supposed to stop somewhere up the line. Still, he listened to my explanation—and I was careful to point out that Dulcer had had no time to listen to my story either when we first met or when we last met. I told him Dulcer and I had agreement whereby if I waited at Banjang, he would stop the first truck and have it take me. This he failed to do. So I arranged for a truck myself and then another. He had canceled my ride with the second truck.

Lane asked me what my plans were next. I had already resigned myself to going on by Nile steamer, not because of current difficulties or of my duress agreement in Khartoum but because when I obtained my visa the officials had said it might be necessary for me to go by steamer; and also because only four days now remained before a steamer was due. Nevertheless, just on a chance I told Lane I should prefer to go on by cycle or lorry. He said cars could not get through then, that it was the rainy season. But I knew the road was still open except for occasional delays of perhaps a day.

Probably one of the reasons why these English officials are so unfriendly is that they have to tell such fibs to support the silly rule against independent travel. No one likes to lie, especially when he knows the other chap knows it. An American official would have said, "Look, old man, you could probably make it, but there's a rule against it and I've got to enforce it." But, of course, in America the situation would never arise. Once you are in the country you can go anywhere you like—right out and bury your head in the desert, and there's no one to stop you. One thing is certain: I had far less trouble in cycling across Soviet Russia than I had with the British in Anglo-Egyptian Sudan. Naturally, among all the peoples I had visited desiring self-rule, I felt the Sudanese ought to have theirs—but quick. But I thought they would be foolish to join up with the Egyptians.

Anyway, Lane did not object when I told him I could probably proceed on the *Nimr* or the post boat, whichever went up the Nile first. He said he had spoken to the Americans about a place for me to stay and he thought they had a spare house. He called them on the phone, but I again felt resentment that someone should request hospitality for me. He asked them if I should come out or would they come down. They chose the latter. When they arrived he went out and talked to them first, leaving me in the office. Soon they came in with apologies that there was some one living in their spare house. Lane said there was a room back of the Town Bench nearby, where I could stay, but there was no accommodation. I very eagerly accepted this because I would not be imposing. However, Lane said they would keep the bicycle there at the Bench, and the Americans supported him by saying the town was small and I would not need it. Hm-m-m! But after all, I realize they had to continue to live under Lane's administration. It turned out that the Bench was just across from the town lockup and a police-post building, into which Jacqueline was put for safekeeping. The Town Bench was a sort of porticoed building where a civilian scribe sat to record complaints leading to civil cases. Back of his table and chair, which were on a platform looking out through the pillars, was a large room, and here I put my stuff. The Americans took their leave of me there, as they were going the twelve miles to Doleib Hill, a big American missionary colony, and would not return until the next day.

They had told me the only place where there was a darkroom to get a film changed was at the Catholic Fathers' in Malakal. I walked out to the edge of town and found Rt. Rev. Monsignor John Hart, Father Owen Kane, and a Catholic handyman in their workshop. The first was English, the second Scottish, and the third Dutch. I was invited by Father Hart to come to the house for a drink. By the time we had reached the door I was asked to stay for dinner and before I had been there five minutes I had been further invited to stay and to eat there until my boat left—this to be two or four days depending on whether I took the *Nimr* or the post boat. Such was the generous good nature and hospitality of John Hart. I say John Hart rather than Father Hart because he always dressed in civilian clothes—shirt open at the neck and gray business trousers—and acted like the young man he looked. I don't recall ever meeting a man for whom I developed more respect and in whose company I felt more downright pleasure. His outstanding trait was unflagging good humor and an ability to make others put a light aspect on aggravations and to keep them happy. During the nearly three days spent at his house, I marveled at the man.

I was given my own large room but had the run of the place. The long screened porch was used as a living room and opened off the rooms of Fathers Hart and Kane. At the far end was the chapel and at the other end— just outside my room—the dining room. Our custom was to gather on the porch for drinks (soft) just before meals and have a pleasant chat. When we were ready to be served, John called the boy from the outside kitchen. John sat at the head of the table, then myself and Father Kane on opposite sides, and the Dutchman at the foot. We were served soup by John in that order, and when the boy passed the serving dishes, usually four in number, the order was adhered to.

So I was content—yes, due to the calming influence of John Hart, content even when a policeman called that evening to say that I was expected to stay at the Town Bench.

"Oh, yes," said the Dutchman. "It's a closed area here, you know, and they are strict about visitors. Remember that chap who came through here from the south a year ago [addressing John]? They took him off the boat and made him stay in one of these houses somewhere near here. They sent him back. He had no special permit. Someone slipped in not telling you to get a special permit."

In spite of the policeman's calling, John Hart's hospitality and faith in me never wavered. He gave me an early dinner—thus accepting a warm-up dinner for themselves, as they had to wait until 9 P.M. for another guest— and told me to be sure to come back for my meals the next day. He gave me a big flashlight, a candle, a candleholder, a box of matches, and a *Saturday Evening Post* to read.

I was not satisfied with my position, though, and upon arrival at the Town Bench had the sergeant bring the submamoor, a Sudanese. The latter said he had written instructions from the D.C. and offered to bring them for me to read. A bit nettled, I assented. They stated that I would sleep at the Town Bench but could roam about the town as I wished. I know the submamoor offered to get these instructions because both he and the mamoor wished me to know they had no part in such ridiculous restriction. But Lane had gone to Kodok for seven days, and so I could not reach him. I shall never be really sure that he meant I *had* to sleep at the Bench. But as I have said, I was content because the sleeping was a small matter when I had a home, good meals, and plenty of books, magazines, and friends to occupy my time. One of the mamoors sent me a bed. To assert my independence I slept outside the building and left early the next morning for the Catholic mission.

The blessing at the Catholic Fathers' table was quite different from that at the table of the American missionaries. At the latter we had a long prayer asking God's blessing on missionaries and their work, myself and journeys, my family, etc., before giving thanks for the food. And this prayer often followed Scripture reading. But the fathers crossed themselves rapidly while still standing, uttered a few brief words even more rapidly, said "Amen" and sat down almost without pausing on their way to the plate.

During the following three days I became quite well acquainted around town. The shoemaker would hail me off the street to sit down and have tea with him. He had charged me only half price on my shoe repair. The tailor did twice as much as he contracted to do in sewing patches on my threadbare overalls. The two Greek merchants knew me well. The post-office and D.C. employees were friendly acquaintances. I met the medical director at the hospital. Two young men in their late twenties bought me a drink and talked politics while we were visiting a store.

When the steamboat *Nimr* arrived from Melut, I caught Bert Ellis coming along the waterfront. He said he was going to be held up on account of fuel and the post boat might leave first. He was on his way to see the governor, per order, and he thought it was about me. Apparently poor Bert was to go on the carpet for offering me a ride.

According to three young men with whom I took breakfast one morning, and according to the two I met at the corner, Sudan had three political parties. One wanted self-government, another self-government as a member of the British Commonwealth of Nations, and another self-government but in close cooperation with Egypt. The last group seemed the strongest. They claimed they did not have freedom of speech, etc., and two went so far as to say they would be arrested if heard talking politics with me. New enterprise was discouraged by rules laid down by the British. The British had had the country for fifty years, I was told, but look at the lack of schools, the awful illiteracy, and the entirely naked natives—even in a provincial capital like Malakal. Most educated Sudanese were really embarrassed about the nakedness of the natives and often mentioned it.

The reason politics played such an important part in Sudanese life is that the country's history has involved three nations instead of the usual two. In 1936 the British made a second alliance with Egypt in the Sudan, and Sudanese feeling ran high because the Sudanese resented their affairs being settled by outsiders. After World War II they thought their excellent war record would merit political recognition, but it looked as though they would be doomed to unite with Egypt or else the British would retire to leave them to another reign of terror under the son of the Mahdi. When it was decided to keep the status quo but eventually give the Sudanese a plebiscite, Egypt objected. The Sudanese then took action, drew up a constitution, kept the governor-general and put six Sudanese and six British on the executive council. So it was a case of so far, so good.

That noon, just before we sat down to eat at the mission, who should drop in but the English chief of police. I had not met that worthy before.

"The governor wanted me to call and suggest you go down and buy your ticket."

"I've already bought it. Would you like to see it?"

"Oh, no! He thinks you should go on the post boat. The *Nimr* doesn't have much accommodation."

"I don't mind that. I am used to sleeping on decks."

"Yes, I know. I should think you would enjoy a bit of luxury," he rejoined.

I did not think about it at the time, but I afterward wondered if the color bar and the Englishman's desire to maintain white prestige did not have somthing to do with his being so interested in my method of travel across the Sudan.

"The D.C. does not mind if I go on the *Nimr*," I continued. "I saw his written order." I figured that would floor him. "Besides, she's a faster boat."

Long pause.

"I guess you were pretty dry the other day when that truck stopped. They said you were out of water in the middle of that long stretch."

"Oh, no, I just asked him for a *cold* drink. Trucks usually carry these water bags, you know. No, I had nearly two canteens of water left. And it was only twenty-five miles between villages. I've had to carry water up to a hundred and thirty miles." I thought it was about time I won a round or two.

However, people usually believe what they want to believe, and I felt that every English official in the Sudan would discourage all future travelers with the account of the American cyclist found perishing from thirst on the road to Paloich.

27

Dress and Undress
on the Upper Nile

While in Malakal I took lunch one day in the home of the postmaster, Abdel Hamid Suliman. Zubeir effendi, another post-office employee with whom I had already lunched, was also a guest. His grandfather was Zubeir Rahama, sultan of Darfur for ten years and quite prominent in Sudanese history.

The platter on which the food was brought had a large round, highly colored basketry cover called a *dhabug*. This is to keep out the dirt. It cost about four pounds ($16). My host said he had seen women use them as hats or umbrellas. Under the dhabug were both mutton and chicken in addition to okra, which I cannot seem to like. The chicken was well fried and delicious, and the mutton was super. I never tasted better.

There was one thing that did not taste good, and that was the bitter, black grounds-filled coffee. But it is such a national institution that I will say more about it and the method of serving it in homes. It is the first and most essential item so far as a guest is concerned. Suppose a man returns to Khartoum after a visit to Malakal. Someone may ask: "Did you see Ibrahim Mohamed effendi in Malakal?"

"Yes, I have met him, but I didn't drink coffee with him."

This is a big insult to the character of Ibrahim Mohamed. If his father should hear of it, he may write him, "You are my son no longer."

The coffee berries are ground by being placed in a big hole on the top end of a long stone. A large stick is lifted up and down in this hole to crush the berries. To brew the concoction graced by the name *coffee*, about two-thirds of a pint of water is put into a dipper with a sharp-cornered spout and boiled. A tiny cupful of coffee—about two heaping tablespoons —is then put in. The spout contains a loose bunch of fibre wadded up like a wad of string, and this is supposed to filter the mixture. It is of no use whatsoever. The coffee is then poured into a coffeepot (*jeb'enah*), a sort of long-spouted little jug. This may be made of tin or silver. Hamid's was made of mud, but it was as thin and dainty as though it were china. It was brown in color and engraved. The unfiltering filter is transferred to the mouth of the pot for a second futile attempt.

Now the pot, a small china bowl of sugar, two tiny china cups, and a little spoon are put into a covered basket called a *kabawtah*. The pot, having no base, is rested on a doughnut-shaped pad called a *weegaiyah*.

Hamid's was red with a red and white band of beads around the outside, worked in a pretty design. His *kabawtah* was about the same basketry as Americans bring back from Mexico. Small palm-tree fibers are dipped in dyes or orange, purple, etc., and then wound tightly around sticks, made into circles and fastened to each other. The round bottom part of the basket was surmounted by a taller "witches' hat" of the same construction. The hat was held on by two light leather straps looping over the peak, where a small carrying loop was fastened to one of them. The kabawtah is used for the pot only if there is but a short distance to go for serving, the sugar bowl and cups being carried on a tray.

The guest (note it is not the host) puts sugar in his own cup first and then asks the host how much sugar he wishes. The guest removes the top of the basket and pours his own coffee first. He drinks first also. If there are several guests, the most important man drinks first. If a new guest arrives after the coffee has been brought into the room, a new basket must be made up and brought in so that he may think it is especially for him.

The guest is always the big cheese. If there is but one bed or one chair, he takes it as a matter of course. But his wish is law. If he says to take the bed out to your wife, he will sleep on the floor with you, the host must do so. If the guest spits melon seeds on the floor, the host must do the same. But if the host urges his guest to eat more even after he is full, it is polite for the guest to comply. All dishes should be emptied.

The postmaster felt that he had the finest Sudanese home in Malakal. He said it was better than the mamoor's next door because it had a veranda on each end. Thus he was comfortable both forenoon and afternoon. Still and all, the roof was thatched and the plasterboard ceiling showed where the water leaked through to the floor. Furnishings were extremely meager. The books he produced for me to read were three volumes of a set covering World War I, and a copy of the Anglo-Egyptian agreement.

The postmaster had no children of his own, but the mamoor, who had six, had loaned him his youngest—a little girl of about three. She was a cute little tyke, and he loved her very dearly.

At one time our conversation turned to the cost of living and wages. A chicken cost 17 cents (4 piastres), a pair of pigeons 22 cents, a sheep $2.40, a bull $16, and a dozen eggs 13 cents. Before the war you could buy a sheep for less than 60 cents, and an entire chicken for 5 cents. As to wages, the Shilluks, like those carrying bricks on the waterfront, received 22 cents per day, but northern Sudanese might get 43 to 65 cents per day. The lowest-grade government employee received $28 (7 pounds) per month; and the highest $56. Schoolteachers' salaries were lower.

I packed up Jacqueline that evening about six o'clock, with enough food for the eight days on the boat. However I had a lot of cans remaining from Khartoum gifts.

The *Rejaf* arrived about 7:30, and I pedaled down and got aboard.

The agent had made things easy for me, and I found that even the mamoor himself, in plain clothes, had come on board to help. He spoke to the chief of the commissary about getting me a good place to sleep and bathe and granting my wish to have bicycle and pack together in a separate place. Meanwhile other Sudanese were working in my behalf. The postmaster spoke to the boat postmaster to make things easy for me and later introduced me to him. We sailed around midnight. I had just found a vacant area for sleeping, when the commissary chap found me and had me move upstairs to a well-screened porch used by second class for recreation.

And so by morning we were well on our way up the Nile. The *Rejaf* was a wood burner and during the voyage had two barges on the starboard side with wood in them. These were to be replenished from stocks placed along the river. The steamboat carried her first-class passengers above her engines and kitchen. The second-class passengers occupied the second floor of the barge she pushed on her nose, the first floor being used for second-class kitchen, post office, commissary, chief's office, and quarters for postmaster and chief of the commissary. On the port side of this barge the third-class passengers held forth on a separate barge, most of them having brought their own beds. There was another barge on the port side of the *Rejaf* fitted out for passengers, but it seemed to be empty. There was no running water, and I washed and shaved by pouring out of my canteen. Other accommodations were similarly primitive, but I did not complain. First class was $37.50; second class, $19; third class (my class), $5.20.

The postmaster had his cook boil my eggs for me. The first afternoon, between rains, we docked at Tonga village and I bought a dozen more eggs. Vendors had a cup of water so that the purchaser could test each egg for freshness by seeing whether it would sink or float. Lacking a cup, the vendor would dig a hole in the mud and the rainwater filling it would provide a place to test.

The government employees running the second-class section, and two second-class passengers, insisted that I take my meals with them. Thus you may say I ate with the upper section of the middle-class Sudanese. We ate native style with plenty of good bread, chicken, and mutton. The location was the front end of the second-class barge, in the screened porch previously referred to.

Eating was great sport, I found. The object of the game was to see who could eat the least with the most effort and the messiest fingers (for of course there was no silverware). Eight of us grouped around the gaming table on which the "boys" (waiters) had just previously placed quarter loaves of bread. They then brought in three or four dishes of food—sometimes different, sometimes the same. No one began eating until all eight people had arrived; it was against the rules. As soon as the last chap touched his chair, everybody pitched in. The first hurdle was to break off a piece of bread from a quarter loaf with one hand—no mean achievement. This was then dipped into the nearest dish of vegetables or meat. Several dips would bring some of the gravy to adhere to the bread and fingers but nothing else. Maximum economy was thus achieved because everybody got filled up on bread. Now, when there was nothing left in the dishes but pure meat and vegetables, the sport really began to get interesting. Of course, one *could* have been allowed to pick up a chicken leg or thigh or a rib of mutton by the bone, but—well, did you ever see anyone run a hurdle race with no hurdles? We were required to pick off bits of meat with bread held between the fingers and using only one hand. There was one thing allowed, however: the player could drag the piece of chicken or whatever out of the dish and onto the table top in front of him. But actually this made the game more interesting because the pieces of meat might skid away across the table when you pinched at them. But a hungry man can accomplish prodigies, and when we eight men had finished, nothing remained but two square feet of bones and three acres of bread crumbs.

Naturally, after the battle was over, one's fingers and mouth were, shall we say, a bit messy. Then came the wash-up process. A boy with a big cup of water and a cake of soap stood ready. The goof always gave you the cake of soap first, then expected you to cup your hands and receive the water he poured. That was possible up to that point—but then what were you supposed to do? I never could figure that one out. The Sudanese not only used soap and water for hands and mouth but rinsed out the inside of the mouth thoroughly as well. I have seen them in cabins, where they had bowls to wash in, use only the water that came from the spout.

One morning a kid and a goat were butchered at the front of the two forward passenger barges. Just about everything was saved but the large intestine. Breakfast was served an hour late that morning. In two dishes were the odds and ends of the goat—tripe, intestines, etc.—but I was saved because a third dish contained some very delicious spareribs. One of the boys asked me if I ate liver raw. I replied in the negative, not dreaming what was back of his question. A little later there came two platefuls of small pieces of raw liver and raw lung. I threw up my hands and selected a piece of garnishing raw onion. They laughed and said I could be excused. But while I was washing they made me come back in and eat bread and jam a boy had brought especially for me.

My hosts spoke to me about many things in which they were interested. Some were surprised to learn that there were Negroes in America. Often our talk would turn to politics. They gave me the usual story about England being there for fifty years and the people still going naked.

"They have done nothing," I was told.

They said the British wanted the south of the Sudan to be separate from the north. The south is very fertile and was a "closed area." Mohammedan merchants who wished to settle were discouraged by the government in every way. Yet Christian missionaries were allowed to go in.

Through the postmaster, my hosts knew that I had had trouble with the British authorities and this was another item to hold against them. And while on the subject I will insert a two-line conversation occurring when an American doctor hurriedly came aboard for the mail at a lonely stop along the river.

"Are you an Englishman?" I queried as he hurried along past me.

"No, thank God," he ejaculated.

There was an honest-to-goodness native prince on board the *Rejaf,* traveling at the expense of the Sudanese government. He was styled His Highness George William Kabango, Prince of Uganda and East Africa. When he learned who I was, he introduced himself and reminded me that we had exchanged greetings outside the passport office in Khartoum. Learning I was going to Uganda, he had said: "I also am going to Uganda. Perhaps I will see you there or on the boat."

So now it had come to pass. He was very friendly and insisted that I take one meal a day as his guest. He wanted to take me to the first-class salon with him, but apparently there was a rule against that, so I was served privately in his first-class stateroom each evening. Here is a sample of a Nile-boat first-class dinner: three good-sized thick pieces of fresh fish with a light lemon sauce and with four patties of lemon-flavored mashed potatoes; on a separate plate eight small boiled potatoes; five pieces of chicken, pan gravy, and beans; three small but solid and filling bread biscuits; and orange sherbet. There was plenty of silverware. All this was a contrast to the second-class Sudanese meals I have been describing and radically different from a few meals I ate as a guest of the third-class passengers. With the latter I squatted on a floor foul with spit and nutshells and dipped *kisra* (native sour, thin bread) into our common pot of gooey, very viscous, green lentils.

It was rather ironic that practically all my meals for the eight days' trip on the *Rejaf* were paid for by the Sudanese government. I considered it just, because that government had cost me a week's time and had practically put me on the boat against my wishes. But even apart from the food, I should really thank the government because the experiences I had and the local color I absorbed on board that Nile steamer were widely different than on land and I would not have missed them for anything.

Prince Kabango had received his education in England and had traveled about Europe. He was a pilot at Cairo during the war. For twenty-two years he had hardly been in his country except for a couple of airplane visits of hardly a day's duration. His younger brother was on the throne following his father's death at Mengo Hill, Kampala. The prince had seen to it that one of his good friends was prime minister. While some of this sounds like the prince was an old man, he was young-appearing—I should judge in the early thirties. Tremendously interested in America, he had made up his mind to go there and frankly admitted he needed to make me his friend so he would have some place to visit when he arrived.

And so we sailed on up the Nile day after day. On both sides of the river was a continuous green monotony of dense, wet-country undergrowth about twice as high as a man. Hour after hour, day after day, the same. Islands of grass and weeds called *sudd* were continually floating past us down the river. These were often ten by fifteen feet in size, and, like an iceberg, most of the mass was supposed to be underneath. They seemed to slide easily under the flat-bottomed barges, however, and did not break the planks in the paddle wheel of the steamer. The only wildlife on the landscape was one lone hippo and some water birds.

One midday I was eating with three natives in third class. We were squatting on the dirty floor around a common pot half full of cooked slimy greens into which we alternately dipped our fingers partly covered with kisra. My back was to an open doorway leading out onto the prow of the barge, the only real entryway into the room being in back of the native squatting opposite me. The only furniture was two bottomless double bunks, near which were some loose boards which had perhaps once made the bunks useful. There was no conversation; all was quiet and peaceful. Without warning, the native opposite me jumped up with a great yell and ran wildly out of the room. Before I could gather my wits, a second native jumped up, yelled, and followed the first. The third jumped backward also but instead of running, grabbed up a long narrow board. I thought to look behind me at last and saw a mottled green snake at least six feet long in back of my bedroll. I moved as fast as the natives but was encouraged by the brave one who had grabbed the board to follow his example. Between us we made it hot for the snake all around the room and finally finished him off. Because of our language barrier all the information I could get was that he was very bad, very bad indeed. I think he had fallen onto the prow from the tall rushes which the front barges plowed into and over when going around some of the Nile's sharper bends.

The importance of the Mohammedan religion to the everyday life of its followers was brought home to me during the voyage. Someone was always chanting in a moderate, though high-pitched voice. Five or six times a day most of the people removed their sandals, faced Mecca, audibly uttered their prayers and at short intervals prostrated themselves until their foreheads touched the floor. That's one thing about the Mohammedan religion—no shelving it until one hour or two on Sunday. I noticed in particular two quiet young men in white turbans and long galabiehs. Their faces were long and narrow with thin noses, pointed chins, small mustaches, and tufts of black beard. Their very dark skins were a great contrast to the whiteness of their dress. Constantly together, they sat and read to each other from the Koran for hours at a time.

Nudity was the common sight anywhere along the upper Nile. All body hair was kept removed. Stark naked natives were to be seen waving on the bank or shooting along the edge of the river in their hollowed-tree-trunk canoes. It can't be that the reason the Sudanese government wanted me to go by boat was to avoid seeing naked natives, because even the major stops disclosed many of them. It was a bit difficult to get accustomed to seeing the big six-foot males stalking around without a stitch; and I presume the women missionary passengers must have felt similarly embarrassed when they saw their first nude native women. I saw one sweet thing with a short grass skirt and asked Prince William to explain why she had decided to be different and wear clothes. He said she was married, but that the nude Mira beside her with a string of beads around her waist was a virgin.

"If any man tries to touch her, it is very dangerous for him. These people respect virginity very highly."

There were two musical instruments in evidence. One was a native banjo made with stretched rawhide and wire. The other was a little affair called a *rebaba*, scarcely larger than one's two hands. It had ten small metal bands or strips placed over a small sound box. The long free ends of the strips were pressed down and released by the fingers to create vibrations and sound. One of my nicest memories is standing on the prow of the third-class barge one evening beside a lad strumming one of these *rebabas*. The Nile was dark, deep, and smooth. The music had a definite beat—the kind I can best appreciate. He played quietly. We glided on toward the darkening horizon, and it seemed to me that our souls became kindred—the black man's and the white's.

Other activities on the front end of the second- and third-class barges included spearing fish with long iron- or wood-pointed unbarbed spears. The catch looked like a small catfish. At this end of the boat the chickens were kept cooped or tied; here the doomed sheep bleated, butted, and ignored their coming fate, though their fellows were butchered before their very eyes; here clothes were washed with water dipped up from the Nile, which was nearly as muddy as our own Missouri.

At night Arabs sleeping on the deck enveloped themselves completely in a sheet or blanket. I don't know how they breathed. Most of them had brought their own woven-rope, wooden-frame beds. Some had mosquito nets the size of the bed which could be suspended three feet above it.

At some stops a naked tribesman would get on. He would make his way to a dirty floor in some out-of-the-way corner and sit there smoking a wooden pipe two and a half feet long. He usually carried his tobacco in a hollowed wood stick about three or four inches in diameter, covered with rawhide and well sewed at the ends and along one side. The only opening was through the handhold in the center. Bits of rag on either side of this held the tobacco in the hollow core. Such a traveler when he became hungry would eat a mush of crushed durra—really coarse flour—and water.

The Sudanese (not the native tribesmen) carried small covered watering cans with long, small spouts during their toilet periods. They had no paper and washed themselves with the left hand. Hot water for any kind of washing was unknown. There was no soap in evidence. Soap was used only after eating to wash fingers messy from having dipped in the common dish.

The three vertical scars on either cheek of most Sudanese were tribal marks. New-generation Sudanese did not show these, nor did the older generation of more enlightened families.

Some stops made by the steamer were interesting. At Shambe the boys and a few girls alongside the ship were encouraged to perform a dance. These young folks clapped their hands in time and in unison, and then one or two of each sex would detach themselves from facing rows and advance toward the other, wiggling hips and bodies just as in any American nightclub or stripteaserie. To a white man these motions seemed sensuous; yet the postmaster told me with a serious countenance that it was the dance of the oxen and that they were trying to imitate the movements of cattle, which they reverence. I could not see the remotest resemblance between the quick, lithe movements of these children and the bovine amble; but then perhaps I did not have the proper imagination.

All steamer stops were by no means as interesting as the one at Shambe. In the place called Bor, Prince William and I strolled up and down and decided we were very definitely bored in Bor.

As we went on south corn could be seen at some places along the Nile. It was in small plots surrounding or near a thatched hut on the river's edge.

When we neared Juba we saw a mountain in the distance. Not only that, but a few trees appeared and occasionally a bit of high ground. We saw a herd of elephants too. The Nile was narrower and more tortuous now. Sometimes the bends were so sharp that we didn't make the turn and would sort of slide along the bank for several hundred feet. The bank, if there really was one, was so low and so covered with tall reeds, grass, and whatnot that it seemed we were taking a boat ride in weeds.

Juba was head of navigation for Nile river steamers, and I disembarked. One hundred and twenty miles of the Anglo-Egyptian Sudan yet separated me from Uganda, my next country. But I was fortunate in securing a ride over nearly all of it in a Greek-owned salt truck with an Italian driver.

What a change to traverse the country south of Juba! Here everything was green and pleasing. Hills, trees, grass, occasional rains, and oceans of pure washed air afterwards. No excessive heat. I could cycle comfortably even at midday. Skies had clouds for a change. Trees occasionally shaded the road even if the sun was equatorial.

A customs post and a river and then "happy Uganda." Almost at once I commenced to see many bicycles, even though it was twenty-five miles to the next town. The road was tarred in stretches, but even where it was just gravel, cycling was excellent. Cyclists were friendly and continued so.

The first thing that struck me as different about Uganda was that people wore clothes. Even little boys and girls had something to cover up with or

An elephant's ears may be seven feet long—Uganda.

Acres of cordwood await the Nile steamer, and both men and women go stark naked—Sudan.

at least to cover what should be covered. Cyclists and those on foot were often dressed in white shirt, khaki shorts, perhaps a khaki jacket, knee-length white or khaki hose, and good shoes. Women did not always have their breasts covered, but as I worked south, occasionally full-length drapes or even real dresses—and bright-colored ones—were to be seen.

I was now in territory inhabited by the Acholis, a tribe related to the Shilluks of the Malakal area. They could often be identified by the designs scarred into their faces and bodies. The Acholis were good hunters with nets and spears and raised sheep, cattle, and goats. In religion they practiced a vague fetishism.

I ate lunch in front of a Public Works Division camp. These P.W.D. camps are very attractive spots. Six or more round, peaked, thatched huts are enclosed by a hedge. Ground between is flat and may be either grassed or bare as a floor.

In no time I had an audience. Every can, every utensil, every move I made, was of great interest. I was interested too—in buying a *lukembe,* the Acholi word for the *rebaba,* the small musical instrument I have already described. There were two visible in the group, and I inquired if they were for sale. One of the chaps offered to sell, setting the price at eighty shillings —or maybe my interpreter erred. Anyway, I offered five shillings, and begorrah, he accepted. Thinking I had been bested in bargaining, and in front of such a big audience, I cast about for ways to redeem myself. I asked for the other chap's instrument and sounded both alternately with an attentive ear. Then I shook my head and told my man four shillings (80 cents) was enough. He accepted, and the deal was closed. My *lukembe* boasted a lovely white feather—which added to its souvenir value. I should have photographed the vendor because he was a regular jungle Tarzan, leopard skin and all.

Cycling across Uganda was an idyll. The climate was comfortable, the people were friendly, the scenery was pleasant, and there was always something of interest. Swahili again became the lingua franca, and Arabic seemed to have been left behind at Juba.

On my first afternoon I posed two young Acholi matrons for a picture. Each mother carried a little child riding pickaback in a cloth strap, but I tried in vain to get the women to turn sideways so that their offspring could get into the picture. The little tykes were cute and clean-looking—no fly-filled eyes or dusty bottoms as in the Somalias. Many babies I saw were covered with the dried hollow shell of a big calabash. Such a shell is used to carry fruit, nuts, grain, and so on and bears a striking design in black and yellow stripes. It was picturesque to see this big shell on mama's back with nothing but a little black bottom just visible underneath followed by a pair of tiny legs.

About ten miles from a Uganda frontier place called Gulu, I was given a ride with an English government official. I mentioned my two weeks' bout

Two Acholi mothers (and offspring on back)—northern Uganda.

The charm of mother and son—Uganda.

with dysentery, and when we reached the town he left me at the immigration and raced off to the hospital before it closed for the day in order to get me some pills. When he returned, he handed them to me "with the compliments of his Majesty's government." This was a radical change in treatment from that received from the British officials in the Sudan.

"They're sulfaguanidine," said my benefactor. "Take three every 4 hours for two days. But for God's sake drink plenty of water or it will kill you. I mean it. We had a chap who tried to treat himself, and the stuff crystallized in his kidneys and he died. You must drink at least six pints of water per day. You're cycling and you must allow for perspiration and drink enough for that, too."

Well, after all this I felt I would try sulfaguanidine only when I felt sure I was going to die anyway.

At a place called Atura I boarded a little pontoon ferry for the journey across the Victoria Nile. I use the word *journey* advisedly because the trip was just that. Long poles were used, and six rowers kept more or less busy helping out the two men on the poles. We maneuvered over an island, then drifted around the lower end, poled and rowed up the other side, and then ventured cautiously out into the main channel. I was the only vehicular passenger. This crossing of the Nile was not too far from its main source at Lake Victoria.

I arrived at Kampala, commercial capital of Uganda, late in the evening. The city is built on seven hills, and I picked out one of them to push up to find a place to sleep. Unfortunately it turned out to be the highest—Navirembe—and it was a long walk to the top. Rain threatened, so I found the tree with the thickest foliage and turned in.

I was awakened in the morning by a native woman hurrying past on the road below.

"Rain, bwana! Rain!"

Yes, it did look bad. I turned out in a hurry. Sprinkles! I got the sleeping bag rolled with only a minute to spare before the downburst. The tree had unusually thick foliage, but I was pretty wet, foliage or no foliage, by the time I was all packed and had my boots, rain hat, and cape all on. I was nearly on the equator, where rains are really rains. Fortunately I was just at the edge of the city and it was only a short block to a porch. Here, while waiting out the rain, I was provided with chair and tea by an Indian family in which there were ten sons.

In Kampala I had the good luck to enjoy the hospitality of both Anglo-Indians and English as a result of chance acquaintances made in shops. The proprietor of a bike shop gave me a box for my lukembe, fixed my bike pedal for free and invited me to his home for dinner. An Indian hardware merchant offered me a free gift of anything in his store. On another occasion I entered the city's large service store. The Indian manager of this store had spoken to me at the barbershop the preceding evening. He had heard I had been in his store. Was there anything he could help me to? Well, yes, I had been trying to find a leather case for my papers. So now he spoke a few words to his chief clerk. They hunted through all the stocks, but the only thing they could unearth anywhere near suitable was a plain two-compartment lady's purse. I accepted it and asked the price. Oh, no, they could not take anything for that! It was no use protesting. I noticed the tag later; it was 27½ shillings (about $5.50). I needed a cork for my water bottle and when they did not find one large enough, they took a jim-dandy from a thermos bottle. No use to protest that robbery either.

Practically every merchant in Kampala—and there seemed to be hundreds of them—was an Indian. There was ill feeling between them and the English. The Indians pointed out that they had come to East Africa at Zanzibar two or three hundred years ago. By 1825 they had come to other parts of Africa. They had come in and developed the country while the Europeans stayed away because of fear of yellow fever. Yet now the English governed. And what did the English say about the Indians? "The Indians are the great festering sore in the side of Africa." I have not heard any elucidation of this statement, only the comment: "They multiply like rabbits."

And an unbiased observer? Well, later on in my Ugandan travels I met a Catholic white father who had this to say: "The Indians in Africa are really a blessing because they handle the entire commercial life of the country. The natives are not up to it, and the English are basically a ruling type."

In one Kampala shop I chatted with a fellow customer and received a gracious invitation for the night. Jack Dailey was an Englishman with a pretty wife, Pansy, and two really beautiful children, Jimmy and Jacqueline. I commented on the last name being the same as my bicycle's. Further, they had an Alsatian pup named Jess, which is my first name. There was also a fine tabby cat, though the term "tabby" as used by the English describes a tiger cat instead of a gray one. The servants included cook, houseboy, laundry boy, and nurse.

The Daileys lived in a little house near the center of town. It was not well designed, as you had to pass through the master bedroom to go from the living room or other bedroom to the bath and dining nook. They complained of a housing shortage. Both worked, but they enjoyed a new Hudson car. Each evening they shared the unpleasant duty of picking great blood-filled fleas off the dog, which sprawled on the davenport. They remarked how nice it was that cats never seemed to have such troubles. The dog was not the only privileged character. The children, four and six years old, were allowed to go off to bed with nearly a full box of chocolates ($1.80). The following morning the first thing young Jimmy did was to stuff one of the few remaining ones into his mouth. Unfortunately mommy and pop were not around to remind him to offer the guest one.

The Daileys went out in the evening.

"The house is yours," they said. "There are drinks in the icebox. When you feel like bed, go into the children's room and any empty bed you see, pile in." I never realized it until later, but now I have been a baby sitter in Africa.

Even with a cook the Daileys did not bother much about food. Tea, cigarettes for Jack, and drinks in moderation were more important. Ham and eggs was the meal, often as not. Theirs was what is termed a modern diet, but for me it was semistarvation.

Neverthless, they were surely hospitable and I liked them. Pansy told me if I was going over to Jinja I should stop on my way back and stay the night with them. But even with all of this, the English reserve was still present. I was there two nights, and the second night they took me to a movie but they rarely addressed me by name. When I left after breakfast, remarking that it had been a pleasure to make their acquaintance, they did not reciprocate with a like expression. Nor did they make any remark when I thanked them for their hospitality. Yet I know I was welcome. Yes, Englishmen are peculiar!

I side-tripped to Jinja to visit Ripon Falls and the source of the Nile at Lake Victoria. Victoria Nyanza is the second largest fresh-water lake in the world and is also unusual in that its shape resembles a square. Where the lake issues into the Nile the Jinja Club had a golf course which is said to be the only golf course in the world where you can pick up a ball without a penalty. This is when it falls into a footprint made by a hippopotamus.

Kampala was the seat of government of the Bugandans, the most advanced tribe of natives in Uganda and indeed in British East Africa. Their government was probably the most modern native government in all Africa. So upon my return to Kampala I decided to visit the Bugandan "Capitol Hill." Prince William had given me the address of a friend who would act as guide, and so I looked up a Mr. Muimbwa. Together we rode our bicycles out to a suburban area and climbed the hill to the government buildings. We first went to the palace, where I met the principal secretary. He personally conducted us about the grounds and explained their form of government. The Bugandans had a good government long before the English arrived. In fact, it was so good that the English kept it. The Bugandans had their own ministers of justice and finance and even a prime minister. They collected taxes and secured revenue by both direct and indirect methods; that is, some taxes were turned over to the British government, which then rebated.

The Bugandans had had thirty-four kings in an unbroken line. Immediately after the death of a king the prime minister called a special meeting of Parliament and presented to it a list of the eligible princes. In recent times, since the Bugandans had become good Catholics, this list included only the legitimate sons of the king. At the entrance to the palace grounds was a sort of rectangular concrete pit covered with ordinary corrugated iron. In it burns a flame which must not go out while a king is reigning. It is extinguished only at his death. I asked the principal secretary what the fire burned and he said, "Wood." One man had the duty of tending it, but he did it very secretly so that no one might see the flame. I did not see any smoke, or man, or any pile of wood about, so the flame remained something of a mystery to me.

We visited the waiting chamber near the palace. This was a thatch-roof affair, very handsomely constructed. The supporting pillars were made of *lubugo*, or elephant reeds. At the sides of the chamber were curtains of dark-dark-brown bark cloth. This was made by beating the bark of a certain tree until it was quite thin and pliable.

In the Parliament building the Standing Committee was in session. The committee arbitrated land encroachments and approved the genuineness of succession to property ownership. If a man died intestate, the committee checked on the distribution of land by the head of the clan. In any case the new property owner was presented to the *Kabaka* (king) by the head of the clan to secure official approval.

The people were clan-minded. The king had a throne on a special dais in Parliament, should he choose to sit in on a session. The carpet on his dias could be touched only by the members of a certain clan.

The secretary wanted me to meet the prime minister of Buganda, but he was in conference. This more or less suited me because, attired only in old, considerably worn clothes, I suddenly felt embarrassed at the prospect of meeting prime ministers and such. The principal secretary, dressed in immaculate striped pants and black tails, had already made me conscious of my travel-stained jeans. When we parted he gave Mr. Muimbwa and me a pass to visit the Tomb of Mutesa, the greatest of the Bugandan kings.

En route to the tomb we passed both church-crowned Rubaga and Navirembe hills. Brother, it really requires devotion to attend church in Kampala! The Protestant cathedral is on Navirembe Hill, the highest hill of the seven around which Kampala is built. I toiled up that hill twice—on foot, of course—during my stay in the city. And when I walked Jacqueline up to the Catholic cathedral on Rubaga Hill, I had one of the stiffest climbs of my career. The last part was almost straight up. I'll bet Sunday attendance is slim. They surely would not dare to put a church on a hill like that in America. The king of Buganda and the royal family had become Catholics, and Rubaga Hill is just opposite Capitol Hill, but if they had to walk up to the cathedral to church every Sunday, I'll bet they wished they had never forsaken their heathen gods.

When Mr. Muimbwa and I arrived on the hill of the Tomb of Mutesa, the aged caretaker first showed us the drums used to announce the end of every month, also the special drum sounded only at the death of a king. The tomb was really a gigantic, round, high-peaked thatched hut of very fine construction and with an artistic arched portico. To enter this we were required to take off our shoes. The floor was covered with hay, on which were raffia mats of great size. Near the center three kings had been buried side by side. Mutesa I was in the center, his son, Danieri Mwanga, was on the left, and his grandson, Daudi Chwaii, rested on the right. Their burial dates were 1884, 1910, and 1939, respectively, and the hut was started in 1882. Brass spears and shields lined the front of the resting places, and a large picture of each king was to be seen. There was also a double-sickle or open-caliper arrangement in brass in front of each. This, like a baton, was a symbol of authority.

From Kampala I went to Entebbe, capital of Uganda, and from Entebbe I went off across country toward the Mountains of the Moon and the interior of Africa. My road was hilly, picturesque, and interesting. I frequently passed native shambas. Some of the homes had whitewashed walls and appeared to be of solid construction. Most were the thatched roof, eaves-supported-by-posts type of thing. The majority had some sort of flowering bush or tree or even a hedge by way of ornamentation. Sometimes the display of flowers was quite outstanding. Surrounding the little hut and front yard were banana trees, small plots of corn, or small plots of young sweet-potato plants, well hilled. Happy, happy Uganda!

There were several different kinds of bananas. The staple article of diet was a big, fat green banana which the natives cook. I had some that night, and they were quite tasty, especially with gravy. Another kind of banana was used in making beer. It is intoxicating, at least when one drinks too much. Three young native chaps will sit down to one of these enormous pumpkin shells full and not leave it till it's gone.

According to Jack Dailey, the natives wouldn't improve their fertile land. He cited the case of a government clerk who owned sixteen square miles, and who got eight shillings per year for every house on it. When he accumulated money on his job, he bought a new car rather than a tractor. Yet the government said native land must remain native land and the white man can't take over.

Their property laws were important. I think it was Jack who told me that an adulterer was fined, not because of the moral crime but because he had transgressed on another man's property.

Realizing that I had not yet had a meal in a native Ugandan home, I stopped at a modest shamba and indicated by signs that I wanted to sit on the "porch" (area under the eaves) and eat from my pack. While I was eating, the young mother of four, charming in her hospitality, selected a long pole and went out among the trees to shortly return with two big papayas, one of which she offered me. Then one of the children brought me a pineapple. This I did not even recognize—for what American would think of pineapple growing anywhere outside of Hawaii? I professed ignorance of how to prepare these fruits, so my hostess and her daughter did it for me. The papaya was opened, the seeds were taken out, the meat was sliced away from the shell, and the long muskmelonlike pieces were placed on a plate for me. The husk of the pineapple was cut off and the main part sliced in four pieces. It was my first taste of papaya, and I found it delicious. The taste is much like that of muskmelon. I was also given a piece of sugar cane.

And so I lazed against a porch post and was served like a potentate. "Happy Uganda," I mused. "Yes, there is nothing to keep one from being happy. The climate is comfortable, the soil is fertile, the fruit trees are productive. I wonder what the Ruwenzori Mountains will be like. Ah, it's good to be alive! H-m-m—looks a little like rain. But what matter? There will be other porches along the way."

28

In the Heart of Africa

So across the hills of Uganda to the Mountains of the Moon I pedaled. These mountains are more properly called the Ruwenzori, and the native name means "rainy mountains." Rain falls there 360 days out of the year, and the high peaks are never free from cloud. Behind the veil of mist are glaciers and eternal snows, in spite of the fact that the range is almost on top of the equator. Safely hidden from mortal eyes, the white peaks show their faces only to their mother, the moon.

This area in the heart of Africa, including Lake Kivu farther south, is probably destined to be the greatest resort area in all Africa. Some enterprisers have foreseen this, and the Mountains of the Moon Hotel (Telephone Romance) is a result. And lo and behold, I, the traveler on a shoestring, arriving in faded overalls and blue workshirt, stayed a night at the resort hotel.

Jack Dailey had instructed me to call on a friend at the hotel named Slag-Molen. I found that Slag was a Dutchman who spoke American. He had traveled by foot in France and Spain and had been on the beach in the Mediterranean. Thus he was sympathetic with what I was doing and insisted I put up at the hotel as his guest.

You would have never recognized the young man in overalls who showed up in the main dining room of the Mountains of the Moon Hotel that evening. I had been provided with a soft gray business suit, a deep-red silk polo shirt, and a brilliant yellow tie. So I felt self-assured, even when we were joined by Slag's good-looking young Australian wife, wearing makeup in a most sophisticated manner. The meal was all right for style, but the servings were so small you could hardly see them. Even my hosts made fun of them. I'm thankful I don't stay in hotels; I'd starve. After the meal we had a long comfortable chat in front of the fireplace. The Molens were going elephant hunting in a few days and wanted me to come along. But I sensed there might be delays, so declined.

In Fort Portal I lost a sack containing my woolen Eisenhower and high rubber overshoes. What irony: after lugging them for months through the hot desert countries of the Sahara, then to lose them just as I entered lands where I could expect wet weather, and further south-winter weather! Well, now I knew—why that native was hollering after me. What a fool I was not to investigate!

Southward I traveled across the equator into a land of lakes and plains.

To the west but near at hand were the shrouded Mountains of the Moon. What secrets did they hold up amongst those equatorial snows? I passed through big-game country and saw signs of elephants. Here also was the land of the Batoro tribe. They had a unique custom whereby a bride-to-be was shaved by a barber and by a female relative so that she was deprived of all hair. Then her entire body was greased with butter and castor oil, and these were well rubbed into the skin.

Beyond the Kazinga Channel between two lakes I climbed a tremendous escarpment and found myself in a different world. Here were timbered mountains, forests, natives, shambas, and banana groves. An interesting country, as set apart from the rest of the world as Grand Mesa.

Beyond a town called Kabale in southwestern Uganda I noticed many natives bringing tobacco to market. Harvested from little individual plots on the steep mountainsides, the tobacco was packed into great oblong-shaped bundles held together by long bamboo sticks and looking like a log raft. Such a raft was easy to carry on a native's head as he walked up and down the steep slopes to the road, where lorries would pick it up for the nicotine factory in Kabale. Men, women, and boys all carried these rafts of tobacco. I tried to get some of them to pose for a picture, but they were too scared of the camera and would shy clear off the road or run past me like frightened chickens. When I finally did get one man to stop, the shutter stuck and the exposure was ruined.

Since the preceding evening I had been worried about a swelling on the lower calf of my leg. Now I noticed that it had puffed up on either side of my pant-leg clasp. I removed the clasp and rolled my pant leg. As I started to ascend a low mountain pass, a native and a small boy, the former carrying a spear, started jogging along beside me in companionship. When I came to a level stretch or a brief descent, they had to run to keep up and once dropped well behind. The boy was puffing like mad but the man ran in a free and easy manner and even found time to whistle between breaths. Near the summit he actually pushed the bike, and it was only by his help that I was able to continue riding. He was smiling all the time and enjoyed making exhibition of his strength and endurance. Fortunately there was a native audience at the top of the pass to witness his prowess. Now, wouldn't the composite have made a good picture!

I descended the other side, enjoying some very fine scenery. Then shortly after starting up again, here came a Vauxhal sedan with Mr. and Mrs. Kerr (pronounced "car"). He was one of those individuals who have lived long enough to understand the worthwhile things in life and to recognize the shams for what they are worth. Which, of course, is a nice way of saying that he was democratic enough to be enthusiastic about giving me a ride. Mr. Kerr had been a successful salvage engineer—the operation is called "salving"—and had also been a planter and knew all about coffee raising. He was enjoying his second honeymoon with an attractive wife, not too

Almost always there are babies up behind.

The jungle must be cleared for beans and manioc.

much his junior. The three of us had a most delightful journey together.

I shared the Kerrs' lunch at a high viewpoint called Kinaba Gap. Just below us was a sheer drop of fifteen hundred feet and since the day was clear, the view was very fine indeed. This was a region of yet active volcanoes and three of them towered above the surrounding valleys. And here at eight thousand feet we were in the region of "eerie forests hung with festoons of lichen, dim vistas through a mist of bamboo, of grotesque tree groundsels and bizarre, obelisk-like giant lobelias, arborescent St. John's worts, tree heaths, intermingling with lovely Helichrysums. . . ."

One of the most interesting things about the drive was the way the natives had their plots of tobacco, beans, etc., stuck on to the precipitous mountainsides. It was marvelous. Some valleys seemed to be entirely cultivated—cultivated clear up to the encompassing summits. Often a native hut would occupy the top of a small summit lying perhaps within the valley and connected by a narrow ridge to adjacent slopes. Very picturesque. And Lake Bunyoni, sixteen miles long, quite narrow and shut in by high hills, was fine to behold. It had an island-mountain which looked for all the world as if it was ready for a second fairy castle of Neuschwanstein to be perched upon it. The scenery to me was reminiscent of Madagascar as well as of southern Germany.

And so we came to Kisoro and the exit customs port. While British Uganda had been nowhere near as bad as British Sudan in the matter of traveler's red tape, yet the exit customs held us up with quadruplicate forms involving the bicycle. But across the frontier, the Belgian officials at Rutchuru cut the red tape to a positive minimum. I was amazed. According to travel literature, I expected a demand for smallpox vaccination, yellow-fever vaccination, statement of a physician as to freedom from contagious and mental diseases and epilepsy, declaration or permit for bicycle, statement of intention of visit, place of destination, etc. But not a thing was asked for. Following Mr. Kerr's lead, I said nothing—never let the immigration chaps know I knew a word of French. If the officer saw my Congo visa as he fingered through my passport, I was unable to detect it. Anyhow, *tout de suite* and we were in the country.

The Congo side of the frontier was flat, but there was a good deal of dense forest—especially after we entered the Parc National Albert. This is a habitat of gorillas, but we were content with a couple of baboons. The tropical flora was profuse and varied with masses of erythyma and wild clematis. Continuing south, we approached a storm. It was an awesome spectacle. The dark gray sky had descended to the surrounding mountaintops. Yet from certain of these a great suffusion of pink arose to finally blend out into the enveloping grayness. There was also a suggestion of green.

"In my country that looks like hail," I remarked.

Sure enough we did get a little hail. But it was mostly just a violent downpour. Mr. Kerr drove on undaunted. The missus and I got a little wet. The rain seemed to come in above my window frame. "No American car would ever let rain in like that," I said to myself.

As if to climax the impressiveness of the storm and the forbidding mountains, we saw a volcano with a great cloud of smoke rising into the blackness from near its summit. Perhaps the pink in the sky had been a reflection of volcanic fires.

Occasionally natives hurried by drenched to the skin or perhaps partly protected by a big banana leaf. These Congo natives, when not in a storm, lift their hats politely to the white man passing them.

When we arrived at Lake Kivu, goal of my honeymoon friends, my ankle was paining me a great deal, so they left me at a doctor's. The doctor was a young chap who spoke no English and so I had to resort to French, largely unemployed since Djibouti. He was of the opinion that I had injured my shin and that I had an infection as well. The leg was extremely tender. He gave me a warm wash for it and invited me to dinner.

After dinner we had an enjoyable evening with the next-door neighbors, who habitually dropped over every evening. They were the district commandant and his wife. Since they had no children of their own, I was not surprised at the affection existing between them and the doctor's two little girls, aged about four and six. When they were ready for bed, they shook hands all around and had a hug and kiss for their foster daddy.

The evening was vivacious as only the French can make it. The doctor's wife was young and pretty. She and the D.C.'s wife sewed and crocheted. All four were simple and unaffected. It was decided that I was to have a room at the D.C.'s in spite of my objections that it was an imposition on account of my leg. Conversation was spirited and full of fun. There is really no experience more refreshing than an evening in a French household. It sparkles.

What better spot to be hospitalized than Lake Kivu, the most beautiful lake in all Africa! And what luck! For in nineteen months of travel I was delayed only once by ill health and this was it. The infection in my ankle laid me up for three days in a place called Goma, but my room was only about three hundred feet from the north shore of the lake. There was plenty of time between shots of penicillin to hobble out and look at the water or to study the nearby volcanoes. The volcanoes were active, and no mistake. Hot lava from a new one had just recently cut the road in two places a few miles away along the shores of the lake. One of these spots had been bridged, although the lava was still hot, but the other required travelers to make a trip by boat across part of the lake. Mount Nyiragonga is Hell in the Ruanda religion and when it erupts it means the souls in torment are struggling to escape from their eternal damnation.

As soon as I was able I pedaled over to visit the Kerrs at their honeymoon hotel in Kisenyi. In doing so I crossed the frontier between Belgian Congo and Ruanda Urundi, a country formerly owned by the Germans but now mandated to the Belgians. My road skirted the shore of the lake and was cut out of lava from the volcanoes. It was called the Corniche Road, and I reminded Jacqueline that we had together traversed the great Corniche Road approaching Monte Carlo a number of years before. The African Corniche is flanked by botanical gardens containing palms, flowering shrubs, and beds of bright-colored flowers. On the hillside away from the lake were a number of homes of modernistic architecture, with terraced lawns, flower beds, and circular driveways from the Corniche. The composite made a Riviera in the heart of Africa.

I found the newlyweds seated on the shore of the lake in front of their hotel. It was a beautiful spot, not noisy, but not completely quiet because the waves splashed against the rocks with sufficient force to occasionally send a few drops of water onto the concrete table in front of them. Kisenyi is called the Bay of Naples of Africa and as I gazed across the bay I was inclined to agree. It was a beautifully clear, sunshiny day and Kivu, Africa's highest lake (4,829 feet), was at her rugged best. The water was "blue as at Capri" even though high waves had been whipped up by a wind which one sensed through sight rather than felt along the protected bay. Mountains and hills rose rather abruptly from the water and tier beyond tier were visible until the shore line faded into purple haze and gray horizon. The surface of the lake also seemed to gradually blend into the horizon in sort of a peculiar commingling of mist and sky. This gave a rather startling effect of unreality. Kivu was like a vast unknown sea from an Edgar Rice Burroughs fantasy.

In Kisenyi, while talking to an Arab trader about a ride south, I was offered a ride by a Portuguese, Rui Cristina. He was driving a truck across Ruanda-Urundi for 260 miles and was glad of an opportunity for company. He was leaving at four the next morning, and I think we both looked forward to the trip. It mattered not that we would have to converse in French, a language not native to either of us.

The road from Kisenyi to Usumbura goes smack through the heart of Ruanda Urundi. It starts off spectacularly with a low gear climb of nearly twenty miles and continues to command attention. It is one of the most spectacular roads I have ever traversed but is off the beaten track—if any track in Africa can yet be said to be beaten—so I will have to sing its praises unaided.

The road had been surveyed by a German engineer, according to Rui, but how he ever wound up at a town (I assumed there was one) after leaving his base, I can't imagine. The area is a maze of mountains and valleys. The road stays on top of the mountain ridges most of the way and I think it was plain that this was necessary so the engineer could see where he thought he wanted to go. For whenever we had to descend into a valley, we were as lost as a farmer in a nightclub. Especially throughout its southern half, the road was bordered on the valley side by a row of tall eu-

Some of the grandest views in all Africa are to be seen on the high road in Ruanda-Urundi. (Rwanda and Burundi.)

calyptus or pine trees. These had been planted four to six feet apart and seemed to have reached full growth. There were no low branches, and it was quite easy to enjoy the view at all times. The row of trees enabled us to frequently pick out segments of the road behind or ahead of us that would otherwise have been overlooked.

However, the comfort and presence of these trees were missing much of the forenoon, and as our road clung to the mountain slopes, high, high up, we could usually enjoy the thrill of looking over the edge and down perhaps 1,500 or 1,800 feet of near-vertical mountain side. Rui had been over the road before, yet he was as enthusiastic as I, and when I took pictures endeavoring to capture "the heart of Africa," he took pictures too. There were about three places on the road where there was a near precipice on both sides of us as we drove over a narrow ridge on a saddle connecting two mountains. I had not been over such saddles since traversing the Lewis and Clark trail across northern Idaho in the States and I also recalled the trail to southeastern Utah's lost town of Boulder.

We had one low-gear pull of six miles and later in the day alternating crests and descents of two or three miles each. Rui would not use gears for braking in spite of my broad hints to do so, and I was in some trepidation as to how long the brakes were going to last. He always had to pump these, a common practice all over Africa. I suppose a good brake mechanic was practically unknown.

In those rare cases where the road crossed a low area, it had been built up with rocks and soil all transported by hand. You could not see from where the material had been taken, and it was like riding atop a wall. On the mountain sections, that is to say, for 95 percent of the route, the gravel was held in place on the road on *both* sides by a tiny willow hedge. I say willow because it must have been some member of the family. It looked as though it was a tiny willow picket fence made from sticks about two feet long projecting about six inches above the ground. These sticks were held in a straight line by long withes placed horizontally and tied through the green sticks. Considering both sides of the road, there must have been hundreds of miles of this picket fence. Beyond the fence was the drainage ditch.

Sometimes this little fence was employed to split the road on the sharp corners. Nearly all the latter were divided, that is, there was a barrier of green sticks and short posts to keep meeting traffic separate on each blind curve. This was a practice common in the Congo, and it seemed so practical I at first wondered why we didn't have the same. But I suppose we are too speed-crazy to put up with anything that might actually prevent our cutting a corner.

Ruanda-Urundi was a country of happenstance. King Leopold of Belgium was interested in the Congo region and at a conference in Berlin in the 1880's he tried to draw a map. Because he was not too familiar with

Central Africa, his outline of the Congo region failed to include Ruanda-Urundi and this gave the Germans a chance to set the country up as a protectorate of German East Africa, later Tanganyika. The Belgians acquired it with British help in World War I. Both the Germans and the Belgians retained the native rule of chiefs and a king since it was honest, well set up, and more or less efficiently operated.

Besides the configuration of the land there was much of interest to be seen. The natives along the way seemed to be frightened of the truck and would always get clear off the road in a big hurry, and frequently look away. If they looked at us, their eyes seemed to be haunting and reproachful. As for costume, most of them wore khaki or gray shorts, often tattered. The women wore only a skirt and had no covering for their long pendulous breasts. Many natives wore a white *galabieh* and a red necklace and carried a long spear or staff. They were the Watusi or ruling class, a people of Hamitic stock who came originally from Ethiopia. The Watusi are exceptionally tall, often attaining seven feet. They are the ones who can accomplish such prodigies in the high jump as pictured by Ripley. The Watusi are also noted for their fancy hairdos; and let no American woman think that her sex has a monopoly on those. Watusi coiffures—and they are by no means alike—simply cannot be described in words, and the men spend long hours in working on each other's hair.

There were thousands of small plots of cultivated land on the mountainsides. This led me to believe there must be a tremendous population of natives, and I found out later that the density went up to 300 per square mile. The plots of cultivation were usually far from the huts, and the system was something like that in much of Europe where the people live in villages and grow things on their own plots in the country. There were no labor-saving machines and the ancient combination-hoe-and-spade was swung like a pick by men and women alike. The land on the valley floors was so wet they were forced to heap up the earth so as to leave deep ditches every ten or fifteen feet. Water was usually to be seen in these, but the raised areas could then be used to grow the staple crop, which was beans. Another staple appeared to be kafir corn, and of course the ever present banana. Sweet potatoes, tobacco, and tapioca were also raised. The soil is of volcanic origin and basically very fertile—rich brown in color in the valleys and often quite red on the mountainsides. We passed a government experimental station.

Paths to the plots and to the villages seemed to go straight up the mountainside. They were worn bare by thousands of feet throughout the centuries. It was a marvel there were no signs of erosion. The natives prevent this by horizontal ditches between rows of plots bordered by a thin strip of grass, or the grass alone may be sufficient. The way they had cultivated on nearly vertical slopes was almost incredible.

Once in a while we passed a fairy church perched on a hilltop—like the

Catholic one at Ngozi. It was of light-tan brick trimmed in white stone or white brick. Pretty red flowers bordered the entrances. The town of Ngozi was an eighth of a mile of brick shops all on one side of the road and situated on top of a mountain ridge.

I noticed white Easter lilies growing wild along the road. At one place a mountainside had been planted to a sort of fernlike evergreen tree.

There were herds of cattle with horns that would have put a Texas longhorn to shame. These cattle were a prized possession, for the Watusi were great herdsmen and figured wealth and social position by the number of cows they owned. Among 3,800,000 people there were between one and two million cattle. Each one had its own name and was much too valuable to be slaughtered for meat. The ordinary Watusi greeting was *Amasho,* "I wish you many cattle," and the reply was *Amasongole,* "I wish you many wives." It is easy to see where the women ranked in relation to the cows.

These, then, were the factors that made up what I enthusiastically referred to in my notes as "the greatest ridge road in the world." With the exception of the Lewis and Clark trail road we do not have ridge roads of such combined length and outlook in this country and I do not recall seeing any in thirty countries of Europe. However, the configuration of the land and the views of range upon range of hills reminded me of eastern Oregon on the road leading north from Bend. It was all thrilling from the word "go" —certainly one of the grandest 250 land-view miles in the world.

After Rui left me in the Usumbura area, I made the acquaintance of a number of American missionaries of the Seventh-Day Adventist and Friends churches. I was interested to see how fellow Middle Westerners adapted themselves to the servant problem. They were having quite a time, and "except for the heavy jobs, I'd rather get along without them" was the concensus. Still, I'll bet if they ever go back home to live, they are going to be spoiled so far as doing their own housework is concerned.

Usumbura was on the north end of Lake Tanganyika, and to go southward it was necessary to proceed by boat. A road had been nearly completed along the east side of the lake, lacking but a bridge or two, it was said; but of course completion of such a road would kill the lake-steamer business, so I supposed nothing would be done for years. I bought a ticket for Kigoma in western Tanganyika.

Jacqueline and I boarded the Belgian Congo steamer *Duc d'Brabant.* There was no purser, and the captain made cabin assignments. I sat down opposite him expecting routine, and was astounded to hear him say, *"Pas de place, monsieur."* He had a short list of reservations, and I did not appear on it. I sat there sort of stunned. This was a new wrinkle—to be sold a ticket and then be told by the captain that I could not go.

"And there's no use to expect cancellations because I have two people bearing letters from the governor on the waiting list," he added in acid French.

Well, I stuck around, still sort of stupefied. It was well that I did. After more than an hour of suspense and commiserating with an acquaintance, the captain called me in and listed me as the last passenger. It was also well that I had my medical certificate and exit stamp from Ruanda-Urundi, because he asked for both.

It was a pleasant, clean little ship. We towed a big barge and by morning had put in at a port called Baraka on the Bay of Burton in the Congo. The ship sailed quite smoothly. Lake Tanganyika is the deepest freshwater lake on the globe with the exception of Lake Baikal. Soundings of 3,190 feet have been taken. The north end of the lake is narrower than the average, and we could usually see the mountains on both sides as the voyage progressed. I enjoyed—really enjoyed—my own meals in my room wrestling with a huge pawpaw (papaya) given me by Indian friends in Usumbura, and good fresh bread. Between times I caught up with my diary, chatted with friends, looked at *Life* magazine, and pored through the 1948 edition of the *Union Castle South and East African Yearbook and Guide*. With no seasickness to worry about, a voyage on a mountain lake is something the doctor should prescribe.

When we docked at Kigoma, I strolled about 150 feet along the pier to inquire about boats south. When I returned, the dear captain was in stitches because I had walked off without—believe it or not—paying for my room. Yes, it seemed that even after you had bought and paid for your ticket, both room and meals were extra. This was a new experience! The meals were nothing to brag about either. (I had one as the guest of my Greek roommate.) The captain missed one way to extract more money from the passengers, however: he forgot to charge for the bicycle.

Kigoma! A pleasant little inland town. Bathed in sunshine but with plenty of shade trees. The main street was on a hill. My shipboard friends were bored as usual—sitting on the veranda of the only hotel, just as I remember them sitting around the hotel in Usumbura. But as for me, I had no time to get bored. There was transportation to be seen to, a watch to be fixed, and when such affairs were over, historic Ujiji to visit, only five miles away.

The *Mwanza*, a tiny freight boat, was to leave the next morning for Mpulungu in northern Rhodesia. She had no cabin accommodations and did not ordinarily carry passengers, so I was doubtful that I could get on. Her Arabian captain, Ibrahim Ali, had no objection to my traveling third class if I desired, but it had to be cleared through the office. Here, as I expected, they said Europeans could not travel third. I put up an argument, and the Indian in charge finally said if I got the consent of the district commissioner and a note saying it was O.K., he would sell me a ticket. This I succeeded in doing, though the D.C. admitted it was none of his business. He said that not long back there had been a delegation of Parliament members passing through the territory. They had felt there should be no distinction between white and black, but, as he recalled, they had been denied the right to travel third class on the railroad. The color bar again!

After dinner I pedaled over to Ujiji to see where Stanley had found Livingstone. A fine monument marks the spot where stood the mango tree under whose branches the historic meeting took place. The monument, however, is, as it should be, a memorial to Livingstone. I felt compelled to remove my cap and utter a silent prayer of thanks to God for this pioneer missionary to the Dark Continent and for all the great host of missionaries who have followed and for all they have done to bring light and hope to the natives.

Ujiji was said to be the largest native village in East Africa. There were many streets and hundreds of mud-walled, thatch-roofed houses. But the town was quite neat and clean. No offensive sights or smells or indications of careless living such as I had seen in Spanish mountain towns, for example. Since it was only mid-afternoon, I passed on through the town to visit the White Fathers Mission. Here I was received in friendship and invited to tea. Before this was over, Father Superior Wesselinghe asked me to spend the night with them. Having no further objective for the day, I accepted.

After tea, two of the five fathers (three were from Germany and two from Holland) showed me about the grounds. The most interesting place was the museum with its native figurines of ebony and other woods, musical instruments, drums, walking sticks, bows, shields, and curious skeletons of heads of hippo, lion, and leopard. That night I slept in a room of the old *boma*, built by the Germans and used for administration by them when Tanganyika was a German colony.

The voyage south in the tiny *Mwanza* along the eastern shore of Lake Tanganyika was not particularly eventful. The lake is the longest fresh-water lake in the world, being 75 miles longer than Lake Michigan. It is 420 miles long and 10 to 50 miles wide. I could always see the Congo shore of the lake even though we traveled near the Tankanyika side. Shores were not as impressive as at the north end.

The officers wanted me to sleep at the prow on what passed for the bridge, as it was clean and separate from the Negro passengers amidships, and they were probably used to seeing the white man separate. But the *Mwanza* was only ninety-nine tons, and I declined in favor of a position near the center of the boat where there was much less pitching and rock-ing. This put me among the sailors, and I slept near the English-speaking clerk and an English-speaking passenger. The only cabin was the captain's, forward under the bridge.

I had borrowed some books and magazines of the White Fathers to be returned later. One of the magazines was the March, 1948, *Geographic*, and great was the interest of the sailors in the colored pictures of the circus; and my stories of it, and of high buildings, and fast motorcars in America.

The clerk knew of America through a Montgomery Ward catalogue he had received before the war.

On the third day of the voyage Mr. Pogson, district commissioner for the Sumbawanga District of Tanganyika, came on board the *Mwanza*. He was a native of Christchurch, New Zealand, a town with which I was well acquainted. It is a lovely city, and I was happy of the chance to reminisce about it.

Mr. Pogson told me that Tanganyika had a form of indirect government. The complete tribal organization had been retained. The chiefs had their own courts and might pass judgments, and sentence within limits. The maximum sentence was six months at hard labor, 200 shillings fine, and eight strokes with the cane. Rape and murder cases must be referred to the district commissioner. He got the court books at the end of each month but said he had quashed only three out of 150 cases. There were 94,000 natives of the Fipa (75 percent), Rungu, and Mambwe tribes, and he had only four in jail. He felt this was proof of a remarkable propensity for law abiding and said thievery was practically unknown.

His area was predominately Catholic, but the Jehovah's Witnesses were established near Kasanga, and there was a Protestant Rungu chief at Kasanga. Natives who became Mohammedan dropped their native tongue and spoke Swahili, which was the official language of the country.

29

"And You Don't Carry a Gun?"

A beach of soft sand and nodding palms, smiling up at a tropical sun. A beach with heavily forested mountains rising close behind and a tiny cargo boat in the water offshore. A beach whereon at least a hundred black-skinned, near-naked natives danced about excitedly. Was this an island in the South Seas? No, it was the beach at Kasanga on Lake Tanganyika, darkest Africa.

The most courageous of the small boys on shore swam out to the ship; the others splashed in the shallows. Two large dugout canoes circulated about my tiny freighter. The sun of early afternoon glistened on the waters. Here was a whole world deep in the heart of Africa, contained in one beach and the end of a valley.

Clearly a bicycle had no place here. There was no road leading from the beach or out of the valley. Undoubtedly no wheel had ever traversed the precincts of the tiny village in back of the strand. So it was not surprising that Jacqueline was handled with the greatest care by the two blacks taking her ashore. One devoted all his time to her while the other stood up and rowed with one oar. I followed in the next dugout and packed up, feeling a little foolish to have a bicycle in a place where you couldn't ride it. The freighter was soon to leave, so I was burning my bridges behind me. There was no place to go but forward—or rather upward into the forested mountains. But I had been told there was a native trail.

The ship's clerk came ashore and got a boy to show me the way in from the beach. We walked through two native villages by way of narrow trails bordered by grass higher than our heads. At last we came to the foot of the escarpment from where a rocky trail went straight up. I went about twenty feet and had to stop and rest. My guide had just taken his leave, but when he saw my lack of progress he returned and gave me a boost. And so I had good help for the first three or four hundred feet of the ascent. It was gratefully received because some of the rock ledges were a foot high, there was loose rock to slip on, and a sprained ankle in my case would have been disastrous. Furthermore, the day was hot and I was green from more than ten days of inactivity. The latter factor especially made me no match for my guide's boyish enthusiasm, and I had to be content with merely guiding the cycle and keeping it upright. When he left I gave him forty cents (8 American cents), for I was down to my last shilling, having only traveler's checks.

The trail was not too bad from then on, but there was plenty of work.

How it reminded me of my experience in the Rocky Mountains at home with the same old bicycle when I had taken a two-week holiday on some of the abandoned mountain trails in Colorado! The trees did not entirely obstruct my views of the shimmering expanse of Lake Tanganyika far below me, and on one occasion I spied the *Mwanza* and the barge she towed. By evening I had attained the top of the escarpment and entered a tiny village.

A native volunteered to show me the way out and continued to follow me in spite of my goodbyes and thank-yous. He knew his stuff, though, because after I had lowered myself down a steep slope over huge boulders, I came to a good-sized mountain stream. It was quite deep and full of great stones, so I welcomed his aid in wheeling the bicycle across and in getting it up on the opposite slope to comparatively level ground. Jacqueline was too heavily loaded to be picked up and carried.

A half-hour further along brought me to an area where many trees had been cut down by the government for tsetse-fly control. This pest is the carrier of sleeping sickness. The trees had not been trimmed or removed, however, and I had to maneuver around and under them. Beyond this area I made camp for the night under a large tree in the forest. I looked up at the bright stars and felt content to be on the road once more instead of on an old steamer.

I struck village number two about breakfast time. After debating whether to enjoy my meal in solitude or eat in the village and learn of the people, I decided on the latter. It was not long after my arrival that I discovered the best English speaker in town—a lad of about sixteen. He got me a little native stool to sit on. It looked as though it was made out of a log, as it was round and of one piece cupped to the shape of the human posterior. He also produced a good wooden folding chair, a strange article for a village reached only by a narrow trail.

Of course I had a big audience. I asked my host—as it was his house I was seated by—to tell me the population of the village. It was sixty and I estimated that to be the size of my audience. Every can I brought out was of great interest. Currently I had three cans for sweets—one lemon and melon jam, one quince jam, and one sugar. Then there was an empty butter can, and I filled this from a newly bought tin. I opened a big tin of fish and put the remainder in a spare food can. My host asked for the two empty tins, and he had scarcely got them when his mother reached over the heads of a couple layers of boys and snatched them. By way of compensation she came back with two eggs. I had to request that these be boiled. I gave my host his first taste of white bread, butter, and jam, and canned fish.

When I left, he and a few others walked a way with me. At my request they pointed out cassava, a small bush like sumac. There were four bushes planted on each of a number of raised mounds about four feet square. One of the tubers—white and jim-dandy—was unearthed for my inspection.

I was able to ride along the trail for many stretches both before and after the village. It took a great deal of balancing, though, as the track twisted around mounds of earth and stumps. I met a cavalcade of women and girls bearing baskets of bright-red fruit and eating some of it as they walked. Midst signs and laughter I learned that the red shell was to be thrown away and only the pulp and seeds eaten. I believe it was pomegranate; it was surely sour and thirst-quenching.

Just before reaching the Rhodesian boundary I found a barrier on the trail and a small open-sided, wood-and-thatch pavilion. A chap in uniform with a net on the end of a short stick scurried about the back of my bicycle. He was a tsetse fly control man. Here at last was a chance to get the lowdown on what the durned things looked like. From his catch box I could see I had been bitten in both Uganda and Tanganyika. Sleeping sickness, here I come!

It was still not yet noon when I reached a third village. On my leaving it, ten boys, big and small, guided me through the tall grass and down a steep dirt declivity to the Kalambo River. Here was the dugout placed there by the government for crossing, but it had water in it and looked decidedly unused. The boys led me farther along to a forked tree. This leaned out over the water in the best "ole swimmin' hole" tradition. One of the guides waded nearly across to show me how deep the water was and then returned to help me carry bike and load. I had carefully explained to the boys how my present financial matters stood, but they indicated it made no difference to them. As we waded across in thigh-deep water, I thought what a picture it would make if only my camera had not just broken. For we were crossing the Kalambo River, just above Kalambo Falls, the highest continuous waterfall in Africa. And not only that, but it was crossing from Tanganyika Territory into northern Rhodesia.

We struggled up the Rhodesian bank, floundering about amongst the tall grasses trying for footholds. Then we packed up and walked beside Jacqueline for a way until we reached the vicinity of Kalambo Falls. Then we crept carefully down to the edge of a mighty canyon. To our right and a little below us the river flung itself into the gorge. One of the lads said it dropped 800 feet, but I recalled seeing the figure of 710 feet in print. The scene was wild and impressive. And very frightening too! For to really see the bottom of the fall it was necessary to stand on the very edge of the abyss. When I looked straight down, not a rock or tree impeded my line of vision. It was worse than a sheer drop; it was an overhang. If I moved my feet eight inches I would fall without touching for 800 feet. Perhaps more, for just below me the river plunged again into a second and narrower gorge. I could not estimate the height of this fall, but I recalled reading that subsequent falls accounted for 500 more feet of drop. The canyon and fall recalled Norway's Voringfoss to my mind. I feel that the Scandinavian wonder has a more impressive setting, but this thought did not mar my enjoyment of the Kalambo. It definitely should not be missed.

My guides had kept farther away from the rim than I and had seen to it that the six little tots—most of them in birthday suits—kept even farther away. When I turned to go, we found that they were picking a sort of red nut from some of the trees. This nut they called *mkunzya*, and I found it agreeable.

We next visited the lip of the falls, and I filled my canteens for the journey to Abercorn. As we sat watching the water start its leap I learned in Swahili from my guide that high water is in February and low water in September. It was then June.

I made my camp that night in a forest of northern Rhodesia. There were stars and a moon. Just when the moon seemed the brightest and over my head was about an hour before daylight. It was plenty cool, and I used all layers of my sleeping bag.

In Abercorn I became acquainted with a Polish youth of twenty—an evacuee. "When the Russians invaded," he said, "they told us, 'Come, you must live our way of life. There is no place for rich people.' So we were put into boxcars and on a train with cattle and were shipped to Siberia. If I were to tell you of all the things we saw, you wouldn't believe me. We were a month getting to Irkutsk. It was February and very cold. We went three days without a speck of food. And this not once, but several times. Then, when Germany invaded Russia, Russia said, 'Oh, you Poles are very nice people. If you would like to go fight the Germans, your family may go wherever it likes.' So my father joined the Polish army, and my mother, sister, and I went to Tashkent, then across the Caspian Sea to Persia. Then by boat to Karachi in India, then to Mombasa, and then to the Polish refugee camp in Abercorn. [I recalled a Polish refugee camp in Kampala.] Now my mother and sister have gone to join my father, who is still in the Polish army in England."

Late that afternoon found me on the trail road to Nyasaland. It was ideal for cycling—long, easy upgrades and long descents. One of the descents was unusually long and steep—down, down, down into the bowels of the mountains. Night overtook me before I reached the bottom, and I encamped in a forested canyon with plenty of boulders on the slope above me. I had seen no native villages or even natives for many, many miles.

"I'll lay five to one this is lion country," I said to myself as I crowded through supper in the fast deepening semidarkness. The feeling was a sort of sixth sense—instinctive—one might say. I thought also of buffalo. Of elephant I had seen no signs, and it was not the sort of country I had learned to associate with them.

I unrolled my sleeping bag so that my head would be at the bole of a large tree. After zipping myself in and snapping the outer covering shut, I lay there wondering how fast I could get out if a lion came sniffing around, and if I should have unscrewed my camp axe from the bicycle in order to have it handy for a battle. While attempting to resolve these problems, I fell asleep and the silence of an African night closed down over the forest.

Morning brought July and a continuation of my excellent cycling road. It occasionally crossed a new superhighway (African), being cut through the bush and anthills. The latter are not the ordinary kind but great mounds of earth fifteen feet deep and twenty or thirty feet in diameter. I said, "Hello" at a couple of road camps along the way but was exasperated when no one seemed to have the remotest conception of the meaning of the word America. Later I was given a ride by Mr. Mathis, the driver of a Public Works Division truck—the first vehicle I had seen all day. Mr. Mathis, the road boss and the only white man in many thousands of square miles, was a witty Swiss who had come to Africa as a Catholic brother in 1934 and had come to be a road engineer. This was not surprising, as these brothers are masters of many trades. He was lonely, and he admitted that he was glad to have me for company and hoped I would stay the night with him and ride on his truck the following day. He tempted me with accounts of how much hillier the road became later on, but he need not have worried very much about my declining.

Like most chaps in lonely places, Mr. Mathis was a great talker.

"I have seen two fellows on motorcycles," he began, "but never anyone on a bicycle. It would take an American to do that. No one else would try it.

"And you don't carry a gun? [Mr. Mathis had three.] Well, I suppose you think the lions won't bother Yanks. That place you slept last night— that's lion country all right. And only today, near there, I saw two buffalo. I thought for a minute they were going to charge my lorry. . . .

"You've got a lot of guts. . . .

"And so you have a wife at home. By George, that does it. . . .

"I've got two brothers in the States, you know. Wine growers. Latrobe, California. . . .

"Say you're lowering the opinion of the natives for Americans. They think all Americans ride in gold and silver automobiles with brass plates three inches thick. And now you come along on an old bicycle. . . .

"No, those road camp lads understood you were an American all right. They just wouldn't believe it. They had never seen one before."

Mr. Mathis had a garden of his own about seventy miles away. And so we each had a huge raw tomato for supper; also a rich, fresh vegetable soup, carrots, potatoes, and cold roast beef, with cucumbers and sliced tomatoes available. We reminisced on Switzerland, and he was anxious to hear my comparison with Norway, New Zealand, and America.

Our location was just a temporary stopover camp, so there was no extra bed. But I had a good brick-floored, white-walled room of my own.

By then I was getting inured to the "And you don't carry a gun?" query. And I noticed that my interrogators usually came around to the admission that they had not seen any game themselves or that there really wasn't much danger. They often spoke of leopards but said they would not attack man. They also said lions would ignore you unless there was a man-eater. Usually they will have known of one of these somewhere in the past and will spin a few tales. Mr. Mathis switched from such a tale to mention a lion that came between his tent and his boys' camp one night.

"I wasn't particularly alarmed because I knew there was plenty of cattle about. But he just stood there and roared. And it's the most frightening noise. The ground fairly shakes with the sound. It makes you tremble in spite of yourself. But I've seen them close in the daytime. And from a bicycle too. But he just walked off. Even these buffalo. I think they were just curious about the lorry. Unless one has a wound from a native or something, I don't think they will charge. Of course, a rhino—they will.

"Still, I think the reason no one spoke to you of game in Abercorn was because they never dreamed of you sleeping out in the bush."

When I finally left him the next day, he admitted there was probably no real danger in sleeping out unless there was a man-eating lion. It would be well to inquire about such.

We finally got the old Chevrolet truck started in the morning and began the assault of the first hill. One-third of the way up we stuck. The boy blew into the nozzle of the gas tank, helped the starter by cranking, and Mr. Mathis pumped the accelerator. Finally we got going. Even at a dollar per gallon there was water in the gas. Of course, the car had had no mechanical attention since land only knew when. But like the people in the outback in Australia, Mr. Mathis swore by American cars and said that the British cars were no good for that country.

It was payday, and we had to stop and pay various groups of road workers. Each group had its own foreman, who timidly approached the car, bent his knees a little to one side, clasped his hands above them and uttered a greeting to the "bwana." Then he presented the work cards for his men. Mr. Mathis initialed these and then went to the cash box on the rear of the truck and paid for the month. Each man received 1 pound, 10 shillings ($6) —a wage of 20 cents per day. But Mr. Mathis said that this was high compared with Nyasaland wages. Road workers not on construction, work only six days a week. All start at 6 A.M. and work until about 2 P.M. Then they go and prepare their food—the first meal of the day. This will be millet flour cooked in boiling water. Mr. Mathis said the result was like concrete and if he or I ate it even a couple days, they would have to chisel it out of us after we were dead. The workers eat again in the evening, rather late, as it has to last them until the following afternoon.

Being the only white man in such a vast area and with about twelve hundred boys working under him, Mr. Mathis was practically a king. He was building this great new road from Tunduma to Abercorn—130 miles— and would have to maintain it after it was built. All construction was by hand labor. The big boulevardlike result looked incongruous for the per-haps-two-times-per-week vehicles that passed over the route. It looked too good to have been built without surveyor's instruments and Le Tourneau earth movers.

I made camp that night in extremely hilly country on a lonely road leading toward Nyasaland, a British protectorate 520 miles long but only about 60 miles wide.

For breakfast I had a table and chair in the sun at a native dispensary along the road. The attendant was pleased to have me visit his establishment and look at his medicine and books. Around noon I stopped at a native village and took a picture. Half the inhabitants stood up as stiff as ramrods for the occasion. By night I stumbled onto Fort Hill, the outpost of Nyasaland. I say stumbled because it was unexpected. There were no mileage posts or signs in most sections of the African bush.

Sunday and the Fourth of July! I determined not to eat alone in the bush on such a day. I hunted up the native in charge of the local P.W.D., deliberately made friends with him and invited myself to dinner but offered to provide my share of the food. The natives were sold on the idea that "native" food is not good for Europeans, and so, while they wanted to do the honors to visitors, they felt that they could not. I always encouraged them by saying I could eat anything, but usually they insisted on preparing something special. So today we had rice and fried chicken. Yes, fried chicken, just as at home on Sundays. A body away from home in the heart of Africa couldn't kick on that, now, could he?

Since it required fully two and a half hours to prepare this dinner, I pedaled quite steadily thereafter; and when I was offered a place to sleep at 5:30, declined in favor of another half-hour's work before dark. This was at a P.W.D. camp where I stopped to get oil for my bike. How did I know they had oil? Well, a *capitao* I met on the road told me. A *capitao* is a sort of boss of a project, the word being borrowed from the Portuguese. This man was in charge of making bricks and of construction work on European resthouses, P.W.D. camps, and the like.

"Where did you learn to make bricks?" I had asked him.

"At the Livingstone Mission [Scotch Presbyterian], sah."

And so it was throughout Africa. Ask a native where he had learned to teach, and he would reply, "At the mission." Ask him where he had learned to speak English: "At the mission school, sah." I felt that when I reached home I would urge our church folk to give more support to their missionaries.

Two days later I got a ride with the first car going in my direction in many days. Salesman Lance Corning had picked up a chunky good-humored pal named Ronnie Grewcock to keep him company in a 1948 Ford coupe. The three of us traveled together to a place called Njakwa Gorge, where we accepted an invitation to the hospitality of the solitary resident, the white road boss. He was absent, but his wife, Mrs. Knight, and a lively young matron guest did us the honors.

One of my problems for some time had been how to see Lake Nyasa. It is a lake about as long (340 miles) as the great Tanganyika and nearly as wide, but it lay about fifty miles off my route to the east. The road over from Njakwa Gorge was the shortest I was likely to find, but at the same time it was quite mountainous. It is no fun to go out of the way at any time on a bicycle because you know you must come back over the same route. But on a mountain road, such procedure often becomes mental torture. Now the road over to Livingstonia and down to the lake was also famous for its daring and its stupendous scenery. Gordon Plant at Mombasa had told me of it, and my guidebook mentioned the great difference in altitude between the mountains surrounding the lake and the surface itself. I had mentioned these descriptions to Ronnie and Lance, but without any real hope that they would swerve from their southern path and take me over. Now, however, I found able allies in Mrs. Knight and her guest. The guest enlarged upon the scenic views and the thrills of the road from Livingstonia down to Florence Bay. The former spoke of the daring driving necessary to get over the road and of her husband's success in improving it. The road dropped from 4,100 feet elevation to 1,145 feet on an estimated seven or eight miles over twenty-two switchbacks. Fourteen of these formerly required reversing to get around, but now her husband had reduced this number to five or six. I pointed out that the mountains around the lake attained heights of 8,565 feet, and over 10,000 feet at the extreme north. Ronnie was all for the side trip too, so we finally got Lance to go.

The trip was all that we had expected. We had switchbacks before we even got to Livingstonia. And the views of the lake after we left that place were quite impressive and awe-inspiring. It was a clear day, and we could easily see across the lake to the mountains and shore on the Portuguese side. The beach was clearly distinguishable. There were no roads along the lake —or hardly even touching it—on that side, and on the Nyasaland side there were only a hundred miles or so. A great lake but with shores mostly a supreme wilderness, just as when Livingstone discovered it in 1859.

When we returned to Livingstonia, we stopped to call on Mr. Watson, the Scottish head of the forty Scottish men and women who run the mission. The mission is handsomely situated on the edge of the escarpment overlooking Lake Nyasa. Buildings and grounds are similar to those of a small Midwestern college, and the establishment was maintained by Protestants in East Africa. However in general appearance it seemed to lack the éclat of the African missions operated by the Catholic White Fathers.

Dinner that evening back at the Knights' was a gala affair. Table repartee was excellent. When it was mentioned that my two children were born just two years apart lacking three hours, the young matron remarked: "That's American precision for you."

Ronnie kept bringing up the subject of my sleeping in the open with the wild animals.

"I'm petrified even sleeping in a resthouse when Lance opens the windows," he remarked on two occasions. "And this chap sleeps right out in the bush miles from anyone." Then, turning to me: "Do you sleep sound?"

"Yes"—I laughed—"though I wake up two or three times as it gets colder in order to crawl into successive layers of my sleeping bag."

"Are you sure it wasn't because some lion or leopard wasn't licking your face?" But before I could answer, he added, "Yes. Did you ever dream anyone was kissing you?"

And so it went on.

The next day I rode south with Lance and Ronnie, but our ways separated in the afternoon. I could have ridden on with them into southern Rhodesia and possibly Victoria Falls, but I did not want to bypass any African countries, so continued south toward Mozambique. Jacqueline and I had some hills to do, but the weather was cool, almost cold—ideal for cycling.

We caught another ride with one of several trucks operated by a district commissioner. He had been transferred to a post in the south. This was a stroke of luck because no one else ever seemed to travel on the central Nyasaland section of the road. The trucks were loaded with natives and household equipment. I rode with them for three days and thus had a chance to observe the same natives over a longer period of time than usual.

The amazing thing to me was how little the native men and women ate. We would travel all day, and they wouldn't have a thing to eat. Of course, I had to have my three squares a day. I was told that the natives sometimes went three days without eating. Also, that although they looked very strong and healthy, they were really quite weak physically.

We stopped at a small village in the center of a tobacco region. It was the tobacco season, June, July, and August, and the town of Mponela had swelled in population. There was a tobacco board set up to ensure the natives' getting good prices for their crop. I found a white man here—a Dane —one of three representatives of a United Nations committee scattered about the world to observe education of the natives. He invited me to spend the evening with him, and after supper we sat around a good fire in the fireplace and appeased our intellectual starvation. From Hamsun and Ibsen we turned to the Russians and the Germans. My host had spent six years working for the government in Rumania, four years under German rule and two under the Russian.

"With two very minor differences the Russians and the Germans are exactly the same," he said. These differences are that the Russians do not have the prejudice against racial groups that the Germans have, and they are not quite so sadistic."

As we progressed southward the interminable bush partly disappeared and the villages became more frequent. These assume the usual East African appearance—cement and brick stores with long porches, their roofs supported by square white pillars. Through the open doors one saw long shelves full of bolts of cloth of all colors, for the African, as I had occasion to observe every time our truck stopped, will spend his money on cloth or blankets or a pretty handkerchief while his stomach continues empty hour after hour. So the merchant stocks dry goods, with perhaps a few boxes of soap, some lanterns, and odds and ends. Ninety percent of the merchants were Indians, dressed in white shirt and trousers. The other 10 percent were Greeks or natives. In front of the stores, or out in the open near them, was the ubiquitous Singer sewing machine, with a black sewing busily. Everything is custom work, you see. What a country for the sewing-machine salesman and the sewing-machine repairman!

About midafternoon of the second day, our driver suddenly decided for the first time that he would like to put something into his stomach. But alas! no tea to be had. Finally he found a wayside native hut with teapot plainly visible, and stopped. There were some little cakes, and two or three of the boys bought up to three each. As they returned with these tidbits, I could see by the gleam in their eyes that they felt they had food enough to last them for another day.

The road continued to be horribly rough, jolting us like fury. I rode in the cab, but the natives on top of the truck, no cushions to sit on, and full in the raw, cold wind, looked anything but comfortable. One lad spoke English, and I often talked to him.

"Aren't you cold?" I asked, noticing the goose flesh on his legs.

"Oh, very cold, sir."

"Haven't you eaten anything all day?"

"Oh no, sir."

"Well, will you have something to eat tonight when we stop?" I pursued.

"I don't know, sir. Maybe we might."

I recalled a Greek telling me that when wild game was killed on a hunting safari, the natives could eat for half a day without stopping but they might not eat again for a long time.

This chap was a member of the Yao tribe and spoke the Chiyao language. The Yaos are of Bantu stock and have worked into southern Nyasaland from northern Mozambique (Portuguese East Africa). Though my friend did not give much evidence of it, the Yaos are supposed to be the tallest and strongest of the Mozambique peoples. In the past they were slave traders, but the English brought them into subjection in 1896.

Later I pursued my interrogations.

"What is your work for Mr. Borman?"

"Houseboy, sir."

"Oh! . . . And how old are you?"

"Twenty, sir."

He seemed so like a little boy of fourteen that I hesitated to ask my next question, yet did so, knowing that natives marry young.

"Are you married?"

"Yes, sir."

"Do you have children?"

"No, sir," with an embarrassed grin.

"Where is your wife?"

"Just here, sir," indicating a pretty girl shrouded in a blanket beside him. She was wearing a red bandanna headpiece and shyly turned her face away as we mentioned her, covering it partly with her blanket.

A bit later I asked, "How long have you been married?"

"Just since July third, sir." This was only six days.

"Oh, you're on your honeymoon trip, then! How does one get married in this country?" I had to explain this new question asking if they went before a minister, just announced it to the village, or what.

"Just tell the parents, sir."

"And then you are married?"

"Yes, sir, you have to pay."

"Oh, you pay a dowry to the wife's father?"

"Yes, sir."

"How much did you have to pay?"

"Six pounds, sir." (About $24.)

"And do you have divorce?"

"Yes, sir."

"How do you do that? Just tell your wife to go home?"

"Yes, sir."

"And supposing the wife does not want the husband. Can she send him away, too?"

"Oh, no, sir."

It would seem that there are definite advantages for the male in the African marriage system.

30

Civilization Again
—and the Color Bar

In the palatial mountain home of a tea planter in southern Nyasaland, I am the weekend guest. The house is nestled high up on the base of Mlanje Mountain, which yet towers over four-thousand feet above us. It is a great, gray granite mountain with a bare rock face like a dome in Yosemite. Down from the summit flows the Likabula River to pass within a few hundred yards of the house, which sits on a fertile shelf above it. From either the open or closed verandas of the house we can see off across a great expanse of rolling plain to a distant mountain ridge, often haloed with a band of cloud in a light-blue sky. A eucalyptus tree neatly bisects the view without disturbing it, because this variety has only very little foliage and that is near the top.

The lawn is attractively landscaped with natural stone, a goldfish pool, dark-red bushes, and a bright-red poinsettia tree. In the open, red-brick pillared patio at the back of the house is a heavenly-blue morning-glory vine, and less than ten feet away a tiny rivulet rushes down from the heights to join the Likabula.

Inside the house the rooms are very comfortably, even luxuriously, furnished. A half dozen black boys flutter silently and quickly about to take care of our slightest wish. The meal tables groan with thick steaks and a variety of good food. No less than fifteen cats sniff the savory odors from various corners of the dining room.

Yes, the Likabula Estate is a paradise for both cat and man. And should man weary of its spacious precincts, two latest-model sedans stand ready on the curving drive. Verily there are rewards for the bicycle traveler who sleeps on the ground and eats bread and "tin" through the more remote regions of the earth.

One forenoon my host, George Hay, drove me down the mountain and across to his tea plantation. He explained the A to Z of tea to me, and here it is.

The tea bush is allowed to grow into a tree when seed is desired. The seeds are put in nursery beds to a depth of three inches, the position being important, for if the stem side is put down, the tree will grow into a knot. George dug up a sprouted seed to demonstrate this. The seed was a little larger than the end of my finger.

When the plant emerges from the ground, it is shaded by a grass-

Likabula, a tea estate in Nyasaland (Malawi), where I spent two pleasant days (along with 15 cats).

covered framework for a period of twelve months. After two years in the nursery the tea bush is about three feet high. It is then cut down to a height of four inches and transplanted to the field with a three-foot space each way. This makes about 3,500 plants to the acre.

The tea bush is trimmed or pruned every year to keep it in umbrella form. The yearly cut is about two fingers' width higher that that of the preceding year, until the plant gets too big and too knotty, when a heavy prune is made to cut it back to eighteen inches. The fields are full-bearing by November, when the rains and the heat come on. The bush reaches full capacity in about five years, and it then lives forever unless white ants or careless cultivation destroy it.

Tea is picked by "pluckers" who take the top three leaves on each shoot. A plucker may take 120 pounds of green leaf per day during the picking season, October to March. The leaf is taken to the factory and dried on hessian racks (sacking on frames) and loses approximately 25 percent of its weight in about eighteen hours. It then proceeds to tea rollers, which have the same action as if you rolled the leaves between the palms of your hands. This is a thirty-minute process for each 400 pounds, and certain juices are expressed. Then a trap door drops the tea into a "trolley" (floor truck) and transfers it to a sifting machine of one-fourth-inch mesh wire. The leaf is by then pulverized enough to go through. That not able to pass through is rolled again.

Meanwhile fermentation has started, and this process continues for about two hours, with the tea spread out on a table covered with tin. The leaf then goes into a drier, where layers of shelving allow fan-driven air at 180 degrees to circulate freely. The tea leaves, now nearly as small as you see them on the market, drop from one layer to the other and out the bottom. A cutter and stalk extractor break the leaves up to smaller sizes.

Another tea sifter, which resembles a farm fanning mill, then takes over. The finest grades come out the bottom. Each grade is next winnowed in a long tubelike box with a fan at the end. This process further classifies the tea by weight, and these classes are segregated in wooden boxes for storage and sale. The final product is in weight one-fifth of the original.

Production was about 700 to 1,000 pounds of made tea per acre. George had 300 acres in his plantation, but apparently some was not cultivated, for he put his production at 80 short tons. The market price was around two shillings (50 cents) per pound.

In George's office were tea-tasting cups and small china "jugs" for the use of inspectors. The leaves were placed in the lids of the jugs for comparison with the liquor in the bowls.

After a fine roast dinner one evening, we motored about twenty-five miles along the base of Mlanje Mountain over to visit a neighbor near Portuguese territory. This was a wonderful drive. The great mountain—

rock-bound and vast in extent—dominated the scene. It is really like Grand Mesa in Colorado, an area of forests and small streams located far above the surrounding country. We could see two fine waterfalls tumbling down the slopes in the distance. Dark clouds hovered overhead. The escarpment was first class from a scenic standpoint and reminded me of great views I had seen elsewhere in the world.

Meanwhile we passed through a number of tea plantations. On some of these were rows of tall trees, supposedly for shade, but the foliage was much too high. When the tea planters decide they are of no value, they are ring-barked and after a year are removed. If taken out when still living, a certain starch in the roots would injure the tea bushes. But when the tree dies first, the starch passes up into the trunk.

Trees of unusual type or rare beauty move me to admiration as much as a fine mountain scene. On our drive we passed down a long lane of closely planted flamboyant trees. This type of tree split into three or four trunks just a few feet above the ground and then flared out away from the center, growing upwards to perhaps fifty or sixty feet. Foliage was confined to the top of the tree so that the trunks, in this instance, formed a symmetrical colonnade for the road, while the foliage made a complete roof overhead. Then there were rows of stately jacaranda trees, and thick groves of Australian blue gum. Since the leaves of the latter are also near the top, the forest sometimes looked like a great battery of telegraph poles. We also passed through a dark-green virgin forest containing a great number of mahogany trees. When we reached our destination, there was a magnificent specimen of a flamboyant tree on the spacious lawn. I snapped a picture with the dark escarpment of Mlanje Mountain in the background. A wonderfully moving sight it was! And as I stayed about the home, the equally magnificent lone mahogany tree grew on my appreciation. It was so dark when I decided I must have a picture that the exposure required five minutes.

Up at six the following morning, and George made an announcement of the seven-o'clock breakfast beforehand.

"Well, fella, I've ordered a good thick steak, a couple of fried eggs, and some fried tomatoes laid on for you. How does that strike you?"

"Sounds fine, George."

I ate too much at every meal. Besides the morning steaks, we had everything from pork and mutton roasts to brawn. One evening we had thick whipped cream for our peach dessert and I introduced the Australian custom of putting the cream on bread, butter and jell. They all liked it. And speaking of customs, we always adjourned to the parlor after the meal to take coffee; and in the mornings, orange juice was served on the closed veranda just before the bell rang for breakfast. The fifteen cats were present at every meal and meowed frequently. When this occurred enough to bother my hosts, they would take long sticks kept especially for the purpose and attempt to chastise the offenders. None were allowed on the table except the old mother cat, who was in her teens.

On Monday George drove me to Blantyre, the commercial center of Nyasaland. He was much taken up with the idea of anyone going through darkest Africa on a bicycle and hastened to introduce me to all and sundry as a chap who was pushing a push bike through Africa.

"He only just came down from Cairo," he would add to completely floor the listener.

And it was useless for "honest Joe Rosdail" to try and interject the fact that he often rode in cars and trucks.

En route home that evening we thrilled to some really amazing sunset effects on the granite precipices of Mlanje Mountain. Dark heavy clouds just over the summit made a striking contrast with the pink and fiery cliffs below it.

The evening was a gala one. Another guest, Warren Blenheim, turned out to be a wit, and both George and I were in good form. Commercial psychology, why earn money, are you afraid of old age, and a lot of other sense and nonsense afforded the subject matter. Ah, who can record these conversations after they are past! Not one brilliant sally now comes to mind, yet how clever we thought they were at the time.

George had arranged for me to ride with Warren all the way to Salisbury, southern Rhodesia, in a jeep station wagon. We started late the following morning. Our road led across Mozambique, sometimes called Portuguese East Africa, a country larger than Texas. The customs men were not troublesome—were quite agreeable in fact. The Portuguese mark all their boundaries, and some of their main-route intersections, with large cement crosses about ten feet high on terraced bases of concrete. These are set in the middle of a small cleared area marked off by stones. Mozambique was quite hilly and the roads were no smoother than they had been in Nyasaland. Some of the country was a tumble of gray boulders like the Silver Gate area in Yellowstone. Bridges were concrete, quite narrow, and without guard rails.

Night found us deep in Mozambique and on the bank of a wide river only about three miles from a place called Tete. I rolled out in warm comfort in my sleeping bag under a tree. Warren shivered and squirmed the night through on a cushion in the jeep, which was minus two windows. So it was no wonder he woke me up at 5 A.M.—before daylight. The ferry lad had promised to take us across then, but it was nearly seven before the boys were ready to load us. Meanwhile Warren fretted and fumed.

"Bloody awful, this. . . . G——, how stupid they are. . . ."

Such ejaculations were made within their hearing. Yet Warren was always ready to let the black boys' willing fingers work at ripping the box off a case of petrol for refueling the jeep. And the previous day he had been proud of the black boys' job of making a cover for the gas tank. But of course no praise had been given direct to them. In Africa, black and white are too far apart for that.

We were slowly poled across the river. Three more miles brought us to the wide, and here placid, waters of the great Zambezi, fourth river of Africa. On the opposite side we could see the yellow and white walls of Tete, a sort of metropolis for a vast region of bush and timber. Extensive deposits of coal lay ready for development in the surrounding area, and other vast natural resources lay practically untouched. We ferried across the Zambezi on a one-car raft on pontoons towed by a wheezy launch which made a circuitous route so as not to buck the current.

By afternoon we were out of Portuguese territory and had entered southern Rhodesia, my fifty-seventh country. Near Salisbury, its capital, there was a little farming and open ranch land. From here I hitched a rough all-night ride on a truck to Bulawayo, railroad junction to the southeast.

Mounted once more, I pedaled Jacqueline out of Bulawayo on the road leading northeast to Victoria Falls. The start in the afternoon sunshine and bush reminded me of the road out of Mount Isa in Queensland, Australia, so many months before. By nightfall I was twenty-seven miles out, and a bush farmer, John Durand, standing by the road, invited me to stop for the night. He said there had been an airplane crash near by and that the ambulance was coming; and he invited me to go along with them to the scene. This was only about an eighth of a mile off the road and was my first view of an airplane crash. The standard phrase, "the wreckage was strewn about," may be trite, but it is the most adequate. I now learned what was meant by "twisted metal" and "force of impact." And this crash had been a long horizontal affair, not a plunge. The pilot had struck a tree or he might have been all right, as the bush was not too heavy. The wings were torn off and the wheels thrown to either side. The engine was the farthest along on the path of crash, but the fuselage had reversed so that the cockpit now faced the opposite direction. The poor pilot lay at right angles to the fuselage about midway of its length. There had been no fire, but his nose had been brushed upwards and he seemed to be partly scalped. There were two great cracks in the side of his head.

No one had heard the crash. One of John's native boys had discovered the wreckage about 4 p.m. and John had phoned Bulawayo for an ambulance at 4:10. The ambulance arrived at 5:45—one hour and forty-five minutes later—so it was just as well that the poor chap had probably been killed instantly. The excuse was that there had been an earlier airplane crash and the ambulance was out. The driver of this ambulance refused to take a dead man, so John, the driver, and myself lifted the body into the back of John's pickup. When I removed the middle sack with which we had lifted it, my hand brought away fresh blood.

Kalambo Falls—one of the highest in Africa (Tanzania-Zambia boundary).

"The bush" in Rhodesia.

Shortly after our reaching the road, a Red Cross ambulance and six or seven young chaps from the airfield arrived. All were dressed in the blue gray of the air force. We transferred the body to the new ambulance, and John drove them up through the bush to the crash. There was conjecture as to why there were not two bodies, as they had expected to find the body of the instructor also. Since there had been no fire, there was talk of failure to refuel before leaving the airport. It was decided to dispense with a guard for the night, and everyone went back to Bulawayo. John and I returned to the house, where Jacqueline had already been taken by one of the black boys.

We had a good supper followed by a dessert of guava sauce. The fresh guava that was shown to me was a yellow fruit about the size of an apricot. It was full of small seeds inside, like a passion fruit. The meat was yellow like the outside and you ate both seeds and meat. With good cream, it was a delicacy reminiscent of our strawberries and cream. Excellent!

But what is the modus operandi of a Rhodesian dairy farm? We have plenty of dairy farms in America, but, as in the case of sawmills and sheep raising, I had to go abroad to see one in operation. So well before daylight I set out with John to make the rounds.

The farm had only recently been turned to dairying, and the beef cattle sold. There were now sixty head of purebred dairy cattle. The bull had cost 625 pounds ($2,500), and the mother had come from Holland. The breed was Friesland. We call it Holstein, or Holstein-Friesian, I believe. Some of the pedigrees were written on standard South African breeders' forms and were therefore in both Dutch and English. Cows were milked at 4:30 A.M., 10:00 A.M., and 4:00 P.M., and fed at those times. Here is the ration: 610 pounds of mealie meal (corn meal), 100 pounds of wheaten bran, 250 pounds of monkeynut meal (peanut meal), 50 pounds of bone meal, 10 pounds of salt, and 10 pounds of limestone. This was fed at the ratio of 4 pounds to a gallon of milk produced averaging 4 percent butter fat. Monkeynut meal being unobtainable, production was down from three gallons per cow to two and one-half, even though sunflower seed was being substituted. Butter fat was running 3.5 percent. Official tests of production ran 300 days. A cow might produce, say 9,000 pounds when three years old and 12,000 pounds at maturity—four years.

There was no milking machine because the natives could not be trusted to run one. I saw how the milk was cooled from 96 or 98 degrees to 50 degrees by running over cold pipes and saw the cooling room where the temperature dropped to 35 degrees.

We took a walk over a few of the 1,300 acres. Truck gardens, oats fields, and lucerne fields were laid out in small plots. John had tractor, plow, disk, and harrow, but I saw two natives working land with an ancient hoe. John said they had tried an American rotary hoe, but it had been a flop. Then they tried a British rotary and it worked perfectly, but it was too expensive, so they had to send that back too.

A plot of oats about four by fifteen rods was being irrigated by the overhead method. A perforated pipe ran the length of the plot and rotated from side to side by water pressure. Water came from several wells about sixty-five feet deep, and modern Fairbanks-Morse pumping units were busy. The lucerne plot was irrigated in normal fashion. It had been sown broadcast and then cut into rows. Near the barn Jim had a long row of bur-fruited strymonium, or *stinkblaa*, supposed to be good for drawing pus from a sore and for asthma sufferers. He also had a plot of small melons resembling a watermelon and bearing the native name of *majordas*. These were fed to stock. In the owner's yard were lemon, grapefruit, and orange trees.

A pleasant forenoon, a fine road—just gently rolling; fine weather for cycling; and bush with trees sufficiently high to provide shade for resting. What could be sweeter! At times like these I felt like continuing my trip entirely by bicycle; but the pressure of prolonged absence from home told me that now I was in railroad country, I should use it for faster progress.

Victoria Falls under a full moon! What could be more appropriate for my first view of probably the world's grandest waterfall? Jacqueline and I approached the spectacle with considerable respect and the tingling of high anticipation. We were in the presence of a scenic great—a Mount Rainier or a Grand Canyon; but this was a scenic great with a voice. We trod softly and studied the moonlit landscape.

Ahead of us were clouds apparently rising from the ground to heights of several hundred feet. I correctly surmised that these were clouds of spray coming from the gorge. As I cycled along I felt that I was leaving some of the roar behind me on my left, yet I knew the falls were visible from the bridge below it, and that, we had not yet reached. The pavement approaching the bridge and the bridge itself were wet as if it had just rained. But from the bridge, sure enough, I could see the falls—or rather a segment of them. For the gorge of the Zambezi is like a giant T with a long top and a short stem. The bridge crosses this short stem and so only a certain central portion of the falls is visible. You see, the water plunges downward all along the far edge of the top of the T.

The falls were almost always hidden by spray, but as I stood on the bridge I found that by patient watching, the spray would sometimes drift away and disclose the beauty of the spectacle. But when the veil was again drawn, there was still plenty left to see. There was the gorge, the boiling river, yellow-green in the moonlight, and the shifting mists filling the space between the walls and often rising high into the air.

This, then, was Mosi-oa-Tunya, "the smoke that thunders" in native language. The spray rises to heights of one thousand to three thousand feet and on clear days can be seen as far as ten miles away.

I picked out a campsite not far from the road and at the same time

Victoria Falls can be a thing of great beauty . . .

. . . or a frightening spectacle . . .

not far from the gorge. The gorge drew me like a magnet, even though the thick grass was quite wet and there was no trail. I made my way cautiously to the brink and peered down in a vain attempt to penetrate the mists below. Here I saw the night counterpart of a rainbow, a lunar bow. Just opposite I could frequently see the brink of the falls with the moon-reflecting water rushing headlong in masses of silver over the edge and down into the unseen depths far below.

My bed had plenty of grass for cushioning that night. I felt that the site was out of the range of the mists as the grass was fairly dry and the mist clouds seemed to stay well away on either side. Still I was not more than fifteen or twenty rods from the brink of the gorge, so I put my raincape over my sleeping bag. It was well that I did because I had two or three Victoria Falls showers during the night.

In the morning I cycled and walked along the path through the rain forest. This path was drenched with rain and spray in many sections but afforded a number of opportunities to get out to the very edge of the abyss. There was a strange fascination about that edge. No matter where you approached it, the drop was apparently absolutely sheer and one single step forward over the long wet grass would send you spinning downward. I say *apparently* sheer because the gorge was so filled with spray and roar that I really felt or sensed the precipice rather than saw it. I was amazed at the quantity of water that ascended the wall below me. It was not a spray —it was drops of water—actual rain—rain falling upward; and then falling again on me—still as rain. I remembered an article by Ripley saying that this was the only place in the world where rain fell upward. It is quite a phenomenon.

And so I stood on the edge at various places and for indeterminate periods, enthralled, peering through the rain into the roaring abyss. If there had been a fairy about, she might have sometimes heard me uttering one of the following very edifying and intelligent ejaculations:

"Ain't dat sumpin?"

"Now whadaya think of that?"

"Broth-er, man!"

As to statistics, the average height of the fall is 353 feet, more than twice that of Niagara. Maximum height is 420 feet. Width is just over a mile, 5,600 feet. The volume varies from dry season, 62 million gallons of water per minute, to wet season, 100 million gallons.

I ate breakfast near the Livingstone Monument, erected to commemorate the famous missionary's discovery of the falls. This was just at the brink of the Devil's Cataract section. I cycled slowly along the footpath that wound through the trees on the very edge of the Zambezi River above the falls. The bank was idyllic in every way. It was so low one was almost on the level of the water. The land was sandy or covered with short grass. Trees were pleasant and afforded shade, but did not restrict the view of the smoothly

. . . or both. Water on the foreground path has rained upward *over 350 feet from the* bottom of the gorge.

flowing blue water and the green wooded islands in the river. I could not see across the river because of these islands, yet having seen the great length of the falls, I knew it must be quite wide. Farther on was the huge baobab tree, supposed to be the largest yet discovered. Its girth is tremendous: 88 feet, 6 inches.

I found a camp ground on the northern Rhodesia side of the falls. It was fairly well tented. To the Dutch family where I stopped to borrow shoe polish, I lamented that the use of tourist cabins in America had much curtailed the number of people camping out. The man showed me a tame cheetah tethered near another tent. I scratched and petted it and found that it purred like a cat. The cheetah is probably the fastest sprinter of all animals. The Dutch family invited me to stay for coffee. Into this we dipped dry chunks of homemade rusks, but I was really more interested in the homemade gingersnaps and cookies. When I left they gave me a large sackful. My hostess was quite anxious to impress me with the fact that the Dutch liked the *real* Englishman but not the one who talked continually of "home" and sent his money there.

"Home is where we live—South Africa," she vociferated. "We are South Africans now—we must forget the other places where we came from."

"You were lucky," added the host, addressing me. "You got your independence; we didn't."

I recrossed to the southern Rhodesia side for the night. On the way, I made rather unsuccessful attempts to photograph the tame monkeys and baboons which take food from the tourists along the rim of the gorge, just as our chipmunks do along the rim of Crater Lake. The monks clambered all over the motorist's car but were slow in learning that it was the chap on the bicycle who really had something to eat.

The next morning fellow campers invited me to a good bacon and egg breakfast. My hosts had no children, and their interest, as usual, had gravitated to other things. Mister had a big bulldog and missus a terrier. Both brought up the subject of religion and told me they had gone beyond orthodoxy and were now interested in yogi and spiritualism. My hosts fortunately spared me a long discourse on the world's "vibrations" but said: "My, there's an awful lot to it."

I finally succeeded in buying a "native" ticket on the train from Victoria Falls back to Bulawayo. This was no easy feat because the color bar is such a strong factor in South Africa. The native fare is supposedly designed for native (black) tribesman and is usually much less than half the price of third class. The railroad men don't like Europeans to travel even third class and permit them to do it at all (and this only in certain countries) only because there are compartments and a certain amount of segregation can be maintained.

In spite of my native ticket I was put in one of the second- or perhaps first-class compartments. These cars were mostly empty because it was a goods train, or, as we would say, a freight train with an accommodation. But when the guard, that is, the conductor, took my ticket, he expressed doubt about the next guard's attitude in allowing me to stay there. "To heck with such worries," I thought, and before guards were changed I piled into the adjoining native car. Not long afterward a porter came in with a broom and ordered every native out of the half of the car where I was. I thought at first it was just because he wanted to sweep, but no, they took their luggage off the racks and vamoosed. Then the white guard and colored assistant came in later, the former took a look at my ticket, grunted, and exploded: "Well, you can't ride in here." Then, to his colored aide, he said: "Take him and put him in a third; and let me know the number!"

But I refused to stay in my prison, and roamed the cars, often sitting in colored compartments to listen to phonograph records. Jimmy somebody, and his songs and yodeling, seemed to be the most popular American record with the blacks.

At 5:30 A.M. after twenty hours of travel for the three hundred miles—some speed, eh?—we arrived at Bulawayo. Later in the morning I succeeded, after much arguing, in buying a native ticket to Johannesburg, far to the south. The chap authorizing the sale of the ticket suggested I might ride in the van. I thought it was all settled and happily stowed the bike and told the guard the suggested arrangement. But woe, how unwise! If I had only hid some place until the train started. He took me back to the ticket office and told them he couldn't take me on a native ticket. Arguments ensued.

"Well, but what do you call a native?" remonstrated a clerk.

"A native is a special class. No, I can't do it. He'll have to go third."

"But colored people ride third too, so where's your color bar?" I asked.

He gave me no reply but said to the clerk, "No, I can't take him. You know it might be found out and we'd both be in trouble."

Unfortunately the guard had us over a barrel because the train was about to leave—it was past time, in fact. So rather than wait all day for another train, I asked for a third-class ticket—but then I had just enough change to get me to Mafeking and they wouldn't change a traveler's check. So I got on the train feeling very sour indeed. I figured that lousy guard had cost me about six dollars. However, I worked my spite around to place it where it really belonged—on the color bar. What a damned nuisance it was! Of course, I felt that I was the one being discriminated against. I was traveling on a shoestring, and why shouldn't *I* be allowed to ride as cheaply as any other human being! Disgruntled, I felt a certain satisfaction when the guard caught me hobnobbing with the colored folk. And at Francistown, the first place of importance in Bechuanaland Protectorate, the stationmaster, or some big shot, squawked about how I shouldn't be in third class.

"You see, we're crowded for room. There are two hundred and seventy men getting on here for the Transvaal diamond mines and you occupy a compartment where we could put six men. Would you want someone in with you?"

Of course, he thought I would say no.

"I would not mind," I said. "I am willing to ride native class. I had a native ticket until the guard there raised a fuss."

"Well, you can go into a coupe," he said. "That's a smaller compartment. You see, you make it difficult for us white people in South Africa. This is speaking quietly, of course."

"Uh-huh," I muttered unsympathetically.

But the colored chap in charge of the labor recruits was a better man than the lot of them. He refused to move me, saying he would tend to it later. After the train had started, he came in and we had quite a chat. He had nine children: one was studying for medicine, another law, and of the remaining two sons, one was to be a carpenter. The father wanted me to give him an address of a good school for medicine in the United States so that his son might be sent there.

The alternate guard later transferred me to the first-class coach. It was very posh. I had the whole car, or salon as they call it, to myself. But I had two African visitors from time to time. One of them was this man in charge of the recruits and the other a lad who had loaned me *Murder in the Vicarage* in exchange for a *Reader's Digest*. This lad had no money and no food, so I helped him out on the food. The recruit chief read the magazine from cover to cover. He told me the color bar was very strong in South Africa and most people would be amazed to see us sitting together. Many jobs were barred to colored folk, and he was worried about the lad, who had trained to be a piano tuner. He said he would not be allowed to visit white homes in Johannesburg.

At about this time I should have tumbled to the fact that the color bar was the reason the Nyasaland district commissioner had never spoken to me. I had ridden in his convoy for nearly three days, having been picked up by part of his all-colored staff traveling in advance. When my truck driver received instructions from time to time, there had been several opportunities for conversation, but the D.C. had treated me as though I were not there. After my first rebuff I had naively assumed he was ignoring me because it was against government rules to carry hitchhikers, or some such. In other words, I figured he was "looking the other way" so I could get a ride he couldn't sanction. I was happy and played the game. But now as I got farther into South Africa, it slowly dawned that he had not spoken to me because I had lowered myself by voluntarily riding with the blacks. So naturally he could not be seen speaking to me in front of his colored help.

Bechuanaland was the first of three British high-commission territories I was to visit in southern Africa. The others were Swaziland and Basutoland. The natives in these protectorates enjoyed a greater measure of freedom than those in the Union of South Africa, which practically enveloped them geographically. The Union government wanted to absorb the three protectorates, and the people in the protectorates were worried the British might not keep their promise to protect them from such absorption. They had reason for their fears because the Union could withdraw from the British Commonwealth of Nations if she did not get her wishes, and this might spell the end of Britain as a world power.

Bechuanaland, larger than Texas, was the largest of the three countries. Most of the land was dry; for five hundred miles I saw nothing but bush, endless bush. How like Australia! Most of the Kalahari Desert lies within Bechuanaland. Due to the unfertile land, the standard of living was hardly at subsistence level. The sewage-disposal plant was the open bush, even for cities holding many thousands of people.

Family organization was strong in Bechuanaland. The huts of each family were clustered together. As the size of the family increased, headmen were appointed, and there was a clan chief. Such chiefs might act with others as counselors to the chief of the tribe. A family did not own a certain section of land, but the chief saw to it that enough food was produced for everyone.

Witchcraft was practiced everywhere, and since there were very few schools, it did not decline. The British had failed to stamp it out by law. When the witch doctor was successful (as he frequently was) in saving people from death by snakebite, the people were impressed. Only widespread education of the natives would remove the evil, and it was said the British were loath to do this for fear their supremacy might be threatened.

The sprawling capital of Bechuanaland, Mafeking, was actually located just inside the adjoining country, the Union of South Africa. Here I completed immigration formalities and again took to the bicycle. On the road I soon realized that it was winter in the Southern Hemisphere. It was cold!

At the edge of the town of Lichtenburg I was cordially received by a young Dutch couple. Willie Lochenberg was a hairdresser and had the usual ruddy complexion of the Dutchman. His wavy hair might have been self-inflicted. His was one of those homes where they first invite you in, set you down, give you something to eat and then let you unfold your business or not, as you wish. They had company during the evening and though Willie spoke English, Afrikaans was spoken. A very attractive little German girl of ten was a member of the household, and I was told there was a German community nearby.

The next day I received a ride through flat open country and over fairly good gravel roads to Johannesburg. It boasted a population of pehaps 700,000, half black, half white, and larger than Cape Town. In fact, it was the largest city in Africa after Cairo and had all the paved streets, traffic, shops, and high buildings one expects to find in a big metropolis. Here are found some of the largest and finest city sights in the world: the City Hall,

City Hall organ, Newton Market, Anglican Cathedral, and great city hospital.

Johannesburg is the gold-mining capital of Africa and the center of the richest gold field in the world. Silent evidence of this is the great white mounds and hills of mine dumps I saw at the edge of the city. The value of the land has increased incalculably since it was first purchased for a song by a few farmers in the 1880s. Gold is South Africa's greatest wealth. The value has been ten times greater than that of diamonds.

The gold mines at Johannesburg were the deepest in the world. I became well acquainted with a young man who worked in these mines 7,000 feet under the city. He had associates working at the 8,000-feet level. Some shafts went down 11,000 to 12,000 feet. The Number 5 shaft in the Crown Mine was the deepest. He said Johannesburg was completely underlaid with mine workings and that by superimposing a surface map upon a mine map they used to figure out what building they were working under. He claimed that when it came to extent, one could walk eighty miles in one direction under the ground. This was from Springs to Krugersdorp, passing under Johannesburg. I noticed the road map did show at least sixty miles for the distance.

In Johannesburg while trying to buy a pair of mittens—South Africans had never heard of the word—I ran across an American, Sam Katzman. After he had pumped me out of my life's history as usual, I managed to get in a question.

"How did you ever happen to come out to South Africa?"

"Well, that's quite a long story," he said. Then, lowering his voice, he added, "You see, I married a South African."

Sam's house was a full and busy one. His daughter was beautiful, and charming as well, and just home for a holiday during her first year of college at Cape Town. A son and little niece enlivened the table. As usual I had to answer so many questions, I could hardly eat—fancy that impossibility. Mrs. Katzman was more vociferous in her surprise at my age than most people. When she was so greatly astonished at learning I was old enough to be married, I could not resist adding: "And what would you say if I told you I even had children?"

"Children! But you can't possibly be more than twenty-one. How old are they?"

"One is five and one is seven."

"How on earth have you kept your youth? I guess I'll have to start cycling."

Dinner included a fish casserole, fried chicken, excellent marrow, peas, candied sweet potatoes, soup, and a superduper dessert of candy eggs bathed in blackberries.

The family had to attend a wedding reception and left me in charge of the big living room with a nice coal fire, a basket of good apples, and a plate of chocolate candy. I stowed away four apples and a lot of candy before I went to bed. An evening like this made up for a lot of nights I'd spent alone on the ground underneath a tree in the equatorial forests.

Incidentally, what well-to-do family in America would leave almost a total stranger in full charge of their home for an evening?

The next morning Sam drove me down to the hospital, where I eventually located the dental clinic. I needed two fillings, and all dentists had full schedules. Still they worked me in. Two Afrikaner patients forfeited their time to me. Surely nice of them. I can hardly imagine an American patient forfeiting his time to a foreigner. The clinic was modern and managed in the approved fashion, but I felt that the work was not up to our standards. The girls at the desk and everyone treated me with great friendliness and interest.

I started out of Johannesburg in sunshine and under a cloudless sky. It was nearly midwinter in South Africa. The weather was cool and the highway rolling, all ideal for cycling. About half way to Pretoria, capital of the Union, I was given a ride with Hans Van Vuren, a public-works mechanic. He invited me to his home for the night.

We unloaded my gear and went on a sightseeing tour. The Union building which corresponds to our Capitol, was quite impressive. It is a great semicircle with long wings, high on the hillside overlooking most of the town. The hillside below it is terraced and planted to flowers. There was a great long bank of yellow flowers, than a massed bank of red, white, and blue flowers, and a bank of pink and red. Hedge trees shaped like seven-foot mushrooms and planted in long rows helped to set off the terraces and flower beds. Before we left this beautiful slope, the lights started to come on in the city below and around us.

Like all Afrikaners, Hans was interested in politics. I recalled Willie Lochenberg's statement: "You know, man [it is a great South African mannerism of speech to address one as "man"] there is more politics per square inch in South Africa than there is per square mile anywhere else."

Paul Kruger, leader of the Boers, lived and was buried in Pretoria. Born in Cape Colony in 1825, he accompanied his parents on the Great Trek to the countries to the north in 1835-40. When he was only thirteen, he took part in the battles in which the Boers crushed Dingaan, king of the Zulus. In his twenties he saw much service in expeditions against neighboring chiefs and aided in establishing the Transvaal as an independent state. He was commandant general of its forces and after the Boer rebellion, became president in 1883. He died in Europe at the age of seventy-nine and was buried in Pretoria on the anniversary of the day of victory over the Zulus. Always stubbornly opposed to the English, he once told them: "This is my country; these are my laws. Those who do not like to obey my laws can leave my country."

I located Kruger's grave in the old cemetery and then visited the house in which he had lived while president of the South African Republic from 1899 to 1902. It reminded me of President Grant's house at Galena, Illinois —not in size and architecture but in the way the rooms were labeled and the way the Krugerana was exhibited. Paul's pipes, his walking sticks, his sashes, etc., have been carefully preserved. Out back was his great wagon, well housed, in a building of its own.

On leaving the city I detoured past the prime minister's palace and invaded the "strictly private" governor-general's grounds to see "probably the finest administrative residence in the Empire." Yeah, man!

Again, a cloudless sky, sunshine, and cool cycling. The coolness was an asset because there were long ascents on the road to the Premier mine, twenty-five miles out of the city. For the last eleven miles I had a Dutch lad for company and so made better time than if I had lazed along by myself. The Premier, one of the largest open workings in the world, is famous for having yielded the Cullinan diamond. This was the largest diamond ever found, weighing one and one-quarter pounds. From it was cut the Star of Africa No. 1, the largest cut diamond in the world, with 74 facets and a weight of 530.2 metric carats.

We pedaled by large well-fenced compounds containing barracks where the native mine workers were housed. I was surprised to hear a loudspeaker giving news, music, and whatnot, in a volume that could be heard for two miles. My companion said this went on every day from 6 A.M. until evening. The purpose was to entertain and educate the natives, who must remain within the compound for three months at a time.

These blacks did practically all the work in the diamond and gold mines of South Africa. They were recruited from tribes all over the Union and nearby countries, and contracted to labor for periods varying from eight to thirteen months. Board and shelter were provided, but only fifty cents a day was paid in wages. White workers got more than ten times as much. This cheap labor the white man sought to preserve at all costs. He kept all supervisory jobs, no matter how apt a native might be—a policy in direct contrast to the Belgian Congo, where even clerical positions might be entrusted to deserving blacks. But the South African felt his white supremacy and economy must be maintained. He could not forget there were only two million whites in a land of eight million blacks, and to promote or educate the blacks might have unfortunate results for him. The white man also realized he was divided against himself, for the Afrikaner had never forgotten his defeat by the English in the Boer War.

But in spite of the lack of opportunity the natives are becoming educated in increasing numbers. And as this occurs dissatisfaction arises because the native becomes conscious of his abilities and how he is being kept at a disadvantage. Then, apart from poor wages and poorer living conditions, he sees that even with four times the population he has only one-eighth of the land, and much of this is worn or eroded. And he realizes he has inadequate representation in the South African Parliament. Equality is bound to come in South Africa, but the Englishman and the Afrikaner will stall it off as long as possible.

Along the road the next morning I kept company for a time with an old colored man who looked as though he had just stepped out of Alabama. He was dressed in dilapidated hat, old army coat, old puttees, and old shoes. He had worked seventeen years for one master, who had brought him up from Durban. Now he had a new boss. He said the native farm hand had to work for three months before receiving any wage, and then it was only eight to twelve dollars per month. He had nine children and couldn't buy meat and other necessities on his salary. I spoke of raising vegetables, but he said farm hands had to work seven days a week and had no time to do anything for themselves.

At a place called Ankton, I chatted with Mr. Sheihch, a breezy chap who spoke frankly and cheerily, like an American. Although anxious to keep on the road, I finally accepted his repeated invitations to lunch. I was glad I did. He greeted his wife and three children with: "Here's an American chap for lunch. I don't know his name, but it really doesn't matter."

It was a fine dinner and all ready for us. Actually it was a Sunday dinner: soup so thick with barley and vegetable you could almost eat it with a fork; salad, plenty of vegetables, roast, and sweet potatoes as good as from my own garden in Illinois.

"We are Jewish people, you know," said my host.

"I am not surprised," I replied. "I find Jews to be most hospitable."

"Well, it is part of our religion. If I meet a stranger, I am compelled to take him to my home and feed him. He graces my table, you see. I consider that you have blessed my table."

When I left they sent along a pair of long, gray woolen socks, six oranges, six apples, a sack of candy ,and two pieces of chocolate cake—the first I had eaten since leaving America fifteen months before.

That afternoon I was given a ride into Middleburg by a colored ex-army chap in a light pickup.

"We're the real natives of this country," he said. "The Afrikaners think they should be in charge, but its really our country. We had it for hundreds of years before the white man ever came."

If I had then known my South African history, I could have reminded him that his own ancestors, the Bantu tribesmen, were themselves invaders against earlier black peoples.

A short distance beyond the town I was given a ride by a young Afrikaner bachelor named Peter Vander Ploeg. When he went to turn off twenty miles farther on, he asked me to spend the night with him. It was only 5 P.M., and his farm was six miles off the road, but I assented because I sensed how lonely he was living alone and that he really wanted me to come.

Peter gave me the same complaint I had heard from the young bachelors in outback Australia. It was very hard to run a farm without a wife, and it was hard to find a suitable one or one who would live out on a farm. Peter had a nice little house, some cattle and chickens, and 320 acres of land—all purchased with money earned as a gold-mine worker. He had been clearing $300 a month on his chickens, but now he was selling out and getting away. He couldn't stand living alone any longer.

For supper Peter whipped up some *vet koek*, or fat cakes. His recipe for these round tasties, which serve to take the place of bread, is as follows: Measure three cups of flour, add salt and baking powder, and mix. Then add two eggs and enough water to make a sloppy dough thicker than cream. Drop a tablespoon at a time into an inch of boiling fat. Leave it until it gets a nice golden brown.

We ate the cakes with scrambled eggs, cheese, and golden syrup. Eggs were Peter's staple article of diet. There was plenty of meat on the place, but he said his heart was too tender to ever kill any of his chickens, pigs, or cattle. When he made this statement, I had to again think of the color bar. For Peter's tenderness did not extend to other animals of his own species Homo. Within the hour he had spoken of the blacks as being just a little above the beasts and had mentioned filling a few full of buckshot when they came prowling around.

I was to have more experience with the color bar.

31

Animals and Abysses

In Nelspruit I looked up Paul Van Vuren, brother of Hans. He was handsome like Hans—wavy hair, features women dream about, and a mustache. Friendly and hospitable, he asked me to spend the night with him, and when I protested that Hans had already done the honors, he said: "Don't be silly, man! Our whole damn family is like that!"

Meanwhile he had been busy on the phone making arrangements for me to be given a free ride through Kruger National Park, world's greatest game reserve. Of course the authorities prohibited riding a bicycle through the park, so a ride was a necessity for me. The result of Paul's planning was too good to be true. Either on the morrow or on the day following, the telephone men would be driving not only to the park but clear across it and then bring me back to Nelspruit. Further, Paul said that after my park tour he could send me off with a ride clear to the border of Swaziland. The combination of these offers sounded like a fairy tale, so I kept my fingers crossed.

All was not hospitality in Nelspruit, however. There was a man in town by the name of Freiden who had married an American woman. I dropped around to his establishment for a chat, but he seemed to avoid me. Meanwhile a bunch of his interested employees and I were talking and joking and one of them even asked me to his house for the night—my second Afrikaner invitation. But it was a long time before Freiden took me around to the office where his wife was doing bookkeeping; and before either one made anything even remotely resembling a friendly overture, they made certain I wasn't going to touch them for a loan or anything. So that had been the trouble! This had never occurred to me, but considering my overalls-and-shirt attire, and knowing their background—he had lived in my hometown of Chicago—I should not have been surprised. Even after I had strongly assured them that I needed no money and already had a place to stay, I did not receive an invitation to call. I spelled "Help Wanted" or some sort of racket to them. Yet what a contrast here in Nelspruit between old-world, untraveled, unspoiled hospitality and flea-bitten, American-city skepticism!

Sundowner time (6 P.M. drinks) at the Paul Van Vuren apartment. Paul's pretty and vivacious wife shared the honors. I noticed that the wife of a guest uttered no word of English even when Paul addressed her in that language. He told me she was so mad the Boers had lost the war that she

371

never spoke a word of English. This was the second or third time I had run across bitter memories of the war. And this young mother could not possibly have been born until twenty years after the end of the war.

One of the reasons for contemporary Dutch antagonism is the British treatment of the Boers during the years following the discovery of gold. The British policy was to burn the farmsteads and send the women and children to concentration camps. Here twenty-six thousand of them died from dysentery and other diseases. In England only one voice was raised in protest, that of Emily Hobhouse. Today she is a heroine to Boer descendants in the Transvaal but is hardly remembered in her own country.

After dinner Paul and his wife took me for a ride in their sidecar motorcycle, and a friend went along as well. We climbed high above the town and looked down at the lights. Later, back in their apartment, we got into a discussion of wages and prices. They both worked and together received about three hundred dollars a month, two hundred of which went for living expenses. Refrigerators, washing machines, and cars were twice as expensive as in America. Radios were three or four times as much. Stoves, modern sinks, and the like could not be secured at any price. The best they could get was an old-fashioned range.

The following day I rode out through the surrounding areas of the Eastern Transvaal as a guest of an electric-service man. He had a new International pickup, and we climbed up and down the mountains and enjoyed some grand sights. Much of the climbing was in low and intermediate gear.

Talk about scenery! But how describe it? We climbed along a high ridge—and I mean *high*—and on up still higher to a village on a flat-top mountain. The place was called Kaapschehoop. Near here was a vantage point disclosing about half the world, or so it seemed. We could look out over a vast open area surrounded in the distance by mountain ranges. I cannot call this area a plain because it was broken country—hilly, eroded in places, farmed in others, but mostly covered with dead grass. Occasionally, there were homestead plots of trees. We were so high above the area that it looked like a plain until you examined it. Offhand, I can recall no similar views in the States unless it is the one from the Bears Ears in southeastern Utah; but parts of the view were reminiscent of Snake River country. I would nominate Kaapschehoop as one of the ten greatest viewpoints in the world.

From the prodigious summit we descended to the other side. The road went through stately, government-planted forests of blue gum, and was definitely reminiscent of the slopes of the Sierra Nevada in south-central California. Incidentally the climate was much the same as that in California for that season—winter. This was a marked change from Johannesburg; but here I was told it was the edge of the low veld—where warmth started.

As we approached Nelspruit again I noted great fields of cabbages and tomatoes, and groves of oranges, tangarines, pawpaws, and grenadillos (passion fruit). My friend claimed that two-thirds of all the fruit and vegetables in South Africa were grown in the area and that three trainloads went out every evening. Some of the vegetables were dehydrated. Orchards were sometimes bordered with beautiful red and purple bougainvillaea.

The day for my visit to Kruger National Park dawned at last. It is the greatest wildlife sanctuary in the world. First conceived by President Paul Kruger around the turn of the century, it was nationalized and enlarged in 1926 by the Union of South Africa. The location is in northeastern Transvaal near Mozambique, and it covers eight thousand square miles of virgin bush and primeval forest. The climate is pleasantly subtropical in winter and is passable even in summer. Game is plentiful, and the variety is tremendous. Rest camps have been provided for the visitor, and some of these offer near-luxury accommodations—with proper segregation for blacks and Asiatics, of course. Visitors are often housed in rondavels—round, high-peaked, thatched-roof huts with white walls. The number of people visiting the park was on the increase, and it was already the Yellowstone of South Africa in this respect.

We started out for the park at 8 A.M. in the telephone service truck with Mike at the wheel, Cranston on the outside, and me in the middle. The boys were as keen on the trip as I was, even though they had been through the preserve before. And what a break it was for me! We drove 212 miles, took circular drives off the beaten track, and all at no cost to yours truly. My admission would have been two dollars if they had not passed me as a telephone serviceman (my overalls came in handy), and I would not have been admitted at all if on the bike. Further, my chance of picking up a ride through on an approach road would have been slender because the tourists were all in their own cars, already loaded to the extreme with people and camping equipment. I was lucky!

In addition to my ride, my luck included an expert guide, and free! Mike knew all the game on sight—a remarkable achievement because oftentimes the quarry was quite a distance from the road and partly hidden by bush. Without someone like Mike a tourist would be absolutely unable to identify the various species even with the aid of the pictures in the guidebook. For to the unpracticed eye the various species of deer look about alike when seen moving through the bush. Furthermore, Mike had an uncanny eye for spotting game which Cranston and I would never have seen at all.

We saw hundreds of impala, which are among the most graceful of antelope. They were the most numerous of all the animals in the park. The beautiful reddish-brown coat pales on the sides to white below. Although not large, the impala are noted for their speed and agility.

Next to the impala the blue wildebeest was the most in evidence. It is a large animal, too big for an antelope, and much resembling a buffalo. One might say that the skin has a bluish cast, but the name is applied chiefly to distinguish the species from a nearly extinct cousin, the black wildebeest. Both males and females are horned.

The kudu, especially the kudu bulls, are probably the handsomest animals in the park. The bull has a thick neck and long horns twisted to combine a double spiral with the letter S. Along his smooth back and sides are a few light pin stripes to give him further elegance.

In contrast was the ugly wart hog, who takes his name from two big warts on either side of his face. Both sexes have a pair of tusks which project upward from the snout. Thus the wart hog's appearance is more frightening than ludicrous, but maybe that was because I saw one scarcely ten feet away. He was busy grubbing out some nuts or roots. When on the move they trot briskly with tiny tails held stiff and erect—no curls like their domestic cousins.

The waterbuck is a fine-looking chap with lyrate horns up to three feet long. He has a posterior ring of white, and his shaggy coat is so long around his neck that it forms a ruff. As his name implies, the waterbuck is never far from water. When pressed by his enemies he will jump into the water for protection and stand in it with only his head out. I wonder if he worries about the crocodiles.

One of man's cousins is, quite naturally, the most intelligent animal in the Kruger National Park. He is the chacma baboon. Like man, he is not so good on the smelling, but his senses of sight and hearing are unusually keen. Troops of chacma baboons had become amazingly tame and sometimes sat close to the road in obvious curiosity about the automobile.

Other animals we saw were zebra, steenbuck, grey duiker, sable antelope, eland, hippopotamus, springbok, vervet monkey, and "zoombie." Mike knew no other name for the last animal.

One giraffe was about the biggest animal I had ever seen. He was actually more impressive than an elephant and was probably a good eighteen feet high. A giraffe can travel about thirty-five miles per hour for a short period, but he does not need to rely entirely on speed to evade his ancient enemy, the lion, for he has a hide an inch thick and can kick like a sledgehammer. Leo respects him.

But even the lion has enemies. After man, his most dangerous enemy is the porcupine. For if he gets a quill in one of his pads it works deeper and deeper and becomes a festering sore. The agony is so great that the lion is unable to hunt and so starves to death. And where is there any Androcles today brave enough to help him out?

Of the birds, the lilac-breasted roller was the most beautiful. Other feathered folk spotted included a secretary bird, a hammerhead, a go-away, a blue jay, and doves. The go-away bird, or gray lourie, takes its name from a harsh cry resembling the words, "'go away'". There are 320 species of birds in Kruger National Park, not counting at least 80 migratory species.

The terrain was quite uninteresting—flat, and all bush. Tourists must stay in their cars—in fact, are not even supposed to open their windows;—but we saw natives on foot in several places. I would not have been afraid to sleep out in the park although there are many lions and leopards there.

By evening we had finished our tour and were back in Nelspruit.

The next forenoon found me in one of Paul's trucks climbing in low gear up out of the rugged country I had observed so far below me from Kaapschehoof. Only now I was on the opposite side of the basin ascending the great range of mountains dividing the eastern Transvaal from Swaziland. The view was tremendous.

Once up the first climb we were really in the mountains—precipitously walled valleys, and all the rest which makes up the best in mountain scenery. Unfortunately there was a heavy mist, so heavy in fact that it mounted to rain. This usually obscured the depths below the road. I accepted the situation philosophically because I had had such good luck in visiting Kruger Park. On the other hand, perhaps I really profited by the fog because it gave the ride a rather eerie and impressive turn. At times we passed under an aerial cable leading to a mine and could look up and see the cars appearing out of the mist and then disappearing again into the mists. The cables themselves not being always visible, you can imagine the spectacle. In the other direction—down—I spent a great deal of time peering into the mists trying to get some idea of the depth of the canyons. With the help of my knowledge of the terrain, my imagination had lots of food to keep it busy. I could feel the depths I couldn't see. I could see the position of the cable cars in the mists above.

When the truck reached its destination, I donned rain hat and cape and, once more on Jacqueline, descended to the Havelock Asbestos Mine, terminus of the aerial cableway. Here at the Swaziland police post I met Harry Pipe, a sixty-seven-year-old young man dressed in army khaki with a nicely kept handlebar mustache and a blaze of colors in the bar on his chest. He had been in the Boer War and in the Great War and had seen forty-seven years in the colonial police force. Hale and hearty, smooth of complexion, frank of tongue, proud of his past—this was Harry Pipe. He stamped my passport and invited me for lunch. Mrs. Pipe was as Scottish as they come. She had been twenty-two years in girl scout work and was proud of her record too.

Both had been decorated for their service records during a visit of the royal family to South Africa, Mr. Pipe by the King and Mrs. Pipe by Princess Elizabeth. I received full details of conversation and position for both presentations. I say this without poking fun because it is such experiences as these in the life of common folk that make old age enjoyable. They remembered every detail of the event and would until their dying day. Their theme was how really commonplace the royal family were.

"They're people, same as you and I," they said.

Later, Harry repeated an earlier statement. "We're going to America to visit you, but we've got to win the Irish Sweep first."

Jacqueline and I found that Swaziland grades were terrific. Riding was often out of the question. Sometimes I was unable to even walk more than thirty feet before stopping for a breather.

I spent the night with American missionaries of the Church of the Nazarene whom I met along the road. One of them was a son of the first missionary in Swaziland. The men wore overalls just like my own. Conversation developed that they knew a good friend of mine back in America—a college classmate, James Garner, nephew of a former Vice-President.

Many of Swaziland's mountainsides were barren. However, they would soon be as green with trees as our own national forests. Private companies had bought up much of the land at $6 per acre. They would put about $100 per acre more into the land by planting trees, erecting houses for European overseers, and so on. But in twelve years' time the land would be worth $1,000 per acre, and in thirty years, $2,000. The capitalization of one company was reported to be $8 million. Seedlings were taken from the nursery when three to five inches high and transplanted to slopes that had been burned off.

Under the government of a high-commission territory the Swazis enjoyed more freedom than their neighbors in the Union of South Africa. However, they did not actually own most of their land. When the gold rush was on in the Transvaal, prospectors and adventurers crossed over the boundary line, believing the deposits continued into Swaziland. The paramount chief of the Swazis at that time, Umbandine, traded continuing mineral and grazing concessions for candy, wine, and gin.

The Swazis stole their rain medicine from the Basutos to the south and gave it to their chief woman, or queen mother, since only women were supposed to have this power. Swazi chiefs pay for the rain-making service with cattle. However, it seems that the Swazis did not get quite all of the medicine from the Basutos, so when there is a long dry spell it is necessary to call on the Basutos for help. The Basutos unfortunately only have enough now to make light rains for themselves.

Back in the Transvaal I found myself on the high veld once more. Gently rolling country with sweeping vistas, it differs from our own plains in the large groves of blue gum of various kinds, planted at intervals by private companies. Otherwise it is our South Dakota or Wyoming all over again. Even the little lakes in their small basins are similar. They contained bass, carp, and other familiar fish; and wild ducks and geese were found in season.

Sheep, cattle, and buck (a collective term for various antelope) were raised by the farmers. Sheep were sent down to the low veld (extreme eastern Transvaal) in the autumn to graze on the green grass. They were driven across country but along certain routes because the farms are all fenced. Low-veld farmers were paid for grazing privileges. The sheep came back in early spring. The burned-over areas I saw in the high veld were part of a sheep raising program. Old grass gets hard and sour, and the sheep will not search out the tender shoots. Nevertheless, certain factions were trying to legislate against burning, as it does lots of damage. Some farmers had springbok, the farms being large enough to provide range for such antelope. Herds were either new or holdovers from olden times. Buck were shot for meat for home use or sale. I saw a herd of blesbok.

Among odds and ends of strange expressions I noticed in South Africa were these: "I will come just now," said by someone leaving, means he will return right away. "He goes right away through to—," means he goes straight through. To "turf in" is to throw in or put in. A pigsty is a hog-house. A "robot" is a stop-and-go light. A "tickee" is threepence (about six cents). "Biltong" is jerky and may be made from wild meat. The "bioscope" is the movies. A "tearoom bioscope" is a place where you pay only twenty cents but get an ice-cream soda, soft drink, or what you like, and the privilege of watching the movie—regular feature—for as long as you like. Remarkable! But it would not do in America, for the regular movies would go broke. Railway-crossing signs may read: "Beware of Engine" or "Danger Loco."

I stopped for the night on a farm where there was an interesting and talented Afrikaner family. Father had been a sort of actor and small play producer. His specialty was imitating Charlie Chaplin. Mother and all three daughters were really fine singers. Little Daupy, aged nine, was anything but dopey, which is, believe it or not, the correct pronunciation of her name. She played Largo, Melody in F, and the *Lohengrin* "Wedding March" for us on the organ. The last number was acquired when the family took her to a wedding. She came home, sat down and played it, having heard it just the once. She, like the rest of the family, could not play notes but played solely by ear. The oldest sister played the guitar, and the middle sister also knew how.

There were two other folks present at the supper table. Grandma was eighty-three but didn't look a day over sixty. Then there was a young man who looked exactly like a card shark out of a Bret Harte gambling hall—narrow-jawed, sharp-chinned, small mustache, dark hair, deep-set eyes, and long agile fingers. But appearances are deceiving. He was the local Baptist minister and was engaged to the oldest daughter in the home. What a contrast! She was both the ruddy-cheeked country girl and the Dutch miss right out of s' Gravenhage. The Dutch women of all ages surely have plump, ruddy cheeks. And they are all plump of build too, and bright-eyed.

After supper the entire family adjourned to the cold company dining

Hippopotami at ease in the world's greatest wild animal reserve—Kruger National Park, South Africa.

Native transportation in the Transvaal. Can you find the bike?

room and sang religious songs, and none other, though I hinted they had words of some old party favorites. The young minister took up the guitar.

"Do you play too?" I asked.

"Yes, a little. I played in a worldly band for a while."

In Afrikaans they all sang "Nearer My God to Thee," "Old Rugged Cross," "Old, Old Story," Have You Counted the Cost?" and "Beautiful City of God." In English they sang "Love Lifted Me" and "The Vacant Chair." Following this, cute little Daupy sat at the big organ and played her pieces. I enjoyed it very much.

At nine o'clock we all returned to the warm family dining room for evening devotions. These lasted a half-hour and were led by the young minister. They found a New Testament in English for me, and I showed my ignorance by confusing I John with St. John. Anyway, I found I could follow the text clear through even though the minister read it in Afrikaans. For prayers, we knelt on the floor. The minister was fervent, sincere, ministerial. He prayed for me and for my wife and children. Some of the devotions were in English.

Two nights later Jacqueline and I were just ready to bed down on the open veld, when we glimpsed a farm home snuggled in a valley. Here Mr. Talanda, a Czech dairy farmer with an Afrikaner wife, made me welcome for the night. I noticed that after supper the children would not go to bed until their father had read from the Bible. The Afrikaner family was rather religious. Grace was given before meals, and a prayer on the knees afterwards was customary.

Mr. Talanda and I talked about farming. He objected to government controls on the price of his milk.

"We get subsidy; but why, if we were allowed a free market, should we get subsidy? Before we got our subsidy, they pegged the price at two and eight [68 cents] per gallon, and it was costing me three and three [81 cents]."

My host also told me something of the native custom of naming children. For example, if a man has five girls, the name of the fifth may mean "Enough girls." If he then has a boy, the name may mean "Where did you come from?" A man lost his first wife and had no children by his second wife. When his third wife had a child, the neighbors looked skeptical. But When she had a second child, the father called it "Witness."

The next day I secured a long ride with a thirtyish man of English stock. Next to politics, I found the South African talked and wrote most about the racial question. In a given newspaper, there were sure to be at least two articles on the color bar. This was also an important part of their politics, but I was unable to decipher what stands the opposing sides took. Apparently there was much talk and no action. One Afrikaner told me that the Englishman says: "We're going to do something for the natives" but does nothing. The Dutchman says: "We're under no obligation to do anything for the native—yet, at least. Don't educate him yet—raise his moral standard first."

My friend said South Africa was a young country and couldn't afford to educate the natives. There were no schools for them in the country except missionary schools. The moral standard was low: there was usually no marriage ceremony in the towns, and the natives traded or bought wives.

The native worked for the farmer for rent—or occasionally for money—and the children took care of the farmer's herds. The farmers treated the natives meanly at times, then again, reasonably, because basically they felt sorry for them. The natives sometimes took advantage of this.

In summing up, this chap said the natives were unhygienic and unable to associate with the whites. I heard this sentiment echoed by others later on.

I visited the South African province of Natal primarily to see the Natal National Park and Tugela Falls, the world's second highest waterfall. The park is on the northeastern face of a mountain uplift known as the Drakensberg, which is the roof of South Africa. The Drakensberg culminates at ten thousand feet in the Mont aux Sources from which the major South African rivers, including the Orange, take their source. This mountain stands as a corner boundary to Natal, Basutoland, and the Orange Free State.

There were some long stiff climbs approaching the park as the veld led up to the mountains. I stopped for the night at a little farmhouse snuggled up against the side of a *koppie* or small mountain. Louis Rencken, of German descent, was home alone, as his wife was in Johannesburg following the birth of a baby daughter. Little Wilma Rencken was, believe it or not, born on my own children's birthday. Talk about coincidence! I might have gone on to the next farmhouse.

Louis fried steak and boiled small potatoes in their jackets for supper. Typical bachelor fare and preparation. But he had also made some custard, and it was good.

Louis and his wife were young pioneers—the type our grandparents were when they settled the prairies and mountain valleys of our own country. They were settling on new land. The little house had just been built. There were two rooms with whitewashed mud walls surmounted by a peaked, thatched roof. In one corner of the living room was a modern type window extending completely along the two sides of the corner.

Just off the kitchen Louis was building a bathroom and had the hot-water plant already in. This was simplicity itself. Back of the house on the hillside he had a supply tank. Buried in the wall above the stove, and extending through the wall to the bathroom (as yet without a roof), was a fifty-gallon drum. A pipe ran into the bottom of this from the supply tank, and gravity filled it with water. Another pipe ran from the bottom of the drum through the stove and doubled back to reenter the drum near its top. This was all there was to it. Cold water sank to the bottom, Louis said, and the warmed water from the stove went to the top of the drum, thus creating circulation until all the water was heated.

Among these primitive conditions one would not expect to find culture, but in the living room was a piano. Mrs. Rencken had a degree in music, and Louis was as well educated as most continentals. He played also—classical music—and could handle Beethoven, Wagner, Schubert, Brahms, and others. I spoke of little Daupy and her playing of Largo and Melody in F. He sat down and played them both from memory. When I commented on the fact that family music was becoming a lost art in my country, he said he thought the reason was that America had made the machine a god.

"It is too easy to turn a button on the wireless or play the phonograph," he added with a smile.

Morning came with clouds of mist over the Drakensberg. "Just my luck," I thought. But by the time Jacqueline and I had negotiated the twelve stiff remaining miles to the park hotel, things had cleared up so that there were many stretches of blue sky and several places on the great wall were bathed in sunshine.

There was no map available, so I copied the one in the hotel lobby. Then I packed a double lunch, and at 11:10 I was off for the heights.

Of several trails, I picked the one of most importance to me—that leading to the inner gorge of the Tugela, the world's second highest waterfall, 3,110 feet. The trail had been constructed for about two-thirds of the distance to the falls, to a place called the Tunnel. The trail was wide and easy and used by horses nearly up to this point. From the horse-tethering point the path bore some resemblance to that in Zion Canyon, Utah, especially when it passed through a fat man's misery and an overhanging rock. As in Zion the trail ended when water touched both sides of a narrow gorge. This was the Tunnel, obviously named because the narrow walls twisted and turned so that you usually could not see sky above you. It is like Pine Creek Canyon in Zion or to some extent like Colorado's Box Canyon. New Zealand's Chasm is also on the same order. At full water, it must have been even more interesting.

At one side of the tunnel entrance was a chain followed by chain steps leading up the near-vertical surface of a rock wall. Beyond, the path led nearly straight up. Wires and tree roots had been so placed or exposed that one could proceed and eventually get to the top of the tunnel, which was perhaps fifty feet high. From this point onward the trail, if there ever was one, was completely lost among the boulders and water-filled potholes which comprised the bed of the Tugela River.

I spent a lot of time trying to find the supposed trail but finally came to my senses and simply clambered up the canyon. Nearly always, natural stone stairs could be found to continue upward, though it was often necessary to cross from one side of the canyon to the other in order to circumvent some particularly large boulders of a near-vertical cascade. These stone stairs required the utmost care on my part, because I was alone, no one knew where I was, and more importantly, a turned ankle would kill my chances for continuing to travel by cycle. In addition I kept alerted to the danger of snakes.

For a pack I had settled on my army jacket in preference to my black bag. How I ever even considered the bag, I don't know, because I'd had enough experience in mountaineering to realize that both hands must be free. A can of meat, five thick slices of bread, four oranges, my large camera, and my canteen of water all fitted into the huge pockets of my jacket. When too hot to wear, the jacket could be carried swung over my shoulders by the arms.

By about 3 P.M. I was in the upper reaches of Tugela Canyon. It was the time I had set for returning, but the wildness of the canyon, the almost inconceivable heights of the precipices above me, the several side canyons about the existence of which I could hardly be sure, the turning of the gorges, the occasional glimpses of the top of the Tugela waterfall or of the towering Sentinel and Beacon Mountains—all these wonder sirens lured me on.

I left my jacket and shirt and proceeded with only the camera. In spite of its size it fit into one of my hip pockets (blessed be a pair of overalls). I was then free to clamber rapidly and without sweating. It was good sport to go on and on, and I never ceased to marvel at the progress I had made when I stopped for a rest and could gaze down into the canyon to the far-away-below place I had been a few minutes before. As I climbed rapidly from boulder to boulder with arms and shoulders bare and free, I attained a feeling of physical exultation, of well-being, of good health, of certain lithe powers. I felt like Haliburton at his best, and in my vanity regretted that there was no motion-picture camera to record my movements.

At one time I chose the wrong canyon and was soon stopped by an insurmountable waterfall. You see, it was not always possible to follow the canyon with the most water because the water often flowed for rods under a mass of boulders. Now when I returned to an alternative canyon, I was pleased to find I could go much farther up.

What a temptation heights are to mortal man! "Just one more bend." "Now one more. It looks as though there is a side chasm from that point. Let's go see!" And with thoughts like these, I kept on. When I came to a twenty-five-foot waterfall, I was happy to discover I could crawl up one side. Vertical though it was, there were enough grass tufts to haul myself up. Once over the top, I was able to proceed for an eighth of a mile measured horizontally and perhaps a like distance measured vertically.

At last I stood at the very base of Tugela Falls. The fact that they showed barely a trickle of water did not diminish my admiration of the scene. No longer were the precipices so far above me as to be inconceivable! Now they were close at hand. But still tremendous, mind you! They still rose sheer between two and three thousand feet. Yet, looking back down the canyon, I could see out over the tops of peaks that had once seemed to tower into the very blue.

These inner gorges of the Tugela are, I believe, the best tenders for the title *abyss* I have ever seen. Their walls are more precipitous than those of the Norwegian or New Zealand gorges because there is no rounding off and recession of the walls at the top. They are sheer to the utmost pinnacle. Even after clambering up several thousand feet, I was still buried in the bowels of the earth. There were only glimpses of blue sky or sunlight shafts. I cannot recall having been in a more awesome spot. Perhaps it is because there is not just one abyss, but several, with knife-edge divisions two thousand feet high and more.

I will vie the abysses of the Tugela with the falls of the Zambezi for the supremacy of the African continent.

And how much more thrilling is the Natal National Park in comparison with the much touted Kruger National Park! Kruger Park has very little scenic attraction; it is flat and nearly all bush. Yet auto highways have been built all over the place, while in Natal Park they have not even built a trail into the inner gorge. Kruger Park is only a zoo wherein the people are in the cages (tourists must not get out of their cars) instead of the animals. In fact, it is not as good as a zoo, because if you do see the animals they are usually two hundred feet to an eighth of a mile away instead of ten feet. But in a modern book Louis Rencken had shown me on South African national parks, about forty pages were devoted to Kruger Park and exactly two lines to Natal.

At 4 P.M. I started to return. This jumping or climbing from rock to rock requires as much mental discipline as physical. If even for a second you start to think of the distance ahead, or to think of turning for another look back up the canyon, you are sure to miscalculate a rock and either slip or be thrown off balance. You *must* think "next rock, next, next—ah, here, and to here—etc."

The mists had returned to the heights even before I started down, so it was an early dusk. Nevertheless, by 5:15 I was on the trail again—that is, I had descended to the tunnel and was walking rapidly along. At 5:40 I stopped and had a good supper, having profited by an experience on the twenty-nine-mile desert hike to Rainbow Bridge in the States. I am not able to finish those last tired miles on an empty stomach. *No, sir!* But with hunger satisfied those last miles are just an evening stroll.

There was no moon, and there were heavy mist clouds overhead. Yet the trail was usually visible. I am fairly immune to the spectral shape of rocks and trees that rise on either side of a lonely night trail, but I did give a thought to snakes and animals. In regard to snakes, I was without either snakebite kit or matches to see the wound. But I did not worry about it too much.

One section of trail I expected to give me trouble, and it did! This was through a dense forest. Brother, was it dark in that forest! The trail just completely disappeared and I had to feel with my feet, sense my way or simply guess. I could not grope in the ordinary sense of using my hands because the tree trunks were too far apart and too far from the edge of the trail. And there were a couple of tiny streams to cross in the depths of the forest too. Dark! Oh, man! Two or three times I thought I was going to have to give up and sleep on the path for the night. But just when I despaired I would think, "Is that a glimmer of white path there, or isn't it?" and I would move on.

I arrived back at the park hotel at about 7:15, and I went around to the kitchen to buy a loaf of bread. It was a teeming, busy place of two dozen blacks, some eating heaping plates of squash, cabbage, and the like. The cook called a waiter; the waiter called the headwaiter; and by the time the headwaiter got the manager and the head of stores, I had repeated my request about five times. The last two "officials" were white women and treated me with considerable frost. Was it because I was not a patron, or because I was standing with the black help? I suspected it was the second.

As I prepared to leave the yard one of the black employees, all huddled up in an overcoat, protested: "Oh, no, boss, don't go out into the night alone like this."

I appreciated his concern but told him I was used to it. I think the only reason he did not protest more was that he thought I might go to the park camp ground. But why pay camp fee when there was ten thousand square miles of veld to choose from? A mile of pedaling, and I was soon asleep.

My morning's work was the road up the Oliver's Hoek Pass leading from Natal into the Orange Free State. It was plenty steep, and I walked most of the way, but the magnificent sweeping views over the area lying toward the Drakensberg gave me the necessary inspiration. Open, high veld country. No forests—just groves or rows of evergreens along the road, and these only occasionally. The country was more like our Western ranch land.

About two miles from the top I stopped for lunch but was picked up almost immediately by a truck. The driver was one of these chain smokers and boasted that he had smoked five packs, or one hundred cigarettes, a day for thirty-five years. His expenditure was five bob or one dollar per day, so in thirty-five years time he had spent no less than thirteen thousand dollars for cigarettes alone. Wow, what I could do with that thirteen thousand! I could take eight trips around the world and buy a new car in the bargain. And my enjoyment would be greater, and through memory, much more enduring.

The driver was an old-timer in the area and told me something of the history of the pass. The first voortrekkers went down the steep descent into Natal without a road. It reminded me of our own Mormon trek into southeastern Utah or of some of the experiences of the northeastern Oregon pioneers. All of these folks had courage to go up and down these mountains, believe me. My friend said fourteen head of oxen could hardly haul an empty wagon up the Oliver's Hoek Pass.

Beyond the top of the pass we saw some large white letters on a mountainside far to the east. These read "Kerkenberg" and marked the place where the first voortrekkers, three or four hundred of them, from the Orange Free State camped in 1836. Their leader, Piet Retief, and sixty men went on down into Natal to buy land from the Zulu chief, Dingaan. Dingaan agreed to give them land provided they would first get back for him some cattle stolen by a lesser chief. This was difficult, but after several months the Boers succeeded. Dingaan then placed his mark on a contract ceding the land but invited Retief and his men to stay overnight and there would be a celebration with drinking and dancing. But in the morning the Boers were set upon, taken to the Hill of Execution and massacred. The Zulus subsequently raided the Boer encampments.

The Boers had to wait ten months to inflict retribution. At that time Andries Pretorius, who gave his name to Pretoria, took a company of 464 and went down against the Zulus, said to number tens of thousands. The Boers promised God that if He would grant them victory, they would erect a church and always keep the day holy. They won, and the Church of the Vow still stands in Pietermaritzburg, Natal.

The date of the Zulu defeat was December 16, and each year a celebration is held by descendants and farmers near the letters "Kerkenberg" on the mountain to the east of Oliver's Hoek Pass.

32

Hottentots, Bushmen, and Lions

I crossed a bridge and found myself in Basutoland—my sixty-first country. Here I turned my back on white farmers, for in Basutoland, a high-commission territory, there were only a few white missionaries, traders, and officials. The natives lived in villages, usually located high on hillsides at the base of some rimrock cliff or on the brow of a hill where there was little or no rock. I reached one of the former by dark and inquired for anyone speaking English. Both women and men were extremely good-natured and accommodating. There were grins reaching from ear to ear, whether they had ever heard of America or not. The neighbor of the chap where I first inquired spoke a little English. They were just deciding where to put me when I asked if anyone at the large stone building just below us spoke English. This was a school, so I asked about the school-teacher. "Of course! Just the thing!" they thought. So the first man escorted me there.

The schoolmaster's house looked about like the others in the village. It was built on a rectangular platform, apparently made of concrete but probably made of mud. The material was certainly doing the job of concrete and was raised well above the surrounding soil. This cleanly swept platform, well elevated and far from its neighbors, made the Basuto villages quite sanitary in appearance. Compare the filthy dirt-floored hovels of the native Egyptian—a white man, if you please. There the mud wall of one windowless hut is the mud wall of the next. "Streets" are narrow lanes where donkeys, cattle, chickens, and children wander at will, and women and tiny girls gather up the still-wet offal in their hands, roll it in the inch-deep dust and put it in wicker baskets carried on their heads.

The walls of the teacher's house were a sort of yellowish brown, the usual Basuto color; other walls were orange. Some were true rondavels, others rectangular. All had thatched roofs. The teacher's house had four windows, but windows were not common.

Mrs. Leketa, a large colored lady by no means old, met us on the platform, which served as a porch in front of the house. A little child was riding comfortably on her back in the blanket wrapped around her ample bosom. I was invited into the house, and my guide and another visitor, the son of a minister, followed me in to await the arrival of the husband, Richard Leketa. The new school term had just opened, and he had taken the roll to the French mission about ten miles away. The missionaries in the neighborhood were really French Canadians.

Nearly all African women had babies on their backs —Oliver's Hoek Pass, Natal.

Jacqueline meets another kind of transportation—Basutoland (Lesotho).

The Leketas had three rooms and a rondavel opposite. The cooking was done in the rondavel and, I suspect, most of the eating, because the nice dining-room table and chairs looked quite unused. In this room there was a wall-filling buffet with dish shelves clear to the ceiling, and at the opposite end of the room a sewing machine. A door led into two small bedrooms.

We had coffee, and I took out my food to help get the stuff down. They inquired if I would wait until they prepared a chicken. I declined but said I would try some of their kafir-corn porridge. Knowing their reluctance to offer their own food to Europeans, I had engineered the conversation in that direction. Their porridge was only sour-milk porridge, they said, and I wouldn't like it. But I found the porridge quite good, needing only a little sugar. They fixed my sleeping quarters at one end of the dining room. When I protested against all this trouble, Mrs. Leketa said they really wanted to make a guest happy and it was not trouble. During all of this meal serving, bed carrying, and whatnot, Junior remained sound asleep, bumping about on the lower part of his mother's back.

Mr. Leketa did not seem to know too much about the details of American life. When I found he had never seen a real motion picture, I could understand this. It was not until later that it dawned on me that the color bar was probably the reason for this. Where could the poor chap go even if he wanted to see a movie?

The Leketa's village was called Hleoheng, a name describing the broken cliff just above it. The word *basuto* means "black man."

There were a few sprinkles during the night, and the day started cloudy and cool. I met many Basutos on horseback. The Basuto ponies were about the size of my old Welsh pony and had the same reddish color. The men were usually wrapped in blankets—brown with red and purple designs in a vertical strip down the front. They seemed to be a happy lot. Some wore old army greatcoats. I chatted with one of these. He said that the government had promised them some nice land if they went off to fight but that they had never received any. Where have I heard this tune before?

The non-Christian Basutos practiced polygamy. A wife was purchased by giving her father a stated number of cattle. If the wife left her husband and went home, father might keep the cattle anyway—alimony, you see. Wives might be bought as an American buys a new car—by paying in installments. Uncompleted contracts had to be made good by the children, so a young man might be faced with the prospect of paying for his grandfather's wives before he could get any of his own. Meanwhile it would do him no good to seduce an unmarried woman, because the penalty for that was the same number of cattle as required for buying a wife.

The first chief of the Basutos was Moshesh, a good organizer and ruler. He realized that the Boers and Zulus were too much for him and in 1868 retired to his mountain stronghold and asked the British for a protectorate.

He is the author of the famous law of Moshesh, whereby in case of theft, an animal must be repaid by an animal.

The country of the Basutos is very mountainous in the interior but rather rolling along the western edge. Atop many of the hills are rimrock formations like those found in our Western states; and haystack buttes dot the landscape. The soil on the mountains is usually reddish, and as there are no trees—mark that, no trees—there is a lot of erosion. The only green vegetation is a kind of a giant yucca that seems to be half designed for hedge protection near houses in the villages.

Most of the Basutos did not understand my greeting unless they had been in the army. But they all addressed me as "boss." Sometimes this became "bossy" and I almost burst out laughing when an old colored mammy said, "Yes, bossy."

I cycled without a shirt, but the Basuto men and women were swathed in their blankets. The occasional English storekeepers thought I was nuts. To them it was winter and very cold. These storekeepers were doing all right, as their stores were crowded with natives wanting to buy something —chiefly dry goods; but the rush was in large part due to the harvest season. Natives husked corn by hand, shelled it, and sold to the trader-storekeeper.

When I got my Basutoland stamp, a friendly policeman inquired about America.

"Is America like this—I mean mountains and so?"

"I hear there is war now between Russia and America."

"We would like to see more Americans out here."

From Basutoland I reentered the Union of South Africa. Again I was sometimes a guest in Dutch, English, and Jewish homes; and British customs drew my attention. The big meal was at noon, and the dessert was a replete combination of pudding, jello, custard, and whatnot. Breakfasts might include "bubble and squeak"—leftover mashed potatoes and green vegetables, mixed and fried. Suppers were starved through with a bowl of soup and bread, butter, jam, and cheese to finish up with. Of course, these people think that as long as they've had their tea, they've had their meal without anything else. But the most exasperating thing to an American was the habit of slicing bread very thin so that spreading it was next to impossible and the result was only a mouthful anyway.

I was now in railroad country, and having been absent from home several months over a year, I decided to take a train southwest to Cape Town. I finally persuaded a lonely stationmaster to read through his regulations to prove that there was no written restriction against selling me a third-class ticket; but on the train they put me into a second-class compartment anyway. The trip took two days, and I ate from a stock of provisions that I had laid up for the purpose.

There was plenty of entertainment en route to Cape Town, and I was usually the only audience. My traveling companion, a young sailor—stone

Young Africa at a country store in Basutoland (Lesotho).

broke and without luggage—was an amateur musician. His only instrument was a comb and a piece of paper, but he could do better than an orchestra. Imitating the saxophone was his specialty, and the result was just as loud, and the rhythm and variations were all that could be asked. He claimed to have won several prizes. Another young chap on the train joined in occasionally with his guitar. The sailor could play guitar and comb at the same time by holding the comb with the pressure of his lips onto his left shoulder. He was minus his two upper front teeth, but I did not ask him if they hindered or helped the exercise of his musical talent.

For much of the trip we traveled across vast plains with small hills scattered here and there. Approaching Cape Town, we passed through picturesque and fairly rugged mountains. It was along this route that the Boers had gone north from Cape Town to escape British rule and to found the republics of Transvaal and the Orange Free State.

The history of the Boers goes back to 1652, when the Dutch East India Company set up Cape Town as a halfway point for supplies on the way to India. In the next 150 years the colony increased to twenty-thousand Dutch and Dutch Huguenots. Then, when Napoleon met his Waterloo, Cape Colony was ceded to the British, and not many years later the Boers started their famous trek northward. They were a combination of Dutch, French, and Germans with Bibles in hand, moving slowly behind oxen and great, lumbering covered wagons to make the first major penetration of the little-known regions beyond the mountains. Paul Kruger was on this trek, though only a boy.

Cape Town! The tip of the continent at last! Eight thousand miles from Cairo. Yes, here I was!

Cape Town was a modern city, commercial, yet a bit old—lacking the sprightly éclat of Johannesburg and the landscaped setting of its twin capital, Pretoria, far to the north. In Cape Town I was more conscious of the peninsular location and the braw weather than of the city itself.

It rained for the first two days I was in Cape Town, and there was plenty of wind for good measure. Typical Cape weather, they called it. And, of course it was winter—sort of California winter weather, only colder. Nights I stayed with a friend of Nyasaland days, Ronnie Grewcock, in a suburb called Constantia.

On the third day Ronnie succeeded in getting the car to take me around the Cape peninsula. The drive is said to be one of the most magnificent in the world. On the peninsula we crossed from the Indian Ocean to the Atlantic by driving only six miles. False Bay on the Indian Ocean has warm water, and it is here that the famous Muizenberg Beach is located. But the Atlantic is too cold for swimming; and the near-sunshiny weather of the Indian Ocean was lost the minute we crossed the peninsula. However, the rock-girt Atlantic side was the more impressive scenically, with its pounding surf and cliffs of the Twelve Apostles rising abruptly into the mists of Table Mountain.

On the tour we visited probably the most famous cottage in South Africa—the house where Rhodes died, March 26, 1902. It seems a bit paradoxical that posterity speaks so much of his loving the land when he died on the very edge of the sea and within sound of the pounding surf.

Later on we drove out to the Kirstenbosch Botanical Gardens, reputedly one of the most magnificently situated in the world. I was a bit disappointed, but at this stage perhaps I had seen too much. Also it was winter. As a windup to our sightseeing tour we visited Groot Constantia, one of the finest remaining examples of the old Cape houses built in the Dutch colonial style of architecture. The property dates from 1685, when it was granted to Governor Simon van der Stet, who established the vineyards which produced the famous Constantia wines. The old wine cellar was still in use, for this is the heart of a great wine district. The house is maintained by the state as a museum and contains a fine collection of antique furniture, glass, china, and pictures.

In Cape Town's main railway station that evening I studied timetables until I was dizzy and then boarded the 11:00 P.M. train to go to Tsumeb, an outpost in the bush some seventeen hundred miles away in northern South West Africa. I was in good spirits, for was not the direction homeward?

Morning found the train leaving the mountains I had seen on my way to Cape Town. We then traveled out over the Great Karoo, a flat semidesert area much like some of our Western ranch country. As we approached Beaufort West, the land was nearly covered with yellow flowers. There was also a sprinkling of desert bushes, something like our sage except that it was dark green like greasewood.

What a tremendous amount of desert country there is in the world! It was desert country when I went to bed, it was desert country when I awoke the following morning. It was desert country when I went to bed the following night, and it was still desert the next morning.

West of Upington, as we proceeded toward South West Africa, there was a stretch of white daisies or perhaps everlasting flowers; also the dark-green sparsely growing desert bush I have mentioned before. Later on we passed through an area of milkbush. This was big and branchy like the Australian desert spinifex, except that the many stems were much coarser. My colored companion—my first since leaving Cape Town—said that if the plant were broken, the milk would come out and congeal like chewing gum. Later on we entered a blue stone desert, and this continued on into South West Africa. Still farther along we came to a sparse grassland, the grass dead as befitted the scenery. Beyond Karasburg there was an actual sand desert with sand drifts in the little traveled road. It would have been tough to cycle through. In all of these types of desert it was always possible to see low mountains, or hills, near at hand or faintly distant. None of these seemed to rise more than five hundred feet above the plain.

And what of the people? I had far better opportunity to study them by riding third class. For the bystanders—in fact, usually the whole population of the desert stations—came up to our coaches to exchange greetings, to laugh, and to be excited. The Hottentots were particularly colorful, and I could have used a color camera to advantage. There were house dresses of gay prints, plaid gingham jackets, and the most gloriously colored turbans —reds, greens, yellows. One in particular was right off the swami at the county fair. Sometimes a girl would wear a sort of shiek's headpiece with a dark-red or dark-green knit beret perched on top of it. One mother had dressed her tiny daughter in a skirt of the same material as her own blouse. Modern, eh? This fad was then current in America. Not only that but the dresses were all of the new look length and had bustles. Paris in the desert-- yes sir. And the wearers were more brown than black and were tall, well proportioned, and graceful—quite pleasing, really. Many of the young men were in civilized attire.

Among the passengers on the train I made the acquaintance of a Wesleyan Methodist native minister wearing the white collar and black garb of his calling. He was traveling second class in the back part of my coach and answered to the name of Van Eck. My colored companion, Norman Swanson, was also a Methodist native minister but was not practic- ing and was not very ministerial. His steady job was labor-union represen- tative for railway workers in the Union. He was making the trip to observe conditions in the mandated territory of South West Africa and also to visit his children scattered along the route. As soon as these two gentlemen understood that the color bar did not worry me, they spent quite a lot of time in my compartment. Swanson was down on the Dutchman and kept us laughing with his pointed remarks. Following is a sample of parts of the conversation.

Swanson had been maltreated or insulted by a Dutchman and was retaliating.

"You can't make a black man. Your father couldn't even make half a black man. I was created black. I was born black—black under the blue sky of Africa. And when I die and lie in my grave, they can say, "There is a true native of Africa.'

"Dutchmen! A-a-a! I wish they were all in the sea. They will be too, one day."

Rev. Mr. Van Eck, too, spoke of experience. While wearing the collar, he had knocked at the door of a Dutch woman's house and she had started to insult him.

"Footscop, you dog. Footscop." (*Footscop* is an epithet not even ap-

The South African veld.

Hottentot belle, Southwest Africa.

plied to one's own dog, only to the neighbor's dog. It is roughly equivalent in meaning to "Be off with you.")

"You don't even know me; why do you address me like that, just because I knock at your door?" remonstrated Mr. Van Eck.

"You've no right to ask questions. Footscop, you dog. What right do you have! Are you a white man?"

Mr. Swanson jibed in. "No Dutchman will ever go to heaven. Dutchmen! A-a-a!"

This gave Mr. Van Eck and myself a long and hearty laugh. Mr. Van Eck went on:

"When we go to a Dutchman's house, we can't go to the front door. No-o, we must go to the back, and we must take off our hats and hold them so. And if it is hot, and the sun shines on us, we must stand so. And even if we are a teacher or a minister, it makes no difference. And if we need a drink—just so very bad, we'll say—well, they will give you tea, but in a tin—never in a cup. They will put it in the tin the servant uses. If they don't have a tin, they'll ask you if you have one and send you to find one. You can't drink it out of a cup, you know. And yet the same black hands will peel their potatoes and their carrots and handle their plates and make their beds. And the black girls will raise their children, and I've seen the children cry if their nanny—that's what they call them—if nanny has to go away."

Here Swanson interposed: "We thank God, yes, we thank God, that the white man brought us Christianity. We are thankful for that—but why doesn't he practice it? Dutchmen! A-a-a!"

As we went westward and northward through South West Africa, the Hottentots dressed more and more like American pioneer mothers. They wore pretty, short aprons over very long flared dresses with two-inch hems. Shoulders were built high and flared, waistlines quite high. The hair was enclosed in a colored cloth and arranged so that there was a sort of crown toward the front. The cloth was held in place by a wool scarf or some similar arrangement. Red rick rack was sometimes used running up the shoulder at the back or over the bodice down the front. Place inside all of this, attractive, light-colored, brown, or almost white faces, well-shaped figures, and pleasing personalities, and you have a partial idea of some of the charm of the country apart from the desert.

The Hottentots call themselves Khoikhoi, which means "men of men." They are believed to be a mixture of the Bushmen and Bantu Negroes but are so much larger than the present-day Bushmen it is hard to see how there could be any connection. The Hottentots were the first known inhabitants of Cape Province and then numbered about two hundred thousand. The Boers fought and killed a good many of them, and now there were only about ninety thousand. They were a nomadic and pastoral people, raising cattle and sheep. The men tended the herds and cured the hides, but the women did most of the heavy work and thus earned the traditional respect of their husbands. The Hottentots provide much to attract the ethnologist, for they have an interesting language and a great fund of myths and legends, often connected with worship of ancestors or fictional heroes endowed according to animistic or personified beliefs.

Sunday I had a colored police sergeant, his assistant, and their captured charge for companions in my compartment. Their charge was not very dangerous, and they soon took off his handcuffs. His only crime was having left his job in an Ovamboland mine before his contract was up, and he was being returned. All three sat around all forenoon without eating. The sergeant ate a little bread and meat about 1 P.M. The other two ate parts of a loaf of bread at six in the evening. The prisoner put some flour and sugar into water, and they drank that to get the bread down. Yet these men were well dressed, with the exception of the charge, and appeared as though they could have whatever food they wanted. Of course the thing that saved them was a cup of kafir-corn beer.

About midafternoon one of the above-described attractive young Hottentots came into our compartment. She wore the usual attire with plenty of red, white, and yellow beads about her neck as a choker, and more hanging downward. Full of fun, she typified the happy-go-lucky friendly disposition common to her people. She had two big parcels tied up in cloths, and we kidded her about the contents. She thereupon produced a two-gallon can with a tight-fitting lid. When she loosened this, it flew off with a tremendous bang, scaring all of us and flying across the compartment. The can contained about a gallon of kafir-corn beer, which is pink in color. A cup was found and a drink poured out. It was offered to me, and I took a few swallows. Not bad, and it did not seem too potent. The lady drank last and made a wry face, then passed it back to the assistant, who thought it great stuff. The fair one apparently preferred her snuff, which she daintily inserted in her nostrils, turning politely aside as she did so.

Sunday night I changed trains to a little narrow-gauge affair running north to Tsumeb. The railway had been built by the Germans to take the copper and other minerals from that area down to the sea, the port at that time being Swakopmund instead of Walvis Bay. The narrow-gauge train chugged us off into the bush, seeming to go very fast because we were so close to the ground.

Morning and the same endless bush—and still in South West Africa, for it is another African country about the size of Texas. The temperature had moderated a great deal since Cape Town, and it was no longer necessary to wear my jacket. In fact, it was quite warm during the middle of the day. Nearing Otjirawongo, a conscientious young conductor said I could not ride third class and put me back in first and second. He said later he had to make out a report to headquarters because Cape Town should never have sold me a third-class ticket. I told him that he would find that it was O.K.

if he looked in the book of rules. He insisted it was wrong. But he agreed to look it up and tell me if it was different at the next stop—Otavi. He did not show up again.

Tsumeb and rail's end at last! This was the last outpost up from Cape Town. Beyond were hundreds of miles of bush, plenty of Bushmen, and a little-visited region known as Ovamboland. Across this area I had plotted my course.

Ovamboland was a native reserve lying between Tsumeb and the Portuguese country of Angola, and a special permit was necessary to cross it. Fortunately I had heard of this added travel hazard—there's always something—before arrival and had telegraphed the native commissioner in Windhoek. The reply—favorable, thank goodness—had just arrived at the local magistrate's desk when I walked into the office. The message required me to have in my possession a visa valid for Angola, and the magistrate could hardly conceal his surprise when I showed it to him—purchased in far-off Australia. He then had an aide type out the permit, a whole page of it. I had to travel by motor and check with the police as I advanced. Shades of the Sudan!

At the railway station I found that on certain days they did run a lorry northward about two-thirds of the way across Ovamboland. This was to pick up or deliver natives who worked in mines to the south. However, the railroad would not sell me a third-class ticket even on this lorry. According to their book of rules, one could not travel third class at all in South West Africa and no third-class ticket should have been issued before. Nor would they even consider second class. They did not have second-class accommodation. Whence, per se, they had first-class accommodations, and first-class rates must be charged. Gad, what a gripe this color-bar business was! I decided to skip the ticket and cycle the seventy miles to Namutoni, on the edge of the reserve.

In Tsumeb there was a copper mine—an old one now made modern by American management. The Ovambos knew of the copper at a very early date. Its location was subsequently referred to as the "green hill." The natives used to smelt the ore with charcoal and use the metal for ornaments. Evidence of the process still remains. The Germans took over the mining about 1905.

At the time of my visit the ore was brought up from levels down to two thousand feet, and put through three crushers which worked on the same principle you would use in crushing an egg between your two hands. After the first crushing the material was elevated by a sloping belt to an adjacent tower so as to use gravity in feeding the next crusher. After the third crusher the stones were the maximum size of a guinea egg and were carried into the main mill. Here two huge rotating drums, a "ball mill" and a "rod mill," reduced the ore to powder and mixed it with water. From here on the stuff was handled as a muddy liquid, 20 or 25 percent solid.

The liquid was pumped up to a sort of vat where great rakes pulled out the coarse stuff for reprocessing. The major part of the fluid proceeded to a place where chemicals were added and then went into a battery of churns. Air was forced down into the middle of these, and the liquid came to the surface as big and small leaden bubbles. The solution then contained about 50 percent lead, 13 to 14 percent copper, and some zinc. The zinc was mostly in a rejected liquid.

Water was next removed by being sucked into huge drums covered with canvas, leaving the lead and copper "cake" on the outside, ready to drop into railway cars below. The zinc was handled on a separate drum. When the cake subsequently dried in the cars, it would be more like a powder.

About five hundred "Europeans" and sixteen hundred natives were employed by the mine. They all lived on mine property. Stores and other places of business were on the same property. Tsumeb was the mine, and the mine was Tsumeb.

There were a good many Germans in Tsumeb, holdovers from the days when Germany governed South West Africa. In some public places German was spoken by young and old alike, and I stayed two nights in a German house. There were two Americans, but the hospitality of my fellow countrymen was the same as I had come to expect: wanting or meager, unless they were missionaries. There were also a number of English families, and I spent a particularly enjoyable evening in the home of a Mr. and Mrs. Theron.

After a good dinner the Therons took me to call on a policeman friend, also named Theron, but no relation. He had had quite a lot of experience in Ovamboland and told the story of a man's encounter with a lion. He told it in such a way that the suspense lasted no less than one and a half hours. I could have really taken it down in longhand. Here is his story:

"I told Hartman that he was getting too old to hunt lions. He was a farmer near the station. He was sixty-four and I told him he'd lost some of his nerve, you know, and he could not see as good as before. The last lion he'd got—I think he had shot about fifty—he'd only wounded the first shot or two. Well, he said maybe he would stop. But then he called me up one day and said that they were around and he thought he'd go after them.

"He and his black boy went out on a Saturday. They wounded a lion, but it was only a flesh wound and he got away before they could track that day. Then Sunday they went out again. They found the lion and Hartman shot, but again it was only a flesh wound. The lion had not gone far, you see, because he was stiff in the leg and sore from the first wound. Well, anyway, the beast attacked Hartman and threw him down and I guess the black—he'd been with him in the bush for about thirty years—tried to help him, because he got a great wound in the thigh. But anyway, he fled—ran away and got back to where there was another black and they both returned to the house. By that time the first Bushman was out of his head, you know, with the pain and all, and couldn't tell anything. And the second one didn't know what had happened either.

"Well, this happened sometime in the afternoon, and it was after dark when I knew anything about it. Here I heard this car drive into the yard tootin' and makin' a noise, you know. Mrs. Hartman and her daughter had come after me. Well, I took my constable, a great big six-foot-four chap, and took their car. We had no car at the station in those days—they're all mechanized now, you know. And there was a leak in the sump—oil a-comin' out, and the car was in bad shape. I couldn't get any speed out of it; it's always that way when you are in a hurry. But we got there anyway and gathered together some stuff—bandages, and a stretcher, and all that. Of course, it was all kind of hectic—the missus and the daughter kept askin' me what I thought had happened and all that.

" 'Well,' I says, 'I don't know of course, but frankly don't hold out much hope.'

"Well, we let the black go—lying there at the house. No time to take care of *him*. We drove out as far as we could with the car—three or four miles—then we tried to drive about a mile farther into the bush. But we might as well have walked for all the progress we made. Then we followed the trackers, but couldn't do anything at night, you know. We just stumbled around in an area where he might have been. But then, finally, we found a water hole where we thought he might have dragged himself. He knew the country like a book, you know. Well, the black said it was impossible to go on—couldn't do anything until daylight. It was about three A.M. then, so we sat around and waited an hour or so until it got light, then set off to try and find where they had tracked the lion to, on Saturday. For we knew they would have had to pick up the trail when they started out again Sunday.

"Well, we finally got it and followed slowly through the bush. Those Bushmen are wonderful when it comes to tracking. They see things a white man would never see. There were three of them. They march a few yards apart, each a little in advance of the one behind. After a couple of hours, I said to them, 'Where the bloody hell are we now? I don't see any trail.'

" 'Here, boss,' one of 'em said. 'See this!' and he showed where one claw of the lion had made a little hole—not as big around as a lead pencil. Then he showed me the back part of the print of a man's heel. And so we went on. Finally they stopped.

" 'Where the bloody hell are we now?' I asked.

" 'This is where they shot the lion on Saturday, boss. Now we—'

" 'You bloody bastard,' I said, 'tellin' me we're only up to Saturday! All this time and we're only up to Saturday! Where in bloody hell did they start out on Sunday?'

" 'Now we have to follow the lion,' he said.

"And so we went on. Then I jumped him again about bein' on the trail.

" 'Here, boss, see this,' he said. And it was only a tiny drop of blood—
from the wounded lion, you know. Then he smelled it, got right down and
sniffed it like a dog. They can tell how old it is, you know. He said it was
dropped about Saturday night.

"Well, we went on and on. Then we found where Hartman had picked
up the trail again on Sunday morning. And so we followed him for two or
three hours. My constable wasn't too keen on this stuff. He kept behind me
about fifty yards.

" 'I don't like this bloody business,' he said.

" 'Well, what did you sign on for?' I asked him.

"So we went on a ways. Then all of a sudden those blacks straightened
up. All three of 'em. They sensed something, you know. They didn't see
anything, but they felt it. We went pretty slow after that. Then there was a
noise and the bushes parted and a big lion jumped out and the boys turned
and ran back past me and my constable right with them. Well, I couldn't
do anything there alone without trackers or anything, so I had to go back,
too. And they went a long way before they stopped. Then we heard the
dogs bark. Just once they barked."

"Did you have dogs with you?" I asked.

"No, those were the old man's dogs, you know. Anyway, the blacks
wouldn't take the lead any more. You couldn't hire them to go ahead. And
my constable, 'I'm not going ahead. Not on your bloody life,' he said.

" 'Well, somebody's got to,' I said, and started off. I was so sure I could
go to where those dogs had barked that I walked right towards the spot.
But the bush was awful thick. I went very, very slowly."

"And I'll bet you looked on either side as well as ahead, eh?" I asked.

"You're dammed right! And then finally I saw the lion—under a tree,
off about a hundred yards. I could see him. Well, I stopped.

" 'There's a lion,' I said to my constable.

He had already gotten himself under a good-sized tree. He was under
a bare branch and I could see he'd gotten it all figured out how he could
swing himself up in a hurry.

" 'I'm not going up there,' he said.

"But I could see that the lion had his leg lying out in front of him—not
at right angles to his body, you know. And he never moved. Not a muscle.
So I figured in that position he must be dead. So I went very slowly, with
my rifle cocked, you know."

Just at that crucial moment in the tale the womenfolk announced tea
from the other room. I thought this might encourage the storyteller to rush
on to the conclusion. But he was not to be hurried. So we had tea before
he continued.

"Well, I got nearly up to the lion and I could see he was dead. And
then I smelled something. I don't know what it is, but there is something
about a dead person that makes a smell different from any other."

"Yes, you're right," said Mr. Theron, my host. I could see that both were thinking back to the days when they had lost buddies in World War I.

"And then we found the body—about twenty yards away—and the two dogs beside it. One leg had been bitten nearly off, and the bone was sticking out. The leg was actually back along his side. And his left hand—the flesh was all off the inside, and the second finger of his right hand had been bitten off. But other than that there was nothing—oh, a few little marks on his forehead. And his chest was bruised a little, like from the butt of a gun. But if he had had a native who had some sense or had any help, he needn't have died. He bled to death, you see. The jugular in his leg was hanging loose and empty. He'd tried to stop it; there was a handkerchief around his leg, but it was all loose."

"Well, why was the lion so far away?" I asked.

"Oh, they do that. That's the cat in them, you know. They seem to sense when their prey has been mortally wounded and they lay off to watch it. It gives them a sense of satisfaction and pride."

"But had he shot the lion after it had attacked him or before?"

"That we had no means of knowing."

33

Wherein I Learn
to Like the Portuguese

When I told Boris, my host, that I was going on in the morning by bicycle, he begged me not to.

"There are too many lions, and it's dangerous," he said.

I had to admit that my route was right through the area where the lion had killed Mr. Hartman.

Another man in Tsumeb had also been concerned about my safety, asserting that two hundred natives were killed by lions every year in Ovamboland.

One has to sort out the truth from all these stories and worries. The men who really know the country do not tell me I take a risk. I have not heard one authentic account yet where a man was attacked unless he had wounded the lion or was deliberately out in the bush stalking one. Boris had never been over the road.

It was after 9 A.M. when I cycled out of Tsumeb—loaded with bread and supplies for the great open spaces. I had a nice wind behind me, but the trail was rough and rocky.

By dusk I was in the vicinity of the Hartman farm and wondering if I was anywhere near where the lion had killed Mr. Hartman. I spent the night in the Hartman home but of course said nothing of the unfortunate affair to Mrs. Hartman. The farmstead was not too different from that on an Australian sheep or cattle station. About thirty natives were attached to it —some Bushmen, others Ovambos.

Through the hired man I arranged to take a picture the next morning of a Bushman family by its tiny hut. Father had quite a time getting the family all together. He had to shout across the clearings several times before they came running home, big and little. The little ones were arrayed in Tarzan-type loinclothes. The wife, like other Bushman women, was quite petite.

I was surprised to find that the Bushmen, though small, were fairly well proportioned. For I recalled a chautauqua lecturer of my extreme youth who had told of the African Bushmen. I was not above eight or ten at the time and had retained just one thing from his lecture. "A Bushman," he said, "has arms so long he can scratch his heels without bending his knees." So I had envisioned a hulk of a man with all the proportions of a great ape.

In lining up for my pictures the Bushmen were quick to grasp my meaning and to act upon it. Besides being intelligent, they are said to be fiercely loyal to their friends, solicitious about their children, and respectful of the aged.

Other customs are imbedded in superstition. When a Bushman marries, he follows customs not too dissimilar from those of some northern European countries. A big feast is held for all the relatives on both sides of the family. Near the close of festivities the groom starts to drag off the bride but is set upon with sticks by her relatives. It is a game, of course, and the groom is eventually allowed to take the fair lady home with him.

When a Bushman dies, he is buried with his feet toward the west so that the sun will not rise late the next morning. His grave is danced upon and then covered with stones. These are to keep the evil spirits which caused his death from rising and entering the bodies of those still living.

A few hours after I had taken pictures of the Bushman family, Jacqueline and I pedaled into a game preserve. Almost immediately we began to see game—tiny antelope and a herd of zebra. Then after a little we came to Namutoni! A fort in the desert! Whitewashed to a gleaming white, serrated square-corner towers set against a background of drab desert and scattered scrub, Namutoni seemed unreal. It was unreal, for inside I found a beautiful white-walled pool filled with fresh running water, clear and pure, lightly reflecting the azure blue of the desert sky.

The fort had been built by the Germans, and they were responsible for the innovation of the swimming pool. Well-cemented stones surrounded the edge, and there was a cute little pole shelter with a seat for use when changing clothes. The pool walls and bottom had been whitewashed; the water was clean and ran fresh from the pump in a cement channel. Large flowering bushes and a towering palm afforded further privacy and kept off the cool breezes—for this was winter. After lunch I took a swim, *au naturel*. The only lady within umpty-nine miles, the wife of the sergeant in command, was in her home on the opposite side of the fort.

Around 6 P.M. three covered railway trucks drove into the fort packed with standing Ovambos, visible only from the rear. The sarge spoke to a driver about taking me along third class. Meanwhile the head driver agreed to my separate request for third-class transportation, but when I went to the rear to get in with Ovambos, the first driver nearly burst a blood vessel. He piled out of the driver's seat and was up to me in a flash.

"You can't ride back there. No-o-sir! We don't mix white and black in this country. No, sir. You can ride with me." (He had the mail and freight.)

Namutoni was a rest stop, and we all ate lunch before leaving at 8:30 P.M. There was much sand. Two tracks through the bush as I had in Australia. With my bicycle I would have walked a great deal. One of the trucks had engine trouble, and we all lost a lot of time because of that. On one occasion a vitally important ring was lost from the carbureter and we had to look for it with flashlights along the sand-filled tracks. The three drivers and their assistants only looked near and between the trucks, but I walked a long way back. When I returned, they all asked if I was not afraid of wild animals to go so far away. They could not be hired to leave the trucks more than ten feet. However we finally found the part, where I had suggested they look for it in the first place—on the engine supports.

At one stop, when the men in front were working on the truck engine, a wolf, jackal, hyena, or similar-sized animal appeared in the road about fifty yards away. My driver had gone up to the stalled trucks to see what was wrong. He came back on a dead run as though a lion were chasing him.

"There's a bloody big tiger on the road!" he ejaculated.

This aroused my curiosity, and I walked up to see. Sure enough, there was an animal lying on the road, but before I could get too close it bounded leisurely away. My driver meanwhile brought his truck around to flash his lights on the spot. I walked out into the grass a few yards but saw no signs.

The most interesting part of the trip for me was the crossing of part of the great Etosha Pan. This is a dried-up lake bed, flooded in the rainy season. Now it was a great white expanse of alkali and salt, like our Great Salt Lake desert. Picture it under an African moon!

Five A.M., after a cold all-night ride, brought us to a native administration place called Ondangua. Here at seven o'clock I got my Ovamboland permit stamped at the native commissioner's. No objections were raised to my continuing by bicycle. As at Namutoni, officials were friendly and sensible. What a contrast to those officials in the Sudan! Here was a similar restricted area, yet it was properly administered.

The trail north was full of sand, and I walked more than I rode. I had a flat tire, and an Ovambo helped me fix it—that is, he wanted to, but the support was mainly moral.

The country had become more or less green at last. At least the trees and bushes were green, though the grass, if any, was dead. The land was free from undergrowth, and the open spaces enhanced the beauty of the trees, which resembled our oaks. Ovamboland is supposed to be the garden spot of all the vast area of South West Africa, and I believe it. Yet consider! It was nothing more than a desert bearing trees and a few bushes. Still, in the rainy season, nearly all the country is under water.

And so at last I came to Ovambo-Oshikongo, a place made as romantic by its remoteness as by the sound of its name. For two thousand miles I had been traveling toward this mythical spot in the South West Africa wilderness without ever being able to locate it on any map. And now here it was, a tiny frontier post deep in Ovamboland and just a few steps from the border of Angola, sometimes known as Portuguese West Africa.

Although there was a government resthouse, the assistant native commissioner, K.R. Crossman, his charming wife, and three small children invited me to be their guest. He was a South African colonial, and she was born in Ireland. They were one of the ten most hospitable families I met in my nineteen months of travel. A fair sample of their hospitality is how they planned at dinner what they could give me to take along the next day.

"Would you like some butter? We've scads of it. More than we will use."

"Would you like a loaf of bread? I just baked today."

"Would you like some pawpaws? We've got an enormous one. Could you carry it? How about vegetables? We've some carrots that are big enough."

Mr. Crossman, as assistant commissioner, knew a great deal about the Ovambo, and I made good use of the opportunity to learn. "Ovambo is a Herrero name, and the natives call themselves the Aajambo, or "rich ones." The Ovambos were the largest group of natives in all South West Africa. Ovamboland, Mr. Crossman said, was recognized by authorities as being unique among the native reserves of the world.

The Ovamboland administration aimed to keep tribal customs intact and to build on these as a foundation the best self-government possible. A council of eight headmen, one for each district, met once per month under Crossman's supervision. He acted in an advisory capacity, but his suggestions were usually followed. There were four thousand square miles and sixty to seventy thousand natives under his jurisdiction. He said the Portuguese across the border would have twelve men over a similar charge.

Taxes were five shillings ($1) per person per year, payable in money or corn. There were no sanctions for nonpayment. "Corn" was millet, kept stored in tribal baskets. Mr. Crossman showed me a number of these in the kraal back of his yard. They rested on stilts about two feet above the ground, and the mouth was closed with a mud plug. Some of them had thatched roofs. My host said these granaries would keep the grain up to five years, and very rarely would there be any molding, even in wet weather. Grain was given to any worthy native in temporary straits in lean years.

It was desired to instill a love of country in the Ovambo, so he was allowed to contract out for only one year to diamond mines, railroads, and farms in the south. Then he had to stay home for three months.

Inheritance was matrilineal with the Ovambo, and polygamy was practiced extensively. The hoe must be wielded, and twelve wives will make the work go faster than one or two. Thus polygamy was necessary for successful farming. Of course, there was one chap who had the misfortune to be a Christian and therefore had only one wife. The Lord did not desert him, however, and suggested that he get a plow. With this innovation he plowed in one week a plot that would have taken a six-wife man three months. The Ovambo treated his wives well—nothing but the best for them. After all, did not the Iowa farmer give the best corn to his draft horses before he got his tractor?

The Ovambo was basically very honest, and there was no policeman in all of Ovamboland. There were tribal courts to hear cases, but the assistant

Bushman family outside their home in northern Southwest Africa. The German proprietor of this land had been killed by a lion.

This Ovambo belle has just lost her charming smile— Angola.

Road worker in southern Angola. His mallet headed tamper is in his left hand. Basket and blanket are carried across his shoulders on the stick shown.

Milady bends her head to show her coiffure. The rolls are bright yellow.

native commissioner often tempered the sentences, as they were inclined to be too severe. A native might appeal to the commissioner. One chap stole a sewing machine and was fined five head of cattle although he did not have cattle or any other property. Mr. Crossman pointed out the folly of such punishment and suggested they make the man work on the road at a shilling a day. Enough money would be given back to him for subsistence, but the major part would be turned over to the claimant.

"Oh, we never thought of that," said the court.

The Crossmans did not recognize the color bar.

"After all, how could we? My colleagues, the Portuguese officials across the line, have colored wives. They visit us and bring their native wives."

When I spoke of the lack of educational facilities for South African natives, Mr. Crossman said that when they became educated they indulged in antiwhite talk instead of raising the standard of their fellows.

Angola started out very badly. Sand, sand, and more sand. Still, it was not so bad as the worst part of Australia. In a number of places they had put reeds across the road for the traffic (?) to pass over. But I have learned to expect bad roads to and from international borders. Each nation wants to keep its traffic unto itself.

I met several native Ovambo belles—and I do mean belles—attired in nothing but a short "grass skirt" made out of strips of leather and sinew. I took a picture of one and hope my wife won't mind. They were all by their pretty lonesomes out in the bush.

I was a curiosity at the Portuguese frontier post. The authorities had moved from want of business from the actual boundary to a place called Njeva (Villa Pereira de Eca), which I did not reach before midafternoon. Here I was treated with every courtesy and in no way regarded with suspicion as a spy or an undesirable. The man who stamped my passport said something to the others about my courage.

I was invited to stay the night with a Portuguese who quite naturally bore the name of Pereira. He wrote two letters to people along my route asking them to arrange rides for me. Mrs. Pereira was really dark but petite and fairly well groomed. I noted that a continental coiffure is troubled by kinky hair. The baby daughter was quite fair.

At bedtime a cot, sheet, and blankets were tendered me. About midnight I found I had three companions. These were given last rites, bathed in blood, and we all slept happily thereafter.

There was not too much sand on the bush trail next day. I dismounted many times to walk through bad stretches, but it was not enough to dim my enjoyment of travel. I looked forward to mealtime with the same pleasure as had been my good fortune so far. And why not? For breakfast fare I had my choice of bread, butter, spam, jerky, two kinds of cheese, chicken, carrots, peach jam, apple jell, sugar, candy, oranges, and pawpaw.

Ah, those meals in the bush, with my back up against the shady side of a tree trunk, Jacqueline nearby, and my food items spread out around me! I could never seem to catch up on my loaves of bread and kept them well wrapped in paper and sacks. Still, they would dry out.

This was lion country! I had been warned with words and scared faces by nearly everybody. Yet I saw herds of goats and cattle—not often, but often enough to make me feel there was not too much danger from lions. The only startling thing was the frequent "crack" on a tree adjacent to the one under which I ate my lunch. Afterward when cycling along, I heard similar "cracks" and knew what the sound was. It is apparently natural and not caused by bird or animal.

I reached a lonely Portuguese trading post in midafternoon and enjoyed a drink of cold water. Then I borrowed some oil for Jacqueline's chain, recalling as I did so that winter's day many years before when I had done the same thing in a hill town of faraway Portugal, Angola's mother country. Seeing that I liked milk the family sent me off with a quart bottle of the same. Now all these negotiations were conducted without a word of English. Sign language and some Spanish were the media.

Again I found a lot of sand and lonely country. All bush as usual. About camp time I came across three abandoned huts and took over the largest for the night. This was the only one that allowed me to stand up. All three contained foot-high beds of loose two-to-three-inch-diameter poles laid crosswise. Naturally I chose the ground. Similar poles placed upright made the sides of the house. Thus there were plenty of two-inch cracks for me to see out on the moon-drenched land. I read awhile by my bicycle lamp. There were unexplainable noises about outside and there was no door on the hut, but I did not worry, believing that the reason was something similar to that of the "cracking" stick.

Daylight again, and off. The country teemed with guinea fowl and what we would call grouse or partridge. I saw a pretty bird with a yellow tail and a number of big cranes. I also saw antelope.

In a little village in the bush I found Senhor João Evangelista Moutinho and was again plied with Portuguese hospitality. He was dispatching a truck the very next morning all the way to Nova Lisboa (Huambo), proposed capital of Angola. This was a wonderful stroke of luck, for it meant that I would travel almost through the center of the country instead of along the west coast. The ride was to cost me nothing. All arrangements were carried on in the French language, which my host knew. I thanked my lucky stars that I had studied French.

Next day about 11 A.M.—this is Portuguese starting time—my host called "*Sommes prêt.*" My driver was a short, burly Portuguese with a boil on his elbow. We went northward into the bush; and talk about sand, wow! I honestly don't believe an ordinary car could have made it at all. We had

There are just about all ages here—Ovambo village.

Three loafers at the country store—Southwest Angola.

big double wheels and no load, and the new Ford was in excellent condition, yet we often had to shift to intermediate and once had to stay in that
gear for about two miles. At other times the road was a little more than a
trail with trees close in on both sides. Even when there was an obvious
"road," the trees were very close, and in turning corners, it was a big game
of dodge. And bumps, wow! The springs were good, and the springs in the
seat were positively wonderful—so wonderful, in fact, that they sent us
toward the roof at the slightest provocation. Several times I was thrown
completely off the seat and just managed to light back on it.

Toward 2 p.m. we followed our cowpath to the sand-filled, trackless
yard of a native. Four young girls—but perhaps they were the chief's wives
—came out when we honked. One was particularly nice and brought out a
tiny table and two small stools. Also a large cup of water. So there we sat
in the sand in the shade of a bole of a leafless tree and ate our lunch. This
had been sent by Sr. Moutinho, and there were about fifteen pieces of
freshly fried fish and a big roast, tender and well done. I cut off a generous
slice of the roast, but the driver ate about two-thirds of it. How he could
chew and swallow all of it in the short time he took, I'll never know. I gave
my fishbones to three starved-looking dogs. When we left, the driver gave
a piece of fish and some bread to the girl, and I saw one of the others pick
up our orange peelings out of the sand. I wonder what those poor girls
would do with a chocolate sundae or a piece of ground-cherry pie.

We again followed our cowpath to the shores of the Cunene River, the
biggest in Angola. Then we proceeded northward through rather open
country, still following the river. There were tall grass and some really
green trees for a change, set well apart and with very little undergrowth,
instead of the vast forests we had been traversing. Bear in mind that Africa
is not all jungle. In fact, up to this point I had seen very little jungle.

Villages, native or Portuguese, were practically nonexistent; but there
was one called Capelongo. Portuguese colonial buildings are one-storied
and have white walls and red-tile roofs. We continued to follow cowpaths
and trails that didn't exist until 1:30 a.m., when we called a halt. We slept
until six.

Daylight travel brought partridges, great bustards, wart hogs, and something that looked like a kudu. It also brought a road, and it was not long
before we joined the main Mossamedes-Nova Lisboa "highway." The
Portuguese colonial had built his roads by clearing out a minimum of trees,
then digging two parallel straight-sided ditches. In between was the road.

Nova Lisboa was a well-planned inland commercial city, with buildings
of the tropical architecture I have just described. The principal streets were
paved, but barren brown clayish soil was evident everywhere between the
scattered buildings and in the vacant lots. There were no streetcars and no
buses. In fact, Nova Lisboa was more like a town than a city except in
population.

Pereira's letter to a friend in Nova Lisboa netted me a ride north to a place called Villa Teixeira da Silva. Here the driver left me with a letter to the proprietor of a hotel. This chap spoke neither English nor French, but a young man who was there knew Spanish. So I struggled with my memories of that language. I recalled my Spanish teacher saying that if one studied a language for only one year he would forget but that if he studied it for two years, he would never forget. I believe she was right because I still seemed to get along in Spanish. But it was not too easy to go from French to Spanish, especially when fresh words of Portuguese crowded into the picture.

The hotelkeeper invited me to be his guest for dinner and the night. Can't you just picture an American hotelkeeper anywhere doing that for a foreigner who doesn't even speak his own language? Sometimes I have a very small opinion of us Americans. The hotel proprietor, his wife, and the waiters treated me with the greatest interest and respect. My host kept a store and the following morning helped me with the new odds and ends which had lost off Jacqueline due to the terrific beating she took riding in trucks on these roads. They all expected me at breakfast the next morning, but I ate my own tucker in my room.

In the morning I went to the post office to mail a portion of my diary. What fine treatment I received as compared with busy South African post offices! Granted, I was an event. They offered me sealing wax for my letter—I have always had to ask for it before—even at small post offices. Then an assistant took me across the street to a store where they had a stamp that we could put on the wax. Returning to the post office, the postmaster took much time and patience in getting the greatest possible variety of stamps and then put them on my letter for collector friends at home. When I wanted to buy a postcard but lacked change, he, having none, told me to forget it. So there you are!

I left Teixeira on Jacqueline but soon got a long ride with a road acquaintance of the day before. The country was hilly, and as I worked north it became mountainous. The slopes were largely devoid of trees and bush, but I remembered that near Nova Lisboa plantation owners had planted a short bushy evergreen and tree like a Chinese elm for soil conservation. For the most part this countryside had been burned over. Grass fires and smoke were common across the landscape and at night were very picturesque.

Native men were frequently dressed in white or khaki shirt and trousers and some of the more advanced, in white suit coats and hats. At the other extreme many natives wore nothing but rags. Women had a single cloth wraparound garment and were about equally divided in the practice of covering the breasts. Babies were carried pickaback in a tightly wrapped blanket. Both sexes often displayed their fine white teeth in flashing smiles. There seemed to be quite a bit of blindness. The very little boys wore no clothes at all, but the rest had loincloths. Little girls, I seldom saw and I wondered why. No one seemed to work, except the native women, who were often pounding corn beside their houses.

I had many opportunities to note these houses in various stages of construction. Poles about three inches in diameter are set vertically to form walls in the shape of a rectangle. An honest-to-goodness door frame is very frequently set in the long side of the house facing the road. Mud is then forced between the poles, and the long slender wood wands are fastened horizontally to help keep the mud in place. Even after the house is finished, the poles and wands frequently show to the outside. There are no windows, and floors are of dirt. A village consists of about eight or ten houses.

On the faithful Jacqueline or in light trucks I worked into northern Angola. Around Villa Salazar I passed through the first real jungle in many a moon. Near here was a big sisal plantation. The sisal plant looks like a huge pineapple with big yuccalike spikes growing upward. When the bottom spikes are cut, leaving the white cut places, a similarity to the pineapple becomes apparent. I saw a large area where the white fibers had been hung up to dry.

At Lucala, I pedaled down the street between two parked trucks and in less than no time had the offer of two rides north the following morning. Then, by the time I had bought two small loaves of bread at the hotel just by, I had introduced myself sufficiently in French so that the proprietor and hangers-on became interested and I was given an invitation to supper and a bed by the hotel proprietor, and gratis at that. How could I help but like the Portuguese?

When you sit at table in a Portuguese colonial hotel, you find three plates stacked upside down. By turning all three over at once, your soup dish is on top. The ware is heavy crockery. Your knife is on the right, the fork on the left, and the big spoon in front. There is a small glass for wine and a large one for water, both upside down. A small napkin, folded in a triangle, is at the left of the plate. It may be white, or blue, red, and white; and it may be fringed. On one corner of the table is a brown earthenware water jug on its brown platter earthenware base and with a tiny cloth cover. Or there may be a plain bottle for the water. Decanters of vinegar and olive oil may also be present.

A big tureen of soup is brought by the waiter first and you help your-self with the big ladle. The soup is thick with greens and other vegetables and perhaps meat. It is a meal in itself. The second course may be maca-roni mixed with meat, hot with peppers; or perhaps fish mixed with potatoes; or beans mixed with chicken, beef, or fish; and also rice. The third course is usually steak, roasted potatoes, and lettuce. The fourth course is fruit, usually bananas or tangerines. Coffee follows. Wine is used throughout the meal but may be thinned with water. If salt is desired, it must be asked for. At only one meal in the different hotels in which I have eaten has there been a dessert. This was something like plum jell and eaten with bread. Lunch and dinner are alike. Breakfast is only one course—an omelet and potatoes, or meat and potatoes, the meat being usually fresh fried fish.

My host saw to it personally that I had plenty to eat for breakfast. Then I left Lucala on a combined freight and passenger bus that ran the mail. The driver intimated that he was taking me because he wanted company. His name was Alberto Duarte, and he was courteous and friendly as were the half dozen other young men to whom I had talked in French at the hotel the night before. Altogether I was favorably impressed with the young Portuguese colonials, and the older ones too. They were not overly inquisitive and seemed to tend to their own affairs with little fuss or bother. Alberto was not handsome, but his heart was in the right place and he was very kind to me, insisting on paying my expenses during our two days' travel into the north.

Along the way I noticed a few changes. Native houses started to show windows. These were easily made: the native simply did not put mud over the lattice work where a window was wanted. The framework for the thatched roof was made like the walls, only of smaller strips of wood. The roof had a long overhang supported by vertical poles. The soil had changed to red, so the houses were red instead of brown. The village granaries differed from those of the Ovambo. They were baskets shaped like an immense elongated top with an unusually long center stick at the bottom to keep them well up from the ground. A half dozen of these were frequently to be seen in the center of a village.

The children who ran to the roadside to wave and yell, *"Bom dia"* had exchanged their nudity or loincloth for odds and ends of manufactured material. Some wore a shirt only, others only khaki shorts and others only a piece of cloth wrapped around the body to look like a skirt.

As we rode along, looking out over range after range of hills, I was often awed by the vastness of Africa, and how much, yet how little, I had seen of it. For beyond these ranges I knew, there were other ranges unseen, where there were no roads at all. What did those ranges look like?

By dusk we had reached a place called 'N'gase, and darkness found us well out on a side trip to Uije. We topped one hill, and there on the road was a big black leopard. He was a most impressive beast and instantly reminded me of some sculpture I had seen of a leopard couchant. Coal-black he was, lithe, sleek, powerful. He took his time, too, about turning and slinking off to the side, his belly low, his haunches higher than his back, his great tail curved smoothly upward toward the end. How like a giant housecat he was! I had a big thrill, as it was the first I had seen of this type. I seemed to recall that the black leopard is rare. He was quite close to a native village, and I suppose more than one dog, kid, full-grown goat, or chicken had found its way into his hungry maw.

We ate dinner at Uije. Blacks, whites, and mulattoes were all eating in the same dining room. Conversation had no color bar. Uije was quite a town. Coffee growing was the principal occupation.

The native population increased as we went north. Every hill along the road was topped by a native village. Clean, hard-packed dirt surrounded all the houses. Some villages had a half dozen huts, some two dozen. Construction had improved, and the horizonal withes were so slender and evenly spaced as to make the walls look like fine latticework. I have remarked earlier that no one seems to work, but there was plenty of activity in this region. Women and sometimes men had head burdens of wide, cone-shaped baskets containing ear corn or manioc roots. Some had baskets strapped to their backs. And on the road I occasionally saw work gangs of women and children, carrying head baskets full of dirt to fill up the holes. I recalled a woman's work gang in southern Angola. They were wielding huge hoes to remove grass, and others were using stick brushes to smooth things off. Their bosoms were bare, but these women wore wraparound prints, often gaily colored. Indeed, as we approached Maquela do Zombo, some prints were positively brilliant. I saw one work gang under the supervision of an armed soldier, but the women did not look very criminal to me.

At the end of the run I left Alberto and the mail truck and continued on Jacqueline. The first night I slept in a native village where I was surprised to find a chap who spoke excellent French, as well as Portuguese, some English, and the native tongue. He and the village chief fixed me up with a house and a spring mesh bed on which had been laid a clean cane mat. Another such mat rested on the dirt floor beside the bed. With a tiny one-candlepower lamp and a board for a table, I wrote for a couple hours before turning in.

Daylight, and I was on the road at 5:45. It was cloudy and misty, as a reminder that the rains were due soon. I tried to get cooperation for a picture in a native village but failed except for one man who obligingly stopped his roof thatching and helped me try and round up some women. But they were too shy. At the next village I asked for eggs and found a bashful vendor who would sell me eight for five angolares. The five-angolar notes were unusually worn, and so she insisted on choosing the best of the three I had. But then it developed that she had no pan in which to cook the eggs. In fact, there was not a pan in the whole village. So I had to return my purchase. Lacking pans, the natives must make their corn or manioc flour-and-water concoctions with cold water, using gourds.

At a third village I ate breakfast surrounded by the usual bunch of native children. I asked my host what the population of the village was and if these were all of them. He said that they were all his brothers and sisters. My eyes widened, and I looked at pa, sitting in a dressing gown on a pile of wood. (I see these gowns occasionally; they are worn all day.)

"Mon père a cinq femmes [My father has five wives]," he explained.

Belgian Congo again! This time my entry far to the east marked an important point in my journeyings, for the Congo lies solidly athwart the heart of Africa. It is a country of tremendous potentiality. In area it then ranked no less than twelfth among the world's countries. King Leopold gave all 921,000 square miles of it to the Belgians in 1908 in the greatest private real-estate deal ever consumated. The Congo was estimated to have two and one-half times the potential waterpower of any other country in the world. The Congo River, second mightiest, contributes much of this power with its great cataracts and falls as it descends from the western highlands. In these highlands are some of the most valuable copper mines in the world—a resource most people never suspect of a country traditionally jungle. And there is gold, and diamonds, and coal—all apart from the enormous forest value. The latter is manifest in rubber, quinine, and palm oil, more than in use of the woods themselves. Lever Brothers had a million acres of palm-oil plantations in the Congo—land purchased from the native chiefs with the consent of the colonial government. Cotton and coffee are grown in the Congo, and I passed through an enormous sugar cane plantation.

Late one afternoon Jacqueline and I were given a ride by a jovial, bombastic Portuguese named Avany. Driving a new Ford utility, he was up from Luanda on the Angola coast and bound for Leopoldville, the Congo capital, my own destination. Avany understood Spanish, but not French, so I had to switch to that language. Words of Spanish and French spluttered and fizzed all over the place while I went through mental gymnastics amounting to torture trying to recall my dormant Spanish. Nevertheless, I never regretted all the time spent in studying five languages. The knowledge is a great help in travel.

Avany drove like hell, and I've never seen a worse road. There was sand, sand, and more sand. The Belgians had decided the only way to keep the road passable was to scrape the sand to one side. This process had been continued through the years until the road was a deep trench. The sides were usually vertical in spite of the sandy nature of the soil, and about as high as the car—frequently twice as high. Sand slides had made the bottom of the road a continual series of cross trenches each the width of the diameter of an automobile tire. Imagine traveling over that at any speed.

After dark the headlights of the car reflected against the white sides of the trench. At one point they picked up an odd-looking animal resembling a porcupine or anteater, quite streamlined at the back. He was light-gray in color with small, short black bars along his sides and a black streak up his spine.

We reached the Congo River about 10 P.M. It was not far from Leopoldville, so Avany let me out and I slept on the bank of a tiny stream flowing quietly over to the river. The Congo, incidentally, drains a basin whose area is surpassed only by the Amazon.

I found Leopoldville to be nearly level, clinging tightly to the south

They are clapping their hands in greeting—Congo.

The vastness that is Africa.

There are fish in Congo rivers.

Lunchtime in the Congo.

bank of its mother Congo for several miles. About 8,000 Europeans and 120,000 natives made up the population. Some of the main streets were paved, and there was one high building of ten or twelve stories. A neat city, and most of the buildings and the hotels were quite modern. Of course, Leopoldville would have looked good to me in any event because the dentist filled my teeth for free, the barber cut my hair for nothing, and the garage man fixed up Jacqueline without charge. At the post office I was given preferred attention by both clerks and waiting customers, and when I returned to my bicycle no less than four native policemen were keeping off the usual crowd.

34

Steaming Jungle
and Gravied Taroc

The ferry for Brazzaville, across the Congo in French Equatorial Africa, was quite crowded. I sat with the natives, not noticing that most of the whites sat up in front. It made no difference to me anyway, and I found that in Belgian and French colonies there was no more worry about the color bar than there had been in Portuguese Angola.

Proof of this was my experience in buying a railroad ticket. French Equatorial Africa had one line of about 250 miles running from Brazzaville to the coast, and I found I could make use of it for about two-thirds of its length. The only train available was a goods train. The ticket chap was very friendly. He explained that it was forbidden to ride on such a train, even though the passenger train ran only once a week. But without explanation he understood my anxiety to keep traveling and went to consult the manager. The manager readily gave his consent, and in jig time I had a fourth-class ticket costing only 343 francs—about $1.70. The head ticket seller shrugged his shoulders when the bicycle was mentioned. I wish things were that easy and friendly in all countries.

As I mentioned in an earlier chapter the attitude toward the Negro in the Congo River countries was much different than in the Union of South Africa. There the Negro was feared because of his numerical superiority and education, and advancement was kept from him so that he could not make his advantage effective. But in the Congo the line was drawn almost unconsciously on a social basis only. If a Negro showed promise, he was given a more responsible position. Efforts were made to raise his standard of living and give him knowledge and tools to increase his production. However, there was criticism that this forced impact of civilization was too much for the native's happy-go-lucky nature and he had become confused and uncertain. This I can believe because my own experience showed me that most natives were often incapable of following the simplest instructions. Still, in my estimation the race situation was healthier in the Congo River regions than in the Union because a start must be made, and the Belgian and French administrations were attempting it.

My train ride was not soon forgotten. The van was as dark as the face of the *chef du tren*. It was a big boxcarlike affair with one end partitioned off for the sorting of the mail. I was invited to sit at the mail shelf to eat my supper. There was a lantern, and after eating, I read awhile. Then the mail clerk, or perhaps it was the assistant *chef du tren,* found a place for me to throw my sleeping bag by moving a woman and two sleeping children. The children never stirred as he lifted them and again laid them down on their mats. I slept soundly and awoke refreshed to read or enjoy the scenery. I noticed some small mountain ranges and felt that I was getting beyond the sand of the river.

French Equatorial Africa was the thirteenth largest country in the world and about one-third the size of the United States. The first French settlements on the Atlantic Coast were designed to secure a place where men-of-war could revictual. The first city was founded in 1849 with Negroes from a slave ship, but it was not until an expedition of 1875-78 by Savorgnan de Brazza that the interior was brought under French influence. Vast areas to the north and east were taken over when the French beat the Belgians in a race for the regions of the Upper Nile in the 1890s.

Leaving my little railroad at a place called Dolisie, I met a young chap of the Transports l'Église who said I could ride north with him the next day for 600 kilometers. Later it developed I had to see his boss. The boss turned out to be a fat chap, all business, and *très riche,* as I learned later. He wanted 6,000 francs—about $47 ($32 even at black-market rates)—to carry me the 360 miles, more than thirteen cents per mile. He did not want much, did he? I almost laughed in his face. By his actions I could tell he thought he had me, as he had not sufficient imagination to conceive that anyone would attempt to ride a bicycle so far.

Giving Jacqueline a little pat of appreciation, I headed north over a road which probably saw a car about once a week. My first night in French territory was spent in a little hut of my own in a Bapanou village. I passed the evening writing, but a group of four young men, one of them the chief of the village, kept me respectful company. They were nice young men, and I liked them. When they bothered me with questions, it was in a polite manner and not too frequently. They were interested in conditions in America, especially wages, and when I had given them the picture, the most simple of the four was all for accompanying me right away. Cooks for *les blancs* (white folk) got 35 or 40 francs, or about 20 cents per day in Gabon. Workers with their hands got about 950 francs, or $4.75 per month.

I had traveled about six miles the following morning, when I was offered a ride by a Frenchman and his wife. About eleven o'clock we stopped at madame's brother's. Here monsieur said we were to eat lunch and then go on. I envisioned a wait until noon at least, and was not too keen on the delay, but he assured me we would eat right away. Since we were seated at the table by eleven, I stopped worrying. But believe it or not, we had a nine-course meal which lasted until 1:15 P.M. At that time I really felt full, not just stuffed; and since I like to eat, I rather enjoyed it. We first had Dubonnet as an aperitif. Then bread, butter, and radishes; third, bread, butter, and tomatoes tastily fixed in *huile d'arachid* (peanut oil); then

This young Congo belle is a little doubtful about the camera.

How many million do you guess?

bread, butter, and fish. Since we had been given only three plates, I figured, fool that I was, that this was the last course. Having had seconds on
all courses to date, I was feeling quite comfortable. But alas, we were only
just getting around to the main course. This was steak of the water buffalo
—juicy, tender, and well done, served with plenty of macaroni and more
bread and butter. The butter was a concession to me, as the French do not
use it. Course six was endive salad. Course seven (clean plates for each
course, naturally) was canned peaches and bread. Then came homemade
peanut brittle, still soft. Lastly there was coffee. Eating time: two hours and
fifteen minutes.

It was after dark that evening when I pedaled into the yard of a Swedish
mission to which I had been referred by friends farther south. It was good
to speak English once more and to eat Swedish bread, the most delicious in
the world. After supper the missionary's wife showed me how the ants had
just invaded the wardrobe. Her nice embroidered bedspread and other
keepsakes were ruined beyond repair. All those hours and hours of handiwork for nothing. What a pity! Such are the difficulties of life in the
Congo.

The next afternoon found me cycling through alternate patches of near
jungle and open spaces, recently burned off. These were large enough, and
the soil looked fertile enough, for a good big field of corn. I visualized what
I could do with some modern equipment. The land was free from rocks too.
That night I camped in the open.

The next. day the scenery remained about the same. The road was a
trail, but it had once been put to grade. Often it was so full of stones that
even the natives had deserted it in favor of a footpath alongside. I could
tell how the trail ahead would be by noticing if the little smooth footpath
diverged from it. The stones were too much for Jacqueline too, so for many,
many miles I twisted and turned along the footpath.

There were quite a few native villages, and I stopped at one of these for
the night. I was curious to know what the natives ate and wanted to taste
everything. There were only a few words of French in the whole village,
but they got the idea. The meal was very tasty and quite enjoyable. First
was a soup plate full of *taroc*, i.e. manioc. This was cooked in some kind
of fat and looked and tasted like chicken, or breaded tenderloin, or sweet
potatoes, mixed in a very good, thick meat gravy. Then there were two eggs,
prepared in such a way that they were not recognizable in either taste or
appearance. It was something like an omelet, yet like white fish or meat. If
I had not seen the eggs beforehand, I would not have believed it. Then
there was a plate of baked bananas—the large green kind, mealy and good.
I also was given *les bananes douces*, the only kind of bananas we know in
the States. I elected to take these along for my pack.

Shortly after eating, a truck came along, which would ordinarily have
meant a ride. The Frenchman in charge gave me a lot of palaver which I

could not understand other than that I couldn't ride with him. He was the first Frenchman I had not been able to understand, but I think he was not interested in whether I understood or not. His lack of generosity was a big surprise, but I accepted it philosophically, thinking perhaps he was some government official. Shortly afterward another truck came along. There were colored lads in charge of this, so I was given a ride. By the time we arrived at their destination for the night, I gathered that they were with the *blanc* who had refused me a ride; and I think they had decided that he had done just that, and did not want him to know they had picked me up. They mentioned they might be going on to Lambarené the following day but I would have to see their patron. I decided that would be a waste of time.

The next day, Tuesday, September 8, was my first complete day in the jungle. This was not much different from certain big tree areas in Tasmania, Australia, or Nyasaland. The big trees looked like the same giant eucalyptus to me. There were plenty of ferns along the trail, and these reminded me of New Zealand. Creeks were numerous, and occasionally there were rivers. The amazing thing was that nearly all of them flowed free and clear, many with sandy bottoms. I did not feel afraid to take water from them for drinking. The bridges varied in construction, but most of them were made of great logs flattened on one side, with planks, not always side by side, for cross sleepers. On top was a runway of three six-inch or eight-inch planks. Since these were usually warped, or apart in some way, I had to dismount and walk across. It was impossible to keep Jacqueline on an eight-inch plank, and a fall into a crack would be disastrous. Some of the very short bridges were simply made of flattened logs paralleling the road. Since these were up to eighteen inches wide, I did not have to dismount. But I got off and on the bike a good many times that day. If it was not for the bridges, it was for a rocky stretch too rough to ride over; or perhaps a little grade too steep to top. With my gear shift, though, there were not too many of these.

I was now in the steaming jungles of Africa. Skies were usually cloudy, and I crossed sections where it had recently rained heavily. I rode into heavy sprinkles myself. The humidity was very high. My overalls were heavy with moisture, and even when traversing dry sections, they were reluctant to dry. I recalled my health hints that sweating is more difficult under jungle conditions and that plenty of salt should be taken. Also, something about being more cautious in respect to sunstroke. I occasionally felt of my bare head and realized that although I was almost on top of the equator, the clouds were sufficient to keep me from any danger of the sun.

As for wildlife along the way, I was first conscious of a bird that laughed like an Australian kookaburra, only louder. I often thought I was back in Australia. Then there was a great black bird that made a very loud rustling or squeaking noise when it flew. The sound was like a hundredfold magnification of the rustling of a heavy taffeta dress. I dubbed the bird "old

Central Africa. Will all this ever really be explored?

Many an African river did I cross in a native pirogue. This is the Ogooué, Trader Horn's River (Gabon).

squeaky wings." Often I would look up and see him leisurely flapping from one tree to another, way, way up at the two-hundred-foot level. There were monkeys in the jungle too. I could spot them sometimes midst the hanging vines, perhaps a hundred feet or more above my head. There was a variety of smaller birds and some sort of bird or beast that uttered a loud shriek every once in a while.

Shortly after noon lunch, I heard a truck and held up my thumb, but it turned out to be my *blanc* friend of the night before. He told his driver not to stop, made a gesture toward me and uttered something, plainly indicating that I was to get the hell further off the road. Behind him was the other truck, and of course it did not dare stop when the boss did not. This treatment was unusual and seemed rather mean, so I muttered to myself that I would not go so far as to wish that his truck would have a flat tire or fall through a bridge, but I'll bet if my old pal Bill Hurteau had been along, he would not have hesitated to yell such a wish. Now, you can believe this or not, but in less than thirty minutes I had my revenge. The colored driver who had given me a lift the preceding evening met me on foot and laughingly told me that a bridge was out just around the bend. I could see he was happy in the retribution meted out to his master. Sure enough, all the planks were off the bridge, but I could cross easily on the main sleepers. During this process, my "friend" was trying to keep out of sight below the bridge. He felt like two cents, I hope. The bridge held him up for at least two hours, and when he passed me again, I was nonchalantly sitting by the roadside reading. I casually waved to the rascal as though nothing had happened.

Just at dusk that evening I passed over the crest of a hill on which were two native huts. As usual a native walked toward the road to get a better look at me, and I asked him if he spoke French. By the time he answered I was well past but stopped anyway, as I understood him to say yes. Almost at once another native came tumbling out of somewhere and down the bank to the road. He ran down to me, trying en route to wrap a white, really white, sheet around himself. When he stopped breathless in front of me, he wore the sheet just as my Indian friends had done in East Africa.

This chap wanted me to stay the night, and I accepted. I was given a big kettle of hot water to take a bath and a clean towel and washcloth. A chair and a table were placed in the open for me to write, and a pitch torch was provided for light. I think we would call it a pitch torch. It was a natural product which looked like convoluted strips of light-gray wood or heavy leaves. If it burned low, you squeezed it near the top, or took a stick and poked about in the punklike stuff which seemed located near the center. The light which it gave off was definitely below candlepower measure.

Supper, also eaten in the open, consisted of all the gravied *taroc* I wanted and sweet bananas for dessert. The sky had cleared so that a near-full moon floated serenely above the 250-foot giants surrounding the tiny clearing. Here was a jungle moon, and I was tempted to put on paper all the romance and poetry of the scene, but I ran out of paper, so you, my lucky reader, are spared, because when I wrote the following evening, the mood had deserted me.

I was on the road by daylight, and several hours later I arrived at the bank of the great river Ogooué—the river of Trader Horn. Here was one of my white friend's trucks, not yet to its destination at Lambaréné on the other side. The native driver told me that his master had been very angry with him for giving me a lift the second evening before. I was surprised to find out that this Frenchman was only a mechanic of some sort instead of a government official with a conscience. And upon later consideration I came to believe that he was a friend of, or probably a driver for, the old fat "Transports l'Église" guy who had wanted thirteen cents a mile from me back in Dolisie. And here, with the luck of a few rides (the Swedish missionary had given me a long lift), I had made the 360 miles in the same time as the transports. No wonder his henchman was mad.

A long pirogue took me across the widest part of the river to the island on which the town of Lambaréné was situated. A pirogue is a huge log which has been hollowed out and shaped like a canoe.

It was a pleasure to find that Lambaréné was a good-sized supply point, since Jacqueline was badly in need of a tire. I was amazed at the low prices in a country where everything is high. I found bicycle tires for sixty-five cents. Think of it! Inner tubes were about thirty-five cents. The clerk assigned two young chaps to help me change tires, but it would take a long time to tell what they did not know. One tried and tried to take the old tire off without letting out the air. I don't suppose he knew how anyway. The other chap attempted to screw the pump connection on a valve stem by holding it on one corner, and so, all in all, I had to do most of the work. I was in a steam too, all that precious daylight being wasted, and found it hard to be patient. My lack of knowledge of French technical terms made my temper even shorter. Mechanical difficulties with the rear wheel cropped up, and I had my hands full for three and a half hours.

After crossing the island from Lambaréné, I took another pirogue to the east bank of the Ogooué. Just nearby and in full view were the hospital and mission of the world's famous missionary-doctor, Albert Schweitzer. It had been my intention to call, but when I got across I found there was no road connection and another pirogue trip would be necessary. It was already 5 P.M., so I gave it up.

Bicycle travel in Congo "Equatoria" is not as pleasant as in other areas. I was usually sticky with perspiration, and any skin areas normally covered by clothing itched the minute they were exposed to the air. Tiny flying bugs became mired in sweat and were deucedly uncomfortable. My overalls were soggy with the constant humidity, but I was grateful for the added protection they afforded my legs and ankles. It was bad enough to slap at the

Boy musician with homemade xylophone and arbalest—French Equatorial Africa (Gabon).

Young Africa: She is holding an avocado.

One of my prize pictures; mama usually carries the baby also—French Equatorial Af
(Gabon).

flies on my arms and shoulders, which I had to leave bare because of the heat. The heat, strangely enough, was most noticeable in the evening when the sun was down. This was due to the daily protection of a moist-looking gray overcast, which gave no indication that there were such things as sun or sky, and to a total absence of any sort of breeze in the evenings. This lack of breeze made it more comfortable to keep pedaling, because unless there was a clearing, I perspired just sitting still; and if I rode I stirred up my own breeze and discouraged the flies. Even during the day I often elected to keep riding, though my bones cried for a rest.

At dusk one day I slowed up in front of a native village called Mbalembe and soon had an invitation for the night. They fixed me up with a bed in a tiny hut, complete with *mousquitaire* (mosquito netting), table, chair, and little lamp. The lamp was really a generous move on the part of one lad, who seemed to have the only petrol lamp in the village. He had hesitated to produce it when my host requested it, because petrol is apparently very hard to get. It was a treat to have this in place of the usual torch, even though the tiny petrol flame was inadequate by modern standards.

For my supper one native contributed an egg, another a bunch of eight bananas, another five bananas, and one—wonder of wonders—a big pineapple. This I did not recognize until it was cut open. My host boiled the egg and brought it back with a piece of fish and a plate of baked bananas. I find that the bananas really take the place of bread and are nice and mealy. I stored most of the sweet bananas in my pack. Two dozen of these could be purchased in Equatoria for about two and a half cents, and they are far better than any I have eaten in the United States.

Although there were a few mosquitoes about and my host insisted one could not sleep without a net, I almost lifted it from the bed because of the heat. I kept wishing I was out on the ground in the open instead of inside a bolted door, even though there were cracks between all the sticks constituting the walls. But I found that by opening the door and putting my head at the opposite end of the bed, I was more comfortable. To help me off to sleep, a man had the temerity to start arguing with his wife. Apparently there are just as big fools in Africa as in America. Of course he was worsted.

I finally arrived in a village called N'Djolé. Here there were two missions: the Catholic, in full view across the river, and the Protestant, somewhat hidden in the hills back of the town. I found my way up to the latter with the aid of a pretty native nurse who came out from the hospital voluntarily as I passed by. It was a narrow, hilly trail she led me over, and the perspiration ran off me in little rivers.

Though it was already 10 A.M., it was cloudy, and I had not yet donned my cap when we arrived. The missionaries were aghast at my lack of protection, because we were right on the equator. And when they saw the little cap I wore in place of a helmet, they were quite amazed.

The Alsatian missionary, wife, and little girl gave me cordial welcome and invited me to dinner. I noticed that quinine is always on the French colonial table, and this brings up the subject of health. People were always surprised I had no fever in my journey around Africa.

My hostess arranged for my washing and when my shorts were dry did some mending for me on the sewing machine. Meanwhile I was sewing on my pack, and she saw to it that I was provided with all the necessary tools. I had a comfortable place on the veranda overlooking the river Ogooué, wide and fairly rapid; the wooded slopes opposite, with the Catholic church and a wide expanse of sandy shore ideal for bathing; and the scattered stores and homes of the white inhabitants amongst the trees at the foot of the hills on which the mission was situated. My host's house was surely in the most advantageous spot possible, for in Equatoria the humidity is usually oppressive and the air still. If any sort of wind should decide to come into being, the house with its plentiful screening would receive full benefit.

As I worked northward not far from Spanish Guinea, the number of villages increased, and travel became more interesting. If I wanted to rest a bit while walking up a long hill, I had a whole village around me for company in a minute. This was sometimes embarrassing because there were always a lot of questions and I might be ready to move on before the palaver was finished. Then, too, anytime after 3 P.M. my black friends could not understand why I did not stop and pass the night with them. When I insisted on continuing on in one instance, the whole village following me, I was told the chief forbade my continuing. This threw a scare into me, and I broke away in a hurry. But the beating on native drums in the next three villages left me with the knowledge that my passing was well known. This continual drumming had a most eerie effect on my nerves—and I thought I was pretty well inured to everything.

I stopped to eat lunch in a village where the young men were nicely dressed in white shirts and shorts and seemed to be very friendly. However, this turned out to be mostly curiosity, and no special courtesies were extended. While I was eating, an important-looking young man came in carrying a stick of authority and wearing a white shirt and long khaki trousers. He asked me where I was going and said it was his duty to report my passing to the *chef* of the district.

Passing one village, I was asked to wait for the chief. I feared trouble, but he was just a kindly old chap, grizzled and dressed in only a skirt, who wanted to give me an egg. It was not boiled, and of course I could not carry it, yet I would not have refused the gift for worlds. The chief's face and demeanor reflected a world of understanding. After leaving him, I went over a hill or two and decided to try the egg raw. I broke open one end, sipped the contents gently, and was surprised to find I did not gag or choke as expected. You see, I was one of the many who had never eaten a raw egg.

As I idled past one village a young mother carrying a light-skinned

Boys in "Equatoria" can build their own scooter.

baby came down to the edge of the high bank above the road. She apparently knew in advance that I would be interested, for she descended without hesitation and came up close for inspection. The little chap had blue eyes. She was obviously proud to have mothered a baby by a white father. Who knows—perhaps she thought to augment her family by me.

In this country I noticed the natives had various deformities or diseases of the legs and feet. Some had club feet, others shriveled limbs; quite a few, elephantiasis; and others had feet with open sores and were limping. However, the percentage of deformed or diseased natives was not high.

Women take a back seat in French Equatorial Africa. If I said, "Bon jour" to a native woman on the road, she was so surprised I seldom got a response. The girls, however, were sometimes quite bold, and smiled and laughed responses. I got a smile and a wave from an old grandmother. She was so crippled up she could hardly move, but she could still smile. Not a stitch did she wear except the tiniest of loincloths. The men, on the other hand, returned my greeting or even volunteered one in advance. If they were wearing a beret or hat, they lifted it; if not, they saluted—usually stopping in either case. Some of the young men who had acquired a little education were not so respectful. When I was entertained in native homes, the wife was just part of the menage. If she went clear to the river to get a bucket of water for me to wash in or drink from, and I said, "Thank you," she made no reply, but the husband was quick to say, "Oh it was nothing." Any need of mine was supplied by the wife, but the husband expected the thanks.

As I observed firsthand this native African portion of humanity, I sometimes smiled to myself with a bit of philosophy. For I carried *Reader's Digests* and read during rest periods. At the time, I was reading a long story about the native American, the Navaho, and finding it very interesting. So why travel? Still, would the story have been as interesting if I had not traveled a lot in the land of the Navaho?

By nightfall I had entered a little village called Nkout. There was a tiny native church, and I soon found out there was a second, both Catholics and Protestants being active. The Protestants usually seemed to have the most churches. A smart lad took me to the Protestant catechist for the night. He is the man who teaches the children their ABC's and instructs them in religious matters before they go to a regular school. At the catechist's I was provided with a table and a couple of lanterns for writing, but I had not been at it long before the *chef de ville* and the *chef de terre* crowded into the already well filled room. The former was the old generation, the latter the new. I arose and shook hands, noting that the young generation sat down. The chef de ville did not speak French, so after a bit I sat down and went on writing. But a young man soon came in who could speak French and who had traveled to a nearby country, thus enlarging his understanding and increasing his village prestige. In politeness to him and to my host and

Any design, any color.

Washday on a jungle stream. Clothes are thrown up the stream to drift slowly down for further attention.

to the others, I told them to interrupt my writing anytime they had something to say. They took advantage of this, and we all had quite a talk. I was amazed that nearly all of them did not know their own age.

One man put two eggs on the table, so I brought up the subject of supper. They said they had potatoes and would go search for them, and also for bananas, and so on. Yes, someone would prepare the food. No, they did not want pay. How did I want the food prepared? I would leave that to them. So in due course I had my potatoes, *taroc*, omelet, and baked bananas. This *taroc* was not in gravy but was hot, good, and mealy. Before preparation it resembles beets but afterwards looks like short, white sweet potatoes. While I was waiting, someone brought in a live hen, which I declined on the grounds that I already had had enough to eat. But, no, they thought perhaps I could take it with me on the morrow and they would be glad to prepare it. I did not pass up this opportunity, since it was to be done by the same cook who had just fixed my tasty supper.

When I was leaving shortly after daylight, there came the cook with my hen just fresh fried and still quite warm. He must have risen very early to prepare it. He also had some fresh baked bananas, having heard me say that they took the place of bread. And so I turned into the road with a very warm spot in my heart for the Bekoué people of the village of Nkout.

The country continued to be well populated, with a village at the top of nearly every hill. Each had a signboard bearing its name. Each had one or two men's council huts out front near the road. The "council hut" appellation is my own, because there were usually one or two dozen men sitting in them. The huts were really no more than a roof over pole uprights. Low benches made of poles ran along both sides, and on these the men sat. Sometimes they deigned to work—weaving open baskets or arranging a strip of thatching for a roof.

And then my first equatorial rainstorm! It was weathered not alone huddled under a jungle giant, as were most of my later ones, but with a bunch of young natives under an old tarpaulin in the back of a truck.

The truck was bound for a place called Bitam, and the natives, believe it or not, were all in civilized dress. The driver had two beautiful young belles in the front seat with him, one probably his sweetheart, so there was no room for the white man in the customary place. With a knowledge of civilized customs, you see, comes the knowledge that really the white man is no better than you are. But I was just as happy in the back with eight other young Africans, including two more pretty girls.

In overalls and colored shirt I was better prepared to meet the deluge promised by the black sky than were my companions. The girls were dressed in skirts and light blouses or dark dresses and white shoes, just about as you would see a colored girl in Chicago on the first warm day of spring. One young man with a carefully cropped mustache wore khaki knee socks, white shorts, and a white helmet, and carefully seated himself on a dainty white handkerchief with green embroidery work.

When it started to rain, the circus began! The front half of the truck bottom was filled with enough odds and ends of cargo for us to sit on, facing backward. But the only protection we had against the rain was a filthy old tarpaulin smeared with crushed bananas and having several holes and a big rip near the middle. I put on my sou'wester to keep the banana out of my hair but could not keep it off my shoulders, especially since the tarp was being pulled down on top of us by everyone who could hold a rope, including myself. My companions were careful to give me the preferred position and were genuinely concerned that some of my possessions might get wet. A crippled chap was elected to sit on my pack to keep it dry, but he was near the edge of the tarpaulin and was soon so soaked from the deluge that I could not see where he was doing any good. We were all so busy trying to keep our seats against the lurchings of the truck and also hold the tarp and keep dry that there was no time to think of carsickness. The truck was a laughing, jolly melee of arms, legs, and aching necks. The climax came when the driver suddenly shifted into fourth and one of the girls and I were thrown in a scramble to the bottom of the truck.

35

One More River to Cross

From Afrique Equatoriale Française a ponderous pirogue took me across a river into Spanish Guinea. This country was the southernmost of Spain's African possessions and was divided into an island section called Fernando Po and a continental section called Rio Muni, many times the area of the island. Rio Muni, which I now entered, was bounded on the east and south by A.E.F., on the west by the Atlantic Ocean, and on the north by French Cameroun.

Where I entered the country, there had once been a road, but apparently the Spaniards had only intended to impress the French because all resemblance to a road disappeared the minute I got out of sight of the frontier. There was then only a narrow trail with high tropical growth on either side.

Ebebiyin! A sleepy little Spanish town in a clearing on a hillside just south of the equator! A few white-walled government buildings with red-tile roofs, some white-plastered brick walls, a sort of parade ground, a flagpole. A few houses for officials, a school for the natives, a frontier barricade across the road. This was Ebebiyin.

I was most courteously received by the leading Spanish official. And why not? Undoubtedly I was the first round-the-world traveler on a bicycle ever to disturb his contemplation of afternoon siesta. In fact, I was probably the first globetrotter to ever enter the place by any method of transportation. And so I stumbled over my half-forgotten Spanish, received the proper stamps in my passport, passed the time of day, said my adios and departed on the road toward Cameroun.

My first afternoon in French Cameroun found me on the bank of the River Ntem, one of the principal constituents of the Rio Campo. Here a truck was being loaded with bags of palm seeds from a ferry which had just completed a crossing with the truck aboard. Part of the cargo had been unloaded to better balance the ferry. The owner of the truck was M. Juan, "À votre disposition," a Spaniard who spoke French as the Spaniards speak Spanish. It was most pleasing to the ear to hear him say, "Monsieur Juan, à votre disposition," because he made a rhyming couplet out of it.

Quite a few natives rode the ferry with Jacqueline and me. One lad passed the time by fishing with a plant tied to the end of a line. I noticed some of the women had designs worked into their faces in horizontal stripes where the skin had been darkened. This is done by making cuts in the skin and impregnating them with mud.

Roadside group of eight.

The trail in Rio Muni.
Jacqueline at right. Little did
I dream someday we'd have
to go through the tall weeds
too.

When I entered a town called Ambam, although it was after hours, I saw from the remarks of the natives from whom I inquired the way that there would be no peace for me until I had cleared the customs authorities. Having been inspected by the *douanes* on the frontier, I did not stop at the Ambam douanes, passing both the patrol post and the house of the douanes farther on, and made my way direct to the office of the *chef* of the district. I had hardly introduced myself and found out that he spoke English, when there came several excited douanes and an audience of four or five natives. But I noticed they were quiet and courteous in deportment. The *chef* told them I had cleared the customs already, and they departed satisfied.

The *chef* was quite young and spoke English well, but slowly. Like many other Frenchmen I met, he had served in the French army and trained in America, seeing New York, Washington, and New Orleans. His wife was in France, and he did not talk as though she was coming out to join him. He lived alone in a big, old red-tile-roofed house built by the Germans and containing an immense cellar underneath, where they had held out for a long time during World War I.

The *chef* personally conducted me to the *case de passage*. These are well-built and exceedingly well furnished guest houses, a far cry from those of that unhappy English administration in the Sudan. The furniture was modern and solid. There was a private shower place, a nice lavatory with running water, and a private *cabinet*. The boys fixed me up with a tub of hot water, and I had a bath before returning to the *chef's* house for dinner. His boys were laboring in the dark near the front stairway, trying to get an engine to go so that we might have electric lights to eat by. But in the end we ate by lantern light.

Some of the furniture was made of the "wood of Ambam," a beautiful wood resembling dark oak. Ebony and mahogany were common in the region, and, switching the subject slightly, there were gorillas. My host said Bushman had been taken not far away.

It was a rare moonlight night—rare because it was now the rainy season. Fleecy clouds scurried about trying in vain to cover up the moon; and there were palm trees to make the scene more romantic.

I slept soundly in a wide bed, nicely made, and awoke to customary sounds, which I suddenly realized were the same morning sounds I would hear at home in spring. Birds were chirruping, a light rain was pattering on the roof, and the roosters were crowing. But when the drums started beating the hour for rising, I knew I was in Africa.

As I decended the hill out of town I spied a couple of storekeepers dressed Arab style.

"Salaam alaykum," I waved.

"Alaykum salaam" came back at me with smiles. Truly I was getting back into North Africa.

I took my time this forenoon because I sort of expected "M. Juan, à votre disposition" to come along and give me a lift. Sure enough, he showed up about noon and talked the daylights out of me in French. The Spanish civil war, conditions in Spanish Guinea—he covered everything.

It was nearly one o'clock when I arrived at Ebolowa, a town of fair size. I wanted to get some mechanical work done on the bike, but it seemed that everything mechanical, everything religious, everything medical, everything everything, was done at the American mission. But it was too near mealtime to call, so I decided to eat; and to eat alone, being somewhat tired of native curiosity and questions. So when I came alongside a wood of well-spaced palms, I chose an unobserved moment and ducked way in. I did better than I expected, for my meal was half eaten before the first group came in from the road. I pretended not to notice, and it was a little while before they had courage to come around to where I could not help but see them. I stood about twenty-three questions before politely suggesting that if they wished to talk with me further, they could wait until I had finished eating. They were prompt to take the hint and go away.

The second group was a little more difficult.

"The American mission is very near here."

"I know it well," I replied.

"Why don't you go there?"

"It is not polite, just now."

"Why do you eat sitting on the ground like that?"

"In the United States many people eat like this when traveling."

Later, at the mission, I was guided to the house of the director of the repair shops. Mr. Cozzens was absent, but Mrs. C. invited me to stay the night. She was quite familiar with Wheaton, a few miles from my home, and her mother lived there. She sent me to the shop with a teacher, but we had hardly left the door before the arrival of a French official in a big truck followed by a great swarm of natives, most of whom had hung around after I had entered the Cozzens house. The official was evidently prepared to find some sort of escapee and invited me inside the house. He thawed after a little but was too excited at first to realize he was looking at the proper visa in my passport. Mrs. Cozzens was a bit flurried too. I managed to take my leave for the shops a little ahead of the officer and his truck, so that the crowd could see the American was not being taken into custody.

But we had been working on the bike only about a half-hour, when Mrs. C. showed up with a note from the police to her requesting I accompany a native in a truck to headquarters. I was not surprised. As Bill Egan (an old office friend) used to say, "Everybody wants to be in the act"; and the big shot wanted to see me himself. At headquarters I was greeted rather apologetically by the officer who had examined my passport at the mission, but I put him at ease. He was polite and friendly. The chief of police asked me no questions and did not even want to see my passport. We had a short friendly chat. I really could not feel angry with these French officials, especially when I discovered the reports they had received from the native police. Mrs. C. told me that I had been reported as hiding away in the wood and sitting on the ground, which was bad for the health and something no one normally would do.

"And besides, he wasn't dressed like other Americans."

In addition it seemed that the French had been having trouble with Spanish ne'er-do-wells from the Guinea frontier sneaking into the country. Ah, well!

While with the missionaries in the Ebolowa area I was surprised to learn that there were about seventy Americans with the Presbyterian mission in French Cameroun. About twenty were stationed at a large hospital at Elat. I met one woman doctor, single, about forty, who had seen many years' service since coming out from Cincinnati. She told me that most of her operations were for hernia and that appendectomies were practically unknown. Leprosy had a very high incidence—perhaps twenty out of every thousand—and there were a number of leper colonies.

Traveling northward again, I noticed that even the primitive dirt and mud villages had set up chambers of commerce. At least somone had erected large tombstone markers on the broad fronts of which had been carved in huge block letters, painted red, the name of the village.

Yaoundé, capital of French Cameroun! A city of hills, and I at once marked the similarity to Kampala, the Buganda capital in Kenya far to the east. Kampala has seven hills, and Yaounde, five. In Kampala the Protestant and Catholic missions were located on the two highest hills near the opposite ends of town. In Yaoundé the Catholic mission was on a hill on the opposite side of town from the Protestant and on an absolute north-south line.

Following the advice of a friend, I looked up M. Mullender, Chef du Service de l' Information, Gouvernement. He was supposed to be able to tell me if there was a road across the southern part of British Cameroun into Nigeria or if I would have to go north by way of Fort Lamy. No map showed a connection across the former regions. Mullender was a young chap who had charge of white and native newspapers, press service, publicity, motion pictures, and the like. He took me in his jeep to the Geographical Institute. No map there. Then to Mr. Green, head of a big English firm, and to Mr. Drinkwater of John Holt Company. This chap knew of a route across southern British Cameroun and gave me full information. He had been in the States and wanted to know, as we munched a tart, if I wouldn't like to have a big piece of juicy mince pie—or of pumpkin pie—right now. I nearly killed the man. He fixed me up with a truck ride nearly to the frontier, starting in two days, on Sunday. With reluctance I agreed to wait.

I figured I had better not eat on the ground that evening or I might be arrested again, so I went up to the American mission.

Here Dr. Goode, retiring in six months after forty years of service, received me. His father had been the first American missionary in Cameroun, and the natives have a yearly Thanksgiving Day to celebrate the anniversary of his arrival. Dr. Goode had another guest—Marlin Perkins, director of the Lincoln Park Zoo in Chicago. Imagine that! Mr. Perkins had flown out to get four young gorillas to keep the famous Bushman company. Dinner was noteworthy for its sour-sop sherbet—a native product greatly resembling ice cream or sherbet. The fruit of a certain tree is broken open; the white milky contents are poured out, a bit of sugar is added, and then it is placed in the refrigerator to freeze. Dr. Goode and I had two helpings of this and two pieces of cake to go with it. A real treat!

After dinner Mr. Perkins and I walked about the mission. A native dance attracted us, and we watched the clapping and dancing and enjoyed the singing. The moon, though covered with fleecy clouds, gave us enough light. We visited the mission church and took especial notice of the windows the money from Bushman had bought. Mr. Perkins flashed his lamp on the outside, while I stayed inside so I could appreciate the coloring in the glass. Aided also by his lamp, I had a few free natural-history lessons on the toad, the millipede, and the lizard.

In the morning I stayed long enough to get a preview of the gorillas thousands of my fellow Chicagoans would see later. One of the gorillas was still very much a baby, and I snapped a picture of Mr. Perkins giving it its bottle. He held it tenderly in his arms, bubbled it over his shoulder and patted its back as though it were a human baby. In fact, both he and the baby acted like mother and child. This amazed me because Mr. Perkins was so much the quietly debonair, well-dressed business executive with mustache, iron-gray hair, and all that, that he was the last person in the world I ever expected to see playing nursemaid to a gorilla.

While in the capital I spent quite a bit of time with M. Mullender and his associates. Government officials, post-office clerks, and the like worked Sunday mornings and afternoons, the same as on weekdays. The majority worked from 7:30 A.M. to 12:30 P.M. and from 2:30 to 5:30 P.M. The only recompense for the slavery of this seven-day, fifty-six-hour week was a six-month vacation in France after a couple years of it. (Of course the Frenchman needs the two-hour lunch period to handle that eight-course meal.)

The color bar seemed to be lacking in the French Cameroun. One day I saw a colored man on a motorcycle behind a white man, his hands on the latter's shoulders. Mullender took me to one of the biweekly movies, and I noticed that there was no segregation in the seating. White officials sat on the same benches as the natives, and there was one instance of marked friendliness. Incidentally, only French movies, with their painfully obvious technical inferiority, were seen, because of the money-exchange situation.

Marlin Perkins in Cameroon, with Irving, one of four young gorillas he was taking back to Chicago's Lincoln Park Zoo to replace Bushman.

Jacqueline and I left Yaoundé on the truck as arranged. The jungle was left behind, and there was now much open country. The road was usually bordered by giant palms, and everything was green and happy-looking due to a rain the night before. It struck me that the "rainy season" of the maps and literature which had prepared me for continuous downpours day after day were no different than late spring in Iowa or Illinois. There may be a short rain, but then the sun comes out and it clears off.

We arrived on the shore of the Sanaga River about noon. It was wide, deep, in flood, and very swift. Just above the crossing the river was divided into three parts by two islands. It emerged from these wooded channels over foaming, roaring cascades. Below these it rushed over boulders sufficient to make good-sized waves. As I studied the speed of the river beyond the ferry landing and looked over to the distant shore, I thought, "Brother, how do they ever get across that?" There was a truck ahead of us and while waiting for it to cross I wrote in my diary. A bit later I happened to look up, and there was the truck and ferry out in the middle of the river. It was being carried along at a high speed with a crew of rowers battling to get the craft across the main current. Soon they were lost to view, but it looked as though they were going to be carried about ten miles downstream.

At around 1:30 P.M. it was our turn, there being two ferries in operation. The ferry was a raft supported by five large pirogues. It took some time to get the gangplank off and propped up. Then a line of eight men took a big cable attached to the boat and started to walk up along shore with it. Three men on the ferry pushed with poles against the river bottom. The water was up to the thighs of the waders, but so far as I could see they were just exerting enough effort to carry the cable and no more. Yet even when the three polers slacked off we continued to move upstream in close to the bank and out of the current. Sometimes the shore pirogue (pontoon) stuck on the sand; then the polers would have to pile out and pry the boat loose with a piece of four-by-six. It sounded as though they blamed the chaps with the cable, but these remained serenely unperturbed. When we reached the apex of the quiet water, the cable men left the cable to be hauled aboard and piled onto the raft to take positions at the oars. There were no less than eighteen men with short oblong-bladed oars—four in the first pirogue, four in the next, three in the next, three in the next, and four in the last. These were all on one side of the truck. The boss ferryman stood in front of them and called the plays and exhorted them to their best effort. I soon saw why. The current was strong and swept us downstream at a terrific clip. The eighteen men plied their oars at top speed, and not one shirker did I see. At the boss's order they changed oars from one side of their pirogue to the other and at certain times slapped their oars against the wooden side. The sound of wood upon wood of eighteen oars in unison was quite unusual. As we breasted the current the speed of rowing increased and the boss's commands and exhortations came faster and faster as he looked ahead at some imaginary point and seemed to say, "If we don't make that, we're goners." I stood on the deck rooting like the army cheerleader at a navy game with the score tied. Sweat poured from the rowers; excitement spread to a crashing crescendo. But at last we passed into quieter waters close to shore and came to rest at the bank. After a while the cable boys got out and commenced their leisurely walk upstream to a point opposite our disembarkation point. And so, after three hours, we got across the Sanaga.

Later that afternoon we had another river to cross. Though it was only a little after five, the ferrymen were not going to take us until the following morning at six. When they finally consented to do so, I thought it was out of deference to me but found out later that the driver had given them extra money. The N'Djin River was not as wide or as fast as the Sanaga, but the crossing was nevertheless interesting. The sun was low, and the silhouettes of the rowers, the dark forest, and the darkening waters composed a memorable picture.

The driver of my truck and his assistant, as well as the natives up behind, all spoke pidgin English. Now, I had always thought that pidgin English was a sort of simple English, like "me do dat," for example, and would be easily understandable. Yet I sat in the cab with these two men for a solid day without recognizing a word of English in their talk. Until I found out, their language was just another dialect so far as I was concerned. After that I listened with greater attention and could understand some of it—if I knew the subject, and the sentences were very short.

About 1 A.M. I was awakened by the stopping of the truck. A bridge had partly broken, and we would have to unload our cargo of salt and carry it over. The first thing everyone did was to have a good scratch. This is a popular pastime in the Camerouns, for the *moute-moute*, which is like our sand fly, is quite active. They are so small as to be virtually unnoticed in the air. The first day after being bitten the skin breaks out in red spots about a quarter inch in diameter, and you think, "Well, what tropical disease have I got now?" After twenty-four hours the spots fade, become little pimples and start itching! And it is the kind of itch that scratching only makes worse.

After we had scratched awhile, we went to work. When the load was about half off, the bridge guards got sleepy and said we could go across now. The bridge was a two-part log and plank structure with a stone center pier leading down twenty-five feet to a rushing torrent. We crossed safely, loaded up and went on, but in about half an hour arrived at a road barrier, requiring us to wait for 8 A.M. police control. At this time I found Jacqueline's front rim, already partly broken by careless handling in the Union, had been nearly broken in two by the carelessness of the boys up back. I couldn't go to bed with my beloved in that condition, so I tightened spokes and fussed around in the moonlight for an hour and a half, finally going to sleep on top of the salt.

The morning came unusually clear, and as we surmounted a range of small mountains we could see Mount Cameroun off on the horizon to the southwest. Over 13,000 feet, it is the highest mountain between the Atlas and the Ruwenzori Mountains.

Journey's end for me came about 9 A.M. at a country market called Ban Bjoum. The road on either side was filled with natives going to the market to buy or sell, or both. Though the country was quite hilly, a few bicycles were to be seen. Native homes through here were more like individual farm homes, and the native villages I had become accustomed to had disappeared. Each little farm had a very tight fence made of long slender poles laced together like latticework until even a cat could not get through without effort. For entry to the farm, one went over a sty, or through a sort of door, down a lane, and through another door. The long fence poles were a staple article, and I saw many being carried along the roads. They were fifteen to twenty feet long and two to three inches in diameter. I sometimes saw small boys of eight or ten years with a half dozen of these on their heads. Throughout Africa everything is carried on the head, but it always gave me the shivers to see a big basket of corn, or of small mixed vegetables, carried serenely on the head. And if I was meeting said head, it was almost always turned to look back after me.

Not far from the market I met the fourth male white native I had seen since Yaoundé. These poor albinos must live a miserable life. They are horrible-looking creatures—really horrible. Red kinky hair, strawberry blond eyebrows, pale, light skin, sunburned on the more exposed surfaces, teeth spread apart or crooked. No white man would think of owning one for a brother, although the natives are more considerate. But it looks very odd to suddenly see a white man with a burden on his head midway in a string of blacks with similar loads.

The passing parade, always of interest whether it is the beau monde of Michigan Avenue or the natives of primitive Africa! On the edge of a culvert not far from the British Cameroun frontier, I sat down one morning to eat breakfast and watch the passing parade!

Everyone was bound for market. The boys raced by on horses at a hard gallop followed by a little whinnying colt. The boys had whistles in their mouths to get folks off the road. They guided their mounts by rope bits, and a great coil of rope was wound around each horse's neck. Women walked by carrying large baskets full of African corn, for it was harvest time. The ears, still retaining most of their husks, were about two-thirds the size of Iowa corn and rather uniform. Stalks in the nearby fields looked pretty good too. Quite a few men were taking pigs to market. Most of the pigs were young, but those nearly grown, while not up to Iowa standards, were good enough to suit most people. The men had less trouble leading and driving their porkers than you might expect, for the native rope was cleverly arranged. Some men were leading goats. The Cameroun goat is quite small—not over eighteen inches high, black and white in color, and nearly as cute as the kids. Grown chickens were carried with the heads down, and little ones in the large or small handbags carried by the men. These bags were of woven work, tan in color, and equipped with a long handle so that they could be draped over the arm or shoulder or carried in the hand in the manner of the American woman's handbag.

And speaking of women, they surely did not bother much about clothes in this section of Cameroun. The only thing they had on was a sort of double loincloth. A cord was tied low around the waist, and a piece of cloth, perhaps two to three inches wide and four inches long, appended thereto. This hung from a usually pendulous abdomen and so was completely inadequate for its purpose. A larger piece of cloth was suspended from the string behind and covered the top center area of the usually well-rounded buttocks. Now, with this lack of attire, I can't help but be conscious of the defects extant in the "female form divine." Huge swaying abdomens, some with a big navel-knot bump, pendulous breasts, little breasts, fat breasts, shriveled-up ones—egad! And I'll wager anything that if we lined up a bunch of American women, à la nude, without the aid of corsets and uplift bras, there wouldn't be a heck of a lot of difference. There was one woman with four breasts. Some of the African young ladies had smeared themselves with red juice or powder, on the legs and above the waist.

The men, strangely enough, were quite well covered. A cloth skirt of fairly attractive design was wrapped around their hips and the surplus of the tie allowed to fall in front. A jacket or tattered shirt covered the upper part of the body.

The frontier region between French and British Cameroun turned out to be very mountainous, with tremendous climbs and descents. In this respect and also in its agriculture, the land resembled Ruanda-Urundi. Potatoes, yams (*taroc*, i.e. manioc), peanuts, maize, pumpkins, melons, and gourds were all in evidence. The last three products were usually planted in the rows of corn. Cultivation of the yams was carried out in small beds, raised nearly two feet above the in-between trenches. These beds were located on mountainsides so steep they looked like they would fall off. Still, heavy rains had not caused erosion. Certainly an unusual soil.

Near the base of a great escarpment in British Cameroun I enjoyed a night of unsurpassed hospitality in the home of Mr. and Mrs. Gebauer, Baptist missionaries from Oregon. Mr. Gebauer was an ex-military man and spoke in matter-of-fact sentences, short and to the point, and seemed totally unlike a missionary. There was another guest at dinner, a spacious Negro woman of culture. Born and raised in the United States and a resident of London for over ten years, she was now touring up and down West Africa, meeting natives, giving lectures, and gathering information for a book to be titled "Mother Africa." She couldn't stand native food or living conditions, so the Gebauers were putting her up in their guest house.

In the morning my host showed me his front-steps view of a splendid waterfall high on the face of the escarpment above. Later he drove me up past it to Bamenda Post, admirably situated on the edge of a near precipice overlooking about half the country. The post was located in the old German fort, complete with moat and inner fortress. Mr. Gebauer was very popular with the British officials. I could have been the veriest criminal and still received my passport stamp as long as he walked in with me.

Westward ho into West Africa. British roads I found to be delightful. Although they were not wide enough for two-way traffic, they were smooth, gravelly, pleasing to the eye and to the seat. A fringe of green grass about a foot wide and with straight tailored edges was left between the road and the ditch. And on such a road Jacqueline and I wound up hill and down dale, over little bridges, and through the dense jungle for many a mile in the British West African possessions.

Bali! Of course I have been to Bali. It is a good-sized native village in British Cameroun, and the girls wear far less clothing than in the far-famed tropic isle. Not only that but many of the girls have fully as much sex appeal.

The men of Bali were interested in other things besides girls. American watches, rings, shoes, lanterns—how could they get those?

Bali was also near the commencement of a cyclist's paradise— a stretch of fifty-six miles—all downhill. But it rains even in paradise, and for some of the descent I had to don sou'wester, rain cape, and my New Zealand rain leggings.

The rain did not stop the native markets, but it considerably dampened them. Some natives had large head burdens to keep off a little of the rain; some used big banana leaves; a few even had umbrellas. The rank and file of the women used nature's own protection, bare skin, and had no worries about getting their clothes wet. But the poor men in shirts and shorts or perhaps even with a sweater or an overcoat—well, they got wet. The overcoat I mention is no joke, and the few I saw were as heavy as any American winter coat. "A land of contrasts," they say in the travel books of this land or that; and I would say there were contrasts in Cameroun when I met a man in hat and heavy overcoat and twenty feet behind him a woman nude as anything except for that useless two-inch square of cloth high on her stomach.

Breezing around the curves, I eventually reached lower levels on my 5,000-foot drop from Bamenda. The rain gradually lessened, but the peaks above remained shrouded in mist. The dripping jungle, the leaden sky, and the mists, and the slowly rising smoke from native villages vying with the mists—all this made a very impressive picture.

Night and a native village shaped like a U. Eggs and peanuts for supper. My hosts shelled the nuts for me.

We are so often not thankful enough for small favors and many blessings. Just as I was preparing my pack for leaving the next morning, the rear inner tube blew out right at the back of my neck. Now it had sat all night under the usual pressure and I had not even so much as breathed at the bike that morning; but there she blew, permitting me to fix it without having to unload the bicycle. It could have blown ten minutes after I was on the road.

In Mamfe young Mr. Hilton, the A.D.C., invited me home to lunch. He and his young and pretty South African wife were most hospitable. I shaved, shined my shoes, and washed up. The boy washed my socks, and in the heat (90 degrees inside the house) they were dry by the time lunch was over. Mamfe is connected with the sea by river transportation, and the palm kernels the people gather were shipped out that way.

The next afternoon I saw my first girl albino and was stopped by a heavy rain. Luckily I was passing through a village and could take shelter on the loafer's bench in front of a house. Invited inside, I wrote by the open back door for an hour and a half while the rain poured down outside. There was nary a leak in the well-thatched roof.

My chance host was a good one. Since I obviously had to stay the night, he offered his own bed; and shortly after 5 P.M. he brought in a plate of broken-open, still-hot *taroc,* and some blue-looking objects like oversize damson plums. As I bit into the *taroc*—white, mealy, and quite dry—I thought, "Oh, boy, how good these will taste with butter and salt!" But before I could get these articles from my pack, my host explained that the plum affairs in the dish were butterfruit. Well, by George, he was sure right. The skin and the yellowish pulp around the big seed tasted something like butter and filled the need 100 percent. I really enjoyed my butter and yams. A little later my host brought in a plate of oranges, and water clear as crystal served in a spotlessly clean mug. Later in the evening he served me two baked bananas and a masterpiece made of beans. They showed me one of the beans—a slender, quarter-inch-diameter affair about eight inches long. The finished product on the plate resembled a huge chunk of light-brown meat loaf. It looked and smelled good, but when I tasted it—wow! It was liquid fire. I could eat only tiny bits of it after carefully working out some of the red pepper, and mixing it with liberal quantities of water, banana, and orange. When I returned the bulk of the bean loaf to my host, he ate it all in large spoonfuls without batting an eye.

The people of this village impressed me with being more polite than any I had recently encountered. My host kept the house free from onlookers except for a few friends. To these I showed my map of Africa, and although

*Witch doctor or village chief?
Congo.*

*Many were the ferries in
Africa.*

they could not read, I think they understood the relative distances. When I wanted to write, they respected my wishes, and my host left the lantern with me when he went off to bed. As a nightcap I was given African wine, a ferment from the juice of the palm.

Here is a side note on goats and dogs. Goats were very tiny and often encumbered by cute little pokes. The dogs in western Africa were exceedingly well behaved and the most unobtrusive dogs I had ever seen. They practically never barked, and if they so much as looked as though they might like to chase me on the bicycle, they got a word of reprimand from a native. If a dog was lying in the center of a village street, I could come within a few feet of him before he would obligingly get up and quietly move a foot or two to one side. I wonder to what extent a quiet, good-natured dog reflects his master's character. But I am probably being idealistic. It's so darn hot in this part of the world, the dogs just have no ambition. In fact, later in my travels I actually stumbled over a dog too lazy to move. I set Jacqueline right over him at the door of a shop.

The next day I traversed an unimproved section of the Cameroun-Nigeria road on either side of the Mfum River. Hills were often terrifically steep—so steep that even on foot I could only push Jacqueline up a few yards before resting. Often the trail was overgrown with grass and weeds, and to make things easier, it rained. The eastern descent to the Mfum, just abandoned, was a hair-raiser. It was cut as a trench with vertical walls twenty or thirty feet deep, wide enough for only one car and in an absolutely straight line. Another absolutely straight line could be drawn on the floor of the road from the water's edge to the top of the mountain. The grade was at least 45 percent, and a descending car would go straight into deep water if the brakes failed.

About two miles west of the Mfum I came to a completed road, but Jacqueline started giving me trouble. First a broken rear spoke. The nipple did not fit well on the new spoke, and in turning it I blew the tube. I had to unpack and repair. About two miles farther the tube blew in a different place. Unpack again. The rip was so long I had to change tubes. On the rear wheel this meant releasing both brakes and three-speed mechanisms, carrier and fender attachments, special attachments, and whatnot. Chain, wheel, brake, and three-speed must all be readjusted afterward. I had been sweating bucketfuls all day and this didn't help. The weather had cleared, but that only made it the hotter. When I had repacked, I found the tube had a slow leak. Curses! I unpacked again but knew it was too slow a leak to find; and it was. I guessed at a place and patched it, but then remembered I had had trouble with the tube's valve stem, and tightened it. A native lad was helping me by this time. Leaving here, I was so mad over all the time lost that I did the eleven miles to the Cross River in nothing flat, leaving the native, who was also on a bicycle and with no pack, far behind.

36

The Bull With the Missing Tail

The Cross River looked to be very, very deep, and yet the current was very swift. The dark water swirled about a snag near the bank and boiled deeply in swirls all along the Cameroun bank—for on the other side was Nigeria. The river lay in a deep channel, with the dark jungle crowding it closely on either side. Ah, these mysterious, somber, jungle rivers! What secrets do your lonely courses hold? How I would like to explore you!

Many times I shouted out across the lonely somber flood, trying to raise the unseen ferrymen. There was no sign of life, no house, no landing. Not even a boat was visible. Perhaps there wasn't any. Horrible thought! When the native caught up with me, we shouted together. Finally six men and a giant pirogue shot out from the opposite bank, and in due time we landed in Nigeria. The head ferryman invited us to spend the night, and since it was dark I readily accepted. There was one huge house and sort of separate small living booths inside the bare framework supporting the roof. All the ferrymen lived here and I think had families. I had a big plate of white yams for supper. These were sliced like pineapple but were half again the diameter and three times the thickness. I used my own butter and salt. It was a delicious treat. A heavy rain had started outside, but shelter was good, and despite my damp clothes, I wrote in my diary at ease. The chief brought in his daughters and lined them up for my inspection should I want company for the night.

Daybreak and a nice road to put me in love with Nigeria. The affection continued, for I found the British officials as friendly and hospitable as those in Cameroun. They saw to the washing of my clothes and the needs of my bicycle and loaded me up with provisions, heat-rash powders, and whatnot. A big contrast to the chilly reception I had received from the British in the Sudan!

America is always paradise to the semieducated native. One Nigerian ferryman wanted to quit his job right then and there and follow me to America as my boy. He was no silly soul either. He spoke English well and had been four years in the army. I declined the offer out of politeness to the next traveler—it was a one-man ferry.

More rain that evening, but there was *fu-fu* for supper. What? You've never eaten fu-fu? Well, the Boki people of eastern Nigeria make fu-fu by first peeling cassava (*taroc*/yams). The root is then grated, put into a raffia bag, and squeezed by the use of sticks until the liquid is all out. The cassava is then left for three or four days so that it will be completely dry. Next it is put into a dry pot which is placed over the fire, and the grains are turned so they will not scorch. It is then ready for use and is called *gari.* When mealtime comes, two cups of *gari* are put in a cup of boiling water. The mixture becomes thick right away and is ready to eat as *fu-fu.*

I ate breakfast one hot, muggy morning with a British trader at a lonely outpost. He sent a boy with an order to the cook.

"Tell him to be quick. This master is in a big hurry. And tell him I want a big breakfast—none of this one-egg business."

Thus, you see, white men are masters and the boys are eager to serve, eager to help move the bicycle, polish shoes or do whatever the master wishes. If I travel in this country much longer, I will be ordering the boys myself, and neglecting "please" and "thank you" in the same way.

That morning I passed about thirty native porters bearing heavily laden baskets on their heads. I stopped to take a picture of three of them, one having two chickens perched on top of his load. Later Jacqueline's front wheel tightened up and I had to stop again. A native mechanic had put the wheel on backside to, and though I had noticed it at the time, I thought it made no difference. It's easy to see that even after twenty thousand miles I still am learning about that bicycle. But these two stops enabled me to observe the porters more carefully and to be reasonably certain that in a stretch of at least ten miles, they did not put down their heavy burdens for a rest. I suppose they couldn't really, for who would help the last man reload? The poor chaps could hardly get along. The sweat ran down their faces and bodies in little rivers. Their legs almost seemed to buckle under the strain. Neck muscles were bulged, calves were hard. The poor chaps could not turn their heads and could only roll their eyes toward me as I passed. One, and often both hands, were used to help balance the load. The men might as well have been in straitjackets and ball and chain for all the freedom they had in those ten heartbreaking miles.

The sky cleared. Sunshine. Open country with a smattering of green bush—savannah. At 3 P.M. dark-blue rain clouds closed in, and I stopped for shelter at two round thatched native huts. But I had anticipated this rain, so after a short wait, I donned all rain gear and headed out, only to get caught smack in the middle of a downpour and not a speck of shelter to be seen, not even a tree. By the time I reached the first house I was pretty wet. Come with me as I enter.

The path runs in from the road about forty feet and is partly under water. At the end is a gate in a high stick stockade running completely around an enclosure which we see contains two houses. The sticks run vertically, are fairly close together and reach up well over our heads. We attempt the gate, noticing it has no hinges and must be picked up and set to one side for entrance. With the top heavy bicycle to balance and with the necessity of lifting the gate, in front of the front wheel, the task seems impossible, but we do it because we must. We shift it one way and find the gate channel blocked, so we move it the other way. Once inside we don't bother about closing but streak it for the house which seems to have the highest entrance of the two. As we expected, the entrance is far too low for the bicycle. We hastily scan the structure five feet in front of it. This is built of great branches of trees averaging six or eight inches in diameter. Vertical branches form the walls, which are about five feet high. But the entrances are too narrow for the bicycle and since there is only a tree-trunk roof, it is just as wet inside as outside. So we lean the bike against the wall by the house, and stooping to waist height, manage to struggle under the overhanging thatching into the house.

Here it is dry. That is fine. But that is about all that can be said. We find ourselves in a sort of antechamber three feet wide, seven feet long, and not high enough to stand upright even on the side nearest the center of the peaked roof. On the right, resting horizontally just off the dirt floor, on sticks, is a thick plank about four feet long. Beside it is the end of a log which has been tapered to a flat-sided oval and resembles a fish lying on its side. At the end of the plank is a log stool about six inches high with a concave top. This has just been placed there by a boy of about ten, who is seated at the left of the entrance on the short side of the anteroom. Sinking to the stool, we stretch our legs out across the path leading into the house proper. Our rain cape we take off and place on the log; then with a sudden inspiration we hand our raincape to the boy, indicating by signs that he is to place it over the pack on the bicycle to keep off the rain. He takes the cape gingerly, as though it were a piece of cake ready to fall apart, goes out and starts laying it on wrong side out. By signs we get it through his head to turn the cape over. But then he fails to spread it out and we, laughing to keep our sense of humor, move out, seat touching heels en route to the exit, to spread the waterproof properly. Returning, we bring our purse in order to have something to read.

Now we are wet with a new wetness, but we are amazed to see how quickly our bare arms and shoulders dry off. And before starting to read, we look around a bit more.

Apparently this anteroom is the scene of whatever culinary work is done. There are some things hanging against the inner wall which seem to suggest this, although we actually cannot identify them; but opposite us, near the log, is a place where fires have been built. We notice that the walls of the anteroom are very thick, made of mud, but hard and smooth.

By this time our eyes are sufficiently accustomed to the darkness to see a little way through the door or hole leading into the black interior. Here, sitting on the earth floor just inside, are two children, perhaps three and six. They are naked, but the ten-year-old wears a loincloth.

We read awhile from *Reader's Digest* about life in faraway lands. Suddenly we look up, struck by a thought. What these poor children are missing in the world about them! No picture books for them to look at on rainy days. No color books with bright-colored crayons. No fond parents to guide the little hands or fix a slice of bread, butter, and strawberry jam. No school to look forward to, no teachers to love, no movies or prettily dressed dolls. They had never seen, would never see, a mountain, a sky-scraper, a firecracker. Here they sat on a rainy day, staring into the dark-ness or at the open doorway. No toys—and no light to see them by if they did have them. Father and mother were either not home or dead; I could not make out which from the boy. The other house we noticed when entering the yard does not seem to be occupied.

Meanwhile it rains steadily on. It does not seem to be raining so hard now. We wish we could see out so as to look at the sky—but no windows. Here comes a chicken—not too wet. We recall our rainy days on the farm in Iowa. Usually the chickens did not come out until the rain was nearly over. Another chicken shows up and comes into the house. We scrootch out, seat on heels; the sky seems to give promise. We grab the cape and scrootch back in to get purse and cap.

As we guide the bicycle towards the gate the rain seems to increase. We look at the sky. There is no promise there, after all. We laugh aloud to keep from muttering darkly, and, reparking the bike, we scrootch back into the shelter. We sit and think a little while, then we decide, "Oh what the heck," and hit the road.

Three hours later we are so far removed from this scene of ignorance and near-savage existence as it is possible to get and still stay in the same country. We are in the home of the district commissioner of the area, firmly ensconced by a letter of introduction and, no doubt, our own wonder-ful personality. We are seated at a long table, fully appointed, in a long dining room. It is a dinner party. On our left is nicely dressed Mrs. Gorman, wife of the district chief of police. On her left is our host, Mr. Campbell. Next to them and opposite us is Mr. Gorman. Then Mr. Rist, assistant D.C., and at the head of the table is our charming hostess. On our left is Major Ford, ranking officer of the miltary barracks at the city of Enugu fifty miles away along my route. On our right is Mr. Jordan, chief of police of that city. We look at each other over beautiful bouquets of flowers—two pink, the center one pale purple. We have fine white napkins. Immaculate servants, attired in white suits with brass buttons, hover about.

We have had our before-dinner drinks and witty sallies in the living room. There has been an hour of astonishment expressed at our feats of travel.

"We thought we had something to talk about when we crossed the Sahara by motorcar," said the city chief of police to the district commis-sioner. "Now I feel like crawling into a hole."

"Yes," chimed in Mrs. Campbell. "And when we go on safari we have about sixteen porters and enough equipment—and he gets all his equipment

Nigerian road transport—no rest for ten miles.

Man and wife, Ibos near Abakaliki, Nigeria. Her legs, red skirt, and stomach are plastered a brilliant yellow.

on a bicycle. I must see that in the morning."

Our passport has been admired, and we have answered all the stock questions. Now the pressure is off, and we can expect to eat with very little interruption. We will relax, listen, eat, and laugh.

But hold! What is this? A waiter is at our elbow with a tray bearing two dark-green earthenware pots or bowls. We shake our beclouded brains. Is this tea? What on earth! There is no cup. There is no help from the waiter. He makes no move whatsoever. Finally we mutter low, "No, thank you." He still stands there. Fortunately conversation is brilliant, and no one is watching us. We have already noticed the green two-handled bowls sitting in our soup plates and have covertly observed the chief of police upset his into his plate. Good gosh! That's it. These bowls on the tray are just like ours. The bloke is waiting for our empty bowl.

All this makes us a little self-conscious. Perhaps we have been sitting around in native huts too long. Our soup spoon is enormous. We suddenly wonder if we are using it properly. But we are relieved to see Mr. Rist sipping from the side of the spoon. We remember Emily saying that the soup spoon should be moved away from us when in the plate. Out of the corner of our eye we see the major is not using his properly and we are content once more.

The Campbells, it seems, are noted for their exotic desserts. This one, in two deep Pyrex plates, has a white top decorated with red half-cherries. We help ourselves to the limit of hungry traveler politeness and then sample. Delicious! But not perfect for our taste because they have added sherry; but who could possibly analyze the other six or eight ingredients. There must be everything that is sweet and good in the field of fruit and pastry.

We move to the living room for coffee. We get a chance to pump the others for a few experiences. The party finally breaks up, and we retire.

The road the next morning brought me back to realities. The native women were as nude as ever. In this area they wore a strip of cloth perhaps two inches wide tied tightly through the crotch from front waistline to back. In the rear it was frequently buried from view.

Enugu was a good-sized city. I called on my friend, the chief of police. He was engaged in bawling out the native officer in charge because the native police football team had returned from a neighboring town two hours late and now there was absenteeism due to overindulgence.

"What!" vociferated the chief, looking over the roster. "There are thirty-five men sick. Thirty-five out of two hundred and fifty—fifteen percent. Fifteen percent. Incredible. Well, there'll be no more leaves, that's all. That's all there is to it. We can't have this."

My English host in Enugu, the young manager of a store, left me in charge of the house for the evening, as he had a prior engagement. This I appreciated for the experience of dining in solitary splendor. Now I had the chance to see just how it felt to live as a bachelor English colonial. Cook and servant and wash boy were mine to command. If I wanted a grapefruit cold drink, the boy brought the ingredients on a tray and let me mix it as I wished while I sat at the writing desk. When dinner was announced, I decided whether I was ready to eat or not. I was. I rang the bell at the end of the courses. I cleaned out the vegetable dish and ate two-thirds of a very commendable meat pie. The pastry was perfect, and lightly browned strips ornamented the top. I called for and was given plenty of bread with jam and sugar—sweet things dear to an American's heart. There was also a pudding for dessert. With a good cook and a houseboy, why should a young man wish to marry? Still it was a rather lonely life, I mused.

East of Enugu, central Nigeria, the country was different from any I had seen heretofore. To begin with, it was much more thickly populated. But the main visual differences lay in the fences. In places of vertical sticks, the fences were of red earth, well overgrown with vines. Being of earth, they were wide at the bottom, and this tended to restrict living space. The one or two huts within an enclosure looked like they were in a well. Paths leading off the road, themselves raised from ground level, were often hemmed closely by these red-earth, vine-covered walls. There were palms or other trees every ten or fifteen feet in any direction. And in the tiny places or earth-fenced plots between the houses were the huge green leaves of cocoa yams. The whole picture gave the impression of a big population suddenly plunked down into the jungle and living and farming there without disturbing the trees.

Girls in this area, even near babies, had their bodies ornately marked with black or blue stripes—perhaps by the juice of some nut. They wore two ropes of pink and blue beads low around the hips—that was all. But the color contrast was very effective. Little boys did not even have the beads. But this was an area where the women wore clothes and the men often very little. It seemed that either one or the other sex must be in a state of undress.

Nearing the metropolis of Onitsha, I was surprised to find a number of two-story, palatial stone structures and was further impressed to learn they were the private dwellings of natives. They were rectangular structures with low roofs and with noticeable bizarre designs around the windows. A number of large stone churches were to be seen.

Entering Onitsha, I caught a glimpse of the Niger, the fourth and last of the four great African rivers on my tour. A little later I was thrilled by the clouds-and-sunset view over the river. The dark clouds were piled up in great clusters like huge blobs of whipped cream, those behind higher than those in front. At the north of these were two plain masses of cloud formed like the mouth of a dragon. Back of them was a splash of red and fiery pink that seemed to have no connection with the horizon or any other part of the sky. This magnificence was a backdrop for a huge city market, the lumber section being immediately in front of me. Here the workers were trying to utilize the light of departing day to the very last.

In Onitsha I was the guest of an official of the United African Corporation. This was the same as Kingsway Stores, Unilever Company, and Lever Brothers. It was the largest business "organization" in the world and was usually referred to as the octopus. *Fortune* magazine wrote it up in three issues.

After dinner we called on an American doctor and his wife. He was building a hospital at the Southern Baptist mission, situated down toward the sea and a number of miles away. The doctor was one of the greatest talkers I have ever met and another one of these natural-born cards. He talked all the time, even when his resthouse neighbors, Mr. and Mrs. G.R. Gray, dropped in. His wife sat quietly, never getting a chance to say anything. Since he was obviously good-natured, I pointed a remark concern-this difference. He picked it up at once.

"Oh, yes, my wife does all the talking in our family. That's how we got married. She talked me into it."

The doctor's stories were all playfully exaggerated and he kept us quite bemused until around eleven o'clock. Something came up about Lagos, Nigeria's biggest port, and the scenery there.

"The best view of Lagos," instantly chimed in the doctor, "is from the back end of a boat."

When the laughter receded he told us of the wonderful things he was going to do to the Statue of Liberty when he saw it again and how anxious he was "to leave darkest Africa in the dark." He had been out two years and had a year to go.

"The reason I came out—well, I heard all about the needs for hospitals and that kind of stuff, and I thought, what the heck, I can give 'em three years, I reckon. And then I came out here and found they had more hospitals than we had in the States."

> There was a young lady of Niger
> Who went for a ride on a tiger . . .

I softly sang these lines as I ferried across Africa's third greatest river with the Grays the next morning. Taking its rise far to the west near Sierra Leone, the Niger makes a sweeping arc to the east through French West Africa, and south across Nigeria, and 2,600 miles from its source flows through a broad delta into the Gulf of Guinea. The Niger is very wide at Onitsha. I noticed a great number of houseboat pirogues, a round thatched roof having been erected over about three-fourths the length of the boat as a permanent residence for the family or families. Another unusual sight was a very large fish net resting upright on the water like a great fan with a sort of basket near its base.

Riding with the Grays in their pickup, Jacqueline and I were carried westward. The day's driving—or most of it—was down a beautiful lane carved out of the jungle—green grass along the road, jungle greenery of vines and trees on both sides and overhanging the road from above. To complete the picture were the happy, grinning natives who shouted, ran toward us, or waved, extending the palm of the hand vertically in our direction.

The Grays were newlyweds, aged thirty-seven and thirty-one, returning from a honeymoon trip of 1,300 miles. I rode with them for two and a half days, and was very grateful, yet the English auto traveler has his peculiarities. England is a small country, the distances are short, and the roads are oiled. So the Grays felt that 170 miles was a good day's drive and worried about every little hill, rut in the road, or culvert detour. With their new Ford no American driver would have given the road a second thought, but every time Glen or Sue Gray saw a little hill or a few feet of wet gravel they shifted to intermediate and pressed the foot feed way down. Eighty percent of the conversation was devoted to analyzing the road and their driving.

The Grays treated me royally. For once I had found someone who enjoyed eating more than I did. Both Glen and Sue started planning the next meal as soon as the last one was over and would send their cook and houseboy into the next market. Nights we stayed in resthouses—more elaborately equipped than the French, and quite comparable to contemporary American motels except that there was no running hot water. There were cooking facilities in a little room at one end; then a sort of storage room; a bathroom with tub, towel racks, and chair; a small room for the toilet; a big bedroom with two beds, dresser, mosquito nets, lavatory, wardrobe; then the living room with table and chairs for dining, two comfy armchairs, coffee table, lamp shelf, another shelf, and a small stand. A number of French windows in both living and bed rooms provided plenty of cross ventilation.

Glen worked for the Nigerian Department of Agriculture and was making a survey of native fowl, his specialty. En route one morning, we took breakfast with an associate employee, young Mr. Smith. He seemed little more than a boy and the English shorts heightened this illusion. But he was already doing his second eighteen-month tour—as the English call a term of duty away from home—after receiving a Bachelor of Science in agriculture at Edinburgh. Here in Africa, though only twenty-four, he was the sole master of a very palatial mansion, cook, houseboys, clerks, and a late-model firewagon-red Ford pickup, or "kit wagon." He could roam his province at will, visiting nurseries and agricultural farms. In fact, after breakfast he led us to a farm at Ado Ekiti, thirty miles north.

He and I arrived first.

"Where are the chickens?" he asked his native supervisor.

"There they are, sir," pointing to a hen and four baby chicks in a pen.

"But where are the rest of them? I gave you three settings of nine eggs each."

"There they are," he repeated.

"But what happened to the others?"

"They died the first day."

"Died! Why?"

"Lice, sir! And the hen died too."

The chap did not seem to know about the third setting.

Smith later confided, "I'd really like to know what happened."

When the Grays arrived, Glen, Smith, and I walked over the nursery. One of the items raised was *awusa*, the Yoruba name for the only known substitute for linseed oil. The awusa tree starts producing in four or five years, and the seeds are baked like chestnuts before packing and shipping. The natives cook and eat them. Then we walked around to the concrete-floored pigpens. Two of the four or five boars had what appeared to be the mange. Smith did not know what it was, and the government veterinary never called. In the barn was an ungovernable bull, horns and all, and evil-tempered.

"What is he tied up for?" queried Smith of the supervisor.

"Oh, he bad!"

"But he will just get worse if you leave him tied up. Who tied him?"

"He tied himself up. When we unload from lorry, it was tug of war. His rope got caught. God tied him up." This with a grin.

Meanwhile we noticed half of the bull's tail was missing.

"Who cut off his tail?" asked Smith.

"No one. He cut it off."

"Who cut off his tail" asked Smith for the second time.

"No one. He cut it off," again came the same answer.

While we were looking at the bull with our nerves on edge, he gave a snort and made a plunge in the direction of the door. We bolted through the door and made for the fence, but fast as we were, the natives were ahead of us.

Still later, Smith remonstrated, "Now, look, that's ridiculous. You know, someone—probably the herdsman—cut off the bull's tail with his machete."

"Yes; he probably got peeved and took a swing at it," I chimed in.

"Who told you he cut off his tail?" pursued Smith.

"The herdsman."

"I thought so."

"He say he running around yard and caught tail in mouth."

"Now, that's impossible. He has no teeth for cutting. Untie him and let him run around the yard. [I tried to form a mental picture of a native brave enough to untie the beast—and failed.] And get a Falani herdsman over to look at him. They have cattle. He'll know what to do. And I think you had better get another herdsman. These stories he tells! Get a Falani man. Understand?"

"Yes, massuh, I look for him."

37

Life on a Mammy Wagon

After leaving the Grays, I became more personally acquainted with that most important of British West African institutions, the mammy wagon. A mammy wagon is a native bus usually loaded to the hilt with Negroes of both sexes and all ages, among whom the mammies predominate. The buses are either Ford, Chevrolet, or English Bedford trucks with a wide wagon box back of the cab and side posts supporting a flat wooden roof. Six or seven six-inch planks running across the box fit into slots at the ends. Five or six natives crowd onto every plank, and since the cab is wide enough to let people sit on both sides of the driver, there may be forty or fifty people on one mammy wagon. Each has at least one basket which is shoved under the planks in a veritable forest of feet and legs. Sheets of canvas hang from the top in case of rain, but are never rolled up high enough in good weather so that occupants can see out comfortably.

Mammy wagons are either careening across the country at high speed or parked beside the road (on a curve) with little-understood mechanical difficulties. The Grays told me in all seriousness that in one hundred miles of travel they had passed no less than thirty-five stalled mammy wagons. They had assured me I would make just as good progress by bike, and it would be a lot safer than if I traveled by native bus.

Deep in Nigeria's Yorubaland, I visited Ibadan, largest Negro city in all Africa. More than 175,000 people lived in the city proper, but the farm suburbs increased the population to nearly 400,000. It was a chimneyless, flat-roofed, unappealing city sprawling over low hills with crooked streets running in all directions. The houses were thatched, had mud walls, and a mud-walled yard with one doorway. There were a few modern buildings, mostly British offices and garages.

Because of its size I thought Ibadan would be a good place to get Jacqueline's brake relined. But even her bicycle shops were only sheds in the open—no floors or walls. There were no workbenches or vises—only a bunch of bikes, some upside down. A few young chaps, hardly more than boys, were usually puttering about. Whatever tools or parts existed were kept locked by the owner in small boxes and taken home at night. You can imagine my feelings when taking a complicated job like Jacqueline's three-speed hub into one of these sheds for repair. When I did finally find a lad who knew his business, he wound up with a broken cable and the brake no better than before.

The Niger, great river of west Africa.

That great institution—the mammy wagon. If you are unhappy with "What God has Wrought," take "WHAT ARE GIRLS."

Near Ibadan you could buy a bushel basket of oranges for thirty-five cents.

When I stopped for lunch along the road one day, a mammy wagon loaded with curiosity pulled up. They wanted me for a passenger and even without pay. There were about forty souls in the back, so I piled into the front seat with the driver, two other men, and two most attractive Yoruba girls. Jacqueline was roped to the side as usual, and I turned the handlebars so they would not project and catch the trees along the way. So off we went, the old Bedford groaning along and requiring fourth gear for the slightest grade.

We made a long stop at a very colorful market that afternoon, and how I regretted my long-time inability to find films for my camera! The girls in this area wore blouses, sort of sarong type skirts, and partly draped turbans. The prints were of various designs but much on the order of a flowery bandanna handkerchief or one of those fancy scarves so often given as gifts in the United States. The men, too, often wore gaily colored pieces of goods. Shades of blue and purple seemed to be the most popular with both sexes. I also noticed items of Mohammedan dress on the men: the small white, sometimes embroidered fez, the flowing white dress with tremendous sleeves, the low sandals. Added to the picture were narrow faces and shaven heads, to remind me of the Sudanese of Anglo-Egyptian Sudan.

Everybody seemed to be a merchant. I was told that everybody wants to be one. Each had a little stall, usually just under a thatched roof supported by bare poles. In the larger towns there were often several blocks of these structures in the marketplace. Different towns had different times for market—say early morn, 10 A.M., or 2 P.M.—but some individual enterprisers were there early and late. White bread, fried fish, fresh meat, trinkets of all kinds, toilet goods, varicolored piece goods— all of these and a hundred more were there for inspection, practically in the open.

Another international boundary! Another country! Again my oft-be-stamped passport was imprinted with exit and entrance stamps. French West Africa this time. Another large country—area 1,815,000 square miles, eighth largest in the world. And this was the first of no less than five entrances I was to make into the country. In entering French territory I again noticed the lack of emphasis on travel control as compared to the British. The native chaps on the French frontier seemed concerned only with what kind of money I had. As an afterthought, one asked to see my passport, examined a few pages upside down, and solemnly returned it.

The first province was Dahomey. First impressions left me with the thought that the natives were more enterprising than in Nigeria. There seemed to be cultivation everywhere, and all underbrush had been cleared away, leaving only the palms. The dark-brown soil was carefully hilled, and bright-green stalks of corn a few inches high showed up squarely in the top of the freshly cultivated mounds. Distance between mounds was about three feet, and one could row diagonally.

In Dahomey I came back at last to the seacoast and saw the Atlantic for the first time since Cape Town. White sands, palms, and frequent estuaries led out to sea. The southern part of all West Africa is divided into four regions. This was the Slave Coast, and as I worked westward I would pass successively through the Gold Coast, the Ivory Coast, and the Grain Coast.

I was given a lift on a sort of cross-country mammy wagon from Nigeria bound for Lomé deep in French Togoland. There were the driver, the mechanic, "the boy," the chap in charge of the car, a native, a United Africa Corporation employee, his oversize mammy, his grown daughter, and a baby daughter of about four. The car was only a light pickup, but eight of us rode in the back on two hard benches facing each other. Normally our number would not have been too great, but mammy bulked and weighed more than all the rest put together—including the truck.

The car was a 1937 Ford in fair condition. We had some carburetor or fuel trouble but nothing really serious until the rear spring (there was only *one*), encouraged by very rough roads and mammy's weight, did a complete collapse. We all piled out to discover that one of the two main spring bolts was gone. Then it developed that there was no jack and no spare bolt. Everyone, including the driver and mechanic, sat down and looked hopeless. Not seeing any advantage in that, I took the camp axe from my bicycle and cut a good-sized green branch from a tree to use as a lever. I had not used that axe since cutting windbreak one night deep in the Australian bush, and had threatened to send it home several times. With the branch as a lever we got one end of the axle up on a U.S. Army petrol can. Then, by good luck, a mammy wagon came along and I hailed it for a jack to push the spring over in place and to see if I could get a bolt. My party spoke no French, so it turned out I could help them a great deal. The other driver said he had no bolt but I poked around in his tool box and soon same up with the proper bolt, and nut and washers in the bargain. The camp axe came in handy again to cut chocks for our wheels. Even with all the man power now available, we had to use my pry to force the big spring into place.

Once this was done and our help and jack departed, the driver decided he ought to change a tire which was showing a great rip in its outer plies. They wanted to cut another pry so as to put one on both sides of the tire and lift the wheel onto a petrol tin; but they changed their minds and tied the tire up with rope. This I had never seen done before, but I refrained from laughing. After all, we live to learn.

The rope was still holding when we arrived at the city of Ouidah, located on the north bank of a lagoon about two miles from the sea. The surf is so heavy at this point that only special small boats can come into the mouth of the lagoon. There are thousands of orange and citron trees in Ouidah, and these have won for it the title of the Garden of Dahomey.

The city was founded by the Portuguese, those pioneer explorers and traders of the West African coast. In 1680 they erected the fortress of S. João Batista d' Ajuda and nearby a residence for the *avogá*, or governor. Ajuda was very important in the days when slave trading was at its height and thousands of blacks were shipped out to the Portuguese plantations in Brazil. The location has always been favorable for the manufacture of palm oil. But control of Ajuda largely passed to the French and today the green flag of Portugal flies over a tiny area described to me by a Frenchman as a "petit, petit enclave." However, this was another country, and I paid it a visit. The governor gave me audience, and his residency officials stamped my passport.

Meanwhile the driver had decided to interchange front and rear wheels. The chap in charge of the pickup had been out trying to borrow a jack but had failed, not knowing how to speak French. I went out and although there were signs of only two or three cars in the whole town, succeeded in getting a jack. We put this under the front, having been able to lift the rear by drafted manpower. Then the driver decided to take off a tire in order to mount the spare, but it developed his tire tools were improvisations and could not manage the job. We all wrestled in vain until I hailed a jeep going by. It held the two ranking officials of two different branches of the police department, and they set about supplying tools right away. One of them drove off in the jeep to get some patches and patching material for a leaky tube, for of course the driver of our mammy wagon carried no such superfluities. The police chaps than took me off to the nearest bar and bought me a soft drink. How different from most English officials, who would have asked me questions and looked at my passport before thinking about my needs!

It was nearly dark when we left Ouidah, but we traveled on until about 9:30, when we reached a barrier of twin ferries at Grand Popo. Here we fought the night. I cannot well say "passed the night." We endured. You see, there were mosquitoes! Ordinarily this would pose no insuperable obstacle to me because I have a sleeping bag and a net for my face. But it was too hot to sleep even in the top layer. Sweating and scratching, plus psychological hum outside and the lure of an occasional breeze—this was all too much for me, and for the first time in my life I gave up after a couple hours, dressed and took a walk. The driver, more sensible than the rest of us, knew he couldn't sleep, so was hunting crabs with a flashlight. He caught about fifteen before morning. I sat on the hood of the truck for a while and dozed with my mosquito net over my cap and head, but if I dozed too much and lay back, the net would swing against my face and the bombers would attack. Later I happened to stroll out onto the end of the pier of the uncompleted bridge. Here was a fairly brisk breeze, so I returned and got my bag, passing on the way the U.A.C. employee and his family lying by the dying embers of a fire. I placed my bag at the end of the pier, undressed and crawled in. As I dozed off I could hear the groans and slapping of two members of my party who had followed me out to see if there was a better place to rest. I could also hear the sounds made by a fisherman in a nearby boat. I slept from 2 A.M. until 5:30, daylight. Mammy told me later that she did not sleep at all; so even the African cannot cope successfully with the mosquitoes. But honestly, even this night—my worst in Africa—there were not the number or size of mosquitoes that I have seen in certain Illinois state parks or in my own back yard in Elmhurst, Illinois. Civilization! Hah! We can't even control a mosquito!

We crossed our two estuaries about eight o'clock. The second crossing was by cable ferry. The boys beat time with their feet as they slowly walked along the deck pulling on the cable. Some sang, then the others followed with a response.

At Anecho, in French Togo, it was announced that we were nearly out of gas and could go no further. Lomé, where I expected to get my first mail in a month, was only twenty-six miles away, so I did not like this idea. The chap in charge of the truck was too tired to care, and so there we sat. I was told two other lorries had left Nigeria at the same time as our truck and would probably arrive by evening, bringing petrol. Nevertheless, knowing something of the way the African mind worked, I decided to wait about a bit before transferring to Jacqueline. Sure enough, after a half-hour or so in the heat, the driver said we would go on if we could get a gallon of petrol. He claimed to have put in six gallons and we had only come about twenty miles, but when I pointed this out he said the car wasn't working right anyway.

"Well, it is doing as well as when we started," I remonstrated.

But to humor him I set out to get his gallon of gasoline. It was not rationed, a storekeeper said, so the driver, the boy, with a can, and I walked several blocks in the heat, only to find that "l'essence" was rationed after all. On the way back to the car the driver decided he would go on anyway and if we ran out of gas we would just stop where we found ourselves.

But mammy had had enough of delays. This was too much for even African patience, so she departed for the shade of a store's covered walk with her entire family and their gear. The chap in charge of the car, lying on some sacks, got his box and elected to stay also. He was not going to risk another mosquito-plagued night in the bush. The rest of us pushed off—we always had to push the car for a start—with a much lighter load. It was just as well we lost mammy; she had been slowly reducing one of the benches to rubble.

I learned much of the African character while traveling on this mammy wagon. The African has never neard that whatever is worth doing at all is worth doing well. When we lost the gas cap and I made for wood to cut a plug, I was told: "Leave it; the boy will fix something."

Yes, he fixed it all right—by carelessly wadding a piece of cloth and putting it in the mouth. This lasted less than two miles, but no one joined me in worrying whether the cloth had fallen into the gas tank or fallen outside. The rear bumper cracked nearly through and left its support, due largely to the use of manpower for a jack and to mammy's weight in her frequent climbings in and out. The boy wired it back on, but as I expected, the job lasted about five miles.

It would also seem that the African has very little sense of responsibility. For example, when the decision to stop at Anecho was made, they ignored the obligation to their passengers—especially to two new ones they had just taken on for prompt transport to Lomé.

The whole point was that these chaps had lost sleep the night before and wanted to rest, passengers or no passengers. So when halfway to Lomé, we suddenly "ran out of gas." This was timed for the moment of meeting another lorry, and none of the usual running-out-of-gas symptoms could be heard. Well, I could not have chosen a better spot for sleeping myself. We had left the heat of the town and were traveling along the sea among many palm trees.

Jacqueline and I, alone once more, enjoyed our journey into Lomé along the Slave Coast beach. What tremendous breakers there were! The sun shone brightly, and the white water sometimes reflected it into my eyes. The wind often brought the salt spray across the road in clouds. Palms on either side of the road were spaced as though they had been planted. Native villages and their people clearly indicated that living came from both sea and palms. Nets and boats were being prepared and piles of coconuts sorted. As I cycled along I watched for ships at sea, but this coast, I believe, is very little frequented.

I reached the post office at Lomé, but no mail! What a bitter disappointment after a month of expectation! But there had been a strike and the mail held up.

When I left French Togoland, there was practically no formality, but across the line was the British Gold Coast. This was quite different, and for twenty-four hours as I cycled near the frontier I was subjected to all sorts of control checks by police chiefs, district commissioners, and native policemen. The last were attired in red fezzes with tassels, black woolen, turtleneck sweaters, shorts, and belts with big police buckles. How they could endure those sweaters in a climate as hot and breezeless as the interior of the Slave and Gold coasts was a mystery to me. Across the chest was printed "British Preventive Service." This referred to smuggling.

The road continued good as I entered British Togoland. But then I had eight miles of mud. Next a big rain came up, and I raced like fury for the last five miles into Ho, just beating the first big drops to the door of the Protestant mission. Here I stayed the night, having pedaled seventy-four miles, the biggest day of my trip.

The Ho mission was founded by the Germans. After World War I, although Togoland was mandated away from the Germans, the missionaries were allowed to return. When Hitler came into power, no money was allowed to come out from Germany, so the German missionaries appealed to the Scots and later to the Americans.

Besides the church there were schools at Ho mission. Candidates for the most advanced school might be as many as six hundred, but of these only sixty could be accommodated. These of course would be selected from the best grades on the entrance examinations. What a pity to deny education to so many! Graduates of this school had an education equivalent to junior college in the states. Several were ready to go there for further study. It had taken months to clear the red tape, so only one month remained before the term began. Then they could not get a boat.

From British Togo I reentered the Gold Coast and before long ferried across the Volta River, one of Africa's giants. Mammy wagons were lined up for a quarter mile waiting for the single ferry, even though it was motor-driven. One driver told me he had waited from 10 A.M. until 4 P.M. The ferry stops at 6 P.M., so all night might be spent in line. But for Jacqueline and me there was no delay.

Learning of a mission called Agomanya where there were Americans, I stopped to say hello. Amazingly I found two men from my home areas in Iowa and Illinois. It was a Catholic mission, and as always there was plenty of good food and a sufficient staff to provide much jollity. But they had difficulties with the local government. It had agreed to build certain houses for the teaching staff but had never done anything about it. The mission was building its own. Mission requests were always received graciously, but nothing ever happened. Just then they were trying to get free transport for the student teachers, over fifty in number.

"But the permanent chief went off to London and told us to get our answer from the treasury department," said my Iowa friend.

"What! You mean you are dealing with natives in all this business?"

"Oh, yes. Of course, the British have their own government. But we deal with the chiefs here. Oh, they're pretty powerful men. They have cars, nice houses, live like we do, and all that."

"But what have they got to do with free transport?"

"Oh, everything! They own the trucks we want to use. We've been giving them chits for our boys' transportation. So when the treasury department said, 'Why, we can't give you an answer—we've had no instructions,' we said we'd just hang onto the chits until we got an answer.

But they're smart, though. We sent a truck up north to get some lumber, and before they would load it, they demanded payment in advance. They're foxy."

It was the final evening of a Boy Scout jamboree. A big bonfire was blazing skyward, and one of the fathers—the best humorist—was in charge. There was singing, chain dancing, and a general good time with four or five hundred boys seated in a huge circle.

"Oh, we're pushing this very much," the father said to me. "The government backs us on scouts, you see. It's an English-born organization. [I thought of a recent article giving part or half credit to William Thompson Seton, Canadian Scotsman.] We are also pushing the Girl Guides."

And so to Accra, capital and chief metropolis of the Gold Coast. The name comes from *Nkran*, a Fanti word meaning "an ant," which was used to designate the tribe inhabiting the area. The city grew up around three forts set up on the Gold Coast—one built by the British, one by the Danes, and one by the Dutch. The last two were ceded to the British in 1850 and 1871, respectively. Of the three the Danish is the finest, and I could understand why the governor of the Gold Coast had chosen this one, called Christiansborg Castle, for a residence.

Travel is often a revelation. Who today ever dreams that the Danes once established themselves on the west coast of Africa? It's a long way from Greenland and Iceland.

The city proper was bustling and commercial, and there were even big department stores. New and modern construction was in progress, and some streets were littered with it. Native policemen were both official and helpful. In some areas native markets struck an almost anachronistic note as they overflowed the sidewalks and narrowed the streets. The petrol-driven power grinder has invaded both French and English markets along the Gold Coast, and natives were busy with these, grinding corn and cassava. There was supposed to be a shortage of regular flour, and bread was expensive, but loaves of all sizes were being displayed on the heads of native women vendors. In Accra one could buy tempting tidbits such as light-brown cake, hard candy, soft gaily-striped "African toffee," and ice cream.

By previous invitation I spent another night at a Gold Coast Catholic mission. Talk at the supper table centered about native customs. Human sacrifices were still made, although rarely. An eight-year-old girl was sacrificed because the *juju* said it was necessary for the election of a certain candidate for office. They tried to grab her little brother, but he escaped. Certain parts of the body—eyes, heart, skin—were used in the rituals. I had already witnessed two witch-doctor dances along the way— caricature costumes with high, waving, black plumes above the head, drums, and the calabash filled with seeds. The rhythm of these two instruments was such that I could sense how emotions could be worked up to frenzies to commit any atrocity.

When a big chief dies, it is fitting that he have someone accompany him into the other world. So his family sets out to find a victim, preferably a stranger, because no one objects. While the hunt is on, other chiefs have their people stay off bush paths at night, mothers keep their children close, and general trepidation marches. There was a double murder for one deceased chief who complained through his witch doctor that the first chap did not speak his language.

The natives sometimes cut a man's cheek and let the blood run onto a stool in place of paint if some important person is to sit on it.

Mammy wagons were plentiful on the roads, and I rode on several. The Gold Coast wagons, I noticed, usually had religious inscriptions in large white or yellow letters on front or back. Sometimes these were in native language. "God's time is the Best," "Jehovah Jire," "God is Love," "Still in the service of Jesus," and "All days are not equal" are fair examples.

The mammy wagons tore across the country at a great rate. Speed is important, and besides, it's deucedly exhilarating, don't you know. And what a thrill the native gets out of coasting—speed her up at the slightest hill, turn off the gas, and whoopee, here we go! If there is a ferry ahead and a wait is possible, all the buses hold a great race to get there. It is a wonder there are not more accidents, because we always rounded a curve or topped a hill expecting to see a parked bus.

Another reason for speed in the mind of the driver is to make up time for his frequent stops—every couple miles or thereabouts. You see, competition for patronage is so intense that any innocent-looking pedestrian, even with a great pan or gourd filled with food on her head, must be propositioned for a ride, and this means stopping the truck. If a stop is not made for a passenger, the driver thinks up something. Putting in some extra gas is the most common excuse.

There are many mammy wagons taking part in the competition for passengers. Towns are big, and on some roads there is a bus about every five minutes. In one wagon I was riding, we heard a rumor that there were passengers to be had down a side road. We turned frantically, only to find another wagon there ahead of us. Still it looked as though both buses were out of luck because no one was about except a few people going down the side road away from town. Our boys—there are usually two on every bus beside the driver—tore down the road on a dead run in a footrace with the boys from the other truck. The first to arrive grabbed the poor pedestrians bodily and propelled them toward their truck. Alas, all but one bewildered chap succeeded in extricating themselves and continuing their peaceful way down the road. This one chap

—well, I'm not sure, but perhaps he also escaped later.

Then it was noised about that the real prospects were out of sight even farther down the side road. We took off again and after a mile or so found about six women and men who suffered high and wide head-burdens to be torn from their heads and put into the truck by our gleeful boys. During this process the other truck dashed by on the quest for further passengers, and presently we succeeded in passing it. Great sport!

There is another kind of competition on a mammy wagon ride. The wagon no sooner comes to any more or less scheduled stop than the food vendors are about it like swarms of bees. On the heads of fair young maids and matrons, in great calabash or gourd bowls, are oranges (two or three for 2 cents), bananas (six to nine for 2 cents), peanuts (handful for 2 cents), bread, and a number of 4- or 6- inch-diameter flat-sided balls of corn—a flour product wrapped in green plantain leaves. In making the last the natives put the corn flour in cold water to soak for a day, then boil the mixture and wrap the result in plantain leaves. The stuff is then boiled again, leaves and all. The leaves are taken from the tree of the large banana I have mentioned before. They are not eaten, but the banana itself is delicious, and I often saw natives frying it, split or whole, along the way. They used palm oil brought to a boil in a deep or shallow vessel, placed over a fire built in a small kettle with a hole broken in one side.

There is plenty of variety in the dress of mammy-wagon passengers. The men wear full-length draped cloths, as in the pictures you see of old Roman togas. The women wear blouses and skirts with a wraparound outer skirt. This invariably comes unwrapped and falls nearly off when madame gets into or out of a bus, and she frantically rewraps it—very inadequately in keeping with the way all things are done in Africa. It will fall down again in a few minutes. All these pieces of clothing are in zigzag or broad stripes of color. There are blues, greens, yellows, and rusts, in about that order of preference. What a field for the motion-picture color camera, all this welter of color and excitement!

For excitement always prevails. The whistle blows far in the back where the conductor hangs desperately to the outside. The wagon plunges to a stop with the driver muttering, "What now?" and the passengers all craning to see. Maybe it's a new passenger, maybe not. Maybe it's a recently disembarked passenger tearing madly up the road yelling that he or she has been short-changed. If such is the case, the driver piles out, and argument and gesticulation ensues. He seems to handle the money but seldom makes any effort to collect, being too busy with starting and stopping the bus and blowing the two horns, one of which may be the old-fashioned bulb-type honker. Fares are paid by passengers at will at the end of the ride. The driver can't possibly keep track of when they got

Where is the American, male or female, who could carry that load (and the baby) for five miles?

Great mounds for planting must be made before the rains come.

on so as to assess proper fare. Most of the faces he sees for the first time when they come forward at the end of the journey. I never found out why one of the two chaps at the back could not handle the money. Even the one with the whistle did not blow it all the time.

When the mammy wagon arrives in a big town, it stops at three or four different places. If someone wants to get off on a side street four blocks away, the driver obligingly takes him there. Many have difficulty in making up their minds where to get off. The whistle blows, the bus stops, the mind is changed, two minutes are lost in vociferation and argument, the bus moves on. Yes, indeed, there is plenty of excitement on a mammy wagon.

Signs along the road were indicative of both human nature and the progress of darkest Africa through the throes of enlightenment. Here are a few samples:

"Happy Bar—Don't mind your wife"

"Coronation Bar Most Delicious in Taste"

"The Famous Fitter"

"Latrine for Male—Bafie Kroum—Date 12-4-47" (Bafie Kroum was the town)

> "I Have Here a Medicine
> Given to Me by God
> Called the Sain Law Ointment
> It will Cure Nearly All Diseases."

But the sign to end all signs was one of the before-mentioned religious inscriptions on the front of a mammy wagon. And having risked my life in a number of these race buggies, I thought this particular inscription was quite appropriate. It read:

"The Future Is Unknown."

38

Moonlight and Music
on the Ivory Coast

At a place called Cape Coast, Jacqueline and I decided we had had enough of mammy-wagon travel. We packed up at a sort of terminal surrounded by ferry boys and drivers who wanted us for passengers. Other hangers-on helped to swell a big half-circle of the curious.

"Are you going by bicycle to Sekondi?" There was almost a ridiculous-idea curl to the lip of my questioner.

"Yes."

"It's forty-seven miles. How can you do that?"

The unbelief in the faces about me was too much for my equanimity.

"I've ridden this bicycle many thousands of miles. Forty-seven miles— it is nothing."

What an exemplification these people made of the fact that anything beyond the experience of a particular human being is often doubted by that human being. My trip was so far beyond their experience that comprehension did not even dawn. Glen Gray had repeatedly mentioned this in regard to the resthouse boys and other natives to whom he had attempted explanations in their own tongue. Even to tell them that I came from the countries to the east and go to those of the west, was useless. They could only conceive of a few adjacent towns.

The Portuguese have left their mark on the Gold Coast as well as the Slave Coast, and I side-tripped to visit Elmina Castle, perhaps the most interesting of their old forts. It is located on an elevated rock just at a slight point of land and thus overlooks the sea and those long, long stretches of West African coastline I had come to know. There were thick walls and crenated battlements, a great moat running around, and a high bridge across to a narrow entryway under a tower. Outside, the pounding of the surf on the rocks. Romantic? Yes, indeed!

Fernão Gomez, "honest and respected citizen" of Portugal, discovered the place in 1471. When the Portuguese found that trade in gold could be carried on with the natives, they gave the region the name Costa da Mina, or Gold Coast. In allowing Gomez to trade there, the government of Portugal decreed that he must explore 300 miles of coast each year for five years so that at the end of that time 1500 miles of coast would be brought under Portuguese sovereignty. Gomez completed his assignment and with his appetite for adventure thus whetted sailed off again in 1486 in company with an adventurer named João Alfonso do Estreito. In two ships they set out to find Ilha das Sete de Cidadeo ("Island of the Seven Cities"). Their search must have been just as futile as Coronado's quest for the seven golden cities of Cibola, but we will never know for sure because both adventurers and all their crews disappeared from the annals of mankind.

During the usurpation of Spain, the castle and town of St. Jorge da Mina (Elmina) were taken over by the Dutch. They made it the capital of their coastal possessions, which totaled, in the 1850's about 5,000 square miles and 100,000 people. The climate being unsavory for European women, the Dutchmen took the only women available and the streets of the town were embellished by shapely "jaffrouws," or mistresses, who looked after their children and the household interests of Mynheer, to whom they were devoted. But who can say that broken hearts remained when the Dutch in turn were supplanted by the British on the Gold Coast?

From Elmina Castle, I cycled west, passing many fisherman and their families busy on the beaches. Nets sometimes ran for half a mile. There were ropes and coils of more rope. In one place about twenty men were pulling on two ropes running through the surf into deeper water. There two two-man boats were tending the net just outside the breakers.

My last evening in the Gold Coast was spent sitting on the second-floor veranda of a British residence in a place called Axim. It was a fitting climax, for I was on a hilltop and while sipping the cold lemon squash the boy placed at my elbow, I could command all the breeze possible. Below me were the town and the sea, still visible in the semi-darkness. Not since Merca in Italian Somaliland had I sat on a second-story veranda overlooking the sea. How far away was Merca? I did not know. Several thousand miles anyway. But it was certainly on the diametrically opposite side of the African continent. How long ago was it? More than six months; and when at the former, how could I have foretold my present comfort at Axim?

I could not resist visiting the town's old fort before leaving the next morning. I prowled upstairs and down and walked along the battlements past the old rusty guns still in place. Below on three sides was the sea beating away at the rocks. On the landward side the gray weather-beaten walls were offset by a street of the sleepy village and a grove of palm trees. Axim, too, had been Portuguese and then Dutch before coming into the British Empire.

Along the road that mornings I met two white road contractors, both claiming to be Swiss. I often suspect that it is easy to explain German speech by claiming Swiss nationality. Isn't it strange, or is it, how people respect citizens from countries such as Switzerland and Sweden which have brains enough to remain neutral in wars?

My last seven miles to the French frontier were on foot in deep sand amongst palm trees and thick bush. Palm leaves had been placed on the sand for passage of occasional autos, and they recalled my entry into Angola. At a village called Jewi I entered a pirogue for an hour's row across a great lagoon. This was a real experience and the longest pirogue ride I had in Africa. As we rolled about in a choppy sea the water occasionally splashed over the boat and I felt a little uncertain more than once. Oy! It was a long, long way to shore. If we upset, should I hang onto Jacqueline or my baggage? I decided to hang onto Jacqueline.

It was dark when we landed at Frambo, the first point on my second entry into French West Africa. With the police chief, also the chief of the village, I climbed the hill to the house of the immigration officer in charge, a native.

"Is there anything you need—water, food?" I was asked.

"No, thank you; but did you want to look at my passport?"

"Oh, we can look at that in the morning, or now, or whenever you wish."

The chief said he had a place for me to spend the night, and between the two they worked to make me comfortable. The officer provided a chair and filtered water, and the chief took me down to a house near the lagoon, where he provided lantern, table, room, and bed. I list these in their order of importance to me. I moved the bed outside so as to get the benefit of the breeze, and there, just within the shelter of the roof, I spent the night. As I drifted off to sleep I could see the palms in the brilliant equatorial moonlight, and the lagoon beyond. There was no road out of Frambo, so I hired a native to take me by canoe to a place where there was one. My boatman had two oars but no assistant. He needed none, for he well knew the white man would be too impatient with the slow progress of just one oar. I picked up the second oar before we had gone five rods and never put it down until we reached Ebobo, three miles away, lying along a narrow branch of the lagoon. It was quite romantic to think of starting into the interior of Africa by canoe. But believe me, I did my full share of the rowing. Occasionally I would hear no signs of activity behind me, but when I looked around the oar would suddenly move and for the next four or five strokes there would be the sound of tremendous swishings of the water behind me.

En route we passed fisherman in other pirogues, usually naked and in pairs. The one behind rowed and the other stood erect in front ready to cast the net held in his hands. They were finely built, well-muscled chaps, black as ebony and with very short curly hair. Speaking of hair, I noticed that in this part of Africa the heads of most children were kept shaved. Sometimes a patch of hair about four inches in diameter would be left on the head of a girl, and this would be arranged in two tiny braids. But there were all sorts of variations, for African mothers were no different than American. Some shaved the little heads so that there were four patches of hair left; some shaved only down the center, leaving two.

After landing at Ebobo, I found the road was only a jungle trail used about once a year to haul coffee. Now it was overgrown with weeds and grass two feet high, and I had to follow a winding native path which sometimes disappeared. And then it rained! Brother, it really poured! I thought that my sou'wester and large, heavy rain cape were adequate for any downpour, so I was really amazed to find that the water got through, and even when I stood still under a tree. But it was not too bad, and I was able to keep my pack dry by standing close and keeping it under the cape.

When the rain slackened, I traveled on, but it was two o'clock before the sky had cleared and I felt it was safe to lay out my food for a meal. Then I had to hunt for a spot where the sun could penetrate the trees, for this was a real jungle, and most of the trail was as dark as dusk.

Night and a native village where the chief's daughter offered her company. Another noon and another downpour, but this time there was a shelter beside the road, and I joined the lone woodcutter sitting underneath. The skies failed to clear, but the rain was light and intermittent. I wrote, the woodcutter just sat, but we both listened to the steady chop, chop of a machete on a big tree in the nearby forest. Finally a great crash indicated a forest giant had fallen, and my companion went to join his brother, who had apparently been doing the chopping. I started to eat dinner but was interrupted—as usual, it seemed—by a truck loaded with pineapples, sisal, and natives. I hailed it for a ride.

Americans have no conception—indeed, can never have any conception —of the condition of most African trucks. The are run until they stop, are fixed a little, then run until they stop again; and the process is repeated about a dozen times. They wheeze, cough, spit and mutter along on about half of their cylinders. Smoke rises through great holes in the floor along with heat from an exhaust without a muffler, or at least with a broken one. You can see the body warping about on the front axle and feel its wild twistings on the seat where you bounce. I said "bounce," not "sit." You touch the seat only between times. When you do, the projecting springs tear at your shoulders and derriere. The radiator has great holes in it, and water has to be added every few miles. Oil drips from the engine into the water-filled holes in the road. The oil gauge is always low and the oil black and thin, even though No. 50 is put in quite often. The hood is tied down with native rope, or else left to flop skyward at every bump. Cab windows, handles, and door latches have long since ceased to exist. Doors are kept closed with a piece of rope. Engines knock and springs break. Spare parts are practically impossible to get. Gas-tank caps are invariably tin cans or other improvisions. All in all, Ford, General Motors, and International would never in the world be able to recognize their offspring.

Cycling over a bad road near Grand Bassam, I saw a boy carrying two dead monkeys or baboons on a pole. The faces were fringed with a circle of white. Other lads had a big *civet*, as the French say, an animal resembling a small hyena, black with many vertical white side stripes. And speaking of animals, I again noticed a small cow which stood only about three feet high but was round and healthy looking. Then, just to show that the Ivory Coast was a real land of opposites, I saw a lot of sheep as tall as the cows. The sheep were rather skinny and unappetizing in appearance.

Beyond Abijan, capital of Ivory Coast Province, I turned inland away from the sea. Two good-natured Lebanese offered me an all-night ride on their truck. The road was so rough I was nearly knocked out trying to sleep, but one of my hosts compensated by taking me to the home of a friend for a big supper about 11 P.M. These folks were all Arabic-speaking Lebanese, and the fact that I remembered a few words of Arabic pleased them immensely. The food was excellent— fried hamburger, pancake bread like I had enjoyed in Egypt, cookies, and good cake. Plenty of water to drink, and no one bothered me with offers of wine.

On the road again, I alternated between lying and sitting, but sleep would not come. It was a beautiful moonlit night, and the great jungle giants spread their branches perhaps two hundred feet above us across the face of the moon. Magnificent! These are thrills that only the traveler knows!

I cycled well into the interior of the Côte d'Ivoire, wondering at the jungle and the customs of its people. Some of the natives had white porcelain clay smeared on their bodies. A woman had it on her forehead and the upper part of her breasts; a boy had it on his face in vertical oval lines. This clay is used when there is pain in the eyes or head, and it can be bought in the market and stored in the hut for such emergencies. Another custom was for certain matrons to have all their upper front teeth pulled except three, which were pulled out part way and trained to slant upward. The appearance of these three tusks may be beautiful to some Africans, but you can imagine the effect on a white man.

There were a number of large coffee and cacao plantations north of Gagnoa, and I stopped at one of these for water. I noticed large grapefruit going to waste on the ground and ate one. In so doing I made the surprising discovery that really good grapefruit needs no sugar; also that just one of these grapefruit made me feel as full as though I had eaten a meal. As I finished its thirst-quenching goodness a young matron passed by and opened a conversation in French. She sent me away with all the grapefruit I could carry.

Not far away, near a small stream, three native workers reclined at ease under a crude shelter. Two of them had native violins, the third an empty half-calabash, and they were making music. I opened negotiations for one of the violins as a souvenir for mother and succeeded in buying it for about eighty cents. I was well pleased with my purchase.

One day I found a giant tree had fallen across the road. A crew of choppers—they had axes, believe it or not—and a lot of onlookers were at work making two cuts in the huge trunk, which rested shoulder high. There was shouting in rhythm, and laughter and excitement. I decided to use one of my two precious remaining exposures. Everyone posed beautifully. When the last cut was completed, all hands laid to in order to roll the log to one side.

"Ya-ho, ya-ho, ya-ho, huf," shouted the leader. He and others varied the "huf," which meant "heave," with trills, whistles and the like. Everyone seemed to have a general good time.

At a place called Daloa I pedaled to the edge of town to visit a young French doctor to whom I had been referred by a friend. I was greeted by slender, attractive, tall Madame Fourton. It seems wrong to call her "madame" since to me this connotes someone not young or vivacious. She spoke to me in fairly good English, having spent six months in the United States with friends in Manchester, New Hampshire, and Philadelphia. She impressed me immediately as being practical, frank, busy, and interesting. Her husband had not arrived home, and she was pouring gasoline into the light plant and getting ready to start that.

The Fourtons were one of those unusual couples you remember. Briefly speaking, the doctor had put his fingers into about everything, and she had adopted his interests and was right in there pitching beside him.

One of his avocations was snakes. About twenty-five feet from the house were two cages made of wood and wire netting and full of snakes. As Mrs. Fourton and I approached, a huge black cobra inflated its neck and reared up more than two feet. Some of the snakes were the ugliest things I had ever seen.

"See that nice one in the corner," said Mrs. F., pointing into one of the cages. "Isn't he a beauty?"

"Uh-huh," I said. I could say no more.

"This one over here has recently changed his skin. You can't really see how nice his new skin is because they are in sand, you see."

I ignored this observation and opened a new line. "And I suppose you take care of them right along with your husband?"

"Oh, yes. We put them into water and bathe them once every week. I don't like catching them, though. But I have had one around my neck."

"No, really!"

There was a pause during which I tried to envision one of the things encircling the lovely's neck.

"What do they eat?" I asked

"Meat. We have to feed them."

"Isn't it dangerous?"

"Oh, yes, the spitting cobra throws poison into your eyes. My husband has had that happen to him."

I casually managed to step back from the cages a couple feet.

"Does your husband get his snakes from natives?"

"No, he catches them himself."

"Don't you worry about him?"

Well, I don't like it when he goes after the green mamba."

I casually examined the fastenings on the cage doors. The green mamba, I was told, is one of the most dangerous snakes. Its poison, which attacks the nerves and brain, is so lethal that a man may die within three minutes after having been bitten. The mamba is a marvelous climber, incredibly swift, and is often at home in vines or trees so that natives on jungle trails may be bitten on the face or neck. Other snakes might run when disturbed, but not the mamba—it attacks at once.

Later that evening the Fourtons showed me paintings the doctor had made of various snakes in the Ivory Coast. They showed painstaking detail. A given inch of skin must show the exact number and arrangement of the scales, also the coloring and shading. It is the doctor's ambition to put his paintings into a book he hopes to write on snakes.

"But it is now ten months that I have not been able to touch it. You see, I must make a living, so I have had to take a position as doctor."

A second interest of this couple was masks. They showed me what I thought to be a fine collection of witch doctors' masks—grotesque things for the most part—worn in a certain area of the Ivory Coast. The collection was housed in an outbuilding, and it was just after midnight when we took a flashlight and went out to have a look. White-rimmed eyes, red and white and black faces, beards of women's hair—it was all a bit eerie. One ebony face had a long, narrow nose and almond-shaped eyes. The doctor thought this indicated an Indian or oriental influence and said his studies of ethnology bore this out.

A third hobby was a collection of brass weights used on small scales. These had been gathered in an area to the north where each merchant seemed to have his own system of weights. The weights were shaped like small animals, although there were a few elephants and the like; and there were also a native bellows, a crane, and a reptile. These miniatures would have delighted any collector's heart. Mrs. Fourton had drawn pictures of each in a little pamphlet and had them all numbered and the actual weights shown in grams. There was no duplication in actual weight, so the natives must have had a bad time determining which merchant gave them most for their money. The Fourtons would like to get their collection into a museum in Switzerland or the United States.

A fourth hobby was a technical vocabulary of four or five native

Grotesque mask used on the Ivory Coast.

Clearing a tree from the road on the Ivory Coast.

languages. You cannot imagine the work this entails unless you stop and think of all the many parts of a tree or the words involved in the process of weaving cloth.

"It isn't an easy thing to do," said the doctor. "Each word must be checked with five or six different people. And after you have talked to a native for perhaps two hours, his attention wanders, and he gives you careless answers; so it is necessary for you to return to the village another time.

"I wanted to work for the government on some of these things, but I couldn't get them interested, and so—well, I come here and practice as a doctor. One must take care of eating, you know. And so I am building a clinic here."

A fifth hobby was bugs, particularly giant beetles, and they had a nice collection.

A sixth hobby was photography, but mainly technical photography, connected with other hobbies. The doctor talked of his efforts to obtain a motion-picture camera and how expensive was color film.

For a white housekeeper with servants, Mrs. Fourton was unusual among African residents I met because she relied on her boys very little. She made her own cheese and her own butter and worked on her own laundry. I don't think she had prepared the gravy for supper, however, as it was full of ants.

"Oh, don't mind the ants," she said in her rapid French. "I think they must have fallen in from the ceiling, but anyway they are all properly sterilized."

Two well-behaved, chocolate-consuming children, a cute little monkey, a dog, and a cat completed the household.

One night I stayed in a native village where there was a medical dispensary. This was a large, white, thatched-roof building bearing a red cross, and my host was one of the two native dispensers. He let me clean up in a little bathhouse constructed like a temporary outdoor, lath corn crib, except that the laths were round sticks very close together. The wall was high enough for privacy. One could stand on large flat-sided stones if he wanted a *douche*, as they call a shower here. Towel and soap were provided. Supper consisted of a big dish of rice with pieces of chicken, fried as only the African knows how. I suppose Africa was the origin of our famous southern fried chicken.

After supper the sound of drums brought me away from my writing. I wandered among the white-walled, peaked-roof houses until I came to a little open space. Here were drums, dancers, and an audience. The African moon, even through veiled in fleecy clouds, gave quite enough light for me to see all details of the scene. It was incredibly interesting and romantic.

There were three musicians, two drummers, and one who made with seeds in a calabash—or so it sounded. He was so surrounded by people I could not be sure. The drummer with the biggest drum gave it some awful bams with his stick every once in a while in order to keep things going. I had to wait a bit before any real dancing started. Then a feminine voice called out, "Ah gan yey ho," and in a moment half a dozen other voices caught up the same refrain. Soon most of the people were circling slowly, snake fashion, about the musicians. Sometimes they faced them, but more often they moved about in a circle, each one close upon the heels of his predecessor. The movement was what might be called a shuffle. It consisted of sort of skip step forward and a skip step back. There was some hip-wiggling, and usually the body was bent slightly forward.

"Ah gan yey ho, ah, gan yey ho," they sang over and over. The musicians also moved about, shuffling and swaying hips.

Participants were more interesting than the dance. All ages from the cradle up to middle life participated. Yes, from the cradle! Two young mothers had their cute little babies fastened to their backs in the usual fashion, supporting the tiny shoulders with a great cloth tightly wrapped around mama's bosom. When mama moved her hips from side to side, baby, who sat just over her buttocks, moved from side to side also. His little head and tiny arms moved too. He was enjoying it, I am sure. Why shouldn't he? He was right at home. I have seen mothers leaning way over when at work, with baby still supported on the back; and when mama performs a necessary function, baby stays right in the cradle.

Then there were about ten little girls and boys of all sizes who formed the tail of the string of people. They arranged themselves stair-step fashion and shuffled and swung hips as cutely as could be. The little girls had a string of beads around their waists; otherwise all were naked. But one little girl had a long flap of cloth hanging behind just to be different.

There were four big girls, two in short skirts only, and two with a wraparound dress up to the armpits.

"Are all those girls married?" I asked my host, who fortunately spoke French.

"Oh, yes."

"Well, what are their ages?"

"Thirteen to seventeen, but a girl cannot get really married until she is fifteen. Arrangements can be made earlier, but they must not have babies before they are fifteen."

The young men provided most of the noise and activity. Some were in white shorts, and with black skins darkened by night this made a very striking color contrast, especially when they wore no shirt. One chap had affixed a long tail to his behind, and when he swung his hips, he brought forth lots of laughter.

The most interesting figure was a little boy of about five shrouded in a pure white head-and-body garment like the rain capes we put on our little American children. The little black face in the midst of all that whiteness—well, I hope you can imagine the picture. And when he rolled his eyes away from the dancers and toward me, boy, that was a sight.

"A shiek of Araby," I commented to my host.

Morning time again, and breakfast, seated beside Jacqueline in the jungle. As usual there were natural-history lessons all around. A big monkey made a hair-raising leap across the road perhaps a hundred feet above me, and others dropped dizzily as much as twenty feet to small branches which bent suddenly down and let them off on other branches. Close about me were the jungle odors. Unfortunately humans have not developed a method of categorizing and recognizing odors as we have in the case of colors, but the smells were most pleasing. Nor were they directly identifiable with the flowers along the road. There were yellow flowers and pink flowers, but my favorite was a deep-purple flower resembling a morning-glory—a gorgeous thing with a yellow-bordered center. And the trees along the way—the big ones, that is—were magnificent. In girth, in the height to the first branches, in overall height, and in general majesty they did not fall far short of our big trees. They had narrow buttresses about their bases. Sometimes the center of the tree was gone—perhaps burned out at the base—but the tree was still well supported by its buttresses. And of course there were beautiful butterflies, and some notorious flies—the vicious tsetse fly in particular. I had been bitten by this chap in every sleeping-sickness area in Africa, and this area was especially bad. His bite hurts, and afterwards it itches like heck. Nor should I forget to comment on the ants. I found out all about them. They came to eat with me three times a day, the big ones over an inch long. Then there were the driver ants that swarmed in myriads across the road in long, dark-brown, crooked channels. The channels are brown because they are filled with brown ants in high-speed traverse. The channel is usually about an inch wide and is enclosed with earth or with a single row of stationary ants.

In French West Africa I passed quite a few coffee plantations, large and small. Sometimes I saw the freshly picked green and red berries, but usually it was the brown beans drying in large, clean flat areas near the center of the villages. I somehow got the impression that the French had developed their colonies more than the British.

In this land of heavy rains I much preferred a thatched roof at night to my little tent. So each evening found me going through a mental debate as to whether to stop at the village I was then passing or risk finding another one before dark. The best procedure, I finally decided, was merely to stop out front and let things take their course. If it developed that someone in the village knew how to speak French, I stopped. If not, I went on. But imagine my surprise on this particular evening to

In central and west Africa I had many miles of lonely road.

find a native who spoke English, and fairly well at that. He had learned during eleven years with the Firestone Company in Liberia, and said I would find no one else in any village along the way that could speak English. He was worried for fear I would go on, but he need not have been disturbed, because I was so tickled to hear my native tongue I would probably have stayed on the road all night just to talk. He made me at home in an empty house beside the road. There always seemed to be an empty house in every village.

Supper was late, but it was worth the delay: plantain fried in palm oil, a big gourd of rice, and a nice gravy. Each of the three was served in a clean gourd, while a fourth gourd held clean drinking water in which was a small gourd ladle. The plantain was excellent and surprisingly sweet.

My host had a little girl of two who was not well. He told me of his experiences with her and of his own experience with native medical dispensers. He had taken her to a white doctor who had prescribed an injection. The father had carried his baby many miles to receive a subsequent injection from a native dispenser. The injection had been badly given and had not spread, remaining in one place.

"And my little girl, she cry and cry, and I know the pain she had. When I was in Liberia, the same thing happen to me. And my arm was so sore I had to hold it like that. [He held up his arm in a half-bent position.] And it was six months before my little girl's arm got better."

Just before I went to sleep that night I happened to glance on the dirt wall of my two-by-four cubicle. The tiny lamp (a string in a bowl of palm oil) disclosed a most enormous spider. Woof! With a native broom I encouraged his passage to a dark corner where I could not see him anyway. Then I lay down content with my courage. But hold! What was that directly above my face on the flat-stick ceiling. A different kind of spider—as big as my extended hand. Well, I encouraged his passing to a point past the edge of my bed, and then blew out the lamp before I could see any more things of interest.

39

In Which We Are Hailed
by the Multitudes

"Guinée Française." A boundary marker by a stream in hilly, forested country of French West Africa informed me that I was entering another province. Shortly thereafter I passed a sleeping-sickness control post, and a native doctor felt of the glands in my neck. Many in the area were ill from the disease, and I recalled with qualms that tsetse flies had bitten me a number of times.

By noon I emerged on a grassy little plateau where I could see some good-sized mountains close at hand on my left. These marked the boundary between French West Africa and Liberia, the only original independent country in the entire continent besides Ethiopia. I paralleled this frontier for some time.

Late that afternoon, just at the beginning of a very steep descent, Jacqueline's brake cable came apart. I relied on the old German front wheel brake to save my life as it had done once before near Barcelona, Spain. But the tire was wet, and there was not enough friction to stop me. The road was badly washed, and I could not see the bottom of the hill. In a split-second decision I decided to take a spill and turned the bicycle across the road. I got the spill all right, but luckily there was no material damage. Only an hour of light remained, and it looked rainy, so I worked at my cable and brake, trying desperately to keep cool and not do anything rash under the excitement and pressure of the moment. When darkness came, I was still without a brake and very troubled as to how I was going to get it fixed. Since there were rumblings of rain about, I decided the only thing to do was to walk back to the last village I had seen, for no telling how far it would be to the next one. But before arriving there, I met that rare article, a truck, loaded to the gills with humanity and all its belongings. It looked as though there simply wasn't any place for me and mine, but of course there's always room for one more. The chap in charge was a young Lebanese, and when we arrived at N'Zerékéré, his Lebanese friends took me in and plied me with hospitality.

On my second evening in N'Zerékéré, I took dinner with five other guests at the home of a Frenchman, M. Drablier. It was one of those French dinners that I like to rave about, and I do not mean just about the food. For in spite of all the food and many courses, the real French dinner is still 50 percent vivacity, and of this 25 percent is sparkling conversation as only the French know how to make it sparkle, and the other 25 percent is gesturing and general tom-foolery. Completely at ease, quite unreserved, the Frenchman (and I mean to include his wife) is really lovable. There is no word that fits him better. You would never dream of using "lovable" in connection with the Englishman—he is too reserved and has an exterior that you are seldom able to pierce. This evening my French enabled me to follow most of the conversation, but I could not make repartee as quickly as I wanted, and came away firmly resolved to spend still more time along the road with my French book. I also looked forward to lecturing young American students to be sure to acquire a basic knowledge of French above all other languages.

As for the food that evening, there was so much I honestly did not know what I was eating half the time. Oh, yes, there was chicken! I remember that because they kept me talking during that course and I was late in finishing. And I remember there was beef because I succumbed to the importunity of a big tiger cat that spent most of the mealtime with her head and paws on my lap.

One-thirty A.M.! At this outlandish hour I got up to join a convoy driving into Liberia. The man in charge, M. Barbey, a Swiss, had a transport service to Monrovia, the capital, and both French and Liberian interests were mixed up in it. Palm kernel was taken from French Guinea to Monrovia for export. Although Barbey was paid in dollars (Liberia uses U.S. money), he was required to send them to Dakar, a capital of French West Africa, for legal exchange into francs.

We arrived at the Liberian border, here marked by the Mani River, at daybreak. Barbey could not take me across, so I exchanged the convoy for Jacqueline and ferried over independently.

Liberia, a country of 40,000 square miles, dates from 1821, when the American Colonization Society sent over a group of Negroes to liberate them from American slavery. The colonists had trouble with the natives but defeated them under the leadership of an American white man, Jehudi Ashmun, considered the founder of the country. A white associate, Dr. Robert Gurley, coined the name Liberia.

Although the United States is usually believed to be the all-time patron saint of Liberia, we did not give it official recognition until 1862, fifteen years after it proclaimed itself an independent republic and was recognized by other great powers. We have played our most important part since 1908, when we rescued the country from collapse by reorganizing its finances and setting up a police force.

In Liberia I noticed that due to American influence it was possible to buy almost everything in the way of food. But prices were high, and since my larder was low I had to pay sixty cents for an eight-ounce tin of cheese and the same for a tin of beef. Perhaps I should have waited because later I was a guest at an American Methodist mission and my pack was replenished there for free.

"What else can we give him, mama?" asked the little girl at the mission after her mother had filled one of my tins with margarine. Then she added, "Oh, I know! We can give him some chocolate bars."

"Oh, no," I protested. "You save those for yourself."

But she went off and soon returned with two Hershey bars.

"I think that is very generous of you, but I will just take half of one and then you can eat the rest," I said.

"Oh, take them," said her mother. "We've got more. We are just able to get them now for the first time."

This was Alabama hospitality way down in Liberia.

I also called on the wife of an American doctor. He held a high post with the Liberian Foundation, an organization working for the country's improvement. There was an American economic mission working in the area also. The doctor's wife, in overall shorts and with cigarette, seemed too cosmopolitan for Africa. She took me on a tour and sent me off with bananas and grapefruit. As we stood at the door a native came up with a skull, which she looked over critically.

"I guess that would be worth fifty cents," she said to him. "But here's a broken tooth. That will be ten cents off, bub."

The native just looked bewildered.

"We buy these occasionally," explained my hostess.

"Where do they come from?"

"Oh, we don't know. A little man pops up with some every once in a while."

When I thanked her for the bananas, she said: "Oh, that's nothing. The way we get bananas around here is to say, 'Boy, what, no bananas!' and presto, he returns with some."

I could well believe this, for my two grapefruit were taken from the hands of a small boy who had just brought them, apparently as a gift.

Liberia is nearly all forested, and this surprised me because it is the principal country of Africa's Grain Coast and presumably there should be extensive fields of wheat or oats. But the Grain Coast, I learned, was so called because of the old trade in the "grains of paradise," or *Amomum* pepper.

Returning from Liberia to N'Zérékéré on Jacqueline gave me a chance to observe the native life I had missed when traveling the road before. The women, I noticed, bunched their hair at the sides in front of the ears, and this often gave them the appearance of having two stiff horns, points down. Hair designs on children's skulls continued to be diverse. I saw one child with a two-inch strip of hair down the middle of the skull, front to back, a quarter-inch fringe running down both sides of the skull just in back of the forehead, and a two-inch diameter circle of hair on either side well toward the back.

The natives had adopted the white man's habit of shaking hands for greeting. Of course the Frenchman also shakes hands on retiring and on arising, on arriving, and on leaving. The native women especially seemed to think that handshaking was quite the thing. But after they had extended their hands, that was the end of it so far as they were concerned. When I took a hand, there was no corresponding pressure. It was like picking up the hand of an unconscious person. When a lady who was only a casual passer-by extended her hand to me—as I was pumping up a tire, for example—I suspected her motives. But this may be unjust, for even respectable native wives with children and husbands en route also presented their hands, after their husbands had interpreted who I was.

Baby bonnets on African natives! Yes, someone had started the fad in the big village of Karema, and how I wished for more film! Little boys, little girls, big boys, big girls, and even young men wore white baby bonnets with a feathery fringe over the forehead. You can imagine the effect, especially since most natives wore a single white dress not reaching to the knees. But I saw one man wearing a baby bonnet with a European summer suit. In addition many of the younger folk had smeared their bodies with white clay, especially about the eyes, with rather gruesome effect.

Natives chewed a red nut called kola nut, a great deal. It was supposed to satisfy hunger, quench thirst, and be a sort of stimulant. I found it rather tasteless.

I shaved by a jungle stream with a luscious belle for company. Her demeanor gave me the impression that she was not unconscious of her charms. She had 'em too. But I really meant to comment on jungle streams. They are not always deep and muddy. Often as not, they are clear and quick-flowing, with a nice sandy bed.

My French friends in N'Zérékéré arranged a ride for me to an American mission along my route and then fixed it up so that a mail truck would pick me up there the following day. While I was at the mission two American women from a mission station in Liberia came for a visit. It had taken them two hours to drive a jeep over a jungle trail to get to the French border and a road.

And what do Americans in Africa talk about when they get together in the bush? I'll give you three guesses. Ice cream, pie, and cake, and how much they are going to eat when they get home. Postal-service inadequacies and red tape, and thefts of imported goods, are usually discussed, and someone is certain to remark, "You sure never really appreciate the United States until you leave it."

The mail truck arranged for by my N'Zérékéré friends turned out to be an old French army wagon without doors or top. The toplessness was O.K. because there was a mountain range to cross and I could enjoy the glorious views. This particular region was supposed to contain the finest scenery in all the vast, vast area of French West Africa, a country three-fifths the size of the United States.

I had been given a letter of introduction to a family by the name of Ratzloff at a place called Macenta. The Ratzloffs were missionaries of the Christian Missionary Alliance and hailed from near Worthington, Minnesota. They dined me nicely on fare which included homemade bread, buns, cinnamon rolls, and cake. Meanwhile I seized the opportunity to learn more about the mission and the natives to which it ministered.

The Macenta mission was founded by a native who had become a Christian. He asked for a missionary, and in a year or so one was sent, but he departed after one and a half years. Then, for eighteen years, the native carried on alone, always asking for a white missionary. So when the Ratzloffs arrived, they received a royal welcome.

The people with whom they worked were called the Toma, and their language had never been reduced to writing. The Ratzloffs were hard at work on that project. However, they spoke the language and told me some things about it and about the fetish worship and superstitions of the people.

The bicycle is an "iron horse"; kerosene is "fire water"; gasoline is "car fire water"; a post office is a "wire house," so called from the wires leading to it. Peace of mind is "peace of liver."

The Toma worship stones or fish, often feeding the fish. Mr. Ratzloff was bathing in a stream one time and a big fish swam right up to him.

Superstitions are many. In one village they let all the bananas rot because they believe that if they eat bananas, no children will be born. Certain other edibles are taboo for certain families; for example, people named Gudawougie will not eat dogs, people named Polawougie will not eat fowl; and so on.

When a boy is eleven or twelve years of age, he is taken out into the bush for initiation into manhood. He is tatooed, given certain instructions, and finally circumcised. Then they have a man who occasionally dresses in full regalia and is known as the bird of death. His calls and appearances are known to the men and the circumcised boys. When he approaches a village, all the women and uncircumcised boys must go inside. If they look out, they will be killed.

Children among the Toma are well spaced. It is considered a disgrace to have a second child in less than four years. There is no particular method of birth control, but the husband takes another wife. The first wife lives in a separate hut with her child, probably quite close by. Indeed, the husband may eat her rice, but he will not live with her.

It is a real trial for a Christian to give up a second wife. In one case where the man did this, he wanted his daughter to go to a Christian school. According to tribal custom or law, the children belonged to the father, so he had the right to send her; but the chief and all the villagers were against him. Mr. Ratzloff considered getting a writ from the government compelling the chief to comply with the law but finally decided not to interfere.

Mr. Ratzloff said, and his wife did not deny that the women were very ready to have relations with the men. Upon questioning, the men admitted that the scanty attire of their associates did affect them.

Sunday, October 24, I put in a long hard day. There were plenty of mountain grades to climb, and I did a great deal of walking. Gradually I was emerging from the continuous jungle. Entire hillsides were now often free of trees except for a scattering of palms. Sometimes I saw natives climbing these to get palm nuts.

By this time I had worked into an area where the native huts were round, as they had been in the Sudan. My abode for the night was one of these, closely surrounded by a dozen neighbors just like it. The floor was raised perhaps two feet above the surrounding land, and there was only one small door. One side of the floor was raised another foot to form the bed, which was further set off by two heavy vertical posts. The floor beyond the headpost had again been raised perhaps two feet, so that when I went to bed, there was a ledge or shelf at my head. A low wall hemmed in my feet at the opposite end. A round, slightly raised place in the center of the floor indicated where a fire might be laid. Over my head was a low ceiling constructed of coarse wickerwork, so I could not see up to the conelike peak of the house. From the sounds, some good-sized four-legged animal occupied my particular attic.

One native had presented me with a new mat to lie on, and another, with a sort of blanket resembling very heavy linen. Since entering the Ivory Coast, I had occasionally noticed this cloth being woven on crude hand looms. These looms are hard to describe; they are operated with foot pedals, and the shuttle is put through by hand.

There were mosquitoes about that night, and I had to use my net. But the African mosquito has a bark worse than his bite. He whines enough to wake you up, but I never received a good itching mosquito bite like we get in the States.

By 10 A.M. the next day I had toiled over the remaining miles to Guékédou, seat of the last "circle" of government I would pass through before entering Sierra Leone. The French *circle* is a division of a province in West Africa and corresponds to our county. At Guékédou, when getting my passport stamped, I could tell by the size of the audience and their questions, that Mullender's article about me in the French African newspapers had been widely read.

From the ferry across the Makona River I ascended my first hill in the

English country of Sierra Leone. The name was given by Pedro de Cintra, Portuguese discoverer in 1462, either because of the "lionlike" thunder on the hilltops or because of their resemblance to the form of a lion. Like Liberia, Sierra Leone was founded as a sanctuary for American Negroes, and four hundred of them, augmented by sixty white women of questionable repute, started the colony in 1786. Tropical diseases exacted a heavy toll in the land, and the term "white man's grave," often generally used for West Africa, was first specifically applied to Sierra Leone. The climate seemed to be particularly hard on governors—there were seventeen in twenty-two years—and Sydney Smith jested that Sierra Leone always had two governors: one just arrived in the colony and one just arrived in England.

While traveling I occasionally felt my throat for signs of sleeping sickness. The missionaries had told me that white people do get it and spoke with personal knowledge of fellow missionaries who had died with it. Toward the end cerebral hemorrhage occurs, and the mind wanders. However, the disease can be cured if noticed in time.

A native who spoke English kept me company on his bicycle one afternoon. He was amazed that I had married as young as twenty-five.

"Here young men don't get married until they're thirty or thirty-two."

"And how old are the girls then?" I asked.

"Oh, they can be seventeen," and after a pause he asked, "How many wives do you have?"

"Only one. In America we have only one wife."

"Oh, here you can have as many wives as you want."

The road, always nicely graveled, became more level and quite attractive. Tall palms and jungle giants and a sort of coarse green grass lined the roadway. The grass was kept trimmed almost like a lawn, largely by the many goats. Not too many trees permitted occasional views. Low areas were somewhat under water and were devoted to raising rice. I decided that Sierra Leone was a very pretty country.

A ride on a truck brought me the acquaintance of a colored chap who had come over from America in 1932. He had the idea of using American hurry-up and enterprise to make money in slow old Africa, but it had not worked out as expected. As we drove along he told me some things about the country and the people.

The government encouraged the people, mostly in vain, to grow rice in the low swampy ground and leave the uphill ground for other crops. Crop rotation is not practiced as we know it. Rice is planted on a plot, and the following year a different plot is selected. After four or five years the natives return to the first plot, clear off the brush again, and plant anew.

Deaths and funeral services for Christians are much the same as at home. However the first or second Sunday after burial is set as the commencement of "regular mourning." Folks wear black to church, and thereafter, every day for a year, wear at least one black item as a token.

When a native wants palm wine, he cuts off the lower branches of the tree first and makes a cut in the trunk. He then inserts a tap and affixes an empty gourd. By night his gourd may be full of palm wine, which is either drunk or used for yeast.

Nuts for palm oil grow in clusters at the level of the lower branches. They are golden brown when ready, and are taken, washed, and boiled. The oil comes to the top and is skimmed off. This is the palm oil used by the natives for cooking and in their lamps. However there is also kernel oil, and for this the nuts are dried and then broken. Inside is the famous commercial product, palm kernel, which is shipped to other countries, where presses extract the kernel oil.

We sidetracked to visit a chromite mine—a surface working high on a mountainside. The view seemed to include half of Sierra Leone. Chromite, which is part chromium, is used in steel hardening and for refractory bricks.

Another albino! He was the head man at a Sierra Leone ferry, and I had the opportunity to examine him closely. An albino is a "pigmentless individual of a pigmented race." The pigment is composed of minute granules of an ingredient called melanin, really sepia in color, but which is in masses and absorbs the light so completely as to appear black. But our ferryman was lighter than any Swede you ever saw. His eyebrows were light yellow, and his complexion was red and white. He had a towel around his shoulders and used it to wipe the perspiration from his face and neck. To me his nostrils seemed less thick than is usual with the African, but his mouth was certainly that of a native. We discussed his albinism, and he said the worst thing about it was that he suffered with the heat much more than his associates.

It was nearly dark that evening when I called for my passport stamp at the last Sierra Leone district commissioner's. He invited me to stay to dinner, and two English ex-service men showed up a little later. All four of us, I judged, were in our early thirties. English conversation, as usual, was careful and precise. Still, there was some good-natured, rival area bantering and quite a bit of gossip. It is hard to decide whether you like an Englishman or not. I found myself observing and comparing. It seemed to me it would take a long time to build up a real friendship with an Englishman.

Lucky me, you say, to come out of the jungle at six in the evening and get all these invitations to dinner prepared for a white man's table. But wait, all is not gold that glitters. These dinners were almost invariably late, and I had yet to eat a meal that was worth waiting for. When a man has pedaled a bicycle up hill and down dale for five consecutive hours, he is hungry! Make no mistake about that. Beyond time for a good wash he has no patience to brook delays for baths, drinks, and idle chitchat. He wants to eat!

But inflict on such a man the English colonial regimen. He is given a chance to wash but then is invited to have drinks in the parlor. Now he has already drunk a couple quarts of water on the road, as required to balance his losses by perspiration, and the very thought of more liquid—even water—is repugnant to him. But he accepts the rum or whatever to be sociable and sits an hour or two with his stomach growling and aching at this desecration of its emptiness.

At about 7:30 your thoughtful host orders a bath prepared for you. It makes no difference that you may have just had a bath the night before and would much prefer to pass the time by reading or talking. One might take another bath with better grace if he felt the host was honestly worried about keeping his sheets clean; but you know the boys will wash the sheets anyway. Resignedly you rush through the bath as fast as possible and return to the living room thinking that now, surely, you will eat.

But no, you are asked to sit down and are given another drink. There is more conversation while you inwardly fume. Hasn't the English colonial official ever heard the philosopher's remark about conversation profiting more from a full stomach than an empty one. And hold! What is that your host is shouting? Oh, no, it can't be!

"Buoy! Next bawth!"

Yes, sir. Each one of those three blokes is going to have a bath, and each one is going to take his sweet time about it. Your stomach collapses in sheer horror at the thought and pains you no more. You scrootch deeper into the big easy chair and mutter into your beard how you should have spent the night in the jungle again and then your stomach would be full and you would already be in bed.

Around ten o'clock dinner is at last announced. Your appetite, long since dead, is aroused by soup and morsels of chicken. But one last ignominy is in store for your benighted stomach. An African chicken is only about the size of a small American pullet, and there are four men to share it. Your host stands at the sideboard and carves in utter silence, as well he might, though of course it's only his English reserve. And so at last around 11 P.M. you carry your again unhappy stomach to the living room to be plagued by coffee.

I left Sierra Leone the next forenoon, appropriately by ferry. In 352 miles of Sierra Leone travel I had to use ferries no less than thirteen times, an average of one every 27 miles. What an opportunity for an American bridge builder!

Under the French tricolor once again, I found that some French officials can be as fussy about passport stamps as the British. In this circle they insisted at three different places on stamping my passport, in contrast to other parts of French West Africa where they had not been concerned at all. But for this slight nuisance I was well recompensed.

On the road I passed a heavyset colored policeman on a light motorcycle, resplendent in a big grin, brilliant red fez, light khaki coat and shorts, belt, buckles, straps, white knee socks, and shoes. He was parked beside the road and I didn't associate him with my arrival at all. So I was quite surprised when I approached a little village a mile or so further and found the inhabitants—nearly all adults—lining both sides of the road. This looked funny. Could they be there to see me? No! Probably some official. Still the commandant knew I was coming and perhaps he had read the article on my travels in the French papers. Sure enough, as I drew between the two lines of people, all raised their hands and started clapping. Of course I was as pleased as punch, and though it was on the upslope of a hill, I stopped for acknowledgment of their salute. The leader was well dressed with a white full-length underdress and a sleeveless full-length overcape of blue material bearing a black pin stripe. On his head was a short red fez with tassel. He gave me a long encomium in faultless French, and I impromptued a reply in the same language.

Shortly afterward the motorcycle cop overtook me, beaming jovially. I finally got it through my head that the commandant at Forecariah was waiting lunch for me and that the town was close by. Just by chance I was late on my meal schedule that day—the first time in months—and so I had not eaten even though it was 1:30 P.M. Ah, well! A free dinner and a French one at that. This was different.

When we entered the town, people lined the street. The cop was a little ahead of me, and all were clapping. And so I smiled at this group and that, waved and nodded, trying to look at everyone. Some were on their verandas or steps, some were hurrying up side streets. Oh, boy, I thought, me and Lindbergh and wrong-way Corrigan! (I had seen Corrigan on his escorted ride around Chicago and recalled it at once.) Yes, sir, on this day Rosdail came into his own! By George, one woman even had a French flag on a long pole that she waved out in front of me.

The commandant had two other guests and had been compelled to start lunch. But he came out on the steps with a friendly glad hand, showed me the place to wash and welcomed me to the table. One of his guests was an elderly French artist touring throughout the A.O.F. for subject material. He painted landscapes, fruit, women. The other guest was a young local planter who raised banánas.

"Il est très riche," said the commandant.

"Oh, naturellement," I replied, and we all had a good laugh.

Our meal had all the usual French vivacity. What a contrast to my dinner with the three Englishmen—the English commandant and his two guests—only the night before! At that affair no one questioned anyone else on anything relative to the other's life. It simply was not done. But we four at the French table knew each other's history and future plans within the half-hour. Moreover, we knew the extent of each other's families and had shown each other pictures of the same. The artist's son was a fencer, and his snapshot showed him in action. It also developed that the artist was a recent grandfather, and we congratulated him. He thought the pictures of my children were exceptionally well done. Anyhow, we all had a good time—laughter, gay sallies, and comradeship. After dinner we retired to the living room for conversation and champagne—the only drink that does not taste like bad medicine, in my estimation.

The commandant pressed me to stay for a day, but I declined on the excuse of time. He then got into his car and personally escorted me to the ferry at the edge of town. Here he secured a boat in a hurry and gave instructions to the head ferryman to tell any truck coming along to stop and pick me up.

A Lebanese planter did pick me up later on, and I passed the night with him. He was a really intelligent and sympathetic chap with a colored wife and three children. The two oldest were away at a Negro school, but the youngest was at home and sat at table with us. He was the apple of his father's eye, and that proud parent displayed great patience in instructing his son in certain French words.

One of the planter's crops was bananas—the species *sinensis*. It takes six and one-half months for the tree to reach maturity and eighty or ninety days more for the fruit to grow and mature. When new trees are wanted, the old are cut down and the stump sprouts are transplanted. My French was not technical enough to set down in writing all he told me about leaves and planting.

My road the next morning lay between a high but not continuous escarpment and the sea far to the south. This escarpment was quite inspiring. From a long, steep wooded slope sprang a white cliff to a further height of several hundred feet. It resembled Knife Edge at Mesa Verde National Park. The escarpment sometimes took the shape of a giant amphitheater, similar to that in the Colorado National Monument. Near the road were palm trees, and the trees of the many banana plantings.

Streams in this land were quite clear, even when sluggish—an unusual condition. The water was so clear you could see to the bottom in depths which sometimes appeared a good ten feet. Often, long grass nearly filled the stream with the rich green color that one can find nowhere else. Other streams had beds of gravel or boulders, and both kinds were very attractive. There were still patches of jungle about, and where the stream left the road, if it was not too big, the trees would completely cover it. Long lianas, perhaps one or two inches in diameter, sometimes formed a wide swing just above the water.

There were a number of good-looking women in this area with figures quite the Hollywood type. But these were the exception. I sometimes saw them washing clothes in the clear streams.

At dark I received a nice welcome at a small village, and the paramount chief gave me his home for the night. No one spoke French, but fortunately a visitor from atop the escarpment spoke perfect French. He was tall and wore a long blue dress, sandals, and a short fez of dark material with a yellow embroidery band near the top. He was forty-four and had seen four years of service with the French army.

When I was offered food, I spoke of payment.

"Monsieur," said my interpreter in French, "here the white man and the black man are like this," and he clasped his hands together. "You need not pay."

My host brought two eggs, a bowl of peanuts boiled with the hulls on, an enormous dish of rice, and a dish of fish in pimento and palm-oil sauce. The fish looked like they had been baked without cleaning, but I made out a good meal.

Through the visitor-interpreter I offered thanks for these gifts and for the fine bed.

"Monsieur, we are Mussulmen," he said simply.

This, he felt, was quite sufficient to explain that whatever a Mohammedan had, it was at the complete service of the stranger. Can't you just see an American giving up his bed or his whole house to a stranger who could not speak a word of his language? Or giving it up to one who knew his language but spoke with a foreign accent? Can you imagine it? He probably would not even give him something to eat at the back door. However, the trouble is not that Christianity is inferior to Mohammedanism; it is just the way we practice it.

The chief's house was a nice one, and I noticed that in general the natives in the area were better housed and more prosperous than any I had seen since central Nigeria. The chief, as usual in this region, lived some little distance from the rest of the village. His was a sort of house within a house—the outer one oval in shape and the inner one square. Or it might be better described as a small square house completely covered by an oval-roofed porch, nearly enclosed with high walls and broad pillars. The bed, table, and chairs were located in the inner sanctum. On my bed I had pillows, a mattress with a red and white coverlet, and a mosquito net. Native luxury!

40

Romance and a Lost Trail

The following afternoon I skirted the tidal extremity of a number of streams. It was low tide, and judging from the height of the mud on stones and banks, the tide must approach in height that of the Bay of Fundy. I sat out a big rainstorm in a rude roadside shelter with only a native woman for company. The road was atrocious because the ascents and descents to cross the streams were ruts filled with sharp rocks and coarse, deep gravel. The crude bridges were of poles laid lengthwise, often loose and strayed.

This was the country of the Baga and the Susu peoples. The Baga have the more negroid features and work scars into their skin. Polygamy is allowed, but there are certain requirements. The brothers of the husband must take his wife's sisters in marriage whether they are good-looking or not. When a man dies, his younger brother or nephew must marry his widow. The first wife chosen, if there is more than one, has the preferred standing in the village, and property is inherited through the women rather than the men. After death a man's house and some of his personal possessions are burned. The Baga believe that plants, stones, and the like have a conscious life, and fetishism is part of their religion.

Dark found me at a little village opposite a native mosque—only a roof over a concrete floor with perhaps a two-foot wall supporting most of it. These structures are round or oblong in shape and have a dais at one side or end. I saw one mosque where the thatching came clear to the ground and the only door was a rectangular hole two feet high, no doubt to eliminate the danger of nonreverent entry.

The mosque and the oval friendly faces of the villagers gave evidence that the people were Susus, of the great Mandingan race. Though fetishism and spirit worship have not disappeared, the Susus are generally more advanced than other tribes in this part of Africa. The members of a family live close together within the village, and marriage between cousins is common. Polygamy is practiced, but inheritance is in the male line.

The chief of the village was absent, but a young chap educated at a Catholic mission took care of me. He and his friends put me in a tiny room, one of several surrounding the inner sanctum of a large house. There was a bed but not much room for anything else. We squeezed in the bike and then two chairs so that I might write. Supper consisted of rice and the most excellent fish, cooked to a nicety in palm oil. For the first time in any native village I was given regular bread. The meal was good, and I expressed my appreciation. Afterward the cook herself showed up to receive my thanks. She took special pains to arrange and tie the mat which fell from the ceiling to cover my short doorway. I did not suspect any ulterior motives at this time. She was attractively dressed and had an intelligent face and flashing eye.

Later on my cook returned with the young host-interpreter and offered me chicken and rice for the morning. This was to be a gift if I would return a gift; but I told them I had only money. After some palaver they set a price of thirty or forty francs, a bargain considering the price of canned stuff. Behind the girl's back my handsome interpreter indicated by laying two fingers side by side that what she really wanted was to sleep with me. I laughed and said I had a wife at home and two children in the bargain. Both left at this, but after a little palaver outside the interpreter popped back with the news she would pass the night with me for 700 francs ($3.50). His eyes shone, and his grin plainly told me he was enjoying his role. He had such a predilection for the idea that I naturally would want a companion for the night that my statement of a wife at home had had no effect; or perhaps in this land of many wives he didn't consider it mattered. I now drove it home to him that my religion prohibited being untrue to my wife. He got the idea and departed.

I now expected a big frost, and no chicken and rice the following morning. But when I arose, both were in process of preparation.

The sun was very hot, and by noon I was unusually tired. So I joined the sleepy noonday picture of the house nearest the road in a tiny village.

There was an empty chair on the dirt veranda, well shaded by the low overhang of the steep round roof. Near the chair and seated on one leg was a scholar in khaki shirt and shorts, barefooted, and shaven-headed. He was copying Arabic with ink and heavy pen, using for a table a polished board bearing Arabic characters. Sheets of paper he had finished were kept in a little notebook with a goatskin cover. A youth lazed on the other end of the porch, reclining in a dirty-looking skin hammock. Near him was one of the big round pots or jugs of water I had been observing along the road for the benefit of passers-by. Incidentally, this was a custom I had not noticed since Egypt, and it betokened a return to Mohammedan lands. Although in this instance the pot rested on the ground, I usually saw them on a worn-out mortar—the vase-shaped tree-trunk affair in which they hammer grain. The jugs had a cover of wood and a can or half-gourd on top to drink from.

With the scholar's consent I sank gratefully into the chair, where I dozed for half an hour.

When it was time to eat, I asked for a table. The scholar entered the house and after several minutes, during which I could see him removing sundry articles and quantities of dust, he emerged with a rickety affair to answer my purpose. Through the door I could also see a bed with a mosquito netting, dusty and aged.

While eating I saw a woman come up to turn the grains of rice spread out to dry in the sunshine near the porch. As she leaned over, her pendulous breasts, at least a foot long, flapped against her arms and belly. She gathered some rice from the mat and put it in an enormous bowl. Nearby were a naked little boy and a little girl. The girl wore a tiny skirt in addition to the customary three strings of red, white, and purple beads. The skirt was fashioned with four pieces of cloth about five inches wide, the two over the hips being several inches shorter than the other two, which came nearly to her knees. One eye was swelled completely shut, the other partly so. For a remedy, yellowish-gray mud had been put all over her face above the level of the mouth, and a narrow reed band had been placed around her head. The little tyke was not more than four years old. So here, with the scholar, were ignorance and learning contrasted.

Passers-by were greeted by the scholar just as our American forebears used to do from their front porches. The continued return of salutations showed the Mohammedan influence.

My route improved somewhat on this day. There were very long level stretches, slightly sandy, and hemmed in by grass taller than my head. On one such stretch I overtook *her!*

She was positively the prettiest, most charming girl I had seen in 22,000 miles of African travel. I suppose she was eighteen or thereabouts. Her face was as round as a rose, her lips and nostrils were as thin and sweet as any American girl's of the same age, her breasts were as perfect in every respect as any pretty girl could have wished. She had slender hips and slender ankles, the ankles visible below a long skirt with a pattern of big white squares. On her head she carried a big gourd bowl in which was a smaller bowl containing some kind of nut.

My camera startled her at first, and she fled a few steps down the trail. All I had to halt her was my smile and a gesture or two. I also used the French word *photographie* and then shortened it to *photo*. This registered, and she took a few steps in my direction. But on account of the sun I wanted her to pass me a little. This she refused to do, and no amount of persuasion—even the offer of money—would cause her to forfeit her opportunity for a quick escape down the road. Perhaps she knew a wolf when she saw one. But she did come closer. Luck was with me, and the sun went under a cloud. I got all set. She had started nervously to hull and eat nuts, totally unconscious, I am sure, of what she was doing. When I was ready to snap the picture, her lovely smile disappeared. But I had learned my lesson from previous picture-taking and indicated that the smile was to remain. To be sure that it did, I looked at her while snapping.

I had been feeling a little tired of it all and a bit despondent. This encounter was just the romantic medicine I needed.

At the next town, Boké, I visited the native hospital to have the sores on my lower legs dressed. They may have been started by scratching and were loath to heal, perhaps due to a lowered resistance after eighteen months of travel. But I am more inclined to attribute it to continual sweating and the chafing of my overalls. In this humid hot climate I was almost tempted to buy shorts. But when a tsetse fly bit my exposed ankles I was glad I did not have to fight them off legs as well. The native doctor had his "dresser" fix me up, and I bore away with me some gauze and adhesive tape, so rare in this part of Africa. My query as to fee was met with, "Nothing at all. Just think of me after you arrive in America."

Leaving Boké, I took a pirogue across a river and commenced a long trek to the frontier of Portuguese Guinea. I had no map, but at one time a dry-season route for trucks had been cleared. This had been left to revert to its natural state, and boy, had it reverted!

At first I was able to ride because the natives had made a trail. But the grass was higher than my head and the trail usually hidden from view. Once dismounted I was helpless until I could reach an open space where I could mount again. There were streams and low marshy places to cross. At the first, a man bathing carried me over and then returned for Jacqueline. She was too heavy for carrying but could be wheeled, although it was difficult for anyone not used to the balance of her weight. At the second crossing there was no one in sight but a young mother who came and moved stones to make me a walk, a job I couldn't do because there was no place to lean Jacqueline. I didn't want to wade because of my fresh bandages. If there hadn't been a wee baby on mama's back, I might have been tempted to ask for a ride myself. When mama was arranging the stones, poor baby stood almost on his head. In getting across I used mama's shoulder for balancing. At the third crossing I came to an impasse where I was clinging to Jacqueline and trying to keep my feet dry by stepping on clumps of grass. Two men threw down their head burdens and came to my rescue.

Apart from these water hazards, the road grew worse and worse. The two faint tracks descended and crossed an open field of high ripe grass, at the other side absolutely disappearing in a seemingly impenetrable wall. There was nothing for me to do but to battle on through. One of the original two tracks could be sensed underfoot—or even seen when I got down on my hands and knees and hunted. Even with a bike one can get through grass nine feet high if it is standing up nice and straight, but most of this had lodged. I worked for a couple hours fighting my way through, sweat running off me in streams. At some places I tried to ride, but the grass and weeds would wrap around the pedals and throw me off.

I had been on trails where a weed or grass stem would slap my face and it would be necessary to watch out for the next one. But now there was a constant tattoo of them, and my eyes were closed to the merest slits. These grasses were all ripe and showered me with seeds, some of which had sharp points and beards approximately four inches long. They even got through my overalls, while the lighter seeds worked inside my undershirt. (I hadn't worn a shirt for months.) With the sweat, and the vicious tsetse flies, my misery was complete. But no, not quite! Even though it was four o'clock in the afternoon, the sun had not yet dried out the lower parts of the tangle and I was soaked with water from the grass and weeds.

I began to think I was lost. Surely no road could be so bad and untraversed as this. But I recalled other times when I had thought myself lost: in the Norwegian mountains and in the Australian bush. In the first instance I kept on; in the second I turned around and later found I should have persevered. So now I continued.

Crossing an open area where the golden grass was only waist high, I heard a shout, so far away that I could not see the native. All I could do was to point ahead and shout, "Sansalé?" the name of a village on the frontier. There was an answer of some kind, but I didn't even know the native word for yes. I repeated the question but got silence. Then I shouted, "Sansalé *oui*," and "Sansalé, *non?*" This netted no response. After two or three more tries I started on. Again I was arrested by a shout from the same quarter. I repeated my interrogations. No result. Naught to do but go on.

Not long afterward I descended a hill to a stream. Just across the bridge a native trail turned off to the left—cleared and, to me, looking like a boulevard. But dead ahead on the truck trail was a solid wall of seven-foot weeds, through which I probably should continue. Nearby a native girl was getting water. "Sansalé?" I questioned, pointing alternately over the weeds and then along the trail. She waved her hand along the trail up a steep hill and started to ascend. I tried to get her to stop, but she just turned enough to smile. For a minute I was panicky. The first human being I had seen in ages was about to leave me.

"Wait! Don't leave me!" I implored, even forgetting to speak French.

I hurriedly ascended the hill after her, bicycle and all. And on the hill, praise heaven, were a native village and a man who spoke a little French. He soon assured me that I was on the route and took me to where the road, having curved around the base of the hill, could again be followed.

Farther on I spent the night in a native hut beside the road. For the first time in my African experience the women spent a social evening in the same room as the men. We had a fire of several large slow-burning pieces of wood at one side, although cooking was done in a separate shelter. Nearly over the fire was a cord hammock and on the opposite side of the hut a crude bed. When I eventually sought rest on the bed, I put my clothes and shoes in the hammock to dry.

The day dawned and I departed, dressed in my waterproof leggings for the usual heavy dew. I missed the overshoes I had lost in Uganda. The road had short intervals where it had been cleared, detouring usually near and into a village. I unknowingly detoured through two of these. In recovering the road from the second I had a little experience I wouldn't care to repeat. In many places my trail had been under water but with a good gravelly bottom. Thus I was in the habit of riding in water often to the depth of the lowest pedal. I now entered one of these traverses, although a turn in the trail kept me from seeing the end. When I rounded this turn in six inches of water and with three feet of it on either side of me, what should I find but a young river flowing rapidly and heaven alone knew how deep! On the opposite shore the trail continued. When one is already struggling—and I do mean struggling—in low gear through water and coarse gravel, there is no time to stop and make decisions. The very instinct of self-preservation keeps one going. If you lose motion, you lose balance and over you go into the water, passport, camera, papers, and all. So I pushed deeper and deeper. Finally my shoes and ankles were under water at each stroke. If there had been boulders, they might have twisted and thrown me, but there weren't. Still, as I was about to emerge my wheels passed within inches of a sudden drop into a hole two or three feet deep. It raised the hair on my head for a minute. Would I have been better off on the truck trail with all its weeds? I shall never know.

Then it happened! Toward noon I suddenly hit a submerged stump—submerged under the weeds, that is. My pedal arm—a right solid piece of metal—was bent and twisted to such an angle I could hardly put my foot on it. I had no wrench big enough for straightening, and it seemed ages since I had seen any rocks. But I struggled along until I came to some. The pedal pin wouldn't drive out, so I had to unpack and lay the bike down while I hammered the arm back in position. I sweat bucketfuls. Finally the pedal was navigable, though still on an angle. I felt I had pulled a Flood and Wilson. Meanwhile the vicious tsetse flies made things interesting. Sleeping sickness, here I come!

Speaking of pests, I now know definitely what it is to have ants in your pants, and African ants at that. Needing water, I stopped after crossing a long bridge over a clear, deep, swiftly flowing stream. Searching for means to reach the water, I noticed a great log had fallen or been placed completely across the river just below the bridge. With an eye out for snakes, spiders, and whatnot, I moved cautiously out to the middle of the stream where the log sank low enough for me to reach the water with my canteen. The log was slippery with moisture, and I was very careful, keeping one hand on the bridge when I could. Then I crouched and filled my canteen, holding it by cork and string as usual. I noticed ants on the log and saw one or two run over my shoe—yes, even felt one bite. And almost before my canteen was full, I felt bites in several places on my legs. Since only my shoes were in contact with the log I didn't see how I could have acquired very many ants. But before I could walk the log back to shore, they were biting me in a hundred places from the waist down. I was on fire. In no time they were on my shoulders. For the next few minutes I was a very busy man. I pinched ants to death, first here, then there, as the pain moved me—and it moved me pretty fast. They were all standing on their heads to get in a good bite before their demise. I had to shed nearly all my clothes before I got 'em all killed.

I ate lunch at noon on the banks of a little stream where, if I had been so immodest as to look, I could have watched a native woman doing her washing à la nude. On leaving, a sudden push on the pedal broke the weakened grip of the threads, and from then on I put in an afternoon of the most futile and exasperating efforts to make the pedal stay on. I tried canvas, wire, and whatnot. It would stay from a few strokes to a quarter of a mile. And all of these devisings were accomplished to the usual tune of streaming sweat, eight-foot grass and weeds, millions of seeds, and tsetse flies. The flies are underhanded cusses. They rarely attack from above, and as a rule I didn't worry about my shoulders. Only my ankles, or the undersides of my chin, arms, or hands!

To add to my modest troubles my front tire went flat. This would ordinarily have been fixed in a jiffy, but that durn weed seed had gotten into the valve and was so tough I couldn't even pull it out with the pliers. Fortunately I had another valve.

Three natives passed me as I was finishing. A bit later I descended a long hill, where water was running in the track, and came to a great river. Here the three natives were waiting for a boat they had hailed. The company of these humans on the bank of this lonely river barrier made me stop, in spite of all the trouble I was having, to count my blessings. For one thing the country was fairly level; and best of all there was no rain. I shuddered to think of struggling through that forest of grass in the face of an approaching rainstorm. And if I had come to this broad river alone, with no pedal, and with no boat in sight, I would have been sunk in the depths for sure.

After quite a wait a chap came to the pirogue on the other side of the river. He was so far away as to be hardly distinguishable, and it was a long, long time before he had paddled upstream and then across to our side. By that time a fourth native had shown up to be taken across.

Though facing the prospect of walking through fifteen miles of weeds, I was moved by the scene surrounding me. How powerfully the river moved! How wide! How very, very deep! It put our own Mississippi in the shade. Yet I had never heard of it before, and it was not even numbered among the great rivers of Africa. In fact, my map of Africa didn't even show it. How symbolic this was of the vastness of the Dark Continent. And there we were—six puny specks in a tiny boat lost on the bosom of the water. On either side of us was a black rim of trees. And down the river the sun sank darkly behind a black rim of cloud. What a scene it all made: the two straight banks of trees, the somber, powerful flood, the blood-red sun, sunk too low to brighten the water, and four silent men sitting in a canoe with two more quietly rowing, one standing, the other sitting!

Once across we climbed the muddy slope of the unused road. The river had recently been ten or twelve feet higher judging from the mud. The ferryman offered me accommodations for the night, and the village chief brought a lamp for me to use when writing. The natives who had crossed with me had a separate hut and found a small poisonous snake inside. But it was the heat rather than the fear of snakes which made me abandon my host's house and bed for my own sleeping bag in open air. This made me conscious of another travel blessing—practically no mosquitoes.

This was a land inhabited by the Tendas, a people with a rather different type of organization. Each village is a separate unit, religiously and politically, and is one of a confederation. But the people are also divided into groups according to age, and the women are organized into societies. There are three age groups with a chief over each one, then a sort of commissioner over all of them, and he is responsible to the paramount chief. Marriage between close relatives is not allowed, but second cousins may marry and often do. Mother's consent is essential for any marriage. In figuring succession the maternal line is the important one.

The next morning I was chagrined to find that the native travelers were on the road before me. I set out soon after with every intention of walking the remaining distance to Sansalé, since the pedal now refused to stay on at all. But I found I could ride Jacqueline with only one pedal. It was difficult, but with a little concentration it could be managed. Of course, when my one good pedal would get tangled up in the weeds I had less chance of fighting through. But by midmorning I was in the native village of Sansalé.

Beyond were two swampy stretches. These I did not mind because my feet were continually soaked anyway. Then another stretch of eight-foot grass and weeds, mostly weeds this time. But at last, all of a sudden, I emerged from the weeds onto a wide road, not too old, where there was not a blade of grass or weed of any description. I burst out from this wall of eight-foot weeds so suddenly that my last push on even the one pedal carried me two miles down the road in the clear before I could stop. I then placed my two feet on actual dry earth and took my first grass-seed-free, fly-free, clear breath in several days.

There was no doubt about the demarcation of the Portuguese Guinean frontier!

41

Tsetse Flies and Airplanes

Jacqueline! My beloved Jacqueline was still broken. True, I had found a road at the Portuguese Guinea frontier, but how could it be put to any real use when Jacqueline was minus a pedal?

But somehow we staggered into a place called Gadamael, one of the most lonesome posts I have known white men to occupy. Off the road and on the banks of a lonely river, there were two "civilized" houses and three or four native houses. That was Gadamael!

In the house nearest the river lived two young Lebanese, born in Africa of mixed white, though predominantly Lebanese, parents. Now they were starting families of their own. They made me welcome, fed me, and then took me up the hill to the smith.

The village smithy, African style! On the bare dirt under a tree, crosslegged, sat a very old black man with a short beard. No American-equipped smithy, this, even judged by early pioneering days. Two crude hammers, a tong or two, a big mass of iron for an anvil, and a box with pieces of iron in it—this was his list of auxiliaries. His main piece of equipment was a two-pouch bellows. The top parts of these were of goatskin, and when he inserted his hands into the tops and raised and lowered them alternately, the wind came out of a sort of funnel leading from the bottoms. The air fanned the flame into a tiny pile of coals. It has always been a mystery to me how a smith can get so much out of so few coals.

We commenced Operation Jacqueline. The whole population watched and gave advice. We heated the arm, inserted the pedal, and hammered the arm around it. When the job was finished I made a short trial run and discovered the arm moved slightly. But everyone had done his best, and though I hinted to the Lebanese that it ought to be done over, I got no support. I did not press the matter but felt sure that the pedal would be off again within three kilometers. I was wrong! It never came off.

Just at dark that night I came to a little cluster of huts called Gam Dimbel. No one spoke Portuguese, French, or English, but the sign language is always effective. I had a bath, and one of the women washed my underclothes. There was no lamp, but I wrote in the open by candlelight. When I insisted on sleeping outside under a little round roof used for a cookhouse and gathering place, the women came with small whisk brooms and swept the floor clean. It was hard for them to understand why I would not sleep inside, but honestly, it was so hot I would not have slept a wink. The mosquitoes woke me up around midnight, and I had to fix my net.

The first three hours the next morning were a nightmare that I hate to think about. Gooseflesh breaks out all over me when I do. There was a long uncleared section of the road, and brother, it was as bad as the French Guinea route to Sansalé had been. Only here I was unlucky enough to catch a morning after a day when it should have rained but didn't, and all the rain had come down as dew. The ten-foot grass dripped miserably, and I blasted through it like a meteor with my new pedal. The grass beat at my face so much that sometimes I could not open my eyes at all except for the merest of slits. And the water ran off my face, or was beaten off, and even got into my mouth. I was soon soaked even with my rain leggings, and as for grass seed, my bare arms and shoulders were just plastered with it. I also had the dear, dear tsetse fly to contend with. Honestly, he is fierce! If a man had told me there was a fork in the road ahead and down one branch were two hungry lions, and down the other two hungry tsetse flies, I would have taken the road with the lions. The tsetse flies were really vicious and were the worst when I hit stretches of grass only three feet high. Thus if I did not have weeds in my face, I had to fight the tsetse flies. If I raised one hand from the handlebar on the suspicion that there was a tsetse fly under the wrist —and there was—and just at that instant his bite registered, the sudden pain drew my other hand from the handlebars without any hesitation, even though it almost certainly meant a spill.

I noticed that even on cleared roads there were plenty of these tsetse flies. When I stopped, a swarm of them were onto me like savages. My first concern was my ankles, but I had only a second to scratch off a pant clasp so that my pant leg would drop and give protection, because by that time I had to tear the flies from my face. Then a snatch at the other clasp and three minutes of waving my handkerchief about my face before I could get a drink of water from my bottle, or whatever else I had stopped for.

About one o'clock I arrived at a place called Buba and was dragged off the street by a servant at the only real residence in town. Here I was welcomed by the owner, a Portuguese doctor, and his wife, and the wife of the *chef de post*, whose husband was then absent. The doctor gave me a much needed map of the country and a very substantial dinner. We enjoyed the dinner in solid comfort because of one of the servants stood outside the room pulling a rope which moved an enormous fan just over the table.

The doctor's specialty was tsetse flies and sleeping sickness. But not one tsetse fly did I encounter in the town. He should have been with me that morning or again in the afternoon. I would have shown him a few things about the pests. Sometimes there were fifty riding along on the back of my pack. When I stopped I of course brought my leg over the pack, and this stirred 'em up to take delicious chunks out of me. It was a long time before I discovered why there were so many about me when I stopped. Here the buggers were getting a free ride. How they did like to bite me on the underside of my fingers or under my chin! Tsetse flies are about five times as big as a housefly.

At dusk there was a river to ford. The village chief on my side of it was a racketeer preying on travelers just as some villages had speed traps in the Chicago vicinity until the automobile clubs got busy. The *chef* of the canton was about, and he was more sensible as to charges but apparently had no power in the matter of service. This money-grasping chief wanted fifty escudos to row me about one and a half miles to a point very near X'tole, a town where he said there were Europeans. But he did not want to leave until morning. The alternative was a short canoe trip across the river and porters to carry my stuff through water hip deep (I was told). But this would cost only thirty escudos. It was fast growing dark, and no one was in a hurry except me. They wanted me to stay in their village for the night as a curiosity anyway. I took the thirty-escudo ride, and old Shylock could not get his hands on the money fast enough. I wanted to pay half at either end, but it was only his boys who were going with me, it seemed, so I had to pay him all.

It was quite dark when we arrived at the other side of the river. Then we started out across a huge rice field, following little narrow paths that went at right angles every three rods or so. While there was no hip-deep water, we walked on very narrow ridges with water on either side. It was true that I could not have negotiated it alone, for one could not walk on the ridge and wheel the bike at the same time. Sometimes the ridge almost failed, and I slipped toward the water. At one place a tree was squarely in the path, and it took some negotiating even empty handed, as I was. The boys were also necessary as guides because it was difficult to find paths that would lead us out where we wanted to go. Even the chap in advance became confused on two occasions.

This was another one of those really memorable experiences of travel! There we were, four silent figures threading an African rice field by moonlight! Picture it! First was the head guide with my bedroll and two shopping bags. Then myself, followed by a boy with my saddle bags on his head. The man with Jacqueline on his shoulder brought up the rear.

We at last reached high ground and soon arrived at a native village only two kilometers from X'tole. Here my boys turned back. It was too dark to negotiate any more native trails alone, so I spent the night in the village.

I had trouble with the trail the next morning. There were two different and difficult water crossings, but fortunately I overtook a native who volunteered to help me. At one crossing we had to balance the bike on a narrow log over deep water and make a transfer to another log in mid-stream.

From X'tole to Bambadinca I was given a ride. The little old truck was the kind rural American chicken buyers used in the middle twenties, but it ran excellently and I began to wonder if Portuguese Guinean cars were in better shape than those elsewhere. But this would be hard to say, for I only saw about a half dozen in the whole country.

Portuguese and Lebanese traders did much less business than their brother merchants in the French and English possessions. Their towns were sleepy and deserted. But they treated me royally and wanted me to stay awhile and keep them company. It has always seemed to me that the Portuguese through long years of neutrality really practice the golden rule. Or perhaps it is because they practice the golden rule that they have had long years of neutrality.

I should say something about the animals. On my first afternoon in the country I was startled to see a big black gorilla cross the road about thirty feet ahead of me. Further along a herd of brown baboons crossed the road. I saw several of these herds. One crossed just behind me and sat there barking at me to come back and fight, and on another occasion a bunch barked their defiance from the treetops. There were all kinds of monkeys, but gray monkeys and golden-brown monkeys seemed to be in the majority. And the way these chaps traveled in the treetops took my breath away. They will drop from a branch one hundred feet up onto a tree only about sixty feet tall, catching a small branch. I have seen one of these branches give downward from five to ten feet with their weight, but before it could bounce back upward the monks had climbed to stouter branches. Along the road I also saw a small tailless antelope, a squirrel that scuttled ahead of me for a long distance, and a lizard with orange coloring on its underbody.

And for the ornithologist there were guineas, a kind of big quail, birds that looked like herons, birds dressed in fine violet, little red birds with gray wings, doves, and various other birds of all sorts of sizes and colors.

There were fish in the streams too, some very large.

Incidentally, the word Guinea as a place name for sections and countries of the African coast did not have its origin with the guinea fowl. It was quite the reverse. The name, as might be expected, originated with the Portuguese, who called the land Guine after a native kingdom with a similar name. Fowls of a certain kind naturally became "guinea fowl"; the standard English coin of twenty-one shillings, became a "guinea" because it was supposedly first struck out of gold from Guinea; the guinea pig was probably so called because it was brought from South America to England on slave ships from African Guinea; and the worm which entered a West African's stomach and eventually took up residence—all five inches of it—in his leg, was naturally called the Guinea worm.

Portuguese Guinea road workers were provided with long metal-edged tools resembling oars in every way except that there was an angle near the middle. With this oar a worker scooped mud from the water along the road and enforced the shoulders, patting it down with the same oar. Humps were taken out of the road itself by the same instrument, and I think they grubbed out the grass with it, too. Of course you can imagine how smooth was the finished job—just one little chuckhole after the other; and it surely made for a sore seat. But at least the Portuguese worked their roads, which was often in contrast to the French. The Portuguese road gangs that I saw might number more than fifty men and boys. Sometimes, as in Angola, there was a bunch of women workers. When the dirt got sandy or washed, new dirt was put on. This was taken from beside the road, and the hole was usually large enough to contain three men, who operated like a rabbit digging a burrow. They scraped the dirt from the sides to the center, thus loosening it. Other workers took the dirt in baskets carried on their heads to wherever it was needed.

In a place called Mansoa I stopped at a store where four young fellows were playing cards. One of them spoke a little English—self-taught—and almost immediately invited me to his house for dinner. This was notable for its "African potatoes," actually the roots of the manioc. I thought them very good. My host's native wife did not sit at the table with us, but he embraced her at other times, so her absence at table was due to custom rather than any lack of affection. He said that he had seven children, four boys and three girls, but only one small boy shared our meal.

The curse of Mansoa was the mosquito.

"Without a net, you wouldn't sleep five minutes," said my host.

He went to two of his neighbors to borrow a net for me, and his neighbor lady fixed it up that evening with hammer and nails. She also gave my overalls a much needed washing.

It was too hot to wear a shirt around the house even with the windows and doors open, yet the mosquitoes prevented my writing without it. The problem was partly solved by my thoughtful host, who put one of his boys to work shaking a cloth over my neck and shoulders. Under such a luxury I wrote like fury, but the weak little carbide lamp nearly drove my eyes from my head. Life in West Africa was becoming more and more difficult. Still, I slept well.

In the morning, the missus brought out a pair of twins—a boy and a girl—for my inspection. I expressed approval, and thinking to be complimentary, said, "And my, you have seven!"

"Oh, no," said my host, "only four. You see, I have two other houses."

Well that was that.

I followed an attractive road that morning. The Portuguese had a row of trees along each side and had recently planted a second row. Natives could be seen harvesting rice but apparently only for their current needs.

I also noticed what I took to be broom corn—a tall cornlike plant with a sort of cattail on top. Examination of the top showed a complete covering of brown pollen and some small cereallike grains underneath. As elsewhere on the Guinea coast, small boys and men were posted on high platforms or along the road to keep birds and animals from eating the crops. There was often a lot of shouting, and since there were so many monkeys about, I wondered if they stole from the fields as well as the birds.

At a Portuguese police post the assistant commandant showed me a murderer, his only prisoner. He looked harmless enough but he had slit the throat of a native of French Guinea—in fact, had nearly cut off his head. I was told he would be sentenced to twenty-five years in prison in Angola. (Apparently Portuguese Guinea had no penal institution of its own.) It would seem that the penalty for murder was not as heavy in Africa as in America, but perhaps this was true only for natives.

French West Africa for the fifth time! This was the Casamanche, part of the province of Senegal. The Casamanche is only a finger of territory running down to the sea, and it took me hardly a day and a half to cross it.

At Ziguinchor, while waiting for a ferry, a request for permission to eat my lunch on an apartment-house porch netted me an invitation to dine upstairs. The thing I thought interesting here was the hospitality and ready acceptance of the stranger on the part of two people who were well past middle age and had obviously never had any children of their own to induce hospitality. You know the type I mean: madame in paint and powder and dressing-gown portliness; monsieur, a devoted husband. The type that keep a dog and are self-sufficient. Imagine their American counterparts taking a travel-stained, undershirted foreigner with Mercurochrome-covered sores on the back of his hands and in need of a shave, inviting him in and seating him at the table with a clean plate on a place mat with napkin to match and serving him with food.

French roads had been worse than the Portuguese, and I expected an improvement when entering British Gambia. But no, it was worse. Sand just like back in Australia, ruts a foot deep or more, and weeds on either side. Finally I came to a place called Bikama and two white people—an English veterinary called Wilson and his assistant, Tony. The vet took me to his home for supper and on the way I met Tony, almost a genuine American, since he had spent twenty-two years in the States.

Tony and I hit it off in grand style.

"I've already eaten," said Tony. "I'm not like these guys. They don't eat until eight or nine or ten o'clock. I eat as six P.M. and then I'm through with it. My cook has gone already."

Tony was originally a Basque from Bilbao. At sixteen he had left home and gone to America. He had been a sheep shearer in the Western states

I meet a forest nymph in Guinea.

A west African village huddles among the big trees.

and knew Los Angeles, Stockton, Marysville, Elko, Reno, Boise, Pocatello, Salt Lake City, and Butte quite well. Since I love the Western country we had much to talk about.

In the early thirties Tony had hearkened to the call of an aging mother in Spain and gone home for a visit. But he had never thought about taking out citizenship papers in the United States and so had to go back to Spain on a Spanish passport. Then he stayed too long and got mixed up in politics on the wrong side. So Franco took him prisoner, and he spent a lot of time in concentration camp. His mother and sister were killed in a bombing. Eventually he was allowed to load ships, and one of these was American, bound for the Gold Coast. About twenty Spaniards planned on stowing away on this ship, but only Tony and a friend made any real preparations. Working at night, they built planks into a hiding place and were not found when the vessel sailed. For four days they stayed low without food or water and then gave themselves up. Tony was put to dishwashing.

"I was happy as hell," he related. "Then we were off the Gambia coast here one day and I was whistling away in the galley and all of a sudden we got torpedoed!"

"Torpedoed!" I echoed. "By the Germans?"

"Oh yes! World War II had started by this time. And so we spent a couple days on a raft and then landed in Bathhurst, and I've been here ever since. Oh of course we get furloughs home to England!"

Gambia is a country comprising two strips of land about ten miles wide on either side of a river with the same name. The country's narrowness multiplied the problems of Wilson's agricultural department. He was telling me that if it was thought he was going to make an anti-anthrax injection, the Gambian natives would temporarily transfer their cows over the border. A native's cows are his wealth, and he counts them just as we count dollars. He has no particular interest in increasing their milk production as long as he gets at least three pints a day. On the other hand, Gambia's biggest chief was then in England and would come home full of ideas on infusion of new blood by using top-notich bulls at once. However, this could not be done, according to Wilson, until the present cattle were gradually built up by selection.

Transportation accidents and General Rust had at last finished my front wheel, which had turned 21,000 miles under my pushing and who knows how many more before my time! A section of the rim had been gradually pushing out and now endangered the tire. So in Bathhurst, capital of Gambia, I was sent to Mr. Reed, a friendly Scot, who managed marine repairs and was the harbormaster. He was dubious about welding the wheel but thought maybe he could find me an old one. Though bike wheels were scarce, I heard him say over the phone: "I thought we could dash him that one."

"Dash" means to give free of charge. A new one cost £1-17-10, or nearly ten dollars.

The wheel turned out to be usable, and Reed saw to it that I was provided with the proper nuts to hold it. Having thus fixed up the steed, he turned his attention to the rider and called the hospital to arrange for new dressings for my hand and leg sores.

The doctor at the hospital was—well, the less said the better. I had not met his like since that assistant district commissioner in the Sudan. He was late for lunch and could not afford to wait for me, he said. He was there to attend to the natives, not to travelers. But come on, he would order my dressings, as he did not want me to write in a book that I could not get dressings at the Bathhurst hospital. That chap in the Sudan, I recalled, had expressed a similar fear of what I might write in my book. When fears instead of kindness motivate men, how quickly they lose ground. Or have they already lost it?

On the Gambia, Jacqueline and I went to sea but never left the river. The stream at Bathhurst is more like an estuary and is several miles wide. The crossing was both long and rough. The ferry had a barge in tow bearing Jacqueline and an object of lesser value, an automobile. The tow line was very long, and I spent a lot of time looking back to see if Jacqueline was riding safely. Four of the ten natives in the launch with me became seasick. The engine had an unhealthy habit of slipping out of gear just when the waves were the biggest, and when this happened we lost headway at once and rolled mercilessly while the engineman struggled with the gear lever. It was pretty rugged.

My personal condition did not improve much after landing. I had arisen long before daylight and was tired. Gambia sand was ankle deep, and dragging the bike was hard work. The sores on my hands and legs were not healing and were discouraging to look at, and those I could not see at the base of my back worried me more. I decided that I must be run down and felt very, very tired with my long journey.

I stopped early, too tired to proceed, and decided to sleep out for a change because there was not a cloud in the sky. The moon came out, and I ate by its light. I almost never lost my appetite on the entire trip. Alone with nature for the first time in many nights. I felt more tranquil than I could remember without thinking back a long way.

Morning came with its first sounds: the roosters crowing in the nearest native village, then the beat, beat, beat of the mortar and pestle of the women making flour. This starts nearly an hour before daylight. Finally the chirping of the birds.

I slept out again the next night—back in Senegal Province, French West Africa, once more.

The following morning was a bad one. The rear tire was nearly done for anyway, but it had the misfortune to run into a bunch of burrs. You

One oar and one arm gets all across the Gambia.

Africa with charm—on the Gambia.

can't win. There was too much sand in the center, and so I was running on the sides of the road and there I met the burrs. While I was changing the rear tire to the front, along came a car and gave me a fourteen-kilometer ride into a small village. There were probably five women in the back of the truck, and the minute the truck stopped they all burst into wild wails and tears. The men explained that a woman had just died at the house where we had stopped. There was certainly wailing and gnashing of teeth, and a couple of the women had to be helped from the truck, they were so suddenly and completely overcome by grief.

I took Jacqueline and my gear to the concrete-floored, shaded porch of the school and there, surrounded by umpty-nine kids, labored for four hours. Talk about trouble!! Gad! Leaks at the base of the valve stem were the big bugaboo. It was heart rending to fix a tube, test it in the water, mount it, pump it up and then in five minutes find it down. I fixed four leaks in the thorn-punctured tube before I gave that up and changed tubes.

And so finally I came to Dakar, western gateway to the continent. It was a typical French colonial city—blocks of yellow and white walls, wide paved streets, and a plentiful scattering of green palms. I picked up my mail, at long last, and cycled in the moonlight out along the ocean drive to hunt a cool place to sleep. I found a jim-dandy, perhaps two hundred feet above the sea where the breeze blew full and free. And I jolly well needed such a place because it was surely warm. And there I slept with the breakers far below and a hedge for privacy.

The next day was Sunday, but all offices were open as usual. My hunt for a land route available to the north for Morocco was in vain, so I had to make arrangements to go by ship.

Sailing was scheduled for Tuesday, so imagine my surprise on Monday noon to be told that the *Hoggar* sailed in four hours. Sailings are always hectic even when you know about them in ample time for preparations. In this case I started off well because they sold me a fourth-class ticket without any fuss or argument. What a pleasure it was to travel in a country where there was no government color bar! I then scurried around, made some last-minute purchases, ate lunch and got Jacqueline and her pack into an out-of-the-way spot on board ship by 2 P.M. Just to safeguard against not being stopped at the last minute I went back on shore and around to the immigration. They were a little chagrined, I think, to learn I had been around Dakar for two days without an arrival stamp. I got a little tired of these city officials. Their star rises and sets in their city, and they behave as though it were a nation. I travel nations, not cities. Perhaps they had never had an international traveler by land. Anyway, one cranked that he did not think I could go because I had no visa for Morocco. Such a statement by an officer in a position to keep me from going, and made less than one hour before sailing—well, you can imagine how my heartbeat quickened. I had to explain that visas for Morocco were not required for Americans because of an old treaty between the two countries. Explaining something in a foreign language is never easy, and under the pressure of both importance and time it becomes downright difficult. But luck was with me, and I raised enough doubt in the official mind so that he consulted higher authorities, who confirmed my assertion.

No one paid me the least bit of attention as I went back on board the ship. It would certainly have been a cinch to stow away. We pushed off at four o'clock on my first ocean voyage since the Red Sea seven months before. I expected to fight nausea for a while but was agreeably surprised to find that the boat, well loaded, cut through the water with pitch and roll almost imperceptible.

There were a lot of favors shown me on the *Hoggar.* The table boys and kitchen help were always smuggling me apples, oranges, cheese, cake and the like. Sometimes I was served the same food as the first-class passengers. You see, we fourth-class passengers were given a plate and silverware, and at 10:30 A.M. and 5:30 P.M. we went around to the kitchen and got our meals. In addition we went forward to the bread baker's to get our bread and then amidship to get our oranges and bananas. What a blessing fruit is on board a ship! For queasy stomachs it is the one thing that goes down easily. The food tasted O.K. the first two days, but then I commenced to sense how greasy it was, and my stomach lost its happiness. However, I was not feeling up to par so the fault was partly mine.

Our sleeping quarters were in the first hold forward—rather stuffy and none too clean. We had the usual double-tiered canvas beds. There were two whites besides myself and perhaps twenty blacks. The blacks were mostly Mohammedans and had the habit of spitting on the floor. Seeds and orange peelings went the same place. I often slept on the deck where I could get a breeze, and this was a marvel to the blacks because there was quite a wind, which to them was like a blast from the North Pole. We were working north into the winter season of the Northern Hemishere.

The Mohammedan's method of personal cleanliness had improved somewhat over those followed in Egypt and the Anglo-Egyptian Sudan. He still took his little teapot of cold water when he went to the toilet but in addition a bunch of fibers like long excelsior, and a cake of soap. The fibers were used over and over, and he did not use paper. Then in the next few minutes I would see him with his fore-fingers in his mouth as far as they would go—washing his teeth. Yet he had had no opportunity to wash his hands in soap and hot water meantime. Many of the blacks went barefooted and walked where others had spit.

As for passengers on board the boat, whom should I meet but the police chap who chased after me at the American mission at Ebolowa, French Cameroun. He was most pleased to see me and treated to a lemonade.

Then there was Mabel! Mabel was a dyed blonde and the mother of a very dark mulatto child, a little girl of about four. Mabel was the only one on board whose language was English, so we talked together. Born and raised in England, she married a Frenchman and had four children, not including the little mulatto. She told me the girl was the result of a rank indiscretion at a wild party she had attended. Her French husband had divorced her, but his mother had given her the money to visit him in Brazzaville, French Equatorial Africa, to arrange alimony. She took the little girl with her. Her trip had been unsuccessful, and out of funds, she had worked her way north by this ship and that, getting help from British consuls and getting chased by French police for vagabondage. Her experiences in and out of hotels, sleeping in a spare bed in a hospital, and the like were laughable, yet unhappy. Finally she stowed away on a boat called the *Canada* and so got to Dakar. Here the authorities refused to let her land but packed her aboard the *Hoggar*. She had luggage stored in Dakar, but they would not let her get it. Although traveling second class now, she was penniless and had wired the British consul to meet her at Casablanca. I was surprised that they would help her, for she was really a French citizen.

Mabel had a real mother's love for her child, mulatto or no, and swore to stick by her no matter what happened.

"If they try to take her away from me, I don't know what I'll do," she said. "I'll kick and bite and scratch . . . Oh, I'll never leave her."

That is real mother love, I reckon, because black and white alike talked about her, and I noticed she ate with the blacks in the dining salon.

I had a short bout with malaria on the *Hoggar*. Now I can sympathize with the Europeans in Africa who had complained, "I've got a touch of fever today." It was strange that I was free until after leaving Dakar, my last malarious port. In fact, I had started my sign-off period dosage of atabrine—four tablets a day for seven days instead of the daily preventative tablet I had been taking for nearly a year. I presume this sign-off dosage is designed to knock out of you any malaria that might have sneaked in between tablets. But in spite of these precautions I had all the symptoms of malaria—headache, loss of appetite, chills, and hot feverish spells. I was dizzy too—but perhaps that was partly caused by the increased use of atabrine. Incidentally, the drug is a bright yellow and my skin had acquired a hue that would do credit to any Chinese.

The *Hoggar* had a cargo of bananas and *miel de Guines*. The latter was in fifty-gallon drums all over the decks. I could not believe it was

The casbah, Casablanca, Morocco.

Oil merchant in Casablanca.

really honey. Who ever heard of honey in fifty-gallon drums?

We ran close to the shores of Rio de Oro and Morocco. Some averred that we also saw the Canary Islands. Fishing vessels enlivened the landscape near the Moroccan shores.

We arrived at Casablanca on the morning of November 20. (I started to write my diary in French. I had been so long in French territories that I even thought in French. Imagine that!)

I was astonished at the size and modernity of Casablanca. There were new American cars as in Cairo. There were horse-drawn, open carriages, each with two black or two brown horses in good condition. There were nice boulevards lined with palms and occasionally high buildings. I felt at once that here I could get American products like films and ice cream.

There was a railroad leading out of Casablanca, and I was too long away from home to resist the temptation. Jacqueline and I boarded the 9:00 P.M train and awoke the next morning to enjoy the landscape of Morocco. We were in the region of the Middle Atlas Mountains, and the country resembled New Zealand—long rows of tall, very green poplars, oiled roads, and small farms on the more gentle slopes. Wheat fields gave evidence of modern cultivation, but they were stony and reminded me of Spain. Streams showed plenty of water, but the hills were brown with short dead grass. There were some clumps of scrub evergreens.

Beyond Taourirt I noticed Bedouin tents on the open plains. These were like a circus tent, but rectangular in shape. Sometimes, about halfway between the peak and the edge, a triangular opening could be seen where the tent seemed to be propped open by a stick. Near some tents were little piles of grass, and I wondered where on earth that came from. Not far away were small enclosures for sheep and goats made by a low brush hedge. Nomad girls in long yellow dresses and beads added pleasing color to the picture. These Bedouins were Berbers like most native Moroccans, whether nomadic or city-dwelling, and probably spoke a Berber dialect rather than Arabic.

Algeria! A country three and one-half times the size of Texas. And really fine scenery near the frontiers! Railway curves and tunnels and at least one bridge reminded me of Switzerland. I noticed contour farming and some terracing.

Tlemcen, a city in the mountains, was a reminder that Algerian history runs far into the past. For Tlemcen and its environs date from the time of the Romans, who expanded slowly through this part of Africa in the first centuries following the birth of Christ. They were replaced in the Middle Ages by the Arabs and Berbers. In the thirteenth century even Algiers was still considered part of the sultanate of Tlemcen, whose population increased to 125,000. Then came the Turks from 1500 to 1800, and finally the French. Near modern Tlemcen is the minaret of a mosque dating back to 1200 and built in part of large hewn stones from the Roman Pomaria. At Tlemcen I saw magnificent ruins of an aqueduct 1,300 years old. The city of today probably resembles its ancient counterpart. Water is still brought into the city by aqueducts, and I saw vineyards, olive groves, ripe oranges (French possessions have a marvelous seedless orange), apple trees, and lemon trees.

Beyond Tlemcen were red rim-rocked canyons, and through one of these passed a fine oiled highway. The scene was just like parts of our West, and gray and red outcroppings of rock, evergreen scrub, and some trees enhanced the similarity. Later there was a more open sweep of landscape with red soil and red-tiled roofs in the towns, just as in Spain.

Meanwhile I had plenty to occupy me inside with the befezzed natives. Such arguments over seats! And then, crowded as we were, a chap got on with eight gunny sacks full of coffee beans. Most of these were handed in to him through the windows. He filled one seat and then piled them in the doorway of our compartment. My seatmate said the beans were contraband but would not enlarge on his statement. Finally our friend was persuaded to take his sacks elsewhere, but the sounds of a big argument came back to us from down the aisle before he got settled.

At Algiers, capital of Algeria, I detrained. Once more I was back on the north coast of Africa, having now traveled two and a half times the length of the continent and entirely across it. My trip was practically completed as planned, and I spent the day visiting shipping companies to see about passage home. It was late November, and I definitely wanted to be home for Christmas. But just as in Australia, it looked as though a ship was going to be hard to get. Curses! I didn't want to spend six weeks waiting in another port. But the second trip to the post office netted me a new idea.

I was long overdue on a letter from the good wife. There was nothing at my first post-office visit, but just as an afterthought, on my second call, I asked the General Delivery clerk to look under my middle name. Sure enough here was the wife's letter. It had been written early in August and sent to Kano, Nigeria. Returned, she had resent it October 20 to Dakar, and it had been forwarded to me from there. She wanted me to come home, and considering the age of the letter, I got the idea of flying home!

Now I really could not afford such shenanigans, but I had carried temptation in my pocket for no less than nineteen months and I might be excused for giving in now. This temptation was the refund check for the unused Sydney-San Francisco airplane ticket, which had been required by the British consulate before I could leave America. I had kept the check for a cushion upon my return, but now I decided to use it for an air passage home.

This check was made out by Pan American World Airways, no less, yet I spent an entire day trying to cash it and was still unsuccessful. The Algiers airlines' offices—Air France and Trans World Airlines—refused to take it on the ticket. The banks in the city would not cash it because they could not verify the signature of the Pan American treasurer who had signed it. (Of course my passport vouched for me.) The American consulate as usual was sympathetic but uncooperative. They were tied up by rules forbidding endorsement of checks either officially or personally. So there I was! I had just enough money in traveler's checks to get me to Paris, and the T.W.A. manager decided to accept that and send me there on the chance I could get out on a flight to Chicago.

"Perhaps you can get your check cashed in Paris," he said. "Pan American has an office there."

I went to the city park and sorted out the nonessentials from my pack in order not to exceed the sixty-six pound weight limit. The manager had arranged to take the bike and this was an unexpected stroke of good luck. I had been worried how to get it back, for to leave my beloved steed was unthinkable. But all I had to do at the air office that evening was to take off the front wheel and tie it on the side of the frame.

A bus drove us to the airport, and we cleared immigration and customs. The takeoff was about midnight. It was my first flight by air, but I did not feel nervous about it; everything seemed to be done so simply. I did not even know when we left the ground. When we got out to sea a little way and the great amphitheater of lights that is Algiers faded from view, I went to sleep. Four hours later, when it was yet dark, I was awakened and told we were over Paris. And what a sight the lights of that city presented!

French customs were easily cleared, and a big bus took us into the city. I packed up and pedaled along the still dark Champs Élysées toward the Arc de Triomphe. I mused that this was the second time Jacqueline and I had been in Paris.

My day in Paris was a combination of business and pleasure. Believe it or not, but the Pan American Airways office could not cash their own company's check. The manager was most embarrassed, but realizing some obligation, he persuaded T.W.A. by phone to accept the check for my transatlantic passage to Chicago. The only reason they agreed was to avoid a rebate of 7 percent to Pan American which they would have to pay if Pan American sold me the ticket—or some such folderol. Anyway, I got my ticket and a refund draft for the balance payable in America in dollars. In the afternoon I changed some French moneys, went to a show, and went shopping.

And then, sheer fantasy!! It could not be real—or if it was, could I possibly be a part? The time was three o'clock in the morning. From the second-floor windows of the Paris airport I gazed out at a great aircraft—

long, gray, cold, unreal—under the floodlights. It was ready for a takeoff. This towering behemoth, this thing from another world, was going to lift itself into the sky and cross a great ocean—and with me on it. I suddenly felt like a voyager in the first spaceship.

I climbed aboard and found myself seated inside one of that long row of round windows I had seen. At twenty minutes after three in the morning we commenced to move, effortlessly and rather quietly. In a few moments we were airborne. And not long after daybreak we landed at Shannon, Ireland, for a substantial breakfast. It was as simple as that.

Then the long flight over the Atlantic Ocean. My place was over the wing, and I could see both ahead and behind. Far, far below lay the sea, and the miracle was that we could see it most of the way. The day was bright, and the clouds were light. Often there were fairy worlds of white cloud masses and in the distance great ranges of cloud mountains. It was all a strange new world—my first experience with the wild blue yonder by daylight.

Tirelessly we flew onward, hour after hour. The plane was a four-engined Constellation, and there were forty-six passengers besides Jacqueline. Ships post logs for their passengers sometimes, so I was not too surprised to receive typed news sheets showing our progress. We had a headwind of forty miles per hour, and our net speed was 210 miles per hour. Our altitude was about eight thousand feet. Two weather ships were stationed along the route to provide up-to-the-minute reports to aircraft, and I had the luck to get a clear view of the weather ship *Charlie,* riding the waves far below. She sure looked lonely. At another time the airplane turned slowly off to the right, and then slowly off to the left. My seatmate, a flight engineer, told me the crew was taking a double drift on the wind to see if we were being taken off course.

We were served a good hot meal aloft at noon. Around 6 P.M. Paris time, we sighted the many little lakes and rock outcroppings of Newfoundland. This was just fifteen hours out of Paris! I thought back to the days when Leif Ericson had made the first crossing of the Atlantic in the year 1000. How long had it taken him in his open longboat? Or for that matter, how long had it taken my own great-grandparents on the tiny *Norwegian Mayflower* of 1825? They had bobbed about on the waves for ninety-eight days, as I recalled.

When the ship landed and I walked into the waiting room at Gander, I was surprised to find that it was only one o'clock in the afternoon. We had gained five hours. Then, when we were airborne again, we had our second hot dinner of the day. It was Thanksgiving, and how or where else could one ever get two Thanksgiving dinners on the same day? Turkey, cranberry sauce, and the rest were served to us in our places.

Then Detroit and the good old U.S.A. about 9 P.M. And into Chicago by 11:30 for a fine landing at journey's end. We had been about twenty-seven hours from Paris, but due to time changes we arrived the same day we departed. Again I marveled! It had taken me thirty-five days to get to Australia. Now I had returned from Africa in less than two days.

U.S. Customs procedure made us returning Americans blush. They herded us like sheep into a tiny room, with all windows closed, not enough chairs, and scarcely standing room for the balance. To add insult to injury they locked the door on us as though we were a bunch of criminals. When they got around to it, Immigration called us by name, one at a time. Once we were past Immigration, Customs examined our baggage thoroughly. We were all held up in an even smaller room than before. Three customs men took care of each inspection. This was a contrast to Europe, where the customs bench is long and the two customs men handle travelers with such dispatch that there are almost no delays. Some of my fellow travelers arriving at Chicago would be in Customs for two or three hours.

I packed up Jacqueline and pedaled through the early morning hours out to suburban Elmhurst, my home. It seemed such a long way—much, much longer than I had dreamed—and there was a head wind and a leaky tire. But finally I arrived. How happy and excited we all were!

Epilogue

And so the trip was over. One year and seven months of almost continuous travel had covered 67,062 miles: 11,626 by bicycle, 16,529 by car and truck, 27,783 by ship, 5,364 by rail, and 5,760 by air. I had made a practically complete tour of two continents, Australia and Africa, and visited 46 countries. There were 127 visas and entrance and exit stamps in my passport, in which five sets of additional sheets had been placed.

My total outlay for the trip was $1,507, of which no less than $1,213 had been necessary to conquer those uninteresting yet beneficial barriers to world travel—the oceans. Rail travel had cost me $88; bus, $25; mountain-climbing and sea excursions, $43; food, $36; lodging, nil; passport and visas, $34; films, $31; postage, $20; tires, tubes, and bicycle repairs, $17. To have lived at home without traveling at all for 19 months would have cost me at least $800. So perhaps the net cost of the trip was only $700.

I had eaten or slept in 380 different homes, black as well as white. Desert and mountain and jungle had fallen behind the wheels of my bicycle. And I had visited such world wonders as the Great Barrier Reef and Victoria Falls. People without end and scenery without duplication!

In short, I had been around the world and collected enough memories of people and places, hardships and thrills, to fill all my idle hours in all my remaining days.

The contented traveler had come home!

Except for a different hub mechanism the faithful Jacqueline looked the same as when we had departed more than a year and half before.

She would probably like to go again!

Appendix

The Australian Vocabulary

after: afterwards
ant bed: ant hill
arm bands: sleeve holders
attending: taking part in a neighbor's muster and drafting to spot one's own cattle
Aussie: an Australian

back chat: repartee.
bagman: tramp
ballies: baldfaced cattle, Herefords
balloon buster: meteorologist
barrack(v.): cheer for
bach: hut; summer cottage
battens: fence uprights between posts
beano: modern party
berloola: same as *pie*
billabong: pool in dried-up streambed
billy: tin can, pot, etc., used to heat water
binging: beefing in a sort of sly way
bingye/bings: Aborigine domestics
biscuit: cookie
bitzer: machine made of bits and parts of other machines
blister: cop's ticket; summons
bloke: a chap about the place
bloody: "by Our Lady (impolite, common adjective)
bloomer: a mistake
blown: spoiled meat (fly eggs; maggots)
bludger (v.): live off generosity of others; (n.) one who does so
blue: fight; argument
blue/bluey: blonde, or even a red-headed man
blue: trouble ("a bit of a blue")
bobby: calf (esp. one for sale)
bod: person
bods: people
bogey: sledge with wheels (on a wharf for transport)

bogged: stopped
bogie: bath
bolting: galloping
bonnet: hood of a car
bonza (adj.) hospitable; OK
boot: high-topped shoe; trunk of car; tire sleeve
borehead: where artesian water comes out of ground
bot: tuberculosis
bottling: canning
bowser: filling station pump
boxing: mixing oneself up
Boxing Day: day after Christmas
break: paddock of eight to ten acres
breakdown service: tow truck service
brick: ten pounds (money)
Briton: courageous chap
broncho(v.): to rope
bronchoing: roping and tying up an animal for dehorning, etc.
broncho horse: horse steady enough for the act
broncho panel: heavy ten-foot section of fence for holding cattle
brum: penny
brumby: wild horse
bubble and squeak: leftover spuds and cabbage fried for breakfast
buck jumping, buck jumper: bucking broncho
buggered: damned
buggerize: gum up
bull: highway patrolman; cop
bullock: steer; pl. cattle; also bullock driver
bullockies: drivers of bullock carts
bullocking: working very hard
bullock's joy: syrup
bully beef: canned beef
bung (n.): black fellow
bung (adj.): bad (e.g. "bung eyes")
bung it: put it out; throw it away

529

cabin: cab of a truck
call it on: undertake
callithumpian: bush Baptist; near atheist
camp: mob (of cattle or sheep); herd
camp draft: rodeo
cargo boat: freight boat
caravan: house trailer
carting: hauling gravel
chappie: fellow
chemist: drugstore (medicine only)
chit: ticket
chook: grown chicken
chooks: chickens
Chow: Chinaman
claypan: a billabong
cleanskin mick: maverick
cobber: a buddy
cockey: small dairy farmer
cockey's delight: syrup
cooee: call; within hailing distance ("within cooee")
comforter: a baby's nipple pacifier
commo: communist
cook bacon: fry bacon
copper top: red-headed man
corduroy road: one made with logs
corn: oats, barley, wheat, etc.
corrugations: washboard road
cot: baby's crib
counter jumper: store clerk
cove: a chap about the place; fellow; joker
cover: tire
cowboy: one who milks cows, makes butter, gardens, carries wood; handy man on the ranch
credit(v.): believe ("You wouldn't credit it.")
creeper: vine
crib: weekend hut; hut
crib time: lunch time
crib pail: lunch pail (from cribbage, game played at lunch time)
crock: unfit, delicate person; an old horse
crook(adj.): bad; sick ("I'm bloody crook.")
crooked on: mad at; disgusted with
crop(v.): to farm
cushy: easy ("a cushy job")

damper: mixture of flour and water

deener: same as *dinar*
diddle: fool around with in a nice way ("She'll diddle [dance] with you.")
digger: soldier
dinar: bob (shilling)
dingo: anyone who shows cowardice
dinkie die/dinky: real ("a dinkie die American," i.e., born in the U.S.)
dinky: serious ("I'm dinky.")
docket: sales ticket
donkey's years: coon's age
donnybrook: fight; underhanded activity
doss(v.): to throw
downs: wide open spaces
drafting: sorting out cattle
drain: ditch
draw post: anchor post in Western Australian sheep fence
dray: two-wheeled wagon
driver: railroad engineer
duffing: cattle rustling
dust bin: garbage can
done in: killed; died of accident or disease

ear bashing: good gabfest
ears: heads of wheat
eiderdown: bed covering
exhibition: county fair

fair dinkum: real; really
fettler: section hand
fiddly: pound
fiddly did: half pound
fitter: railway mechanic
flash: a show-off
flat: down ("The battery is flat.")
flat out: tired out
float(v.): transport by truck
floorfinder: floor buttons in an elevator
flying fox: aerial tramway
fodder: hay
footballer: one who plays football
footwalk: a walk
forestaller: sub-wholesaler
fortnight: two weeks (much used term)
fountain: big samovar on a stove

gaiter: boot for tire
galoshes: rubbers
ganger: boss of section hands or road workers

gas pliers: pliers
geegee: horse
gidgee tree: umbrella
gin: Aborigine domestic
glass house: greenhouse
good-oh: OK, I'll do that for you
grafter: worker (in Tasmania)
green box: coffin
grid: bike
grizzling: grouching; beefing
guard: conductor on train

half-dollar: two shillings, six pence
hard-up party: hard time party
head rope: lasso
holiday: vacation
hood: top of a car

ice creams: ice cream cones
iron: motorcycle
irons: stirrups
ironstone: iron ore

jackaroo: tenderfoot; an apprentice overseer
jelly: Jell-O
jetting: spraying sheep
jib (v.): move (as a lever); squawk ("He'll jib at it.")
jib(n.): balky horse
jig: (v.) stub ("I had a jig on my toe.")
jinkey: buggy
John: policeman
jug: pitcher
jumbuck: sheep
Joey: baby kangaroo

kicker: engine
killer: bullock to be killed (esp. for a ranch)
king dick: small monkey wrench
kings of labor: sheep shearers
kite: airplane
knocked: killed; peeved

lace (v.): spike (a drink)
land of wait-a-while: Australia
lap(v.): gallop
larrikin: mischievous boy
laughing sides: riding boots
leg rope: lasso
leg up: windfall
lengthsman: section hand

life preserver: truncheon; billy club
lift: elevator
liverish: owly
load up: a load on
lolly/lollies: candy
lorry: big enclosed truck
lounge: living room
lumpers: longshoremen

m-m-m: yes
mad: mad person
maize: corn
Matilda: same as *swag*
me: my
mercery: socks, shirts, underwear, etc.
metal: crushed rock for and on roads
mick: unbranded bull calf; a Catholic
middy: glass half the size of a schooner
milk bar: soda and ice cream place
mincemeat: hamburger
mo: mustache
motor: car
motorbike: motorcycle
mud guard: fender
mulga country: way-out bush country
mummy: a nipple babies suck
munger: food
murphies: spuds (potatoes)

nap: bedcovers (collectively)
netting: chicken wire
never-never country: Australian outback
nick: condition
nip: step along; pass quickly
nipper: baby
noughts and crosses: old cat
nurse: trainee nurse

out: ready ("Breakfast is out.")
outback: land away from cities

pack (v.) *stakes:* set fence posts
paddock: large fenced area for stock
paddy: temper
pannikin: cup
pear jump: to buck (refers to pear cactus)
peckish: hungry
peg: clothespin
petrol: gasoline

pie: steak covered with flour, salted, and fried in beef fat

pikelet: little pancake

pinch: hill

pindown country: land of bush and sand

pink(v.): to balk

pip: seed of fruit

plant: blacks, horses, gear, and man in charge

pliers: wire cutters

poddy: underfed calf with pot belly

poler ("pawler"): one who imposes on another

popsie: a dame

porridge: any hot cereal

ports: portmanteaux

posey ("pawsey"): place where one sits

pot(v.): tell ("She'll pot on you.")

pot(n.): schooner

pottle: circular cardboard container

presser: one who puts wool into bales

publican: keeper of a pub

puftaloon: gob of dough dropped in fat and fried

pumper: handcar

pumpkin: squash (or proper pumpkin)

quilt: any bedcover

quilting: whipping

race: irrigation or mining ditch

rag: weakness; weak card (in cards: "I had a rag in that.")

rat (v.): go through (She rats his pockets.")

ratbag: crazy person (bicycle rider in outback Australia)

reel: spool

repository: warehouse

rick: to wrench (one's back)

Rickety Islands: New Zealand

right: OK ("Are you right? Yes, she's right.")

ringer: cowboy

robe: bed blankets

rock hole: hole in riverbed with rock bottom—holds water longer

rock melon: cantaloupe

root(v.): buck

rubbish tip: garbage dump

rug: blanket

run through: opening in a stock fence

sand groper: West Australian

scarp: scoot

scissors: shears

scoop: dirt scraper

scrub: wide open spaces with few trees

scrub off: write off (as a loss)

service car: bus

settled: finished; in a bad way ("If it breaks, we're settled.")

shades: lamp shades, not window shades

shanks pony: shanks horses

sheaves: bundles of grain

sheep run: place running only a few thousand sheep

sheila: a dame

shift(v.): move people or cattle between stations; also move a nut (mechanic's talk)

shingle: gravel from a river bed

shook: sold ("I'm not shook on him.")

show: county fair

singelet: undershirt

sister: qualified nurse

skillet: skewer

skittle(v.): knock to one side

slewed: out of balance; mixed up; lost

slippery slides: chute-the-chutes

smoko: mid-morning or mid-afternoon tea with cake or scones

snow raking: tramping paths to trapped sheep

soak: hole dug in creek beds for water to seep in

spanner: any wrench not having movable jaws

speed-o: speedometer

spin: five pounds

squatter: one living on a small sheep ranch

squirt: gun, i.e., pistol or revolver

station: ranch

stockboy: stockman or cowboy

stockyard: corral

stook(v., n.): shock (of grain)

store: lean bullock sent to fattening

strainer post: anchor post

stretcher: cot

strides: jeans

stripper: combine
sump: pan of car
swag: bed roll, tucker, billy, etc., altogether
swaggie; swagman: man with a pack
swat: to cram (for an exam)
sweets: dessert

ta: thank you
tack: food
tap: faucet
tar seal: blacktop or bitumen road
tart: girl
tea: either tea and cakes or full meal
tellie: television set
tick off (v.): reprimand
tilly: utility truck
timber up: shore up
tin dog: tin of bully beef
tin-pot town: dead burg
tin opener: can opener
toffs: society folk
top: a Beau Brummel, a swell
top end: end (of a street)
to muster: to ride herd
torch: flashlight
townie: fellow countryman
tram: streetcar
tramped: fired
tray: body of truck
treacle: a dark cane syrup (molasses)
trey: three pence
tricked up: mixed up
trolley: sledge (on wharf for transport)
trucking yards: railway yards (refers to railroad car trucks)
tucker: food
tucker box: railway man's lunch box

valve: tube in radio set
van: caravan; house trailer

wadgy: stick
"Wait": Stop (highway sign)
washer: washcloth
washcloth: dishcloth
weaner: a little pig
wharfie: longshoreman
willy willy: tiny cyclone; gust of wind
windscreen: windshield
wireless: radio
wonky: broken up, apart

wowser: goody-goody chap; grouch
wrench: wrench with movable jaws

yacka: work
yandy: to hunt for something (esp. tin)
yike: brawl

zac: six pence
zed: zee
ziff: beard
zig-zags: switchbacks
zwei: two shillings

UNKNOWN TERMS

cookies
crackers (are they lentils?)
potato salad
sauerkraut ("must be a disagreeable German")

PRONUNCIATIONS

Australian: "aus tryl yin"
clerk: "clark"
mail: "mile"
mate: "mite"
station: "styshun"
Wave Hill: "Wyeville"

AUSTRALIAN EXPRESSIONS

an American afternoon: afternoon party to which you must take a gift
ah well: "guess we'd better be going"
are you away? have you gone?
bash(v.): to talk to one ("She's bashing his ear.")
be away: to pass (in cards)
beg yours: beg your pardon
bit of a bloom: bit of a row
bog in: "set to" at the table
boil the billy: prepare tea or meal
budget of news: collection of news items
do a bunk: run away
get a crib together: do up a lunch
get done: wear out ("The mantel's gettin' done.")
give it in: give it up
go bush: run away
go bung: go broke
go off: stop ("Rain has gone off.")

good on ya: good luck to you

hang of a . . . : whale of a . . .

"how ya poppin?": "how are you getting on?"

humping my bluey: waltzing Matilda in Western Australia

in a bit of a flat: excited, worried

jack to it: wise to it

keep knit: keep watch

keep your pecker up: keep your chin up

knock up: cut up ("knock a heap of wood up")

much of a muchness: alike; the same

next block: next building

nick through: squeeze through

on the bash: on the drunk

on the square: on the wagon

on the trek/on the wallaby: on the road

one for the gutter: a final drink

over the road: across the road

real hard case: real good scout

ride cavvy: be boss of horses in a cattle *plant* (q.v.)

ripping the cat: beefing; in the dumps

rough as bags: rugged; dressed roughly

see a bloke about a dog: see a man about a horse

she's sweet: it's OK

sleep in: sleep out

squib it: chuck it up, give it up

take a pitch with him: have a chat with him

to be shot: not to know what to do

tuck in: same as *bog in*

turn it in: give it up

unroll the knot: unroll the bedroll

up to the knocker: up to snuff

waltzing Matilda: roaming, the swag bouncing on the back

Note: This list of words and expressions is from my own experiences and should not be viewed as the work of a professional skilled in linguistics. The list also covers New Zealand. Some words are undoubtedly localized in their use. A number of words are common to other members of the British Commonwealth, and a few may be familiar to Americans.